Praise for Robert Stinnett's DAY OF DECEIT

"There is plenty of news value to Stinnett's book. Why? Because he has amassed evidence that yields...a far more precise knowledge of who knew what and when than any previous author has presented."

—Steve Weinberg, *The San Francisco Chronicle*

"It is difficult, after reading this copiously documented book, not to wonder about previously unchallenged assumptions about Pearl Harbor."

—Richard Bernstein, *The New York Times Book Review*

"A fascinating and readable book that is exceptionally well-presented."

—Bruce Bartlett, *The Wall Street Journal*

"Stinnett has made a sickening discovery through the Freedom of Information Act...FDR must have known....*Day of Deceit* is perhaps the most revelatory document of our time."   —Tom Roeser, *Chicago Sun-Times*

"Thanks to Stinnett's thorough research, those who will debate this topic in the future will have a fuller picture of the real story behind the 'Day of Infamy.' "   —Ed Halloran, *Rocky Mountain News*

"Backed by seventeen years of research and using more than two hundred thousand interviews and newly declassified documents, Stinnett makes devastating revelations.... [He is] a model researcher.... December 7, 1941, is indeed 'a date which will live in infamy.' Thanks to Stinnett, we now know where the infamy really lay. A sobering blockbuster, an absorbing read, and a model of revisionist history, *Day of Deceit* does much to unmask the awful truth about Pearl Harbor. All Americans interested in our entry into World War II—or concerned with our government's trustworthiness—should read it."   —John Attarian, *The Detroit News*

"Stinnett makes points that disturb conventional thinking about the Pearl Harbor attack." —Lynwood Abram, *Houston Chronicle*

"Explosive, revealing, and disturbing, *Day of Deceit* gets to the heart of the debate about America's leadership as the nation was swept into the war. A triumph of historical scholarship and a valuable contribution to the record of World War II." —Michael D. Hull, *World War II* magazine

"Robert Stinnett has come as close as any mortal will to proving not only that the president had a pretty shrewd idea the Japanese planned to attack, but that he did everything in his power, short of declaring war, to make sure they would. After almost sixty years—and the destruction of intelligence documents—a single 'smoking gun' will never be found. But the case put together by Stinnett during thirteen years of research, painstaking use of the Freedom of Information Act, and interviews with participants, is more than persuasive." —Rupert Corwell, *The London Independent*

"An explosive, well-written look at the events leading up to the Japanese raid on Pearl Harbor, including FDR's provocation of the attack, by a WWII veteran and longtime journalist. . . . Stinnett has left no stone unturned in this account, which should rewrite the historical record of WWII." —*Kirkus Reviews*

"Stinnett provides overwhelming evidence that FDR and his top advisers knew that Japanese warships were heading towards Hawaii. The heart of his argument is even more inflammatory: Stinnett argues that FDR, who desired to sway public opinion in support of U.S. entry into WWII, instigated a policy intended to provoke a Japanese attack. . . . If Stinnett is right, FDR has a lot to answer for—namely, the lives of those Americans who perished at Pearl Harbor. Stinnett establishes almost beyond question that the U.S. Navy could have at least anticipated the attack."
—*Publishers Weekly* (starred review)

"Pearl Harbor holds fewer secrets because of Stinnett's research."
—*Booklist*

ALSO BY ROBERT B. STINNETT

George Bush: His World War II Years

TOUCHSTONE
PUBLISHED BY SIMON & SCHUSTER
NEW YORK   LONDON   TORONTO   SYDNEY   SINGAPORE

DAY OF DECEIT

THE TRUTH ABOUT

— FDR —

AND PEARL HARBOR

ROBERT B. STINNETT

TOUCHSTONE
Rockefeller Center
1230 Avenue of the Americas
New York, NY 10020

First Touchstone Edition 2001

TOUCHSTONE and colophon are registered trademarks
of Simon & Schuster, Inc.

Designed by Carla Bolte

Manufactured in the United States of America

10   9   8   7   6   5   4   3   2   1

The Library of Congress has cataloged the Free Press edition as follows:

Stinnett, Robert B.
    Day of deceit : the truth about FDR and Pearl Harbor /
Robert B. Stinnett.
        p.   cm.
    Includes bibliographical references and index.
    1. Pearl Harbor (Hawaii), Attack on, 1941.   2. Intelligence service—
United States.   3. Roosevelt, Franklin D. (Franklin Delano), 1882–1945.
4. World War, 1939–1945—Diplomatic history.   I. Title.
D767.92.S837   1999
940.54'26—dc21   99-38402
                                                              CIP

    ISBN 0-684-85339-6
        0-7432-0129-9 (Pbk)

THIS BOOK IS DEDICATED TO THE LATE UNITED STATES CONGRESSMAN John Moss (D., CA), the author of America's Freedom of Information Act. Without the FOIA the information revealed in this book would never have surfaced. I was able to express my gratitude to the Congressman when he was honored by the Society of Professional Journalists during an awards dinner in San Francisco, March 18, 1997.

CONTENTS

CONTENTS

PRINCIPAL CHARACTERS

The following are listed in the order of their appearance in the book. Rank/status is as of December 1, 1941.

FRANKLIN D. ROOSEVELT, President of the United States.

LIEUTENANT COMMANDER ARTHUR MCCOLLUM, Head, Far East Desk, Navy Intelligence, Washington.

REAR ADMIRAL WALTER S. ANDERSON, Commander of Battleships, Pacific Fleet.

ADMIRAL HUSBAND E. KIMMEL, Commander-in-Chief, Pacific Fleet.

VICE ADMIRAL JAMES O. RICHARDSON, former Commander-in-Chief, United States Fleet.

ADMIRAL HAROLD STARK, Chief of Naval Operations, Washington, DC.

ADMIRAL THOMAS HART, Commander-in-Chief, US Asiatic Fleet, Manila.

LIEUTENANT COMMANDER JOSEPH JOHN ROCHEFORT, Commander, Station HYPO, Pearl Harbor.

LIEUTENANT COMMANDER EDWIN LAYTON, Intelligence Officer, Pacific Fleet, Pearl Harbor.

ADMIRAL ISOROKU YAMAMOTO, Commander-in-Chief, Imperial Japanese Navy (Operational command).

ADOLF A. BERLE, JR., Assistant Secretary of State, Washington, DC.

J. EDGAR HOOVER, Director of Federal Bureau of Investigation.

COMMANDER VINCENT R. MURPHY, War Plans Officer for US Fleet.

LIEUTENANT GENERAL WALTER SHORT, Commander of US Army's Hawaiian Department, Fort Shafter, Oahu.

CHIEF RADIOMAN HOMER KISNER, Radio Traffic Chief, Station H, Oahu.

TADASHI MORIMURA, Assumed name of Japanese naval spy assigned to Hawaii, March–December 1941. His true name, Ensign Takeo Yoshikawa.

LIEUTENANT GENERAL DOUGLAS MACARTHUR, Commander of Far East Forces, US Army, Manila.

COMMANDER LAURANCE SAFFORD, Officer-in-Charge, Station US.

AGNES MEYER DRISCOLL, Chief Civilian Navy Cryptographer at Station US.

GENERAL GEORGE MARSHALL, Chief of Staff (Operational Command) of US Army.

DUANE WHITLOCK, Radioman First Class. One of three radio traffic analysts at Station CAST.

LIEUTENANT COMMANDER THOMAS DYER. Chief Cryptanalyst, Station HYPO, Pearl Harbor.

PREFACE

THIS BOOK CONTRADICTS AND QUESTIONS MUCH OF WHAT HAS BEEN written about the events and decisions that led to Japan's attack on Pearl Harbor on December 7, 1941. My sole purpose is to uncover the true story of events leading up to the devastating attack on the naval base and adjoining Army facilities, and to document that it was not a surprise to President Franklin Delano Roosevelt and many of his top military and policy advisors.

This is an unvarnished account of how the United States got into a bloody conflict that threatened the free world. It is not an attempt to question the wisdom of America's entry into the war.

As a veteran of the Pacific War, I felt a sense of outrage as I uncovered secrets that had been hidden from Americans for more than fifty years. But I understood the agonizing dilemma faced by President Roosevelt. He was forced to find circuitous means to persuade an isolationist America to join in a fight for freedom. He knew this would cost lives. How many, he could not have known.

The country was disillusioned by the failure of America's idealistic commitment to make "the world safe for democracy" in World War I. Many Americans had chosen isolationism to shelter their young from the horrors of another war, and believed that Roosevelt would "not send their sons to fight in foreign wars." Roosevelt believed that his countrymen would rally only to oppose an overt act of war on the United States. The decision he made, in concert with his advisors, was to provoke Japan through a series of actions into an overt act: the Pearl Harbor attack.

As I have discovered in the course of seventeen years of archival research and personal interviews with US Navy cryptographers, the answer to Roosevelt's dilemma is found in an extraordinary number of documents whose release I have been able to obtain through Freedom of Information

Act requests. These papers outline deliberate steps that were planned and implemented to elicit the overt action that catapulted America into the war, and devastated military forces at Pearl Harbor and other Pacific bases. Eight steps were suggested to provoke a Japanese attack. Shortly after reviewing these, Roosevelt put them into effect. After the eighth provocation had been taken, Japan responded. On November 27 and 28, 1941, US military commanders were given this order: "The United States desires that Japan commit the first overt act." According to Secretary of War Henry L. Stimson, the order came directly from President Roosevelt.

There has been a controversy over American foreknowledge of the events of December 7, 1941. We have long known that Japanese diplomatic cables—which pointed toward hostilities—were intercepted and decoded. What I have discovered, however, is that we knew much more. Not only did we undertake provocative steps, we intercepted and decoded military cables. We knew the attack was coming.

By provoking the attack, Roosevelt accepted the terrible truth that America's military forces—including the Pacific Fleet and the civilian population in the Pacific—would sit squarely in harm's way, exposed to enormous risks. The commanders in Hawaii, Admiral Husband Kimmel and Lieutenant General Walter Short, were deprived of intelligence that might have made them more alert to the risks entailed in Roosevelt's policy, but they obeyed his direct order: "The United States desires that Japan commit the first overt act." More than 200,000 documents and interviews have led me to these conclusions. I am indebted to the Freedom of Information Act and its author, the late Congressman John Moss (D., CA) for making it possible for me to tell this story.

Painful though they surely were, Roosevelt's decisions were strategically calculated to lead to the ultimate victory of allied forces over the Axis nations that threatened the liberties we all cherish. The advisors who formulated the provocative policies were staunch in their support though aware of the risks. I am mindful that it is easier to take a critical view of this policy a half century removed than to understand fully what went on in Roosevelt's mind in the year prior to Pearl Harbor. Yet history asks questions and makes judgments. Historians must grapple with what is knowable, and as documented as human action and thought can be. It is in this spirit that I offer the fruits of my research.

CHAPTER 1

THE BIGGEST STORY OF MY LIFE

WASHINGTON

DECEMBER 8, 1941

ABOUT 1:00 A.M.

EDWARD R. MURROW COULDN'T SLEEP. HIS WIFE, JANET, WATCHED him pace in their hotel room. He was chain-smoking. Murrow, the CBS radio newsman, had just returned from a midnight meeting with President Franklin D. Roosevelt in the White House. Japan's carrier and submarine raid on Pearl Harbor had taken place twelve hours earlier, and the full impact of the military disaster was slowly sinking in for FDR and the American people.[1]

During their twenty-five-minute discussion in the second-floor Oval Study, the President provided Murrow with something—we will never know exactly what—that any reporter would kill for. That night he told his wife, "It's the biggest story of my life, but I don't know if it's my duty to tell it or forget it." Long after the war ended, Murrow was asked about this meeting by author-journalist John Gunther. After a long pause, Murrow replied: "That story would send Casey Murrow through college, and if you think I'm going to give it to you, you're out of your mind."

1

Earlier in the week, the Murrows had accepted a personal dinner invitation from the Roosevelts. First Lady Eleanor Roosevelt personally prepared, cooked, and served supper for two dozen guests. Her specialty was scrambled eggs and sausage, cooked in an electric chafing dish that sat atop a long buffet table in the family dining room. It was the invariable menu. Since the regular White House staff was given Sunday off, she did the cooking while the President mixed the cocktails.[2]

After he heard the first news flashes about the Pearl Harbor raid, Murrow checked with the White House to see if the supper was still on. Told that it was, he and Janet then walked across Lafayette Park, crossed Pennsylvania Avenue, and entered the mansion through the North Portico. After the Murrows were ushered into the dining room, Mrs. Roosevelt explained that the President was meeting with congressional leaders and military officers and could not join them for supper.

Outside on Pennsylvania Avenue a small crowd had gathered. The White House was ablaze with light. No one inside the mansion thought to pull the window shades or institute blackouts on the first day of war—that would came later. An Associated Press photographer took a picture from Lafayette Park. It shows a window in the family dining room with a silhouette of a tall figure—probably the First Lady—presiding over her scrambled eggs.

During the dinner, White House chief usher Howell Crim asked Murrow to remain for an informal meeting with FDR. After Janet Murrow returned to their hotel, her husband went to the second floor and waited outside Roosevelt's Oval Study—not to be confused with the Oval Office—in the West Wing of the White House. Soon Murrow was joined by William "Wild Bill" Donovan, Roosevelt's Coordinator of Information and later founder of the wartime Office of Strategic Services, the forerunner of the CIA.

Donovan had not been present at dinner but had been summoned by the President from New York, where he had been watching a football game at the Polo Grounds. Football fans heard an unusual announcement over the public address system about 2:30 that afternoon: "Colonel William Donovan, come to the box office at once. There is an important phone message." The message was from James Roosevelt, the President's son and a member of Donovan's staff; he told Donovan about the Japanese attack.[3]

Throughout the evening of December 7, Roosevelt conferred with congressional and military leaders. He decided his first wartime move would come the next morning, December 8, when he would ask Congress to declare that a state of war existed between Japan and the United States. He prepared a rough draft of what later became his "Day of Infamy" speech. Then he invited Murrow and Donovan into the study for a midnight snack of sandwiches and cold beer. Chief Usher Crim noted that the three men spent twenty-five minutes together in the study before Roosevelt retired to his adjoining bedroom. Crim's arrival and departure notations in the Usher Book comprise the only official record; there were no official minutes of the meeting.

Only Donovan has hinted at what went on: the conversation was mostly about public reaction to the attack. He sensed that this was FDR's overriding concern. In 1953, while he served as ambassador to Thailand, Donovan disclosed the details of the meeting to his executive assistant, William J. vanden Heuvel, who summarized the recollections in his diary. The President asked Murrow and Donovan whether they thought the attack was a clear case of a first Japanese move that would unite Americans behind a declaration of war against the Axis powers. Both guests thought it would indeed have that effect.

Donovan believed that Roosevelt welcomed the attack and that it was less of a surprise to him than it was to others in the White House. FDR claimed he sent an advance warning to Pearl Harbor that an attack by Japan was imminent. "They caught our ships like lame ducks! Lame ducks, Bill. We told them, at Pearl Harbor and everywhere else, to have the lookouts manned. But they still took us by surprise."[4]

Still not convinced that America's isolationist sentiments would change after this attack, FDR then read to the two men from a message he had received from a British Foreign Office official, T. North Whitehead: "The dictator powers have presented us with a united America." Roosevelt wondered whether Whitehead's assessment was correct. Again he asked, would America now support a declaration of war? Donovan and Murrow again replied in the affirmative.

Whitehead was an influential member of the Foreign Office and an advisor to Prime Minister Winston Churchill on matters affecting America's aid to the British in 1940 and 1941. He evaluated American public opinion and "read" FDR's mind for the Prime Minister. In written comments to Churchill in the fall of 1940, Whitehead had warned of continued United States isolationism, but predicted it could be overcome: "America is not in the bag. However, the President is engaged in carefully calculated steps to give us full assistance."[5]

Several years later Murrow made a brief, circumspect broadcast that in part addressed the question of what the President had known before the Japanese hit Pearl Harbor. According to Murrow's biographer Ann Sperber, "The broadcast itself was a response to an article by John Chamberlain in *LIFE* magazine charging Roosevelt with foreknowledge of the attack. Murrow did not believe it and said so on the air, making it clear that he had only his instinct to go on."[6]

In the end, Murrow's big story remained unwritten and unbroadcast. Sperber believed that the meeting concerned damage reports. Whatever it was, it weighed heavily on Murrow's mind. "But he couldn't forget it either, blaming himself at times thereafter for not going with the story, never determining to his satisfaction where his duties lay that night or what had been in the subtle mind of FDR," Sperber wrote. Murrow took the story to his grave. He died April 7, 1965, two days past his fifty-seventh birthday.[7]

Had FDR revealed something that night about his foreknowledge? Damage reports emerged immediately in local Hawaii papers, though the full details of the American losses were not released to the nation's news media until December 16, 1941, by Secretary of the Navy Frank Knox. He confirmed the initial report by the Honolulu *Star-Bulletin*. Secretary Knox named the seven warships sunk: USS *Arizona*, USS *Utah*, USS *Oklahoma*, USS *Cassin*, USS *Downes*, USS *Shaw*, and USS *Oglala*. He said the human toll on Oahu was 2897 Americans killed, 879 wounded, and 26 missing. There was severe damage to the Army's aircraft and hangars on Oahu. Knox said the Japanese planes came from aircraft carriers and had the "most tremendously detailed" information of the naval layout at Pearl Harbor. He listed Japan's losses at forty-one planes shot down, and disclosed the American capture of a Japanese two-man midget submarine that had gone aground on an Oahu beach and the sinking of four other Japanese midget subs.[8]

Once the nation's news media reported the attack details on December 16, 1941, there was no "big story" left to report on the main events at Pearl

Harbor. None—except speculation about Roosevelt's foreknowledge. Certain words and phrases cited by Donovan hinted at what he and Murrow were told by FDR. William vanden Heuvel's diary, according to author Anthony Cave Brown, is tantalizing: "The President's surprise was not as great as that of other men around him. Nor was the attack unwelcome. It had ended the past months of uncertainty caused by FDR's decision that Japan must be seen to make the first overt move."[9]

Any conclusion about the Murrow meeting must remain speculative, because the participants refused to tell the story. However, there are many more direct pieces of evidence from the days and weeks leading up to December 7 that put the question of FDR's foreknowledge definitively to rest. Previous accounts have claimed that the United States had not cracked Japanese military codes prior to the attack. We now know this is wrong. Previous accounts have insisted that the Japanese fleet maintained strict radio silence. This, too, is wrong. The truth is clear: FDR knew.

The real question is even more intriguing: did he deliberately provoke the attack? Were there earlier covert moves by the United States? According to a secret strategy memo, dated October 7, 1940, and adopted by the President, there were.

CHAPTER 2

FDR'S BACK DOOR
TO WAR

NAVY HEADQUARTERS

WASHINGTON

OCTOBER 7, 1940

As WARFARE RAGED IN EUROPE AND PORTIONS OF AFRICA AND
Japan, Germany and Italy threatened countries in three continents, a
memorandum circulated in Washington. Originating in the Office of Naval
Intelligence and addressed to two of FDR's most trusted advisors, it sug-
gested a shocking new American foreign policy. It called for provoking
Japan into an overt act of war against the United States. It was written by
Lieutenant Commander Arthur H. McCollum, head of the Far East desk of
the Office of Naval Intelligence (ONI) (see Appendix A).[1]

McCollum had a unique background for formulating American tactics
and strategy against Japan. Born to Baptist missionary parents in Nagasaki in 1898, McCollum spent his youth in various Japanese cities. He
understood the Japanese culture, and spoke the language before learning
English. After the death of his father in Japan, the McCollum family returned to Alabama. At eighteen McCollum was appointed to the Naval
Academy. After graduation, the twenty-two-year-old ensign was posted to

the US embassy in Tokyo as a naval attaché and took a refresher course in Japanese there. McCollum was no stuffed shirt. He enjoyed parties and the favorite drink of Japan's naval community—Johnny Walker Black Label Scotch. He was never at a loss for words. After telling a long story, he'd pause with his favorite phrases, "In other words," then go into an even longer version.

In 1923, as the fads of the Roaring Twenties swept the world, members of the Japanese imperial household were anxious to learn the Charleston. McCollum knew the latest dance routines, so the embassy assigned him to instruct Crown Prince Hirohito, the future Emperor, in slapping his knees to those jazz-age rhythms. Later that year, McCollum helped coordinate the US Navy relief operations following the great Tokyo earthquake. Though the American assistance was well intentioned, McCollum learned that the proud, self-sufficient Japanese resented the *ijin* (foreign) relief operations. Nearly twenty years later, McCollum took it upon himself to multiply this resentment a hundredfold by pushing for American interference in Japan's brutal policies of domination in the Pacific.[2]

Lieutenant Commander McCollum's five-page memorandum of October 1940 (hereafter referred to as the eight-action memo) put forward a startling plan—a plan intended to engineer a situation that would mobilize a reluctant America into joining Britain's struggle against the German armed forces then overrunning Europe. Its eight actions called for virtually inciting a Japanese attack on American ground, air, and naval forces in Hawaii, as well as on British and Dutch colonial outposts in the Pacific region.

Opinion polls in the summer of 1940 indicated that a majority of Americans did not want the country involved in Europe's wars. Yet FDR's military and State Department leaders agreed that a victorious Nazi Germany would threaten the national security of the United States. They felt that Americans needed a call to action.

McCollum would be an essential part of this plan. His code name was F-2.[3] He oversaw the routing of communications intelligence to FDR from early 1940 to December 7, 1941, and provided the President with intelligence reports on Japanese military and diplomatic strategy. Every intercepted and decoded Japanese military and diplomatic report destined for the White House went through the Far East Asia section of ONI, which he oversaw. The section served as a clearinghouse for all categories of intelligence reports, not only on Japan but on all the other nations of eastern Asia.

Each report prepared by McCollum for the President was based on radio intercepts gathered and decoded by a worldwide network of American military cryptographers and radio intercept operators. McCollum's office was an element of Station US, a secret American cryptographic center located at the main naval headquarters at 18th Street and Constitution Avenue N.W., about four blocks from the White House.

Few people in America's government or military knew as much about Japan's activities and intentions as Lieutenant Commander Arthur H. McCollum. He felt that war with Japan was inevitable and that the United States should provoke it at a time which suited US interests. In his October 1940 memorandum McCollum advocated eight actions that he predicted would lead to a Japanese attack on the United States:

A. Make an arrangement with Britain for the use of British bases in the Pacific, particularly Singapore.

B. Make an arrangement with Holland for the use of base facilities and acquisition of supplies in the Dutch East Indies [now Indonesia].

C. Give all possible aid to the Chinese government of Chiang Kai-shek.

D. Send a division of long-range heavy cruisers to the Orient, Philippines, or Singapore.

E. Send two divisions of submarines to the Orient.

F. Keep the main strength of the US Fleet, now in the Pacific, in the vicinity of the Hawaiian Islands.

G. Insist that the Dutch refuse to grant Japanese demands for undue economic concessions, particularly oil.

H. Completely embargo all trade with Japan, in collaboration with a similar embargo imposed by the British Empire.[4]

McCollum's eight-action memo was dated October 7, 1940, and was addressed and forwarded to two of Roosevelt's most trusted military advisors: Navy captains Walter S. Anderson and Dudley W. Knox. Anderson was the Director of the Office of Naval Intelligence and had direct White House access to FDR. Knox was a naval strategist and chief of the ONI library. He served as mentor to Admiral Ernest J. King, another of the President's military advisors in 1940–41 and commander of the Navy's Atlantic Squadron (later the Atlantic Fleet). Knox agreed with McCollum's eight actions and immediately forwarded the memorandum to Anderson with this restrained comment: "I concur in your courses of action. We must be ready on both sides and probably strong enough to care for both."[5] He recognized Britain's precarious military position: "It is unquestionably to our general interest that Britain be not licked. Just now she has a stalemate and probably can't do better." Knox did not discuss maneuvering Japan into committing an overt act of war, though he cautioned: "We should not precipitate anything in the Orient."[6]

The paper trail of the McCollum memo ends with the Knox endorsement. Although the proposal was addressed to Anderson, no specific record has been found by the author indicating whether he or Roosevelt actually ever saw it.[7] However, a series of secret presidential routing logs plus collateral intelligence information in Navy files offer conclusive evidence that they did see it.[8] Beginning the very next day, with FDR's involvement, McCollum's proposals were systematically put into effect.

Throughout 1941, it seems, provoking Japan into an overt act of war was the principal policy that guided FDR's actions toward Japan. Army and Navy directives containing the "overt act" phrase were sent to Pacific commanders. Roosevelt's cabinet members, most notably Secretary of War Henry Stimson, are on record favoring the policy, according to Stimson's diary.[9] Stimson's diary entries of 1941 place him with nine other Americans who knew or were associated with this policy of provocation during 1941.[10]

Roosevelt's "fingerprints" can be found on each of McCollum's proposals. One of the most shocking was Action D, the deliberate deployment of American warships within or adjacent to the territorial waters of Japan.[11] During secret White House meetings, Roosevelt personally took charge of Action D. He called the provocations "pop-up" cruises: "I just want them to keep popping up here and there and keep the Japs guessing. I don't mind losing one or two cruisers, but do not take a chance on losing five or six."[12] Admiral Husband Kimmel, the Pacific Fleet commander, objected to the pop-up cruises, saying: "It is ill-advised and will result in war if we make this move."[13]

One of the catalysts for Action D may have been British Prime Minister

Winston Churchill. On October 4, 1940, he requested that a squadron of US cruisers be sent to Singapore. McCollum included the request as a suggestion in his eight-action memo. As it turned out, however, no cruisers were sent to Singapore.[14]

From March through July 1941, White House records show that FDR ignored international law and dispatched naval task groups into Japanese waters on three such pop-up cruises.[15] One of the most provocative was a sortie into the Bungo Strait southeast of Honshu, the principal access to Japan's Inland Sea.[16] The strait separates the home islands of Kyushu and Shikoku, and was a favored operational area for the warships of the Imperial Japanese Navy in 1941.

Japan's naval ministry registered a protest with Ambassador Joseph Grew in Tokyo: "On the night of July 31, 1941, Japanese fleet units at anchor in Sukumo Bay (in the Bungo Strait, off the island of Shikoku) picked up the sound of propellers approaching Bungo Channel from the eastward. Duty destroyers of the Japanese navy investigated and sighted two darkened cruisers that disappeared in a southerly direction behind a smoke screen when they were challenged." The protest concluded: "Japanese naval officers believe the vessels were United States cruisers."[17]

Action D was very risky and could have resulted in a loss of American lives approaching that of Pearl Harbor. In the end, however, no shots were fired during the cruises. It would take not just one, but all eight of McCollum's proposals to accomplish that.

Two major decisions involving Japan and the Far East took place on October 8, 1940—the day after McCollum wrote his memo. First, the State Department told Americans to evacuate Far East countries as quickly as possible.[18] Then President Roosevelt brought about Action F—keep the United States Fleet based in Hawaiian waters—during an extended Oval Office luncheon with the fleet's commander, Admiral James O. Richardson, and former Chief of Naval Operations Admiral William D. Leahy, a favored presidential confidant.[19] When Richardson heard the proposal, he exploded: "Mr. President, senior officers of the Navy do not have the trust and confidence in the civilian leadership of this country that is essential for the successful prosecution of a war in the Pacific."[20] Richardson did not approve of Roosevelt's plan to place the fleet in harm's way. He strongly disagreed with two of FDR's lunchtime points: 1. FDR's willingness to sacrifice a ship of the Navy in order to provoke what he called a Japanese "mistake," and 2. Richardson quoted the President as saying: "Sooner or later the Japanese would commit an overt act against the United States and the nation would be willing to enter the war."[21]

After Richardson and Leahy left the Oval Office luncheon, dishes were cleared and reporters were ushered in for a 4:00 P.M. press conference. The ever-affable FDR used humor to lead reporters astray:

> Q: Can you tell us anything, Mr. President, about your conference this afternoon with Admiral Richardson and Admiral Leahy?
>
> THE PRESIDENT: Oh, we were just studying maps.
>
> Q: Did the conference touch upon frontiers in the Far East?
>
> THE PRESIDENT: We studied maps.
>
> Q: Pacific maps?
>
> THE PRESIDENT: We studied maps and are learning geography.
>
> Q: Were they mostly in the Eastern Hemisphere?
>
> THE PRESIDENT: What?
>
> Q: We thought mostly maps of the Eastern Hemisphere.
>
> THE PRESIDENT: All three hemispheres.
>
> Q: O.K. *(Laughter)*[22]

For Richardson, the safety of his men and warships was paramount and the policy was no laughing matter. Richardson stood up to Roosevelt. Doing so ended his naval career. On October 26, 1940, a White House leak to the Washington-based *Kiplinger Newsletter* predicted that Richardson would be removed as commander-in-chief.[23]

The admiral was relieved of his command on February 1, 1941, during a major restructuring of the Navy. The sea command held by Richardson—Commander in Chief, United States Fleet (CINCUS)—was modified. In his restructuring, Roosevelt approved a two-ocean Navy and created the Atlantic Fleet and the Pacific Fleet. Skipping over more senior naval officers the President picked Rear Admiral Husband Kimmel to head the Pacific Fleet and promoted him to four-star rank. The job had been offered to Rear Admiral Chester Nimitz in the fall of 1940, but Nimitz "begged off" because he lacked seniority.[24]

Roosevelt had carefully selected and placed naval officers in key fleet-command positions who would not obstruct his provocation policies. One of them was Admiral Harold Stark, his chief of naval operations since August 1939, an all too faithful servant of the President. Outgoing Admiral Richardson criticized Stark as "professionally negligent" for kowtowing to FDR and agreeing to place the fleet in jeopardy. He said Stark had been derelict and had suffered a major professional lapse due to "taking orders from above." In Richardson's opinion, Stark could have protested the orders to keep the fleet at Pearl Harbor or at least questioned the policy in proper but forceful fashion. After the success of the December 7 attack, Richardson claimed FDR turned his back on Stark: "The President said that he did not give a damn what happened to Stark so long as he was gotten out of Washington as soon as practical."[25]

There is no evidence that Admiral Kimmel knew of the action plans advocated by McCollum, because Admiral Richardson never told him of them. "The Roosevelt strategy of maneuvering the Japanese into striking the first blow at America was unknown to us," Kimmel wrote in his book, *Admiral Kimmel's Story*, published in 1954. His first suspicions that someone in high office in Washington had consciously pursued a policy that led straight to Pearl Harbor "did not occur to him until after December 7, 1941." Kimmel said he accepted the command of the Pacific Fleet "in the firm belief that the Navy Department would supply me promptly with all pertinent information available and particularly with all information that indicated an attack on the fleet at Pearl Harbor."[26]

Not until Japan surrendered in 1945 did Richardson break his four-year vow of silence and turn on Stark. He said he shared Kimmel's belief and he denounced Stark's failure in harsh terms: "I consider 'Betty' Stark, in failing to ensure that Kimmel was furnished all the information available from the breaking of Japanese dispatches, to have been to a marked degree professionally negligent in carrying out his duties as Chief of Naval Operations."[27] Richardson continued: "This offense compounded, since in writing Stark had assured the Commander-in-Chief of the United States Fleet twice that the Commander-in-Chief was being kept advised on all matters within his own knowledge." Richardson cited Stark's promise: "You may rest assured that just as soon as I get anything of definite interest, I shall fire it along."[28]

Kimmel received his promotion to admiral and was designated CINC-PAC (Commander in Chief, Pacific Fleet). Then, depending upon their missions, forces were either assigned to the Atlantic Fleet, whose commander was Admiral Ernest J. King as CINCLANT, to the Pacific Fleet with Kimmel as CINCPAC, or to the small Asiatic Fleet, commanded by Admiral Thomas Hart in Manila as CINCAF.

Richardson's removal on February 1, 1941, strengthened the position of McCollum. Only five months earlier, in mid-September 1940, Germany and her Axis partner, Italy, had signed a mutual-assistance alliance with Japan. The Tripartite Pact committed the three partners to assist each other in the event of an attack on any one of them. McCollum saw the alliance as a golden opportunity. If Japan could be provoked into committing an overt act of war against the United States, then the Pact's mutual assistance provisions would kick in. It was a back-door approach: Germany and Italy would come to Japan's aid and thus directly involve the United States in the European war.[29]

McCollum predicted a domino effect if Germany overwhelmed Britain. He was certain that Canada and the British territories in Central and South America and in the Caribbean would succumb to some degree of Nazi control. The strategic danger to the United States was from Germany, not Japan. In his eight-action memorandum, McCollum cited these six military factors in promoting his proposals:

1. All of continental Europe was under the military control of the German-Italian Axis.
2. Only the British Empire actively opposed the growing world dominance of the Axis powers.
3. Axis propaganda successfully promoted American indifference to the European war.
4. United States security in the Western Hemisphere was threatened by the Axis fomenting revolution in Central and South American countries.
5. Upon the defeat of England, the United States could expect an immediate attack from Germany.
6. Warships of the Royal Navy would fall under the control of the Axis when the British were defeated.[30]

His dire predictions were undoubtedly right. The number one problem for the United States, according to McCollum, was mobilizing public support for a declaration of war against the Axis powers. He saw little chance that Congress would send American troops to Europe. Over the objections of the majority of the populace, who still felt that European alarmists were creating much ado about nothing, he called for the Administration to create what he called "more ado": "It is not believed," wrote McCollum, "that in the present state of political opinion the United States government is capable of declaring war against Japan without more ado."[31]

His solution to the political stalemate: use the eight proposed actions to provoke Japan into committing an overt act of war against the United States, thus triggering military responses from the two other signers of the Tripartite Pact. An allusion to McCollum's eight actions was recorded by Assistant Secretary of State Breckenridge Long. He wrote that on October 7, 1940, he learned of a series of steps involving the US Navy and that one included concentrating the fleet at Honolulu to be ready for any eventuality. "It looks to me as if little by little we will face a situation which will bring us into conflict with Japan," Long wrote in his diary.[32]

A link to some of McCollum's provocations surfaced earlier in 1940 but did not produce a written directive. McCollum's proposal, triggered by the Tripartite Pact, is the only verifiable evidence of the American policy. The links started in May 1940, when FDR met with Secretary of State Cordell Hull and Secretary of the Navy Frank Knox and discussed permanently basing the United States Fleet in Hawaii. Their suggestion raised the immediate ire of Richardson, who began a five-month argument to return the fleet to the West Coast.[33] He lost the battle on October 8, a day after McCollum wrote his memorandum.

Earlier in 1940, an influential citizens' group urged withholding war materials from Japan as punishment for what they perceived as her aggression in China. But their embargo advocacy called for stopping the Japan-China conflict—not enticing an overt act of war.[34]

———

Arthur McCollum continued his close ties to Japan. In 1928, the Navy sent him back to Tokyo, this time as a language instructor. The thirty-year-old McCollum taught a Japanese language class that included three other officers of about the same age. All four were destined to provide FDR with secret intelligence on Japanese war preparations during the 1940–41 prelude to Pearl Harbor. They were also to become lifelong friends.[35]

Eventually these four men became leading naval intelligence officers in World War II: Joseph J. Rochefort, cofounder of the Navy's communication intelligence section; Edwin Layton, the intelligence officer for the Pacific Fleet, 1940–45; Lieutenant Commander Ethelbert Watts, as assistant to McCollum in 1940–41; and McCollum himself, head of the Far East desk of the Office of Naval Intelligence. Every pre–Pearl Harbor intercept of Japanese radio communications would pass through their hands. Rochefort became commander of Station HYPO, the combat intelligence center for the Pacific Fleet, one of America's most important cryptographic centers, at the Pearl Harbor Naval Yard. (HYPO, a part of the Navy's phonetic alphabet, stood for the letter H—Hawaii.) McCollum and Watts supervised the communications intelligence pipeline to Roosevelt. Layton directed information to the Pacific Fleet commanders: Richardson in 1940, Kimmel in 1941, and Nimitz in 1942–45.

Naval intelligence established a secret delivery system for Japanese military and diplomatic intelligence for Roosevelt in the winter of 1940. McCollum was the distribution officer on 151 routing slips found by the author in the National Archives. These Navy routing slips provide a trail to a massive collection of Army and Navy documents that resulted from monitoring Japanese communications and that were available to Roosevelt and key members of his Administration between February 1940 and December 7, 1941. Sometimes when he had a hot item McCollum personally delivered the report to FDR;[36] otherwise the President's naval aide made the delivery. This twenty-two-month monitoring program allowed the American government to anticipate and then study Japan's reactions to the provocations advocated by McCollum.

McCollum dispatched his first intelligence reports to the White House on February 23, 1940. There were two, both in a diplomatic code. McCollum marked both: "Original to Aide to President" and sent them to FDR. At the time, the President and seven members of his staff, including naval aide Captain Daniel J. Callaghan, had reached the midpoint of an eighteen-day fishing cruise aboard the cruiser USS *Tuscaloosa* in Pacific waters off the west coast of Panama. Naval seaplanes landed alongside the warship and delivered the documents to Callaghan.

In the first message, Roosevelt learned that Japan was applying diplomatic pressure to obtain oil export rights in Portuguese Timor, a small island east of the Dutch East Indies. The other dealt with Japanese Army plans to send "advisors" to Bolivia, which had vast resources of tin needed by Japan's military-industrial complex. McCollum noted that both reports were based on "highly reliable information," a standard oblique reference to intercepted communications.

Extraordinary secrecy surrounded the delivery system. The Japanese intercepts destined for FDR were placed in special folders. Captain Callaghan as naval aide was responsible for the safety of the documents. Roosevelt read the original copy but did not retain any of the intercepts. Each original was eventually returned to the folder and stored in McCollum's safe at Station US in Washington. There they remained, available for White House review. Shortly after December 7, when Congressional critics began to question the Administration's failure to prevent the Hawaii attack, all records involving the Japanese radio intercept program—including the White House route logs and their secret contents—were locked away in vaults controlled by Navy communications officials.[37]

During the spring and summer of 1940 the diplomatic intercepts provided valuable insights into Japanese foreign policy. Through the intercepts, FDR could follow Japan's continued pressure on Portugal to supply her Empire with raw materials from Timor, its colony in the East Indies. After Nazi armies conquered France in May 1940, Japan expanded her quest for raw materials and pushed for access to the French colony of Indochina, today's Vietnam.

That August, Hitler's Luftwaffe began all-out bombing of England, targeting airfields, aircraft factories, and radar stations. A massive attack by 2500 planes of the Luftwaffe hit London on *Adler Tag* (Eagle Day), August 16. The next day the Führer declared a total blockade of the British Isles. By August 31, Germany claimed victory in the Battle of Britain and Hitler began to assemble barges and ships for Operation Sea Lion, the invasion of Britain, which would never take place.

Roosevelt's third-term nomination heartened internationalist-minded Democrats at the party's convention in Chicago. He was forced to campaign against a Republican antiwar platform led by its nominee, Wendell Willkie. A Gallup Poll taken in early September showed that 88 percent of Americans agreed with the views of an isolationist bloc, led by aviation hero Charles Lindbergh and industrialist Henry Ford, that advocated staying away from Europe's wars. Yet Roosevelt outmaneuvered the isolationists and persuaded Congress to pass (by one vote) the Draft Act, then sent fifty World War I destroyers to England as part of what would become the Lend-Lease program of aid to the allied powers, including the Soviet Union. During the campaign, he promised American mothers and fathers: "Your boys are not going to be sent into any foreign wars." [38] But according to FDR biographer Robert Sherwood, the President assured members of his staff during a campaign swing through New England, "Of course, we'll fight if we are attacked. If somebody attacks us, then it isn't a foreign war, is it?" McCollum's eight-action memo would soon make the President's words a reality. [39]

McCollum's concept for his memo's Action F—keeping the fleet in Hawaiian waters—had its beginning in April 1940, when major portions of the US fleet moved from their West Coast bases and joined warships of the Hawaiian Detachment (later named the Pacific Fleet) for an annual training exercise. Once the exercise was completed, Admiral Richardson planned to send the fleet (less the Hawaiian Detachment) back to the West Coast. [40]

The fleet never returned. Washington slowly put the brakes on Richardson's plan and issued specious explanations for keeping the fleet in Hawaii. Undersecretary of State Sumner Welles answered Richardson's objections by predicting a "diplomatic disaster" [41] if the fleet returned to the Pacific Coast. In late April, Welles' rationale was touched on in a message sent to Richardson by Admiral Stark, who offered his own version of the potential "diplomatic disaster." He told Richardson the fleet might receive instructions to remain in Hawaiian waters "in view of the possibility of Italy becoming an active belligerent and maybe you won't." [42]

There was no adequate explanation for connecting Italian threats to the United States and basing the fleet in Hawaii. The "might" and "maybe" in the dispatches made no sense to Richardson. He requested a meeting directly with Roosevelt. The admiral disagreed with what he sensed was the "Europe First" priority in the White House.[43]

As commander of America's major sea command, Richardson's first duty was to carry out the orders of Roosevelt and his military chiefs. He reluctantly obeyed the orders but stated his objections for the record. He would not sacrifice his ships and men to what he saw as a flawed policy. Richardson listed five objections to basing the fleet in Hawaii:

1. Lack of fundamental training facilities.
2. Lack of large-scale ammunition and fuel supplies.
3. Lack of support craft such as tugs and repair ships.
4. Morale problems of men kept away from their families.
5. Lack of overhaul facilities such as dry docking and machine shops.[44]

He objected in vain. Roosevelt wanted the fleet kept in Hawaiian waters. All Admiral Richardson received from his protests were more indecisive orders from the administration. A dispatch of May 4 is an example:

IT LOOKS PROBABLE BUT NOT FINAL THAT THE FLEET WILL REMAIN IN HAWAIIAN WATERS FOR A SHORT TIME AFTER MAY 9TH.[45]

He was particularly displeased on May 7, 1940, when he was ordered to issue a press release saying that he had asked to keep the fleet in Hawaii. "There was no logical reason for me to make such a request," Richardson wrote. "It made a perfect nitwit out of me."[46]

The rationale behind the directives became even less convincing on May 15, when the warships were ordered to "stay in Hawaiian waters for some time." Richardson thought he had a chance to dissuade Roosevelt and asked for a meeting in the White House. The two met alone for lunch on July 8, 1940. The meeting was a disappointment for Richardson. "I came away with the impression that, despite his spoken word, the President was fully determined to put the United States into the war if Great Britain could hold out until he was reelected." But the admiral gave no details of the White House conversation except to say that FDR had promised not to send the fleet to the Far East under "any foreseeable conditions."[47]

In the "illogical basing of the fleet at Hawaii," Admiral Richardson saw a disaster in the making. He was responsible for 69,000 sailors under his

Pacific command, and he grew increasingly alarmed at using them and his 217 ships in what he saw as a provocative scheme. He asked, "Are we here as a stepping-off place for belligerent activity?"[48] Exasperated, he complained, "The President and Mr. Hull [Secretary of State Cordell Hull] never seem to take it into consideration that Japan is led by military men, who evaluate military moves, largely on a military basis."[49] Richardson missed the point. White House strategy was based precisely on the premise that Japan's militant right wing would push for an act of force against the United States. Though he got nowhere with Roosevelt, Richardson bided his time.

During midsummer of 1940, with his third-term presidential campaign in mind, Roosevelt issued a licensing plan—McCollum's proposals had not yet been adopted—that appeared to curtail Japanese access to petroleum products and scrap iron in America. The San Francisco *Call-Bulletin* photographed stevedores in July and October 1940 at San Francisco docks, loading the Japanese vessels *Tatsukawa Maru* and *Bordeau Maru* with scrap iron, an apparent violation of FDR's embargo. The ships loaded up with tons of scrap iron, slipped out through the Golden Gate, and headed for Japan.

The oil-licensing system was also a sham in that it did not apply to the refineries on America's West Coast. The White House essentially allowed Japan to obtain petroleum supplies sufficient to maintain its ability to make war. Japan's consul-general in San Francisco assured his government that the Roosevelt administration was not enforcing the embargo; oil and gasoline supplies were available. "All our export permits have been granted. These American agencies from whom the oil is bought go ahead and make suitable arrangements with the government authorities at Washington."[50]

The consul-general wrote that he had purchased "special blend crude oil" and easily evaded Roosevelt's embargo. He then detailed Japanese purchases of over 44,000 tons (321,000 barrels) from the Associated Oil Company. In concluding his secret dispatch, the consul-general told Japan's military leaders: "American oil dealers in the San Francisco area selling to Mitsui and Mitsubishi, of which the principal one is the Associated Oil Company, feel that there will be no difficulty about continuing the shipment of ordinary gasoline to Japan."[51]

The consul-general's "no difficulty" dispatch was routed to FDR on September 16, 1940. But no one in the White House enforced the petroleum embargo. Instead, export of oil to Japan received the green light. Japanese oil and gasoline tankers, with the tacit approval of the Administration, rushed back and forth across the Pacific loading up at oil refineries in Pacific Coast ports.[52] Naval radio direction finders, on orders from Washington, tracked the tankers to the Japanese naval oil depot at Tokuyama, located at the southern tip of Honshu on the Suo Nada, an arm of the Inland Sea.[53]

Between July 1940 and April 1941, during a period when American petroleum supplies were supposedly under embargo, nearly 9,200,000 barrels of gasoline were licensed for export to Japan. Approval for 2,000,000 additional barrels was pending late in April 1941. From October 1940 to December 1941, the Japanese tankers were under constant electronic surveillance by the Navy. Washington closely followed the tankers.

Transportation of the petroleum to Japan was monitored at Station SAIL, control center for the Navy's West Coast Communications Intelligence Network (WCCI) near Seattle (SAIL being the Navy phonetic for the letter S—Seattle). Commercial radio facilities of Mackay Radio & Telegraph, Pan American Airways, RCA Communications, and Globe Wireless provided information used in the surveillance. This vast monitoring network extended along the entire West Coast from Imperial Beach, California, to Dutch Harbor, Alaska.[54]

The surveillance yielded important intelligence for the White House by tracing the movement of oil supplies, watching for signs of Japan withdrawing merchant vessels from the world's oceans, and identifying the radio transmitter characteristics of each vessel. Code breakers at SAIL and the West Coast network produced Tracking Chart 1 based on radio-direction-finding reports that traced the Pacific Ocean routes taken by eight of Japan's tankers from October 1 to December 6, 1940. From the tracking chart, US Navy officials learned that most of the petroleum was obtained from the Associated Oil Company refinery at Port Costa, California, and transported directly to Tokuyama—the principal oil storage facility for warships. President Roosevelt obtained his confirmation that Japan was evading his embargo from the consul-general's "no difficulty" intercept.

Naval intercept operators easily followed the tankers. During their round-trip voyages, they diligently used their radio transmitters and provided their positions to the Navy's radio direction finders. Navy intelligence in San Francisco identified all the tankers by their Japanese radio call signs.[55] Two of the tankers, the *Kyokuto Maru* and the HIMJS *Shiriya*, were destined to be included in the Pearl Harbor strike force. Both vessels sailed into San Francisco Bay throughout 1940 and 1941, picked up their cargoes of American oil, and returned to fill the Tokuyama storage facility. A year later, the *Kyokuto Maru*'s radio signal was instantly identified when she became the flagship of the eight-vessel tanker train that refueled the warships of the Pearl Harbor force. *Maru* derives from the Japanese word *maru*, meaning "circle." Merchant ships, but not warships, have the word added to their name for good luck as they encounter the perils of the high seas in the belief that *Marus* complete the voyage to the distant port and return to a joyous homecoming, thus completing the circle. In 1940 and 1941, the *Kyokuto Maru* would make many circles between ports in America and Japan.[56]

During the last days of September and first week of October 1940, a team of Army and Navy cryptographers solved the two principal Japanese government code systems: Purple, the major diplomatic code, and portions of the *Kaigun Ango*, a series of twenty-nine separate Japanese naval operational codes used for radio contact with warships, merchant vessels, naval bases, and personnel in overseas posts, such as naval attachés. Much has been made of the Purple Code and far too little of the navy codes. Historians have made misleading references to the Purple Code by confusing its use and purpose. It was used solely by the Japanese Foreign Ministry for encoding diplomatic messages dispatched by radio between Tokyo and selected overseas embassies and consulates. In the United States, Japan issued the Purple system to its Washington embassy and to its consulate in Manila, but not to the Honolulu consulate. The Purple Code was never used by the Japanese Navy.[57]

Leading historical publications in the United States have confused readers by publishing erroneous details on Purple. The truth of Pearl Harbor is found in the naval codes, not in the diplomatic codes. As recently as December 1997, *Naval History*, a magazine published by the US Naval Institute, printed an article which claimed that the American naval victory at Midway resulted from breaking the Japanese Purple cipher.[58] In fact, however, the Midway victory came about because US Navy cryptographers had broken Japan's Code Book D, one of the twenty-nine code systems in the *Kaigun Ango*. Throughout 1941 and most of 1942, United States naval cryptographers and intercept operators referred to Code Book D as the 5-Num code, because a group of five numbers represented a Japanese word or phrase. Japan's navy assigned thousands of different five-number combinations to represent their language for radio transmission purposes. On November 19, 1941, the five-number group for the carrier *Akagi*, the flagship of Japan's Hawaii force, was 28494. It was up to US Navy code breakers to solve the meaning of 28494 (and subsequent revisions). And they did, starting in October 1940.[59]

Cryptographers have their own jargon. To them, "recovered value" or "solution" means that they had solved and knew the meaning of 28494. In addition to the 5-Num code, American cryptographers solved and could recover values from three other code systems of the *Kaigun Ango:* Merchant Marine Code (Code Book S); radio call signs (*Yobidashi Fugo*) issued to every category of Japanese warships, units, individual officers, and vessels of the Japanese Merchant Marine, known as *Marus;* and Japan's naval movement code in which warships, *Marus,* and individuals reported their arrivals, departures, and destinations. These four naval systems were used by Japan's navy for radio messages in the pre–Pearl Harbor period and throughout the Pacific War. The US success in solving the diplomatic and naval code systems was a closely guarded American secret. President Roosevelt regularly received copies of Japanese messages decoded and translated from both the Purple Code and the *Kaigun Ango*.

Controversy surrounds the timing of the successful decryption of the four code systems of the *Kaigun Ango* by American code breakers. Testimony given to various Pearl Harbor investigations suggests that the navy codes were not solved until Spring 1942. The author's research proves otherwise. Their solution emerged in the early fall of 1940, at about the same time Arthur McCollum's memorandum reached the Oval Office.

Rear Admiral Royal Ingersoll, Assistant Chief of Naval Operations, revealed America's ability to detect and predict Japan's naval war strategy and tactical operations to the US Navy's two Pacific commanders, Admirals James Richardson and Thomas Hart, in a letter dated October 4, 1940. Ingersoll was specific: The Navy began tracking the movement and location of Japanese warships in October 1940. "Every major movement of the Orange (America's code name for Japan) Fleet has been predicted, and a continuous flow of information concerning Orange diplomatic activities has been made available."[60] He said that Navy cryptographers had solved the Japanese naval merchant ship code. "The system itself is 99 percent readable," reported Ingersoll.[61]

Japan's main naval radio system, the "Operations Code" (the 5-Num code) remained a problem for cryptographers. A full solution was expected by April 1941. "Recovery was well defined," wrote Ingersoll, "but demanded laborious work sometimes requiring from only an hour to as many as several days to decode each message."[62] To speed up decryption time, the Navy constructed a special decoding machine. Mystery still surrounds the workings of the machine—as is typical of nearly sixty years of Navy secrecy concerning all aspects of the 5-Num code. The machine has not been turned over to the National Archives. Neither have the original Japanese naval intercepts in the 5-Num code that were obtained by US Navy cryptographers. The author contends that this extraordinary secrecy, which still remains in effect in 1999, is intended to distance the American government and particularly FDR from foreknowledge of Japanese attack plans.

But Ingersoll's 1940 letter sheds a light on the 5-Num system that was never intended by the pre–Pearl Harbor naval censors. Recovery was effected before April. By the end of January 1941, President Roosevelt was on the receiving list of the *Kaigun Ango*, according to the White House route logs prepared by Arthur McCollum.

On January 30, Station CAST, the navy's Philippine cryptographic center on Corregidor Island in Manila Bay, placed the first Japanese military intelligence in FDR's hands. It informed Roosevelt of a large build-up of Japanese warships in the South China Sea off French Indochina. It was an ominous beginning.

CHAPTER 3

THE WHITE HOUSE DECIDES

———

ARTHUR MCCOLLUM WAS NOT CONVINCED THAT THE PUBLIC AND American industry could be mobilized in sufficient time to fight off the Axis powers. His memorandum of October 7, 1940, circulated among Navy and White House officials while a torrent of bad news poured in from the European front. England was nearly on its knees, threatened with invasion and beginning to feel the impact of the German U-boat assault on its shipping lifeline. Hitler had instituted the early stages of what would later be called the Holocaust.

At home, Wendell Willkie, campaigning for the presidency, stumped across America and closed to within a few percentage points of Roosevelt's lead.[1] In early September the President took four steps to move the country toward war:

1. He sent America's first peacetime Draft Act to Congress. The act called for conscripting men into military service and sought the authority to seize industrial plants for defense production.

2. He called up National Guard units to active duty throughout the country.

3. He traded fifty old US Navy destroyers to England in exchange for the lease of bases in Bermuda, the Bahamas, Jamaica, St. Lucia, Trinidad, and British Guiana.

4. He signed $5 billion in legislation, creating a two-ocean Navy that would eventually include 100 aircraft carriers.[2]

Roosevelt haters had a political field day. A fistfight broke out in the House of Representatives when Representative Beverly Vincent (D., KY) tried to trip Representative Martin L. Sweeney (D., OH) in the House aisle. Sweeney had just delivered an anti-FDR speech. The Associated Press reported it as hand-to-hand combat. Each congressman took, and gave, about six blows to the face.[3]

Willkie condemned the destroyer trade as the most "arbitrary and dictatorial action ever taken by a president in the history of the United States."[4] Other Republicans agreed: "The destroyer trade is an "outright declaration of war," said Senator Gerald Nye (R., ND). "It's a belligerent act and will weaken our own defenses. If Britain should be defeated, why should we supply her with destroyers to surrender to Germany?" Republicans continued to snap at FDR's heels during a defense-plant inspection trip. "A cheap publicity stunt to make political capital out of national defense," charged Senator Styles Bridges (R., NH). Major newspapers joined in the fray. "An Act of War," editorialized the *St. Louis Post-Dispatch*. Carl Ackerman, dean of the Columbia University School of Journalism, complained to Willkie: "If the act becomes law the President may classify all education institutions as defense facilities, and our schools will be regimented as they are in Germany, Italy, and Russia."[5]

Throughout the fall of 1940, Roosevelt worked to unite Americans in their country's defense. He rallied public support while traveling by train on "inspection trips" of defense plants throughout the eastern states. Many Americans listening to the President approved of his policies and agreed with the sentiments of his "no foreign war" promise. An audience in Great Smoky Mountain National Park in Tennessee cheered and applauded when FDR asked for American preparedness against "the greatest attack that has ever been launched against freedom of the individual. We must prepare beforehand, not afterward."[6]

The president called for constructing new military bases for the defense of our shores. "Men and women must be taught to create the supplies that we need. Liberty through democracy can, I believe, be preserved in future years if we want to preserve it." Then FDR took aim at his detractors in America: "We must counter the agents of dictators within our country."[7]

Perhaps Roosevelt's most famous call for preparedness came when he proposed lending military supplies and goods to England. This was FDR using his finest communications skills, in a brilliant analogy: when your neighbor's house is on fire, you lend him your garden hose. He made the analogy during a press conference in mid-December when he claimed he had no news for the correspondents, then revealed his ideas and plans for a Lend-Lease program to help the nations fighting the Axis powers. "Suppose my neighbor's home catches fire, and I have got a length of garden hose four or five hundred feet away: but, my Heaven, if he can take my garden hose and connect it up with his hydrant, I may help him put out his fire. Now, what do I do? I don't say to him before that operation, 'Neighbor, my garden hose cost me $15; you have got to pay me $15 for it.' What is the transaction that goes on? I don't want the $15—I want my garden hose back after the fire is over."[8] Though there was opposition from the isolationist bloc, Congress passed the Lend-Lease Act. Military aid went directly to England and later to Russia when Germany invaded that country. But isolationists like Styles Bridges continued to brand the President's call for action as "dragging America to war."[9]

Audio recordings from the Oval Office in the fall of 1940 indicate Roosevelt's concern over the isolationists painting him as a "dictator leading us to war." The recording was done on an RCA photo-film machine secreted in the basement of the West Wing of the White House directly below the Oval Office. Roosevelt planned the recording equipment installation with David Sarnoff, president of RCA, during a thirty-minute meeting in the Oval Office on June 14, 1940. It was in service from mid-August to early November.

RCA engineers hid a voice-activated microphone in a lamp on FDR's desk; wires led to an on/off switch that he controlled from his desk drawer; most of the time he forgot to turn it off. The device was installed because the President had been angered over news accounts which contained mis-quotes from Oval Office press conferences. Arthur Schlesinger, Jr., wrote that FDR's anger stemmed from a report which quoted him as saying that America's frontier was on the Rhine River, implying that Roosevelt planned war with Germany. The President never uttered the remark, ac-cording to Schlesinger's research; to protect himself from future mis-quotes during the third-term election, he installed the recorder.[10]

One recording reveals FDR's animosity toward press baron Roy Howard, who rankled the President by privately furnishing Willkie with a bitter assessment of Administration policies in the Far East. FDR learned that Howard, head of the Scripps-Howard News Alliance, had also deni-grated the Administration's foreign policy in discussions with State De-partment officials in Southeast Asia. On September 2, 1940, Howard met with Hugh G. Grant, the American consul-general in Thailand, and at-tacked the President personally. The news executive charged that FDR was "down and out physically and mentally" and was mishandling US relations with Japan. A loyal Grant wrote a report giving details of Howard's Far East travels to the State Department. Roosevelt read Grant's secret dis-patch to the members of his cabinet during a meeting on September 6. The concealed microphone recorded a furious President seeking advice on ways to handle Howard; FDR wanted to expose the publisher for acting as Willkie's mouthpiece.

One of those present, speaking with a Southern accent—perhaps Sec-retary of State Cordell Hull—cautioned the President: "No sir. I wouldn't say any more. He might do an awful lot of harm and undoubtedly he is gathering this material for Willkie. There is no chance whatsoever of stop-ping Howard. If we tip him off that we know about his actions it might op-erate to his advantage."[11]

Roosevelt believed that American political opposition to his defense plans was directed from Germany, Italy, and Japan. He scornfully de-nounced an editorial in the *New York Times*[12] which expressed doubts that the Axis powers were involved in American politics. Pounding on his desk, FDR blasted the *Times'* comments and asserted: "It's perfectly true the Axis powers will give anything in the world to have me licked on the fifth of November."[13]

Contrasting the *Times'* news reporting with its editorials, Roosevelt

27

said he was quite amused—the editorial-page writers didn't read the front-page news articles. For proof he cited a news report from Herbert L. Matthews, the *Times'* bureau chief in Rome. Matthews reported a meeting between Hitler and Mussolini held at the Brenner Pass, on the border between Austria and Italy, on October 4. "The Axis," wrote Matthews, "is out to defeat President Roosevelt not as a measure of internal policies of the United States but because of the President's foreign policy."[14] McCollum also supplied confidential evidence which confirmed that the two Axis leaders "attempted by every method within their power to foster a continuation of American indifference to the outcome of the struggle in Europe."[15]

While Roosevelt fumed over the *New York Times'* editorial policies, a Tokyo dispatch written by his "old friend" Roy Howard, brought him "more worry than anything else in the world."[16] United Press and the Scripps-Howard News Alliance distributed the publisher's story to its worldwide clients. FDR was startled to read of a Japanese spokesman calling on the United States to "demilitarize its bases at Wake, Midway, and Pearl Harbor."[17] The Oval Office's secret microphone recorded the President's anger in a telephone conversation with an unidentified caller: "God! That's the first time that any damn Jap has told us to get out of Hawaii. And that has me more worried than any other thing in the world."[18]

When the first election returns came in on November 5, they indicated a Willkie victory. FDR retreated to his Hyde Park study and told his Secret Service chief, Mike Reilly, to lock the doors and keep everyone out. But the news soon brightened. Roosevelt won a huge popular vote and his third landslide victory with 429 electoral votes to Willkie's 51.[19] He emerged from his study and told a cheering throng gathered in front of his mansion's portico: "We are facing difficult days in this country, but I think you will find me in the future just the same Franklin Roosevelt you have known a great many years."[20] His only bad news: Republicans continued to control the isolationist agenda. But a different agenda was perceived by the British government of Churchill. Admiral Stark wired Hart in Manila that the British expected the United States to be at war a few days after the reelection of Roosevelt.[21]

As McCollum's eight action proposals began to be applied, relations with Japan deteriorated. With the New Year, three of his actions were in place: Action E, the dispatch of twenty-four US Navy submarines to

Manila; Action F, retaining the US Fleet in Hawaiian waters; and Action G, the Dutch now refusing to supply Japan with oil and raw materials. Navy intelligence detected the new Japanese attitude from an intercepted diplomatic radio message sent by Foreign Minister Yosuke Matsuoka on January 30, 1941: "In view of the critical situation between the two countries we must be prepared for the worst."[22] Matsuoka directed his ambassador in Washington to change from what he called publicity and propaganda work and establish an espionage-gathering network within the United States. He wanted details on the movement of warships and on military maneuvers, and figures for aircraft production and shipbuilding throughout the United States.

The heart of the Japanese policy was an economic strategy called the Greater East Asia Co-Prosperity Sphere—a Japanese economic plan establishing a Yen (¥) monetary bloc comprising the East Asian countries. The plan diminished the economic influence of America, Britain, and the Netherlands for the sake of Japanese economic interests. Its aim was to gain access to the region's vital natural resources, resources nonexistent within Japan. To appease militant nationalist elements within the government, a bottom line was added: if and when worse came to worst Japan would go to war with the United States and her allies.

Foreign Minister Matsuoka's worse-to-worst policy revealed Japan's breaking point.[23] Arthur McCollum knew it would occur whenever the United States tightened the screws by putting his eight actions into effect. They were soon to come: the pop-up US cruises into Japanese territorial waters and the final action, H, the total embargo intended to strangle Japan's economy.

The civilians in Japan's government still wished to do everything possible to avoid war and to negotiate a diplomatic settlement with the United States. But in an effort to gain support Japan's moderates accommodated her military authorities and authorized a fallback position of general war preparations should diplomatic efforts fail to gain access to Southeast Asia resources.

This fallback position included preparation for an attack on the US Fleet and military bases in Hawaii. It was right out of McCollum's proposed Action F. Though some historians have cited talk about Japanese war planning dating to the 1920s, that was only talk. In 1940, the Japanese military bases in the Central Pacific were totally inadequate for warfare. They consisted of deep-water anchorages without any established military installations. There was no oil storage for warships, no dry docks or repair facilities. Air-war-support structures such as hangars, refueling equipment for aircraft, and landing fields were nonexistent. Military communications at these Central Pacific bases were primitive.

Japan's initial planning for the attack began in the fall of 1940, about a month after McCollum's action recommendations were sent to the White House. Naval Minister Admiral Koshiro Oikawa moved quickly. In mid-November he promoted Vice Admiral Isoroku Yamamoto to full admiral and gave him operational command of the Imperial Japanese Navy. Yamamoto was called to the red-brick Victorian building housing the Naval Ministry in downtown Tokyo. The two admirals informally discussed strategy in opening a war with England and America. They agreed that a surprise air raid on Pearl Harbor should start Japan's military offensive.[24]

By mid-January 1941, Yamamoto had secretly sketched out his Pearl Harbor strategy and appointed key staff members to work out the tactical details. Pearl Harbor would be the bottom line when worse finally came to worst.

On January 24, while Admiral Yamamoto initiated planning for the attack, Roosevelt's Secretary of the Navy, Frank Knox, warned of perils to Pearl Harbor. Knox cited the naval base's military vulnerability to air bombing attack, air torpedo-plane attack, sabotage, submarine attack, mining of the waters in Hawaii by Japan, and bombardment by gunfire from Japanese warships.[25]

Soon after Yamamoto began circulating his Pearl Harbor strategy among trusted Japanese naval officers, the general attack plan was leaked to the US embassy in Tokyo. Max W. Bishop, Third Secretary at the embassy, was standing in a teller line in the Tokyo branch of the National City Bank of New York converting some yen to American dollars. A tap on the shoulder caused Bishop to look up; he recognized the face of the Peruvian minister to Japan, Dr. Ricardo Rivera Schreiber. Motioning Bishop to a side alcove, Schreiber revealed "fantastic" information: "Japanese military forces were planning, in the event of trouble with the United States, to attempt a surprise mass attack on Pearl Harbor using all their military resources."

Bishop had confidence in Schreiber. He had met the minister on a number of occasions and had played golf with members of Peru's legation. Bishop writes that the conversation was completely confidential: "I did not think it odd that he took me to one side in the bank for a brief talk. It was the duty of all diplomatic officers to seek and obtain as much information as possible."

Cutting short his noon lunch break, Bishop hurried back to the US embassy and prepared a confidential dispatch for the State Department. Ambassador Joseph Grew approved the draft of the message. By 6:00 P.M. Tokyo Time it was encoded in an unbreakable State Department cryptographic system, taken across the street to the Japanese Telegraph office, and sent via radiotelegraph to Washington.[26]

The next morning, on January 27, Secretary of State Cordell Hull read the message:

MY PERUVIAN COLLEAGUE TOLD A MEMBER OF MY STAFF THAT HE HAD HEARD FROM MANY SOURCES INCLUDING A JAPANESE SOURCE THAT THE JAPANESE MILITARY FORCES PLANNED IN THE EVENT OF TROUBLE WITH THE UNITED STATES, TO ATTEMPT A SURPRISE ATTACK ON PEARL HARBOR USING ALL OF THEIR MILITARY FACILITIES. HE ADDED THAT ALTHOUGH THE PROJECT SEEMED FANTASTIC THE FACT THAT HE HAD HEARD IT FROM MANY SOURCES PROMPTED HIM TO PASS THE INFORMATION. GREW[27]

Hull distributed copies of the Grew cable to Army intelligence and the Office of Naval Intelligence (ONI). Arthur McCollum was directed to provide the ONI's analysis. However, he immediately faced a quandary. By his own analysis as spelled out in his action memo, an attack on Hawaii was just what was needed. As a youngster growing up in Japan, he knew of the Japanese propensity for surprise attacks. As a five-and-one-half-year-old McCollum was living in Japan in February 1904, when Japanese torpedo boats surprised the Russian Fleet at Port Arthur on the Bay of Korea. A stunned world learned of the destruction of the Russian warships, which were ambushed in a surprise attack.

McCollum remembered his history. From his viewpoint, Grew's cable proved the effectiveness of the goad strategy. But instead of alerting the Pacific Fleet that Action F—the American fleet's presence at Pearl—was luring Japan into war, McCollum discounted Grew's information as "rumor." On February 1, 1941, he sent this analysis to the newly appointed commander of the Pacific Fleet, Admiral Husband E. Kimmel: "The Division of Naval Intelligence places no credence in these rumors. Furthermore, based on known data regarding the present disposition and employment of Japanese naval and army forces, no move against Pearl Harbor appears imminent or planned for in the foreseeable future."[28]

Two days earlier, thirty Hollywood movie stars, including Lana Turner, George Raft, and Red Skelton, had been invited to a gala luncheon at the White House to help celebrate the President's birthday. They kicked off a series of fund-raising celebrations held in all forty-eight states to raise money for research on and treatment of polio—a disease that had crippled FDR for nineteen years. It was on the same day that he received his first intelligence based on Japanese naval intercepts.[29]

The President began to track the movement of Japanese ships and command officers to the coastal waters of French Indochina. Two naval units left the Kure naval base and joined other Japanese warships at Hainan Island in the Gulf of Tonkin.

By the time the birthday celebrations began in the forty-eight states that evening, Roosevelt had a clear intelligence picture of an emerging Japanese strategy involving Southeast Asia. McCollum had proposed that Southeast Asian countries controlled by Britain and the Netherlands cut off their exports of natural resources to Japan, which they had done. Now FDR would see the effectiveness of the move.

According to the cryptographer's summary, Japanese Foreign Minister Yosuke Matsuoka had orchestrated border clashes between the Southeast Asia nations of Siam (Thailand) and French Indochina. An armistice–cease fire was proposed, to take effect on January 31, 1941. Japan expected to work out the details during a conference scheduled on the deck of the light cruiser HIJMS *Natori*, in Saigon's harbor. A final peace settlement was scheduled to be signed at Tokyo later in the year.

Japanese warships, including the flattops of Carrier Division Two, were dispatched to the coastal waters off French Indochina (F.I.C.) in a show of force. Their purpose was to ensure that F.I.C., Siam, and and the countries of Southeast Asia would support the yen financial bloc and provide Japan with access to raw materials.

Meanwhile, Roosevelt was celebrating his birthday in the White House with the movie stars at the luncheon, and that evening the First Lady presided at the fund-raising galas in Washington. Afterward, Mrs. Roosevelt and a retinue of movie stars made the rounds of the major hotels and danced to such popular songs as "Frenesi," "I Hear a Rhapsody," and a British favorite that mourned the Nazi bombing of London, "A Nightingale Sang in Berkeley Square."

Just before midnight, Roosevelt concluded his part in the birthday celebration by delivering a radio address to the nation in which he thanked "every man, woman, and child" who had labored to raise funds for polio, the disease that had robbed him of the use of his leg and thigh muscles. After the microphones were turned off, FDR looked over his presents. They were an impressive lot. He received a five-foot-high, 300-pound birthday cake from the nation's labor unions, a "Happy Birthday" editorial from the *New York Times*, and a denunciation of his international policies by Adolf Hitler.

A Gallup Poll released that day measured America's attitude toward war. An overwhelming 79 percent of the nation opposed Charles Lindbergh's proposal for a negotiated peace with Hitler, but an even greater majority, 88 percent, continued to oppose United States entry into the European war.[30]

FDR's overhaul of the Navy's seagoing command structure took effect on February 1, 1941, aboard the USS *Pennsylvania* at Pearl Harbor. Four new silver stars brightened the white dress uniform of Admiral Husband E. Kimmel as he spoke into a CBS News radio microphone, reading the orders authorized by President Franklin D. Roosevelt that placed him in command of the newly created Pacific Fleet. About eight feet away and to the admiral's right stood Admiral James O. Richardson, whom Kimmel was succeeding. Outwardly Richardson bore no enmity toward the President. He realized the commander-in-chief had the right to dismiss officers who didn't agree with White House policies: "The President packed my sea bag for me." Privately, though, he was shocked and "deeply disappointed in my detachment."[31]

Although few on the *Pennsylvania* were aware of the change, a monitor of the unfolding provocation policy was now inserted into the Pacific

Fleet command structure. Roosevelt personally promoted the Director of Naval Intelligence, Captain Walter Anderson, to rear admiral and gave him command of all Pacific Fleet battleships with the title Commander Battleships. Anderson's reputation as a naval officer was less than sterling. A sixty-year-old career officer and a naval-academy graduate, his military service was nearing an end. Though he had served aboard warships from 1912 to 1933, he was not a distinguished sailor.

Admiral Richardson has written that Anderson did not have the respect and confidence of other naval officers.[32] Admiral Stark apologized for sending Anderson to the Pacific Fleet. He wrote to Kimmel: "The appointment was forced on us by the White House. Anderson is a good man to handle the battleships, but I do not commit myself one inch beyond that." He then warned, "Don't promise Anderson a promotion. He's always looking ahead for a new job."[33]

Rear Admiral Chester Nimitz, the Navy's personnel chief, gave Anderson the good news: he was slated to be the number three officer commanding the soon-to-be Pacific Fleet—first as a vice admiral with three stars, then later, in April 1941, a full admiral with four stars. A delighted Captain Anderson ordered new white uniforms for the tropical climate of Hawaii. They were adorned with gold marks on his sleeves and admiral's stars on the shoulders. Gold braid trimmed his new hat.

Then it all crashed. A week later Nimitz broke the bad news: "You're only getting two stars as rear admiral. The other stars are going to Ernie King, who will become commander of the new Atlantic Fleet." Anderson was crushed. "I was unhappy with my rank of rear admiral. All twenty previous commanders of the battleships took over the job as vice admiral, I didn't."[34] But he took the position anyway.

Privately, Anderson did not blame King for the loss of his stars. "I knew Admiral King intimately. We had been friends since 1912 when we both served on Atlantic warships." Instead, Anderson blamed Secretary of the Navy Frank Knox. In 1940, Knox took a dislike to Anderson when the latter refused to send *Chicago Daily News* reporters to North Africa as confidential ONI agents. "The proposal knocked me off balance. Oh, Mr. Secretary, we couldn't do that."[35] Knox, former publisher of the *News*, had planned to scoop the *Chicago Tribune* with eyewitness war accounts from the North Africa front.

Neither Nimitz nor Knox was America's designated admiral maker. That was President Roosevelt's prerogative. In May 1939 the President moved Anderson from the London naval attaché post and made him Director of Naval Intelligence in Washington. Anderson's reign in naval intelligence was marked by poor morale in the agency. "ONI was the haven for the ignorant and well connected," according to Marine Corps Colonel John W. Thomason, Jr., at the time head of the ONI Latin American desk.[36]

At least three times a week, Anderson met with FDR. "It was usually in the late afternoon in the President's private office."[37] Two other officials, Major General Edwin "Pa" Watson, the military aide, and Colonel John Magruder, then the Army intelligence chief, would join them. During his ONI tenure, Anderson also developed very close friendships with FBI director J. Edgar Hoover and Adolf Berle, Jr., FDR's Assistant Secretary of State. Three days before McCollum put his eight action provocations in writing, Anderson met secretly with a group of Roosevelt's staff in the Hay-Adams Hotel, across Lafayette Park from the White House. The group included Berle, Attorney General Francis Biddle, FCC Commissioner James Fly, and Lowell Mellett, a presidential political advisor.

The group, according to Berle's diary entry,[38] discussed the isolationist movement and ways to form an integral mechanism to combat the kind of propaganda spreading across the country. Their concerns echoed those enunciated by Roosevelt on the secret recordings, but, Berle wrote, the group was unable to agree on a policy. Three days later, in his proposal to Anderson, McCollum advocated uniting the country by creating "ado" with its eight provocations. Throughout 1940 and 1941, Anderson lent McCollum to Hoover for consultation and advice.[39]

The new two-star admiral left Washington in mid-January 1941 and assumed command on January 31. Anderson obviously believed in the McCollum strategy and went to Hawaii knowing of the risks inherent in increasing American pressure on a militant Japan. Yet in an oral-history interview conducted by Columbia University in March 1962, he claimed to know nothing of the Richardson-Roosevelt discussion concerning keeping the fleet in Hawaiian waters.[40]

Most of the Pacific Fleet's senior officers and the crew of the *Pennsylvania* watched the Kimmel/Richardson change-of-command ceremony on February 1, unaware of its full significance. Northeast trade winds gently cooled the deck of the big battleship and tempered the brilliant tropical sun. Resplendent in crisp white uniforms, the officers and men were gathered on the fantail's main deck under the battery of No. 4 turret. Many were destined to die in December.[41]

Richardson showed no emotion as he read out to all those assembled the order removing him from America's top naval command. He was reassigned to a relatively insignificant desk job in Washington. Six newsmen stood high atop the turret and looked down on the main deck but probably none guessed the real reason for the ceremony. Richardson had been fired because he would not agree to place the fleet at risk. He promised Admiral Stark not to rock the boat: "I shall keep my lips sealed and my eyes in the boat and put my weight on the oar to any duty assigned."[42] Before leaving Hawaii, Richardson apparently told Kimmel of a "disagreement with authorities in Washington" concerning basing the fleet at Pearl Harbor. There is no record indicating that he ever revealed the details of his confrontation in the Oval Office to Kimmel.[43]

Looking toward the stern of the *Pennsylvania*, both Richardson and Kimmel could see the newly ordained Commander Battleships of the Pacific Fleet, Rear Admiral Walter Stratton Anderson, standing at attention among a group of senior naval officers. During naval ceremonies the previous day, Anderson, the man who would preside over the devastation at Pearl, had read aloud Roosevelt's orders placing him in command of the fleet's nine battleships.[44]

The new Commander Battleships' poor reputation among the Navy's high command was recalled by Richardson and Kimmel. Just days before, Kimmel had been warned to beware of Anderson by Admiral Stark, who did not mince words. The appointment was not Stark's idea. The Anderson promotion was dictated by the White House: "It's their prerogative and believe me the White House decides these days."[45] Stark also told Kimmel that the shake-up of the Fleet was done under duress: "Our hand was forced, we wanted to run this whole schedule differently."[46] In 1939, Richardson told FDR that he had little respect or confidence in Anderson as a naval officer.[47]

Anderson was sent to Hawaii as an intelligence gatekeeper. He had powerful connections in the Navy Department and the FBI. Declining military living quarters on the Pearl Harbor base, he rented a house on Diamond Head Road located on the makai (Hawaiian for "toward the water") side of the famed Waikiki landmark.[48] From his living-room windows, Anderson could see the southern Hawaiian islands of Maui, Molokai, and Lanai. The sky-jutting cliffsides of the Diamond Head crater cut off all views of Pearl Harbor. Battleship Row and his flagship, the USS *Maryland*, were out of Anderson's sight. Kimmel's assigned residence was among his officers and men. He lived on Makalapa Hill, a naval residential area about 600 yards from Pacific Fleet headquarters. From the front lanai of his quarters he had a commanding view of the entire warship anchorage, including Battleship Row.

On December 7, Anderson's eight battleships (the ninth, the USS *Colorado*, was on the West Coast) would receive the brunt of the Japanese attack. Heavy loss of life and injuries were sustained aboard the *Arizona*, *Oklahoma*, *West Virginia*, *Nevada*, *Tennessee*, *California*, *Maryland*, and the Pacific Fleet flagship, the *Pennsylvania*.[49] Anderson was not aboard any of the battleships. He spent that fatal weekend at his Diamond Head Road residence.[50]

As Director of Naval Intelligence from June 1939 to December 1940, Anderson had been at the center of policy making. He had direct access to Roosevelt in the White House and met weekly with FBI Director J. Edgar Hoover. Most important, he knew of the American success in breaking the Japanese military and diplomatic codes. When he arrived on the quarterdeck of Kimmel's flagship Anderson had one moral duty: to inform his commander-in-chief of the cryptographic triumphs. He failed to do so, and deliberately excluded Kimmel from the decryption success. "I can't understand, may never understand why I was deprived of the information available in Washington," a bewildered Kimmel wrote after the war.[51]

Had he been briefed, Kimmel could have requested that Purple decryptions be sent to him from either Washington or Corregidor. But without the machine, he did not have the capability to decode them. Ironically, the Army's monitor station on Hawaii, Station FIVE, was a principal interceptor of Purple code messages; the intercepts were forwarded immediately by radio to Washington, where they were decrypted on the Station US machine for the White House. Decryption was speedy. Most of Station FIVE's intercepts of Purple encoded messages were decoded on the Station US Purple machine and translated within a day's time, according to the White House route logs kept by Arthur McCollum. Incredibly, copies were not sent to Hawaii. Like Admiral Husband Kimmel, Lieutenant General Walter Short, Hawaii's Army commander, was not told of the secrets of Purple, even though the messages were being intercepted just steps from his command post at Fort Shafter.[52]

Both Admiral Anderson and Commander Vincent R. Murphy, Kimmel's assistant war plans officer, knew of McCollum's proposal to keep the fleet in harm's way. Either or both should have told Kimmel everything they knew about America's ability to learn Japan's strategic and tactical intentions from the intercepts. By mid-February, soon after taking command of the Pacific Fleet, Kimmel sensed his exclusion from the intelligence loop. On February 18 he asked Admiral Stark to fix responsibility for disseminating reports of a "secret nature so there will be no misunderstanding."[53]

Kimmel received Stark's answer on March 22: "Naval Intelligence is fully aware of its responsibility in keeping you adequately informed."[54] Determined to plug into the loop, Kimmel tried again. On May 26 he requested the establishment of what he called a "cardinal principle": "Inform the Commander-in-Chief of the Pacific Fleet immediately of all important developments as they occur by the quickest means available."[55] His requests were ignored. What information he got from Washington, for almost the entire time prior to the attack, did not provide him with a full understanding of Japan's intentions. By late July 1941, he had been cut off completely from the communications intelligence generated in Washington.[56]

CHAPTER 4

WE ARE ALERT FOR
AN ATTACK ON
HAWAII

SELABINTANAH RESORT

JAVA

DUTCH EAST INDIES

OCTOBER 16, 1940

===

ROOSEVELT'S REVAMPING OF THE NAVY'S COMMAND STRUCTURE IN
Hawaii lessened the chance that Japanese moves on Hawaii, spurred to action by Arthur McCollum's eight provocations, would be detected. As
events would show, there were Americans ready to put all eight into effect.
Among McCollum's proposals, the key provocations were actions B and G,
which would cut off vital supplies to Japan and force her into a military
mode to regain access. McCollum's action B proposed to "Make an
arrangement with Holland for the use of base facilities and acquisition of
supplies in the Dutch East Indies." Action G proposed that the United
States "insist that the Dutch refuse to grant Japanese demands for undue
economic concessions, particularly oil." [1]

Japan's leaders reacted immediately and attempted to change the

Dutch attitude after both provocations were put into effect in the fall of 1940 and early 1941. Intercepts in the diplomatic code, analyzed in Washington by McCollum, revealed the Japanese strategy; they disclosed that her diplomats speedily attempted to restore access to the Dutch-owned natural resources. But each attempt at reconciliation brought forth a classic case of tightening the screws.

During September 1940 Japan sensed the screw-tightening by the Dutch and arranged for a diplomatic conference in Java in an attempt to keep petroleum products and other natural resources flowing to the Empire. Its delegation was headed by Minister of Commerce Ichizo Kobayashi, who met with H. J. van Mook, Dutch minister for economic affairs. Commander Arthur McCollum's proposed role for the Dutch had not yet been written but his provocations—still at a latent stage—managed to surface during the initial Dutch-Japanese negotiations in late September and early October.

Japan's delegation felt right at home in the Dutch East Indies after their long sea journey. Tea gardens, tumbling waterfalls, and rice fields surrounded the conference site in the forested mountain resort near the hamlet of Selabintanah about 120 km southeast of Batavia. The beauty of the region reminded the diplomats of the heights leading to Mount Fuji in Japan.

But the heated diplomatic interchanges between Kobayashi and van Mook were in sharp contrast to the peaceful surroundings. Japan's diplomats angrily contended that the Netherlands delegates were mere puppets of Washington. On the table were proposals involving Japanese rights to obtain oil and petroleum products from Holland's enormous reserves in the Dutch East Indies. Japan called for the Dutch to provide a minimum of 3,150,000 metric tons of petroleum annually. One of the delegates, Japanese minister of commerce Ichizo Kobayashi, demanded that the Dutch guarantee a delivery schedule covering a five-year period. Kobayashi expressed the attitude of his government: "The Netherlands has been closely co-operating with the United Kingdom and the United States. Now is the time to shake hands with Japan."[2]

Dutch Minister H. J. van Mook reprimanded Kobayashi and labeled the oil demands preposterous. Besides, he said, the Netherlands government's role was only supervisory. Dutch oil firms controlled the production and sale of the petrol products, not the government.[3]

The Kobayashi mission started off on the wrong foot. When the *Nissho Maru,* carrying the Kobayashi delegation, arrived in Batavia Harbor on September 12, 1940, the captain committed a diplomatic faux pas: he failed to hoist the Netherlands flag, as required by protocol. But whether the *Nissho Maru* hoisted the colors or not the Japanese mission was doomed, because the Netherlands government went along with McCollum's actions B and G. Japan was not going to obtain any petroleum from the Dutch, despite her prolonged diplomatic overtures, which lasted until June 1941.

Though not mentioned by name, on October 16 President Roosevelt learned of Kobayashi's mission through a summary of a Purple intercept routed by McCollum to naval aide Captain Callaghan. The report mentioned the Japanese economic mission in the Dutch East Indies and disclosed the Japanese interest in seizing the Dutch East Indies at the earliest opportunity. The Japanese Foreign Office officials including those in Selabintanah urged fast action in seizing Dutch territory, according to the intercept:

THE UNITED STATES IS INCAPABLE OF TAKING ACTION AT THE PRESENT TIME TO PREVENT JAPANESE SEIZURE OF THE DUTCH POSSESSIONS IN THE FAR EAST AND NO TIME SHOULD BE LOST IN EFFECTING SUCH A SEIZURE.[4]

Roosevelt doubted that America would go to war over the Dutch East Indies, for he felt there was little public support for intervention in the Southeastern Asian countries. He expressed his doubts during the October 8 White House luncheon with Admiral Richardson. "I asked the President if we were going to enter the war. He replied that if the Japanese attacked Thailand, or the Kra Peninsula, or the Dutch East Indies we would not enter the war, that if they even attacked the Philippines he doubted whether we would enter the war, but that they could not always avoid making mistakes and that as the war continued and the area of operations expanded, sooner or later they would make a mistake and we would enter the war."[5]

An October 25 intercept provided additional details on the Kobayashi mission. Roosevelt learned that Japan sought a ground lease for the construction of a "technical base" that would be manned by "disguised troops." Once completed, Japan intended to use the base "for military op-

41

erations against the Netherlands." Realizing the importance of the intercept to the Netherlands government, McCollum delivered a copy of the dispatch to the Dutch naval attaché, Captain Johan Ranneft, on the night of October 30, 1940. Ranneft forwarded the message to his government in exile in London. They refused to grant the lease.[6]

McCollum and Ranneft, an experienced naval-communications officer, worked closely together throughout 1940 and '41. The two shared Japanese intercepts obtained by their governments. Dutch cryptographers eavesdropped on the Japanese navy through a cryptographic unit called *Kamer* 14 (Room 14) operated by the Royal Netherlands Army at Bandoeng, Java. There is no doubt of the close cooperation and exchange of naval intelligence between the United States, British, and Dutch forces prior to December 7. Secretary of the Navy Frank Knox assured Cordell Hull, the Secretary of State, that all US Navy intelligence personnel in the Far East were cooperating with British and Dutch naval intelligence by exchange of vital information of a special nature by rapid means. Admiral Hart, of the Asiatic Fleet, confirmed that a Dutch naval officer, Commander H. D. Linder, was assigned to his staff for such a purpose.[7]

Throughout the spring and summer of 1941, the White House manipulated the oil negotiations. On March 19, Roosevelt met with Netherlands Foreign Minister Dr. Eelco van Kleffens in the Oval Office. Van Kleffens, Roosevelt, and Undersecretary of State Sumner Welles conferred for seventy minutes and reiterated the strategy for frustrating Japanese acquisition of petroleum products as advocated by McCollum's actions B and G. When he left the meeting, van Kleffens went even further than his minister, van Mook, and accused Japan of aggressive behavior toward the Netherlands. He told reporters: "We have rejected every attempt by Japan to overstep and we will maintain that attitude."[8]

The Dutch foreign minister then began a long journey to Batavia by way of San Francisco, where he boarded the trans-Pacific China Clipper through Hawaii. Van Kleffens was not shy with the press. His journey was punctuated by interviews in which he continued to aim provocative remarks at Japan. In Honolulu, the Japanese Consulate reported his arrival and departure for Batavia by radio to Tokyo. When he reached Batavia, van Kleffens outlined the current policy to the local Dutch officials. Japan was permitted to obtain oil but at a diminished rate. An extra impediment was added: Japanese tankers would be required for its transportation; there were no Dutch tankers available. "Japan was enraged," reported Hallett Abend of the *New York Times*, "and suspected she had been out-smarted" by van Mook. She blamed him for the irksome provisions under which Japan must haul oil in her own tankers and pay for it in good American dollars.[9]

Van Kleffens and Ranneft maintained a connection with the Roosevelt Administration throughout 1941, exchanging Japanese military and diplomatic intelligence. In early December, Ranneft learned that the Japanese carrier forces were on the move. The reports came from the Office of Naval Intelligence (ONI) in Washington and located two separate movements. According to Ranneft's diary entries, one location was directly west of Hawaii; the other location involved a movement of carriers easterly from Japan. Ranneft did not provide location specifics in his diary. But the oceanic charts of the Pacific can help identify the two separate carrier locations reported by the Dutch naval attaché. The 21° North Latitude meridian leads directly west from Hawaii, past the Mariana Islands, and to the Philippine Sea. In early December 1941, units of Japanese Carrier Divisions Three and Four were in the Philippine Sea area preparing to support the Japanese invasion of Southeast Asia. Scratch Carrier Divisions Three and Four as a threat to Hawaii.

It's Ranneft's positioning of Japanese carriers on an easterly course from Japan that is most revealing—and the danger to Hawaii. As any nautical chart of the Pacific will prove, an easterly ocean course from Japan must originate somewhere from 32 to 45° North Latitude. In early December, Japan's Hawaii raiding force was proceeding easterly from Japan along the 40° North Latitude region of the North Pacific.

During his visit to ONI on December 2, Ranneft saw a naval intelligence plot (i.e., a route on a nautical chart) that placed two Japanese carriers leaving Japan on an easterly course. Again on Saturday, December 6, he saw an update of the Japanese warship plot maintained by ONI. This time Arthur McCollum and his boss, Director of Naval Intelligence Captain Theodore Wilkinson, pointed to and isolated the Japanese flattops west of Honolulu.[10] Although Ranneft has been criticized as a source, his diary account that he provided to historian John Toland is clear. It reads: "December 2, 1941. Meeting at Navy Department, the location of 2 Japanese carriers leaving Japan with eastern course are pointed out to me on the map."

Official United States naval records also support Ranneft's diary entry. Plottings on the naval intelligence map for December 2 were based on intercepted movement reports and radio direction-finder bearings obtained by the Navy's monitoring stations. Each plot reflected intelligence obtained prior to December 2 and isolated two separate Japanese carrier movements from the Empire: Carrier Route 1 extended southwest toward the Philippines and Southeast Asia[11] and Carrier Route 2 continued northeast through waters of the North Pacific Ocean and east to Hawaii. Ranneft's unnamed port could only be Hitokappu Bay on Route 2 on the Kurile island of Etorofu, northeast of the main Japanese islands.

There was no way Ranneft could mistake the southern Japanese carrier movement for an eastern foray. Three light carriers comprising units of Carrier Divisions Three and Four were tracked on Route 1, the southern route from the Empire. Each Japanese carrier division usually included two flattops, but Division Three was split. The light carrier HIJMS *Zuiho* took part in the invasion of the northern Philippines and Malaya while her sister carrier, HIJMS *Hosho*, remained in the Inland Sea. Carrier Division Four, the HIJMS *Ryujo* and HIJMS *Taiyo* (known to America as the *Kasuga Maru*) assembled at Palau and supported invasions on the east coast of the Philippines. Each of the three flattops and their carrier division commands show up constantly on Route 1 in the pre–Pearl Harbor intercepts of Station H, the Pacific Fleet's radio intercept station on Oahu, which monitored Japan's fleet broadcasts.

From mid-November onward, American radio monitors linked Carrier Divisions Three and Four with the Japanese battle force headed for the Southeast Asia region. Their sortie port was Sasebo on the southwest corner of Kyushu, the most westerly of Japan's home islands. Reports issued by the monitor stations were emphatic. The two light carrier divisions were under the command of Japan's Third Fleet and were headed for Southeast Asia. Missing from the southern-movement scenario were the six heavy flattops of Carrier Divisions One, Two, and Five. They were sailing to Pearl Harbor on Route 2.

By using the geographic term "eastern,"[12] Ranneft excluded the port of Sasebo and Japanese Carrier Divisions Three and Four, which were headed to the south. Navigation by sea eastward from Sasebo is impossible due to the Kyushu land-mass. Then where is the mystery sortie port for the eastern movement of "The Carriers" of Divisions One, Two, and Five? The answer came in a series of Japanese naval-radio broadcasts originated by the Hawaii-bound carriers, their commanders, and Admiral Yamamoto between November 18 and December 1, 1941. Most of the broadcasts were intercepted at Station H, one of eleven Navy monitor stations in the Pacific and the principal interceptor for the Pacific Fleet. Station H was part of the Navy's Mid-Pacific Radio Intelligence Network, commanded by Lieutenant Commander Joseph Rochefort from Station HYPO. Both were on Oahu: HYPO in the Pearl Harbor Naval Yard and H at Heeia, a hamlet on the windward side of the island, fronting on Kaneohe Bay. Though their similar names can confuse those uninitiated into the methods of Navy code-breaking, each had separate functions. HYPO was the combat intelligence center for the Pacific Fleet and the Roosevelt Administration. In cryptographic jargon, HYPO processed (decoded and translated) Japanese naval-radio messages obtained by intercept operators listening to the Japanese broadcasts at the monitoring unit, Station H.

These intercepts and the corresponding radio logs of Station H are powerful evidence of American foreknowledge of the attack on Pearl Harbor. Americans do not know these records exist—all were excluded from the many investigations that took place from 1941 to 1946 and the congressional probe of 1995. The most potent evidence is two radio dispatches sent by Admiral Yamamoto to the First Air Fleet on November 25 while the thirty-one warships were anchored at Hitokappu Bay in the Kurile Islands awaiting instruction to sail to Hawaii. In his messages, Yamamoto provides the evidence that contradicts American and Japanese claims of radio silence and exclusion of the words Hawaii and Pearl Harbor from radio transmissions prior to December 7. Both claims are at the heart of the Pearl Harbor surprise-attack lore. Yamamoto broke radio silence and directed the Japanese First Air Fleet to depart Hitokappu Bay on November 26, advance into Hawaiian waters through the North Pacific, and attack the United States Fleet in Hawaii. He even provided the latitude and longitude for portions of Route 2.

In his first dispatch he wrote:

THE TASK FORCE, KEEPING ITS MOVEMENT STRICTLY SECRET, SHALL LEAVE HITOKAPPU BAY ON THE MORNING OF 26TH NOVEMBER AND AD-VANCE TO 42° N. X 170° E. ON THE AFTERNOON OF 3 DECEMBER AND SPEEDILY COMPLETE REFUELING.[13]

In the second dispatch he continued:

THE TASK FORCE, KEEPING ITS MOVEMENT STRICTLY SECRET AND MAIN-TAINING CLOSE GUARD AGAINST SUBMARINES AND AIRCRAFT, SHALL AD-VANCE INTO HAWAIIAN WATERS, AND UPON THE VERY OPENING OF HOSTILITIES SHALL ATTACK THE MAIN FORCE OF THE UNITED STATES FLEET IN HAWAII AND DEAL IT A MORTAL BLOW. THE FIRST AIR RAID IS PLANNED FOR THE DAWN OF X-DAY. EXACT DATE TO BE GIVEN BY LATER ORDER.

UPON COMPLETION OF THE AIR RAID, THE TASK FORCE, KEEPING CLOSE COORDINATION AND GUARDING AGAINST THE ENEMY'S COUNTERATTACK, SHALL SPEEDILY LEAVE THE ENEMY WATERS AND THEN RETURN TO JAPAN.

SHOULD THE NEGOTIATIONS WITH THE UNITED STATES PROVE SUC-CESSFUL, THE TASK FORCE SHALL HOLD ITSELF IN READINESS FORTHWITH TO RETURN AND REASSEMBLE.[14]

Both dispatches, stripped of all Japanese communication data and lacking the source of the intercept, can be found in two US naval histories: *Pearl Harbor* by Vice Admiral Homer N. Wallin and *The Campaigns of the Pacific War* prepared by the Naval Analysis Division of the United States Strategic Bombing Survey.[15] The published text of the two messages fol-lows the general form of intercepted Japanese naval radio dispatches ob-tained by US naval monitoring stations in 1941. Records of Station H indicate that Yamamoto, using the radio call sign RO SE 22, dispatched thirteen radio messages between 1:00 P.M. on November 24 and 3:54 P.M. on November 26. All thirteen are missing from the intercept file of Japan-ese naval messages released to the National Archives by President Jimmy Carter in 1979.[16]

By reconstructing records of Station H and Japanese naval records, the destination and the departure port for Ranneft's mystery force is made clear. Japan's fleet movement to Hawaii fitted into two time frames in late November: (1) assembly at standby locations on November 17–25, and (2) the sortie to the target November 25–December 7.[17]

Hitokappu Bay, an inlet on Etorofu Island in the Kurile Islands group, was the assembly location for the six carriers of the First Air Fleet—the offensive power of the Pearl Harbor raid. Joining the carriers in the anchorage were its support force of two battleships, two heavy cruisers, one light cruiser, eleven destroyers, and three "I" type submarines, plus the crucial supply train of seven tankers. Several warships committed a serious radio security breach during their sortie to the Hitokappu Bay anchorage: each transmitted coded movement reports—reports that could be read by American naval cryptographers in Washington, according to Albert Pelletier one of the Navy's top cryppies at Station US.[18]

These Japanese warship movement reports are substantiated by intercept records of Station H. None of the movement reports were shown to the 1945–46 congressional investigation or to the one in 1995. Instead, Congress was told that American radio intelligence had "lost" the warships because each Japanese naval vessel maintained radio silence. Admiral Kimmel's intelligence chief, Edwin Layton, substantiated this claim. During his Capitol Hill testimony in 1946, he said neither the Japanese carriers nor the carrier commanders were ever addressed or heard on Nippon radio frequencies in the twenty-five days preceding Pearl Harbor. But Layton was covering up. The radio intercept reports were available, but Layton failed to inform Admiral Kimmel of the Japanese movement to Hitokappu Bay.[19]

In fact, Navy radio monitoring stations at Corregidor, Guam, Hawaii, and Dutch Harbor, Alaska, intercepted the transmissions. Japanese warships and the commanding admirals of the thirty-one-ship Hawaii force broke radio silence and were addressed by Tokyo radio during the twenty-five days from about November 12 through the December 7 "surprise attack."

One intercepted message on November 18 defied all security precautions and spelled out H-I-T-O-K-A-P-P-U-B-A-Y. The Roman letters were not even encoded—they were spelled out in clear. Confirmation of this is available from the Station H records, but Captain Duane Whitlock, the radio traffic analyst at CAST, denies that such a message was sent.

Other warships went on the Japanese naval air waves and confirmed that Hitokappu Bay was the standby location for the Hawaii force. British naval monitors at Singapore and their Dutch counterparts in Java heard the same broadcasts.[20] General Hein ter Poorten, commander of the

Netherlands army forces in the DEI, said his cryptologists at *Kamer* 14 had evidence that "showed Japanese naval concentration near the Kuriles."[21]

The plain-language dispatch of the words "Hitokappu Bay," confirmed a prediction made on the basis of radio intercepts on October 22, 1941, by Joseph Rochefort, the commander of Station HYPO on Oahu, who told Admiral Kimmel that Japan was in the midst of a large-scale screening maneuver or operation involving air units. Rochefort laid out the operation for Kimmel.[22] He predicted it would include a vast triangular area of the Pacific Ocean from the Kurile Islands in the north to the Marshall Islands in the south and Marcus Island in the east and extending to the southeast areas of Asia. For emphasis, Rochefort cited the Kurile Islands three times in the prediction. He had discovered Japan's secret sortie port for Route 2.

The contents of the Japanese message spelling out "Hitokappu Bay" were not revealed to Admiral Kimmel by Rochefort's Communication Summary dated November 19—the logical date for disclosure. The plain-language "Hitokappu Bay" reference does not appear in the summary though Rochefort wrote that Japanese naval circuits in the far north were intercepted. Dropping "Hitokappu Bay" from the typewritten summary may have been done deliberately to conceal American success in decoding Japanese naval communications. Admiral Harold Stark's testimony before the joint congressional investigation in 1945–46 indicates that he knew of the Hitokappu Bay rendezvous point prior to December 7, 1941.[23] But the plain-language "Hitokappu Bay" reference in the message of November 18 was never presented. Nor was it made available to the Pearl Harbor inquiry of Senator Strom Thurmond in 1995.[24]

Between November 18 and November 30, some units of the First Air Fleet radioed movement reports as they sailed north in the Pacific from their home ports in Japan. Their route extended off the east coast of Shikoku and Honshu and past Hokkaido, Japan's most northerly home island. Navigating first to the northeast, then north, then northeast again, their course took them to Hitokappu Bay.

Japan's naval communications were controlled by six powerful radio shore stations in the home islands: Sasebo, Kure, Maizuru, Tokyo, Yokosuka, and Ominato. In the Central Pacific, four stations were in control: Chichi Jima, Saipan, Truk, and Jaluit. For the Far East, the navy used

Takao, Formosa; Shanghai, China; and Pusan, Korea, as radio control points. Three were designated super-stations: Sasebo controlled all radio transmissions to Southeast Asia, China and Korea; Yokosuka to the Central Pacific, and Ominato to the north, including the North Pacific.

For supersecret operations, Japan set up special communication zones known only to senior commanders. It was a way to conceal the operation's location from American and allied eavesdroppers. In mid-November, a special communication zone was assigned to the First Air Fleet at Hitokappu Bay in the Kurile Islands. Normally, Japan issued a 5-Num code equivalent for these special locations, but because Hitokappu had been selected at the last minute it was not on the code list. Tokyo had only one choice: they spelled it out.[25]

After transmitting of the initial message, there were no more Hitokappu Bay plain-language radio leaks. But some warships disclosed their

---

HITOKAPPU BAY INTERCEPT

[overleaf]

Two versions of the Hitokappu Bay intercept, with and without blacked-out code numbers. The censored version, left, as released in 1979 under Presidential Executive Order, blacks out the code designator JN-25-B (a later designator for the 1941 version of the 5-Num code) and the five-number code groups in the text. The message was intercepted by an unidentified Station H operator with the initials SN, at 1932 hours (7:32 pm) on November 18, 1941, as indicated by the "TOI" (time of interception) info at top right. (The date, listed in the lower right-hand corner as "Navy Trans 4/24/46" indicates that the document was then translated or transcribed in 1946. Decryption, however, remains the critical question; Rochefort was fluent in Japanese.) SN said the message came in loud and clear in Hawaii; he rated it as G=good, no static. Radio Tokyo, HA FU 6, transmitted the message to all Japanese fleets U MO 2 on 4155 kilocycles. The original of this message has not been released by the US government. Based on the handwritten note by GZ (Navy designator for the translator) the original Japanese text was transmitted in a series of five-number code groups, each representing a Japanese word—except for HITOKAPPU WAN (Bay), which was spelled out in katakana. The intercept operators and Kisner had solved the Japanese naval radio call signs and knew HI N MA was the Operations Section Chief of the Japanese Naval General Staff; I A TO was the Ominato Naval Base and RI TA 358 was the First Air Fleet's Chief of Staff. Some historians have claimed that the original of this message was not even available until after December 7, but the time of interception is explicit. Immediately upon receipt, the source and recipients of this message would have been clear.

~~TOP SECRET ULTRA~~

(cd)

U MO 2 :	All Fleets
DE	
M. FU 6 ·	TOKYO Comm Unit.
L 34	- SU U

From:	HI N M.	(Naval Gene al Staff 1st Section Chief)
Action:	I L TC	(Chief of Staff OMINA1O Guard District)
Info:	HI TA 358	(Chief of Staff 1st Air Fleet)

1220/18 November 1941   (TOI 11/181932 G SN 3155 A) H

62200

Please arrange to have SUZUKI ▓▓▓ who was sent to the
1st Air Fleet ▓▓▓ on business, picked up about 23 or 24 November at
HITOKAPPU Bay by ▓▓▓ unident) *ship* of your secondary Naval Station.

G2 Comment: HITOKAPPU BAY spelled out, not
from single code group.

JN 6   1276 z   (JAPANESE)   (M) Navy Trans 4/24/46
Ju oc   6 May 46

~~TOP SECRET ULTRA~~

DECLASSIFIED per E.O. 12065
by Director, NSA/Chief, CSS
1 June 1979

SRN. NO   116643

50

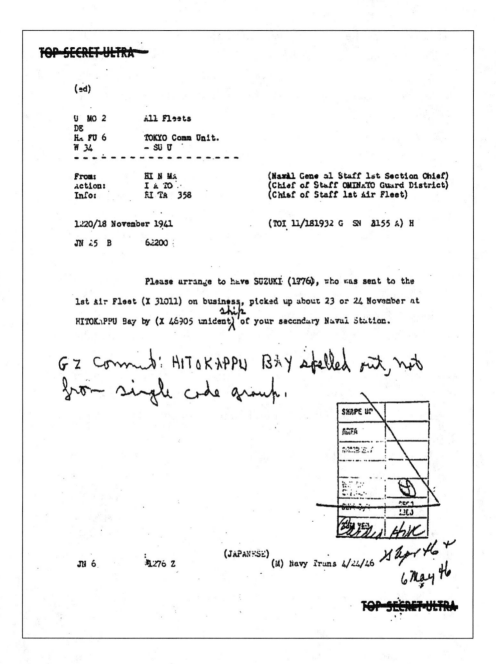

~~TOP SECRET ULTRA~~

(ed)

U MO 2	All Fleets
DE	
Ha FU 6	TOKYO Comm Unit.
W 34	- SU U

- - - - - - - - - - - - - -

From:	HI N MA	(Naval Gene al Staff 1st Section Chief)
Action:	I A TO	(Chief of Staff OMINATO Guard District)
Info:	RI TA 358	(Chief of Staff 1st Air Fleet)

1220/18 November 1941   (TOI 11/181932 G SN 2155 A) H

JN 25 B   62200

Please arrange to have SUZUKI (1776), who was sent to the
1st Air Fleet (X 31011) on business, picked up about 23 or 24 November at
HITOKAPPU Bay by (X 46905 unident) of your secondary Naval Station.

G z Comment: HITOKAPPU BAY spelled out, not
from single code group.

(JAPANESE)

JN 6   1276 Z   (M) Navy Trans 4/24/46

~~TOP SECRET ULTRA~~

locations when they filed movement reports through various Japanese naval-radio communication zones. Their reports provided a dead giveaway to American cryptographers who could read the movement reports solved by Pelletier at Station US. First to leak their zonal locations were three of the long-range I-boat submarines assigned to the First Air Fleet, *I-19*, *I-21*, and *I-23*. Adhering to long-standing orders, the sub commanders reported moving northeast from Kure. Their radio reports indicated an advance through the Yokosuka Communication Zone, then the Ominato Zone, "to the communication zone of the First Air Fleet." The message was clear: The carriers of the First Air Fleet were in their own special communication zone. They could be reached by radio at Hitokappu Bay, northeast of Ominato.

Radio direction finders of the US Navy confirmed the Japanese naval movements. The radio signals were picked up throughout the Pacific Rim. Stations at Corregidor, Guam, and Dutch Harbor provided "fixes" on the carriers *Akagi*, *Hiryu*, and *Shokaku*, and of Carrier Divisions One, Two, and Five. Each flattop was plotted moving north by northeast by the radio operators at CAST on Corregidor. These plots were forwarded to Rochefort at Pearl Harbor's Station HYPO and then to President Roosevelt's routing officer Arthur McCollum in Washington by a special secure Navy radio code circuit called TESTM.[27]

To those uninitiated in the methods of communications intelligence, Japan's radio call-sign system, known as the *Yobidashi Fugo*, looks like alphabet soup. But to the experienced radio intercept operator/cryptographer the call signs, when deciphered, are revealing. The flagship of the First Air Fleet, the 38,000-ton carrier HIJMS *Akagi*, shared triple radio duty. Its radio transmitter served three masters with different radio call signs: Captain Kiichi Hasegawa of the *Akagi*, whose radio code name was 8 YU NA, and Vice Admiral Chuichi Nagumo, who wore two hats: he was both Commander-in-Chief of the First Air Fleet, YO N 7, and Commander of Carrier Division One, SA SO 2.[28]

Vice Admiral Nagumo continually broke radio silence by transmitting messages to his command using the *Akagi*'s radio facilities. But Nagumo was not the only offender. Captain Hasegawa added his transmissions to the traffic. So did Vice Admiral Gunichi Mikawa, the commander of the battleships and cruisers of Nagumo's force. Mikawa was detected by Station CAST using his secret Hawaii call sign, N WA 2. His radio transmissions, according to the CAST radio direction-finder bearings, placed his force off the east coast of Japan. Even worse for Japanese communications security, both admirals used their most secret call signs, which were reserved exclusively for the Hawaii attack.[29]

Japan's navy revised the radio call signs for all warships on November 1, when they put a new radio-call list into effect. Nagumo and Mikawa thought the new coded radio-call signs hid them from detection by US listening posts. They were correct, as long as they kept their radio transmitters silent. But once the warships used the airwaves, the American naval intercept operators solved the new identities quickly.

Transmissions to and from the entire Japanese fleet were in radiotelegraphy, not voice. Radio transmitters emit spurious sounds,[30] which can be identified by "radio fingerprinting." These sounds are unique to the transmitter; that is, no two transmitters sound alike. The US Navy used oscilloscopes to identify the wave patterns of these sounds. Experienced naval intercept operators could sometimes recognize individual Japanese radio operators by their unique use of the radiotelegraph key to send the dots and dashes of their code.

The new call list, List 9, thwarted the American code-breakers for a few days. But once the warships began transmitting, and "fingerprints" could be detected, the code-breakers were able to analyze the meaning of the various calls for individual ships or units. This wide use of radio transmissions was necessitated by the fact that Japan's navy and military operations extended over vast stretches of air, land, and sea. In a Thanksgiving Day assessment of Japanese carrier movements, the Pacific Fleet's radio intercept traffic chief, Homer Kisner,[31] detected a separation of carrier commands. He noted that Carrier Divisions Three and Four were involved in "southern operations" and received their orders from the commander of Japan's Third Fleet, not from the Commander Carriers, Vice Admiral Nagumo. Kisner spotted another movement which he called "the Carrier Divisions": the six big carriers of the Japanese Fleet. These included Carrier Division One, *Akagi* and *Kaga*, commanded by Nagumo; Carrier Division Two, *Hiryu* and *Soryu*, commanded by Rear Admiral Tamon Yamaguchi; and Carrier Division Five, commanded by Rear Admiral Chuichi Hara, with the newest Japanese flattops, *Shokaku* and *Zuikaku*.

Pushing aside his cranberries and turkey, Kisner examined the pile of radio intercepts culled from the Japanese naval airwaves by his 65 radio operators. The thirty-one-year-old Kisner had assumed the duties of radio traffic chief in June 1941. He supervised the interception of all types of Japanese naval radio communications. His headquarters was Station H, a Navy radio receiving facility located at Heeia on Kaneohe Bay on the windward side of Oahu. Homer Kisner had learned to intercept Japanese radio broadcasts in a Navy classroom operated by Station US on the roof of Navy headquarters in Washington in 1933. After graduating from the three-month eavesdropping course, Kisner, then a radioman second class, traveled to Hawaii and placed Station H in operation that summer. In the ensuing years, he served in other monitor stations in the Pacific specializing in the interception of Japan's military and diplomatic radio broadcasts. His unique talent in eavesdropping on Japan's fleet was unsurpassed. His immediate boss, Commander Joseph Rochefort, regarded Kisner as tops in the specialized field of plucking Japanese radio broadcasts from the airwaves. From July 1941 to October 1942 Kisner served as the Pacific Fleet's radio traffic chief. For the next three years Kisner operated with the Pacific Fleet supervising various intercept operations. He observed Japan's early success followed by her defeat. He detected the Japanese advance on Hawaii in 1941 and also intercepted Japan's reaction to the bombing of Hiroshima and Nagasaki and the initial peace feelers in 1945. President Harry Truman in 1946 awarded him the Bronze Star for his expertise. Promoted to full Commander in 1953, Kisner was sent to Korea for communications intelligence and earned a second Bronze Star from President Dwight Eisenhower.[32]

Kisner's daily routine at Station H called for a quick examination of the intercepts for military information. Then he prepared a Daily Chronology and delivered the entire package to Rochefort's basement office at Pearl Harbor, about fifteen miles away on the lee side of Oahu. There were no teleprinters or two-way radio facilities to link the offices. A single telephone line from the Mutual Telephone Company was Kisner's only electronic means of alerting the US government to an emergency. But there was no way Kisner was going to use that telephone. It was a party line.

Every day Kisner packaged the Daily Chronology, intercept message sheets, and radio logs into a neat bundle, strapped a Colt .45 revolver to his hip, and drove to Pearl Harbor in a Navy half-ton pickup truck. He was carrying America's most precious intelligence secrets, and his daily route to Pearl Harbor took him directly past the Japanese Consulate, where a Japanese naval spy, Tadashi Morimura, prepared weekly espionage reports for Tokyo.

Modern freeways bypass Kisner's route today. But in 1941 he drove from Oahu's windward side and up the circuitous Pali Road, which cut through the Koolau Mountains. At the 1100-foot summit, the road became Nuuanu Avenue and followed a steep downhill descent to the Honolulu side. The Japanese Consulate was at the intersection of Nuuanu Avenue and Kuakini Street. One unlucky auto accident at that busy intersection and the Pacific War might have had a different outcome.

Kisner relied on Mama San's Laundry to hide Station H and his daily departures for Pearl Harbor from potential Japanese spies. Her residence, laundry, clotheslines, and huge banana trees fronted the entire side of the Station's property on Kamehameha Highway and cut off views of H from motorists traveling on the highway. He supervised the intercept operations from a large white concrete building with a sixteen-foot-high ceiling. His office view looked out to the turquoise-blue waters of the Royal Fish Pond at Heeia, built and maintained by Hawaiian kings over the centuries as a food source. Inside the building his 65 radio operators split among eight work stations. (The discovery of the two carrier commands was a monumental find, yet neither Kisner nor any of his 65 men nor the remaining hundred-odd intercept operators were ever called before any of the nine Pearl Harbor investigations, including the 1995 probe. The reason, our government would still claim fifty years after the fact, was that their testimony could compromise our national security.) They worked around the clock, including holidays, in rotating eight-hour shifts. Kisner required twenty-four operators for the three shifts every day. Station H logs indicate that in the weeks prior to the attack the work schedule was often junked. Operators doubled up and worked overtime in continuous sixteen-hour shifts. In the US Navy there is no such luxury as overtime pay. As American-Japanese relations deteriorated and approached the breaking point, many radiomen ate their meals and slept on the floor near their monitor positions.

When he wasn't analyzing the Japanese intercepts, Kisner watched his eight men, each at his work station. They sat in swivel chairs before a long bench stacked with radio equipment. Each wore earphones called "cans" connected by wire to banks of radio receivers tuned to the known Japanese naval frequencies. When a message was heard it was transcribed on a special code typewriter called an RIP-5. (RIP stands for Radio Intelligence Publication.) The machine had been secretly developed by the Underwood Typewriter Company[33] to convert the unique dot-dash radiotelegraphy code of the Imperial Japanese Navy to Latin-alphabet equivalents. To the untrained ear, Japan's naval telegraphy procedures sounded like International Morse Code. But each dot and dash had a non-Morse meaning. For example, in Morse Code, dash-dot-dot-dot is the letter B, but in the Japanese naval *katakana* telegraphic system the same sequence means the syllable HA. When an intercept operator typed B on the RIP-5 the *katakana* syllable HA was printed out.

Intercepting and transcribing Japanese fleet messages for FDR and his military leaders was a highly skilled task. In 1941, America had only 165 trained *katakana* operators. Kisner and his 65 operators at H were the best in the business. All had been chosen by Rochefort as the "pick of the crop."[34]

Scanning the Thanksgiving Day intercepts, Kisner looked for Japanese commanders who appeared "bossiest." Kisner first assembled the intercepts in chronological order. He said the interception of "an unusually large number of [radio] messages indicated increased activity or movement of the Carriers." He connected Carrier Division Three with the Third Fleet and associated both commands with a southern movement from Japan toward Southeast Asia.

Kisner discovered other warships. All were destined to attack Pearl Harbor. He placed Destroyer Squadron One and the heavy cruiser HIMJS *Tone* with Carrier Divisions One, Two, and Five. From mid-November to December 6, this placement never changed.[35]

Kisner tracked the Japanese fleet movements with radio direction finders that located Japanese warships when they used their radio transmitters. He included the bearings of Japanese warships obtained by the direction-finder stations in his Daily Chronology. The documentation of Japanese naval broadcasts compiled by Kisner and his radiomen from November 18 through 20 is compelling: Four broadcasts linked warships of the First Air Fleet with the Kurile Islands and Hitokappu Bay—a serious breach of Japanese naval security.

> Nov. 18: Hitokappu Bay appeared in plain language text in a radio dispatch originated by naval headquarters, Tokyo. By using the plain words, the dispatch associated the First Air Fleet with Hitokappu Bay. Intercepted by operator SN at Station H at 7:32 P.M. Tokyo time.
>
> Nov. 19: A Japanese naval submarine transmitted its coded radio call sign of RO TU ØØ and filed a movement report to the flagship of the First Air Fleet in Hitokappu's communication zone. Intercepted at Station H by LF at 2:02 A.M. Tokyo time.
>
> Nov. 20: Japanese naval Submarine Squadron Three reported that sub I-19 was underway from Yokosuka to Ominato, and then to the radio zone of the flagship of the First Air Fleet. Intercepted at Station H by radio operator Merrill Whiting, at 2:35 P.M. Tokyo time.
>
> Nov. 20: Two and a half hours later, Whiting heard a third Japanese sub, TA YU 88, when it filed a movement report to the communication zone of the flagship, First Air Fleet.[36]

Kisner was excluded from every Pearl Harbor investigation, including the 1995 inquiry. His first public comments on the pre–Pearl Harbor communications intelligence were made to the author in April 1988 when he examined the intercepts contained in the President Carter document release. Kisner confirmed their authenticity. He verified that several Japanese intercepts heard by his operators were transmitted in plain language prior to December 7. But after fifty-plus years Kisner could not recall the circumstances of the intercepts or why he failed to flag the plain-language HITOKAPPU BAY in his Daily Chronology on November 19. Emphasizing that he was not excusing himself for overlooking Japan's use of plain language in the radio dispatch, Kisner noted that Joseph Rochefort and his staff of analysts at Station HYPO should have been alerted by the words. On October 22, 1941, HYPO's Communication Summary predicted that Japan was planning a large-scale screening maneuver involving air forces, staged from the Kurile Islands.

In an interview in 1998, Kisner, then eighty-eight years old, was shown McCollum's memo by the author. His reaction to proposal F was the same as Admiral Richardson's—disbelief and outrage: "No one in the Navy would deliberately place warships and sailors in harm's way. If I had known of the plan, I'd have gone direct to Admiral Kimmel and warned him."[37]

During the four years he served with the Pacific Fleet in communications intelligence, Kisner estimated that he and other staff members handled a minimum of 1,460,000 Japanese military intercepts. Kisner's full documentation for the pre-Pearl Harbor period is contained in the message sheets and separate radio intercept logs kept by his 65 operators, including Whiting and the unknown SN and LF. These Station H message sheets and the operator logs are still classified as among America's most secret documents. The Japanese warships and senior admirals of the First Air Fleet gave away their North Pacific Ocean locations during their sorties to Hitokappu Bay. US naval cryptographic monitors as well as their British and Dutch counterparts verified the movements.[38]

Dutch code-breakers at *Kamer* 14 intercepted the same Japanese naval broadcasts and forwarded the information to their government-in-exile in London. These Dutch intercepts placed Japanese warships near the Kuriles toward the end of November 1941. Presumably the *Kamer* facility obtained Admiral Yamamoto's dispatches to the First Air Fleet, for two Dutch military officers, Lieutenant General Hein ter Poorten and Captain J. W. Henning, claim that intercepts of Japanese naval communications by Dutch code-breakers revealed a concentration of warships in the Kuriles. Both officers are credible. General ter Poorten was commander-in-chief of the Netherlands ground forces in the Dutch East Indies; Henning was cryptologist at *Kamer* 14. Adding to the credibility of the two Dutch army officers is the written assurance given November 8, 1941, by Frank Knox to Cordell Hull that there was a full exchange of intelligence information between the Dutch, British, and Americans in the Far East prior to Pearl Harbor.[39]

The Dutch accounts placing the warships in the Kuriles were written in 1960, but they dovetail with the intercepts Kisner gathered in late November 1941. Unfortunately, the military records of the Netherlands East Indies were intentionally destroyed early in 1942 to make sure they would not fall into enemy hands when Japanese invasion forces overran the Dutch colony.

Skeptics argue that the concentration of warships in the Kuriles pointed not to Hawaii but to a Japanese invasion and attack on Russia or the Aleutian Islands of Alaska. But there were no invasion or expeditionary troop components detected in the Japanese warship movement to the Hitokappu Bay–Kuriles region. All the major Japanese expeditionary forces and their commanders were heading south toward Southeast Asia, the Philippines, and Palau. The Kurile concentration was a screening force, which verified Rochefort's October 22 prediction of a Japanese air movement eastward in the North Pacific Ocean.

According to Ranneft's account, the intercepts and chart plots clearly indicated an imminent clash with the United States. "No one among us mentions the possibility of an attack on Honolulu. I myself do not think about it because I believe that everyone in Honolulu is 100 percent on the alert, just like everyone here at ONI."[40]

CHAPTER 5

THE SPLENDID ARRANGEMENT

―――

SINCE THE EARLY 1920S, AMERICA HAD BEEN EAVESDROPPING ON Japanese governmental communications. Roosevelt's military leaders called it a "splendid arrangement," a phrase coined by Admiral Stark.[1] It was America's intelligence backbone. In 1941 it comprised twenty-two Pacific Rim radio intercept stations, including four cryptographic centers that decoded Japanese military and diplomatic messages. Homer Kisner's Station H and Joseph Rochefort's cryptographic center, both on Oahu, Hawaii, were part of it. So were Station CAST on Corregidor Island and Station SAIL near Seattle.[2] Altogether it was an exceptional effort of extraordinary scope and achievement, and for years it had kept American officials aware of every intention and activity of the Japanese government.[3]

Joseph Rochefort[4] and his Station HYPO would play a large part in the Pearl Harbor story and World War II's amazing decryption effort. In 1917, at the height of World War I, the seventeen-year-old Rochefort had joined the Navy while still in high school in Los Angeles. He was called to duty in April 1918 and sent to San Pedro. He wanted to be a naval aviator, but the Navy had different plans and sent him to an engineering school in New York. He graduated an ensign in 1919 and became engineering officer of the USS *Cuyama*, a tanker. In 1924, after five years of uneventful service, a fellow officer noted Rochefort's skills at auction bridge and solving crossword puzzles and recommended him for a Navy cryptanalysis class in Washington. There Rochefort found his true calling. He excelled in the cryptographic work, was promoted to full lieutenant, and was named assistant to Lieutenant Commander Laurance Safford, who was in the initial stages of organizing a communications-intelligence section for the Navy. When Safford was sent to sea duty in late 1924, Joseph Rochefort was named officer-in-charge of the small unit that eventually became Station US.[5]

Like Rochefort, the American military commanders in the Philippines, General Douglas MacArthur and Admiral Thomas Hart, were part of this "splendid arrangement"—but Hawaii's commanders, Lieutenant General Walter Short and Admiral Husband Kimmel, were not. President Roosevelt, British Prime Minister Churchill, and the Netherlands government-in-exile in London used the entire network, which extended from the West Coast of North America to China's east coast and from Dutch Harbor, Alaska, to Batavia on the island of Java in the Dutch East Indies. Seventeen of the monitoring stations were run by the United States, four by the British Royal Navy, and one by the Dutch army.

The US Pacific monitoring operation included thirteen Navy stations and four operated by the Army. Command decisions rested with each service. The Navy controlled its cryptographic operations from Station US, located in Navy Headquarters at 18th Street and Constitution Avenue, N.W., in Washington; the Army's control was centered at the Signal Intelligence Service (SIS) in Army Headquarters, down the street at 20th Street and Constitution Avenue, N.W., known in 1941 as the Munitions Building. The Navy's Japanese monitoring program was the largest by far. SAIL, CAST, and HYPO were the regional control centers. Decoding and translating the intercepts took place at four processing centers: CAST and HYPO in the Pacific and Station US and the Army's SIS in Washington. Station SAIL was limited to intercept operations and dispatched its information by teleprinter to Station US for processing.

Britain's four stations in the Pacific, called WT stations for wireless-telegraph, were controlled from the Far East Combined Bureau, a crypto-graphic processing center in Singapore's Naval Dockyard. Its monitoring station was on Stonecutter's Island in Hong Kong's harbor. Two radio di-rection-finder stations in Canada, at Esquimalt and Ucluelet on British Co-lumbia's Vancouver Island, formed the remainder of Britain's Pacific cryptographic efforts. *Kamer* 14, the Netherlands monitor and processing center at the Bandoeng Army Base in the Dutch East Indies, completed the "splendid arrangement."

America's small Asiatic Fleet, commanded by Admiral Thomas Hart, received its Japanese communications intelligence from CAST,[6] a full-service facility under co-commanders Lieutenants Rudolph J. Fabian and John Lietwiler. The center was manned by 75 trained cryptographic spe-cialists—including intercept operators, radio direction-finder experts, translators, and cryptographers—who monitored Japanese diplomatic and military communications. CAST also served as the exchange center for sharing intercepts with the British and the Dutch.[7]

Rochefort's Station HYPO controlled the Mid-Pacific Network, which was the largest of the Navy's Pacific operations with about 140 radio intel-ligence specialists. Aside from the HYPO staff, 32 specialists manned five RDF stations: at Dutch Harbor, on Midway, on Samoa, and two on Oahu. Coast Guard cryptographers on Oahu also supplied intercepts to HYPO. It was a mammoth job, for about 1000 Japanese military intercepts were pro-duced daily on Oahu and required careful scrutiny. The Mid-Pac Network concentrated only on Japanese naval communications and did not inter-cept diplomatic messages, since that was the mission of CAST and SAIL.

Rochefort created an accurate picture of Japan's preparations despite being unable to see a single warship, sailor, or aircraft of the perceived enemy. The nearest Japanese fleet unit was several thousand miles away. Station HYPO was housed in the basement of the administration building of the Fourteenth Naval District. It was fifteen feet underground in a win-dowless, damp cellar, dug into the volcanic rock and soil of the naval yard. There were no enclosed offices or partitions except for a wall divider that separated the special [and loud] IBM sorting machinery from the rest of the space. From his gray metal desk in the center, Lieutenant Commander Rochefort supervised the entire operation. Tall and lean, with close-cropped dark brown hair, the forty-one-year-old Rochefort was a model naval officer greatly admired by his handpicked staff of officers and enlisted men. The cryptanalysts at HYPO worked in the open around him. The cryptanalysts, or "cryppies," are among the greatest heroes of the war.

Hawaii's tropical temperatures, combined with the heat in the basement generated by the statistical machinery, made working conditions unbearable, so a powerful air conditioner was installed. To endure this chilled air, Rochefort wore a red smoking jacket over his neatly pressed khaki uniform. Then to ease the discomfort caused by the carpetless concrete floor, he wore cushioned slippers. Officially, the smoking jacket and slippers violated naval dress regulations, but whenever he left HYPO's basement to meet with Admiral Kimmel or attend FBI meetings in downtown Honolulu, Rochefort was properly and meticulously dressed.

Although Rochefort was considered the top cryptanalyst in the Navy's officer corps, he preferred sea duty to the draining mental effort that codebreaking demanded. Frustrations associated with the cryptographic chores ate at him twenty-four hours a day. He suffered from ulcers and at the end of the day needed two to three hours to unwind at his home in the Honolulu hills. He missed many meals with his wife Fay and their children, Janet and Joseph, Jr.

Rochefort lived by the credo: "An intelligence officer has one task, one job, one mission. This is to tell his commander, his superior, today, what the Japanese are going to do tomorrow. This is his job. If he doesn't do this, then he's failed." He was proud of his organization. "I would say with all modesty that this was the best communications intelligence organization this world has ever seen. It was due simply to the fact that our people were tops in their particular fields. All worked together as a team. They had been in this business anywhere from five to ten or twelve years. I had been involved in this thing since 1925 and I fancied myself as a translator." True to his mission, Rochefort did more than just translate, he predicted. "I was better prepared to indicate what was in the Japanese mind. That is why we always specified the meaning of Japanese naval operation orders. We also sent in judgments explaining what the Japanese intended to accomplish by the operation orders. That is where I differed from most intelligence organizations at that time."[8]

Rochefort defined the basic concept of communication intelligence

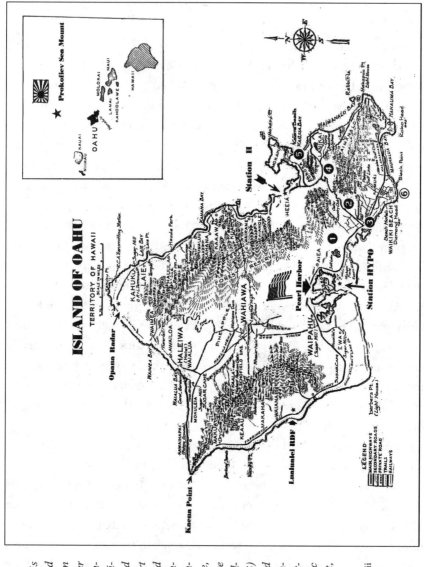

ISLAND OF OAHU

TERRITORY OF HAWAII

Prokofiev Sea Mount

Major sites on Oahu that figure in this book: Pearl Harbor Naval Base and Station HYPO (center right); Station H (center right); Lualualei RDF (center left); Opana Radar, Army early warning site (top center); Kaena Point, navigational base for both Japanese and American forces (upper left); (1) Fort Shafter, US Army Headquarters and site of Station FIVE; (2) Japanese Consulate; (3) Downtown Honolulu includes Aloha Tower, FBI Field office, Army and Navy espionage investigative office; (4) the Pali Road linked windward Oahu (east) with Honolulu; (5) Hamlet of Kalama; (6) Diamond Head residence of Rear Admiral Walter Anderson. Inset: Japan launched its attack on Hawaii from the North Pacific Ocean at the Prokofiev Seamount, about 200 miles north of Oahu.

Source: Map based on map from Hawaii Territorial Planning Board, 1940.

64

thus: "You cannot always count on being able to read these messages forever. Enemy cryptographic systems are constantly changed to avoid detection. You've got to be able to put yourself in a position where you extract a lot of information just from the messages themselves without being able to read them. This generally is known as radio intelligence." Rochefort cited radio direction finding (RDF) as an important part of communications intelligence. He explained: "By means of radio direction finders you ascertain the geographical position of the enemy force. That's called direction finding—DF. That's a part of radio intelligence."[9]

Unlike the interservice cryptographic cooperation in the Philippines, there was no liaison between HYPO and the Army's Station FIVE, an intercept station at Fort Shafter on Oahu. FIVE was under the administrative command of Lieutenant General Walter Short. It was an important link in the "splendid arrangement" but—inexplicably—intercepts were not shared between HYPO and FIVE. Short's operators intercepted Japanese diplomatic messages, including the all-important Purple code, but without the Purple decryption machine or help from CAST or Washington they were unable to decode them.

Apparently General Short learned of the importance of the Japanese radio messages intercepted at Station FIVE. On November 27 he requested that Rochefort instruct the Army's intercept operators at FIVE in solving what Short called the "Japanese telegraphic code." Rochefort received Short's request the next day but details are lacking, for censorship conceals both the text of the request and Rochefort's reaction. Apparently he did nothing to assist the general. A direct link to Short's letter—but not the letter itself—can be found referenced in a Fourteenth Naval District route slip in the National Archives at San Bruno. Rochefort initialed the slip and kept Short's original letter in HYPO's files. On January 1, 1942, a similar request again asked Rochefort's cooperation in the solution of enemy codes and ciphers. Again he acknowledged the request, signed his full signature, J. J. Rochefort, and retained the copy in HYPO's files.

Mysteriously, both the November 27 and January 1 letters have the same Army serial number. Short had been relieved of his duties on December 17, so the date of the second request is suspicious. The identical serial numbers suggest a deliberate attempt to make it appear that the request wasn't received until weeks after the attack. Neither letter has been released by the Navy or the Army. Their existence would not have come to light at all had not the route slips been discovered by the author.[10]

Lieutenant General Short never told Congress of Rochefort's failure to assist him in decrypting the intercepts. Asked directly about the Army's radio intercept facilities in Hawaii, Short told Senator Alben Barkley (D., KY), the chairman of the Joint Congressional Committee established to investigate the disaster in 1945–46, "I had no source of information outside Hawaii, except the War Department."[11]

Short failed to mention Station FIVE or his November 27 request. His discourse with Barkley offered the opportunity to clear his reputation by focusing on the crucial intercepts denied to his command. Traffic encrypted in the two most important Japanese diplomatic code systems, Purple and the J series, passed through Station FIVE's radio receivers at Fort Shafter. These included the Tokyo–Berlin, Tokyo–Batavia, and Tokyo–Washington circuits encoded in the Purple code. FIVE also intercepted the J series, which Japan's Foreign Ministry called the Tsu code. It was the top code assigned to Japan's Honolulu consulate for its radio contact with Tokyo and had been broken by the Americans. The Purple machine was not assigned to the consulate.

To foil Allied code-breakers, the Foreign Ministry changed the Tsu code three times in 1941. The changes were ineffectual and were solved promptly by cryptographers at Station US. Each solution was sent immediately by radio dispatch to both Station CAST and HYPO. The first change, put into effect between January and March, was labeled J-17 by Washington; April through May, J-18. The final change, called J-19, remained in effect for six months—June through December 3. By intercepting the J series, Station FIVE obtained the Tokyo spy orders transmitted in the J-19 code system, which directed preparation of bomb plots for the Pacific Fleet anchorages in Pearl Harbor. Short's intercept operators, unable to decode the bomb plot messages, forwarded them to Washington. They were decoded and, when translated, revealed the bomb plots—but Washington clammed up. Not a word of the bomb plots that targeted Pearl Harbor was sent to Short or to Kimmel.

No record has been found indicating that General Short ever told Admiral Kimmel of the intercept capability at Fort Shafter. Conversely, Kimmel apparently never told Short that the J-19 messages, and the earlier messages of 1941, could be decrypted at Station HYPO.

America's West Coast was served by six Navy stations, which stretched 2400 miles from Sitka, Alaska, to Imperial Beach, near San Diego, California. Of the six, SAIL copied all categories of Japanese naval and diplomatic message text while ITEM, at Imperial Beach, was a special sentinel assigned to locate Japanese fleet units approaching Hawaii and the West Coast. The other four stations were engaged solely in radio direction-finder operations aimed at tracking Japanese merchant vessels and warships throughout the Pacific. It was a "big tent" organization, for the stations received electronic help from America's commercial radio firms such as RCA Communications and Globe Wireless, which transmitted Japanese communications between Tokyo and North, Central, and South America. Canadian stations were also part of the "big tent." Monitor stations at Esquimalt and Ucluelet on British Columbia's Vancouver Island joined in tracking the Japanese vessels.[12] All of these intercept facilities sent intercepted Japanese messages along to Washington by teleprinter for decoding and translating.

The Army had two intercept stations on the West Coast. One was called Station TWO and was situated on the headlands of San Francisco's Army Presidio, overlooking the straits of the Golden Gate. The other was Station FOUR at Quarry Heights, near Balboa in the Panama Canal Zone. Their missions paralleled those of the other two Army stations in the Pacific: the interception of Japanese diplomatic messages. There were no processing facilities, so intercepts were sent by teleprinter to the SIS in the Munitions Building, on the site now occupied by the Vietnam Memorial.

The "splendid arrangement" required a plentiful supply of Japanese intercepts to work. With the vast quantity of diplomatic codes and the naval intercepts, the network had its hands full. Japan's Foreign Ministry used four separate diplomatic codes for contacting overseas missions during 1941: Purple, the J Series, LA, and PA. Five of the intercept stations in the Pacific were focused on these Tokyo diplomatic broadcasts in 1941. The seeming redundancy was crucial; nothing could be left to chance. Radio signals are easily disturbed by outside elements. Solar storms can disrupt broadcasts here on earth. Transmissions intended for short distance sometimes bounce halfway around the world during sun spot activity. Thus

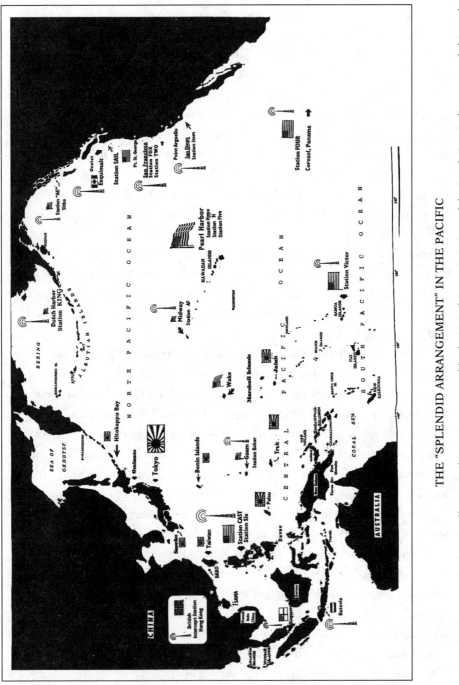

THE "SPLENDID ARRANGEMENT" IN THE PACIFIC

Twenty-two communications intelligence radio stations operated by the United States, Britain, and the Dutch East Indies surrounded Japan's government in the Pacific in 1941.

Army intercept stations in Manila, Honolulu, and San Francisco combined with two Navy facilities—CAST on Corregidor and Seattle's SAIL—as a hedge against a loss.

Of the four code systems, Purple contained messages that involved the most sensitive and important dispatches of the Japanese Foreign Ministry and its overseas ambassadors. Every Purple message yielded strategic decisions involving the Axis nations. In Berlin, Japanese Ambassador Baron Hiroshi Oshima frequently met with Hitler and his lieutenants and learned secret German strategy. Oshima dutifully passed along Hitler's secrets to Tokyo in the Purple Code. In fact, Roosevelt discovered Germany's plans for the invasion of Russia through a Purple intercept on June 14, 1941.[13]

Purple was a two-step encryption system. In the first encryption step, prior to radio dispatch, Ministry code clerks converted the Japanese text to Roman letters. Then the coded text was further encrypted by an electronic cipher machine process that used six rotor wheels to sequentially rearrange the Roman letters.[14]

To further foil American and Allied code-breakers, Japan issued separate ambassadorial codes to her various embassies. For example, the Tokyo–Berlin Purple system always remained cryptographically different from that of Tokyo–Washington. Thus, for the United States to read Purple messages obtained from the Washington and Berlin circuits, cryptographers had to solve each ambassadorial code first, then translate the message into English.

The essential element of the decoding process required reconstructing the cipher machine and its daily wheel sequence. Without the machine and the sequences, messages in the Purple system could not be read. Army cryptographic specialists led by Colonel William Friedman of the SIS solved the intricacies of the Purple machine in 1940 and constructed a prototype.

Friedman's staff produced their first decrypted message on September 25, 1940. When they were satisfied that they had the machine down pat, prototypes were reproduced by naval technicians at the Washington Naval Yard and sent to Station US, to CAST, and to the British government. The machine was not sent to Hawaii because the messages could be decrypted and translated at either CAST or Washington and sent from there to Army and Navy commanders on Oahu. Rear Admiral Leigh Noyes, the Director of Naval Communications, made the decision to exclude Hawaii: "I knew perfectly well that CAST could decipher the diplomatic traffic and send it to Honolulu." Noyes saw no point in a needless duplication of effort.[15]

The first step in decoding Purple messages required setting the daily letter sequences for the six rotor wheels in proper order. Each wheel had letters of the Roman alphabet engraved along the outside of its rim. Japan changed the sequence of the letters every twenty-four hours at midnight. Each day, a different six-letter sequence was used to signal how the alphabet would be encrypted. On a given day, every E would translate to a different set of letter combinations, every P to another, etc. There are billions of possible encryptions of the twenty-six-letter alphabet, according to David Kahn, author of *Codebreakers*.[16]

Ensign Laurance L. MacKallor, who was the Navy's Purple decoding specialist at CAST[17] and who personally guarded and transported the code machine from Washington, explained how he obtained the daily decoding sequences for the Purple code: "Normal traffic required a daily alphabetic sequence which determined the order in which the letters of the electric typewriter were connected into the cipher box. This sequence was usually recovered in the field [at CAST]. Sometimes the sequence could be predicted in advance, as Japs reused a master book which had been partially recovered. The sequence was usually recovered during the current day, but time of recovery varied greatly with depth and quality of traffic." Between November 29 and December 7, Commander Laurance Safford of Station US sent the daily Purple sequences to CAST by radio dispatch. For example, FTNLQB was the setting for the six wheels for November 29 and VUTHLD the sequence for December 5, according to Safford.[18]

A second tier of Foreign Ministry codes—known in America as the J series—played a pivotal role in pre–Pearl Harbor communications intelligence. General Short's Station FIVE intercepted the J system but—as discussed earlier—lacked expertise in decoding and translation. Between January 1 and December 3, Ministry officials, confident that the code had not been compromised, used Tsu for transmission of spy messages between Tokyo and Honolulu. For nearly twelve months a constant flow of Tsu messages between Hawaii and Tokyo reported operations of the Pacific Fleet and provided bomb plots of Battleship Row for Japanese aviators assigned to the forthcoming attack.

American cryptographers knew the code's techniques by heart, for they had first solved the J series in the 1920s. By 1941 Japan, hoping to outwit the code-breakers, introduced minor variants of the code every three months. Each of the three J series put into effect in 1941 was read and translated within a day's time.[19] There was no outwitting America's cryppies.

The J series was originally solved by what is politely referred to in cryptography jargon as the "direct method." This involved things like burglary of the baggage of Japanese Foreign Ministry couriers. Japan's Foreign Ministry preprinted variations of its code systems in separate code books that could be placed in effect at some future date. Then Foreign Ministry couriers delivered dozens of the books to the overseas missions. U.S. Naval intelligence officers learned a courier's route and method of transportation through decryption of radio dispatches such as this one directed to San Francisco: "Courier Fukuda[20] will be aboard the *Yawata Maru* to arrive in your city on April 24, 1941. Please arrange clearance through Customs." Navy men were happy to facilitate the movement of Fukuda and his code books through Customs. They placed officers on the docks, posing as customs agents, who opened the boxes containing the code books, quickly photographed their contents, then resealed the boxes and passed them through. Or the codes were bought outright. Agents in San Francisco paid $40,000 to Chief Radio Officer T. Harada of the *Yawata Maru* for the Japanese merchant-ship code *Shin*.[21]

The most explosive controversy involving America's foreknowledge of Japan's attack on Pearl Harbor centers on the *Kaigun Ango* [Navy Code], a system of twenty-nine separate naval codes. Japan used four of these systems to organize and dispatch her warships to Hawaii by radio. America's "splendid arrangement" had solved each of the four by the fall of 1941. So had the British, the Dutch, and the Chinese government of Chiang Kai-shek. A sixty-year coverup has hidden American and Allied success in obtaining the solutions to the *Kaigun Ango* prior to Pearl Harbor. American naval officers hid key code documents from congressional investigators. Naval intelligence records, deceptively altered, were placed in the US Navy's cryptology files to hide the cryptographic success.[22]

The four primary systems were: (1) Code Book D, known to American cryptographers as the 5-Num code; (2) a radio call sign code assigned to Japanese officials, shore stations, warships, and *Marus;* (3) the Ship Movement code, a system for reporting arrival and departures of naval vessels from Japanese ports and anchorages, known to Americans as the SM code; and (4) the *Shin* code, used for contacting vessels of the merchant marine, known as S code in America.[23]

From July to December 7, 1941, Admiral Isoroku Yamamoto, commander-in-chief of the Imperial Japanese Navy, transmitted his war orders using all four systems. The orders consisted at first of directives organizing the various fleets and assignment of personnel and then progressed to war assignments. Disclosure of Japan's Hawaii plans came during a dramatic sixteen-day period between November 20 and December 6, when Yamamoto and his commanders took to the radio airwaves and revealed that two forces were aimed at Hawaii: a main naval force moving across the North Pacific—six aircraft carriers escorted by battleships, cruisers, and destroyers plus a fuel train of seven tankers grouped together as the First Air Fleet—and a second force composed of thirty submarines and auxiliary vessels moving eastward through the Central Pacific. Both groups were under the tactical command of Vice Admiral Chuichi Nagumo and collectively called the *Kido Butai*, or Strike Force.[24]

Their encoded broadcasts over Japan's naval airwaves were intercepted at HYPO and, by most accounts, at CAST. After fifty-nine years, two essential questions remain: How promptly were the intercepts decoded and translated? Who in the United States received the translations and what was done with the information? Duane Whitlock, a traffic analyst at Station CAST, wrote that his unit was not reading the Japanese naval codes in 1941. "I can assure those messages (Japan's naval) were not read until they were sifted out and read in 1946." By contrast, Admiral Thomas Hart, commander-in-chief of the US Asiatic fleet was reading the intercepted messages obtained by Station CAST, according to his 1941 flag lieutenant Charles Adair.[25] The official answers are no one and nothing, according to the joint congressional investigations of 1945–46 and 1995. Both inquiries found that American cryptographers had not solved Japan's naval codes and that the Japanese warships were on radio silence and consequently were not discovered by American radio direction finders. Congress was told that not even Japan's shore-based radio stations disclosed any details pointing to Hawaii as the target. Congress did not find the truth.

Japan's SM code first disclosed the Hawaii plans early in November.

This code proved a gold mine for American cryptographers. It provided 210 movement reports of Japanese warships between November 2 and December 4. Every class of warship is represented, from mine layers to the carriers of the First Air Fleet. None of the SM dispatches were ever examined by Pearl Harbor investigators.[26]

An example of 5-Num and SM decryption before the attack can be documented through a CAST intercept of November 29. Lieutenant Rudolph J. Fabian, co-commander of CAST, quotes directly from the SM code in a radio dispatch sent by Vice Admiral Nobutake Kondo, commander of Japan's Second Fleet and the leader of naval forces about to conquer the Philippines and overrun the Southeast Asia region: "The Commander-in-Chief SECOND fleet indicates he will shift communications from the Kure Communications Zone at 0400, on the 29th; from the Sasebo Communication Zone at 0000, [on December] 1; and enter the Bako Communication Zone (in the Pescadores Islands west of Formosa) at 0000, on December 2, thus implying a move from Japan proper to the South." Fabian's report was delivered to the Naval Aide to the President, according to McCollum's assistant.[27]

Fabian's report established that CAST's cryptographers were decrypting and translating Japan's SM code as well as the radio call sign code. Cryptographer Albert J. Pelletier, Jr., of Station US verified that the Navy had broken the SM code in 1941. "We were reading ninety percent of the messages," Pelletier wrote in the official publication of the Naval Cryptographic Veterans Association, *Cryptolog*, in the Summer 1992 issue.[28]

The key figure in Roosevelt's "splendid arrangement" and in breaking the 5-Num code was Agnes Meyer Driscoll,[29] the Navy's chief civilian cryptanalyst. From the mid-1920s to 1941, she was instrumental in solving every Japanese naval-operations and ship-movement code. America's success in naval cryptography had its beginnings at the start of World War I. Its roots stem from a Shakespeare commune[30] established in Geneva, Illinois, by a Chicago textile merchant. The commune attracted a young student of genetics just out of Cornell University, William F. Friedman, who was hired by a merchant, George Fabyan, to improve agriculture techniques on the Geneva farm. But another interest of Fabyan's, cryptology, soon became Friedman's lifelong pursuit. Friedman's introduction to cryptology centered on the writings of William Shakespeare and whether they were actually written by Francis Bacon. Fabyan had assembled Shakespeare scholars on the farm and had Friedman, an expert photographer, copy words and phrases from the Bard for comparisons with those of Bacon. Friedman used his photography skills and with his future wife, Elizebeth (detesting Eliza, she substituted the E), developed cryptographic means to pursue the Baconian research. Enormous publicity followed the cryptographic quest and when America entered the war in 1917, Friedman's talent as a cryptographer caught the eye of the US Army, which offered him a commission in the newly formed code-breaking unit.

Agnes May Meyer joined the commune in February 1920 at the age of thirty, when the Navy sent her to Geneva, which by then had evolved into a major training center for military cryptography. She had patriotically joined the Navy Reserve in June 1918 with special qualifications in physics, engineering, math, and statistics earned at Ohio State University. Her skills were wanted by a new Navy unit called the Code and Signal Section. Though fully qualified for an officer's commission, Meyer was given a petty officer rating of Yeomanette. After completing classes at Fabyan's center, she resigned from the Navy and took a job with a firm engaged in developing electronic cipher machines in Oakland, California. Meyer became an expert in the concept of machine cryptography and on August 1, 1924, rejoined the Navy, this time as a civilian. Assigned to the fledgling Codes and Cipher Section, she worked under Laurance Safford and Joseph Rochefort in breaking Japanese codes. She was a fast learner. From 1924 onward through World War II she solved every Japanese naval code system. Rapidly she rose to the top in Navy cryptology and became the principal civilian cryptanalyst. She married Washington attorney William Driscoll in 1924. But among the cryppies of the Code and Cipher Section she was known as Miss Aggie or Madame X.[31]

Edwin Layton, later head of Intelligence for the Pacific Fleet, worked with her in the summer of 1936.[32] Warned that she was touchy, Layton was told not to patronize her because she was sensitive to her role as a woman in a man's world. He noticed that she kept to herself both at work and socially. "None of us were ever invited to social events hosted by the Driscolls," Layton wrote. "She could be warm and friendly but usually affected an air of intense detachment, heightened by her tailored clothes and lack of facial makeup." Sometimes Layton's ears picked out her voice:

"She could curse as fluently as any sailor." Rochefort recalled that she always turned pages with the eraser end of her pencil and never used her fingers as page turners. Eventually the Codes and Ciphers section became Station US, where in June 1939 Driscoll first identified Japan's switch to the 5-Num code and supervised the Navy's efforts at decryption. Of course the Navy could not publicly credit her with the solution. Not to do so was a deliberate decision devised to mask America's success in learning Japanese military secrets.

Driscoll formed a cryptographic team, the first Americans to identify the system. It appeared simple enough—groups of five numbers substituted for a Japanese word, hence the 5-Num code label. Japan tacked on addition or subtraction numbers to the original 5-Num group to confuse American and allied cryptographers. Two change techniques were used—one for the morning, the other for afternoon use. For encrypted messages, 11111 might be added to the basic 5-Num group in the morning and subtracted in the afternoon. Japan believed their 5-Num system to be unbreakable. But Driscoll was able to crack it when she realized it was similar to a code used by the American government in the Spanish-American War.[33]

Documents concerning the 5-Num Code remain classified, but it is clear from Admiral Ingersoll's statement that the code produced intelligible messages as early as October 4, 1940. The FBI confirmed the Navy's decoding success on October 21, 1940, and reported the feat in Department of Justice records.[34]

Driscoll's cryptographic team prepared written instructions for solving the 5-Num system and issued them as Radio Intelligence Publication (RIP) 73. Revisions of RIP 73 were issued by Washington as RIP 80 in March and July 1941.[35] With these revisions, cryptographers at CAST and HYPO had the capability to supply Generals MacArthur and Short and Admirals Hart and Kimmel with Yamamoto's plan of attack.

Some time in the fall of 1941 the latest techniques for solving the 5-Num code were issued from Station US—presumably by Driscoll and her team, headed by Ensign Prescott Currier—and sent to Hawaii so HYPO's cryptographers could produce decodes of Yamamoto's military plans for Admiral Kimmel. Yet the crucial decode details—presumably the latest version of RIP 73 or RIP 80—did not arrive in Hawaii until after the attack. The Department of Defense has refused to release delivery details. Even the 1995 Joint Congressional inquiry failed to probe this question.

This much is known: in the fall of 1941, a revised solution to the 5-Num system was sent to Hawaii on apparently the slowest boat in the Navy.[36] The solution would have let Admiral Kimmel in on Japan's secrets. A Navy document admits that the solution of elements of the 5-Num code was sent to HYPO from Station US in the autumn of 1941. This is an astonishing disclosure, for it directly contradicts postwar claims that the code was not readable until 1942 or early 1943. The Navy's admission, couched in caveats, boils down to this: On an undisclosed date, wrapped in an undisclosed package, carried by an undisclosed officer-courier, the 5-Num secrets were transported to Hawaii on an undisclosed vessel.

Inside the the package(s) were the means to break open Japan's Pearl Harbor plans, which had been transmitted over the airwaves and intercepted by the hundreds at Station H. As of December 6, Admiral Nagumo had originated 844 secret radio messages[37] in the 5-Num code, according to Japanese records. America's Stations CAST and HYPO obtained the messages, but apparently did not issue translated decryptions—nor, incredibly, did Station US, which had the solution to 5-Num that had been prepared by Driscoll and Currier. A total blackout concealed Nagumo's dispatches, and all Kimmel received was silence.

Only on the day when Admiral Husband Kimmel was fired, December 16, 1941, did the head of the Pacific Fleet get access to the intelligence community's most vital information. On that day Kimmel's temporary successor, Vice Admiral William Pye, received Admiral Nagumo's Message 845. In Nagumo's comprehensive radio dispatch to Tokyo, he reported the damage inflicted on the Pacific Fleet during the "surprise attack." Rochefort and his cryptographers at HYPO immediately intercepted and produced a long decryption—too late.[38]

Admiral Kimmel and the Pacific Fleet should have been the principal beneficiaries of the "splendid arrangement." That was the intent of Commander Laurance Safford, head of Station US, who had detailed Rochefort and nearly 140 military cryptographers and radio intercept operators to Kimmel by June 1. Starting on July 15, 1941, the cryptographers of Station HYPO, using intercepts from the four code systems of the *Kaigun Ango*, began providing Admiral Kimmel with a daily summary of Japanese naval operations. By the morning of December 6, when he received his final pre-war summary, at least 112,000 Japanese naval intercepts had been obtained by Station H. But intercepts that indicated a Japanese strike at American territory never appeared in the summary. Nor did any of the 844 messages dispatched by the First Air Fleet as it planned for the Pearl Harbor raid.

During President Roosevelt's fourth-term campaign in 1944, Republican candidate Thomas E. Dewey[39] learned of the "splendid arrangement" and saw in it the political means to defeat Roosevelt. He reasoned, if the White House was reading Japanese messages leading up to the attack, why were our forces in the Pacific caught so woefully unprepared? In the autumn of 1944, Dewey planned a series of stump speeches charging Roosevelt with advance knowledge of Japan's plan to attack Pearl Harbor. Dewey's proof was the intercepted Japanese messages.

His plans were impolitic, to say the least. War was raging in the Pacific and lists of American casualties were printed in the newspapers daily. Japan remained a wounded but formidable enemy. Japanese naval leaders did not realize that the *Kaigun Ango* codes had been solved by US codebreakers. Candidate Dewey risked sacrificing America's code-breaking advantage at a time when learning Japanese strategy was still a powerful factor in major battles. Japan would have immediately changed her code systems. General George Marshall, then chairman of the Joint Chiefs of Staff, persuaded Dewey to call off the code controversy. "American lives are at peril," Marshall aptly warned.

In 1999, almost sixty years later, the government has not released details regarding the delivery of the 5-Num slow-boat package despite the author's FOIA requests. Questions abound. Why weren't Nagumo's 5-Num radio messages detailing the First Air Fleet's advance on Hawaii delivered to Admiral Kimmel? The secrecy surrounding the slow-boat delivery is confounding. The Purple Code delivery to Manila and Churchill has been fully disclosed. When the Purple solutions were shipped to the Philippines for use by General MacArthur and Admiral Hart in January 1941, extraordinary security procedures prescribed by Naval Regulations were scrupulously followed and documented. Ensign MacKallor has told how he took charge of five packages containing RIP 72 and RIP 77—the former, the Navy's secret designation for the Purple Machine, the latter its code solutions and the instructions for its use.[40] According to MacKallor's written report, the shipment contained an instruction book, an electric typewriter connected to a cipher box, and a daily six-Roman-letter sequence that determined the settings of six cipher wheels that, used in combination, unmasked the coded Japanese text.

MacKallor armed himself with a pistol, took his crated packages to Washington's Union Station, and on January 19 boarded a transcontinental train to Los Angeles. He arrived in San Pedro on January 26 and headed for the USS *Sepulga*, an armed Navy tanker anchored in the Los Angeles harbor. MacKallor's chore was not easy. He loaded his crated secrets into a small boat and set out across choppy waters to the gangway of the *Sepulga* for transportation to Station CAST. It was a long trip. En route the tanker developed steering problems and returned to Los Angeles for repairs. She didn't reach Manila until March 25.

At about the same time that courier MacKallor started his journey to CAST, a similar ocean voyage began in Annapolis and transported two Purple machines and the 5-Num solutions to England so that Prime Minister Winston Churchill could share in the "splendid arrangement." On January 24, two auto caravans left Washington for Annapolis Roads in the Chesapeake Bay and the midchannel anchorage of the HMS *King George V*, one of Britain's formidable battleships. Lord Halifax, the new British ambassador to the United States, and his wife were arriving on the battleship. President Roosevelt,[41] in a demonstration of British-American solidarity, headed a reception party that included Secretary of the Navy Frank Knox, presidential military aide Major General Edwin Watson, and presidential naval aide Captain Daniel Callaghan. The presidential group left the White House, drove to Annapolis, boarded the warship, and welcomed the envoy to the United States.

At the same time another caravan, this one made up of Navy station wagons, headed for the *King George V*. Inside the vehicles were two Purple machines, their operating instructions, and solutions to Japanese naval codes including the 5-Num code and the radio call signs.[42] Four American military officers guarded the secret cargo: Major Abraham Sinkov and Captain Leo Rosen of the Army's Signal Intelligence Service, and Lieutenant Robert H. Weeks and Ensign Prescott Currier of Station US. The two Army officers were experts on the Purple Code; they were part of the team that discovered its solution in September 1940. Weeks and Currier were America's specialists in Japanese naval codes, especially the 5-Num. In a driving rainstorm, the four code-breakers loaded their cargo into an open boat and sailed out to the battleship, where the secret cargo and the four officers were brought aboard.

After the Roosevelt party escorted the ambassador ashore the battleship departed for England, arriving at the Scapa Flow Dock Yard February 6. The Americans and their crates were transported to the British code-breaking unit outside London called the Government Codes and Cipher School, where the machines and codes were delivered to Edward Travis, second in command. After instructing the British in the complexities of the code systems the Americans returned to the United States. Travis sent one Purple machine and the solutions of the Japanese naval codes to the British cryptographic unit at Singapore.

Churchill was now plugged into Japanese diplomatic and military strategy. Still the "splendid arrangement" was not in full operation in the Pacific, because experts in solving the 5-Num code remained in Washington. So in March and April 1941 three Navy code-breakers, schooled in the solutions of the 5-Num code at Station US, prepared to leave Washington for fleet assignments—Lieutenant John Lietwiler to Station CAST and Lieutenant Robert Weeks to the Atlantic Fleet's flagship, USS *Augusta*. Ensign Prescott Currier,[43] one of the Navy's brightest code-breakers, got the assignment to Station HYPO and the Pacific Fleet. Directives were issued ordering CAST and HYPO to work on the 5-Num code jointly, and to supply decoded translations to their respective commanders, Admirals Thomas Hart and Husband Kimmel.

In the Atlantic, Lieutenant Robert Weeks was ordered to the USS *Augusta*, and its commander, Admiral Ernest King.[44] The code-breaking plan was indeed a "splendid arrangement." Allied leaders Roosevelt and Churchill were plugged in; so were the British and American naval commands. An additional exchange included General MacArthur in Manila and the Dutch Army and Navy in Batavia.

Suddenly in late April the plans for distributing the solutions to the 5-Num code to America's military leaders crashed. Admiral Kimmel was cut from the loop—but the other major commanders were not. The severance was done this way: Currier was held in Washington and his orders to the Pacific Fleet canceled. But Lietwiler and Weeks continued to their new posts: Lietwiler to CAST and Weeks to the *Augusta*. Cover stories designed to mask the Kimmel cut-off abound. An official history of Navy intercept operations of the Pacific War claims that the 5-Num code was never described to, assigned to, or exploited by HYPO until after December 7. But other Navy records dispute the claim. In November 1940, for example, special IBM sorting equipment for use in decrypting the 5-Num code was ordered for HYPO.

Recoveries of the 5-Num code obtained by Station US and the British Singapore unit were received by CAST in March 1941, according to a secret dispatch sent by Admiral Hart,[45] who described the Singapore decryption activities: "The British employ three officers and twenty clerks on this system alone." A handwritten note on Hart's dispatch indicates that both Singapore and Station US had obtained at least 8200 recoveries in the 5-Num system and expected to obtain more. Another notation disclosed that HYPO would begin solution of 5-Num in July 1941. But the most astonishing disclosure on Hart's typewritten message is a handwritten margin note which directs that the dispatch be removed from Navy files and a dummy message substituted in its place. The order apparently came from Captain Joseph Redman, Assistant Director of Navy Communications. Redman's directive has hidden the contents of Hart's dispatch and the margin notes from every Pearl Harbor investigation. It disclosed the successful British effort aimed at penetrating the 5-Num system and set up a cryptographic red line for Admiral Kimmel: he would receive nothing from either Purple or 5-Num. His Purple Machine went to Singapore, and the 5-Num code was sent to him on the slow boat.

Kimmel's cut-off was orchestrated by Rear Admiral Royal Ingersoll, Assistant Chief of Naval Operations, who ordered CAST to supply intercepts from the Purple and 5-Num codes to Hart and General MacArthur but omitted any reference to Admiral Kimmel. General George Marshall, head of the US Army, knew of the arrangement. So did Captain Alan Kirk, Director of Naval Intelligence, Redman, and Commander Laurance Safford, head of Station US.[46]

In 1988, Prescott Currier[47] declined to give his version of the 5-Num cut-off: "Public disclosure of any aspect of intelligence collection is a bad thing; it calls undue attention to something we would much prefer to pass unnoticed." Currier had been assigned to Kimmel, but his June posting to the Pacific Fleet was canceled by Washington. Lieutenant Weeks and his Japanese code expertise arrived aboard the *Augusta* while the warship docked in Newport, Rhode Island, on June 15. So by the end of June 1941, the major American military commanders and the British government were plugged into the "splendid arrangement"—all except Admiral Kimmel and General Short in Hawaii, where, as far as Japanese intercepts were concerned, mum was the word. This cryptographic blackout was applied only to Hawaii.[48]

Congress tried to obtain details on the 5-Num distribution controversy during the 1945–46 investigation. Senator Homer Ferguson (R., Michigan) asked for the 5-Num intercepts. His request was derailed by Democratic members of the committee. Instead of producing the Japanese naval intercepts for Ferguson, the Democrats introduced the dubious "Winds Code." Supposedly the "Winds Code" was a variation of a proposed Japanese weather-report message that, if dispatched or broadcast on overseas radio channels, indicated a break in diplomatic relations and subsequent war with any or all of three countries: the United States, Great Britain, or Russia. But there is no proof that the "Winds Code" was ever transmitted by Japan.[49]

On November 28 Japan's Foreign Ministry first outlined the now discredited "Winds Code" in a secret radio message to its diplomatic posts and missions. Anticipating that communications would be severed by host countries, the ministry devised phrases with secret meanings to indicate war moves. Wind directions would be the key words in regular Tokyo news broadcasts: "east wind rain" would mean war with the United States, "west wind clear" would mean war with Britain, and "north wind cloudy" would mean war with Russia.[50]

News of the "Winds Code" system created a media sensation during the congressional hearings. Reporters focused on the "Winds Code" and lost interest in the less fantastic naval intercepts. Eventually the controversy was dismissed when Congress learned that the implementing weather message was never transmitted by Japan. By then the 5-Num dispatches had been forgotten.

Every 1941 intercept of the Japanese navy remained sequestered in

American files until 1979, when President Jimmy Carter[51] released a small number of English translations of pre–Pearl Harbor intercepts to the National Archives. These intercepts originated in the fall of 1941 and were obtained by US naval monitoring stations on Guam, Corregidor, and Hawaii. Even Carter's cautious declassification order was circumvented by National Security Agency officials, who blacked out all references to code systems before delivering them to the Archives. The documents released publicly only hid American success in solving Tokyo's encoded naval radio messages prior to the Pearl Harbor raid.

The US National Security Agency (NSA) defended its failure to release information involving American cryptographic success with Japan's naval systems. "It's in the public interest," according to David W. Gaddy, chief historian of NSA. He explained the censorship: "The subject cannot be debated publicly; the government cannot disclose the basis for its position if the basis is itself part of the secret it must protect as part of its obligation to secure the public interest."[52]

A Freedom of Information Act (FOIA) request filed by the author asked the National Archives to restore the blacked-out information on the Japanese intercepts for publication in this book. The request was granted in 1987 for the author's copies but not for the public viewing copies on exhibit at Archives II. Today, most blackouts on the pre–Pearl Harbor intercepts still conceal the 5-Num code designator used by the Japanese navy. These seemingly innocuous five-number sequences continue to hold the secret to understanding Japanese communications during World War II and—far more revealingly—the secrets to American officials' moves to obscure them.

CHAPTER 6

THE OUTSIDE MAN

BY THE CLOSING MONTHS OF 1941, AMERICA WAS INTERCEPTING AND breaking—within a matter of hours—most every code that Japan could produce. When December began, the cryptologists who had labored over the codes were not surprised to learn that some of them originated on American soil: they had long known that there was a spy operating in their midst.

As he strolled down Bishop Street toward the waterfront piers adjacent to Honolulu's Aloha Tower, Chief Yeoman Ted Emanuel checked his image reflected in a storefront window. He had reason to be looking his best. It was Boat Day—the arrival of an overseas passenger liner at Honolulu's Aloha Tower piers. Traditionally, each Boat Day was the occasion for one of Hawaii's most festive ceremonies. It was definitely a dress-up event. Emanuel was proud of his image reflected in the glass—tropical blooms covered every inch of his short-sleeved aloha shirt in a busy design of Hawaiian hibiscus, poinsettia, and bougainvillea. He carried a Leica camera hidden underneath his shirt; he was part of a clandestine naval intelligence team ordered by President Roosevelt to meet and survey every Japanese vessel docking at Honolulu. As early as August 10, 1936, Roosevelt had circulated a secret memorandum declaring: "Every Japanese citizen or noncitizen on the Island of Oahu who meets these Japanese ships or who has any connection with their officers and men should be secretly but definitely identified and his or her name placed on a special list of those who would be the first to be placed in a concentration camp in the event of trouble."

Emanuel was the Navy's senior undercover agent in Hawaii, assigned to maintain surveillance on suspected Japanese agents. On this particular Boat Day, his mission was to obtain a surreptitious photograph of a suspected Japanese navy spy arriving under diplomatic cover on the *Nitta Maru*, a luxurious passenger liner. Satisfied that the camera was obscured but that the lens could capture an image through a small hole cut into his shirt's floral design, Emanuel decided to test the arrangement. When he extended his arms in a waving motion, he could trip the shutter by stretching a concealed cable and wire release. The click of the shutter assured Emanuel that the camera worked. He hurried along Bishop Street to Pier 8. The *Nitta Maru* was scheduled to dock earlier than expected. She had arrived during the night and was anchored offshore in Mamala Bay, awaiting Customs clearance.[1]

Emanuel's target was the Japanese spy Tadashi Morimura, who was scheduled to assume the post of chancellor in the Japanese Consulate. The position was a responsible diplomatic job, usually assigned to seasoned, experienced members of the foreign service. Morimura's posting aroused suspicions within America's intelligence community, because he was young and not listed in the official Japanese Diplomatic Registry. Japan rarely sent twenty-seven-year-olds to fill such important consular posts. His real name was Ensign Takeo Yoshikawa; under the cover name of Morimura he had been detailed to Hawaii for espionage purposes. Yoshikawa had graduated from Japan's naval academy, Eta Jima, in the late 1930s. Japanese naval authorities decided that a navy officer was needed to observe military operations on Oahu and spy on the Pacific Fleet. His job called for him to gather fleet operational details, to obtain Hawaiian maps including photographs, and then to assemble them into an intelligence picture for use by Japanese torpedo and bombing pilots.[2]

Morimura would provide the operational intelligence on Pearl Harbor using the Tsu radio code in the J series of Japanese Foreign Ministry codes. For eight months in 1941, Morimura used the Tsu code and gradually presented Pearl Harbor as the target for Japan's bomber and torpedo pilots. On December 3, he switched to a simple diplomatic code known as PA for his final messages before the attack. American cryptographers had already broken the Tsu system as well as PA and could intercept, decode, and translate the dispatches within a day's time. Morimura's succession of Tsu dispatches, along with the final PA, confirmed that Pearl Harbor was a primary Japanese bombing target.

Morimura was allowed to operate freely throughout 1941. American authorities, including Roosevelt, never curtailed his espionage. Morimura was able to supply Admiral Yamamoto with highly accurate bombing charts of Pearl Harbor and other US Army and Navy targets on Oahu. On December 6 Morimura's work was complete. He notified the Japanese carrier force:

THERE ARE NO BARRAGE BALLOONS AT THESE PLACES—AND A CONSIDERABLE OPPORTUNITY IS LEFT FOR A SURPRISE ATTACK.[3]

From the eve of Morimura's arrival in Honolulu onward, Rear Admiral Walter Anderson placed a protective veil around the espionage conducted from the Japanese consulate. According to a memorandum issued by J. Edgar Hoover, Anderson told the FBI's special agent Robert Shivers, the agent in charge of the Honolulu Field Office, that the Navy would conduct the espionage investigation, not the FBI. Hoover indicated that the admiral had taken over the investigation with the FBI's approval.[4] Anderson was in a unique spot to oversee and control the espionage investigations. Before leaving Washington as Director of Naval Intelligence, he placed Navy intelligence officers in two key Hawaiian posts: he named Lieutenant Commander Edwin Layton as head of intelligence for the Pacific Fleet and Captain Irving Mayfield as director of intelligence investigations for the Fourteenth Naval District, which included all the Hawaiian Islands as well as American-controlled bases throughout the Central Pacific.

After completing two weeks of sea duty training in air raid drills aboard his flagship, the USS West Virginia, Admiral Anderson had arrived back in Pearl Harbor.[5] On March 26, the day before Morimura's arrival, Anderson met with Robert Shivers, the FBI chief in Hawaii, and reiterated the orders from Hoover: Navy Intelligence was in charge of the Morimura surveillance, not the FBI.

Special Agent Shivers supervised sixteen FBI special agents. The group worked out of the second-floor FBI Field Office in the Dillingham Transportation Building in downtown Honolulu. All were eager to investigate espionage involving personnel attached to Japan's Honolulu consulate. About mid-October 1940, shortly after Arthur McCollum proposed his eight actions, the FBI had been asked to refer investigations of Hawaiian espionage to Navy Intelligence. Hoover passed the policy along to Shivers—then sent another letter warning that the Japanese government planned to detail Japanese naval officers, disguised as clerks, to spy on American facilities.[6] Shivers' professional ethics were apparently offended. How was he to investigate espionage by Japanese naval officers and at the same time stand aside?

On October 31 Shivers protested the stand-aside orders to his boss: "This office has acquired considerably more information concerning the Japanese situation and has developed a much larger number of Japanese informants than the office of the Naval Intelligence. We are better equipped with superior investigative personnel."[7] Shivers' response to his order must have exasperated Hoover, for on December 14, 1940, the FBI director tried again: "The Federal Bureau of Investigation is not equipped with translators, interpreters, and informants and cannot undertake the full responsibility for Japanese espionage until it is equipped to do so."[8] Contrary to Hoover's assertions, however, Shivers did employ Japanese translators and informants in Honolulu. The informants were first rate— wiretaps on the consulate's telephones that provided inside ears into the activities taking place.

Hoover's memorandum, filed with the Army's Pearl Harbor investigation, relates a continuing tug-of-war with Shivers over espionage probes in Hawaii. Hoover confirms that he enlisted the aid of Captain Walter Anderson of ONI in trying to curtail Shivers' espionage investigations. Most of what transpired during the Anderson-Shivers meeting aboard the *West Virginia* remains unavailable. Attorney General Janet Reno has refused to declassify secret FBI files on the matter, citing FOIA rules that prohibit

disclosing national defense secrets.[9] But now-retired FBI agent Frederick
G. Tillman, who was the case agent assigned to Morimura in 1941, has
provided some details.[10]

Morimura's journey from Tokyo to Honolulu aboard the *Nitta Maru*
was tracked by American intelligence. The first break had come on March
8, when Foreign Minister Yosuke Matsuoka unwittingly tipped off American intelligence officials in a cablegram to Honolulu: "Secretary Morimura
being sent to Honolulu consulate."[11] The *Nippu Jiji*, a Japanese newspaper
published in Honolulu, reported Morimura's appointment and arrival
date. For the next nineteen days, US intelligence relied on a variety of intelligence data, including clear-text radio messages, J code intercepts, and
State Department correspondence, to track Morimura to Honolulu.[12]

When the *Nitta Maru* arrived in the Mamala Bay quarantine anchorage, Morimura remained in his cabin and awaited the arrival of Otojiro
Okuda, the vice consul. Unlike Morimura, Okuda was a thirty-seven-year-
old career diplomat of the Japanese Foreign Ministry. He had reported to
the consulate post on June 10, 1940, with his wife and two young sons.
Employees of the consulate regarded Okuda as snooty and were overheard
on the wiretap describing him as "disgustingly drunk" at parties. When
Consul General Kiichi Gunji was recalled to Japan in September, Okuda
became acting consul-general and the diplomatic spokesman for Japan in
Hawaii. His speeches were not exactly diplomatic. On Armistice Day, November 11, 1940, Okuda blamed the Western nations for the Japanese-
Chinese conflict and cited as a root cause Commodore Matthew Perry's
1853 expedition to Japan, which had opened up trade with the West:
"Since Japan opened her door against her will, she was compelled to face
and combat Western aggression in Asia."[13] Okuda was more than a
spokesman for his country. According to the Navy wiretaps and FBI reports, he supervised the gathering of military information pertaining to
Army units in the Hawaiian Islands and particularly the operations of the
United States Pacific Fleet at the Pearl Harbor naval base. On August 22,
1941, Tillman had identified Okuda as "the man at the consulate who is
concerned with intelligence matters."[14]

Morimura had been sent to Hawaii to serve as Okuda's "outside
man"—a polite term then used by the intelligence fraternity for a spy. He
was single, a handsome twenty-seven-year-old with somewhat Caucasian

features. His only avocations were wine, women, and song, and a large part of his every day and night was spent in indulging them.

The State Department saw the same puzzling questions in Morimura's background that Navy intelligence saw. They couldn't find his name in the Japanese foreign registry. Nor was Japan precise on Morimura's title. In their application for his diplomatic entry to the United States, the Foreign Ministry listed him as "Chancellor," yet in Honolulu he was announced as a "Secretary." These inconsistencies immediately flagged Morimura as suspicious.

Two naval investigators, Theodore (Ted) Emanuel and Lieutenant Denzel Carr, were on hand for the *Nitta Maru*'s arrival.[15] The US Navy's Inspector-General Captain W. S. Kilpatrick had praised Carr's work as "unequaled by anyone else in the United States naval intelligence service."[16] Carr joined the Customs inspection party posing as a health officer while with his concealed camera Emanuel took up a position on the dock. At six o'clock in the morning Carr and the Customs party climbed up the Jacob's ladder and boarded the ship in the anchorage. Its manifest designated thirty-three passengers debarking at Honolulu. Carr looked it over and spotted Morimura's name. Carr bided his time; he expected Vice Consul Okuda to arrive on board when the ship docked and escort Morimura ashore.[17]

The vessel received permission to dock at Pier 8, alongside the Aloha Tower. Confetti streamed through the air as the gangplank was lowered and secured. The Royal Hawaiian Band struck up "Aloha Oe," the haunting musical greeting composed by Queen Liliuokalani, Hawaii's last monarch.[18] Carr mingled with the Customs officials and watched Okuda bound up the gangway and head for Morimura's cabin. Okuda remained in the cabin for about thirty minutes, then escorted Morimura past the Customs boarding party to the liner's gangway, where both debarked about 8:45 A.M. Emanuel waited dockside and watched for a signal from Carr. As the two Japanese started down the gangway, Carr touched the top of his head. Emanuel saw the signal, began waving his arms as if greeting someone, and triggered his camera.[19] The two naval intelligence officers then returned to their headquarters in the Alexander Young Building, a short distance away. The next day, March 28, Emanuel placed Morimura on the Navy's Group A espionage-suspect list.[20]

Copies of the Navy's espionage alert were delivered to the FBI's Honolulu field office and to the intelligence officers for Admiral Kimmel and General Short. After the war, both Kimmel and Short testified that their intelligence officers did not inform them either of Emanuel's alert or that Morimura was under surveillance. Of the three intelligence agencies headquartered in Hawaii, only Shivers reacted sharply to Morimura's Class A espionage status. Ignoring directives from both Hoover and Anderson, Shivers placed a special watch headed by Tillman on the Japanese consulate.[21]

"We did not put a tight surveillance on him," Tillman said in 1990. "We couldn't do much around the consulate. The State Department told us not to monkey with the consulate. So we didn't. We would have gotten there (into the consulate) a little earlier if it wasn't for that. The consulate members were sacrosanct. Holy, you know."

Morimura didn't do much work in the consulate office, according to Tillman. "It came to our attention that he was the outside man. He spent most of his time outside the consulate. We would see him in the downtown areas and at various locations on Oahu. Once I tailed him to a Honolulu shoe store and watched while he purchased two pairs of shoes. I believed he planned a return to his homeland. Since leather shoes were difficult to obtain in Japan, I thought he was purchasing them to wear back home." Nearly fifty years after Pearl Harbor, Tillman said that the decrypted intercepts that were denied him would have made a crucial difference in curtailing Morimura's activities. "I was not aware or told about the interceptions until after the [Pearl Harbor] attack. Headquarters did send us a picture of him in late November, about two weeks before the raid. But the photo did not justify an arrest. Though we named him as a suspected spy, without the intercepts there was no way we could could prove in court what he was doing. We were not provided the intercept evidence. He had a right to go into the heights that overlooked Pearl Harbor."

Tillman does not believe Morimura was aware of the FBI's scrutiny. "Our eyes met at times, but I don't think he was wise to the loose surveillance." There was also the wiretap on Morimura's personal consulate telephone. The wiretaps gave advance warning of his trips to the country, which were usually followed by telephone calls to RCA or Mackay—both radio cable firms—for a messenger boy. Tillman did not follow Morimura when he went to various parts of the islands. "No need to," said the G-Man. "We knew what he was up to."[22]

Shivers forwarded Emanuel's warning to Hoover. For the next eight months American intelligence officials in Washington monitored Morimura's reports. But none of the Morimura Tsu and PA messages were ever seen by those who needed them most: Kimmel, Short, Hoover, Shivers, or even Tillman.[23]

Morimura was not particularly liked by the consulate's professional diplomats. As aware as US authorities that he was not included in Japan's Diplomatic Register and was using diplomatic cover, they saw him as encroaching on their territory. Kokichi Seki, the consulate's thirty-nine-year-old Third Secretary, was particularly miffed at Morimura. Originally, Seki had been responsible for spy reports on the Pacific Fleet. He was Okuda's first "outside man," from mid-December 1940 to late March 1941. Cautioned not to enter or photograph American military bases, Seki traveled on local roads and identified the best scouting locations. The consulate's 1937 Ford sedan, driven by Richard Kotoshirodo, was used for the trips.

Kotoshirodo, twenty-five, held dual citizenship and worked as a consulate clerk. During the first week of January 1941, Kotoshirodo and Seki went to several of the high vantage points surrounding Pearl Harbor. Rolling down the Ford's window for clear views, the spies took a census of the Pacific Fleet. Their first spy excursion of the New Year counted nearly seventy major warships in the harbor and provided a benchmark for Admiral Yamamoto's future war planning. Distinguishing characteristics of the ships were noted, including the number of scouting aircraft carried by battleships and cruisers. When confronted with his activities in 1943, Kotoshirodo would acknowledge what he had done, though denying responsibility. "I understood that I was gathering naval information for the Japanese government when I made these trips, but I gave no thought as to what my superiors in the consulate were going to do with it."[24]

On January 6, 1941, Acting Consul-General Okuda summarized their observations of the Pacific Fleet in Pearl Harbor in a 191-word report and encoded the message in the J Code. Before telephoning for a messenger from the local office of Mackay Radio & Telegraph, Okuda inserted a designator that meant that the message was intended for delivery to the Imperial Japanese Navy. It was a single five-number group near the beginning of the message, plus a five-letter group positioned at the start of the text. The letter group was distinguished by a consonant-vowel-consonant-vowel-consonant pattern.[25]

By placing the designator groups at the beginning of the message, Okuda unknowingly sent the report to the attention of Roosevelt and Churchill. Since Mackay was British-owned, Churchill had access to these messages. Documents reveal that Mackay's Washington office supplied copies of the spy reports to the White House. Both US and British intelligence knew that these designator patterns signaled espionage reports. American radio intercept stations in the Pacific were directed to send any Japanese spy messages containing the designators to Washington by priority dispatch. The first messages received in Washington disclosed Japan's interest in the number of warships at Pearl Harbor. Later in the year the reports progressed to bombing plots of the anchorage and the eventual recommendation that the American fleet at Pearl represented an opportunity for a surprise attack.

Mackay Radio & Telegraph began transmitting Okuda's text, labeled H-4, to Tokyo. As soon as the message hit Tokyo's airwaves it was intercepted by the US Army Signal Corps in San Francisco.[26] Unknown to Okuda and other Japanese officials, the Honolulu spy reports were at the top of America's watch list. Each report was flagged for American intelligence agencies by the designator system. Okuda radioed eight espionage reports to Tokyo during January 1941. And every radio message was transmitted by Mackay and intercepted by Army monitoring stations. The most successful of these was the intercept facility at Fort Winfield Scott in the San Francisco Presidio, known as Station TWO. Fort Scott operators intercepted seven messages, including H-4 of January 6, 1941. The intercepts were then forwarded to Station US in Washington, where cryptographers and translators confirmed that the messages were in the J series. Decoding and translating took only a day.[27] Each translated message—called a "smooth message" in cryptographic jargon—was distributed by McCollum to officials in the Roosevelt Administration.

Spy message H-4 was fully decoded and translated in Washington on January 10, four days after its interception at Fort Winfield Scott. Admiral Yamamoto received his copy about the same time. He noted that the Seki-Kotoshirodo team admitted errors in a December 1940 spy report and erroneously identified Navy patrol boats anchored in Pearl Harbor as minesweepers. This sloppy reporting was unacceptable to Tokyo and prompted the departure of Ensign Takeo Yoshikawa (as Morimura) to Pearl Harbor.

Once Morimura had arrived on Hawaiian soil, Seki guided him to observation points where Pacific Fleet operations in Pearl Harbor could be observed. Over the weekend of March 29–30, the pair hired a taxicab and scouted the fleet's operations. However, their alliance did not last. Okuda was embarrassed by Seki's past identification errors, and besides, the spies did not work well together. Seki resented the younger and less experienced man. He complained about Morimura's pursuit of after-hours pleasures and his drunken binges. But reining in Morimura was out of the question for Seki. It was Morimura's job to correct Seki's earlier errors. He had come to Hawaii with the backing of the highest levels of the Japanese Navy Ministry and had an expense account to prove it.

Honolulu was Morimura's kind of town. He looked forward to visiting Honolulu's Japanese tea houses, staffed with young waitresses and geishas. He quickly developed a lively social life, and spent his first dollars on a private telephone line. The Mutual Telephone Company installed the phone in his private quarters, located in the rear compound of the consulate—and published his phone number and address in the Hawaii phone book. It was not an auspicious beginning.[28]

Naval intelligence installed a wiretap surveillance on Morimura's telephone. It was an easy job, since the other consulate telephone lines were already tapped. The consulate's telephone conversations were piped to Ted Emanuel's residence three blocks away. Emanuel's home on Pacific Heights Road was selected so that Navy Intelligence could distance itself in the event the wiretap was discovered by the Japanese. A contingency cover story was readied in case of discovery, according to Denzel Carr: "Emanuel was just an overzealous gumshoe operating on his own." The Navy did not want an embarrassing international controversy.[29]

An automatic Dictaphone recorded the conversations on a cylinder. (Such machines preceded tape recorders.) Each morning, Emanuel carried the cylinders to Carr's office for translation. Soon the wiretaps revealed Morimura's activities: his fun-filled nights and trips to the country to gather information. For many days and evenings he combined work and

From: Honolulu (Okuda)
To: Tokyo (Gaimudaijin)
6 January, 1941
(J17–K6)
#002 (in 2 parts—complete)
Re my message #234 of last year.*
Vessels seen in Pearl Harbor on the morning of the 5th were as follows:
Five battleships (New Mexico, Mississippi, and probably the Idaho as well as two of the Texas class); five heavy cruisers (one of the Portland class, three of the ——— class, and one of the New Orleans); nine light cruisers (five) of the Honolulu class and four of the Omaha class); 37 destroyers; five destroyer tenders; two (patrol boats?); several special service ships (of which two seemed to be submarines, but it could not be definitely determined); two heavy cruisers in (dry dock?); one vessel—either a battleship or a cruiser, is outside the harbor.
Key-shaped cranes, similar to those toward the stern of the Idaho class cruisers, are being constructed on the five light cruisers of the Honolulu class, on the extreme end of the after-deck.
It was also noted that the more modern masts have replaced the mainmasts which used to be on the four Omaha class vessels.
The vessels which were previously reported to be mine sweepers are, in reality, patrol boats, so please make corrections.
JD–1: 165   13495   6 January, 1941   Navy Trans. 1–10–41 (2)

*JD–1 74 (SIS #13380).

Source: Pearl Harbor Report Part 12, page 255.

This is the American version of H-4—the first Japanese spy message sent from Honolulu in 1941. When it was introduced in evidence before the Congressional investigation of 1945–46, Okuda's vowel-consonant pattern had been omitted. A full Congressional look at the Morimura spy-grams never occurred.

Acting Honolulu Consul-General Otojiro Okuda dispatched H-4 to Japan's Foreign Minister Yosuke Matsuoka on January 6, 1941 (HST). It was encoded in the Japanese diplomatic Tsu code—known to US cryptographers as J-17.

Army Station TWO at Fort Winfield Scott in San Francisco intercepted the encoded text the same instant it was dispatched by radio to Tokyo. Station TWO personnel forwarded the coded text by air mail to Washington, where it was decoded and translated on January 10, 1941.

pleasure in the Shunchoro Tea House located high in Honolulu's hills; it had direct views of the warships in Pearl Harbor and the flight operations at Army airfields.[30]

Meanwhile, Consul Okuda worked to end the bickering between Seki and Morimura. He replaced Seki with Richard Kotoshirodo—the consular clerk—as the associate on most of Morimura's spy trips. Sometimes Morimura traveled alone—usually in a Packard limousine hired from the Royal Auto Stand. If ever there was a spy whose actions invited attention it was Morimura. The luxurious Packard stood out on Oahu's roads in contrast to the working-class Chevys and Model A Fords driven by the plantation laborers on Hawaii's sugarcane fields.[31]

Throughout April, May, and June, Morimura scouted military installations on Oahu. The Navy's enlisted men's landing at the foot of the Pearl City Peninsula proved to be a productive location. Morimura made friends with Teisaku Eto, whose soft-drink stand did a steady business with Pacific Fleet sailors whose ships were anchored in the lochs that comprise Pearl Harbor. Directly opposite Eto's stand, separated by a narrow stretch of water, was the Naval Air Station, Ford Island. The big carriers USS *Saratoga*, *Enterprise*, and *Lexington* sometimes berthed on the Ewa side of the island; the battleships were always on the Diamond Head side. Cruisers, destroyers, and auxiliary warships were moored to buoys in the various lochs. Morimura thought it amusing that US Navy officials allowed Eto, a Japanese alien, to operate his soft-drink stand right in the middle of the Navy base with clear views of the berthed or anchored warships. A similar situation was unthinkable in Japan—no American would ever be granted a lease near military compounds. America's freedoms enabled the spy to sip a soft drink, take a census of the Pacific Fleet, and eavesdrop on sailors' scuttlebutt as they waited for liberty boats to haul them to their warships.[32]

Cautioned not to break US espionage laws, Morimura and Kotoshirodo never physically entered or took photographs of any military installation. There was no need. Color postcards picturing military bases, and maps published by the US Geodetic Survey, were easily available from local merchants. By mid-May, Morimura's "outside" activities convinced Carr that the Navy's original assessment was correct. Trouble beset Morimura when he tried to establish a local bank account. The Honolulu branch of the Yokohama Specie Bank couldn't find any credit history and balked at setting up an account for him, according to the tap. The nature of Morimura's business in Oahu was clear. On May 16 Carr noted with an underline: "Morimura seems to spend most of his time <u>outside</u> the office. At first I assumed it was a coincidence or that he was sick, but now have decided he is the outside man." Tillman initialed the report and highlighted it for Washington.[33]

Morimura's espionage operations in Hawaii fall into two phases: from March 29 to August 21, 1941, and from August 21 to December 6. In the first phase he sent twenty-two messages to Tokyo. The Army and Navy intercept stations at Corregidor, San Francisco, Fort Hunt, Virginia, and Mackay's Station X in Washington obtained nineteen of the messages. In these intercepts, Morimura reported on types of warships and aircraft he saw operating from Pearl Harbor and at Army airfields.[34]

He located the Navy and Army radio transmitting facilities on Oahu, but missed Station H. Station FIVE, General Short's intercept unit at Fort Shafter, also escaped scrutiny not only by Morimura, but by Japan's new Consul-General Nagao Kita and by Okuda. During a ceremonial visit to Fort Shafter in April to honor Kita's arrival at the diplomatic post, both failed to notice the unit, which was located in an old laundry building near the main gate.

For over fifty years top FBI officials have denied knowledge of Morimura/Yoshikawa's activities prior to December 7, 1941. Their denials are another major Pearl Harbor cover-up. Two dozen FBI and Navy documents dated before the attack link Morimura with espionage in Hawaii. According to these documents, senior American intelligence officials, including the President, knew of Morimura's espionage at the Honolulu consulate. His reports clearly pointed to Pearl Harbor as a prime target of Japanese military planners.[35]

On April 2, seven days after Morimura's arrival at the Honolulu Consulate, various activities of Japanese governmental missions in the United States came under the direct scrutiny of the Joint Intelligence Committee, a group formed by Roosevelt to monitor suspected espionage. Its members included Hoover, the Army and Navy Intelligence directors,[36] and Assistant Secretary of State Adolf Berle, Jr., FDR's personal representative to the J.I.C. The committee noted that Japan had increased personnel at various diplomatic posts in the US "out of all reasonable proportion to the volume of business transacted."[37] Hoover was directed to discuss the matter informally with Berle. Their talks triggered additional surveillance in Honolulu, beginning with the wiretap on Morimura's phone. On April 29 Berle coordinated the FBI team investigating Japanese agents assigned to diplomatic posts.[38] In late May a mail cover[39] was placed on the Honolulu consulate by FBI agent Tillman. It directed the postal service to furnish a listing of all return addresses found on mail delivered to the consulate. In his interview with the author, Tillman said he wanted to identify persons contacting either the consulate or Morimura by mail. Later in the month, FBI interest in Morimura heightened when agents obtained his picture and distributed it to all Field Offices. Finally on June 16 Morimura was named the head Japanese espionage agent in Hawaii by the FBI.

The espionage reports involving foreign consulates triggered immediate reaction in Washington. Somehow rumors reached the press corps. Reporters questioned Roosevelt and asked whether consulates of nations other than Germany were engaged in "doubtful activities." One reporter specifically sought details about subversive characters attached to foreign consulates. Roosevelt dodged the question: "There isn't any news on that today." But questions persisted: "Mr. President, there have been charges made that certain other consuls and countries have also engaged in doubtful activities." Again FDR, who occasionally wrote a column for a Hyde Park weekly, dismissed the question with a joke: "We newspapermen don't speculate."[40]

It is quite possible that Director Hoover learned he was excluded from the Tsu intercepts and, in a state of pique, planted the espionage questions directed at FDR with favored White House reporters. The FBI chief was well known for leaking secrets to friendly newsmen, such as Walter Winchell, the powerful New York gossip columnist and radio broadcaster. Navy communications officials excluded the FBI from the Japanese intelligence loop and Hoover wanted in. A major dispute erupted between Hoover and the Navy on April 15. The prickly FBI director was offended when he was refused access to secret naval communications documents. FBI censorship still veils the full details, but apparently Navy codebreakers refused to share Japanese intercepts, including the Tsu reports, with Hoover.

Hoover was vindictive: "Because of the uncooperative attitude which has been displayed towards the Federal Bureau of Investigation by the Communications Division of the Navy Department it is essential that all Bureau Agents be most circumspect[41] in the handling of any material obtained which may be of interest to the Office of Naval Communications." Every FBI agent knew that Hoover meant there was to be no cooperation with Navy Communications.

A tenacious Hoover kept up the pressure on President Roosevelt. He fought to arrest consulate spies or force their recall to Japan. Berle calmed the FBI chief and said that only Roosevelt could expel Japanese consular agents engaged in espionage: "No expulsion is possible as any charge leading to ouster would reveal American cryptographic success to Japan."[42] Neither Berle nor the President wanted to lose the secret Japanese pipeline. Hoover never gave up and continued compiling evidence. Though there is no proof that he saw the Tsu reports, he continued to forward evidence of the Japanese espionage at Honolulu to Berle. Two reports prepared for Hoover by Tillman found their way to the White House in August.[43] They named Morimura as the "outside man" at the consulate and reported that Consul-General Kita, who signed Morimura's spy reports, had been placed on the FBI's "most dangerous" list.

Soon after Kita earned his place on the FBI's list, Hawaii espionage entered a new period. Morimura began his second phase of activity: preparing bomb plots of the Pearl Harbor naval base.[44]

CHAPTER 7

ALL CLEAR FOR A
SURPRISE
ATTACK

MORIMURA BEGAN PHASE TWO OF HIS REPORTS ON AUGUST 21, 1941. In addition to keeping track of the warships present, Phase Two established grid coordinates for Pearl Harbor so that Tokyo could prepare maps of Pacific Fleet anchorages for the bombing and torpedo pilots of the First Air Fleet.

On August 21, Morimura,[1] using information gathered at Pearl Harbor by Richard Kotoshirodo, identified fifty-three of the Navy's docks, piers, and anchorage areas and designated each by a letter code. He marked the berth of the USS *Arizona* as Ho Ho, and then sent the coordinate details to Ambassador Nomura in Washington, asking that copies of the message be forwarded to Tokyo and the San Francisco consulate. His bomb plot grid details were encoded in the J code and sent by RCA radiograms from Honolulu to Japan's Washington embassy. Censorship has concealed from the American public the details contained in this first bomb map, nor was the map's existence ever revealed to Congress in any of the Pearl Harbor investigations. Even worse, at the time when it was needed most, the report of these J-code intercepts was withheld from both the US Pacific Fleet and the US Army commander on Oahu.

Though the grid details for the bomb plot map are locked in National Archives vaults in College Park, Maryland, it is possible to circumvent most of the censorship. The contents of Morimura's grids can be pieced together using collateral information found in the Navy wiretaps and secret FBI reports obtained through FOIA requests. The plots were based on the best maps that money could buy. According to the Navy wiretaps provided to the FBI, the Japanese consulate had purchased US Geodetic Survey maps earlier in 1941 from a bookstore in Honolulu. Morimura's grid coordinates were probably keyed to those highly accurate maps.[2]

On August 21 John Mikami, whose Packard taxi service was favored by Morimura, drove up the circular driveway leading to the two-story Japanese consulate building, which was adorned with the chrysanthemum seal of the Emperor of Japan and the rising-sun flag. He parked the Packard limousine beneath the Emperor's symbol and awaited his passenger. But instead of Tadashi Morimura, out came Richard Kotoshirodo, who sat alongside Mikami and directed him to proceed north to scenic roadside turnouts that provided views of Pearl Harbor. Kotoshirodo, a $75-per-month clerk in the consulate, was paired with Morimura after Vice Consul Otojiro Okuda dismissed Third Secretary Kokichi Seki from the spy team. Two years younger than Morimura, the twenty-five-year-old Kotoshirodo was an American citizen born in Honolulu. He and his wife, who were childless, lived in Honolulu with his mother and two brothers and two sisters. He began working for the consulate in 1935 and had hopes of joining the Japanese diplomatic service.[3]

Morimura and Kotoshirodo worked well together. Both were young and enjoyed excursions to the nearby islands of Kauai, Maui, and the "Big Island" of Hawaii, where they spent Morimura's generous expense account visiting bars and brothels. In between they scouted the islands for military installations. Kotoshirodo first appears in the wiretaps on December 4, 1940, and about a dozen times in 1941, mostly in conversations with women. Nothing in the wiretaps indicates that he was associated with spying. Though the Navy's espionage file on Kotoshirodo begins on February 18, 1941, he is not mentioned in the pre–Pearl Harbor FBI spy lists. The Navy file does not contain the 1941 documents pertaining to Kotoshirodo.

Driver John Mikami followed the assistant spy's directions. The trip took two hours—a two-dollar charge in Mikami's account book. Upon his return to the consulate, Kotoshirodo reported to Okuda's office. Here he found Morimura drawing a rough sketch of Pearl Harbor. Kotoshirodo was asked to assist in updating the military layout of the naval base. He confirmed the location of battleships alongside Ford Island and of repair facilities and dry docks in the Navy Yard. Morimura labeled each of the fifty-three military targets with a four-letter symbol. Late in the afternoon, RCA's motorcycle messenger picked up the bomb map message and it was dispatched in an unusual roundabout way to the Naval Ministry in Tokyo.

Intercept logs in Station US in Washington traced this message. Two monitoring units, Station CAST on Corregidor and the Army's Station SEVEN at Fort Hunt, Virginia, intercepted its RCA radio signals. Though censorship makes the message difficult to trace today, both units heard and transcribed it. They said that it contained sixty code groups of five letters each in the J system and the subject concerned the movement of US warships.

Navy wiretaps of August 22 show that Morimura celebrated his first bomb map report by going on a binge in several Honolulu bars. At 2:17 A.M., just after the bars closed, he was picked up roaring drunk by the police.

About eight hours later, the wiretap on Okuda's office telephone highlighted the story. At 10:15 A.M. an unidentified man told Okuda that he was greatly worried by a police matter. Okuda immediately telephoned the *Nippu Jiji*, a Japanese-language newspaper in Honolulu, and talked with reporter Zenichi Kawazoe, who confirmed that the Honolulu police had issued a report on Morimura's public drunkenness. On Saturday morning stories about Morimura's behavior reached reporters, who began checking the reports. Lawrence Nakatsuka, of the *Star-Bulletin*, telephoned the consulate for details. The wiretap provides a record of the conversation:

NAKATSUKA: I heard a very bad story about the Japanese consulate that says this Morimura fellow sure runs wild.
CONSULATE: Yeah. How do you know?

NAKATSUKA: A reporter is supposed to know everything. What's the matter with the guy, anyway?

CONSULATE: You know better than I.

NAKATSUKA: I didn't know he would be that wild.

CONSULATE: He's wild already.

NAKATSUKA: Is he still working or have you folks fired him?

CONSULATE: No.

NAKATSUKA: What! You won't fire him?

CONSULATE: No.

NAKATSUKA: If I was Kita, I would fire that guy.

CONSULATE: You would?

NAKATSUKA: Sure. You can't let him make so much trouble as that.

CONSULATE: Too bad. He takes advantage of that.[4]

Morimura's binge also came to the attention of the FBI. A two-page wiretap transcript describing the incident was forwarded to the FBI's Tillman, who saw and initialed the report on August 27. So by the end of August, Morimura's spying on the Pacific Fleet, his first bomb map of Pearl Harbor, and his raucous public behavior were all in America's intelligence pipeline. It led from Tillman in Honolulu to Hoover at the FBI to Adolf Berle, Jr., at the State Department.

In the White House, the messages soon caught the attention of President Roosevelt. Throughout 1941, Berle served as the President's source for espionage activities involving foreign diplomatic missions within the United States. There is no doubt that Berle was aware of Morimura. On August 7, FBI Director Hoover informed Berle that Morimura was Japan's "outside man" in Honolulu. In the next three weeks Hoover sent five more reports by special messenger to Berle. To assure that FDR would see the reports, Hoover sent copies to the President's military aide, Major General Edwin "Pa" Watson. But the content of the reports is unknown. In 1999 the text is blacked out by the FBI as a category B-1 national defense secret.[5]

Captain Theodore Wilkinson, FDR's third Director of Naval Intelligence for 1941 and a colleague of Berle, admitted, "We were cognizant of the fact that espionage on the fleet was underway but we were helpless to

Strictly secret.

Henceforth, we would like to have you make reports concerning vessels along the following lines insofar as possible:

1. The waters (of Pearl Harbor) are to be divided roughly into five sub-areas. (We have no objections to your abreviating as much as you like.)

Area A. Waters between Ford Island and the Arsenal.

Area B. Waters adjacent to the Island south and west of Ford Island. (This area is on the opposite side of the Island from Area A.)

Area C. East Loch.

Area D. Middle Loch.

Area E. West Loch and the communicating water routes.

2. With regard to warships and aircraft carriers, we would like to have you report on those at anchor, (these are not so important) tied up at wharves, buoys and in docks. (Designate types and classes briefly. If possible we would like to have you make mention of the fact when there are two or more vessels along side the same wharf.).

ARMY 23260   Trans. 10/9/41   (S)

Source: PHPT 12, p. 261.

THE BOMB PLOT ORDER

This is the English version of the Tokyo request for the bomb plot order of September 24, 1941, as printed for the Joint Congressional Investigation of 1945–46. It is inaccurate because American censors excised the priority designator contained in the original Japanese text from the Congressional printing (upper left). Such designators, inserted in spy reports by the Japanese, flagged the messages for American intelligence. Gerhard Gesell, Chief Assistant Counsel for the 1945–46 Joint Congressional Investigation, explained why the designators were missing: "They do not appear on our copies of the exhibit because as we advised the committee, we had them stricken off" (Gesell's testimony, December 19, 1945, PHPT 4, p. 1911).

For over fifty-five years, no member of the public has seen the original of this message, which contains the Japanese spy designators. Twice the original message details have been denied to Congress—during the 1945–46 inquiry and during the Thurmond-Spence probe of 1995.

A letter S at lower right confirms that this message was intercepted at Station SAIL, near Seattle. The order originated with the foreign minister of Japan, Admiral Teijiro Toyoda, and was addressed to the Japanese consulate, Honolulu. Toyoda directed the consulate to prepare a coordinate-grid schedule of the Pearl Harbor anchorage and divide the waters into five areas including Battleship Row (Area B). J-19 denotes that the message was encoded in the Japanese diplomatic Tsu system. In 1945, Congress was told that Army cryptographers (Army 23260, lower left) couldn't decode and translate this message until October 9—a delay of fifteen days (lower right). The Army's intelligence chief dismissed this type of communications intelligence as "chitter chat." It was withheld from both Admiral Kimmel and General Short in Hawaii.

stop it. We could not arrest Japanese subjects. There was nothing we could do. All hands knew that espionage was going on all along and reports were going back to Japan."[6]

Hoover complained that the Department of Justice impeded his investigation of the espionage being conducted from the Japanese consulates. Berle's diary entry for June 3, 1941, reports that the FBI director was "unhappy about a lot of things but principally because he gets information about various activities but can never do anything about it." Berle hinted in his diary that Francis Biddle, FDR's Attorney General, had silenced the FBI director: "I think there is some tension there between him and Biddle."[7]

Apparently in late September Hoover, looking for congressional support for the FBI's counter-espionage efforts, leaked some information on Morimura's activity to a Senate committee that included Senator Guy M. Gillette (D., Iowa). The senator was quoted by the Associated Press in an October story alleging that the Japanese consulate in Honolulu was under American espionage surveillance.

On September 24, Tokyo indicated a growing interest in the American fleet's precise anchorage patterns in Pearl Harbor and asked Morimura for more grid details. Station SAIL, the US Navy's monitor station outside Seattle, intercepted the order. Morimura was directed to divide Pearl Harbor into five grid areas and locate the berthing locations of all warships, including aircraft carriers. Morimura lost no time and spent two days scouting the Pacific Fleet. Mikami's Packard once again toured the high roads around the naval base that weekend.

Morimura developed a more intricate grid system for identifying warship berths in his second bomb plot. Battleship Row was designated bombing area FG. Morimura completed the grid details on Monday, September 29, and telephoned for a Mackay messenger. The text was wired to Tokyo and a copy sent to the Washington embassy. The combination of Tokyo's request and Morimura's response was intercepted by four monitor stations: SAIL, CAST, Station TWO, and Station SEVEN at Fort Hunt, Virginia. Officials at Mackay's Station X in Washington permitted Navy photographers to copy the bomb plot messages addressed to the Japanese embassy.[8]

According to testimony given to various Pearl Harbor investigations, the decoded and translated bomb plot messages were greeted with indif-

---

[*13*]   From: Honolulu (Kita)
To: Washington
29 September 1941
(J19)
Circular #041
Honolulu to Tokyo #178
  Re your #083*.
  (Strictly secret.)
  The following codes will be used hereafter to designate the location
of vessels:
  1. Repair dock in Navy Yard (The repair basin referred to in my
message to Washington #48**) : KS.
  2. Navy dock in the Navy Yard (The Ten Ten Pier) : KT.
  3. Moorings in the vicinity of Ford Island: FV.
  4. Alongside in Ford Island: FG. (East and west sides will be
differentiated by A and B respectively.
  Relayed to Washington, San Francisco.

JD–1: 5730 23312   (D) Navy Trans. 10–10–41 (X)

*Not available.
**Available, dated 21 August.

Source: PHPT 12, p. 262.

MORIMURA'S REPLY OF SEPT 29, 1941

Morimura's second bomb map pushed FDR into action. Not content with this intercept from British-owned Mackay Radio, FDR persuaded David Sarnoff, president of RCA—an American-owned wireless firm—to give the Hawaiian Army and Navy intelligence officials copies of the Japanese messages in Hawaii.

This English translation of Morimura's bomb plot grid exposes three false statements by Navy officers:

1. They testified to Congress that cable firms such as RCA and Mackay refused them access to the Morimura espionage messages prior to December 7. The X in the lower right refutes the contention. It indicates this report was photocopied in Mackay's downtown Washington office by Navy photographers on September 29, 1941.

2. The claim that message 83 is not available (lower left) is false. Message 83 is Admiral Toyoda's bomb-plot order to Morimura. It was intercepted by the Navy's Station SAIL, near Seattle, on September 24 and immediately became available to American cryptographers.

3. Congress was not told that this message was also intercepted at Station CAST in the Philippines and was available to General MacArthur and Admiral Hart, the American commanders. Neither informed their counterparts in Hawaii that they had such a message.

ference by Army and Navy intelligence officials in Washington. Brigadier General Sherman Miles, head of Army Intelligence, told Congress in 1945 that he saw the bomb plot intercepts but none impressed him as anything more than "chitter chat." Miles dismissed a question posed to him by congressional investigator Gerhard Gesell: "It was primarily of naval interest." Miles didn't agree with Gesell's position that Morimura prepared a bombing plan for Pearl Harbor. He implied that Japanese agents prepared similar plots locating US warships in harbors and anchorages throughout the world and that they were inconsequential. Gesell asked, "Will you find me one such message, General?"

"Well," responded Miles, "if you mean similar in dividing the harbor into sections, there are no such messages that I know of."[9]

When it came time for Navy intelligence to explain their failure to warn Admiral Husband Kimmel of the bomb plot messages, political pandemonium erupted in the congressional hearing room. Republicans interrupted the testimony of Admiral Theodore Wilkinson and charged that the Navy was "spoon feeding" evidence to Congress. Wilkinson, head of Naval Intelligence between October 15 and December 7, 1941, attempted to deflect Gesell's question about the bomb plot messages:

GESELL: This is a bomb plot message, isn't it, Admiral?
WILKINSON: In general, yes. I discussed the message with other officers in the Navy Department including Captain [sic] McCollum. [In 1941, McCollum was a commander.]
GESELL: Do you recall your conversation?
WILKINSON: It showed an illustration of the nicety of detail of intelligence the Japanese were capable of seeking and getting.
GESELL: What did they say to you?
WILKINSON: I don't recall.[10]

Military officials may claim to have treated the bomb plot grid communique with indifference, but President Roosevelt certainly did not. On October 14 he invited David Sarnoff, founder and president of RCA, to lunch at the White House. The Mackay connection formed the basis for this one-hour Sarnoff-Roosevelt luncheon. If the British-owned Mackay firm supplied bomb map intercepts for the British Prime Minister, then, the President must have reasoned, US-owned RCA should supply copies of the

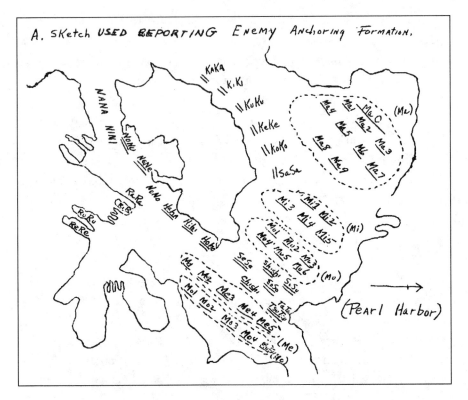

A. Sketch USED REPORTING Enemy Anchoring Formation.

Source: Pacific Fleet Intelligence Bulletin I-42. RG 38, MMRB, Archives II.

This bombing and torpedo plot of Pearl Harbor was recovered by Navy intelligence from a downed Japanese plane on December 7, 1941. Ford Island is shown center; the adjacent Battleship Row is designated as NoNo (top) to HoHo (USS Arizona*). The Navy Yard berths (left) are marked RaRa to ReRe. At the right the M series denotes cruiser and destroyer anchorages in East Loch.*

Hawaiian bomb plot messages direct from its downtown Honolulu office. Sarnoff, who held a general's commission in the Army Reserve, offered to match the Mackay arrangement and left for Hawaii, going by train from Washington to San Francisco, and then taking the SS *Matsonia* to Honolulu. Assistant Secretary of the Navy James Forrestal sent a Navy radio message to Admiral Kimmel asking him to extend every courtesy to Sarnoff.[11]

Sarnoff spent nine days in Hawaii, discussed communications intelligence with Admiral Kimmel, Lieutenant General Short, and Lieutenant Commander Rochefort of HYPO. The Sarnoff visit, but not its true purpose, was well publicized in Hawaii. The *Star-Bulletin* published a news photo of Short conferring with Sarnoff and the local RCA manager, George Street. During his visit, Sarnoff directed that copies of all Japanese consulate messages filed with RCA in downtown Honolulu be provided to Navy intelligence. Rochefort later testified that at Station HYPO he had the facilities to decode and translate the Japanese messages released by Sarnoff, but the early days of December would show that Rochefort failed to do so once they were in his hands.[12]

Before he returned to the mainland on the steamer SS *Matsonia*, Sarnoff sent a direct wire to President Roosevelt: "I am glad to report to you that the heads and the staff of the Army and Navy here are well informed and keenly alive to the latest developments in communications and to their useful possibilities." It appeared that Admiral Kimmel and General Short would now be given copies of the Japanese espionage messages. But they weren't.

The original copies of the messages were obtained from RCA's Honolulu office under the Sarnoff-Roosevelt arrangement. Then, once transmission started, Army and Navy monitoring stations throughout the Pacific Rim plucked the messages off the RCA airwaves and placed their contents into the White House intelligence loop. But deceit took over. Neither Short nor Kimmel received the cables until after the December 7 attack. According to the evidence, it was not a bureaucratic snafu that delayed the cables getting into American hands but Washington deceit—and the Hawaiian commanders, their sailors and troops, and the civilians of Honolulu were the victims.

A series of Navy documents that were hidden from all Pearl Harbor investigations provides the evidence and the trail of deceit. The trail starts with a seemingly innocuous radio dispatch on November 24. Rear Admiral Walter Anderson, Commander, Battleships of the Pacific Fleet, and the original addressee of McCollum's action plans, sent the November 24 dispatch to Captain Irving Mayfield, District Intelligence Officer for the Fourteenth Naval District. Mayfield was ordered to report aboard Anderson's flagship, the USS *West Virginia*, to serve on a court-martial board. The radio orders removed Mayfield from his very important intelligence duties—including supervision of the Sarnoff-Roosevelt arrangement. After Mayfield reported aboard Anderson's flagship, the Sarnoff-Roosevelt arrangement completely failed in Hawaii. Between November 28 and December 6, Morimura's spy messages obtained by American intelligence in Hawaii and Washington were deliberately derailed and mistranslated. There is only one plausible reason for the failure—to keep the information from Kimmel and Short and so ensure an uncontested overt Japanese act of war.

Mayfield's subordinates in the Honolulu naval intelligence office attempted to place the Sarnoff agreement in operation but immediately faced difficult obstacles. Navy intelligence officer Lieutenant Yale Maxon picked up the first batch of spy reports at the RCA office on Monday, December 1. Maxon and his colleague Lieutenant Denzel Carr were skilled Japanese linguists, but not cryptographers, so they were unable to decipher the messages. Maxon knew that Rochefort had the skilled personnel and facilities to decode the messages and requested his help. In 1982 Maxon and Carr vividly remembered alerting Rochefort. "I obtained the RCA messages the morning of December first," Maxon said. "Denzel normally would have taken custody but was ill with the flu. The coded messages on the RCA forms were unreadable. Yet I knew they were important because of the earlier visit of Mr. Sarnoff who met with our boss, Captain Irving Mayfield, head of Navy Intelligence in Honolulu." Maxon decided to send an alert directly to Rochefort; it is known to the author as the Maxon alert.[13]

In his handwritten note to Rochefort, Maxon carefully chose his words. He knew the code-breaking unit was surrounded with secrecy to prevent leaks to the Japanese. Marking the note "SECRET," he alerted Rochefort that "radio checks, from a source you know, are now available." Both Maxon and Carr suspected that the coded messages involved espionage of some sort. The code-breaker had discussed the RCA messages with Sarnoff during his visit and had agreed to assist Maxon and Carr.[14]

Then problems arose. There were no Navy officer couriers available to speed the RCA messages to Rochefort's office, eight miles away in Pearl Harbor. Washington had disallowed a five-cents-a-mile cost for use of officer courier automobiles earlier in September. Though made personally aware of the RCA messages by Sarnoff's visit, neither Kimmel nor Short ever took an interest in them. After the war ended, they would claim that they were unaware of these messages. Rochefort was equally lax. He knew of the spy messages through the Sarnoff meeting and the Maxon alert. And his daily commute to Pearl Harbor from his Honolulu hills home took him directly past the RCA wireless office. He could have personally picked up copies of the messages each day.

On Tuesday, December 2, Morimura informed Tokyo that the naval base at Pearl Harbor was not on the alert for an attack. Commander Mitsuo Fuchida, leader of the air attack, said he received the report aboard the *Akagi*. According to Fuchida, Morimura's message was:

NO CHANGES OBSERVED BY AFTERNOON OF 2 DECEMBER. SO FAR THEY DO NOT SEEM TO HAVE BEEN ALERTED. SHORE LEAVE AS USUAL.

Morimura filed the report with RCA at 4:51 P.M. as consulate outgoing message 357. The message reached Station HYPO on Friday afternoon, December 5, and was in the group that Rochefort's staff deciphered and translated prior to December 7. The consulate log said it concerned "Movement of USN Warships." But the description of the message by Rochefort's diplomatic cryptographer, Farnsley Woodward, conflicts with the Fuchida version. Woodward labeled the text of 357 as "?". Neither Congress nor any Pearl Harbor investigation explored Woodward's contradictions. Morimura's original of 357—filed with RCA—has never been released by the United States.[15]

When Sarnoff left Honolulu on November 14, twenty-three days remained before the attack. Toward the end of the period Morimura disclosed that Pearl Harbor was the target. Each report leading up to his final disclosure was flagged for American intelligence by the telltale designators inserted within the message. Five of America's cryptographic stations in the Pacific region intercepted the spy reports. These were Stations CAST and SIX in the Philippines, Station FIVE in Hawaii, and the two West Coast listening posts, SAIL at Seattle and TWO at San Francisco. But before they could be read and produce meaningful intelligence, each report had to be decoded at a processing center. The decoding procedures worked fine in Manila and Washington, but not in Hawaii. When the opportunity came for direct Hawaii access to the contents of the espionage messages which originated in Honolulu, it was not properly exploited. This intelligence failure came not in the acquisition of the messages but in decoding and translating them.

The cover-up concerning the Japanese consulate's spy messages is another Pearl Harbor deceit. There are major contradictions. Four intelligence officials testified that the Japanese spy messages were unavailable to the United States government because the cable firms, RCA and Mackay, refused to provide copies of each message based on a federal law that prevented interception and disclosure of private communications. Robert Shivers, the FBI bureau chief in Hawaii, detailed the cable firms' refusal in a report to J. Edgar Hoover. "It should be stated here that repeated efforts had been made to enlist the cooperation of the managers of Globe Wireless, R.C.A. Communications, Mackay Radio, and Commercial Pacific Cable companies in Honolulu, T.H. to furnish this office and the Office of Naval Intelligence copies of all communications between the Japanese consulate in Honolulu and the Foreign Office in Japan. The managers of these respective companies flatly refused to cooperate to this extent, notwithstanding the fact that they were even pleaded with and that the seriousness of the situation was pointed out to them so we would know in advance what, if anything, was going to happen against the Hawaiian Islands by the Japanese Government." [16]

Three Navy intelligence officials backed up Shivers: Theodore Wilkinson, FDR's fourth Director of Naval Intelligence in 1941, Edwin Layton, the Pacific Fleet's intelligence officer in 1941, and Joseph Rochefort, commander of Station HYPO. In testimony given to the seventh Pearl Harbor investigation in 1945, Wilkinson said, "the District Intelligence Officer of Hawaii had endeavored to obtain copies of dispatches sent by Japanese diplomatic agents from the local cable companies but had been advised that the law did not permit interference of such messages." Layton said, "the FBI was restricted by law from getting Japanese cables." Rochefort said, "the United States was handicapped because it could not censor Japanese communications." [17]

But the evidence in the Station US papers contradicts the assertions of Wilkinson, Layton, and Rochefort. Washington intelligence officials ignored the federal laws and intercepted the Japanese messages, but kept the information from Admiral Kimmel and General Short. Mackay's Washington DC office allowed Navy photographers to copy the Japanese spy messages. Again, the evidence is overwhelming. There were sixty-nine spy messages transmitted from Honolulu to Tokyo by RCA and Mackay between January 1 and December 6, 1941, according to a log book kept by the consulate and confiscated by the Honolulu police department on December 7. Monitor stations of the United States and England obtained fifty-eight of the messages. Nine were not intercepted, according to US intercept logs found by the author in Archives II.[18]

President Roosevelt shouldn't have bothered with the Sarnoff deal. It was not needed. Fully 84 percent of the spy messages were in American hands without Sarnoff's help. The total was even higher between August 1941—when Morimura began sending his bomb plot messages—and December 6, 1941. American intercept operators and cryptographers ignored federal anti-intercept laws and obtained thirty-four of the thirty-six spy messages sent by Morimura—a success total of 94.4 percent during the five months.

The Sarnoff-Roosevelt arrangement for delivery of the spy messages in Honolulu remains a mystery. A logical explanation focuses on Rear Admiral Anderson. The Honolulu release of the RCA cables can be viewed as an arrangement for Anderson's exclusive use so he would know when to expect the attack. He was not aboard his flagship, the USS *Maryland*, during the weekend of December 6–7, 1941. He left Pearl Harbor Saturday afternoon and went to the safety of his home on the Maui side of Diamond Head—far from the disaster that hit Battleship Row on the morning of Sunday the seventh.

During the final six days of peace, Morimura dispatched ten messages from the RCA office on South King Street. Within minutes the reports were on their way to Tokyo and to American hands, including the important CAST monitoring station in the Philippines. Yet there is no record that General MacArthur or Admiral Hart shared the CAST spy reports with the Hawaiian commanders. Hart had a direct Navy radio dispatch code for contacting Kimmel. It was an electronic cipher machine called COPEK, similar to Japan's Purple and Germany's Enigma, that linked together Hart, Kimmel, Station US, Atlantic Fleet commander Admiral King, HYPO, and CAST. COPEK was the Navy's most secret code system, used exclusively for rapid exchange of intercepted communications intelligence. Access was limited. Commander Laurance Safford, who devised the system, said it was unbreakable. There is no evidence that Japan or Germany ever solved the COPEK system. Captain Theodore Wilkinson, Director of Naval Intelligence at the time of Pearl Harbor told Congress: "I think our (Navy) code was fairly secure."[19]

Robert Dowd, a Navy yeoman in the cryptographic section of Station CAST (see cutaway drawing in photo insert), can trace the dissemination of the Japanese diplomatic messages obtained by CAST. "They were dispatched by radio in our own cryptographic code to Admiral Hart and General MacArthur in Manila. Copies were relayed by the Navy radio station at the Cavite naval base to Honolulu and Washington," Dowd said in a telephone interview with the author in May 1999. He said he had no way of knowing whether these types of messages were delivered to Admiral Kimmel or General Short in Hawaii. But Dowd said he was positive the intelligence information was dispatched. His post in the CAST cryptographic tunnel was next to the Navy's radio transmitter and the cipher machines used to encode the very secret messages. "I could see our electronic cipher machines from my desk," he said.[20] Dowd's recollection is backed up by his boss in 1941, Rear Admiral Leigh Noyes, Director of Naval Communications. During testimony to the Joint Congressional Investigation on Saturday, February 16, 1946, Noyes testified: "I knew perfectly well that they [CAST] could decipher the diplomatic traffic and send it to Honolulu."[21]

Between June 27 and December 3, 1941, Morimura's espionage reports were encoded in the J-19 (Tsu) diplomatic system, which Tokyo believed was impervious to American code-breakers. These J-19 reports were transmitted from Honolulu to Tokyo over either RCA or Mackay radio circuits (November was MacKay, December RCA). All three of the processing centers knew how to decode J-19, because decryption instructions called Radio Intelligence Publications (RIP) had been issued to them from Station US in Washington.[22]

But as an intelligence tool the use of J-19 became moot on December 3, when the Japanese Foreign Ministry directed the Honolulu consulate to destroy all their code systems except Oite (Called PA by Navy cryptographers). At midday the Japanese Foreign Office signaled that war was near. It sent a message via RCA to Japanese diplomatic posts in North America that directed:

BURN YOUR CODE BOOKS EXCEPT FOR "OITE." WHEN DESTRUCTION IS
COMPLETE, WIRE US THE CODE WORD HARUNA.

An exception was made for the embassy in Washington, which was di-
rected to hold on to its Purple machine. In Honolulu the consulate complied. It burned the codebooks including the Tsu code (J-19) and retained
Oite (PA) for last-minute communications. It confirmed the destruction to
Tokyo by dispatching the code word HARUNA in plain language over RCA.
Thereafter, from December 3 to the late afternoon of December 6, all of the
Hawaii messages involving Morimura and Tokyo were encoded in PA and
transmitted by RCA. Duplicate copies were sent by Navy courier to HYPO
for decryption and translation. There was backup; each PA message was
intercepted by American monitoring stations and sent to decoding and
translations centers in Washington.[23]

Chief Yeoman Farnsley Woodward was one of America's top code-
breakers for Japan's diplomatic codes. He had learned to break the diplomatic codes in 1939 while stationed at the Navy's intercept station in
Shanghai. Woodward knew one of the diplomatic systems by heart: the PA
code, used for messages requiring less security. Its wide use by Japan over
her China diplomatic radio network enabled Woodward to become adept
in decrypting the system. His cryptographic know-how was perfect for decoding Morimura's target messages in Hawaii.

Japan's PA messages were startling. On Saturday morning, December 6, Tokyo—using the PA system—ordered Morimura to report on the
current status of the anti-aircraft defenses at the naval base and nearby
Army facilities. Morimura finished his last descriptive report on Pearl Harbor just before noon. Hawaii, he claimed, was ripe for a surprise attack.
His final bit of advice to Japanese bomber and torpedo pilots was explicit:

THERE ARE NO BARRAGE BALLOONS UP AND THERE IS AN OPPORTUNITY
LEFT FOR A SURPRISE ATTACK AGAINST THESE PLACES.

Then Morimura telephoned the RCA office and asked for a motorcycle
messenger. Within minutes his message was in the South King Street office, time-clocked at 12:58 P.M., and dispatched to Tokyo using the PA system. Station TWO, at San Francisco's Presidio, intercepted and forwarded
the all-clear message by teleprinter to Washington. RCA also made a copy

Source: PHPT 38, item 232.

Japan's two-group spy designator pattern appears on the second line, left: 02530 KOKOK. This designator placed this message on top of America's cryptographic want list. Stamp showing that this message arrived at the RCA office in Honolulu at 12:58 P.M. [top] and was transmitted at 1:04 P.M. at bottom is obscured by the consulate's seal.

```
                                # 368
From : Kita
To : F. M. Tokyo
                                                    6 Dec. 41.
Reterring to last paragraph of your No. 123
    1. The Army ordered several nundred balloons for traming at Camp Davis NC
on the American mainland.  They considered (at that time) the practicability
of their employment in the defense of Hawaii and Panama.  Investigation of the
vicinity of Pearl Harbor reveals no locations selected ror their use or any prepara-
tions for constructing moorings.  No evidence of training or personnel preparations
were seen.  It is concluded that their installation would be difficult.  Even if
they were actually provided they would interfere with operations at nearby
Hickam Field, Ewa Field and Ford Island.  The whole matter seems to have been
dropped.
    2. Am continuing in detail the investigation of the non-use of nets for torpedo
defense of battleships and will report further.
    Delivered 1248
    Transmitted 1304
```

Source: PHPT 37, p. 998.

The incorrect translation of Morimura's PA report of December 6, 1941. See last sentence of paragraph 1 (above) for Lieutenant Joseph Finnegan's translation error. Finnegan was a Japanese translator assigned to Station HYPO immediately after the attack on December 7, 1941.

of Morimura's espionage report at the downtown Honolulu office for Station HYPO's Rochefort.[24]

Japan's Pearl Harbor secret was now, finally, fully open to American cryptographers. Yet inexplicably the entire "splendid arrangement" crashed—but only for the intercepts that indicated the specifics of the attack. Twice during the week of December 1 to 6, Morimura indicated that Pearl Harbor would be attacked. On Tuesday, December 2, he stated that the naval base was operating in a normal fashion and not on the alert. His Saturday report was even more specific. Yet these fatal messages sat unexamined by the men who needed them—Admiral Kimmel and General Short.

Joseph Rochefort and his assistant, Farnsley Woodward—America's top military/diplomatic code-breakers—offered contradictory explanations of why they did not solve the RCA messages until after the attack. There were twenty-seven Japanese messages processed by RCA's Honolulu office between December 1 and December 6. Eighteen were spy messages; the remaining nine were routine business-type reports. Each of the routine messages was decoded and translated before the attack. But the spy mes-

From: Honolulu
To: Tokyo

December 6, 1941.

PA–K2
#253   Re the last part of your #123ᵃ.
  1. In the American Continent in October the Army began training barrage balloon troops at Camp Davis, North Carolina. Not only have they ordered four or five hundred balloons, but it is understood that they are considering the us of these balloons in the defense of Hawaii and Panama. In so far as Hawaii is concerned, though investigations have been made in the neighborhood of Pearl Harbor, they have not set up mooring equipment, nor have they selected the troops to man them. Furthermore, there is no indication that any training for the maintenance of balloons is being undertaken. At the present time there are no signs of barrage balloon equipment. In addition, it is difficult to imagine that they have actually any. However, even though they have actually made preparations, because they must control the air over the water and land runways of the airports in the vicinity of Pearl Harbor, Hickam, Ford and Ewa ᵇ, there are limits to the balloon defense of Pearl Harbor. I imagine that in all probability there is considerable opportunity left to take advantage for a surprise attack against these places.
  2. In my opinion the battleships do not have torpedo nets. The details are not known. I will report the results of my investigation.

ᵃ Not available.
ᵇ Kana spelling.

The correct translation, above, has Morimura's "considerable opportunity left to take advantage for a surprise attack against these places" in the last sentence of paragraph 1. Originally Pearl Harbor was mentioned three times by Morimura (above), but only once in the incorrect translation.

sages—in the same PA code system and most containing the designators that placed them on America's most-wanted list—were not. Woodward indicated in a written note that he received the RCA messages in two deliveries: twenty-one messages on the afternoon of Friday, December 5, that were "deciphered and translated prior to December 7, 1941," and six messages intercepted during Saturday, December 6, that were "delivered the night of December 7." [25]

Rochefort withheld the written alert that he had received from Yale Maxon on Monday, December 1, from all Pearl Harbor investigators. It was a crucial piece of evidence that directly placed Rochefort in the decoding pipeline of the Sarnoff-Roosevelt arrangement. The Maxon alert directly placed responsibility on Rochefort for decoding the messages and delivering them forthwith to Admiral Kimmel. By hiding Yale Maxon's alert, Rochefort diverted a thorough examination of the Sarnoff-Roosevelt spy-message deal and made it impossible for Admiral Kimmel to establish

#Ø253Ø Secret "P. A."   (#368)   6 DEC. 41.
From: Kita.
To: Gaimudaijin Tokio.
Kiden (dai .... gō) 123 matsudan nikanshi (Para).

1 Bei how do ni a ri te wa October ko . riku gun wa Beg. Eng KE [c] LA [am]
EK [p] ZI [—] DI [da] YC [vi] IW [s] ZI [—] VY [N] AA [.] KE [c] AA [,]
IØ [End spell] ni oite so sai ki kyū u hei no yō sei ni chaku shu si sū hyaku no
ki kyū wo chū mow se shi nominarazu ki kyū ni yoro ha wa i . Panama pō [Bō]
ei wo mo kō ryo shi wo ru omomu (ki) na ru to koro tō chi ni 9 [KAN] shi te
wa shin zyu wan fu kin wo tan sa se ru mo so re to wo mo wa ru ru ba sho no
sen tei oyobi kei ryū shi se tsu tō na shi wo ra zu ma ta ki kyū fu yō kun ren mo
mi za ru wo niotte i ma no tokoro so sai ki kyū se tsu chi no chō kō su ra mito
(me) zu ka tsu sō kyū ni wa ji tsu geu seraru (ru) mono to wa mito (me) gata
(ku) shi shikashite mo shi ji tsu geu surin to mo shin ju wau ni kin se ku se ru
[hi tsu ka mu] [fu ō do] [e wa] hi kō jō no ri chaku riku su i ni tai suru so ra
no kai gū wo OU—D—K za—Y beikara (zu) yuc (mi) shiu ju wau ki kyū pō
ei—E—F geu Y—a ri kore wo A—ze ki suru ki kai wa sō tō ta buw mi mo ko
sa raru (ru) mono to —N dau seram (ru) (para) (2) kan 1—ku se ru tokoro
sen kan wa gyo rai pō zyo mō wo yū se zu shō sai hikitsuku (ki) chō sa hō—G
ran koto to su.

Source: PHPT 37 p. 999.

The erroneous Japanese-language decryption of Morimura's December 6 PA message was discovered by the seventh Pearl Harbor investigation, conducted by Admiral Henry Kent Hewitt on July 4, 1945. There are eighty-eight decryption errors in this text, according to translators Naemi and Sean McPherson of the University of California at Berkeley. Even the words for Pearl Harbor, Shinju Wan, were misspelled in lines 11, 7, and 5 from the bottom by Lieutenant Joseph Finnegan, the Navy cryptographer/translator.

a logical defense to charges of dereliction of duty. The blame for dereliction of duty belongs on the shoulders of the two cryptographers, not Admiral Kimmel. Rochefort's motive can only be guessed. In his Oral History he told a US Navy interviewer that the carnage at Pearl Harbor on December 7 was a cheap price to pay for the unification of America.[26] His unity observation parallels that of his close friend Arthur McCollum and suggests that Rochefort was aware of or approved of McCollum's eight-action plan that called for America to create "ado" and provoke Japan into committing an overt act of war against the United States.

The apparent do-nothing posture of the personnel at Station HYPO during the week of December 1 to 6, their ignoring Morimura's "all-clear" message, and the false decryption misled Admiral Kimmel. But the look-the-other-way attitude was US policy and it came direct from the White House. None of the other last-minute PA messages decoded and translated at HYPO contained errors.

Navy officials assert that Morimura's all-clear message did not reach

Rochefort until late Sunday afternoon, about seven hours after the attack. Even though the Rochefort effort failed to produce a timely decryption of Morimura's PA report, there was still an opportunity for American cryptographers to uncover the all-clear message and warn the Pacific Fleet. Station TWO sent the message to Washington by teleprinter—but it was ignored by Army and Navy intelligence officials there.

How could such important intelligence pertaining to the Pearl Harbor attack have been shunted aside? Answers—over fifty years late—have come forth in evidence hidden from investigators. The first discovery was the alert sent by Lieutenant Yale Maxon to Rochefort on December 1, telling of Navy access to the RCA intercepts. Maxon's alert was part of a collection of 1941 official Navy communications documents found by the author in Rochefort's personal effects, held by his daughter.

The failure of the Navy's Hawaiian intelligence organization to exploit Morimura's all-clear message has never been satisfactorily examined. After the war, when Kimmel learned of the significance of the message, he did not call for a probe of the circumstances that denied him the vital information before the attack, nor did he complain of the mistranslation. Apparently Woodward deciphered the surprise attack message by December 11, 1941. Then it was handed over to Navy Lieutenant Joseph Finnegan, who produced the misleading translation. His error was not discovered until 1945. In a brief appearance before the seventh official Pearl Harbor inquiry, conducted that June by Admiral Henry Kent Hewitt, Finnegan admitted "without hesitation" that his translation of the Morimura message was not correct. But he could not explain why.[27]

For the six days prior to the attack, Captain Mayfield supervised the handling of the coded radiograms. He had one paramount responsibility, to get the intercepts to Admiral Kimmel. His failure to do so has escaped scrutiny. Morimura's famous final message, filed at 12:58 P.M. on December 6, has been falsely reported to investigators. The differences between the message Morimura sent and the one Finnegan translated tell the real truth of Pearl Harbor.

CHAPTER 8

AN UNMISTAKABLE
PATTERN

Wᴇʀᴇ ɪɴᴅɪᴄᴀᴛɪᴏɴꜱ ᴏꜰ ᴀɴ ᴏᴠᴇʀᴛ ᴀᴛᴛᴀᴄᴋ ᴏɴ Pᴇᴀʀʟ ʜᴀʀʙᴏʀ mistakenly or deliberately ignored? After fifty years it is difficult to impute motives. Even if Anderson, McCollum, Rochefort, Mayfield, et al., were in accord with a general policy decision to provoke a Japanese attack—a not unreasonable position—it is impossible to be certain about what happened to the original Morimura intercepts.

What we can do, however, is to examine a broader array of evidence and look for a pattern. Japan's preparations for war took a definite new turn in July 1941 after President Roosevelt put the last of McCollum's actions in place. That was Action H, which called for a complete embargo on all US trade with Japan in collaboration with a similar embargo imposed by the British Empire.

Diplomatic intercepts shown to President Roosevelt early in July and throughout the summer months disclosed Japanese reaction. It was swift. Three bold new steps suggested that hostile actions were not far off:

(1) 500,000 Japanese males were inducted into the armed services—the largest draft since the China Incident of 1937; (2) Japanese merchant vessels were recalled from the oceans of the world; and (3) Japanese warships and aviation units were recalled from occupation bases in China.[1]

The China Incident started in July 1937, with a skirmish between Japanese troops and forces of Chinese Nationalist Generalissimo Chiang-Kai-shek at the Marco Polo stone bridge near Peking (now spelled Beijing). Japanese troops had been garrisoned in the Peking area as a result of a thirty-seven-year-old agreement that concluded the Boxer Rebellion of 1900. The presence of Japanese troops on China's soil was a sore point and formed a catalyst that united Chiang and the Communist forces led by Mao Tse-tung. The two warlords pledged to drive the Japanese from North China. On July 7, 1937, a minor shooting skirmish on the Marco Polo bridge between a company of Chiang's troops and a Japanese patrol escalated into major warfare. Over the next four years of war between the two Asian nations, public sentiment in America favored the Chinese over Japan. Japanese officials, citing the Communist menace in North China, attempted to persuade the United States to favor their cause but were rebuffed.[2]

By reading the Japanese diplomatic intercepts during the summer of 1941, President Roosevelt could gauge Japan's response to Action H. The three bold steps taken that summer confirmed that Japan was preparing for hostile action. Still there was the possibility of a diplomatic settlement as outlined by Foreign Minister Yosuke Matsuoka's "worst" policy, initially proposed in January 1941. Matsuoka's strategy offered diplomacy as the first option for Japan; war with the United States and her allies would be the last resort—and only when worse came to worst. But conceding to a diplomatic solution does not appear in the President's strategy. His response instead was to tighten the economic screws and encourage the "worst" policy. In July 1941 he closed the Panama Canal to Japanese shipping, seized Japanese assets in the United States, and placed a truly effective embargo on shipments of petroleum products, iron, steel, and metal products—restrictions that were sure to infuriate the military-dominated government in Tokyo.[3]

The earlier embargo of 1940, which had allowed the sale of millions of gallons of petroleum products to Japan, ended. Roosevelt followed McCollum's suggested Action H and embargoed all trade with Japan. Joseph Rochefort, the commander of Station HYPO, regarded the total embargo as an ultimatum: Japan had no recourse but war. "We cut off their money, their fuel and trade. We were just tightening the screws on the Japanese. They could see no way of getting out except going to war."[4] Both Hawaii and the nation's capital grasped the danger. In Honolulu the editors of the *Advertiser* sensed the war clouds hovering over the Pacific and on July 25, 1941, published a feature story on a possible air attack on Pearl Harbor. The article, in the magazine section, featured drawings showing what such an attack might entail.

In Washington, authorization and funding for a two-ocean Navy had been approved by Congress, and by the summer of 1941 construction was underway in the nations' shipyards. In 1941 US naval forces were weak compared to Japan's. America had seven aircraft carriers; Japan had ten flattops. One of the seven in the US Navy, the USS *Ranger*, lacked maneuverability at high speeds and was not considered a front-line carrier. Funding and contracts had been let for construction of a powerful American naval force built around 100 aircraft carriers. Though the goals of the two-ocean navy were laudable, completion of the first phase of the American naval might was not expected until 1943—almost two years away.[5]

With the tightening of the economic screws, Japanese oil tankers unable to load up at American refineries in California returned home. But the Empire was not without oil resources. During the previous year-long limited embargo, the White House issued export permits that allowed Japan to obtain just enough fuel to keep her warships going. Most of the reserve was stored at the major Japanese naval fuel depot at Tokuyama in the Inland Sea. America had quite deliberately put Japan in an untenable position with just enough fuel to fight, but not enough to win. There was only one recourse for Japan: resort to military might and gain access to the petroleum.

In 1941 Japan required 3,500,000 tons of oil for peacetime use and allocated 2,000,000 tons for the Imperial Navy, 500,000 tons for the army and 1,000,000 tons for civilian use. As of July 1941 she had a two years' peacetime supply, or about 7,000,000 tons, according to Lieutenant Maxon.[6]

It was a timetable intended by the United States to expire in 1943 when her petroleum reserves would be exhausted and American war production was predicted to kick into high gear allowing an offensive war operation.[7]

The timetable was a perfect fit as far as United States strategy was concerned. Congress had approved and funded a two-ocean Navy. Although a 1941 tally of each nation's warships gave the edge to Japan—she had ten first-line carriers to America's seven flattops—by mid-1941 United States shipyards had laid down the keels for what would become a fleet of 100 aircraft carriers, built around the heavy carrier design of the *Essex* class, the light carriers of the *Independence* class, and escort carriers called baby flattops.[8]

By September 1, Japan's war planning was proceeding at high speed. Japan's naval radio broadcasts disclosed both its overall strategy and its tactics. American cryptographers learned of major changes in Japanese worldwide shipping assignments. Merchant vessels, which normally operated under civilian control, began receiving their movement orders from the Imperial Navy. At the same time a significant number of warships and naval air units assigned to the war in China were recalled to the Empire for overhaul and reorganization. New expeditionary groups emerged from these recalled forces; the restructured units then trained in beach invasion and landing tactics.[9]

Admiral Yamamoto's war plans called for seizure of the American, British, and Dutch possessions in Southeast Asia. Japan wanted access to the vast natural resources of this huge area. Her planned conquest extended along 100° east longitude from Siam (Thailand), south along the Malay Peninsula to the Netherlands East Indies, then branched eastward to the mid-Pacific Ocean near longitude 180°, the international date line.

To implement this immense campaign, Yamamoto organized his Combined Fleet into eight separate commands. American radio intelligence obtained the details and Rochefort at Station HYPO informed Admiral Kimmel of the reorganization on September 4. Four of the fleet commands were assigned to support the southern offensive—the invasion of Southeast Asia by Japan's army. These fleets were the major firepower of Japan's 1941 navy, but did not include the six major aircraft carriers of the First Air Fleet.

Cryptographers at Station CAST on Corregidor were able to break down the composition and targets of the main forces. Traffic analyst Duane

Whitlock of CAST prepared a Japanese Order of Battle, which apparently was later forwarded to Kimmel and to Washington at the end of October: the Southern Expeditionary Fleet consisted of troop transports, torpedo boats, mine layers, submarines, and other small craft; the Second Fleet served as main support for the other fleets and included battleships, cruisers, and destroyers. The Third Fleet was the invasion fleet of amphibious forces trained for beachhead landings; its supporting vessels included light cruisers and destroyers; finally, Air Fleet-Eleven was made up of land-based air support which combined the major bomber and fighter squadrons of Japan's navy with seaplane tenders and four light aircraft carriers.[10]

With these fleets, Admiral Yamamoto planned to block American interference with Japan's Southeast Asia conquest. He was sure that the United States would react to the invasion of the Philippines by dispatching warships, air units, and military reinforcement to the British and Dutch governments. Part of his plan included invading and seizing Guam and Wake islands, two minor and lightly defended American bases in the Central Pacific. He organized four fleets to counter the American threat and formed a screening force to immobilize the Pacific Fleet through a surprise attack on Pearl Harbor. This screening force consisted of the First Air Fleet with six fast aircraft carriers, protected by a screen of destroyers, cruisers, and battleships and a supply train of seven fuel tankers; the Fourth Fleet based at Truk in the Central Pacific, including cruisers, coastal submarines, air units, destroyers, landing craft, troop transports, and Air Flotilla 24 with its land-based bombers, fighters, and seaplanes; the Fifth Fleet, a patrol force built around trawlers, gunboats, and other small craft capable of making ocean patrols of Japan's northern and eastern coasts to send out early warnings of countermoves by the United States or the USSR; and the Sixth Fleet, a powerful force of 45 oceangoing fleet submarines, some of which carried float planes and midget subs.

Japan's Fast Carrier Force was concentrated in the First Air Fleet, which had been formed on April 1. This force and 30 submarines of the Sixth Fleet would be aimed at Pearl Harbor on December 7. Japan's Fourth Fleet, based at Truk, was assigned to capture Guam and Wake and prevent an American military advance through the Central Pacific.[11]

By organizing these fleets into combat-ready forces using the radio waves, Japanese officials unwittingly disclosed their intentions to Americans, Dutch, and British. These disclosures occurred throughout 1941. Most Japanese and American historians assert that Japan's naval vessels ceased radio broadcasts after November 25 pursuant to an order issued by Admiral Yamamoto. These assertions have been accepted as fact for fifty years. But Yamamoto's order of the twenty-fifth was not all-inclusive—it contained a proviso that permitted radio transmissions. The order was intercepted at Station H by Radioman Second Class Jack Kaye at 8:48 P.M., on November 24. It read, according to a USN translation dated March 18, 1946:

FROM 26 NOVEMBER, SHIPS OF COMBINED FLEET WILL OBSERVE RADIO COMMUNICATION PROCEDURES AS FOLLOWS. (1) EXCEPT IN EXTREME EMERGENCY, THE MAIN FORCE AND ITS ATTACHED FORCES WILL CEASE COMMUNICATING. (2) OTHER FORCES ARE AT DISCRETION OF THEIR RESPECTIVE COMMANDERS. (3) SUPPLY SHIPS, REPAIR SHIPS, HOSPITAL SHIPS, ETC., WILL REPORT DIRECTLY TO PARTIES CONCERNED.[12]

Radio intercepts obtained by US Navy monitoring stations disclosed that the broadcasts continued after the order was issued. Instead of radio silence there was substantial, continuous radio traffic from the Japanese naval ministry, foreign ministry, and warships, most of which American communications intelligence personnel intercepted and understood. It was a major departure from normal Japanese naval communications. Since the late 1920s, Navy intercept operators using IBM statistical machinery maintained an ongoing analysis of Japan's naval broadcasts. The analysis established a norm for all categories of her naval commands and indicated who communicated with whom and how often. When her naval transmissions increased dramatically in 1941 it was a clear indicator of Japan's intent to make war against the United States, according to Homer Kisner of Station H.

Radio intercept operators monitored the eight commands listed above and determined which were the most active, as well as each command's radio association with Japanese warships and the land bases and bureaus of Japan's navy. By analyzing these radio associations, American cryptographers could accurately predict Japan's military moves in 1941.[13] For example, a major source for predicting future Japanese naval operations was Japan's Bureau of Military Preparations. The Bureau provided war supplies such as replacement aircraft, aerial torpedoes, and bombs for the First Air Fleet. When radio communications between the Bureau and the First Air Fleet exceeded normal levels, American cryptographers knew that something was brewing. When information copies of the messages between the Bureau and the First Air Fleet were sent to Japan's Central Pacific bases, the communication pattern revealed a probable destination. Soon the destination was confirmed when Japanese naval post offices in the Central Pacific received directions by radio to forward mail to Saipan, Truk, and other Japanese naval bases in the region.[14]

So far as is known, all of Yamamoto's original orders initiating the naval recall from China were contained in secret letters hand delivered to commanding officers by Japanese naval couriers. No recalls ordered by radio dispatch have been located in American intercept files. Nevertheless, the White House learned of the recall when Japan's naval commanders acknowledged their movement orders by radio.

September 1, 1941, marked the day the Japanese navy unwittingly revealed the secret recall of its forces from China. Rochefort's intercept operators at Station HYPO obtained movement reports, and he informed Admiral Kimmel of the mass arrival of the China units at Sasebo and other homeland ports during a five-day period from September 4 to 8. It appears that the China-recall reports were either in plain language or in the SM (Ship Movement) code.[15]

At about noon on September 1 Admiral Mineichi Koga, commander-in-chief of Japan's naval forces in China, forecast that critical times lay ahead. He even suggested that a huge new operating area for offensive operations required withdrawing forces from the China region. His estimations came in an ominous radio message sent to the commander of Japan's Eleventh Air Fleet, then quartered in China:

ON THIS OCCASION OF DETACHING YOUR FLEET FROM MY COMMAND, I WISH TO THANK ALL HANDS OF THE FLEET, FROM THE COMMANDER IN CHIEF ON DOWN, FOR THEIR ORDEALS, AND ESPECIALLY TO ASK THAT YOU WORK EVEN HARDER TOWARD INCREASING YOUR FIGHTING ABILITY, IN VIEW OF THE CRITICAL TIMES WHICH WE ARE FACING.[16]

Hints of the recall order didn't stop with Admiral Koga. Other commanders of large and small units took to the airwaves during the week. The commander of Base Force One, which consisted of amphibious landing craft and support units, reported,

> SUBCHASER DIVISION I AND II, AOTAKA, HATSUTAKA WILL LEAVE THE PLACE OF THE CHINA INCIDENT AND PROCEED TO HOME PORTS IN ACCORDANCE WITH THIRD FLEET OPERATION ORDER 16.

Later, Koga sent this message to Yamamoto:

> AIR FLOTILLA TWENTY-THREE WILL RETURN TO KANOYA AND SAEKI [Navy airfields on Kyushu].

During the remainder of the week the China exodus continued. The commander of the Eleventh Air Fleet, comprising all of Japan's land-based naval aviation,[17] announced his arrival at Kanoya Air Base after a seven-and-a-half-hour flight from China:

> AT 0900 TODAY THE SECOND, I DEPARTED CHINA AND ARRIVED AT KANOYA AIR STATION AT 1645 VIA BOO AIR BASE. I RETURNED MY FLAG TO KANOYA AIR GROUP.

More China units reported heading for Japan. On September 4, Destroyer Squadron Five reported leaving Amoy for homeland naval bases at Maizuru, Sasebo and Yokosuka:

> THE FOLLOWING SHIPS DEPARTED FROM AMOY: NATORI FOR MAIZURU, DES DIV 22 FOR SASEBO; DES DIV 5 FOR YOKOSUKA.

Submarine Squadron Six transmitted:

> THIS UNIT LESS SUBDIV 9 DEPARTED FOOCHOW OFFING FOR KURE.

The orders continued on September 5. The Commander in Chief of Japan's Third Fleet, Vice Admiral Ibo Takahashi, radioed:

> DEPARTED HANGCHOW IN COMMAND OF CRUDIV 16, LESS KUMA.

At 7 A.M. the next day Takahashi reported his fleet's total removal from China:

> THIRD FLEET IS HEREBY REMOVED FROM OPERATIONAL COMMAND OF CINC, CHINA AREA FLEET. ALL UNITS AND SHIPS WILL PROCEED TO DESIGNATED PLACES FOR UPKEEP.

He sent action orders to his command and thus unwittingly disclosed their identity to American Intelligence: Sea Plane Tender Division 12, Submarine Squadron 6, Destroyer Squadron 5, Base Force 1, the light cruiser *Kuma*. The broadcasts continued as Takahashi's ships kept him (and Station H) informed:

SEA PLANE TENDER DIV 12 AND THE FUJIKAWA MARU ARRIVED SASEBO.[18]

These forces remained in Japan's Third Fleet through December 7, and were never attached to the Hawaii-bound carrier force. This separation was noted by American intelligence and confirmed that Japan had no intention of actually invading Hawaii in the initial stage of the war.

Additional proof of the recall of Japan's amphibious fleet from China's waters continued to come through naval radio transmissions. As September 6 turned into night, Subchaser Division 51 and Seaplane Tender Division 12 reported their arrival at Sasebo. That base, located northwest of Nagasaki, was the naval center for Japan's China and Southeast Asia operations.

The China naval recall, we now know, prepared Japan for the first phase of its war and supported the invasion and occupation of the Philippines, Singapore, Borneo, and Malaya. The warships and units of the Third Fleet headed for dry docks at Sasebo, Maizuru, and Yokosuka for refitting, overhaul, and stripping of flammable materials such as wood, linoleum, etc. Once outfitted for war, every Third Fleet unit remained under the control of one commander.

In October, men of the recalled warships and auxiliaries of the Third Fleet trained in beach landing drills. Their training took place at Tachibana Bay on Kyushu and at Murozumi Bay on the south tip of Honshu. When the forces sailed between the two areas they kept in touch by radio communications, always sending information copies of their dispatches to the Third Fleet commander. These radio exchanges enabled American cryptographers such as Kisner's radiomen to identify the "mother hen" (the Third Fleet) and the "chickens" (the invasion forces).[19]

Since the Japanese warships failed to observe basic communications security, American cryptographers at Station H learned the organizational structure of the Third Fleet. It was a simple procedure to follow the warships to Southeast Asia and to locate and separate vessels headed eastward across the Pacific. Commanders of Third Fleet cruisers, destroyers, and submarine squadrons dutifully reported their positions and arrivals at their home ports, located on one of the four main islands of the Empire. Japan's naval organization was consistent. None of the six flattops of the First Air Fleet was ever associated with the Third Fleet by American radio-monitor operators. The First Air Fleet was always linked with an easterly movement across the Pacific Ocean toward Hawaii, never toward Southeast Asia.[20]

As September ended, Japan had recalled most of its capital warships and military air units from China, and Americans knew it. The move signaled a major change in Japanese military strategy. President Roosevelt and his staff closely watched the developments as the Japanese military intercepts revealed a new theater of operations.

Japan's worldwide recall of its merchant marine paralleled that of the China warship recall. In a matter of hours Japan's world trading operations came to a halt. It was immediately seen in Washington as a prelude to war. Arthur McCollum recognized the importance of the recall: Japan's merchant marine fleet would soon become troop transports and military cargo-handling vessels. McCollum had once written: "It is assumed that prior to any initiation of hostilities, a nation contemplating war probably would withdraw its commercial shipping and detached naval units from those areas where this shipping could be readily seized or destroyed."[21]

American radio intercept operators easily distinguished between Japan's warships and her merchant vessels, called *Marus*. Japan used a different communication procedure in contacting the latter. Commercial vessels communicated through Tokyo in peacetime by using radio call signs issued through the International Radio Tribunal in Berne, Switzerland, known as the Berne List.[22]

Each Japanese *Maru* was assigned four Roman letters beginning with J for Japan. For example, the *Tatsuta Maru*, Japan's premier ocean liner, was known as JFYC. Japanese warships and naval shore stations were addressed in a separate code system that used two *kana* syllabics and a number. For example, the flagship of the Japanese carrier force was the HIJMS *Akagi*, whose secret radio call sign in the fall of 1941 was 8 YU NA. The two different Japanese communications procedures have confused some American World War II historians, who claimed that the vessels could not be distinguished by radio procedures.[23]

The recall of the *Marus* was first noted by American intelligence on July 1, 1941. Eight Japanese merchant vessels were told to depart American East Coast ports immediately. To meet the deadline, officials of the NYK line and other Japanese shipping firms directed American longshoremen working the East Coast docks of Baltimore, New York, Boston, and Philadelphia to "rush-load" supplies into cargo holds. Radio Tokyo ordered the captains of these ships to clear the Atlantic coastal harbors immediately, transit the Panama Canal, and be in the Pacific Ocean by July 22. The schedule called for one ship per day to transit the Canal, starting on July 16th and ending on the 22nd. War planners in Japan badly needed these ships. Most were slated for conversion to troop transports for the invasion of the Philippines and the Kra Isthmus. Others were scheduled for the invasions of Singapore, Malaya, and Borneo. Three of the vessels, *Tokai Maru*, *Amagisan Maru*, and *Kirishima Maru*, were earmarked for the Philippine invasion at Lingayen Gulf on Luzon in mid-December.

The *Amagisan Maru* would play a key part in operations against the US Army Air forces in the Philippines, commanded by General Douglas MacArthur. During the war's opening salvos—just six months away—the vessel would transport elements of the Eleventh Air Fleet from the home islands to air bases in Formosa (today called Taiwan or Chinese Taipei). On December 7, the Eleventh Air Fleet took off from their Formosa bases and destroyed most of MacArthur's bombers and fighters on the ground at Clark Air Field in central Luzon. A fourth merchant vessel, the *Awajisan Maru*, slipped out past New York City's Statue of Liberty on July 4. The 9700-ton passenger/cargo vessel steamed past the Sandy Hook lightship, entered Atlantic waters, and headed for the Panama Canal. New Yorkers who happened to observe her departure were looking at a doomed ship. The *Awajisan Maru*, assigned to the Japanese Third Fleet, was sunk on the first day of the war by Australian bombers during Japan's amphibious operations at Khota Bharu, north of Singapore.

From Boston, New York, Philadelphia, and Baltimore Japan's East Coast merchant fleet sailed for home. July 22 was fast approaching. But the ships found the Panama Canal closed to them. Because President Roosevelt knew of the planned exodus from the intercepts he had ordered that Japanese merchant shipping be denied the right to use the Canal.

Most of the American intercept operators were Navy men, trained for a job in a concrete classroom built on the roof of the Sixth Wing of the Navy Department headquarters on Washington's Constitution Avenue. All were regular noncommissioned radiomen. They called themselves the "On-the-Roof Gang." Every Roof Gang member was sworn to a lifetime of secrecy. To protect the security of the intercept stations, only the commandant of a Navy District was allowed aboard them. Even the admiral's staff was kept off the stations.[24]

Radio orders to the captains of the *Marus* were intercepted by the Roof Gang personnel. By July 3, the message sheets containing the Japanese encrypted text had been decoded and translated by cryptologists in Washington. While celebrating the Fourth of July at Hyde Park, President Roosevelt read the reports and closed the Canal effective July 5. A cover story was concocted. Major General Daniel van Voorhis of the Panama Canal Zone Command issued a press release claiming that the emergency closure was caused by water leaks in the transit locks of the canal. Japan had no choice. Denied the Panama Canal transit, the vessels were routed back to Japan the long way—via the Straits of Magellan at the southern tip of South America.

At 7:39 P.M. on July 3, just minutes after Radio Tokyo's dispatches had been translated, Admiral Stark sent a war warning to Admirals Kimmel and Hart: "Japan's policy probably involves war in the near future. They have ordered all Jap vessels in the Atlantic ports to be west of the Panama Canal by August 1."[25]

By late summer, the oil embargo stopped the flow of American oil products into the bunkers of Japanese tankers and merchant ships then waiting for refills on the West Coast. On August 14, Admiral Stark, as CNO, sent additional details to the Navy's Pacific commands: "Japanese rapidly completing withdrawal from world shipping routes. Scheduled sailings canceled and the majority of ships other than (those in) China and Japan sea areas are homeward bound." It was the last meaningful message based on communications intelligence that Stark sent to Kimmel. In Hawaii, although Kimmel had been denied crucial communications intercepts from Washington, he learned about the merchant vessel exodus from

Rochefort's cryptographers. But as we shall see, the Rochefort source was eventually curtailed.[26]

Admiral Kimmel knew these ships were likely to be part of Japanese invasion forces. Beginning in the late summer, Kimmel requested, received, and initialed the recall position reports of various Japanese *Marus* obtained by the US Navy's West Coast intercept network (WCCI). These documents show the admiral's direct interest in the matter. For example, on September 27 Kimmel saw the radio direction finder position of the merchant ship *Heiyo Maru*. Kimmel read the report obtained by the WCCI and directed his intelligence officer Edwin Layton "to bring these late reports to me." According to the intercepted Japanese broadcasts decoded and translated in Washington, DC but not sent to Kimmel, the vessel was returning to Japan from Manzanillo, Mexico.[27]

As Pacific Fleet commander and as an experienced naval officer, Kimmel would have fully grasped the import of Japanese merchant vessels being abruptly placed under military control. Such ships were essential components of invasion and occupation forces. Layton passed Kimmel's order to the US Navy's intercept operators, who began tracking the *Heiyo Maru* and other ships. The tracking paid off. In the two week period following Kimmel's directive, Rochefort's intercept operators and those on the West Coast reported that 45 vessels were pouring military troops, laborers, and supplies into Japanese naval bases in the Central Pacific. One of the most active was the *Heiyo Maru*.[28]

Rochefort's Daily Communication Summary of September 24 called Kimmel's attention to a "peculiar" 5-Num coded dispatch involving the Maizuru naval base and special guard units. Kimmel was told that the naval base and the guard units were associated with Japan's Central Pacific command—the Fourth Fleet. According to Rochefort's alert to Kimmel, Maizuru rarely sent radio messages concerning personnel. He said the communication procedure was highly unusual. Rochefort promised to follow up.

Rochefort[29] sorted out the 5-Numeral dispatch and wrote that it was a peculiar dispatch originating with the Maizuru naval base's supplies and accounts section. Six days earlier, on September 18, he had advised Kimmel that Maizuru's personnel bureau had changed radio communication tactics. Instead of receiving radio messages involving transfer of personnel, Maizuru was actively engaged in moving military personnel away from the base—an unusual communication procedure for Maizuru, according to Rochefort. US Naval intelligence knew that Maizuru was one of the amphibious landing training centers for the Imperial Japanese Navy— similar to US Marine Corps amphibious centers. Though he didn't predict the intent of the movement away from Maizuru, Rochefort had discovered the Japanese force that eventually invaded and seized Wake Island in late December 1941.

It is not clear how much of the 5-Num message text he could decipher, translate, and read. But Rochefort's 1941 admission concerning the 5-Num code is startling. It uncovers another Pearl Harbor deceit—because when questioned by Senator Homer Ferguson (R., MI) of the Joint Congressional Investigation Committee on February 16, 1946, Rochefort claimed that neither he nor other Station HYPO cryptographers worked on the 5-Num code until after December 7, 1941: "We were specifically told to keep away or not to exploit that so-called five-number system, which was a naval system. That was being done elsewhere."[30]

Rochefort's Communication Summary of September 24, 1941, directly contradicts his statement to Senator Ferguson. He told Kimmel he obtained information from the intercepted 5-Num code dispatch. Obviously he exploited the code system and did not keep away from it, as he claimed to Ferguson. Rochefort identified three Japanese units for Kimmel that he predicted merited future watching: *Keibii* 51, *Keibii* 52, and *Keibii* 53.[31]

Kimmel read and initialed Rochefort's informative report culled from the 5-Num dispatch: "For purposes of future reference, the following peculiar despatch [*sic*] heading is noted: 52 *Keibii* 32 at Maizuru originated a 5 numeral dispatch (SMS 001-NR 690) for action 4th fleet staff officer info to 52 *Keibii* 32 at Sasebo and 53 *Keibii* at Yokosuka. The suffix 32 is generally associated with Supplies or Accounts and the *Keibii* is something similar to the meaning for guard ship." Four days later, on September 28, Rochefort developed additional information from the 5-Num code for Kimmel and wrote that "a 4th fleet staff officer originated a dispatch to 51 *Keibitai* believed at Sasebo, 52 *Keibitai* at Maizuru and 53 *Keibitai* believed at Yokosuka."[32]

Rochefort's identification for Kimmel was right on. He had detected Landing Force 51, 52, and 53 which—three months in the future—would supply Japanese military reinforcements for the Battle of Wake Island. Clearly the two 5-Num dispatches indicated a close association between the three amphibious landing forces and the Central Pacific (Fourth Fleet).

Rochefort implied that he would keep Kimmel informed of any later movements of the three *Keibii* units. There is no record that he did. A Japanese radio dispatch from Kwajalein did provide the destination information on November 29, 1941. The dispatch, in the 5-Num code, was intercepted at Station H. It listed *Keibii* 51, 52, and 53 in the heading of the message and firmly connected the units with the Japanese expeditionary forces gathering in the Central Pacific. Normally Rochefort, after a quick analysis of the communications components of a message, summarized the information found in the headings of 5-Num dispatches. In cryptology jargon an addressee anywhere in the heading of the message reveals vital location information. It is like reading an address on the front of a postal envelope.

Two weeks later on December 11, US Marines on Wake Island, under command of Major James Devereux, drove off an initial Japanese landing attempt, sank the destroyer HIJMS *Hayate*, and damaged the light cruisers HIJMS *Tenryu* and HIJMS *Tatsuta*, a transport, the *Kongo Maru*, and two patrol boats. The Japanese force—temporarily defeated—limped back to Kwajalein, regrouped by adding the troops of *Keibii*, 51, 52, and 53, and returned on December 23, 1941. The US Navy commander of Wake Island, Commander Winfield Cunningham, radioed Pearl Harbor:

ENEMY ON ISLAND. ISSUE IN DOUBT.

He surrendered to Japan that afternoon. Wake Island was a costly battle for the Japanese. In the sixteen days of fighting, a total of 820 Japanese were killed and 333 wounded. American casualties totaled 120 killed, 49 wounded, and two missing. Taken prisoners of war by the Japanese military, the American survivors were brutalized by their captors.[33]

Joseph Rochefort's public testimony in the Pearl Harbor investigations of 1944 to 1946 and his own Oral History of 1969 challenge his and the US Navy's credibility regarding the pre–Pearl Harbor Japanese naval code interceptions. At issue is the 5-Num code and whether Rochefort provided the Pacific Fleet with all the essential intelligence he had gathered and collated. He clearly informed Admiral Kimmel that Station HYPO's cryptographic staff had intercepted the 5-Num code. On seven different occasions between September 4 and November 16, he specifically informed Kimmel that his staff had obtained intercepts in the 5-Num code.[34]

On September 4, Rochefort called Kimmel's attention to "a short 5-Num dispatch originated by the Naval Minister." By October 1, he noted: "5-Num messages are increasing in volume." And he reiterated on the fourth, "Messages in the 5-Num system slightly greater than normal." The reason for the increased frequency of 5-Num traffic would soon be painfully clear. But unaccountably, Rochefort ceased mentioning 5-Num to Kimmel on November 16—the day Japanese naval forces headed for assembly points to begin their assault on America and her allies. For the Hawaii air attack, the assembly point was Hitokappu Bay. His next mention of a 5-Num report would come on December 19, when he intercepted, decoded, and translated Admiral Nagumo's report on his devastating attack on the Pacific Fleet.

Between September 24 and mid-November, significant portions of the Japanese naval code systems revealed much about the composition of the Japanese amphibious force being sent to the Central Pacific for the invasions of Wake and Guam. How much was disclosed to Admiral Kimmel and the White House is obscured by continued US censorship. But it is clear that the merchant vessels were steadily tracked through the Central Pacific; radio direction finders located them when they transmitted movement reports to Tokyo. Each fix provided a precise location. These position reports were included in daily summaries furnished directly to Kimmel and to Arthur McCollum in Washington. The concentration of Japanese warships and invasion forces was an obvious threat to US bases at Guam, Midway, and Wake Island, if not to Pearl Harbor itself.[35]

It is ironic that Admiral Kimmel singled out the *Heiyo Maru* for electronic monitoring. It is one of the "what if" questions of Pearl Harbor. What if Rochefort had followed through on his promise and reported tracking the Special Landing Forces to the Marshall Islands, south of Wake? Would Admiral Kimmel have sounded the alarm and saved his reputation and naval career? Just days after Kimmel ordered Edwin Layton, his intelligence chief, to track the *Heiyo Maru*, she arrived in Japan and was converted to an armed merchant vessel. Shipyard workmen installed anti-aircraft guns and other armament. In two war preparation voyages in October and November, the 9800-ton vessel traveled to Maizuru naval base on Japan's west coast, took on Special Landing Forces that were slated to seize Wake Island, and transported them to Central Pacific bases.

The movements of the *Heiyo Maru* throughout the two months can be traced through communication intelligence records of Station H (Hawaii), Station SAIL (Seattle), Station ITEM (Imperial Beach, California), and Station AE (Sitka, Alaska). The four intercept stations obtained RDF bearings and reported her precise locations to Admiral Kimmel. Her first war preparation voyage began on October 19. Significantly, each radio order linked the Bureau of War Preparations office in Tokyo with the commander of Japan's Fourth Fleet based at Truk in the Central Pacific, who commanded all Japanese naval forces in Micronesia. The Bureau's radio messages heralded a major change. The *Heiyo Maru* no longer received sailing instructions from the passenger agents of the civilian NYK line. Her new boss was Vice Admiral Shigeyoshi Inoue, the Fourth Fleet commander, who directed the vessel to ferry military forces to various bases in the Mandate Islands of the Central Pacific.[36]

During the two months of war preparation voyages the *Heiyo Maru* broke radio silence on at least eleven occasions. Her bearings left no doubt; she was positioned by US Navy direction finders traveling eastward past the Bonin Islands, Iwo Jima, and to the Marshall Islands—carrying troops and war materials slated for Wake. The captain of the ship originated the transmissions and was heard by Navy monitoring stations throughout the Pacific.[37]

They came in loud and clear at Station H in Hawaii. Though Japan issued new radio call signs for its naval ships on October 1 and November 1, they were solved by cryptographers at Station H. One of the first to be solved was the coded call sign of the *Heiyo Maru*, whose captain broke radio silence on November 22 and reported that he was departing the Maizuru naval docks and heading for Saipan. His arrival at the Central Pacific base was set for 0600 hours on November 26. His radio messages said nothing about an invasion of American territory, but there were plenty of indications that would alert a vigilant American radio intelligence officer just by analyzing the radio call signs found in the address headings of the intercepts. In October, the military radio call sign of the *Heiyo Maru* was SA TE 0. Her radio contacts were with the Maizuru naval base and Japanese forces in the Central Pacific, including Vice Admiral Shigeyoshi Inoue, the commander of Japan's Fourth Fleet at Truk, and advance bases in the Marshall Islands. The radio association listed in the heading addresses, combined with the RDF bearings, confirmed the route. Japan changed her naval radio call signs on November 1 for the forces afloat—but not those of the shore stations. They kept their former call signs. By November 4, US Navy cryptographers unmasked the *Heiyo Maru*. Her new call sign was HE NU 2.[38]

The passenger/cargo ship was directed to pick up amphibious forces at Maizuru base and transport them to Saipan in the Central Pacific. Then Japanese radio operators firmly linked the Maizuru forces with the Central Pacific by sending copies of the radio orders to Japan's naval base at Kwajalein in the eastern Marshall Islands, about 600 miles south of Wake. On November 20, the Special Landing Force boarded the ship at the Maizuru docks and the vessel headed for Saipan, radioing that it would arrive on the morning of the 26th.[39]

Admiral Kimmel's war plans staff should have been alarmed by the arrival of a Japanese invasion force south of Wake Island. The man who was responsible for evaluating Japanese intentions was Commander Vincent R. Murphy, assistant war plans officer for Kimmel. Murphy was a holdover from Admiral Richardson's staff, and accompanied Richardson to Washington in October 1940 for the tumultuous meeting in the White House. Murphy attended major meetings with America's top naval brass while in Washington in late 1940, which suggests that he learned of FDR's policy of "let Japan commit the first act of war." It is unreasonable to believe Richardson did not convey Roosevelt's policy to his top aide—Murphy.[40]

Though he promised to continue monitoring the movements of the Maizuru landing force, Rochefort dropped the forces from his Daily Summary and did not suggest to Kimmel that the destination of the Maizuru force was Wake. He did warn Kimmel that Japan was concentrating "far greater" naval forces east of Saipan in the Marshall Islands.[41]

Kimmel picked up on the warning and, after conferring with Rochefort, alerted Washington to the dangers posed by Japan's growing military force in the Central Pacific. The admiral's response was proper military procedure—he sought authority from Washington to confront Japan's military moves in the Marshall Islands, particularly at the Jaluit naval base.[42] But General George Marshall, Army Chief of Staff, wanted physical proof and dispatched two B-24 photo planes from California for a reconnaissance mission over the Japanese bases. General Marshall directed that the mission take off from Wake Island, photograph Jaluit and Truk from high altitude, then provide photographic prints for Kimmel and Short with copies to MacArthur and Hart in Manila.[43]

On December 5 one of those B-24 photo planes, lacking machine guns for its defense, landed in Hawaii. General Short kept the plane on the tarmac at Hickam Field awaiting installation of its machine guns. But it was destroyed two days later by the First Air Fleet. The second B-24 never arrived. After the attack, Kimmel and Short were accused, in part, of gross failure to institute reconnaissance. But it was Washington that had deliberately failed to provide the proper equipment for the reconnaissance.[44]

Kimmel and the intercept network watched closely while the *Heiyo Maru* and other former merchant vessels delivered war materials and troops to the Central Pacific. They continued to watch helplessly while the ships steamed into position. Ultimately, tragically, they could do little but stand aside and obey the orders from the White House as it followed its policy of war.

CHAPTER 9

WATCH THE
WIDE SEA

———

JAPANESE FLEET MOVEMENTS POINTED TOWARD AN ACT OF WAR.
Intercepted messages did the same. Spies reconnoitered Pearl Harbor
while they themselves were under surveillance. The question begged by
this is not so much whether some Americans knew it and welcomed an attack, but what would men do who needed to defend against it? Could Admiral Husband Kimmel, the commander-in-chief of the Pacific Fleet, be
stopped from doing his job of preventing a Japanese strike?

Consider the plight of Lieutenant Commander Joseph John Rochefort
in October 1941. He was certain war between Japan and the United States
was imminent. The tone and sheer volume of intercepted Japanese naval
dispatches piling up on his desk at Station HYPO on Oahu alarmed him.
He was sure that the heavy radio traffic between warships, navy yards, air
squadrons, and shore facilities meant that the entire Japanese navy was organizing for a major offensive. Rochefort had no illusions about a peaceful
1941 or 1942. The only question was when and where Japan would strike.

Rochefort answered those questions for both Admiral Kimmel and President Roosevelt. They read his Daily Communication Summary, which detailed Japanese war preparations. But FDR and Kimmel were at cross purposes. America's top fleet commander was not aware that FDR might choose to place the Pacific Fleet and himself in harm's way. Kimmel looked for military ways to interdict Japanese hostile acts aimed at Hawaii.

The Japanese intercepts piling up on Rochefort's desk during the first week of October sounded a Klaxon of alarm. Since midsummer of 1941 Rochefort's cryptographic staff had been listening in on a major reorganization of the Japanese navy. He puzzled over the pile of intercepts. What was Japan up to? The requisitioning of the entire Japanese merchant fleet and placing it under military control was first detected in July and recognized throughout the US command as an initial step toward war preparation. Rochefort sought more information. About noon on October 8, Rochefort sent a message to his entire command, the Mid-Pacific Communications Intelligence Network: they were placed on an "eight-day" week and ordered to monitor every Japanese radio signal originating in the Pacific basin. The order was unprecedented for the Navy. Rochefort produced his eighth day by adding a scoop watch to the radio-monitoring schedule. The extra watch would scoop up every Japanese radio transmission in the Pacific Basin. The order applied to Navy radio listening posts in the Central Pacific, Alaska, and the West Coast of the United States. Everywhere it meant the same thing: locate all categories of Japanese vessels.[1]

Rochefort established a priority list for the scoop watch. Topping the list were the flagships of the Imperial Japanese Navy. Next on the list were the battleships, carriers, and detached units. The last were important for predicting Japanese naval movements, since they included oil tankers and supply ships. A naval armada sails with its oil tankers serving as mobile gas stations. Replenishing fuel is mandatory for voyages of over 1000 miles; no naval captain wants his ship low on fuel on the high seas. Carrier task groups gulped fuel. Support vessels—particularly destroyers—needed refueling every three or four days. The high-speed maneuvering of carrier groups during launching and recovery of aircraft consumed enormous amounts of fuel. The tracking of Japan's naval tankers was a high priority for the scoop watch and provided a fall-back intelligence source if the carriers' location became elusive. When Rochefort's staff issued their first

Communication Summary on July 15, 1941, they promised Admiral Kimmel that they would keep on the lookout for Japanese naval tankers.[2]

Japanese naval communication procedures unwittingly made tracking easy. During their voyages the tankers reported their latitude and longitude position to Tokyo. These reports were transmitted by radio every day at 8:00 A.M., noon, and 4:00 P.M. in the navy's dot-dash *kana* system. Sloppiness made things even easier. Civilian crews on the tankers irritated the naval personnel who operated the guns aboard each vessel. *"Gunzoku!"* sneered the navy gunners, contemptuous of the lack of military discipline shown by the civilians. In Japanese naval slang the term equated to "scum." Included among the *gunzoku* were the civilian radio operators of the tankers, who enjoyed "talking" with marine radio operators of other nations in the dot-dash language of International Morse Code.

American intelligence could track the Japanese ships through Radio Direction Finding (RDF). The more radio signals available, the better. A typical 1941 shore-based direction finder was a radio receiver set and antenna, mounted in a wooden housing in the center of a twelve-foot-diameter wooden circle. Each point of the compass from zero to 360 degrees was marked on the circle. The RDF device locked on a Japanese naval transmission as the operator moved the receiver's antenna on the compass in the direction of the targeted radio signal. At a certain point, called a "null," the signal disappears. When matched with the compass reading, the null point establishes the bearing in a straight line from the RDF housing.

For example, in October, Kisner's direction finder unit at Station H identified and tracked the Japanese survey ship HIJMS *Katsuriki* to the Gilbert Islands by monitoring her radio transmissions as KE RO 8 in Japan's naval call sign system. In the first part of the month, the vessel's bearings obtained at Station H indicated she sailed in the vicinity of 9.4° N, 172° E to 5.3° N, 169° E. Then in late October she moved to 10°N, 169° E. After obtaining these fixes on KE RO 8 it was easy to locate her in the Central Pacific. Though RDF bearings must be recorded on a Great Circle chart for accuracy, a simple reading of a Mercator-projection (typical flat) map will show that the *Katsuriki* operated at Tarawa 5° N, 172° E, then returned to her base at Kwajalein in the Marshalls [169° E × 10° N] by the end of the month. The nulls established that the *Katsuriki* was in the vicinity of Tarawa performing oceanic surveys. Kisner said US Navy intelligence knew the ship was a precursor for a future Japanese invasion, for her naval role called for taking soundings and mapping out the Tarawa atoll and other islands in the Gilbert Group. Japanese troops invaded the Gilberts in the spring of 1942.[3]

Rochefort used this sort of direction finding to gather information on Japanese fleet movements. It provides instant intelligence—no code-breaking is required except for knowing the radio call sign. Admiral Kimmel needed this information most urgently of all and he received it daily from Rochefort. Why didn't he make use of it? The question is all the more compelling because Kimmel's predecessor, Admiral Richardson, had placed Station HYPO on a wartime basis as a full decryption site precisely in order to have a source of information independent of Washington.

In the late fall of 1940 Admiral Richardson had decided, soon after his fractious lunch with Roosevelt on October 8, to take steps to protect his warships and men from a surprise Japanese attack. Richardson did not trust the "kowtowing" [his word] White House brass to supply him with accurate intelligence information on Japanese intentions and preparations. Richardson wanted his own information on Japan's naval activities. He decided the best protection for himself and the United States Fleet was Station HYPO.

The admiral believed that the fleet could be denied vital information if the White House controlled the intelligence flow. As a backstop, he decided to bypass the White House and directed that HYPO be brought to immediate war strength and provide continuous intelligence information direct to the fleet. When Richardson's request reached Station US early in 1941, it was approved by Commander Laurance Safford, boss of Navy radio intelligence activities. Safford knew just the man to supervise the expansion of HYPO and take charge of the unit—Lieutenant Commander Joseph J. Rochefort.

Richardson, however, was unable to exploit Rochefort's skills. FDR fired the admiral in January, and put Kimmel in command in his place. But the requested expansion of HYPO went forward. That May, Rochefort was transferred from a staff command position with the Scouting Force of the Pacific Fleet (later called the Fast Carrier Forces) and took charge of the rapidly expanding cryptographic-analytic center.

On July 15 his handpicked staff, using the RDF reports and intercepts from Station H, produced the first Daily Communication Summary for Kimmel. Copies went to McCollum at Station US, where a presidential monograph was prepared for the White House. Rochefort's crew rapidly sized up Japan's move toward war. In late August they identified a new carrier division and its flattops, the HIJMS *Shokaku* and HIJMS *Zuikaku*. In September they discovered the China recall and the military buildup in the Central Pacific using Japan's merchant fleet. By October 8, Rochefort's operations were on the highest priority—the scoop watch. It produced results within two weeks, when Rochefort's cryptographers discovered the scope of an emerging Japanese two-pronged military strategy: (1) the Southeast Asia Invasion and, (2) the screening maneuver involving air forces in the North and Central Pacific that became the Pearl Harbor raid.

Citing an intercept from Vice Admiral Nishizo Tsukuhara, commander of the Eleventh Air Fleet, Rochefort[4] scoped out the massive invasion for Kimmel on October 21: "It would appear from this message that whatever the Combined Air Force intends to do will interest the China Fleet. It is apparent," Rochefort continued, "that he had already located parts of his command from TAIWAN northward at least as far as GENZAN [Korea]. The fact that he has had Carriers added to his force (Carriers are not normally part of the Combined Air Force) indicates a large-scale operation over a long distance." [Parentheses and capitalization by Rochefort] In the summary, Rochefort said Carrier Divisions Three and Four were part of the operation.

By the next day, October 22, Rochefort had discovered the formation of a separate Japanese air operation that he said was focused on the Kurile Islands and would extend eastward and south over a vast area of the North and Central Pacific. "With nothing definite to point to, the impression grows that a large-scale screening maneuver or operation, at least, is in progress, involving mainly air units in the Mandates, Takao-Hainan Indo China area, the Kuriles, the Submarines, Marcus and Chichi Jima to the Kuriles. Identification of Horomushiro as an Air Base the other day places operations up to the Northern Kuriles."[5]

Major collateral evidence concerning Japanese plans for hostile action came from Ambassador Joseph Grew in Tokyo. He seems to have planted an informant inside the Imperial Palace. On November 5, an Imperial

Conference with Emperor Hirohito present decided on war with America and her Allies. Japan's military was given the go-ahead for invasion and occupation of Southeast Asia targets. Admiral Yamamoto received the OK for his screening movement. He was authorized to attack Pearl Harbor, knock out the Pacific Fleet, and prevent its interference with the invasion.

The general tenor of the Palace meeting reached the United States. "War with the United States may come with dramatic and dangerous suddenness," was the closing sentence of a lengthy report sent by Grew to Secretary of State Cordell Hull the next day.[6] Grew cautioned that in the event diplomatic conversations failed, the United States should not underestimate Japan's obvious preparations for war. He felt that the risk and danger of war was very great and was increasing. Quoting the unnamed informant, Grew said the decision for war was presented to Hirohito by Prime Minister General Hideki Tojo, Naval Minister Admiral Shigetaro Shimada, and Japanese Foreign Minister Shigenori Togo.[7]

To confirm the Japanese naval war preparations reported by the Imperial Palace informant, Grew sent his naval attaché, Lieutenant Commander Henri Smith-Hutton, on a railroad observation trip to the Inland Sea naval operating areas of the Japanese fleet. First Grew filed a transit application with Japan's naval minister, saying that Smith-Hutton and his wife Jane were taking a brief vacation.[8] The couple sought approval for a daylight round trip to view the beauty of the Inland Sea, according to the application. Their rail route provided an overnight stopover at Miyajima on November 3. Two days, November 5 and 6, were scheduled for the Beppu area, a site of the Japanese Pearl Harbor carrier training operations. The rail journey and overnight stay at Miyajima on the south shore of the Hiroshima Bay region offered operational intelligence of the nerve center of Japanese naval war preparations. The train passed near the Kure Naval Base—a beehive of activity.

After lunch on November 4, the Smith-Huttons left Miyajima and boarded the train for Beppu. The rail journey took them past the Tokuyama oil depot, whose storage tanks brimmed with aviation fuel from American oil refineries. At nearby Murozumi Bay, Japanese amphibious forces of the Third Fleet practiced invasion landing techniques. Both ports front on the Suo-Nada, a southern branch of the Inland Sea.

Night approached as the Smith-Huttons arrived at Beppu's rail station on November 4. Darkness prevented any sightseeing, but their vacation plans for the following days permitted a day and a half for viewing the scenery of the Japanese naval operating areas surrounding Beppu. Yamamoto's flagship, HIJMS *Nagato*, was anchored south of Beppu at Saheki Bay. Aboard the battleship, the admiral's staff busily prepared the final operational orders for attacks on Pearl Harbor, Wake, Guam, the Philippines, and Southeast Asia. Nearby were Japan's naval air stations at Oita and Usa, important home bases for the aircraft squadrons of the First Air Fleet. Warships, including carriers, rode at anchor in Beppu Bay. The sky buzzed with Zero fighters and torpedo planes practicing war maneuvers. Departing Beppu at 2:30 P.M. on November 6, the Smith-Huttons retraced their rail route back to Kobe's Sannomiya Station, then transferred to the express train for the return to Tokyo.

Soon after the attaché and his wife returned, Ambassador Grew sent a much stronger warning to Washington. On November 17, he again predicted a sudden military or naval action by Japan's armed forces. Grew was specific. He was referring not to China but to other areas available to Japan for a surprise attack. Be alert, Grew emphasized to Hull, "We cannot give substantial warning."[9]

When Rochefort's estimates and Grew's warnings were received in Washington they triggered another astonishing event. Navy officials declared the North Pacific Ocean a "Vacant Sea" and ordered all US and allied shipping out of the waters. An alternate trans-Pacific route was authorized through the Torres Strait, in the South Pacific between Australia and New Guinea. Rear Admiral Richmond K. Turner, War Plans officer for the United States Navy in 1941, explained the reasoning with a startling admission: "We were prepared to divert traffic when we believed that war was imminent. We sent the traffic down via Torres Strait, so that the track of the Japanese task force would be clear of any traffic."[10] On November 25, the day that the Japanese carrier force sailed for Pearl Harbor, Navy headquarters sent this message to Kimmel and San Francisco's Twelfth Naval District:

ROUTE ALL TRANSPACIFIC SHIPPING THRU TORRES STRAITS. CINCPAC AND CINCAF PROVIDE NECESSARY ESCORT. REFER YOUR DISPATCH 230258.

The order was dispatched about an hour after Admiral Nagumo's carrier force departed Hitokappu Bay and entered the North Pacific.

The Vacant Sea order dramatizes Admiral Kimmel's helplessness in the face of FDR's desires. The admiral tried on a number of occasions to do something to defend Pearl Harbor, based on Rochefort's troubling intercepts. Exactly two weeks prior to the attack, Kimmel ordered a search for a Japanese carrier force north of Hawaii. Without White House approval, he moved the Pacific Fleet into the North Pacific Ocean in the precise area where Japan planned to launch her carrier attack on Pearl Harbor. But his laudable efforts came to naught. When White House military officials learned Kimmel's warships were in the area of what turned out to be the intended Japanese launch site, they issued directives that caused Kimmel to quickly order the Pacific Fleet out of the North Pacific and back to its anchorages in Pearl Harbor.[11]

This unfortunate reversal of direction has been ignored by every Pearl Harbor investigation. It was never discussed during the original series of inquiries held from 1941 to 1946. It escaped scrutiny during the 1995 Congressional probe by Senator Strom Thurmond and Congressman Floyd Spence. Congress opened the 1995 Pearl Harbor probe at the request of Husband Kimmel's surviving family members. But neither Admiral Kimmel nor his family ever mentioned the mysterious sortie and the sudden recall from the North Pacific waters. Yet it provides exculpatory evidence which proves that Kimmel vigorously reconnoitered the waters north of Hawaii. After the attack, Kimmel was accused of failure to conduct precisely this type of reconnaissance.

Robinson Jeffers, one of the few American poets to oppose America's entrance into World War II, described the effect of the Vacant Sea order in "Pearl Harbor," which he published in 1948.

> Meanwhile our prudent officers
> Have cleared the coast-long ocean of ships and
> fishing craft, the sky of planes, the windows of
> light these
> clearings
> Make a great beauty. Watch the wide sea; there
> is nothing human; its gulls have it. Watch

the wide sky
All day clean of machines; only at dawn and
dusk one military hawk passes
High on patrol. Walk at night in the blackout.[12]

On Sunday, November 23, the Pacific Fleet was at sea north of Hawaii looking for a Japanese carrier force. Officially the sortie into the North Pacific waters was named Exercise 191. The object of the exercise called for Force Black [Japan] to conduct an air raid on Force White [USA]. Exercise 191 would prove eerily similar to Admiral Isoroku Yamamoto's Operation Order No. 1 which set forth Japan's naval plans for the Hawaii raid. Both Exercise 191 and OPORD 1 called for a Japanese carrier force to advance on Hawaii from the North Pacific in an operational area between 158° and 157° west longitude—the approach to Oahu and Pearl Harbor.

In a bizarre series of coincidences, Yamamoto and Kimmel selected the identical launch area—the Prokofiev Seamount, an extinct underwater volcano about 200 miles north of Oahu. Their timing and planning borders on mutual clairvoyance. Each used Kaena Point, a promontory on Oahu's north shore, as the benchmark, decided on Sunday for an early-morning launch time, and marked two Oahu targets: Pearl Harbor Naval Base and Kaneohe Naval Air Station on Oahu's windward side. They differed only in their calendar choice: Kimmel began his search on November 23, two weeks before the actual attack. Radio intelligence gathered by Rochefort seems to have generated Kimmel's North Pacific sortie. Grew's information, gathered from sources in Japan, parallels that of Rochefort, but there is no proof that the ambassador's dispatches were ever sent to Hawaii.

Earlier in August, Admiral Kimmel had prepared a 1941–42 Fiscal Year employment schedule for routine fleet training in the Hawaii region.[13] It involved all classes of warships from small patrol craft to the battleships and carriers and set a schedule intended to last through June 1942. One portion of the schedule set aside the dates November 23–25 for what Kimmel called Fleet Tactics, but he gave no specifics. Some portions of the schedule called for ship upkeep in dry docks; others were assigned to buoy tending. Revisions were adopted in late October, soon after Kimmel read Rochefort's prediction of a two-pronged Japanese attack. His August schedule, calling for October operations in Hawaii, appears to have been junked, for about a third of the fleet was then anchored on the West Coast in San Francisco and San Pedro for upkeep and training.

By the end of October, Yamamoto added the final touches to the Hawaii raid plan. So did Kimmel. Yamamoto issued his plan on November 5. So did Kimmel. Both admirals distributed their plans by officer courier to major fleet commanders. Kimmel's choice for his raid was not the regular fleet training area. For the previous several years most fleet training operations and employment schedules were conducted southwest of Oahu—an area off-limits to merchant shipping.

American naval war planning had always contemplated a Japanese carrier raid aimed at Hawaii from the North Pacific. Rear Admiral Richmond K. Turner testified that the theory of such an attack had been discussed among senior naval officials for at least the prior twenty-five years.[14] In 1938, Vice Admiral Ernest J. King, using his flagship, the aircraft carrier USS *Saratoga*, conducted a simulated air raid on Pearl Harbor from the North Pacific, but it differed from Kimmel's concept in that King's exercise hit at midday. King's raid was described by Admiral Alan Kirk, who served as FDR's third ONI director briefly in 1941: "King headed the Black Fleet [Japan]. His tactics were exactly those employed by the Japanese on the 7th of December, except King's attack was later in the day not early morning. By golly, he took his carriers north of Oahu, launched his airplanes in bad weather, swooped through the favoring storm clouds and appeared over the Blue Fleet [USA] to the startled consternation of everyone concerned."[15]

Kimmel's operation order was explicit. Exercise 191 was not to be an ordinary exercise. Every vessel was warned that hostile warships might be discovered at any moment. A code phrase would indicate the presence of the enemy. The warning would be sent via a signal flag dispatch:

EASY CAST EASY.

He did not want to use the fleet's radio system and tip off the Japanese.[16]

Pacific Fleet warships were moved from Hawaii and California ports to the North Pacific. It was not a routine training exercise. As they sped toward Hawaii from ports in San Francisco and Los Angeles the warships sailed under wartime conditions. Daily gunnery and anti-aircraft drills imbued each sailor with a sense of wartime. The peacetime operating conditions for the West Coast vessels changed when they entered Hawaiian waters on the morning of November 7. A predawn general quarters was sounded, according to Lieutenant F. W. Purdy of the battleship USS *California*.[17]

Admiral Kimmel assigned 46 warships and about 126 aircraft to the North Pacific. Five battleships and the carrier USS *Lexington*, plus cruisers, destroyers, submarines, and various auxiliary ships formed the surface force. For air support he grouped the *Lexington*'s 60 planes plus 54 aircraft from Marine Air Group 21 into a fighting unit. Kimmel meant business— the aircraft included both bombers and fighters. Twelve long-distance Catalina flying boats of Patrol Squadron 12 were detailed to search the entire "classical-composer" sea lanes from the Prokofiev Seamount at 157° W to the Chopin and Mendelssohn Seamounts at 162° W.[18]

The search area was narrow—a 65-degree arc originating on Kaena Point on Oahu's North Shore and curving out 600 miles. Admiral Kimmel did not assign search planes to the west, south, or east quadrants from Kaena Point. No responsible naval officer ever contemplated a Japanese approach from the other quadrants, for those courses involved the main shippings lanes and risked discovery. "Black" would be found in the small search arc north of Oahu. Round-the-clock radar surveillance was included in the operation orders. No one could fault Kimmel's strategic and tactical plans. Every naval discovery tactic was used in the reconnaissance plans for the search of the North Pacific: distance air search and radar on a twenty-four-hour basis. All were sound naval procedures, whether for an exercise or the real thing.

Secret orders directed warship and air unit commanders to attend an urgent conference at Pacific Fleet headquarters on Thanksgiving eve, November 19. The summons was sent by blinker light on Kimmel's orders. Radio transmissions were not used—he did not want Japanese monitoring operations to detect the sortie.[19] At the conference, Kimmel laid out his war-game scenario for his officers and men, doing his best to simulate the reality that might soon occur. It was an exact forecast of Sunday, December 7. The White commander was notified by his Navy Department that war was momentarily expected with Black and that Black's raiding force was definitely known to be at sea in vicinity of Base X-Ray [Pearl Harbor]. Black submarines might be encountered, and White could not muster full naval strength due to Atlantic commitments (escorting of convoys to Britain).[20]

Kimmel's plans for Exercise 191 required last-minute adjustments that were not on the original employment schedule. First he canceled all leaves for the Thanksgiving weekend. Exercise 191 was planned as a four-day operation starting at 0600 on Friday, November 21, to 0600 on Tuesday, November 25. He concentrated his ships and aircraft in the most likely approach route for a Japanese raiding force. Early dawn hours on a Sunday were set for the start of the operation. Aircraft were poised for long- and short-distance aerial scouting of the North Pacific sea lanes. Kimmel's plans indicate that he was thoroughly prepared for action if he encountered a Japanese carrier force. Upon its discovery he would send his warning signal by blinker light and signal flags indicating that hostile action between America and Japan had begun.

Kimmel mailed ten copies of the operation details to the Navy Department in Washington and on November 19 briefed his fleet commanders. Rear Admiral Walter Anderson—Commander Battleships—filed a written objection to the 600-mile-wide aerial reconnaissance area outlined by the plan. He wanted to scuttle the search plan because the long aerial flights assigned to the float planes of his battleships jeopardized the safety of the pilots—they would run out of fuel. He raised his objections to the commander of the White Force, Vice Admiral William S. Pye, after learning of the search plan. His complaint alleged that the battleship aircraft could not carry enough fuel for the 600-mile round trip reconnaissance flight. (The aircraft's fuel capacity was rated at 745 miles). But his objection can be seen as another move to support Washington's Vacant Sea policy and clear the North Pacific of US aircraft and ships. Based on Rochefort's intercepts and Grew's warnings, there was an outside chance that Japanese warships had advanced in the North Pacific and might be discovered before they committed an overt act of war.

Shaken by Anderson's charge, Pye asked his Force aviation officer, Lieutenant Commander C. F. Greber, for advice.[21] Greber argued that Anderson's objections overstated the fuel problem and cited records from the Navy's Bureau of Aeronautics showing that the battleships' scout planes could carry fuel for up to 745-mile flights. Kimmel's search strategy, Greber told Pye, was designed to prevent an enemy carrier force from entering the 600-mile search area undetected. But Anderson did not think that his battleship's search planes carried enough fuel to constantly monitor a large area and advised against the wide-ranging aerial patrol. Kimmel, aware of Anderson's White House clout, overruled Pye and Greber. Anderson won. Exercise 191 went forward as planned, but long-range reconnaissance of the North Pacific was curtailed.[22]

On Sunday, November 23, Kimmel had both Black and White forces positioned over the Classical Composer Seamounts of the North Pacific. West longitude 157° was the general route selected for the approach to Hawaii by Black forces. A strong storm in the Gulf of Alaska sent pulses of inclement weather throughout the North Pacific. The early morning attack on Base X-Ray was delayed. Stormy weather restricted aerial reconnaissance. Heavy seas pounded the warships and a number of sailors were injured. Several hours passed, and the pounding seas subsided. By noon the skies cleared. Finally at 12:55 P.M. one of the search planes sighted the *Lexington*'s Black Force at 27° 17' N, 157° 55' W, nearly over the Prokofiev Seamount—the exact location of the launch site of the Japanese Navy's First Air Fleet, then just two weeks in the future.

The war games between the two forces continued throughout Sunday and into Monday, November 24, as the warships and aircraft chased one another over the submerged volcanoes of the Handel, Ravel, Scarlatti, and Mozart Seamounts. Suddenly at 3:30 P.M., though the exercise was intended to last another fifteen hours, Kimmel called it off. He issued orders to the Task Groups:

CEASE PRESENT EXERCISES.[23]

The *Lexington* recalled its fighters and bombers, which were about to attack White. The warships returned either to their anchorages inside Pearl Harbor or to patrols off Oahu's southwest coast. The North Pacific was again a Vacant Sea.

Kimmel's premature cancellation of the exercise came several hours after Washington sent him specific action orders. He was warned to expect a surprise aggressive movement by Japan in any direction, but not to place the Pacific Fleet in a position that would precipitate Japanese action. Rear Admiral Ingersoll sent the message:

CHANCES OF FAVORABLE OUTCOME OF NEGOTIATIONS WITH JAPAN VERY DOUBTFUL X THIS SITUATION COUPLED WITH STATEMENTS OF JAPANESE GOVERNMENT AND MOVEMENTS THEIR NAVAL AND MILITARY FORCES INDICATE IN OUR OPINION THAT A SURPRISE AGGRESSIVE MOVEMENT IN ANY DIRECTION INCLUDING ATTACK ON PHILIPPINES OR GUAM IS A POSSIBILITY. CHIEF OF STAFF HAS SEEN THIS DISPATCH CONCURS AND REQUESTS ACTION ADEES [ADDRESSEES] TO INFORM SENIOR ARMY OFFICERS THEIR AREAS X UTMOST SECRECY NECESSARY IN ORDER NOT TO COMPLICATE AN ALREADY TENSE SITUATION OR PRECIPITATE JAPANESE ACTION X GUAM WILL BE INFORMED SEPARATELY.[24]

Kimmel said he regarded Ingersoll's message as an injunction directing him not to take provocative action against Japan. He recalled a Roosevelt directive that Stark passed on to him in late September: "At the present time, the President has issued shooting orders only for the Atlantic and Southwest Pacific sub-area." In emphasizing the presidential directive, Stark said that US Navy Regulations backed it up—implying a court-martial if disobeyed.[25]

At the time, of course, Kimmel did not know of Washington's eight-action policy. If McCollum's action policy was to succeed in uniting America, Japan must be seen as the aggressor and must commit the first overt act of war on an unsuspecting Pacific Fleet, not the other way around. FDR and his highest-level commanders gambled on Japan committing the first overt act of war, and knew from intercepted messages that it was near.[26] An open sea engagement between Japan's carrier force and the Pacific Fleet would have been far less effective at establishing American outrage. Japan could claim that its right to sail the open seas had been deliberately challenged by American warships if Kimmel attacked first.

Despite the early cancellation of Exercise 191, Kimmel wasn't quite ready to give up. Though the naval brass in Washington forced him to pull the warships from the North Pacific, he approved two new missions intended to discover a Japanese carrier force: on November 24, shortly after 191 was canceled, Vice Admiral William "Bull" Halsey, Kimmel's carrier chief, issued operation plans for a 25-warship task group to guard against an "enemy air and submarine" attack on Pearl Harbor.[27] The force was built around the carrier USS *Enterprise* and the battleship USS *Arizona*.

Halsey's directive said the operation would last seven days, from November 28 to December 5. His proposal was similar to Exercise 191. If a true enemy was located he planned to issue the same EASY CAST EASY signal established for 191. But Halsey's plan was never put into effect. During the late afternoon of Thursday, November 26, Admiral Stark directed Admiral Kimmel to use aircraft carriers and deliver Army pursuit planes to Wake and Midway islands.

Early the next morning Kimmel called a conference with General Short, Halsey, and other Army and Navy officers. After hearing the Washington plan, they decided it was faulty.[28] Army pursuit pilots were not trained for carrier operations, could not land on a carrier since the planes had no tail hooks, and were unable to navigate over widespread areas of the ocean. Oahu-based Marine Corps pilots, who had the training and whose planes were equipped for carrier operations, were substituted. Halsey agreed to transport twelve Marine fighter planes to Wake Island and canceled his "look for the enemy" operation. He left early on the twenty-eighth aboard the carrier USS *Enterprise*, with the fighters on the flight deck, escorted by eleven of the fleet's newest warships. The *Arizona* was left behind at Pearl.

A second delivery of eighteen fighters to Midway was delayed a week. On December 5, the carrier USS *Lexington*, accompanied by eight modern warships, departed Pearl Harbor and, according to her deck log, headed for an unnamed "assigned area." The fighter planes were never delivered. On December 7, as his force neared Midway and prepared to launch the aircraft for a flight to the island, the Task Group commander learned of the Pearl Harbor attack shortly after 8:00 A.M. and cancelled the flight.[29]

On orders from Washington, Kimmel left his oldest vessels inside Pearl Harbor and sent twenty-one modern warships, including his two aircraft carriers, west toward Wake and Midway. Those were strange orders, for they dispatched American forces directly into the path of the oncoming Japanese fleet of thirty submarines. The last-minute circumstances that moved the warships out of Pearl Harbor were discussed during the 1945–46 Congressional inquiry. Members wondered whether the sorties were genuine efforts to reinforce Wake Island and Midway or merely ploys to move all the modern warships from the Pearl Harbor anchorages prior to the attack so they would not be hit by the First Air Fleet. Senator Alben Barkley,

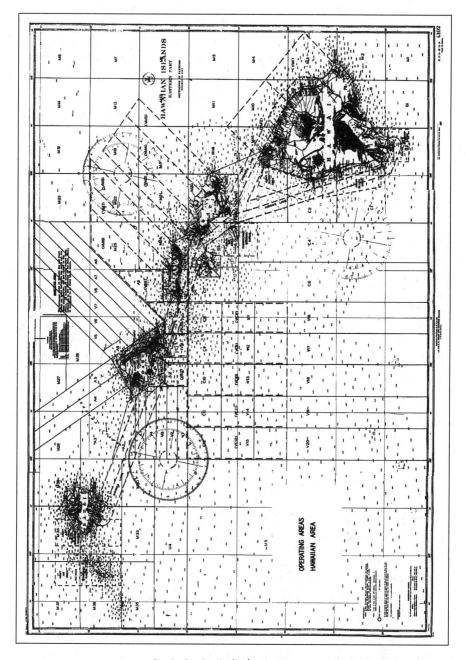

HAWAIIAN FLEET TRAINING AREAS

The Pacific Fleet's designated operational/training areas were located southwest of Oahu in 1941. There were none designated for north of the Hawaiian Islands on this 1941 Navy map.

Source: Walter Short's papers, Hoover Institution Archives, Stanford University, Stanford, California.

153

the chairman, questioned Admiral Stark about the sortie of the two carrier forces:[30] "It is not clear in my mind whether they were sent." Stark replied, "Yes sir; they were sent. The dates were set by Admiral Kimmel. We gave no specific dates." Stark stumbled over the facts: he set the date, not Kimmel. According to Navy records, Stark set the date on November 26:

IT WILL BE NECESSARY FOR YOU TO TRANSPORT THESE PLANES AND GROUNDS CREW FROM OAHU TO THESE STATIONS ON AN AIRCRAFT CARRIER.[31]

With the departure of the *Lexington* and *Enterprise* groups, the warships remaining in Pearl Harbor were mostly 27-year-old relics of World War I.

While Washington pulled Kimmel's fleet around the Pacific on invisible strings, the admiral still searched for the Japanese carriers that Rochefort had spotted in the Kuriles. Kimmel asked for Rochefort's cryptographic help in a terse order on November 24: "Find The Carriers." According to Edwin Layton, Kimmel's intelligence chief, the admiral wondered if other Pacific monitoring stations had also obtained bearings of the Japanese warships.[32]

From November 18 to November 24, both Station CAST and Station HYPO tracked the carriers north to Hitokappu Bay. The evidence that was hidden from every Pearl Harbor investigation is overwhelming: on November 19 a Japanese submarine, using the radio call sign RO TU ØØ, headed toward the First Air Fleet Communication Zone, north of Ominato. The next day subs *I-19* and TA YU 88 reported entering the First Air Fleet Communication Zone north of Ominato, according to an intercept by Merrill F. Whiting at Station H. The heavy cruiser HIJMS *Tone* and Destroyer Squadron One joined the carrier divisions. On November 21, Rochefort informed Kimmel that most of the other Japanese fleet submarines were at sea, moving east in the Pacific. On the following day, November 22, the carrier *Akagi*, flagship of the First Air Fleet and Carrier Division One, was heard using a tactical call sign of 8 YU NA.[33] It was located by radio direction finder at a bearing of 028 degrees from Corregidor. The 028-degree bearing placed the *Akagi* on a great circle line with Hitokappu Bay. (See chart on p. 191 of this book.) More radio transmissions emerged during November 22 and 23 as the vessels of the First Air Fleet traveled to the rendezvous point. At the same time that CAST heard the *Akagi*, Admiral

Chuichi Nagumo, commander-in-chief of the First Air Fleet, initiated a radio message using his secret Hawaii radio call sign of SA SO 2, which was reserved for radio contact during the Pearl Harbor attack. His transmission was long enough for Station CAST to obtain a radio direction finder bearing that placed Nagumo on a line of 040° from CAST—a position consistent with the Hitokappu Bay locale. Nagumo's RDF fix—about 12 degrees of longitude from the *Akagi*—indicates that he must have traveled aboard one of the other warships enroute to Hitokappu, perhaps the *Kaga*, sister of the *Akagi*. The 040° bearing would have been reached when the vessels passed Cape Inubo—a point of land on Honshu that juts far out into the western Pacific.

The carrier *Zuikaku* of Carrier Division Five was also located by radio direction finder at 030° from Corregidor, placing her off the east coast of Japan enroute to Hitokappu Bay. The next fixes from CAST came at 10:00 A.M. on November 27 and placed the *Akagi*, *Shokaku*, and *Hiryu* at 030°. This position is also consistent with their journey to Hawaii, for it would place the flattops about 500 miles east of the Kuriles in the North Pacific. That is where they were on November 27, according to Japanese records. In Bandoeng, Java, Dutch cryptographers at *Kamer* 14 provided collateral evidence to Washington and reported hearing similar Japanese naval broadcasts originating from near the Kuriles.[34]

Beginning with the cancellation of Kimmel's exercise, and continuing through the final days before the attack, conclusive cryptographic evidence indicates that FDR shared McCollum's intentions and left the Pacific Fleet in harm's way. The dispatch containing the plain-language words HITOKAPPU BAY was delivered to Rochefort by Kisner and provided a major clue to the location of Japan's fast carriers—the First Air Fleet. Now the carriers appeared to be moving to a position where they could threaten American forces. Their radio direction finder bearings traced a north-by-east course in the North Pacific. None were associated with the southern movement of the Japanese naval expeditionary force. As of November 23, this information was available to Kimmel. The same cryptographic information was transmitted over secure radio circuits to Station US, in Washington, where Arthur McCollum and his staff prepared a daily monograph for President Roosevelt.

Grew's November reports, coupled with the Station H intercepts tracing the movement of the First Air Fleet to Hitokappu Bay, were just what Arthur McCollum had waited to read. The eight provocative actions that he advocated had now fallen into place. Japanese access to fuel and natural resources in Southeast Asia had been interdicted; American heavy cruisers had entered Japanese territorial waters; increased military aid had been granted to Chiang Kai-shek and a US Army Commission headed by Major General John Magruder[35] had gone to China in October 1941; twenty-four US submarines had been transferred to Admiral Hart in Manila; the Pacific Fleet remained in Hawaiian waters; a complete embargo of all US trade with Japan was in force; the Dutch refused to grant concessions to Japan; and the British had granted the United States use of military bases in the Pacific in accord with McCollum's eight-action memorandum. One of the bases was Rabaul in the Bismarck Archipelago, north of Australia.[36]

With the recall of the Pacific Fleet from the North Pacific on November 24 and the cessation of aerial reconnaissance over the ocean, America had no effective means of locating the advance of an enemy force on Hawaii except through the intercepts obtained by the monitoring stations. But the cryptographic reports obtained by Stations CAST and H did not appear in the Daily Communication Summaries shown to Kimmel in 1941.

Kimmel, alone and outmaneuvered, would make one last-ditch effort to convince Washington that a critical situation faced the Pacific Fleet.

CHAPTER 10

A NIGHT WITH
A PRINCESS

———

BY NOVEMBER 25, AN ATMOSPHERE OF CRISIS PERVADED THE WHITE
House. During a meeting with his Cabinet, President Roosevelt announced
that America might be in a shooting war with Japan in a few days. The
President echoed a forecast made ten days earlier by General George C.
Marshall, Army Chief of Staff: "The United States is on the brink of war
with the Japanese." Marshall delivered the warning during a strictly secret
press briefing.[1]

Marshall's briefing coincided with the start of phase two of Japan's
war preparations, which began on November 15 when she moved forces
toward American territory. During the briefing, Marshall alluded to one
of America's most vital secrets when he revealed that the United States
could read Japan's encrypted messages. He told the correspondents that
his war assessment was based on access to a leak from the Japanese:
"We know what they know and they don't know we know it." Marshall
then predicted that a Japan-America war would break out during the

"first ten days of December," according to the notes of one correspondent present.

Marshall invited seven newspaper correspondents (radio reporters were not invited) to his office in the Munitions Building. He explained his embarrassment in calling the secret conference and said anyone who did not care to share secrets was at liberty to leave before he started talking. Though the function of the press is to publicize, none left. They kept Marshall's secret from their readers, who included many of the officers and sailors manning the warships on Pearl Harbor's Battleship Row.

Two ethical questions are raised by Marshall's secret conference with the reporters: (1) Instead of the press conference on November 15, 1941, why didn't he confer with Lieutenant General Walter Short on November 15, 1941, and disclose that he had learned from secret Japanese sources that war with the United States would break out within the first ten days of December? Ethical questions abound. Who deserved the very secret information, the reporters or Short? General Short raised the ethics question during testimony before the 1945–46 Joint Congressional Investigation Committee: "After October 28, 1941, with the War Department receiving information almost daily which indicated that war was imminent, he [Marshall] communicated to me none of those personal messages containing the inside information." (2) What was the responsibility of the reporters, their editors, and their publishers? In the land of the First Amendment, Americans expect journalists to abide by strict ethics and report the news, not hide secrets. Yet four of the nation's major news media—the *New York Times, New York Herald Tribune, Time,* and *Newsweek*—and the three major wire services—Associated Press, United Press, and International News Service—were let in on secrets denied to General Short and Admiral Kimmel in Hawaii.[2]

On the 25th, seeking a diversion from matters pertaining to war, Roosevelt invited Crown Princess Martha of Norway for cocktails and dinner in his second-floor suite in the White House. She and her royal family had been granted refuge in the United States following the Nazi occupation of their country. FDR's private quarters overlooked the south lawn, the Ellipse, and in the distance the Washington monument. Motorists or strollers on the Ellipse could see the lights of the presidential suite to the left as they faced the south portal of the mansion. On wintry nights, smoke swirled out the White House chimney from the wood-burning fireplace in FDR's Oval Study.

Always a genial host, Roosevelt enjoyed serving what he called "yummy" cocktails to his dinner guests. The cocktail hour was usually only a thirty-minute affair beginning at seven o'clock. On most occasions, drinks ended when the family cook, Mary Campbell, was ready to serve dinner. Roosevelt measured the drinks himself in a sterling silver shaker, then poured the mixture into silver goblets. The ritual could be extended if he declared a "dividend"—usually proclaimed when he lost count of the martinis.

Crown Princess Martha was a frequent visitor to the White House. The thirty-nine-year-old princess and her three children—Princesses Ragnhild and Astrid and Prince Harald, heir apparent to the Norwegian throne— were given asylum in the United States by the President following the Nazi invasion of Norway in April 1940. Her husband, Crown Prince Olav—the future King of Norway—remained in London. In 1999 their son Harald is King of Norway. On many occasions in 1941, Princess Martha turned up at the White House on the eve of momentous world events—most often when First Lady Eleanor Roosevelt was out of town. On June 15, 1941, Martha was with FDR just days before the German invasion of Russia. And it was the princess who traveled with Roosevelt aboard the presidential yacht, USS *Potomac,* in August when FDR sailed to Newfoundland and the Atlantic Charter conference with Winston Churchill.[3]

Eleanor Roosevelt's two-room suite was dark on the night of the 25th. Her quarters were part of a series of suites on the second floor that open onto the east-west corridor. Mrs. Roosevelt had left the presidential mansion for National Airport in midafternoon to catch a 4:00 P.M. flight to New York. She was active in the Office of Civil Defense, and her duties required frequent flights to Manhattan and conferences with Mayor Fiorello La Guardia, head of the OCD.

Just as Mrs. Roosevelt's plane became airborne, the President met with reporters at a news conference in the Oval Office. Questioning lasted only fifteen minutes. At 4:15, the traditional "Thank you, Mr. President" ended the conference. Shortly after, Roosevelt called for the White House limousine and, escorted by Secret Service men, was driven to Pooks Hill, the Bethesda, Maryland, estate of Crown Princess Martha.

———

As the presidential motorcade left the White House, another departure was taking place half a world away in Hitokappu Bay. Dawn was breaking over the vast anchorage. Leaden skies obscured the sun and barely allowed daylight to fall on the snow-covered mountains of isolated Etorofu Island in the Kurile archipelago about 200 miles northeast of Hokkaido, Japan's northernmost home island.

Vice Admiral Chuichi Nagumo, commander-in-chief of the First Air Fleet, ordered the "Get Underway" signal flag hoisted from the mainmast of his flagship, the Japanese aircraft carrier HIJMS *Akagi*. Through the early morning mist, the signalmen attached to the vessels of the First Air Fleet saw the order. Blinker signal lights reflected off the bouncing waves as the warships flashed messages between vessels. The waters of the bay slowly sprang to life as three fleet submarines churned their way into the North Pacific. As the vanguard of the Hawaii force, the subs took position fifty miles ahead. Their mission was to intercept any vessels on the route that might discover and report the movements of the main force.

Nagumo was unaware of the Vacant Sea order issued by the United States that cleared the North Pacific of shipping. He had nothing to fear from the American Navy. There was little chance his sortie would be discovered by ships at sea. There wasn't a United States merchant vessel, warship, or aircraft patrolling in the North Pacific. Japanese naval headquarters erroneously thought that two Russian merchant vessels, the *Uritski* and the *Azerbaidjan*, which were reported en route from San Francisco to Russian ports, might cross Nagumo's route, but it didn't happen.[4]

One of those ships, the *Uritski*, departed from the Golden Gate on November 28, headed for Petropavlosk on the Kamchatka Peninsula. Heeding the Vacant Sea orders from Washington, San Francisco's Twelfth Naval District directed the *Uritski* to proceed instead to Astoria, Oregon, a small anchorage at the mouth of the Columbia River. She anchored there on December 1. On December 5, after the Japanese carriers had cleared the North Pacific, the *Uritski* sailed from Astoria and resumed her journey to Petropavlosk. Records of the San Francisco Maritime Museum indicate that the *Azerbaidjan*, a Russian tanker, sailed from the Golden Gate for Vladivostok on November 14 but was "diverted south."

Meanwhile, back on the East Coast the red lights of the Secret Service escort began flashing as the presidential convoy prepared to depart Pooks Hill. Roosevelt waited in the rear seat of the Packard as the Princess stepped up onto the running board, entered the tonneau, and sat next to him. On a signal from the President, the motorcade circled the driveway and then retraced its route back to the White House. Roosevelt was assisted from the limo and, following his regular practice, was wheeled to the White House doctor's office for a fifteen-minute rubdown by Lieutenant Commander George Fox, a Navy physical therapist and the White House pharmacist. Princess Martha went to the second-floor living quarters.

At 7:00 P.M., Roosevelt was ready for the cocktail hour, his favorite time of the day. He asked his guest, "Child, what would you like in the way of a cocktail this evening?" Princess Martha, enthralled by the president's attentiveness, answered, addressing him, at his request, as "dear godfather."[5]

At Etorofu Island, the smaller warships of the First Air Fleet weighed anchor and headed into the Pacific, setting a course that generally moved toward the fortieth parallel of north latitude. Once they reached the choppy ocean, they formed into a giant protective circle and waited for the six big carriers to join the force. Admiral Nagumo supervised the operation from the flag bridge of the *Akagi*.[6]

Following years of Japanese naval communication procedures, some of the vessels transmitted an encrypted movement report to their home-port harbor-control master. But supposedly all Japanese warships and aircraft were maintaining complete radio silence. Admiral Isoroku Yamamoto, commander of all Japanese naval forces, had ordered that radio silence commence at midnight November 26, 1941 (Tokyo Time). A proviso inserted into the order permitted fleet commanders to break radio silence for emergency purposes or at their option.[7]

Yamamoto's radio silence order was sound military procedure. If all the Japanese warships observed radio silence, British, Dutch, and American radio direction finders could not locate them. Any radio transmission would give away their location if identified by those communications facilities. Japanese naval officers and historians are unanimous: the First Air Fleet remained a silent force from November 26 to December 8, 1941. Radio transmitters were sealed and telegraph keys were bolted shut. No radio messages or transmitter sounds were possible from the vessels of the First Air Fleet. Commander Minoru Genda, air officer of the First Air Fleet, who stood at the side of Admiral Nagumo aboard the flagship, HIJMS *Akagi*, reported after the war, "The fleet maintained absolute radio silence from the time of departure from Japan to time of attack. All orders concerning the fleet's voyage to mid-Pacific were decided before departure. Consequently, no direct order was given from Yamamoto to Admiral Nagumo of the Task Force."[8]

American intelligence officers, both Army and Navy, have agreed with Genda. Edwin T. Layton,[9] Kimmel's intelligence officer, concurred: "The Hawaii force was on super radio silence." So did retired Brigadier General Telford Taylor,[10] an Army intelligence officer in World War II: "All sources in Japan insist that the Pearl Harbor task force observed absolute radio silence throughout its approach to Oahu." Respected names in journalism have accepted this assertion. Don Whitehead, twice a Pulitzer Prize winner, wrote, "All radios were silent as the pack headed eastward toward Hawaii."[11]

A key aide to Admiral Ernest J. King also subscribed to the radio silence doctrine: "The Striking Force as it moved north to the sortie point in the Kuriles, and thence to the Eastern Pacific, was operating under strict injunctions to maintain radio silence to help assure the secrecy of its movement and mission." So wrote Commander W. J. Sebald, who was King's communications intelligence aide during the war.[12]

After sixty years it is clear that the US Navy, the Army, and the press were all wrong. Admiral Yamamoto did send radio messages to the Pearl Harbor force during its eleven-day sortie to Hawaii. Overwhelming evidence proves that Yamamoto, as well as the commanders of the Task Force warships, broke radio silence and that their ships were located by American communication intelligence units. First to ignore Yamamoto's silence order was Vice Admiral Nagumo. As he departed Hitokappu Bay at 6:00 A.M. on November 26 (Tokyo Time) he held extensive radio exchanges with

Japan's Central Pacific commander and the submarine force commander. Their three-way conversations were intercepted by Station H operators at midmorning on Tuesday, November 25.

Joseph Rochefort revealed the Nagumo broadcasts directly to Admiral Kimmel in the Communication Summary dated November 25 but delivered to the admiral the next morning: "Commander Carriers was in extensive communications with the submarine commander and Central Pacific Forces."[13] Rochefort's source was the intercept operators at Station H, who overheard Nagumo using the *Akagi*'s radio transmitter and coordinating war tactics with Vice Admiral Shigeyoshi Inoue, Japan's Central Pacific commander (Fourth Fleet), and Vice Admiral Mitsumi Shimizu, commander of Japanese submarines (Sixth Fleet). Admiral Inoue, whose headquarters was at Truk in the Central Pacific, commanded the Guam and Wake invasion forces and the aerial operations of Air Flotilla 24—composed mainly of seaplane squadrons used for long-range search missions. None of these "extensive communications" intercepts have been released by US censors.

All three admirals were under British, American, and Dutch radio surveillance, including radio direction finders (RDF). Admiral Shimizu was aboard his flagship, HIJMS *Katori*, leading thirty fleet-type submarines and their sub tenders toward Hawaii. Shimizu continuously violated the radio silence orders as he headed on a southeastern course from Japan. Naval radio direction finders followed his route past the Bonin Islands and Iwo Jima. South of Saipan the sub force turned east toward Hawaii. Refueling stops were made in the Marshall Islands.[14]

Every message intercepted at H was examined for military information by at least three experienced radio intelligence experts: the intercept operator; his watch supervisor; and Homer Kisner, the radio traffic chief for the Pacific Fleet. Though not cryptologists, the operators could decipher parts of messages. Kisner flagged and analyzed the communication data contained in the most important messages, and every twenty-four hours issued a Daily Chronology, which he sent to Rochefort.[15]

November 25 was another typical day for Kisner. He bundled all the Japanese naval message sheets, supervisor reports, and the Chronology into a package and personally drove the secrets over the Pali Road, past the Japanese Consulate, to Station HYPO in the Pearl Harbor Naval Yard.

The bundle contained crucial intelligence about Japanese naval war preparations. Kisner knew his reports reached Admiral Kimmel in summary form, but he had not been told that the President also received the information.[16] The reports and intercepts contained important information for the safety of the Pacific Fleet. At the top of his bundle were the code movement reports transmitted by units of the First Air Fleet from Hitokappu Bay.

At 7:20 A.M. the commander of Carrier Division Five (*Zuikaku* and *Shokaku*) filed a radio movement report from Hitokappu Bay. Admiral Nagumo continued his extensive radio communications with the commanders of the Japanese Central Pacific force and the submarine force. Then at about midmorning, when they were 120 miles east of the Kurile coastline, Japanese aircraft carriers were heard transmitting on 4963 kilocycles by Kisner's operators at Station H.[17]

Additional confirmation of the transmissions came from Dutch Harbor, Alaska, where radio direction finder personnel heard the *Akagi* transmitting on 4960 kilocycles. Harry Hood was one of the Navy intercept operators posted to Dutch Harbor in September 1941. In 1986, Hood confirmed to the author that he and other members of the RDF crew located Japanese warships in the southern Kuriles around November 25. "I recall very intensive Japanese navy traffic taking place around 25 November 1941 that lasted several days followed by a period of very light or no radio activity. Bearings pointed to the southern Kuriles." Hood said that these RDF positions were reported directly to Rochefort in Pearl Harbor by priority radio dispatch from Dutch Harbor. Hood did not testify at either of the Pearl Harbor congressional investigations.[18]

Rochefort's month-old prediction that Japanese naval forces would use the Kurile Islands for an advance toward Hawaii was now confirmed. On October 22 he had warned Admiral Kimmel of Japanese military plans for a "broad range of air operations" involving most of the Pacific Ocean. By "broad range," Rochefort meant land-based reconnaissance planes and aircraft carrier operations. Now he had evidence to prove it.[19]

The danger facing the Pacific Fleet in its Hawaii bases grew by the hour. After his morning intelligence briefing on November 25, Admiral Kimmel knew from reading Rochefort's communication summary that a large Japanese force of fleet subs and long-range patrol aircraft was heading eastward toward Hawaii from Japan. Kimmel had a right to be alarmed. Naval doctrine held that the presence of enemy submarines forecast a carrier attack: "If you detect submarines, then look for carriers" was straight out of naval textbooks.[20]

The massive movement toward Hawaii was unprecedented—not a training exercise and on a war footing. Kimmel learned that it included the commander and staff of the Sixth Fleet (submarines) aboard its flagship, *Katori*, in company with support vessels and nine subs of Submarine Squadron Three. Reading on, he saw that "a large number of submarines from the Submarine Force are in the Marshall area" (Central Pacific).[21]

What was Kimmel to do? He had complied with the November 24 order and pulled the Pacific Fleet from the now-Vacant Sea. Looking out his office window, he could see the warships had returned to the safety of their Pearl Harbor anchorages. He knew that he could not fire the first shot. About midmorning, deeply concerned by the implications in the Communication Summary, Kimmel decided to discuss the situation directly with Rochefort and his staff. Alone and without his intelligence officer, Edwin Layton, Kimmel left his office at the submarine base and drove to the Administration Building of the Fourteenth Naval District for a conference. En route, he joined up with Rear Admiral Claude Bloch, the commandant. Both admirals descended the concrete steps that led to the basement quarters of Station HYPO in the Pearl Harbor Navy Yard. For security purposes, a massive six-inch-thick steel bank-vault door barred all visitors. No one was admitted into the basement unless they were known to Chief Yeoman Durwood Rorie, HYPO's security head. Naval identification cards and security passes were not enough. At 10:30 A.M., they went over the intercepted Japanese messages brought in that morning by Kisner which represented Japanese naval intercepts through the evening of November 24. Though it was midday on the 25th in Hawaii, it was now 6:00 A.M. on November 26 across the international date line at Hitokappu Bay, and the First Air Fleet was on the move.

By noon, Rochefort convinced Kimmel and Bloch that the two-pronged Japanese military operation—which he had discovered in October—was now in operation. It was aimed at countries containing nearly a billion people who resided in the Southeast Asian nations and in the United States. The admirals agreed and directed Rochefort to summarize the dangers posed by the Japanese military advance. His summary was then transmitted by priority radio to Washington. He said the Southeast Asia movement was led by the commander of Japan's powerful Second Fleet, contained invasion components, and was protected by the 500 aircraft of the land-based Combined Air Force:

FOR PAST MONTH COMMANDER SECOND FLEET HAS BEEN ORGANIZING A TASK FORCE WHICH COMPRISES FOLLOWING UNITS: SECOND FLEET, THIRD FLEET, INCLUDING FIRST AND SECOND BASE FORCES, AND FIRST DEFENSE DIVISION, COMBINED AIR FORCE, DESRON THREE, AIRRON SEVEN, SUBRON FIVE AND POSSIBLY UNITS OF BATDIV THREE.[22]

It said that the units were heading in the direction of Takao Navy Base (Formosa), Bako Navy Base in the Pescadores Islands in the South China Sea, and Sama Naval Base on the island of Hainan in the Gulf of Tonkin. There was no mention of carrier divisions in this force.

Rochefort then closed his summary by identifying the eastward submarine advance in the Central Pacific and linked it with a carrier division unit—not necessarily a flattop:

THERE IS BELIEVED TO BE STRONG CONCENTRATION OF SUBMARINES AND AIR GROUPS IN THE MARSHALLS WHICH COMPRISE AIRRON TWENTY FOUR, AT LEAST ONE CARRIER DIVISION UNIT PLUS PROBABLY ONE THIRD OF THE SUBMARINE FLEET.

Then, fulfilling his promise to reveal Japanese military strategy to his commander, Rochefort closed his dispatch:

EVALUATE ABOVE TO INDICATE STRONG FORCE COMPONENT MAY BE PREPARING TO OPERATE IN SOUTH EASTERN ASIA WHILE PARTS MAY OPERATE FROM PALAO AND MARSHALLS.

His reference to at least one carrier division unit lacks specificity. Kisner's operators at Station H had previously linked Carrier Divisions Three and Four with the Palao/Mandates region and said both divisions were under the command of the Third Fleet. Another omission can be detected in Rochefort's dispatch: the six carriers of the First Air Fleet, which were preparing to depart Hitokappu Bay for Hawaii. Earlier that morning, Kimmel had learned from the Communication Summary that Rochefort had intercepted extensive radio broadcasts between Admiral Nagumo and the submarine force.

At 2:40 P.M., the 224-word dispatch was marked PRIORITY, encoded in a highly secure Navy cipher system, and sent to Station US. It arrived in Washington at the office of the Chief of Naval Operations soon after 8:10 P.M. Eastern Standard Time. Laurance Safford, commander of Station US, was on duty. He initialed the dispatch and sent copies to the Navy high command, including Lieutenant Commander Arthur McCollum, Roosevelt's routing officer. At that moment in the White House the President and Princess Martha had finished their cocktails and started on the first course of their dinner.

Roosevelt's dinner with Princess Martha continued for nearly five hours. Courses were prepared in a third-floor kitchen, placed on trays, then brought to the Oval Study. FDR, according to historian William Seale, usually ate at his desk, and guests from a folding card table. Sometimes on her White House visits Princess Martha brought along a bottle of aquavit, the schnapps-like Norwegian national drink, according to Grace Tully, the President's secretary. The White House Usher Book indicates that the dinner ended at midnight and FDR retired at 12:15, but does not list the departure of the Princess.[23]

The Kimmel-Bloch-Rochefort alert of November 25 is the only intelligence report generated by Station HYPO that can be linked to President Roosevelt. It can be traced by documentation from Hawaii to McCollum's office in the Navy Department. It received priority attention from the duty officer, Lieutenant Commander Ethelbert Watts, one of McCollum's assistants. A presidential monograph was prepared, numbered 65, and addressed: "Aide to President—Show." Watts directed delivery to the White House through the President's naval aide, Captain Beardall. Officer couriers rushed additional copies to the communications intelligence distribution list which included Secretary of War Henry Stimson. The list was tightly controlled. Only a handful of officials were allowed access to the Japanese intercepts.[24]

In the two weeks prior to the attack, Roosevelt's access to Japanese naval intercepts is documented by a series of radio intelligence bulletins, called monographs, that were prepared by McCollum. According to his numbering system, McCollum had prepared seventy-four radio intelligence monographs as of December 3. Their delivery to the White House was assured when the route slip was checkmarked, "Aide to the President—Show." Five monographs were marked for FDR's attention between November 26 and December 3 and can be found in Navy files. But sixty-seven in the series are missing—a major concern to National Archives historians Richard A. von Doenhoff and Barry Zerby, who could not locate the documents. "We can confirm the monographs are missing from the Navy files but have no explanation for their removal," said von Doenhoff.[25]

The Rochefort-Kimmel-Bloch alert is the sole HYPO monograph that has been located; the other four available monographs were originated by CAST. It is of immense historical importance. Forty-five hours after it was slated for White House delivery, Roosevelt placed America's military on a war footing. Tracing the Navy's copy of the HYPO message to the White House during this time frame is difficult. It was scheduled to be delivered by Beardall, the naval aide, on the night of the 25th. Extraordinary secrecy surrounds his delivery of presidential monographs. Beardall's White House visits between November 26 and December 3 are not recorded in the Usher Books kept by Chief Usher Howell Crim. Roosevelt's early-morning schedule bypassed Crim; early visitors to the President's second-floor bedroom saw him off the record, still in his pajamas, propped up in bed. Most days Crim's visitor list didn't start recording until FDR entered the Oval Office.[26]

More information is available concerning the delivery of the Army's copy. Some time after 8:10 P.M., but before midnight, an Army courier delivered the monograph to Stimson's palatial Southern-colonial-style mansion, Woodley, which was situated on the high ground overlooking Rock Creek Park in northwest Washington. Acting swiftly, Stimson ordered an extra copy sent to the White House. Unknown to Stimson, the dinner in progress at the White House delayed the delivery of the Army's copy of the monograph to FDR.

The next morning, Stimson telephoned the President and reached him in his bedroom: "I talked to the President over the telephone and I asked him whether he had received the paper which I had sent him over last night about the Japanese having started a new expedition from Shanghai down toward Indochina. He fairly blew up—jumped up into the air, so to speak, and said he hadn't seen it and that changed the whole situation because it was an evidence of bad faith on the part of the Japanese that while they were negotiating for an entire truce—which would require an entire withdrawal [from China]—they should be sending this expedition down there to Indochina. I told him that it was a fact that had come to me through G-2 [Army intelligence] and the Navy Secret Service [sic] and I at once got another copy of the paper I had sent last night and sent it over to him by special messenger."[27]

Roosevelt's denial to Stimson concerning the monograph appears to be classic Washington distancing. His denial contradicts earlier orders he issued. On November 12, according to the congressional evidence, FDR directed that Beardall bring him every intercept.[28] Specific contents of the Japanese intercepts delivered to President Roosevelt by Navy couriers are hazy. Administration officials referred to the intercepts as Magic; it appears their reference was to diplomatic messages in the Purple code system. About November 1, 1941, Roosevelt objected to the summaries of communications intelligence being brought to him by his naval aide Captain John Beardall.[29] Instead he wanted to see the "raw intercepts," not condensed interpretations written by Army or Navy intelligence officers. On November 12, Beardall followed orders and began delivery of the "raw intercepts" to FDR. Each delivery contained at least three to fifteen pieces of data, according to Major General Ralph C. Smith, executive officer for the US Army's military intelligence division in 1941. The delivery procedure was elegant. The raw intercepts were placed in a leather pouch with gold lettering, especially constructed for the White House by Camalier and Buckley, one of Washington's swank stationery firms. A zipper and a small padlock on the pouch, designed by Navy officials, guaranteed security. Gold lettering on the pouch announced its destination, "For the PRESIDENT," and smaller lettering directed finders to "Return to Room 2711, Navy Department." The White House Usher Book meticulously detailed Beardall's visits with FDR between May 15 and November 11, but none thereafter. During the Pearl Harbor Joint Committee investigation, Beardall confirmed delivering the intercepts—which he termed Magic—to Roosevelt in the White House.

MR. RICHARDSON: And when that Magic was brought there it was for the purpose of giving it to the President?

BEARDALL: Yes, sir.

MR. RICHARDSON: What would be done with it in the ordinary routine way if it was brought for delivery to the President?

BEARDALL: It would be delivered to him.

MR. RICHARDSON: By whom?

BEARDALL: By me, normally.[30]

In his briefing of FDR, Stimson did not stress or even discuss the Japanese submarine advance on Hawaii reported by what he called the Navy's "secret service." As the civilian head of the Army, he understood the expeditionary nature of the Japanese troop movement toward Southeast Asia, but he apparently failed to fully grasp the dangers of the naval movement of warships toward Hawaii. FDR, an Assistant Secretary of the Navy in World War I, fully understood naval operational strategy and tactics, for he loved sailing, the Navy, and warships. Rochefort's assessment of a two-pronged attack aimed at America was not lost on Roosevelt. The might of the Japanese navy was on the move, heading for US territory in the Philippines, Wake Island, Guam, and Hawaii.

Even after Stimson's phone call, FDR evaded answering Admiral Kimmel. Thirty-two hours went by. The Pacific Fleet commander was left dangling as Roosevelt tended to political matters. In the North Pacific, the First Air Fleet continued its journey—nothing would stop the warships. Then at 3:45 P.M., Thursday, November 27, the President met with the Navy's Atlantic Fleet commander, Admiral Ernest J. King, in the Oval Office. After two hours with Roosevelt, King left the White House and returned to Navy headquarters. FDR went swimming in the White House pool with his daughter-in-law, Betsey Roosevelt.[31]

Forty-seven minutes after King left the White House, Kimmel finally got his answer. It came in a radiogram sent from Navy headquarters: the Pacific Fleet and America's entire military forces were placed on a war alert. The radiogram was Roosevelt's reply to Kimmel's alert of November 25. The war warning was authorized by the President and was transmitted immediately, according to Secretary Stimson, who dispatched the Army alerts in the absence of General Marshall. "Normally I didn't meddle with military staff matters. I did so on this occasion because I felt I was convey-ing a message from the President. Since General Marshall was away for the day on maneuvers, I wanted to make certain that the President's orders were carried out accurately," Stimson wrote in his diary.[32]

Fifteen Army and four Navy commands were on the distribution list. The group comprised the entire American military command structure. Secretary Stimson approved the wording of the Army warning, signed General George Marshall's name, and sent the message to four Army gen-erals—Short in Hawaii, MacArthur in Manila, Frank Andrews in Panama, and John DeWitt in San Francisco. Eleven additional Army posts in the continental United States received abbreviated alerts from Marshall's in-telligence chief, Sherman Miles.

The Assistant Chief of Naval Operations, Rear Admiral Royal Inger-soll, dispatched the war warning to America's naval commands on Novem-ber 27.[33] Ingersoll, substituting for Admiral Stark, who was ill with the flu, sent the war warning to four naval commands, including Admiral Kimmel. In effect, it was Roosevelt's answer to Kimmel's forecast of November 25, in which the admiral warned of dangerous Japanese hostilities. Ingersoll noted that the dispatch was "to be considered as a war warning." Copies went to Admiral Thomas Hart in Manila, to Admiral Ernest King of the Atlantic Fleet, and to Admiral Robert Ghormley, the American naval liaison ob-server in London. It begins and ends with padding designed to foil Japanese code-breakers. (See Appendix C for copies of the original war warnings.)

HELLS MM THIS DISPATCH IS TO BE CONSIDERED A WAR WARNING X NEGO-TIATIONS WITH JAPAN LOOKING TOWARD STABILIZATION OF CONDITIONS IN THE PACIFIC HAVE CEASED AND AN AGGRESSIVE MOVE BY JAPAN IS EX-PECTED WITHIN THE NEXT FEW DAYS X THE NUMBER AND EQUIPMENT OF JAPANESE TROOPS AND THE ORGANIZATIONS OF NAVAL TASK FORCES INDI-CATES AN AMPHIBIOUS EXPEDITION AGAINST EITHER THE PHILIPPINES OR KRA PENINSULA OR POSSIBLY BORNEO X EXECUTE AN APPROPRIATE DE-FENSIVE DEPLOYMENT PREPARATORY TO CARRYING OUT TASK ASSIGNED IN WPL46 X INFORM DISTRICT AND ARMY AUTHORITIES X A SIMILAR WARNING IS BEING SENT BY WAR DEPARTMENT X SPENAVO INFORM BRITISH X CONTI-NENTAL DISTRICTS GUAM SAMOA DIRECTED TAKE APPROPRIATE MEASURES AGAINST SABOTAGE X MM LOOSE

But Ingersoll made a major goof in his text: he failed to include the stand-aside sanction approved by the President, calling for Japan to "commit the first overt act." Stark, recovered from his illness, corrected the omission in a revised message he sent out the next day, November 28.[34] The revision was sent PRIORITY to Admiral Kimmel and the commanders of the Pacific Coast Naval Frontiers, a sea and coastal region that extended from Panama to the Territory of Alaska. Stark was direct:

> IF HOSTILITIES CANNOT REPEAT CANNOT BE AVOIDED THE UNITED STATES DESIRES THAT JAPAN COMMIT THE FIRST OVERT ACT.

Admiral Stark's revised message, with its padding, was received at Pearl Harbor after 2:40 P.M. November 28:

> HOT ZZ REFER TO MY 272338 X ARMY HAS SENT FOLLOWING TO COMMANDER WESTERN DEFENSE COMMAND QUOTE NEGOTIATIONS WITH JAPAN APPEAR TO BE TERMINATED TO ALL PRACTICAL PURPOSES WITH ONLY THE BAREST POSSIBILITIES THAT THE JAPANESE GOVERNMENT MIGHT COME BACK AND OFFER TO CONTINUE X JAPANESE FUTURE ACTION UNPREDICTABLE BUT HOSTILE ACTION POSSIBLE AT ANY MOMENT X IF HOSTILITIES CANNOT REPEAT NOT BE AVOIDED THE UNITED STATES DESIRES THAT JAPAN COMMIT THE FIRST OVERT ACT X THIS POLICY SHOULD NOT REPEAT NOT BE CONSTRUED AS RESTRICTING YOU TO A COURSE OF ACTION THAT MIGHT JEOPARDIZE YOUR DEFENSE X PRIOR TO HOSTILE JAPANESE ACTION YOU ARE DIRECTED TO UNDERTAKE SUCH RECONNAISSANCE AND OTHER MEASURES AS YOU DEEM NECESSARY BUT THESE MEASURES SHOULD BE CARRIED OUT SO AS NOT REPEAT NOT TO ALARM CIVIL POPULATION OR DISCLOSE INTENT X REPORT MEASURES TAKEN X A SEPARATE MESSAGE IS BEING SENT TO NINTH CORPS AREA RE SUBVERSIVE ACTIVITIES IN UNITED STATES X SHOULD HOSTILITIES OCCUR YOU WILL CARRY OUT THE TASKS ASSIGNED IN RAINBOW FIVE SO FAR AS THEY PERTAIN TO JAPAN X LIMIT DISSEMINATION OF THIS HIGHLY SECRET INFORMATION TO MINIMUM ESSENTIAL OFFICERS UNQUOTE XX WPL52 IS NOT APPLICABLE TO PACIFIC AREA AND WILL NOT BE PLACED IN EFFECT IN THAT AREA EXCEPT AS NOW IN FORCE IN SOUTHEAST PACIFIC SUB AREA AND PANAMA NAVAL COASTAL FRONTIER X UNDERTAKE NO OFFENSIVE ACTION UNTIL JAPAN HAS COMMITTED AN OVERT ACT X BE PREPARED TO CARRY OUT TASKS ASSIGNED IN WPL46 SO FAR AS THEY APPLY TO JAPAN IN CASE HOSTILITIES OCCUR ZZ BABY

The Army message and the two sent by the Navy contained eight major directives that Stimson said originated with FDR: (1) A war warning; (2) Negotiations with Japan have ceased; (3) An aggressive move by Japan in any direction is expected in a few days; (4) Invasion of the Philippines, the Kra Peninsula, or Borneo expected; (5) Execute an appropriate defensive deployment; (6) United States policy calls for Japan to commit the first overt act [stressed twice]; (7) Before Japan strikes undertake necessary reconnaissance; and (8) Do not alarm the civilian population or disclose intent.

The Ingersoll and Stark messages handcuffed the Pacific Fleet. It is hard to see how Kimmel could disobey Stark's message, already stressed by the President and repeated again in Stark's next-to-last sentence. But because he followed these orders Kimmel would later take the blame for Pearl Harbor.

Nine American military commanders are on record as receiving the warning of pending hostile action by Japan. Seven of them immediately placed their units on a wartime footing. Hawaii—including Pearl Harbor—was the only exception. Neither Admiral Kimmel nor General Short took the war warnings seriously—or at least that was the conclusion reached by the Pearl Harbor investigations conducted between 1941 and 1946.

In the Philippines, the politically savvy American military chiefs, General Douglas MacArthur and Admiral Thomas Hart, read the meaning intended by Washington in the war warnings correctly. MacArthur wired: "Everything is in readiness for the conduct of a successful defense." When the Japanese bombers arrived over Luzon, MacArthur's pursuit fighters of the Far East Air Force, alerted by radar, rose to meet them but could not find the enemy, according to evidence given to the Joint Investigating Committee. Clark Field in central Luzon and Iba Field at the north were destroyed in the ensuing attack. Hart sent US Asiatic Fleet units south to link up with Dutch warships. Though Hart had nearly two dozen submarines that could have attacked Japanese invasions forces swooping down on the Philippines, he kept the subs in port. None interfered with Japan's move toward war.[35]

Later, once the attack succeeded and Japanese troops overran the

Philippines, Roosevelt approved orders detaching both commanders from the Philippines. A Navy PT boat evacuated MacArthur, his family, and selected staff members from Corregidor and took them to the southern Philippines, where they boarded aircraft for Australia. Before his escape, MacArthur transferred the Philippine Army command to General Jonathan Wainwright, who later surrendered and was taken prisoner by Japan.

Admiral Hart withdrew to Australia. He had sent about ten of his warships south after receiving approval from Washington on November 25. Eight of those ships were destroyed by Japanese forces in the opening weeks of war. Thomas Hart returned to the United States and the backwaters of the Navy and never again received a combat command. In 1945, he was appointed US Senator from Connecticut to fill the term of Francis T. Maloney, who died in office. Hart served for two years but did not seek reelection in 1947.

On America's West Coast, General Frank Andrews of the Panama Command and General John DeWitt of the Western Defense Command placed their troops on an instant war footing. DeWitt was specific in his message to Washington: "This command now ready to carry out tasks assigned." He relayed copies of the Stimson/Marshall order to the Naval Districts in California and Oregon. In Panama, General Andrews assured Marshall that all was in readiness to defend the Panama Canal. Every troop unit was on a continuous watch and Navy vessels patrolled the Pacific sea lanes leading to the canal. He emphasized that Army radar operations were working around the clock on a mission to detect hostile aircraft.[36]

A different military situation prevailed in Hawaii. Though ordering Short to conduct reconnaissance and not to jeopardize his defensive measures, the Stimson/Marshall message had specifically told Short: "Do not alarm the civil population or disclose intent." When he read these orders, Short was baffled. How was he to conduct reconnaissance or place his 25,000 troops on a war footing without alarming a civilian population intimately connected to life at the massive US base? There was no way to hide the troop movement or fighters and bombers engaged in a massive air search. Hillside home sites above Honolulu looked down on all the Army posts as well as on Pearl Harbor. General Short complained, "I couldn't possibly order my troops on an all-out alert without telling them who to shoot at."[37]

Short was also well aware of the intense scrutiny of Hawaii's news media. The two daily papers, the *Advertiser* and the *Star-Bulletin,* covered military activities with determination. Putting Oahu's troops on full alert would have been front-page news. Both newspapers owned broadcast stations in Honolulu, affiliated respectively with the NBC and CBS radio news networks. Short saw only one military option: he placed his troops on a low-alert status, a sabotage/espionage watch that did little to actually raise the level of military readiness. Soldiers continued their daily routines. Guns and ammunition were stowed away in padlocked cabinets. He did order a secret predawn surveillance by the radar operations of the Army's Aircraft Warning Service. Hawaii's excellent Army radar facilities could detect aircraft at 130 miles' distance and provide at least a forty-minute warning to the approach of hostile aircraft.

In midafternoon on November 27, Short wired General Marshall:

DEPARTMENT ALERTED TO PREVENT SABOTAGE. LIAISON WITH NAVY.

The word "liaison" should have meant that Short had exchanged combat information with Admiral Kimmel. But there was no liaison. The Navy officers assigned to Short's radar unit never reported for duty. His eight-word message was the least responsive of all those of the sixteen Army commanders who acknowledged Marshall's alert. But those eight words were just what Marshall wanted to hear from Hawaii. Short and his soldiers were in no position to prevent a Japanese attack. Just to be sure that Short didn't adopt a more aggressive response, Marshall's adjutant general, Emory S. Adams, sent another message the next day. It pushed Short toward an anti-sabotage mode and away from the placement of the troops on a full alert which the available intelligence had shown so clearly was needed:[38]

CRITICAL SITUATION DEMANDS THAT ALL PRECAUTIONS BE TAKEN IMMEDI-
ATELY AGAINST SUBVERSIVE ACTIVITIES WITHIN FIELD OF INVESTIGATIVE
RESPONSIBILITY OF WAR DEPARTMENT PAREN SEE PARAGRAPH THREE MID
SC THIRTY DASH FORTY FIVE END PAREN STOP ALSO DESIRED THAT YOU
INITIATE FORTHWITH ALL ADDITIONAL MEASURES NECESSARY TO PROVIDE
FOR PROTECTION OF YOUR ESTABLISHMENTS COMMA PROPERTY COMMA

AND EQUIPMENT AGAINST SABOTAGE COMMA PROTECTION OF YOUR PERSONNEL AGAINST SUBVERSIVE PROPAGANDA AND PROTECTION OF ALL ACTIVITIES AGAINST ESPIONAGE STOP THIS DOES NOT REPEAT NOT MEAN THAT ANY ILLEGAL MEASURES ARE AUTHORIZED STOP PROTECTIVE MEASURES SHOULD BE CONFINED TO THOSE ESSENTIAL TO SECURITY COMMA AVOIDING UNNECESSARY PUBLICITY AND ALARM STOP TO INSURE SPEED OF TRANSMISSION IDENTICAL TELEGRAMS ARE BEING SENT TO ALL AIR STATIONS BUT THIS DOES NOT REPEAT NOT AFFECT YOUR RESPONSIBILITY UNDER EXISTING INSTRUCTIONS X ADAMS.

General Short placed full trust in his "old friend of forty years," General Marshall. Admiral Kimmel did the same. Kimmel had been friends with his boss, Admiral Harold Stark, since their Naval Academy days. But after the successful Japanese raid on December 7, Marshall would go on to be lauded for his direction of World War II in his role as chairman of the Joint Chiefs of Staff. Kimmel and Short would be fired.

CHAPTER 11

WAR MAY COME QUICKER
THAN ANYONE
DREAMS

———

ON FRIDAY AFTERNOON, NOVEMBER 28TH, WITH THE STRENGTH OF the Japanese carrier and submarine fleet headed for Pearl Harbor, President Roosevelt decided to leave the nation's capital and head for Georgia. To keep the President up-to-date on the crisis, a new communication official was added to the White House staff who would play an important role in delivering communications intelligence to the President during the last week of peace. He was Navy Lieutenant Lester R. Schulz,[1] who—because of the suddenness of the trip—wasn't fully prepared for the journey. Schulz had just one hour to pack his suitcase and jump aboard US Number One, the special presidential railroad train. Even worse, he had no train ticket. Just days before, Schulz had completed a training course in Navy radio communication methods given by instructors at Station US. Upon finishing the course, he was assigned as assistant naval aide to the President of the United States, to be used as a communications courier. His job: custodian of the presidential leather

177

pouch that contained the secret Japanese radio intercepts and the intelligence monographs.

The presidential party was en route to Warm Springs, Georgia, for a delayed Thanksgiving holiday celebration with patients of the Polio Institute.[2] Before leaving, FDR held a fifty-minute White House meeting with William Donovan and Secretary of War Henry Stimson in the upstairs Oval Study. After Donovan departed, the President and Stimson moved to the Oval Office, where they were joined by the "War Cabinet" (Stimson's term) of Cordell Hull, Frank Knox, General Marshall, and Admiral Stark in a noon conference.[3]

Stimson's morning meeting in FDR's bedroom centered on strategies involving Japan. According to Stimson, "He branched into an analysis of the situation himself as he sat there on his bed saying there were three alternatives and only three that he could see before us. His alternatives were—first, to do nothing; second, to make something in the nature of an ultimatum again, stating a point beyond which we would fight; third, to fight at once. I told him my only two were the last two, because I did not think anyone would do nothing in this situation, and he agreed with me."[4]

Stimson's account of the Oval Study discussion was disingenuous. Alternative number one *was* the policy. The military orders placing the policy in effect had been sent to America's admirals and generals the previous afternoon: do nothing militarily that could be regarded as a posture of offense; let Japan commit the first overt act. The morality issue of placing US servicemen and civilians in harm's way was discussed three days earlier at a noon meeting in the White House. It was a troublesome issue for the policy-makers, who included FDR, Stimson, Secretary of the Navy Knox, Secretary of State Hull, General Marshall, and Admiral Stark. Stimson's diary entry discussed the morality issue, "One problem troubled us very much. If you know your enemy is going to strike you, it is not usually wise to wait until he gets the jump on you by taking the initiative. The question was how we should maneuver them into the position of firing the first shot without allowing too much danger to ourselves. It was a difficult proposition," Stimson wrote.[5]

The catalyst behind the White House discussion was overcoming America's opposition to war. Opinion polls—watched by the cabinet members—said that Americans, while favoring military aid to Great Britain, were opposed to sending troops overseas to participate in another world war. Pros and cons of the policy were recorded by Stimson in his diary. "In spite of the risk involved, however, in letting the Japanese fire the first shot, we realized that in order to have the full support of the American people, it was desirable to make sure that the Japanese be the ones to do this, so that there should remain no doubt in anyone's mind as to who were the aggressors." A policy of doing nothing to oppose Japan militarily—it can be argued—had been firmly adopted.

The adoption came at noon on Tuesday, November 25, in Washington; across the international date line the time at Hitokappu Bay was 1:00 A.M. on Wednesday, November 26. Buglers were about to sound reveille for the crews of the thirty-one warships and awaken them for their journey to Hawaii, which was set to start at 6:00 A.M.

As the week drew to a close, more subtle diplomatic alternatives surfaced in Washington that appear to be cover stories designed—once Pearl Harbor was history—to take the focus off the stand-aside policy. During the November 28 White House meeting, the War Cabinet agreed with another presidential suggestion—that a special telegram[6] be dispatched to Emperor Hirohito warning that "disastrous events would be set afoot" if a severe blow was aimed at the Allied powers of Britain, Holland, and America by Japan. Roosevelt addressed the message to the Emperor but delayed its transmission for over a week, until the night of December 6. In the 816-word cablegram, FDR said he was concerned about situations of extraordinary importance to both countries.

THE PEOPLE OF THE UNITED STATES, BELIEVING IN PEACE AND IN THE RIGHT OF NATIONS TO LIVE AND LET LIVE, HAVE EAGERLY WATCHED THE CONVERSATIONS BETWEEN OUR TWO GOVERNMENTS DURING THESE PAST MONTHS. WE HAVE HOPED FOR A TERMINATION OF THE PRESENT CONFLICT BETWEEN JAPAN AND CHINA. WE HAVE HOPED THAT A PEACE OF THE PACIFIC COULD BE CONSUMMATED IN SUCH A WAY THAT NATIONALITIES OF MANY DIVERSE PEOPLES COULD EXIST SIDE BY SIDE WITHOUT FEAR OF INVASION; THAT UNBEARABLE BURDENS OF ARMAMENTS COULD BE LIFTED FOR THEM ALL; AND THAT ALL PEOPLES WOULD RESUME COMMERCE WITHOUT DISCRIMINATION AGAINST OR IN FAVOR OF ANY NATION.

Roosevelt closed the message by asking the Emperor to

GIVE THOUGHT IN THIS DEFINITE EMERGENCY TO A WAY OF DISPELLING
THE DARK CLOUDS.

Roosevelt held up this message and didn't dispatch it to Tokyo until 8:00 P.M. on December 6 (EST). It was sent to Hirohito by way of Ambassador Joseph Grew. At 12:15 A.M, on December 8, Tokyo Time, Grew met with Foreign Minister Shigenori Togo and requested an audience with the Emperor. Togo replied, saying he would present the matter to the Throne, but made no definite commitment. Grew returned to the embassy. An audience was never granted. Launch time of the First Air Fleet was about three hours away.[7]

After Friday's War Cabinet concluded, the President headed for Union Station and went aboard his special railroad car, the *Ferdinand Magellan*, for the Georgia trip. If FDR was anxious about the worsening crisis, he covered it well. On Saturday afternoon, November 29, he drove his Ford roadster (equipped with hand controls, since his legs were paralyzed by polio) through Warm Springs and the beautiful grounds of the Institute greeting patients and well-wishers. The car's radio was tuned to the Army-Navy football game. He stopped at the cottage of his former secretary, Marguerite "Missy" Le Hand, who was recuperating from a stroke and neuritis suffered in 1940 while she was living in her third-floor White House suite.

Later that evening, Roosevelt was relaxed as he carved the roasted tom turkey. He sliced chunks of white meat for his guests in Georgia Hall, the spa's grand dining room. The chefs had prepared a twenty-four-course meal including a choice of seven desserts. After dinner, the patients entertained the presidential party with a skit in which the leading character in a dream sequence heard the voice of the President appoint himself Dictator of Warm Springs. FDR picked up the skit's theme when he addressed the gathering. He commented that much of the world was owned and controlled by real live dictators, and ended his remarks with this prophesy: "United States soldiers, sailors, and marines might be fighting in defense of this country's institutions by next Thanksgiving."[8]

Upon returning to the Little White House, FDR held a long conversation on the phone with Secretary of State Cordell Hull. Both agreed that the President should return to Washington immediately because of press accounts reporting bellicose statements by Japan's Premier, General Hideki Tojo. They set an arrival deadline of "before noon on Monday" (December 1), according to Press Secretary Steve Early.[9]

The President's personal car, the *Ferdinand Magellan*, and the rest of the railroad train were recalled from Atlanta to be ready for the President's return.[10] A. C. Spencer, the Southern Railroad official in charge of the train, passed orders to control towers. Along the nearly 700 miles of track between Newnan, Georgia, and the nation's capital, Southern tower operators hoisted a dark gray ball—a railroad signal that ordered the tracks cleared. As the President's train sped on its way, troop and military supply trains were shunted to sidings to permit its swift passage to Washington.[11]

Upon his return to the White House on December 1, Roosevelt met for over an hour with Secretary of the Navy Knox, Secretary of State Hull, and Admiral Stark, who was the only military officer present. At least four diplomatic messages between Japan and Germany awaited the President. In the last week of peace, Japan's Foreign Minister, Shigenori Togo, her ambassador to Germany, Baron Hiroshi Oshima, and Ambassador Kichisaburo Nomura in Washington were as talkative on their dot-dash transmissions as Admiral Nagumo.[12] Through these four intercepts, Roosevelt learned that Japanese military action was near. All four intercepts were obtained by one of the Pacific listening posts, Station SAIL at Seattle, which eavesdropped on the Foreign Ministry radio circuits transmitting the Purple diplomatic code, Japan's high-security cryptic system for overseas diplomatic missions. A November 28 Station SAIL intercept read:

IN A FEW DAYS US-JAPAN NEGOTIATIONS WILL BE DE FACTO RUPTURED. DO NOT GIVE THE IMPRESSION THAT NEGOTIATIONS ARE BROKEN OFF.

Two of Togo's other dispatches followed; they contained instructions to Ambassador Oshima in Berlin that added clarification to the foreign minister's intentions. They were directed at Adolf Hitler and Germany's Foreign Minister Joachim von Ribbentrop. One of the dispatches read:

SAY VERY SECRETLY TO THEM THERE IS EXTREME DANGER THAT WAR MAY SUDDENLY BREAK OUT BETWEEN THE ANGLO SAXON NATIONS AND JAPAN THROUGH SOME CLASH OF ARMS. THIS MAY COME QUICKER THAN ANYONE DREAMS.

Roosevelt asked for a copy of the "extreme danger" dispatch for his personal files.[13]

Although none of the Purple dispatches cited above mentioned Pearl Harbor as a target, a fifth intercept received midweek should have eliminated all doubt. It disclosed that Tokyo planned "last-minute" instructions for Washington and Honolulu. On December 3, Japanese diplomatic missions located in the United States, Great Britain, and the Netherlands East Indies received orders to destroy all their code systems. Japan's embassy in Washington and its Honolulu consulate were exempted; they were directed to retain certain code systems for eleventh-hour orders. If nothing else, these diplomatic intercepts and the massive submarine advance on Hawaii revealed by the naval intercepts signaled war in a matter of days.

In Washington, military officials recognized that Japan's code-destruction order meant war. Rear Admiral Richmond Turner, the Navy's war-plans officer, said, "Destruction of codes is a definite and sure indication of war."[14] To Rochefort in Pearl Harbor, the code destruction "looked damn bad" and he personally warned Admiral Bloch, the Commandant of the Fourteenth Naval District, "We ought to take whatever steps we can."[15]

Admiral Kimmel received similar information from his assistant Edwin Layton, but failed to interpret the code-destruction order as meaning immediate war with the United States. Kimmel seems to have been influenced by his two war-plans officers, Captain Charles McMorris and Commander Vincent Murphy. Between December 1 and 6, both told Kimmel that a Japanese raid on Hawaii was unlikely.[16]

On December 3, as the crisis worsened, the Navy Department ordered Station SAIL to concentrate on the Tokyo–Washington radio circuits of RCA and Mackay and to forward the dispatches on a high-speed teleprinter circuit to the Navy Department. Almost all of the messages intercepted by SAIL were in the Purple diplomatic system. When they reached Washington, Army and Navy code-breakers decoded and translated the intercepts the same day, usually within a few hours. By December 4, a paper trail of Japanese intercepts had found its way to the White House. Japan's diplomatic messages, Japanese navy communications, and RDF bearings locating Japanese warships heading toward American territory in the Western, North, and Central Pacific were all in the pipeline and available to Roosevelt.[17]

Remarkable intelligence work by the cryptanalysts at Station CAST discovered most but not all of Japan's Hawaii force. Though Japan's navy reassigned radio call signs for her 200 warships and commanders at midnight of November 30, the CAST cryptographers detected the ruse. By switching radio identities Japan hoped to confuse American intelligence agencies and derail efforts in tracking the warships toward Hawaii. It didn't work. By constant monitoring of the naval broadcasts on December 1 to 5, CAST obtained the revised radio code names for all the vessels, including the carriers. The cryptographers also identified new radio call signs for Admiral Nagumo and Admiral Yamamoto, the commander-in-chief of the Japanese fleet. (See TESTM dispatch of Dec. 5, 1941, in Appendix D.)

CAST had developed the list of new call signs and quickly sent copies to HYPO at Pearl Harbor. But instead of reporting the crucial evidence of Japanese carrier radio transmissions to Admiral Kimmel, Rochefort ignored the CAST reports. In his Daily Communication Summaries of December 1 to 5,[18] he wrote that there was no information on the carriers of the First Air Fleet: "Not one carrier has been identified." His next summary, based on intercepts of December 5 and delivered to Kimmel on Saturday morning, December 6, modified the statement. In six words, Rochefort informed Kimmel that Admiral Yamamoto had "originated several [radio] messages to the Carriers."[19] There were more than "several." Station H operator logs list ten messages to fleet units that were dispatched by Yamamoto on December 5. Seven of those broadcasts were directed to the Hawaii force and were intercepted by radio operators Maynard Albertson, Henry F. Garstka, and Joseph C. Howard. In his log entry, Garstka said he copied one broadcast on the long-distance frequency of 16,620 kilocycles. All three operators obtained Yamamoto's call signs, which had been identified by CAST earlier in the week. Obviously Rochefort had received the information, was able to recognize the admiral's new call signs, and informed Kimmel.

By 1:00 P.M. on December 5, Homer Kisner at Station H had delivered Yamamoto's ten messages to Rochefort's office at Pearl Harbor. The full details of these crucial intercepts remain hidden by Navy censors. None were released by President Carter in his declassification order of 1979. John Taylor, the archivist in charge of Japanese naval intercepts, confirmed to the author in 1996 that they were not found in the Archives II files.

Rochefort should have identified the carriers by name, and fully discussed the seven intercepts with Admiral Kimmel on Saturday morning, December 6, but he did not. America's top naval code-breaker failed to follow the creed: "Tell your commander today of Japan's plan for tomorrow." Instead Rochefort ignored the report from CAST and gave no communication details of the messages intercepted from Japan's naval chief. Such details are crucial in communications intelligence—and especially in this case, for they indicated a progressive movement away from Japan in an eastward direction. The move from 12,330 kilocycles to the 16,000-kilocycle spectrum detected by Henry Garstka represented a big jump in distance. Kisner's chronology set the stage for recognizing the jump the previous day, December 5, when he reported that Radio Tokyo was heard broadcasting simultaneously on dual frequencies[20] to ships at a great distance from Japan. He told Rochefort the frequencies used by Tokyo were 32 kilocycles and 12,330 kilocycles.

Kisner later explained the significance of the dual broadcasts during interviews with the author in 1988 and 1998. "Tokyo and Radio Ominato in north Japan wanted to reach the First Air Fleet's vessels and its escorting submarines in the North Pacific. So they chose two frequencies: the daytime long-distance frequency of 12,330 kilocycles, which bounces off the ionosphere, and the ground-wave frequency of 32 kilocycles, which travels over the surface of the earth and is ideal for reaching submerged (or half-submerged) submarines. The dual-frequency transmission was a well known communication technique in 1941 and necessary to communicate with a full fleet across a great distance." He pointed out that Garstka's discovery of a higher frequency of 16,620 kilocycles indicated a further progression of the warships from Tokyo. The powerful antenna systems and radio receivers of the battleships and carriers of Japan's First Air Fleet picked up the sky wave from the ionosphere, whereas the ground wave was perfect for the subs, which lacked the powerful radio facilities.[21]

Kimmel was entitled to know if Yamamoto was using the great-distance frequency to reach "the Carriers," which at the time were about 900 miles north of Oahu. There is no record that Kimmel and Layton discussed Yamamoto's radio contact with the flattops during their morning meeting on December 6. None of the original Station CAST reports that identified Japan's Hawaii force, nor Kisner's "great distance" intercepts,

were ever introduced or discussed by any of the Pearl Harbor investigations, including the 1995 inquiry headed by Senator Thurmond.

Since the CAST reports directly contradict both American and Japanese claims that the Hawaii raiding force was on radio silence and never
originated or received radio messages, the author sought verification of the
reports from Navy Captain Duane Whitlock,[22] who was one of the radio
traffic analysts at CAST in the fall of 1941. When shown the reports by the
author during a 1993 interview, Whitlock confirmed their authenticity.
"Our radio direction finder was located on Corregidor Island and operated
day and night on Japanese warships and military units. Not only did we
furnish copies to Admiral Hart and General MacArthur, copies were sent
by radio dispatch to HYPO," he told the author. In 1941, Whitlock believed
that the copies sent to HYPO would be shown to Admiral Kimmel. "All of
our COMINT was available to Admiral Hart. I assumed our copies were
shown to Kimmel; that was Navy policy." Whitlock explained that the reports were first encoded in a Navy code system called TESTM before being
dispatched to Hawaii.[23] The TESTM system was used exclusively for radio
direction finder (RDF) data and could only be decoded at CAST, HYPO, or
Station US in Washington. "No one else in the Navy could decipher
TESTM or any of the other radio intelligence circuits we controlled. We
didn't want our cryptographic success to leak out," Whitlock said. He had
been posted to CAST as radioman first class for over a year and had extensive prior intercept experience at Navy radio stations in China. Six feet tall,
slim, and with excellent language skills, Whitlock commanded attention.
He had graduated from the Navy's intercept school at Station US in 1938.
He knew and respected Kisner. Both had worked together at CAST until
June 1941, when Rochefort picked Kisner to supervise the intercept operation at Station H in Hawaii.[24]

During the eighteen days between November 16 and December 4, Station CAST identified and located the Japanese carriers *Akagi*, *Zuikaku*, and
Hiryu, the battleship *Kirishima*,[25] and Cruiser Division Eight, according to
Whitlock. On December 4, CAST succeeded in identifying Japan's top-
secret radio call signs for both Nagumo and Yamamoto. Their ID came directly off the naval airwaves and indicates a wide disregard for radio
silence by the Japanese navy. "We sent this information direct to Kimmel
and Washington by radio dispatch and copies were sent to General

MacArthur at his headquarters in Manila," Whitlock told the author.[26] According to the TESTM files, after December 4 neither Nagumo nor his warships were heard, though CAST continued to intercept messages involving the forces surrounding the Philippines and heading for areas of Southeast Asia.[27]

"Our facilities intercepted both Japanese diplomatic and naval broadcasts. We had the Purple machine and the means to intercept, decode, and translate its messages. Radio receivers were tuned to every major Japanese diplomatic circuit," he continued. Their coverage included the entire diplomatic network serving China, the Pacific, and points in Europe and South America. "Since we were so near to Japan and its naval operation area we were in an excellent position to intercept radio broadcasts."

Station CAST's cryptographers, intercept operators, and linguists worked in Tunnel Affirm, dug and blasted from the rock of Corregidor, a rock island at the entrance to Manila Bay about thirty miles west of Manila.[28] The intercept facilities were forty feet underground, part of a military compound the Navy shared with Army troops stationed at Fort Mills. Intercept antennae and the radio direction finder were topside. Radio wire leads carrying the Japanese *katakana* message sounds were fed to receiving sets in the 20-foot-wide tunnel. Four radio traffic analysts analyzed intercepts obtained by 63 operators organized in eight-hour shifts, copying Japanese diplomatic and naval broadcasts 24 hours a day. Unlike the Navy's Hawaii intercept operation, which was divided between Pearl Harbor and the windward side of Oahu, on Corregidor the CAST enlisted personnel and eleven officers all worked from the same quarters, producing the TESTM dispatches that should have then been sent to the Admiral.[29]

None of the nine Pearl Harbor investigations examined the TESTM dispatches or questioned why their crucial data were cut from Kimmel's intelligence loop. Since he was never told, the admiral could not raise the question in his own defense. It was impossible for him to surface the TESTM records; they were locked in Navy vaults until December 1986, when a FOIA released them to the author. In April 1995, Congress reopened the Pearl Harbor probe at the request of Kimmel's family, and directed that the Department of Defense conduct an investigation. But the TESTM documents were not produced by the DOD, even though they had been released by the FOIA. Captain Duane Whitlock—one of America's most honored and heroic code-breakers—was available to explain and identify the dispatches in both 1945 and 1995. He was never asked to testify.

Kimmel's isolation from the intelligence loop can be traced to numerous directives issued from Washington. Explanations for the cut-off varied: His need to know did not apply to diplomatic negotiations since he was a military commander; providing him information from the intercepts would have risked revealing American code-breaking success. The crash of Hawaii's intelligence loop distribution started on November 24 shortly after the Pacific Fleet was pulled from the Vacant Sea. Commander Arthur McCollum contributed to the crash when he issued a new directive, which called a halt to the distribution of Rochefort's Communication Summaries (COMSUMs) and those of other monitoring stations that compiled Japanese naval movements. With the approval of the Director of Naval Intelligence, Captain Theodore S. Wilkinson, McCollum sent this directive to Kimmel [COM 16 was the cover name for CAST; OPNAV for Station US]:

ORANGE NAVAL MOVEMENTS AS REPORTED FROM INDIVIDUAL INFORMATION ADDRESSES ARE OFTEN CONFLICTING BECAUSE OF NECESSARILY FRAGMENTARY NATURE X SINCE COM 16 INTERCEPTS ARE CONSIDERED MOST RELIABLE SUGGEST OTHER REPORTS CAREFULLY EVALUATED BE SENT TO COM 16 FOR ACTION OPNAV FOR INFORMATION X AFTER COMBINING ALL INCOMING REPORTS COM 16 DIRECT DISPATCHES TO OPNAV INFO CINCPAC BASED ON ALL INFORMATION RECEIVED INDICATING OWN EVALUATION AND PROVIDING BEST POSSIBLE CONTINUITY X REQUEST CINCAF ISSUE DIRECTIVE AS NECESSARY TO FULFILL GENERAL OBJECTIVE X[30]

McCollum's reasoning behind the order is highly suspect and can be seen as a means to distance Roosevelt from Rochefort's warnings. Kimmel's personal alert to the White House on November 25—during FDR's dinner with Princess Martha—was the last Hawaii-originated monograph prepared for FDR.

Hawaii's radio traffic chief Homer Kisner bristled fifty years later when the author told him of McCollum's "most reliable" pronouncement. Kisner dismissed the assertion. "Our reports were not fragmentary. We had very little reception difficulties in Hawaii," he said. "We intercepted at least a thousand Japanese naval messages every twenty-four hours. That's a minimum of about forty-two per hour. Yes, at times there were reception difficulties, but never significant, because Japan's radio facilities constantly repeated messages and we obtained missing broadcasts from the repeats."[31]

After November 26, the reports detailing the Japanese military advance on Hawaii were excised from the Presidential monographs. Decrypts about the movement of two-thirds of the Japanese fleet's submarines toward Hawaii, and the location of the *Akagi* and oil tankers in the Vacant Sea directly north of Oahu, were kept from the usual distribution by McCollum's order. So were the TESTM reports from the "most reliable" CAST. FDR's monographs were stripped of all the information that mattered.

When he returned from Warm Springs on December 1, President Roosevelt received the first "cleansed" monographs. They were monographs 70 and 71 and were based on Japanese naval intercepts and movement reports obtained and analyzed by CAST personnel. Roosevelt's final monograph, prior to the attack, was routed to him on December 3. No mention was made of locating in a communication zone at Hitokappu Bay the First Air Fleet and the carriers—the force that would soon arrive off Oahu.[32]

But the American intelligence network was a complex and multifaceted one. If one channel was blocked, vital information could still flow through many others. The Japanese were coming and Roosevelt knew.

CHAPTER 12

THE JAPS ARE BLASTING AWAY ON THE FREQUENCIES

TWELFTH NAVAL DISTRICT

INTELLIGENCE OFFICE

717 MARKET STREET

SAN FRANCISCO

NOVEMBER 28–DECEMBER 4, 1941

As the thanksgiving weekend ended and the month of Novem-ber drew to a close, FDR was obtaining the intelligence data that he needed to best serve his interests. Recent research has shown that the most conclusive evidence of the upcoming Japanese attack did reach the White House but has been withheld from public discussion.

In his book *Infamy*, published in 1982, John Toland wrote that San Francisco's Twelfth Naval District obtained radio direction finder bearings that placed Japanese warships in the Pacific Ocean north of Hawaii from about November 30 to December 4, 1941.[1] Toland's source was Robert Ogg, who in 1941 was on the staff of the naval district intelligence office (DIO) as a special investigator. Ogg remembered that during a five-day period from about November 30 to December 4, his boss, Lieutenant Ellsworth Hosmer, obtained radio direction finder bearings on Japanese warships. Hosmer asked Ogg to enter the bearings on a great-circle chart of the North Pacific Ocean that was kept in the intelligence office on Market Street in San Francisco. Once Ogg plotted them on the chart, the bearings disclosed Japanese warships in the North Pacific.[2] In his account to Toland and later to US Navy historian Commander Irwin Newman, Ogg said he remembered that the bearings came from commercial sources such as RCA Radio and Globe Wireless and from the Navy's radio direction finder station at Dutch Harbor, Alaska. Ogg stated that verification of his account could be found in Dutch Harbor records. Today, over fifty years later, those records have been found.

When Ogg plotted the locations of Japanese warships on the DIO's nautical chart, he noticed that they were moving eastward from the international date line toward the United States mainland. On about December 3 the eastward movement stopped. Then the warships turned south toward Hawaii. At that point, no more RDF bearings were obtained. Based on the distinctive communications procedures of the vessels reported to the DIO, Hosmer felt certain the RDF bearings came from Japanese warships and alerted Captain Richard McCullough, the District's intelligence chief. McCullough told Ogg that he forwarded the alert over a secure radio circuit to Washington, where the information reached the White House.

Robert Ogg has strong ties to America's military; generations of his family served in command positions in both the Army and the Navy.[3] Through these connections, Ogg found a close family friend in the commandant of the Twelfth Naval District, Vice Admiral John Greenslade. After Robert Ogg had completed his day's work, he often joined the admiral at his quarters on Yerba Buena island in San Francisco Bay. Over a cocktail the admiral called a "williwaw," the two left work behind and discussed personal matters.[4]

A portion of Greenslade's command included joint administration of the West Coast Communications Intelligence Network. The WCCI was anchored at its southern end by Station ITEM at Imperial Beach (San Diego), California, and extended 3000 miles north along the Pacific Coast to Station KING at Dutch Harbor. In between were RDF coastal facilities at Sitka, Alaska; Bainbridge Island, Washington; plus Point St. George, the

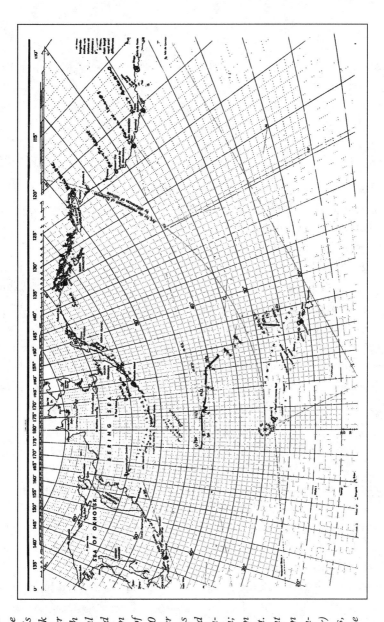

In 1987 Robert Ogg reconstructed the great-circle chart bearings he prepared for San Francisco's Twelfth Naval District (dark line). He used the dates November 30 to December 3, 1941. Though it was not part of his original 1941 information, he also traced a Navy RDF bearing, based on Station CAST, locating units of the First Air Fleet on a line of 030 degrees from Corregidor (upper left). The line shows the warships off the Kurile Islands. Ogg added locations of the Navy's RDF stations at Dutch Harbor; Sitka; Bainbridge, Washington (Station SAIL); and California's Point St. George, Farallon Islands, Point Arguello, and San Diego Station ITEM, on the chart. The December 6 positions (lower center) were part of his original bearings, and show the final route of the Japanese warships.

Source: Robert Ogg.

Farallon Islands, and Point Arguello in California. Greenslade held the keys to GUPID, a Navy code system that enabled him to copy and exchange communications intelligence with CAST, HYPO, and Station US. GUPID was similar to other highly secret systems such as TESTM and COPEK.

Additional sources for the WCCI included direct liaison with Canadian RDF operations and input from Pan American Airways Clippers, RCA Communications, Mackay Radio & Telegraph, American Telephone & Telegraph, and Globe Wireless. San Francisco was the hub of Pacific Rim commercial communications. All Tokyo diplomatic messages intended for Japanese missions in America passed through the RCA-Mackay-ATT communication funnel in San Francisco. Voice telephone service to and from Japan went through American Telephone & Telegraph offices near Market Street. All Japan–USA commercial wireless messages were routed over RCA and Mackay transmitters and receiving apparatus in the headlands north and south of the Golden Gate. Radio messages for Japanese merchant marine vessels originated in San Francisco at Globe Wireless.

Through this vast network, Greenslade's intelligence crew could listen in all along the Pacific Rim. They purchased Japanese navy code books from Japanese naval communication officers assigned to *Marus* calling at San Francisco, and placed "bugs" inside the Japanese Consulate. Thus Japan's government secrets sent through the Golden Gate, both military and diplomatic, were readily available to the highest officials in Washington, including Roosevelt in the White House.

Robert Ogg's expertise was in electronics and navigation; it was his superior, Ellsworth Hosmer, who assembled communications intelligence for the Twelfth Naval District from the San Francisco cable (telegraph) and telephone firms and the Navy's intercept stations. Then he and Commander Frank Venzel, the District's communications officer, coordinated the flow of Japanese intelligence data obtained from the Navy's West Coast network to Station US in Washington. Hosmer was known in Navy intelligence as the San Francisco contact man, and he had a direct link to Arthur McCollum at Station US.[5]

Over the November 28–30 weekend, US Navy intercept facilities were told to be on the lookout for the Japanese carrier force.[6] About Sunday November 30, according to Ogg, commercial radio firms supplied Hosmer with RDF bearings that placed Japanese warships in the North Pacific. The report of vessels in the North Pacific surprised Ogg and Hosmer, for both were aware of the Vacant Sea orders. Ogg said the RDF bearings that he plotted were obtained from the Japanese navy's four-megacycle radio band of 4000 kilocycles.[7]

Vice Admiral John Greenslade, who was both the District's commandant and the commander of the Western Sea Frontier, wore a third hat as naval convoy director for American controlled shipping proceeding west across the Pacific Ocean. Under provisions of the National Emergency Declaration, President Roosevelt had designated two ocean areas off the West Coast as Sea Frontiers: The Panama Sea Frontier and the Western Sea Frontier. Both frontiers extended United States sea authority to about the international date line. One purpose was to exclude German raiders from the areas and to protect British shipping in the Pacific Ocean, principally in the South Pacific. Another was to comply with the Vacant Sea orders from Washington, which rerouted trans-Pacific shipping via the Torres Strait between Australia and New Guinea in the South Pacific.

According to Ogg, Hosmer identified the radio transmissions as Japanese, since the vessels used the unique *kana* telegraphic code of Japan's navy.[8] He was certain that the radio signals did not originate with American or Allied vessels, for there were none at sea in the area. Two separate bearings were obtained. One took off from north of San Francisco, the other south. When Ogg traced the two bearings on his chart they intersected in the North Pacific, north of Hawaii. Hosmer was sure that the bearings plotted by Ogg had located warships heading for Hawaii.

Captain Richard McCullough, the District Intelligence Officer, sent these findings in a report to the Navy Department. Most likely it was sent in the GUPID system, which had been assigned to Admiral Greenslade for supersecret contact with Station US and Arthur McCollum. As this book went to press in 1999, censorship prevented a look at the GUPID system. In 1946 the Joint Committee investigating the Pearl Harbor attack was asked to delete all reference of GUPID from the official record of the investigation by the Chief Assistant Counsel Gerhard A. Gesell.[9]

Once received in the nation's capital, the Japanese warship locations were delivered to President Roosevelt in the White House, according to district intelligence chief McCullough.[10] In a handwritten memo filed by Hosmer with the Twelfth Naval District's intelligence office, Hosmer wrote that around November 28 he learned that: "at least six, possibly eight Jap [*sic*] units were operating between Hawaii and the Aleutians and clearly indicated that a force was to steal out on a secret [mission] and attempt to obtain mastery of the air."[11] Hosmer's account differs from Ogg's. Ogg recalled the source as commercial radio facilities; Hosmer said the information was contained in an intercept obtained by a Navy operator from the "Jap *Kana* code." Asked about the conflicting accounts in 1998, Ogg said there was not really a conflict. "After fifty years, I did not recall the Navy intercepts. It is quite possible Lieutenant Hosmer obtained the bearings from both commercial and Navy sources for he had extensive contacts within the radio industry."[12]

Ogg never testified before any Pearl Harbor investigation, including the 1995 probe. He first disclosed his role in locating the Japanese force north of Hawaii to writer John Toland. Soon after Toland's book appeared, Ogg's statements were challenged by prominent historians, who cited Japanese claims that the Pearl Harbor warships were on radio silence and could not possibly have been intercepted by Americans. Ogg admitted he had no tangible proof of his assertions, since Navy intelligence personnel were forbidden to retain classified documents. But he assured skeptics that confirmation could be found in the records of the Navy's intercept station at Dutch Harbor, Alaska. "Look in the four-megacycle records [4000 kilocycles]. I recall the Japanese broadcasts reported to us were on an odd frequency in that radio spectrum," Ogg said.[13] But no one looked.

In 1984, all original Japanese intercept records of the Pacific Theater were classified TOP SECRET CODEWORD and held in the custody of the Naval Security Group Command in Washington. The author's requests to the Navy to see the 4000-kilocycle records of Dutch Harbor for November and December 1941 were turned down. Navy historians George W. Henriksen and Commander Irwin Newman told the author that there were no such records in the NSGC files.

Trying a different tack, the author learned of a Navy radio direction finder station at Dutch Harbor known as Station KING, which was a unit of Rochefort's Mid-Pacific Direction Finder Network in 1941. Since KING came under the administration of the Commandant of the Thirteenth Naval District in Seattle, the author checked with the National Archives and in October of 1985 discovered the 4000-kilocycle Dutch Harbor reports.[14] They irrefutably confirm Ogg's intercept details. According to a secret report issued in November 1941 by Chief Radioman Robert Fox, the traffic chief for KING, the *Akagi* was heard on 4960 kilocycles in tactical communication with several merchant vessels. Fox wrote that the broadcasts were transmitted on a rarely used Japanese naval radio frequency, but did not list the date. The records of Station H provided the last piece in the puzzle and revealed that Hawaii also intercepted an *Akagi* broadcast on November 26, when the carrier used 4963 kilocycles.[15]

The series of intercepted Japanese broadcasts centering in the North Pacific have been overlooked by every Pearl Harbor investigation. They are described here for the first time. Each report is compelling evidence for Ogg's assertions. As of December 3, the number of Japanese warship broadcasts in the North Pacific was significant. In addition to the Hosmer-Ogg source, five Navy listening posts—Stations ITEM, CAST, H, KING, and SAIL—and a Matson liner, the SS *Lurline*, heard the broadcasts and placed the information in the intelligence pipeline intended for the White House. This vital information obtained by the five units was logged in official Navy reports and forwarded to Washington, but was withheld from Admiral Kimmel and the Pacific Fleet. CAST's identification of the carriers and of Admiral Yamamoto occurred at the same time as and parallels the reports given to Hosmer.

About mid-November, Japan's navy assumed control of overseas civilian broadcast operations. High-powered Japanese radio stations normally used for worldwide commercial overseas broadcasts aimed their signals at the North and Central Pacific. Instead of transmitting to civilian/commercial radio addresses in North or South America or Europe, each broadcast was now directed to Japanese warships, using the secret *Yobidashi Fugo* address system of radio call signs. Long-distance frequencies beamed the broadcasts from shore stations in Osaka and Tokyo. Immediately, the powerful transmissions reached the American West Coast and disrupted Navy transmissions. Station SAIL at Seattle and Station ITEM at Imperial Beach, California, reported the interference. Station US in Washington requested details of the disruptive Japanese transmissions. One of the first stations to reply was Station ITEM. Chief Radioman Martin Vandenberg, ITEM's traffic chief, investigated the interference and said it was coming from Japanese naval radio stations in Tokyo and Osaka. He wrote that all classes of navy traffic were noted and that the "reception at Station I is very good." Vandenberg gave an example of one intercept. It was addressed to the radio call sign of the Japanese battleship HIJMS *Kirishima*, part of the Hawaii raid force, in the urgent special cipher code.[16]

The broadcasts to and from the North Pacific grew in intensity and reached the radio room of the American liner *Lurline*, plying the Pacific between California and Hawaii.

Captain C. W. Berndtson headed the SS *Lurline* toward Honolulu. The luxury liner, pride of the Matson Line and synonymous with cruises to Hawaii, departed San Francisco on Saturday, November 29, slid under the Golden Gate Bridge, sailed south along the California coast, and picked up more passengers from the docks at Long Beach, the harbor for Los Angeles. The *Lurline*'s staterooms were filled with civilian workers headed for Hawaii and Pacific isles to build up American defenses.

Leslie Grogan, the *Lurline*'s first assistant radio operator, had little to do. Yearning for more radio work during his midnight-to-morning watch, Grogan moved the dial of his radio receiver—and discovered unusual transmissions from Japan. "The Japs are blasting away on the lower marine radio frequencies. All in the Japanese code and continues for several hours," Grogan wrote in the *Lurline*'s radio log.[17] He noted that the broadcasts originated from shore stations in Japan and were beamed toward the Northwestern Pacific.

Grogan's next log entry is startling. He reported that Japanese ships in the North Pacific repeated the messages from the shore stations. "We noted that signals were being repeated back possibly for copying by craft with small antennas [sic]."[18] The broadcasts continued for the next two nights, December 1 and 2. "We continue to pick up the bold Japanese general order signals—it can't be anything else. We got good radio direction finder bearings, mostly coming from a Northwesterly direction from our position. The Jap floating units continue their bold repetition of wireless signals, presumably for the smaller craft in their vanguard of ships. Floating units repeat the signals from JCS, the shore station."[19]

Commercial radio call signs such as JCS were not normally used by Japan to address warships, but rather for commercial ships.[20] When Japan addressed warships, radio station JCS switched procedure and used the call sign of HA FU 6. Grogan's intercepts appear to coincide with Japanese naval messages originated by HA FU 6 (the same transmitter as JCS) and addressed to units of the Hawaii strike force, which were then proceeding eastward across the North Pacific. Grogan's account of hearing warships repeat radio messages fits in with Admiral Nagumo's radio communication plan, which called for repeating the Tokyo broadcasts for the smaller warships within the task force. The intercepted radio signals from JCS only indicated a land-based station near Tokyo. Each separate vessel had to transmit signals in order to be located by the *Lurline*'s direction finder. Grogan understood the implications of the Japanese naval broadcasts: "We are now making a concise record to turn into the Naval Intelligence when we arrive in Honolulu, Wednesday, December 3, 1941." Immediately upon docking at the Aloha Tower, Grogan presented his transcript of the broadcasts and the RDF bearings to Lieutenant Commander George Pease of Naval Intelligence. According to Grogan's account, Pease was a "good listener but showed little outward reflection as to what we felt was a mighty serious situation."[21]

If Pease, who died in a plane crash in 1945, ever submitted a report on the *Lurline*'s locating Japanese warships north of Hawaii by RDF, it has disappeared. So has the *Lurline*'s original radio log. On December 10, the liner returned to San Francisco and Lieutenant Commander Preston Allen boarded the ship and confiscated the radio log. Allen, a member of the Twelfth Naval District intelligence unit, took the log containing the details of Grogan's interceptions to his District office. It has never been seen since. Grogan's account, quoted in this book, is based on a reconstruction of the missing log that he prepared for Matson Lines after Allen took possession of the log.

During research for this book, the author uncovered details of the *Lurline* log's disappearance. In the late 1970s, shortly after John Toland began research for his book, he filed an FOIA with the Navy asking to see the log. The Navy said there was no record of such a log, but a withdrawal slip in the National Archives, San Bruno, California, tells another story.[22] After he took possession of the log, Lieutenant Commander Allen did not return it to Matson Lines. Instead he filed it in the voluminous records of the Port Director, Twelfth Naval District. There it remained, unknown to all Pearl Harbor investigations. In 1958, the Port Director files were turned over to the Federal Records Center [FRC] in San Bruno, a division of the National Archives.

Sometime in the 1970s someone removed the log from the National Archives and left a withdrawal slip form in its place. The caption on the slip refers to the *Lurline*'s radio log, but it is not dated or signed—a possible violation of National Archives procedures. "It had to be someone connected with the Navy," said Kathleen O'Connor, who discovered the withdrawal slip in August 1991. O'Connor, an archivist at San Bruno, told the author that the white withdrawal slip is yellowed, indicating deterioration based on a storage period of about twenty or more years—from the time that Toland made his FOIA request. At the time the *Lurline*'s log was in the physical custody of the Center but under the legal control of the Navy. The FRC is a government records center where both temporary and permanent Federal records are kept. Permanent records are eventually transferred to the National Archives' custody and opened for public research. Most FRC records are not open for public inspection. "Only naval personnel had access," explained O'Connor.[23]

She noted the "curious coincidence" of the above events. "Customary procedures pertaining to the care and preservation of archival documents were neglected," O'Connor said. "There is no date of withdrawal, nor any signature of the person who removed these highly significant records."

The *Lurline*'s radio operators weren't the only ones recording the Japanese radio "blasts." Station SAIL at Seattle confirmed the reports of Hosmer/Ogg and the *Lurline*. On December 3, operators at SAIL said that strong radio signals were originating in the North Pacific. By the next day three other Navy intercept stations reported the same signals. But 98 percent of the intercepts acquired by the four Navy facilities have been hidden from public view. Included are radio messages to and from the Pearl Harbor-bound warships *Kirishima*, *Akagi*, and *Tone* and Admiral Nagumo, commander of the raiding force.[24] Radio logs of the three monitoring stations found by the author in Archives II provide the evidence.

December 4, 1941, was a busy day for Japan's powerful radio transmitters. Broadcasts to three vessels of the Hawaii-bound carrier force were detected by three US Navy monitoring stations—ITEM, CAST, and H.[25] Each broadcast was transmitted on long-distance frequencies. Messages to the battleship *Kirishima* were intercepted at Stations ITEM (San Diego) and H (Oahu). On Corregidor, Station CAST intercepted messages to the First Air Fleet and its flagship, the *Akagi*. At Station H radio intercept operator Henry F. Garstka wrote in his operator log that he intercepted two messages to a warship with the radio call signal of NU TO 4. According to Garstka's log entry,[26] the message came from Radio Yokosuka, who kept asking, "Kan?, Kan?," which was a Japanese naval communication procedure meaning: "Can you hear me, and if so, please answer." The warship did not answer and for a good reason. NU TO 4 was the heavy cruiser HIJMS *Tone*, and the supersecret call sign was reserved for the Hawaii attack. The cruiser was part of the First Air Fleet—Japan's Pearl Harbor raiding force. The *Tone*'s captain wisely did not answer, for Radio Yokosuka violated Japanese communication security. It made a mistake in jump-starting the secret Hawaii list—it was not to be used, presumably, until the day of the attack. While Garstka did not identify NU TO 4 as the *Tone*, it proves Radio Yokosuka was a gross violator of Yamamoto's radio silence order. And Henry Garstka's intercept of NU TO 4 provides firm evidence that warships of the Pearl Harbor force were addressed by radio before the raid started and intercepted by US Navy monitoring stations.

Garstka intercepted the broadcast on a long-distance radio frequency used by Japan to contact individual ships and shore stations.[27] It was one of many Japanese communication procedures that enabled US intercept operators to estimate the warships' general location. Three distinct communication procedures were generally used: (1) "All Points" broadcasts for the entire Japanese navy; (2) shore to ship and vice versa; and (3) ship to ship.

The "All Points" broadcasts were sent over a vast radio network used by Tokyo to issue orders to commands in the Western and Central Pacific Ocean regions and areas of the Far East under Japanese naval control. Regular time schedules were maintained and Japanese radio operators assigned to diverse units copied the broadcasts, which contained general information for various commands. American cryptographers called these transmissions the "UTU Broadcasts." Japan set aside the frequencies of 4155, 8310, and 16,620 kilocycles for the exclusive use of the UTU transmissions. Prime time started at midnight on 4155 kilocycles, then switched to 8310 for the predawn hours and continued throughout daylight on 16,620 kilocycles. As twilight approached the switch was made to 8310, then 4155, etc. These UTU schedules continued twenty-four hours a day, seven days a week. Every Japanese naval command received general orders from the UTU broadcasts. Other eager listeners were the US Navy's intercept operators at CAST and H. As war neared, Japan set up additional UTU frequencies when the regular radio circuits became overloaded. Although the overload broadcasts did not necessarily provide locations for the warships or air units, they did indicate that her navy was gearing up for some kind of drastic operation, as Homer Kisner dutifully reported in his Chronology of December 4, 1941.[28]

An entirely different communication procedure provided US Navy intercept operators with the general location of warships and merchant vessels. This procedure is called point-to-point broadcasting and involved reserved frequencies. Each major Japanese naval base had its own set of frequencies. So when intercept operator Henry Garstka of Station H intercepted radio transmissions from the Yokosuka naval base's point-to-point broadcast, that intercept disclosed that the *Tone* was a great distance away in the North Pacific. Garstka noted that Yokosuka beamed the message on the long-distance frequency of 12,690 kilocycles. There was no other rational analysis in determining her location. If she had been in the Western or Central Pacific, naval radio station transmitters at Sasebo, Saipan, or Takao would have been used to contact the warship. It was a communication intelligence error by Radio Yokosuka and was recognized as such by the captain of the cruiser, who did not respond.[29]

In the same December 4 Chronology where he predicted Japan's navy was preparing for drastic action, Homer Kisner of Station H reported that "The Carriers are believed to have remained in the vicinity of Kyushu [the southernmost of the main islands of Japan]."[30] But which carriers? The Third Fleet carriers of Carrier Divisions Three and Four or the First Air Fleet's Carrier Divisions One, Two and Five—which, at the time, were in the North Pacific headed for Hawaii? Those questions were posed to Kisner by the author during interviews in April 1988 and April 1998.[31] "I was locating the Third Fleet carriers," Kisner said of the December 4 Chronology. He maintained that his locations were consistent. Since early

November 1941 his daily Chronology linked Carrier Divisions Three and Four with the Southeast Asia movement organized by the commander of the Third Fleet in the area of Kyushu and the port of Sasebo.

Kisner pointed to his Chronology of November 20, where he placed the warships of Cruiser Division Eight, Destroyer Squadron One, with the Carrier Commands [Kisner's capitalization].[32] He admitted that by late in the day of Friday, December 5, the locations of the Japanese warships had been obscured by Japan's communication procedures. But the obfuscation didn't fool Kisner. He analyzed the broadcasts of Radio Saipan (Central Pacific), Radio Takao (Philippines and Southeast Asia), and Radio Ominato (North Pacific) and wrote that the "method of delivering the [Japanese fleet] messages tends to keep unknown the position of vessels afloat." He predicted that "Japan's navy operations were near a war-time basis."[33] It was the unknown positions of the vessels afloat between Hawaii, Saipan, and Ominato that worried Kisner, according to his April 1998 interview with the author. "I came to the conclusion they were going to jump us."[34]

Japanese navy officers involved in the Pearl Harbor attack insist that the carrier fleet of Divisions One, Two, and Five were on total radio silence and developed a fallback position to deflect questions on their location. They say American monitoring stations heard deceptive broadcasts originated by Japanese naval air stations that pretended to be the *Akagi* and other vessels. Captain Sadatoshi Tomioka provided details. "The Main Force in the Inland Sea and land-based air units carried out deceptive communication to indicate the carriers were training in the Kyushu area."[35]

Tomioka's assertions were backed by the first witness before the 1945–46 Congressional investigation. On November 15, 1945, Admiral T. B. Inglis said Japan used deceptive[36] radio broadcasts and simulated the presence of carriers in the Inland Sea prior to the attack. But he gave no details and did not produce a single intercept indicating deceptive messages. Admiral Kimmel's intelligence chief Edwin Layton gave Congress two contradictory stories. He told the Army Board in 1944 that "the Japanese practiced radio deception." Then in his 1985 book he wrote, "Contrary to popular myth and the assumption of many historians, there was no sustained deception plan put into operation by Japan." Layton had gotten it right the second time. No real examples have ever been located. If radio deception was attempted by Japan, it was inept and soon discovered.[37]

Radioman First Class Paul E. Seaward of Station H reported hearing naval air stations at Kanoya, Omura, and Yokosuka in radio contact with a call sign of 1 NI KU on December 5 and 6. Whoever they were attempting to contact—or whether it was an attempt at deception—remains a mystery. The call sign was not assigned to any of Japan's aircraft carriers, battleships, or cruisers with the First Air Fleet.[38]

American intercept operators were not duped. The ruse (if it occurred) was recognized instantly. On America's West Coast, Navy interception operations at Station SAIL and Station AE at Sitka, Alaska, discovered the false signals. Radioman First Class Fred R. Thomson, the Navy's Sitka traffic chief, wrote that they came from the radio station attached to the Japanese naval air base at Kasumigaura, 34 miles northwest of Tokyo. The air station sent a radio message to a fleet unit, then pretended to receive a reply.[39] Thomson detected the sham when Kasumigaura used the same transmitter for the response. In effect, Kasumigaura was talking to itself. In his oral history interview, Joseph Rochefort said that none of his officers or operators were fooled by Japanese radio deception: "It is awfully difficult to deceive a trained counter-communications intelligence organization, awfully difficult."[40]

CHAPTER 13

A PRETTY CHEAP
PRICE

DECEMBER 1–6, 1941

IN HIS POSTWAR TESTIMONY TO CONGRESS, ADMIRAL HUSBAND Kimmel maintained that he would have been ready to defend Pearl Harbor . . . "if I had anything which indicated to me the probability of an attack on Hawaii."[1] The information that Kimmel needed was available—so available, in fact, that it often appears as though the Japanese had made few efforts to conceal it. As we now know, Lieutenant Commanders Joseph Rochefort and Edwin Layton could have provided that indication, but they did not do so.

Their failure allowed Japan's First Air Fleet to make its surprise attack and then to escape to Japan. In a postwar assessment of the attack Rochefort said, "It was a pretty cheap price to pay for unifying the country." But others would angrily question that conclusion.[2]

Seven Japanese naval broadcasts intercepted between November 28 and December 6 confirmed that Japan intended to start the war and that it would begin at Pearl Harbor. The evidence that poured into American in-

203

telligence stations is overpowering. All the broadcasts have one common denominator: none ever reached Admiral Kimmel. The Navy's head cryptographer in Hawaii developed an excuse. It is a powerful statement that has assured the American and Japanese people that indeed Japan's navy observed radio silence and never divulged in any manner that Pearl Harbor was the target. "There is not the slightest reason to believe that JN-25 or any other navy system contained anything that would have forecast the attack." This assurance came from Lieutenant Commander Thomas Dyer, second in command and chief cryptographer at Station HYPO, in a letter to the author on June 4, 1983.[3] But in the Station H records there were plenty of indicators found, in the form of intercepted Japanese broadcasts.

The first of these came on November 28, when Tokyo Naval Radio transmitted a message in the 5-Num code to the First Air Fleet. It warned that the warships could expect a powerful winter storm in their path. Aerographers of the Imperial Navy had located several low-pressure centers in the North Pacific.[4] Each low indicated the presence of storm conditions that were steering Siberian polar winds in a southerly direction to meet up with the Kuroshio Current—Japan's Gulf Stream.[5] For centuries, mariners knew that the warm waters of the Kuroshio or Black Current, which originated in the East China Sea, became storm catapults once they reached the North Pacific and clashed with cold Arctic air south of the Kamchatka Peninsula and Alaska's Aleutian Islands. Carried eastward by the high-altitude winds of the jet stream, these storm systems deliver heavy rains and snow packs to the United States and Canada. The intensity of the storms can be ferocious, often resulting in the monstrous forty-foot waves that break on the north-facing shores of all the Hawaiian Islands.

Radio operators within the Japanese First Air Fleet didn't need the warning—the storm was already roiling the stomachs of many crew members. Soon the storm slowed the forward speed of the entire thirty-one-vessel fleet and scattered the warships over a fifty-mile area at 42 degrees of north latitude near the international date line. From the deck of the light cruiser *Abukuma*, flagship of Destroyer Squadron One, Petty Officer Iki Kuromoti described the scene in near-*haiku* style: "The weather grows worse, a gale blows, the seas rage, a dense fog descends. In this bitter weather, a show of actual force, a test by the gods. Though tossed about in their struggle with the elements, the ships continue on their glorious way."

Kuromoti said men were washed overboard and signal flags were blown away. "Without sleep, and by the silent struggle with nature every man was completely exhausted by continuous watches. Our spirits were buoyed that we were soon to strike the first blow in this greatest of all wars."[6]

By November 30, the storm's fury had subsided and Admiral Chuichi Nagumo decided to round up his warships. Blinker light signals were out of the question. Driven off course by the typhoon-force winds, warships and tankers were scattered beyond the fifteen-mile horizon line, out of sight and unreachable by light signals. Radio was the only means to return the First Air Fleet to its tight formation. With the *Akagi's* transmitter tuned to 4960 kilocycles, the carrier sent out broadcasts to the strays and directed them back to the task force. Since the broadcasts were intended for ships relatively close by, the radio operators set the transmitters on low power—a communication procedure that limited their signal range to about a hundred miles.[7]

But another storm was forming millions of miles away on the surface of the sun. In a sunstorm or solar storm, ions created on the sun's surface bombard the earth's atmosphere, wreaking havoc with radio transmissions.[8] These sunstorms distort electronic communications and create what is called the northern lights or aurora borealis, which can be observed in the earth's higher latitudes. (The southern counterpart is called the southern lights or aurora australis.) Radio signals—even those generated by low transmitter power—can be bounced halfway across the earth's surface by the quirks of solar storms. A radio receiver thousands of miles from a transmitter can sometimes clearly hear a broadcast while a similar receiver a short distance away draws a blank.

The *Akagi* radiomen were not aware that one of the largest solar storms of the century was taking place as they continued on their glorious journey. They were confident that low-power tactical frequencies, limited to a few miles, would be secure. There was no way, they believed, that American, English, and Dutch eavesdroppers would hear the messages.

Admiral Nagumo's round-up directions were transmitted to the flagships within the First Air Fleet. There was a designated command flagship for each type of vessel—battleships and cruisers, destroyers, and the oil tankers. Each flagship, known as a type commander, served as a communications sentinel for its type of vessel. The *Kirishima* was the flagship for the battleships and heavy cruisers, the *Akagi* for the carriers. The destroyers relied on radio orders from the *Abukuma;* the oil tankers, from the *Kyokuto Maru.* Homer Kisner of Station H told the author that the type of the broadcasts provided clues to his staff that enabled them to penetrate Japan's hostile plans. He referred to the flagship system as the "mother hen and chickens" breakthrough. "It enabled us to first identify who was bossiest, then who was being bossed," Kisner said. He gave the *Abukuma* as an example. "If a single warship continually talks to the same vessels, obviously it is the controlling authority."[9]

Nagumo's orders to gather the scattered task force were first transmitted to the command flagships within the First Air Fleet. Then the orders were repeated to the "chicks." An important vessel was the *Kyokuto Maru,* flagship of the seven-tanker fuel train. The tanker was first spotted for Admiral Kimmel in Rochefort's Communications Summary (COMSUM) of October 9, 1941. In the summary the tanker was associated with what became the thirty-one vessels of the Japanese Pearl Harbor force. Writing that the warships had been fairly prominent during the last part of September and early October 1941, Rochefort identified the commands (the mother hens): Battleship Division 3, Commander Carriers (Admiral Nagumo), Destroyer Squadron 1, Cruiser Division 8, and the *Kyukuto Maru.* He also listed the Commander of the First and Second Fleets and the oiler *Tsurumi,* which eventually were attached to the opening salvos of the Southeast Asia campaign.[10] By mid-November, the staff had solved the tanker's code-movement reports and associated the vessel with the First Air Fleet.[11] In what Kisner later called "a remarkable bit of intelligence," he placed the commanding officer of the *Kyokuto Maru* aboard the carrier *Kaga* on October 27. Admiral Kimmel saw and initialed the unusual report the next morning.[12]

Throughout the weekend of November 28–30, the solar storm bounced the *Akagi's* radio transmissions across the Pacific to US Navy intercept stations on Oahu, Alaska, and America's West Coast and to the SS *Lurline.* Kimmel was informed of the *Akagi* broadcasts by Rochefort's report dated November 30. The admiral read the warning on the morning of December 2 and asked his intelligence officer, Edwin Layton: "Where are the carriers?" Layton said he didn't know. With a twinkle in his eye, Kimmel asked,

"Could they be rounding Diamond Head?" Layton's reply was, "I hope they would have been discovered before then."[13] But Layton may not have been completely frank. He said that Japan's Carrier Divisions One and Two had not been heard from for at least fifteen to twenty-five days—starting from mid-November. He then expanded the falsification: "Neither the carriers, carrier division commanders or the carrier commander-in-chief [Nagumo] had been addressed in any of the thousands of messages that came out of the Naval General Staff. In addition, no traffic [radio transmissions] had been originated by the carriers."[14]

Joseph Rochefort of Station HYPO backed up Layton, claiming that from December 1 onward "We lost our knowledge of their activities and their position because they had gone on radio silence." On the eve of the attack he told Kimmel, "Carriers are lost, carriers not heard." Later in 1946, during the Pearl Harbor investigation, Rochefort modified his statement, testifying on February 15, 1946, that he had "located them in a negative sense."[15]

Homer Kisner told the author that bearing locations obtained by the radio direction finder operators were part of the complete intelligence bundle he delivered each day to Station HYPO. Until the end of October, RDF reports were included in intelligence summaries sent to both Kimmel and the White House. But beginning November 1, the RDF reports were omitted from the summaries delivered to Kimmel. When shown the omissions by the author in 1988, Kisner was astounded. "Who held them back? They should have gone to the admiral!" he said.

Why were the RDF reports missing from Admiral Kimmel's copy? Rochefort's original Communications Summaries were found by the author stored among Navy records in the National Archives, but all the RDF reports for November and December 1941 were crudely cut from the copy of each report that had been prepared for Kimmel. Every RDF fix had been excised some time after Kisner delivered the complete reports to Station HYPO. No one at the National Archives could explain the deletions. When were they cut? Before they were delivered to the admiral? Did the deletions trigger the "Where are the carriers" question Kimmel directed to Layton?

In 1993, the deletion questions were posed to Richard A. von Doenhoff, a specialist in the Pearl Harbor section of the National Archives. He confirmed that more than sixty-five of Rochefort's November and December Summaries intended for Kimmel had been mutilated. Von Doenhoff wrote the author that the RDF pages which listed Japanese warship locations had been cut prior to the start of the 1945 Congressional Hearings. "We examined the Fourteenth Naval District Communication Summaries and found that those summaries had indeed been cut off from the bottom of the pages. We have no idea why this was done, but it appears that the documents were entered into evidence during 1945 and 46 in this manner."[16]

So began the myth of the radio silence of the Japanese carrier force. It is a myth that has endured for over fifty years and that continues to baffle historians. In 1995 Stephen Ambrose, one of America's most distinguished historians, excoriated the pre–Pearl Harbor intelligence when he wrote: "It was simply terrible. In late November, intelligence 'lost' the Japanese aircraft carrier fleet," Ambrose wrote. He repeated this charge in the *Wall Street Journal* in May 1999.[17]

Layton's claim about the carrier commands' radio silence does not hold up to scrutiny. There were 129 Japanese naval intercepts obtained by US naval monitor stations between November 15 and December 6 that directly contradict Layton's figures. The intercept rate can be documented from the records of Stations CAST and H. For the 21-day period, it averages 6.3 intercepts per day. All categories of Japanese carriers and carrier commands cited by Layton as on radio silence either originated radio broadcasts or received messages during the three-week period, according to an analysis of the intercepts conducted by the Navy's 1941 radio traffic experts, Captain Duane Whitlock of Station CAST and Homer Kisner of Station H.[18]

Kisner's reports and intercepts collected in Hawaii have been preserved. The intercepts gathered by Whitlock's operators after mid-November 1941 were burned so they would not fall into the hands of the Japanese troops that were advancing on Corregidor in the spring of 1942. An exception was Station CAST's radio direction finder reports, which were sent to Hawaii over the US Navy's TESTM radio circuit before the attack.[19]

During separate interviews with the author, Kisner and Whitlock identified the 129 intercepts that refute Layton's claim of radio silence. Whit-

Franklin Delano Roosevelt favors photographers with his famous smile. *FDR Library, Hyde Park, New York*

Edward R. Murrow, CBS news correspondent extraordinaire, got the news story of his life when President Roosevelt called him in to the White House for a meeting immediately following the Pearl Harbor attack. *Photo courtesy CBS.*

Blackouts did not apply to the White House on the night of December 7, 1941. Most of the crowd's interest is directed toward the photographer instead of the mansion, where Eleanor Roosevelt was preparing a Sunday dinner for invited guests in the first-floor family dining room just above the taxi's rear lights. *Photo courtesy Library of Congress.*

Admiral Thomas Hart, commander-in-chief, US Asiatic Fleet, in 1941 with his flag lieutenant, Leo W. Nilon, on his left. *US Navy photo.*

Admiral Husband E. Kimmel, commander-in-chief, US Pacific Fleet, 1941. *US Navy photo.*

Captain Walter S. Anderson, Director of Navy Intelligence, 1940. *US Navy photo.*

Captain Arthur H. McCollum, FDR's routing officer, shown here at Port Moresby in 1943. McCollum's memorandum, dated October 7, 1940, detailed eight specific actions that should be taken to provoke Japan to war. It was endorsed by Dudley W. Knox, one of Roosevelt's most trusted naval advisors. *Courtesy US Navy Historical Center.*

Admiral Harold R. Stark, Chief of Naval Operations, 1941. *US Navy photo.*

Florence Short pins Lieutenant General stars on her husband, (now) Lieutenant General Walter Short at Fort Shafter in February, 1941. *Walter Short Collection, Hoover Archives, Stanford University, Stanford, California.*

Angry, feared, and highly intelligent: Admiral Ernest J. King, Commander-in-Chief of the Atlantic Fleet in 1941, met frequently with FDR. *US Navy photo.*

Patriotic San Franciscans heartily endorsed FDR's embargo—called for in McCollum's October 1941 memorandum—of exports to Japan during a July demonstration at the NYK Line pier. San Francisco *Call-Bulletin photo by Jack Fay. Bancroft Library Collection.*

But the embargo was not so effective that it prevented Japan from fighting. Japanese naval tankers had little difficulty obtaining oil from America's West Coast refineries. In spring 1941, the *Nisshin Maru* filled up its holds at the Associated Oil refinery in Port Costa, California. *US Navy photo.*

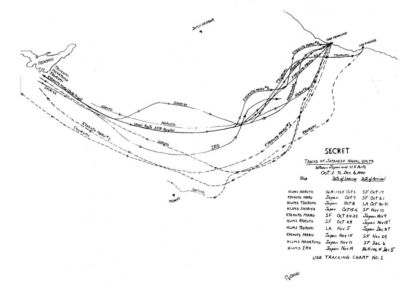

US Navy radio direction finders tracked tankers like the *Nisshin Maru* across the Pacific beginning October 1, 1940. One of the tankers whose track is shown here, the *Kyokuto Maru,* was later assigned as flagship for the eight tankers that would refuel the First Air Fleet during their voyage to and from the Pearl Harbor assault. *National Archives, Seattle, Washington.*

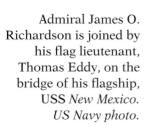

Admiral James O. Richardson is joined by his flag lieutenant, Thomas Eddy, on the bridge of his flagship, USS *New Mexico*. *US Navy photo.*

It would not last. Aboard the USS *Pennsylvania* Admiral Kimmel (standing at the microphone beneath the rightmost fourteen-inch gun) reads the orders that make him the commander of the Pacific Fleet. Riochardson, fired by President Roosevelt, stands to Kimmel's right. *US Navy photo.*

Agnes Meyer Driscoll, the Navy's legendary civilian chief cryptographer and the solver of Japan's 5-Num code. *Courtesy National Security Agency.*

The interceptors. The "On the Roof Gang" intercept operator class of June 1933. From left to right, Orville Jones, Homer Kisner, E. H. Marks, and Thomas Hoover. In the rear, W. C. Rathsack, Donald Barnum, Benjamin Groundwater, and John Gelineau. In 1941 Kisner and Jones were at Station HYPO on Hawaii; Hoover and Gelineau at CAST; and Barnum on Guam, where he evaded capture by Japanese units by hiding until US forces retook the island in 1944. *US Navy photo.*

Traffic chief Homer Kisner (at left) is joined at the entry to the Station H operations building by fellow decrypters Orville L. Jones, L. F. Myers, and William Knefley (front). Kisner would be promoted to commander and placed on the Navy's cryptographic honor roll for his work on Japanese communications between July 1941 and June 1942. *Courtesy Captain Homer Kisner, USN*

The same Captain Homer Kisner nearly a half century later holds up the daily chronology he wrote on the morning of December 6, 1941. In it, towards the bottom of the page displayed, he warned that Japan had taken "the first steps towards placing the operations of the Navy on a wartime basis." Kisner's warning was not heeded. *Photo by Robert Stinnett.*

The machine. The keyboard of a RIP-5 code typewriter, made by Underwood, showing the difference between Morse Code and Japanese naval *kana*. Note, for example, that Morse Code "B" is "HA" in *kana*. *Photo by Robert Stinnett.*

The eccentric Lieutenant Commander Joseph J. Rochefort (with raised hand) commanded station HYPO in 1941. He is shown here in a game of dominoes aboard the USS *Indianapolis* in 1940. *Photo by Carl Mydans, © Life Magazine.*

Where they worked. Station HYPO occupied a portion of the basement of the Administration Building of the Fourteenth Naval District in the Pearl Harbor Navy Yard in 1941. Rochefort supervised the cryptographic operations from the center of the large interior space. Sorting and statistical machinery (at right) aided in solving the Japanese naval 5-Num code. *Photo by Robert Stinnett; art by Frank Pennock, Jr., based on a plot furnished by Captain Thomas Dyer.*

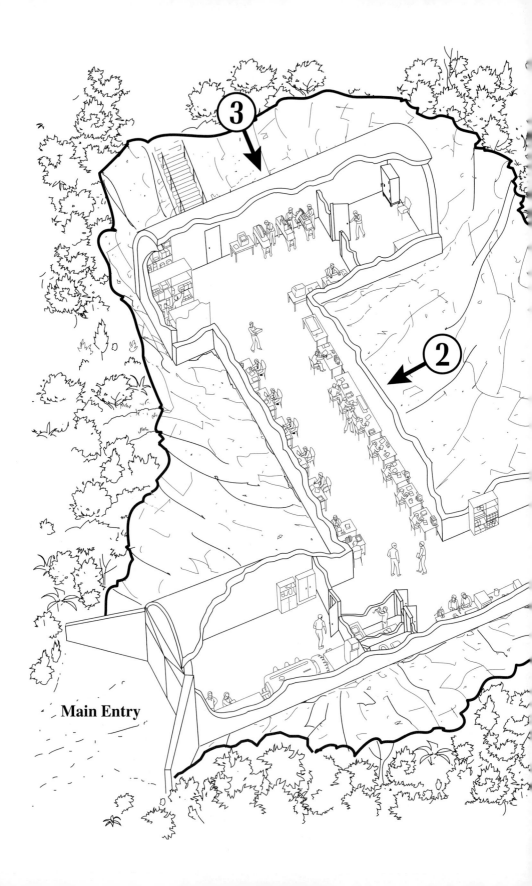

Main Entry

STATION CAST
Corregidor Island, Philippines
December 1941

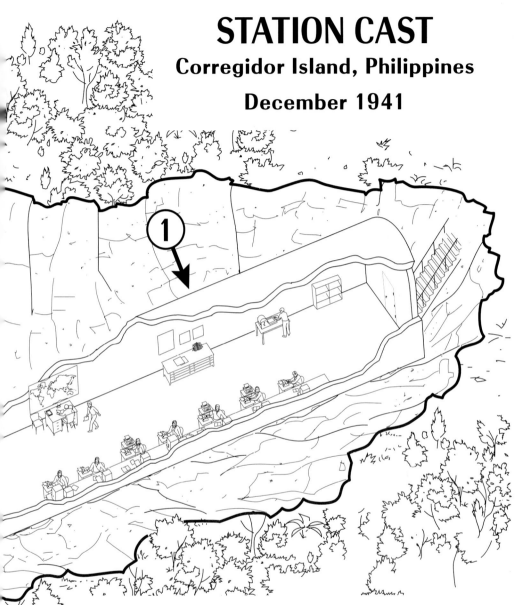

Station CAST was one of the links in the chain of American intelligence. Cryptology and intercept operations involving Japanese military and diplomatic codes were forty feet underground, centered in these three tunnels carved from the rock of Corregidor. Intercept operators worked in area (1) lower, supervised by Anton Novak from his desk on opposite wall. Cryptographers and radio traffic analysts worked in area (2), supervised by co-commanders, John Lietwiler and Rudolph Fabian, at facing desks at lower left. In the machine area (3), Robert Doud managed the Purple machine that sat alongside his desk. On the opposite wall, near an emergency exit leading to top side, were IBM statistical machines used for the 5-Num code. *Drawing by Dan Siculan, based on description furnished by Duane Whitlock, Jack Kaye, and Robert Doud.*

Tadashi Morimura was really Ensign Takeo Yoshikawa of the Imperial Japanese Navy; he came to Hawaii for espionage purposes. Morimura came to Hawaii under diplomatic auspices, but the ruse did not fool US officials. Rear Admiral Walter Anderson made it clear the to the FBI's Robert Shivers that the Navy, not the FBI, was in charge of the Morimura investigation. They carefully monitored Morimura's every move—but did nothing.

Richard Kotoshirodo assisted Morimura in gathering intelligence information for the Japanese navy. Kotoshirodo, an American citizen, was later sent to a Utah internment camp at Topaz, but was never charged with espionage. *Photo from FBI files.*

The Japanese Consulate at Nuuanu Avenue and Kuakini Street in Honolulu. Morimura lived in the residential quarters at right rear. *Photo from FBI files.*

Admiral Osami Nagano, Chief of the Navy General Staff. *Imperial Japanese Navy photo.*

The attackers. Admiral Isoroku Yamamoto held Japan's major afloat command in 1941 as Commander-in-Chief of the Imperial Japanese Navy. *Imperial Japanese Navy photo.*

Vice-Admiral Chuichi Nagumo, commander of the First Air Fleet. *Imperial Japanese Navy photo.*

The Japanese First Air Fleet, commanded by Admiral Nagumo, departed from Hitokappu Bay for Pearl Harbor on November 26 (Tokyo Time), 1941. Contrary to popular belief, Nagumo broke radio silence during the voyage, carrying on extensive radio communications with other Japanese admirals. His signals were heard in Hawaii, Alaska, and on America's West Coast. In the photograph, a lone Japanese sailor dressed for the cold weather of the North Pacific watches the HIJMS *Kaga* (left) and the HIJMS *Zuikaku* follow in the *Akagi*'s wake. *Imperial Japanese Navy photo.*

Evidence available today says otherwise, but Lieutenant Commander Edwin Layton, Intelligence officer of the Pacific Fleet in 1941, claimed that Japan's Hawaii force was on "super radio silence." *Official US Navy photo.*

Robert Ogg, a special Navy investigator for San Francisco's Twelfth Naval District, holds up a piece of the proof. Ogg located Japanese warships in the North Pacific by radio-direction-finder bearings in the week before Pearl Harbor. Some historians have discounted Ogg's claim, but here he points to confirmation that the flagship of Japan's Pearl Harbor force, the carrier HIMJS *Akagi*, broke radio silence on November 30 to contact ships in the tanker train. In doing so, the *Akagi* revealed its position to the US Navy's intercept operators. "The only tactical circuit heard today," reads the report, "was one with AKAGI and several MARUS." On that day the *Akagi* was near the international date line in the North Pacific. *Photo by Robert Stinnett.*

According to Robert Ogg, Lieutenant Ellsworth Hosmer, shown here, obtained the radio-direction-finder bearings of Japan's Pearl Harbor force. Hosmer headed the radio intelligence section of the Twelfth Naval District and had direct lines to Arthur McCollum in Washington. *Photo courtesy Robert Ogg.*

The Japanese attack on Pearl Harbor begins. The time is about 7:55 A.M. as the opening salvos of the assault are photographed from a Japanese plane. The large geyser of water in the center just aft of the USS *Oklahoma* is probably a torpedo hit. The battleships (from the left, on the far side of Ford island) are the *Nevada, Arizona* with repair ship *Vestal, Tennessee* and *West Virginia, Maryland* and *Oklahoma,* oiler *Neosho,* and *California.* On the Ewa side of Ford island (the lower left of the photograph) are the *Detroit, Raleigh, Utah,* and *Tangier.* Japan ignored the Navy's oil reserves, stored in the tanks that can be seen at upper right. Weather conditions are ideal. There is no cloud cover over the Koolau Mountains. *Imperial Japanese Navy photo.*

By 1:00 P.M. devastation reigned over Battleship Row and Pearl Harbor. The repair ship USS *Vestal* has beached at Aeia Bay (in the lower right), and the *Nevada,* which attempted to reach open water, can be dimly seen in the center channel. The photograph was taken from near the Aeia Elementary-Intermediate School at Kaimakani and Ulune Streets. The school can be seen in the foreground. *National Archives.*

The USS *Shaw*, hit by Japanese bombs while in dry dock, presented one of the most dramatic photographs of the attack. *US Navy photo.*

Rescue squads work on the capsized hull of the USS *Oklahoma* in an attempt to rescue trapped sailors. Lawrence McCutcheon, the first American believed to have been killed in the raid, died at his post high on the mainmast of the *Maryland* (top*). US Navy photo.*

Tragedy left its mark that day in Oahu. A victim of the Day of Deceit on the shore of Kaneohe Bay. *US Navy photo, National Archives.*

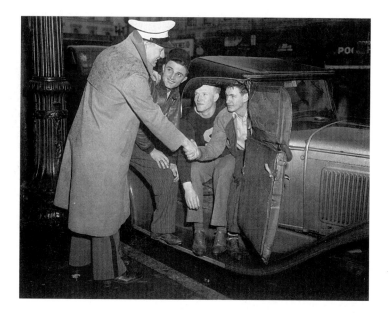

The raid served its purpose. Outrage did what FDR's more subtle machinations did not. Americans rushed to Army, Navy, and Marine Corps recruiting stations immediately after news of the attack. Here, on a rainy Monday, December 8, these young men gave up their Model A Ford and joined the Marine Corps in Oakland, California. *Oakland Tribune photo.*

At the urging of the families of Admiral Kimmel and General Short, Congress reopened the Pearl Harbor inquiry in 1995. Again the Army and Navy did not disclose to Congress the 1941 military and naval intercepts. Shown here are (from left to right) Admiral Thomas Moorer, former Chief of Naval Operations and chairman of the Joint Chiefs of Staff, and Admiral Husband Kimmel's descendants, grandson Thomas K. Kimmel, Jr., sons Thomas and Edward Kimmel, and grandson Manning Kimmel. In the rear is grandson Husband E. Kimmel II. *Wide World Photo.*

Like the 1945–46 investigations, the 1995 inquiry failed to disclose the truth. This cartoon ridicules the former but could apply to the latter. *Cartoon by Batchelor, © 1945 News Syndicate Co., Inc.*

lock analyzed the radio direction finder reports obtained by Station CAST, and Kisner analyzed the intercepts obtained by his operators at Station H. The 129 reports, dated during the 21-day period, were compiled by the author from three sources found in Archives II: (1) Japanese naval intercepts, (2) Japanese code movement reports filed by warships, and (3) the TESTM radio direction finder reports obtained by Station CAST. Admiral Nagumo, the commander-in-chief of the Hawaii-bound force, was the most talkative. He originated nearly half of all Japanese naval radio broadcasts intercepted by the US Navy monitoring stations. The author compiled the seven categories of intercepts:

A. Radio transmissions by Admiral Nagumo:	60
B. Tokyo radio to the vessels of the First Air Fleet:	24
C. Broadcasts originated by carriers:	20
D. Broadcasts originated by Carrier Division Commanders:	12
E. Messages originated by vessels attached to the First Air Fleet, but were not carriers:	8
F. Messages originated by the Midway Neutralization Unit:	4
G. Tokyo radio to individual Carrier Division Commanders:	1
	129[20]

Radio silence was ignored as more Japanese naval broadcasts hit the airwaves. The first military intercept that specified Pearl Harbor as the target came from Japan's highest naval commander, Admiral Osami Nagano, Chief of the Imperial Navy General Headquarters. He breached security in a radio broadcast and disclosed that a Japanese carrier strike force would attack Hawaii. The broadcast was beamed from Tokyo to the communications officer of the Eleventh Air Fleet, a powerful naval air command based on Formosa, composed of 500 bombers and fighters that had been massed for an aerial attack on General MacArthur's command in the Philippines and other objectives in Southeast Asia.

Nagano's broadcast was first publicly disclosed in a postwar article written by Commander Koiichi Shimada, an air officer of the Eleventh Air Fleet, who wrote that his command received a radio dispatch from Imperial General Headquarters packed with highly secret information. The message said:

IMPERIAL HEADQUARTERS IS QUITE CONFIDENT OF SUCCESS IN JAMMING
THE ENEMY'S RADIO FREQUENCIES SO THAT ANY WARNING DISPATCHED TO
THE PHILIPPINES AS A RESULT OF THE CARRIER STRIKING FORCE'S ATTACK
ON HAWAII WILL NOT GET THROUGH. MEANWHILE, IN ORDER TO ASSURE
SUCCESS OF THE HAWAII ATTACK, IT IS IMPERATIVE THAT ELEVENTH AIR
FLEET IN FORMOSA TAKE EVERY PRECAUTION TO GUARD AGAINST THE
ENEMY'S LEARNING OF OUR MILITARY MOVEMENTS BEFORE THE ATTACK
TAKES PLACE.[21]

The disclosures contained in this Tokyo-to-Formosa broadcast are confounding. Why would Japan's top naval officer abandon basic radio security? An even more important question for the Pacific Fleet: Was the broadcast intercepted by US Navy cryptographers, or was Commander Dyer of HYPO correct in asserting that Japan did not transmit a single message naming Pearl Harbor as the target?

Although Shimada provided few communication details of Nagano's broadcast, he indicated that it was received on a Tokyo–Formosa radio circuit before the attack. He suggested the date was before December 5, 1941, Formosa Time. The broadcast is another of Pearl Harbor's mysteries. No transcript of it was found in President Carter's 1979 release of Japanese naval intercepts, nor was it discussed by any Pearl Harbor investigation. Since the message dealt with Japanese plans to disrupt American radio-receiving facilities of General MacArthur and Admiral Hart, the author looked for Tokyo radio messages directed to the Eleventh Air Fleet's communication officer in Formosa. Station H in Hawaii kept a daily log of messages dispatched to Japanese commands. These messages are listed in that log as the UTU broadcast schedule. Each UTU log discloses Japanese communications details, but not the message text. The text—in either navy code or plain language—was recorded on a separate message sheet. Entries in the UTU log contain the Japanese originator and the intended receiver of each message, as well as the radio frequency, the time of the intercept in Tokyo Time, and the initials of the Station H intercept operator.

In the Japanese navy's radio-address code (Yobidashi Fugo), the suffix 49 always designated the staff communications (radiotelegraphy) officer of each command. The suffix code never changed. The November 1941 radio code address for the communications officer of the Eleventh Air Fleet was

SU YO 449; it changed to SI HA 149 on December 1. Japanese attempts to mask the change didn't work. American cryptographers at CAST saw through Japan's disguise and instantly identified the new name for the Eleventh Air Fleet. They sent a TESTM dispatch to Hawaii on December 4 (Manila Time) and named the five new radio call signs: "Idents for Eleventh Air Fleet: HI ME 6, MO NO 1, RE HE 8, SI HA 1, YO NO 1."[22]

A message sent by Radio Tokyo to SI HA 149 in the UTU log for December 4 (Formosa Time; December 3 in Hawaii) used the same radio call—"idents"—provided by Station CAST. The log tells this story: on December 3, Station H operator CU heard a message sent to the communications staff officer of the Eleventh Air Fleet. CU intercepted the message at 7:45 A.M., entered the communication details of the message in the UTU log book, typed the Japanese text on a separate message sheet, and sent both on their way to Admiral Kimmel.[23]

As with the other crucial intercepts of the week, there is no record that the message ever reached Kimmel. Yet there is firm evidence that Nagano's message was intercepted in Hawaii. In his Chronology for December 4, Homer Kisner noted that the Communications Division in Tokyo sent high-precedence messages to "general collective calls." One was SI HA 149, the communication officer of the Eleventh Air Fleet. Except for CU and Commander Shimada, no one in America has admitted seeing the original message that names Pearl Harbor as the target for a carrier attack. Extraordinary secrecy surrounds the intercept. None of the SI HA 149 intercepts have been released.

There were many more clues. Another radio broadcast placed the Japanese submarine *I-10* off American Samoa in the South Pacific. On December 4, Tokyo Time, the sub reconnoitered the small US Navy base at Pago Pago on American Samoa, a United States possession of several islands about 1500 miles east of Australia in the South Pacific, and launched a small scouting aircraft on a reconnaissance mission. When the plane, believed to be a float plane converted for submarine operation, failed to return, *I-10* broke radio silence, contacted the commander of the submarine fleet, and reported it missing.[24] The broadcast originated within easy intercept range of Station VICTOR, a Navy direction finder station at Pago Pago. VICTOR, named for the small village of Vaitogi, operated around the clock, obtaining radio direction finder fixes of Japanese naval units in the

South and Central Pacific. RDF fixes obtained by VICTOR were radioed immediately to Joseph Rochefort's office at HYPO in Pearl Harbor. Yet Rochefort testified that he never received anything from VICTOR. National Archives documents in San Bruno, California, contradict him. So does one of his assistants, Lieutenant Commander Thomas Huckins, who wrote that VICTOR "has been giving excellent service as a strategic DF station." [25]

There are 300 pages of RDF fixes that were originated by VICTOR between July and December 1941 locked in Archives II vaults at College Park, Maryland. Another set of documents at San Bruno traces them to Rochefort's office in Hawaii. But neither set of VICTOR documents has been released as of the writing of this book.

The *I-10* transmission demonstrates the wide disregard of radio silence by Japan's navy. A captured Japanese communication document obtained in 1944 by the Pacific Strategic Intelligence Section is the source. According to the translation by PSIS, the broadcast reporting the loss of the scout plane was transmitted by the sub on December 4, but gave no communication details. Confirmation of the broadcast can be attributed to the commander of the Japanese submarine fleet, Vice Admiral Mitsumi Shimizu, who used the radio call sign FU NE 44 to contact Tokyo, according to Station H records. Admiral Shimizu, who at the time was aboard his flagship in the Marshall Islands at Jaluit Atoll, used the UTU long-distance daytime frequency of 16,620 kilocycles. His message was intercepted by Stanley Gramblin, Radioman Second Class, at 2:59 P.M. Wednesday, December 3, at Station H in Hawaii. There is no mention of the *I-10* broadcast in Rochefort's Communication Summary presented to Kimmel on December 4 or 5. Nor was Gramblin's intercept found in President Carter's release. [26]

Not all of the information available to the intelligence community was mysterious or subtle. Contrary to cryptologist Dyer's assertions, Japanese naval messages did confirm that war was near. Two such messages were on Dyer's desk or inside the HYPO office on December 6, Hawaii Time. Vice Admiral Shigeyoshi Inoue, commander of the Fourth Fleet in the Central Pacific, informed his forces by radio that a declaration of war was imminent. His radio message was intercepted by Henry F. Garstka at Station H at 8:40 P.M. on Friday, December 5, and included in Kisner's bundle, which was given to Dyer at 1:00 P.M. the next day, but was never delivered to Admiral Kimmel. According to Garstka's intercept, Inoue sent the war message as high-precedence information to ten of his Central Pacific commands including the Maizuru Special Landing Force, an amphibious unit of Japanese marines scheduled to invade and seize Wake Island. A 1946 English translation of the intercept indicates that it was encoded in JN-25-B. But in 1941 there was no such American or Japanese code designator. Verification of the code system is impossible because of American censorship of Garstka's original documents.[27]

Inoue began:

A SPECIAL MESSAGE ON THE OCCASION OF THE DECLARATION OF WAR, TO ALL UNDER MY COMMAND.

About two hours later, Inoue repeated the war declaration dispatch. Again it was intercepted in Hawaii by a different operator, LF, and included in the Kisner intelligence bundle delivered to Dyer.[28]

Most Japanese naval intercepts in President Carter's 1979 release contain interception details, but not Inoue's war message. Two omissions—which appear deliberate—wipe out the intercept's link to Hawaii before the attack: (1) There is no record that the message was intercepted at Station H, and (2) the initials of the intercept operator are missing. Without these two details for guidance, the Pearl Harbor investigators had no way to learn that Inoue's war declaration dispatch was intercepted in Hawaii. The author learned the intercept details from Garstka's radio log after it was declassified in January 1995.

Another radio message, issued jointly by Admiral Yamamoto and Emperor Hirohito, announced Japanese war intentions during the early morning hours of Saturday, December 6, Hawaii Time. Similar to the Inoue dispatch, it was intercepted in Hawaii but never delivered to Kimmel. It was dispatched in two parts, twenty-four hours prior to the Hawaii attack, and directly links Emperor Hirohito with the Japanese war moves. An English version of the message, released by President Carter in 1979, lists the intercept date as December 7, 1941—but that date is per Tokyo Time. American censors have not released the original two parts nor disclosed whether the messages are in code or in plain language.

The true intercept details of the Hirohito–Yamamoto dispatch can be found in the Station H logs. Emperor Hirohito issued an Imperial Rescript, which was transmitted to the Combined Fleet, urging the officers and men to "annihilate the enemy." Admiral Yamamoto told the Combined Fleet that he received the Rescript from the Emperor on Tuesday, December 2 (Hawaii Time), and was passing it on to every officer and man "prior to declaration of war." True to his word, Yamamoto set the broadcast release time of the Rescript at midnight, December 7, Tokyo Time, about twenty-four hours before the war's scheduled start. (Midnight Tokyo Time on December 7 was 4:30 A.M. on Saturday, December 6, in Hawaii.) Due to a mix-up his chief of staff, Rear Admiral Matome Ugaki, authorized the first broadcast two hours early, at 2:45 A.M. Hawaii Time.[29] It was transmitted throughout the Pacific to Japanese units. The cruiser *Aoba* confirmed receiving the message on December 7, Tokyo Time, while anchored in the Bonin Islands.[30]

Radio operators at Station H intercepted the Hirohito–Yamamoto messages directly off the naval airwaves during the five-hour period. Admiral Ugaki's premature broadcast was obtained by operator Maynard Albertson, a Radioman Second Class. Two hours later, at 4:45 A.M. on December 6, Hawaii Time, Yamamoto took over the airwaves and repeated the dispatches to the Combined Fleet and the carriers of the First Air Fleet.

By 8:30 A.M. on December 6, Hawaii Time, seven duplicates of the Hirohito–Yamamoto message had been intercepted and transcribed at Station H in Hawaii by Albertson and his relief, Radioman Third Class Jesse Randle. The four that Albertson intercepted entered America's communication pipeline around 9:00 A.M. when they were turned in to Kisner. Randle's intercepts (repeats of Albertson's) didn't enter the pipeline until the following morning, at the height of the attack.

As is the case with a huge amount of intercepts and documents still sequestered by Secret classification, the Defense Department continues to deny access to the seven Hirohito–Yamamoto messages. Only the one English version with the misleading December 7 date has been publicly released. None of the seven message sheets prepared by Albertson and Randle at Station H before the attack have been declassified.[31]

By late morning on December 6, Hawaii Time, Captain Homer Kisner had finished his analysis of the intercepts, including Albertson's report of Hirohito's declaration of war, and prepared a two-page report which warned that Japan's navy was on a wartime footing. Kisner accurately identified three areas of potential hostile Japanese action: (1) massing of Japanese warships and aircraft of the Eleventh Air Fleet around the Philippines and Southeast Asia, (2) arrival of the Japanese submarine force, including its commander, at Jaluit in the Marshall Islands, and (3) two identical Tokyo naval broadcasts that were aimed at ships a great distance from Japan.

Kisner did not mention any of the Japanese carriers in the report. Asked why by the author in 1988, Kisner said his policy was to stick with verified communication data of the carriers. His last verification took place on December 2 before Pearl Harbor and involved the three carriers associated with the invasion forces heading for Southeast Asia. That estimate held until new information came over the airwaves. As for the six carriers of the First Air Fleet, Kisner said he placed them operating with Destroyer Squadron One and Cruiser Division Eight on November 20, and since he had no contradictory evidence, left them there as he prepared his report on the morning of December 6.[32]

Kisner grasped the full impact of Japan's communication procedures disclosed in the overnight naval broadcasts. After completing his analysis about noon on December 6, he prepared his daily written report. He fully expected that what turned out as his last peacetime report would be delivered to Admiral Kimmel. It included this prophesy based on Japan's naval broadcasts: "The use of this method of delivering messages tends to keep unknown the positions of vessels afloat, and is probably one of the first steps toward placing the operations of the [Japanese] Navy on a war-time basis." In 1998, Kisner explained the "wartime" comment in a video interview: "From reading the messages between radio stations and ships which were between us and Tokyo, I came to the conclusion based on leaked words in the message that the Japanese were moving toward Pearl Harbor and were going to jump us." By "leaked words" Kisner meant that he and the radiocryptographers at H were able to understand enough of the coded Japanese naval text to make sense of the messages—but after fifty-seven years he could not recall the exact details. "One thing is for sure," he said. "That's the only time I ever forecast war with Japan."[33]

Following his usual custom, Kisner jumped into his pick-up truck and drove the intelligence bundle to Station HYPO. On the way he passed by the Japanese consulate, where spy Tadashi Morimura had just sent his message indicating that Pearl Harbor lay helpless before a surprise attack. When Kisner delivered his intelligence bundle to the basement cryptology center for the Pacific Fleet, he noted that Joseph Rochefort had left. In his place stood Lieutenant Commander Thomas Dyer, second in command at the station. Joseph Rochefort, exhausted by the week's work, had left HYPO at noon; he returned to his home in the Honolulu hills behind the University of Hawaii, about ten miles from Pearl Harbor, and took the rest of the weekend off.

Kisner left the intelligence bundle containing his war warning on Dyer's desk. The bundle went no further. Though it was on the top of the package, Dyer did not pass the war warning to Kimmel. Instead, the bundle of 900 intercepts, including the four "annihilate the enemy" and declaration-of-war messages originated by Emperor Hirohito and Admiral Yamamoto, remained untouched. Dyer later claimed in a letter to the author that only he and a yeoman staffed Station HYPO after the weekend liberty began at noon. The other twenty-six cryptographers and linguists were given the weekend off. "There were not enough warm bodies left," he wrote to the author in 1983.[34]

Granted the station was short of staff, it still seems clear that Dyer should have read Kisner's war warning and passed it on to Kimmel and the fleet. A phone call to the weekend duty officer of the fleet, reciting Kisner's war warning, might have changed the course of events. Reminded of his war warning in 1998, Kisner said that if he had to do it all over again he would have personally notified Kimmel's duty officer.

As Japanese warships headed eastward through the Pacific toward the Pacific Fleet, there were more disclosures of the Japanese fleet's destination, including one from the oil tanker HIJMS *Shiriya*. During the evening watch on Sunday, November 30, Hawaii Time, a radio operator at Station H intercepted a movement-report message from the *Shiriya*'s captain: "This ship is proceeding direct to a position 30-00 North, 154-20 East. Expect to arrive that point at 1800 on December 3. Thereafter, will proceed eastward along the 30-degree north latitude line at a speed of 7 knots." As every chart of the Pacific Ocean shows, the 30th degree of north latitude leads directly to Midway Island.[35]

The *Shiriya*'s original radio message is difficult to trace in American records. Though it was intercepted at Station H, it is impossible to identify the intercept operator. His initials have been removed from an English version released by President Carter's 1979 executive order. The code system used by the *Shiriya*'s captain is also blacked out, but since the radio dispatch is essentially a movement report it is presumably in Japan's naval-movement code system. Vice Admiral William "Bull" Halsey was not too far from the tanker. Halsey was aboard the USS *Enterprise,* about 500 miles south of the *Shiriya,* on December 3, delivering twelve fighter planes to Wake Island as a reinforcement for the Marine air group protecting the island. Though Halsey conducted aerial searches out to 300 miles from his Task Group, his scout planes missed the *Shiriya* and her destroyer escort.[36]

Following the radio exchange between the *Akagi* and her tankers on November 30, Station H operators began an intense search for more broadcasts. Radio transmissions to the tankers appear prominently in the log books of H starting December 3, Hawaii Time. Radio Tokyo attempted to contact the ships on the great-distance frequency but none responded. However, the powerful transmissions directed to the tankers' radio receivers carried throughout the Pacific Basin and were intercepted at Station SAIL near Seattle.

Tokyo's broadcast to the tankers disclosed important intelligence for Admiral Kimmel. According to Kisner, "We didn't need to fully decrypt messages. As long as we had the ship's identity, Japan's communication procedure to the tankers told the story. Stepping up the daytime radio frequencies from 11,000 kilocycles to above 16,000 kilocycles indicated a progressive eastern movement from Japan."[37]

The long-distance frequency showed that Japan's navy was refueling warships at sea—far from local oil reserves available in the Empire or at naval bases in the Formosa region. Earlier in November, the tankers had been linked with all six carriers of the First Air Fleet in radio dispatches. Kimmel was told that Kisner's operators placed the captain of the *Kyokuto Maru* (the flagship of the tankers) in conferences held aboard the carrier *Kaga.* Though it is obvious that the tankers practiced refueling at sea with the six flattops of Carrier Divisions One, Two, and Five in early November, the idea that the real thing was underway in early December north of Hawaii never occurred to Admiral Kimmel and his staff.

Over the weekend of November 28–30 diplomatic negotiations between America and Japan collapsed when the United States presented a calculated ten-point proposal that called for settling relations. Japan, according to Rochefort, was backed into a corner with no place to go—a situation forecast by Arthur McCollum fourteen months earlier. In Hawaii, Rochefort recognized Japan's dilemma. "Anyone who knew anything about the Japanese or things Japanese would have said that when we sent the November 26 letter you better run up the red flag. I believe sincerely that the November 26 message was an actual ultimatum the Japanese could not accept and their only alternative was to go to war."[38]

The American proposal insisted that Japan renounce the war with China, renounce their Tripartite Pact with Germany and Italy, and renounce the economic plan for Southeast Asia called the Greater East Asia Co-Prosperity Sphere. Secretary of State Cordell Hull presented the proposal to Ambassador Nomura late in the afternoon of November 26. It contained ten points that Hull called a *modus vivendi* (temporary agreement).[39] Two of the points angered Japan: point 3, "The Government of Japan will withdraw all military, naval, air and police forces from China and from Indo-China," and point 4, "The Government of the United States and the Government of Japan will not support—militarily, politically, economically—any government or regime in China other than the National Government of the Republic of China with the capital temporarily at Chungking." FDR held views similar to Rochefort's on Japan's reaction. In a handwritten note to Hull, the President said he regarded the proposal as fair but did not believe that Japan would agree. "I am not very hopeful and we must all be prepared for real trouble, possibly soon."[40]

From Japan's point of view, renouncing the war in China was impossible. It would have turned the nation's back on hundreds of thousands of Japanese military personnel who had been killed or wounded in the four years of fighting there. To abandon either the Tripartite Pact or the Greater East Asia Co-Prosperity Sphere would have been equally difficult for Japan. Japanese officials felt that their nation's survival depended upon access to the natural resources of Southeast Asia. And her only governmental friends in the world were Germany and Italy.

Emperor Hirohito and his council of advisors, the Liaison Conference, responded to the ultimatum by giving the go-ahead to Admiral Yamamoto: start the war on Monday, December 8, 1941—Tokyo Time. Yamamoto then sent a message using a prearranged phrase to the Combined Fleet. According to American sources and most Japanese accounts the phrase was broadcast in plain Japanese in the *katakana* naval syllabary. It read:

NIITAKA YAMA NOBORE, 1208.

In English:

CLIMB MOUNT NIITAKA, 1208 REPEAT 1208.[41]

At 1:30 A.M. on December 2, the message reached Hawaii. One of Kisner's operators at Station H, Joseph Christie Howard,[42] intercepted the order. He had started his midnight watch and had been on intercept duty ninety minutes when he heard the familiar dot-dash of Japan's navy *kana* on his earphones. Like most of the bachelor radiocryptographers, Howard lived on the base of Station H in a large open-porch barracks and walked to the radio shack—the operations center. He transcribed the message on his code typewriter, entered it in the log book, and put it in the intelligence pipeline. But in the next step of the pipeline, deceit took over. According to Edwin Layton, Hawaii never received the NIITAKA transmission. He developed four different stories that implied that the message was never intercepted or received in Hawaii.[43]

But the stories were flawed, for the message was intercepted by Joseph Howard at Station H. For 58 years Howard's account of intercepting Yamamoto's war start message never became public. Howard never testified before any Pearl Harbor investigation, including the Thurmond-Spence inquiry of 1995. During most of Layton's postwar lifetime, the Navy intercept records of Station H remained in locked vaults, classified TOP SECRET CODEWORD, unavailable to the public. Layton certainly had reason to believe that the intercepts would never be declassified and would never be used to contradict the assertions he made about the NIITAKA messages. Most of all no one could foresee that Joseph Howard would outlive Layton. But Edwin Layton died on April 12, 1984. And as this book goes to press in 1999, Howard is alive and well and living in Kent, Washington.[44]

In truth, the message was intercepted by three Navy listening posts—on Corregidor, Guam, and Hawaii—and was available by December 3 Hawaii Time for delivery to Admiral Hart and General MacArthur in

Manila, Admiral Kimmel and General Short in Hawaii, and President Roosevelt's military staff in Washington. But there is no record indicating that any of the officials saw the intercept. None of the Pearl Harbor investigations followed the paper trail of the NIITAKA dispatch that led from Stations CAST, HYPO, or BAKER on Guam.

Japanese naval historians are split on the broadcast details of the CLIMB NIITAKA message. Two authoritative Japanese historians say the message was transmitted in plain language, while Yamamoto's biographer, Hiroyuki Agawa, writes, "The message was encoded syllable by syllable using the five-digit, random numbers code."[45]

President Carter first released an English-language version of the infamous intercept in 1979. The original American interception documents that provide the complete details of the text have not been declassified by the United States. The original Japanese intercept, obtained by Joseph Christie Howard, produced at least two official Navy documents on $8^1/_2 \times 11$ paper. The Navy has censored Howard and his original records. Though he was America's expert witness to the CLIMB NIITAKA message, he never testified before any Pearl Harbor investigation.[46]

Beginning in 1988, the author filed FOIA requests with the Navy, the National Security Agency (NSA), and the National Archives asking to examine Howard's original documents.[47] Nothing was released. Instead, three officials supervised a ten-year blackout and denied the author access. From 1988 to 1997, FOIA appeals were made to NSA officials including Vice Admirals William Studemann, John McConnell, and the Navy's communications intelligence head, Rear Admiral Thomas Stevens. All replied with a firm No.

The last person believed to have seen the records was Homer Kisner, the traffic chief at Station H. Asked by the author whether he or Howard could translate the plain-language Japanese *kana* of the NIITAKA message, Kisner said he could not recall Howard's language skills because he had been aboard for only a few months. But the more senior personnel could read simple Japanese *kana* text. "All of us who had been in the organization since the mid-thirties knew the word *yama* meant mountain." Did he understand the message's significance? He said he could not recall but added, "The original intercept and working papers of the message would disclose my reaction." Did he believe the message was withheld from Ad-

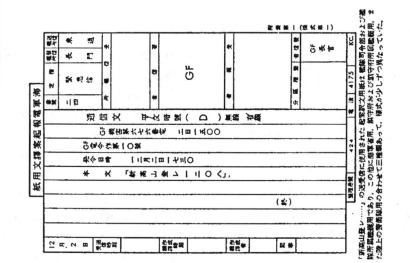

Both versions of the NIITAKA message released by the United States (left) and Japan (right) are suspect. The US version asserts that Tokyo Radio, HA FU 6, transmitted the message on 4155 kilocycles and used Yamamoto's personal radio call sign YO WI ØØ. Japan's version appears to be a postwar reconstruction and contradicts Joseph Howard's version by claiming the frequency was 4175 kilocycles. Neither version clarifies whether the original transmission is in plain Japanese. Japanese translators at the University of California, Berkeley, could not find any radio-call signs listed in Japan's version.

Source: USA=SRN #115376 in RG 457, Archives II; Japan, Miyauchi p. 11.

221

miral Kimmel? "I have no way of determining what happened to the message once I delivered it to HYPO. Our organization's primary purpose was to provide information to the admiral, not withhold."[48]

Since none of the original documents were presented to the congressional investigations, no official determination has been made whether the message is in plain Japanese. If Japanese historians are correct, Yamamoto chose his phrase from the "hidden-word" code book devised by Japan's naval cryptographers, not the more sophisticated Code Book D, which used a five-number system to encode messages. The hidden-word code is from Code Book A, which contained scores of phrases with hidden meanings.

Words with hidden meanings might intrigue Japanese scholars but they are a disaster when used for communications intelligence. Even a relatively inexperienced communication intelligence specialist could discern their meaning—and did. When the English version of the message was prepared (but never introduced into evidence) for Congress in 1945, a cryptographer whose Navy initials are RK interpreted the meaning of NIITAKA YAMA NOBORE, 1208. RK wrote: "This was undoubtedly the prearranged signal for specifying the date for opening hostilities. However, the significance of the phrase is interesting in that it is so appropriately used in this connection. Niitaka Yama is the highest mountain in the Japanese Empire. To climb Niitaka Yama is to accomplish one of the greatest feats—in other words, undertake the task (for carrying out assigned operations). 1208 signifies the 12 month, 8th day, Item time."[49]

Howard used his Elliott-Underwood code typewriter to convert the Japanese naval *kana* dot-dash to message text. He spent about five minutes typing the short message, finished his shift about 8:00 A.M., and filed his logs and message sheets with watch supervisor Elliott Okins.[50]

Howard intercepted at least eight Japanese naval messages, including the NIITAKA dispatch, during his shift. Two messages involved the aircraft carrier *Kasuga Maru* (a.k.a. HIJMS *Taiyo*), Carrier Division Four, and Air Flotilla Twenty-Two, the powerful land-based navy air force that sank Britain's HMS *Prince of Wales* and HMS *Repulse* during the first week of hostilities. Okins analyzed Howard's intercepts but did not include the CLIMB NIITAKA dispatch or those involving the *Kasuga Maru* and Carrier Division Four in his report to Kisner.[51]

After he received Okins' analysis at about 8:30 A.M., Kisner prepared his Daily Chronology for December 2. He noted the Carrier Division Four report but failed to mention the *Kasuga Maru* and the remarkable CLIMB NIITAKA dispatch. Kisner then took the intercepts gathered by Howard and other radio operators to Rochefort's office. His intelligence bundle contained radio direction finder and code movement reports of the Japanese fleet. About 1000 intercepts were in the bundle, representing reports from the previous twenty-four hours. Kisner believes that Rochefort would have spotted Yamamoto's NIITAKA message and recognized the importance. "He was an expert Japanese translator and was assisted by four other language officers attached to HYPO," Kisner told the author.

Rochefort and his staff distilled the bundle into the Daily Communication Intelligence Summary and delivered it to Admiral Kimmel for his scheduled 8:00 A.M. briefing by Edwin Layton on December 3. The Summary's contents had nothing to say about the NIITAKA dispatch or Howard's intercepts of the carrier *Kasuga Maru* and Carrier Division Four, whose mission was to attack American bases in the Philippines. Under the heading "CARRIERS," Rochefort wrote, "Almost a complete blank of information on the Carriers today. Lack of identification has somewhat promoted this lack of information. However, since over two hundred service calls have been partially identified since the change on the first of December and not one carrier call is at a low ebb."[52]

Admiral Thomas Hart, the Asiatic Fleet commander, saw decoded and translated copies of most intercepts produced at Station CAST. On orders from Washington, Hart normally shared them with General MacArthur.[53] Circumstances suggest that Hart learned of the message—for speedy military action in the Philippines followed soon after NIITAKA hit the airwaves. Hart cleared all his warships from Manila Bay on December 3 (Manila Time) and sent them south to Dutch naval bases. MacArthur ordered his construction engineers to enlarge an airstrip used by the Del Monte pineapple plantation on Mindanao Island in the southern Philippines for use by B-17 bombers.[54]

The evidence available today is plentiful, but circumstantial. Until the Navy comes clean, the true fate of the NIITAKA message will remain a mystery.

Captain Charles Horatio McMorris, Kimmel's war plans officer, assured the admiral that there wasn't a chance of a Japanese air raid on

Pearl Harbor: "The admiral asked me when I thought there would be an attack on Pearl Harbor by air and I said, Never." [55]

Was Kimmel convinced by McMorris' answer? On December 5, he had McMorris draw up a secret action plan for the fleet in case war broke out within the next forty-eight hours. McMorris prepared twelve war-action recommendations that essentially kept the fleet's aircraft carriers, *Enterprise* and *Lexington*, together with their escorts of six cruisers and thirteen destroyers, out of Pearl Harbor. The third carrier, *Saratoga*, was held on the West Coast of California. Then, after approving the weekend war-action plan, Kimmel returned to a peacetime routine. He accepted a Saturday-night invitation to a luau at the Halekulani Hotel on Waikiki beach and scheduled a round of golf with General Short for Sunday morning, December 7.

CHAPTER 14

THIS MEANS
WAR

CBS RADIO BUREAU

SINGAPORE

DECEMBER 6, 1941, HAWAII TIME

ADMIRAL HUSBAND KIMMEL MIGHT NOT HAVE GONE TO THE LUAU AND might have canceled his golf game if he had heard Cecil Brown's radio broadcast from Singapore: "The British military is prepared for a Japanese surprise move over the weekend. Soldiers and sailors have been recalled to their barracks and ships." Brown reported that American reconnaissance planes had sighted a strong force of Japanese warships and troop transports heading for invasion beaches in central Malaya.[1]

But despite the many indications of an attack that had been received over the airwaves, Kimmel wasn't looking for carriers or anticipating a surprise move by Japan. Though he had seven aircraft in the air on local patrol, fifty-four of his long-range PBY scout planes were grounded.[2]

The paradox of the White House ordering Kimmel to stand aside, all the while denying him full access to Japanese communications intelligence, is further illustrated by another cryptographic channel that revealed Japanese war moves. Japan's military wasn't the only organization divulging secrets. On December 5, Japanese Foreign Ministry officials transmitted two messages which disclosed that war between Japan and America would start December 7. Stations US, CAST, and FIVE obtained two intercepts. They were in the Purple Code; interception of the messages went fine, but there's no evidence that Stations US and CAST forwarded the intercepts to Hawaii—even though both cryptographic centers knew the keys to Purple and decoded such messages in hours.

Neither message was decoded until after the attack. This was true of every Japanese military and diplomatic message obtained during the week of December 1–6, which stated that Hawaii was the target of a carrier attack, set the date for the war's start, or named the enemy as Britain and America.

The American policy of noninterference with Japan's first overt act of war can be further documented through four diplomatic intercepts that

---

[Secret]

From: Tokyo
To: Bangkok
December 6, 1941
Purple (Urgent)
(CA)
#852.

The (——)ᵃ day (X Day) decided by the ——ᵇ liaison conference on the *6th (?)*ᶜ is the 8th and the day on which the notice is to be given is the 7th (?) (Sunday). As soon as you have received this message, please reply to that effect.

Army 25881   Trans. 12/8/41 NR)

Translator's assumptions:
ᵃ "Proclamation" or "declaration."
ᵇ "Ambassadorial" or "China."
ᶜ This word is garbled and could be either the word "6th" or the word "November."

Source: PHPT 12, p. 247.

This is the Station CAST intercept that assigns a date to "X Day." It is the first of two Japanese Foreign Ministry messages in Purple Code dated December 5, 1941, Tokyo Time.

According to the intercept shown above, Foreign Minister Togo notified his Bangkok ambassador that "X Day" would be December 8 Tokyo Time. His message, sent in the Purple Code, was intercepted at Station CAST, but neither the C designator nor the time of interception was included in this document, presented to the Joint Congressional Investigating Committee in 1945–46. Cryptographers at CAST said they could decode Purple messages in one day or less but "trans" took two days, according to the notation above.[3]

```
                              [Secret]
From: Peking
To: Tokyo
5 December 1941
(Purple)
Cir #625—(Circular Number)   To be handled in government code.
   Re my secret military communication #262* of November 30th.
   1. Concurrent with opening war on Britain and America we have
considered Holland as a semi-belligerent and have exercised strict
surveillance over her consulates and prohibited all communication
between them and the enemy countries.
   2. Coincident with the beginning of the war against Britain and
America we have taken steps to prohibit the use of code messages
and the use of wireless by the Holland consulates.
   3. In case war breaks out with Holland we will take the same steps
toward that country that we have taken in the case of Britain and
America.
26108
JD-1: 7335                          (H) Navy Trans. 12–11–41 (AR)
*Not available.
```

Source: PHPT 12, p. 236.

The beginning of the war on Britain and America is plainly stated in this Purple message sent from Japan's minister in Peking to Tokyo. General Short's interception unit at Fort Shafter, Station FIVE, obtained this all-telling message on December 4, Hawaii Time. Congress was not told that this message was intercepted in Hawaii; neither was Short. The designator 5 has been omitted and AR [Army Radio] substituted. There is no explanation for why it took eight days for a "Navy trans." Both Army and Navy cryptographers commonly produced decodes of Purple Code intercepts for FDR within hours.

were obtained December 6 and 7, before the Pearl Harbor raid, and that reveal the speedy decryption service provided to President Roosevelt. Japan transmitted the messages in four parts over a twenty-four-hour period—a time frame that permitted American cryptographers ample opportunity for rapid decoding and translation. First Tokyo sent a "pilot" message, known as Part 1, to Ambassador Kichisaburo Nomura in Washington, which said that Japan would reply to nearly one year of diplomatic negotiations with America. The reply was arranged in two messages. Tokyo outlined the subject of both, saying Part 2 would contain thirteen parts and Part 3 would contain the final fourteenth part. Nomura was told that Part 4 would be dispatched last and would set the time of presentation of the reply to the United States.

Unknown to Japan, US Army and Navy cryptographers intercepted, decoded, and translated the four messages before they reached Ambassador Nomura. In essence, the four intercepts directed the ambassador to present a fourteen-part memorandum that severed Japanese relations with the United States government and set a presentation deadline of 1:00 P.M. EST for Sunday, December 7. Though the deadline message lacked specificity, Washington's senior military leaders realized that 1:00 P.M. corresponded to 7:30 A.M. in Hawaii and that some hostile action by Japan could occur then or shortly thereafter.

All four intercepted cablegrams were decoded, translated, and delivered promptly to President Roosevelt over a twelve-hour period starting at 9:30 P.M Saturday, December 6, and ending at 10:00 A.M. December 7. But for reasons that are difficult to accept, direct delivery of the messages to Army Chief of Staff General George Marshall was delayed for fifteen hours. During the 1945–46 Pearl Harbor investigation, Republicans would wonder aloud: was the delay deliberate, to forestall American military interference with Japan's attack?

Instead of picking up his scrambler telephone and tipping off General Short to the 1:00 P.M. deadline, Marshall sent the warning to Hawaii using a combination of Western Union and RCA, a slower method.[4] A bizarre paper trail follows the four intercepts from Tokyo to the Oval Study in the White House. It includes a later attempt to distance Pearl Harbor investigators from Marshall and the 1:00 P.M. deadline and involves coercion of a US Army colonel to alter his testimony. It even reaches to post-surrender Germany in 1945 when that colonel, Rufus Bratton, was flagged down on the Berlin Autobahn and persuaded to "modify" evidence against Marshall.

The first of Foreign Minister Togo's four orders, which preceded the 14-part message breaking off relations and declaring war, is known as the "pilot" message. It laid out Japan's plans for war notification. On December 5, Togo demanded that secrecy be maintained and messaged Nomura to be on the lookout for a fourteen-part memorandum that would be sent "tomorrow" (December 6, EST). Togo said that the last part of the message—the time of delivery to the Americans—would be sent later. In the meantime, Nomura was to prepare the memorandum "in nicely drafted form and make every preparation to present it to the Americans just as soon as you receive instructions."[5]

By 3:00 P.M. December 6 (EST), the first thirteen parts of Togo's war scenario notification were intercepted at Station SAIL and sent to Station US by teleprinter for decoding. Commander Laurance Safford, head of Station US, supervised the decryption and, to speed up decoding, sent six parts of the memo to the Army's cryptographic section in the adjoining Munitions Building. By about 4:00 P.M., with the Army's help, all thirteen parts had been converted to English except for minor garbles. Upon reading all thirteen parts, Safford knew war was coming; he notified the White House. He asked FDR's naval aide, Captain Beardall, to alert the President to expect delivery of very important intelligence that evening. Safford then worked out a delivery schedule with his principal Japanese translator and thirty-eight-year-old aide, Lieutenant Commander Alwin Kramer. The schedule called for delivery of the message to the White House and separate copies to go to Secretary of the Navy Frank Knox and other top naval officers. Kramer then took extraordinary steps to get the intercept to Roosevelt. He telephoned his wife at home and explained the emergency. She agreed to act as chauffeur and drive her courier husband on his delivery rounds. Mrs. Kramer pulled up to the gates of the White House at 9:00 P.M. Her husband jumped out, passed through the Secret Service checkpoint, and raced to the small basement office of the naval aide. Here he found Lieutenant Lester Schulz, who had been alerted to the delivery by Beardall.[6]

Schulz phoned the White House ushers' office and was told to come over, the President is expecting you. By 9:30 P.M. he was ushered into Roosevelt's Oval Study in the second-floor residential quarters. Schulz quickly opened the leather pouch and handed the secret documents to the commander-in-chief, pointing out that the set of messages was incomplete. Two more messages were expected from Japan: Part Fourteen and a delivery deadline. Schulz recognized Harry Hopkins, FDR's confidant and former secretary of commerce, pacing back and forth in the room.

The President spent about ten minutes reading all thirteen parts, according to Schulz's testimony before the Joint Congressional Investigations Committee. The long message conveying Japan's official reasons for making war charged America with obstructionist tactics aimed at Japan's economy and favoring the side of Chiang Kai-shek in the China War, and it alleged that the American government wanted to extend the war:

THE JAPANESE GOVERNMENT CANNOT TOLERATE THE PERPETUATION OF
SUCH A SITUATION SINCE IT DIRECTLY RUNS COUNTER TO JAPAN'S FUNDA-
MENTAL POLICY TO ENABLE ALL NATIONS TO EACH ENJOY ITS PROPER
PLACE IN THE WORLD.[7]

Schulz remembered that FDR finished the last page of the memorandum, turned to Hopkins, and pronounced the famous utterance: "This
means war." It was 9:45 P.M. Neither the President nor Hopkins discussed
Pearl Harbor as the Japanese target, nor did they mention any date for the
war's start. While he waited in the study, Schulz overheard Hopkins express the view that since war was going to come at the convenience of the
Japanese, it was too bad we couldn't strike the first blow to prevent our
being surprised. "The President nodded and then said, in effect, 'No, we
can't do that. We are a democracy and a peaceful people.' Then he raised
his voice, and this much I remember definitely. He said, 'But we have a
good record.' "[8]

Schulz said that FDR then picked up the telephone and tried to reach
Admiral Stark. Told that the admiral was attending a performance of the
Sigmund Romberg operetta *The Student Prince* at the National Theater,
Roosevelt decided to wait. "He did not want to cause public concern by
having the admiral paged inside the theater, for if he left suddenly it would
have been seen by the audience and cause undue alarm," Schulz testified.
Stark's hasty departure would have been reported by news media and
could have tipped off Tokyo that America anticipated hostile action.

At about 10:00 P.M., FDR handed the documents back to Schulz, who
then returned to his small office and gave them to the waiting Kramer. For
the next three hours, the Kramers traveled about the District of Columbia
and the Virginia suburbs of Alexandria and Arlington showing the top
brass the memorandum that Roosevelt had called a declaration of war. Except for the Kramers and President Roosevelt, Washington's senior military brass were all involved in social activities on Saturday night,
December 6. Admiral Stark, the Navy's operational boss, was at the theater and Secretary of the Navy Knox was entertaining officials of the
Chicago Daily News in his Wardman Park Hotel suite. The Kramers found
Captain Theodore Wilkinson, Director of Naval Intelligence, hosting a
gathering in his Arlington, Virginia, residence that included Captain John

Beardall and Brigadier General Sherman Miles, head of Army Intelligence. After showing the Japanese memorandum to a select few of Wilkinson's military guests, Kramer returned to Station US and placed the secret document in its safe. Lieutenant Commander Watts, the duty officer, told Kramer that the two crucial elements of the memorandum, the fourteenth part and the deadline instructions, had not yet been intercepted. Kramer then left for his home, assuring Watts he would return at 7:30 in the morning when Commander Arthur McCollum took over as duty officer.[9]

A few hours later, a highly unusual Japanese communication procedure caught the eye of intercept operators at Station SAIL. Just before midnight, Pacific Standard Time, Radio Tokyo, using Morse code, contacted RCA Wireless and Mackay Radio & Telegraph in San Francisco. The contact was in plain English and alerted both firms to expect two very important messages addressed to KOSHI (Minister) in Washington. Transmitting messages over the dual facilities was a rare procedure for Radio Tokyo and served as a special alarm to the intercept operators at SAIL. At five minutes past midnight, the Tokyo–San Francisco circuit sprang to life with the arrival of the delayed fourteenth part of Togo's memorandum. Then at 1:37 A.M. the final part of the message—the deadline—arrived. SAIL operators instantly intercepted the messages and verified that "VERY IMPORTANT"—in English—prefaced each. By 2:00 A.M. both messages were entered on the SAIL logs as intercepts 380 and 381 and sent by teleprinter to Station US in the nation's capital.

The time was about 5:00 A.M. in Washington and 11:30 P.M. Saturday night in Hawaii when watch officer Lieutenant Francis M. Brotherhood pulled the two messages off the printer. Brotherhood was part of the Navy's cryptographic team that had solved Japan's main Navy code, the 5-Num system. He was also adept at decoding the Purple machine's diplomatic code. He noted that both intercepts were in the Purple system. When he ran it through the machine, 380 turned out in English. "It was perfectly clear to me," Brotherhood said. "It was the missing part fourteen and I readied it for dissemination through the customary channels."

OBVIOUSLY IT IS THE INTENTION OF THE AMERICAN GOVERNMENT TO CONSPIRE WITH GREAT BRITAIN AND OTHER COUNTRIES TO OBSTRUCT JAPAN'S EFFORTS TOWARD THE ESTABLISHMENT OF PEACE THROUGH THE CRE-

ATION OF A NEW ORDER IN EAST ASIA, AND ESPECIALLY TO PRESERVE ANGLO AMERICAN RIGHTS AND INTERESTS BY KEEPING JAPAN AND CHINA AT WAR. THIS INTENTION HAS BEEN REVEALED CLEARLY DURING THE COURSE OF THE PRESENT NEGOTIATIONS. THUS, THE EARNEST HOPE OF THE JAPANESE GOVERNMENT TO ADJUST JAPANESE-AMERICAN RELATIONS AND TO PRESERVE AND PROMOTE PEACE OF THE PACIFIC THROUGH COOPERATION WITH THE AMERICAN GOVERNMENT HAS FINALLY BEEN LOST.

THE JAPANESE GOVERNMENT REGRETS TO HAVE TO NOTIFY HEREBY THE AMERICAN GOVERNMENT THAT IN VIEW OF THE ATTITUDE OF THE AMERICAN GOVERNMENT IT CANNOT BUT CONSIDER THAT IT IS IMPOSSIBLE TO REACH AN AGREEMENT THROUGH FURTHER NEGOTIATIONS.

Message 381 was in Japanese, so Brotherhood, who was not a translator, walked the intercept to the nearby Munitions Building, where Army translators were on duty. It was the deadline message:

VERY IMPORTANT. WILL THE AMBASSADOR PLEASE SUBMIT TO THE UNITED STATES GOVERNMENT (IF POSSIBLE THE SECRETARY OF STATE) OUR REPLY TO THE UNITED STATES AT 1:00 P.M. ON THE 7TH YOUR TIME.[10]

It was nearly seven o'clock in the morning and the end of Brotherhood's shift. Before going off duty, he placed the decoded and translated SAIL messages on the desk of Alwin Kramer, who Brotherhood knew was expected in at about 7:30 A.M. Now it was up to the "runner," Kramer, to get both messages into the hands of Roosevelt and his top military and diplomatic advisors. Kramer reported to his office at 7:30 promptly, picked up the two SAIL messages, and realized their import: Japan planned to end diplomatic relations with the United States and directed that the rupture notice be delivered at 1:00 P.M. local time, which was 7:30 A.M. in Hawaii. Kramer discussed the two intercepts with Commander Arthur McCollum, who had just arrived. Both realized the significance of the 7:30 A.M. time in the Pacific, but neither had authority to transmit any warnings. Only Stark or Marshall could issue war warnings. The time was now about 8:00 A.M. in Washington and 2:30 A.M. in Hawaii. After assuring himself that Army intelligence officials were aware of the 1:00 P.M. deadline, Lieutenant Commander Kramer set off to deliver both messages to the White House while McCollum took copies of the messages to Admiral Stark. The time was now about 9:30 A.M. EST. In Hawaiian waters,

Japan's First Air Fleet was speeding along the 157 degree meridian of longitude and nearing the Prokofiev Seamount. In two hours the carriers were scheduled to launch their first bombers.

The paper trail of the deadline message is fully documented in Navy files. It was intercepted in the early morning hours of Sunday and delivered to the White House by Commander Kramer at 10:00 A.M.—4:30 A.M. in Pearl Harbor. Instead of relying on his wife as chauffeur, Kramer ran the four blocks to the White House. There Captain Beardall, the naval aide, handed the message to Roosevelt in his bedroom. According to Beardall, the President read the intercept but made no comment on the 1:00 P.M. deadline. "I had no sense that he was alarmed," Beardall said.[11]

Even though the night before FDR had said that the earlier Japanese intercept "meant war," Navy officials in Washington continued to delay sending war warnings to the Pacific. After the curtain came down on *The Student Prince*, Stark returned home and about midnight discussed the memorandum with Roosevelt by telephone. According to Stark's account, Roosevelt stated that "our affairs with Japan were in a very critical condition" but did not suggest any action be taken. Stark went to sleep.[12]

Tracing the Army's delivery of the identical set of Foreign Minister Togo's intercepts during the weekend is labyrinthine. Evasive accounts from some of the Army's top generals of World War II contribute to the complexity. The trail is obscured by charges of intimidation, perjured testimony, coercion of witnesses, and obstruction of justice. Two of the most famous and respected American generals of World War II—General George C. Marshall and Lieutenant General Walter Bedell Smith—are involved. Controversy reached into the congressional investigation of 1945–46 when two congressmen verbally battled over whether or not changes in Army testimony involving the 1:00 P.M. message were coerced by "small-town police court tactics."

These charges and countercharges focused on the Army's "runner," Colonel Rufus Bratton, and whether he delivered Togo's four intercepted messages to General Marshall in a timely manner. Bratton's duties paralleled those of Kramer. He worked for Army Intelligence and distributed the secret intelligence reports to a select list that included Secretary of State

Cordell Hull and Marshall. Bratton never delivered intelligence messages to the White House; that was a Navy responsibility, by presidential edict.

Bratton said he obtained the first two messages—the pilot and the first thirteen parts—from Kramer at about 4:00 P.M. Saturday. He read and recognized their importance and placed them in two locked leather pouches, one for Marshall and the other for Secretary of State Hull. Then he began delivery, leaving the pouch intended for Marshall with the Secretary of the Army's General Staff, Colonel Walter Bedell Smith, who promised immediate delivery to the general's residence in Fort Myer, Virginia, about a ten-minute drive from the War Department. Between 9:00 and 10:00 P.M., Colonel Bratton reached the State Department and delivered the pouch to Hull's office, then went off duty.

The delivery intended for General Marshall was delayed fifteen hours and did not reach him until about 11:00 A.M. EST on December 7, when it appeared on his desk in the War Department. Japan's 1:00 P.M. deadline message was turned over to Bratton on Sunday morning around 9:00 A.M. Bratton, like his Navy counterpart, realized the significance of the time-frame and frantically tried to reach Marshall at his home. Told the general was out riding horseback, Bratton asked that an orderly be sent out to the bridle paths of Fort Myer to locate the Army chief and advise him of the emergency. More delay ensued. Finally, at about 10:00 A.M., Marshall returned Bratton's phone calls and learned of the emergency. Bratton offered to come immediately to Fort Myer. Marshall declined the offer and said he would drive directly to his office—a ten-minute drive.

Marshall didn't arrive in his office, however, until about 11:15, a 75-minute delay. The thirteen-part message was on the top of his desk. Marshall spent 30 minutes with it. Bratton repeatedly tried to interrupt Marshall and show him the 1:00 P.M. deadline message but was rebuffed. But by 11:45, Marshall apparently realized its significance, and wrote out a warning to the Army's Pacific commanders. He checked by telephone with Stark, who asked that naval commanders also be notified and offered the use of the powerful Navy radio stations to broadcast the message to the Pacific. Marshall declined the offer and sent this message to four Army commands:

JAPANESE ARE PRESENTING AT ONE P.M. EASTERN STANDARD TIME TODAY WHAT AMOUNTS TO AN ULTIMATUM ALSO THEY ARE UNDER ORDERS TO DE-

STROY THEIR CODE MACHINE IMMEDIATELY STOP JUST WHAT SIGNIFI-
CANCE THE HOUR SET MAY HAVE WE DO NOT KNOW BUT BE ON ALERT
ACCORDINGLY STOP INFORM NAVAL AUTHORITIES OF THIS COMMUNICA-
TION. /SS/ MARSHALL

At 11:52 A.M. in Washington and 6:22 A.M. in Hawaii, the Army's radio station WAR began transmitting Marshall's handwritten alert to the Caribbean Defense Command in Panama, General MacArthur in Manila, and the Western Defense Command in San Francisco. Last on the list was Hawaii, where at 12:17 P.M. [EST] WAR tried to contact General Short's command at Fort Shafter. The radio signals failed to reach from Washington to Hawaii, so the message to Short was sent via the Western Union land lines between Washington and San Francisco, then by RCA radio to Honolulu. The transmission delay has never been adequately explained. Just twelve minutes earlier, at 12:05 P.M., WAR had successfully relayed Marshall's alert to MacArthur in Manila through the Fort Shafter radio.

According to Bratton's testimony, he spent nearly three hours, from 9:00 to 11:45 on Sunday morning, December 7, attempting to convince Marshall to act on the emergency. This delay was investigated in 1944 by the principal Army inquiry into the Pearl Harbor disaster. Three Army generals determined that the delay began on Saturday night, December 6, and ended at eleven o'clock the next morning, a time lag of fifteen hours.[13]

Their investigation, authorized by Congress and called the Army Pearl Harbor Board, coincided with the fall 1944 presidential contest between Roosevelt and Thomas Dewey. After concluding their three-month investigation on October 6, 1944, the three generals issued a report that damaged the reputation of General Marshall. One finding concluded that Marshall failed in his communications with Short over the weekend of December 6–7. They found that "[Marshall failed] to get to General Short on the evening of December 6 and the early morning of December 7, the critical information indicating an almost immediate break with Japan, though there was ample time to have accomplished this."[14]

Marshall quickly sought to counter the charge and, with the approval of Henry Stimson, Secretary of War, dispatched an Army major on a 55,000-mile aerial journey throughout the European and Pacific war theaters to gather affidavits and testimony that contradicted Bratton's account. Hostilities were still raging over the entire globe, as Major [Later Lieutenant Colonel] Henry Clausen began the sixth Pearl Harbor investigation in March 1945.

Clausen, an Army reservist and a lawyer in civilian life, obtained affidavits from ten Army officers during 1945 who disputed Bratton's account of the evening of December 6, but with the caveat, "to the best of my memory." Most important was the sworn affidavit given by Lieutenant General Walter Bedell Smith, by then chief of staff to General Dwight Eisenhower. Smith confirmed that Bratton brought intercepts to him in a locked pouch on various occasions in the fall of 1941, but did not recall seeing him on the night of December 6. "To the best of my recollection, I left the office at around seven P.M. that night." Neither Smith nor the other nine officers actually denied Bratton's assertion that he dropped off the thirteen-part message for delivery to Marshall's residence at Smith's office that evening. Their affidavits contain the numerous qualifications easily recognized in military circles as passing the buck.[15]

In what might be the most bizarre episode in the Pearl Harbor raid's story, Henry Clausen confronted Rufus Bratton with the ten affidavits. Clausen traveled to Berlin after the German surrender, tailed Bratton's automobile, and flagged it to the shoulder of the Autobahn. As military vehicular traffic whizzed by, Clausen persuaded Bratton to "modify" his recollection concerning his intended delivery to General Marshall on December 6, 1941. Both then flew to the Hotel Prince of Wales in Paris, where the text of the modification was drawn up. Bratton then "made some statement to Colonel Clausen to the effect that in light of the evidence before me now it seems advisable for me to modify some of the statements that I gave before the Grunert Board" [the Army Pearl Harbor Board].

But despite Clausen's efforts, Bratton never changed his original testimony. The Army Board's assignment of failure to General Marshall stood. During the congressional investigation of 1945–46, Republicans and Democrats verbally clashed over whether Bratton's affidavit was coerced under pressure from America's top generals. Republican Congressman Frank Keefe of Wisconsin, in a quarrel with Democrat John Murphy of Pennsylvania, complained that "There have been so many changes of testimony relative to this matter, produced by the Clausen report, and testimony under oath in the Army and Navy reports and so on that I am having difficulty finding out what the fact is." [16]

Even after the countless American missteps in the early morning hours of December 7, there was still an opportunity to alert the American fleet to the raid. Between 6:50 A.M. and 7:15 A.M. Hawaii Time two Army radar operators detected the first wave of Japanese aircraft closing in on Oahu. Two large blips appeared on their radar screen during that twenty-five-minute period. As the blips became progressively larger, indicating an approach to Oahu, the operators became concerned and telephoned warnings to the Army's Aircraft Warning Service (AWS) at Fort Shafter. Neither operator identified the mass of aircraft as either friendly or hostile, just that "it was the largest group of planes I ever saw on the oscilloscope."

Privates Joseph Lockard and George Elliott focused the electronic beam of the radar's set directly north along the 157th meridian of longitude. They were part of an Army signal battalion that operated several radar sites in Hawaii. [17] Both privates were in their early twenties, had had at least four months of training in radar operations, and were considered experienced in this still-new technology. As they stared at the radarscope, images appeared indicating that large groups of aircraft were heading toward their vantage point on 700-foot Opana Hill, on Oahu's north shore near Kahuku Point. Both privates checked their instruments and antennae to be sure the radar beam was not reporting a flight of birds or false echoes off the water. Certain that their evaluation was correct, Elliott used a direct telephone link to the AWS center and reported the bearings. No interest was shown by the duty officer, Lieutenant Kermit Tyler, an Army fighter pilot who was learning basic intercept operations. It was his first day on the radar post and he knew nothing about AWS skills. Tyler told Elliott to "forget it." As the planes continued to move from 130 miles out and closed in on Oahu, Lockard got on the phone again, but he could only reach the switchboard operator, Private Joseph McDonald. McDonald was as experienced in radar technology as Elliott and Lockard, even though the Army only gave him a lowly private's rating. The threesome knew far more about radar operations than the very inexperienced Tyler. McDonald had been working at the AWS center since August, first installing the radar-plotting equipment, then manning the telephone switchboard. Like the other trained enlisted personnel, McDonald worked every day, including weekends.

Lockard pleaded to be connected with Tyler. He told McDonald, "It's the first time I have ever received anything like this. It's an awfully big flight. Large number of planes coming in from the north, three points east. I am really excited." Twice McDonald tried to get Tyler to answer the phone: "Sir, I would appreciate it very much if you would answer the phone."[18]

Tyler gave in about 7:20 A.M., and talked with Lockard, but dismissed his radar report as "nothing." In testimony he gave to the prime Army investigation of Pearl Harbor, McDonald said he had wanted to send a message to General Short and had showed it to Tyler. But the inexperienced Tyler would not allow the message to be sent; he closed down the center and released the radar crews for breakfast. Tyler believed the planes to be Army B-17 bombers en route to Hawaii from California. Earlier, as he drove to the AWS center for his four-to-eight-o'clock shift, Tyler had heard traditional Hawaiian music on his car radio. He offered the less-than-compelling explanation that a bomber pilot friend had told him that whenever Hawaiian music was played on the radio during the early morning hours it meant that flights of bombers were due to arrive from the mainland. Tyler said he thought the pilots used the music as a directional guide to Hawaii.[19]

Lieutenant General Short had acted on the November 27 orders from Washington directing that he establish reconnaissance operations and had directed that the Army radar detection search start two hours before sunrise and continue until 11:00 A.M. daily. He specifically stated that the operation was to include Sundays and holidays. He added an order that "all radar reports of aircraft involved with carriers come directly to me and keep the Commanding General and all interested staff officers informed regarding the enemy situation."[20]

Five Army radar stations were placed in operation by the order, three on Oahu and two on Kauai. All five aimed their radar beams toward the North Pacific. General Short said his staff decided that the most dangerous time for hostile action was the two hours before dawn.[21] Thirty men, headed by an Army major and assisted by a Navy and an Air Corps officer, were detailed to the control center during the danger period. Then for the remainder of the morning a training schedule went into effect.

When Tyler arrived at the center at 4:00 A.M. he found seven or eight enlisted men whose job entailed plotting radar reports on a large map of the Hawaiian Islands. There was no Army major to be seen. None of the promised Army, Navy, or Air Corps controllers were there either. Tyler was the only officer present.[22] None of the others showed up until after the attack was in progress. Later, the commanding officer of the radar unit, Major Kenneth Berquist, testified that he was "not alert" that morning and not on duty at the time of the attack.[23] He never faced disciplinary action by Short. According to Tyler, there was no radar activity reported to him until about 6:10 A.M. when a radar station on Kauai reported several aircraft flying around Oahu (probably the scout planes from the *Tone* and the *Chikuma*). Radar was still in its infancy and there was no way to distinguish enemy from friendly aircraft. Tyler assumed that all radar reports were friendly and took no action. Besides, he didn't know whom to call in an emergency.

When he heard the full details of the Opana Hill radar site debacle in 1944, Lieutenant General George Grunert, president of the Army's Pearl Harbor investigating board, said the entire organization was faulty, its instruction faulty, and lacked common sense and reasoning. "There was nobody to do the work," Grunert said. "The Navy liaison man wasn't there, then at seven A.M. everybody disappeared except the telephone operator." Grunert summed up the Opana situation: "It seems all cock-eyed to me—and that, on the record."[24]

The confusion in the air was mirrored by pandemonium on the water. During the early morning hours of December 7, crewmen of a minesweeper, USS *Condor*, sighted the periscope and conning tower of a Japanese submarine about one and three quarters miles off the Pearl Harbor entrance. At 3:42 A.M., a fluorescent wake near the *Condor's* port bow caught the attention of Ensign Russell McCloy. He focused his binoculars on the wake and discovered that it was caused by a periscope that was moving at about nine knots and stirring the waters to a brilliant glow. On closer examination, McCloy detected a conning tower of a partially submerged submarine. Two crewmen standing watch alongside him confirmed the sighting and realized it was not a US sub; they were forbidden to be submerged in the entrance channel and adjacent waters, which were in a Defensive Sea Area, a ten-square-mile zone where submerged vessels were prohibited. Admiral Kimmel had previously issued standing orders directing Navy vessels to attack submerged vessels in the zone.

When sighted, the sub was proceeding toward the Pearl Harbor entrance and was on a collision course with the *Condor*. Apparently it sighted the minesweeper and turned sharply to port. McCloy then sent a visual blinker light message to a destroyer, the USS *Ward*, patrolling the Defensive Zone: "Sighted submerged submarine on westerly course, speed nine knots." After receiving the visual signal, the *Ward* made a sonar search for about an hour and a half, without result. Meanwhile the *Condor* returned inside the Pearl Harbor anchorage after an antisubmarine net that stretched across the entrance was retracted. The entry remained opened, for another Navy vessel—the USS *Antares*, with a 500-ton steel barge in tow—was expected at about 6:00 A.M.[25]

During this period at least two Japanese midget submarines passed through the opened entrance and entered the Pacific Fleet's anchorage. They were part of a force of five midget submarines transported from Japan while strapped to the top decks of mother subs. Between 2:00 and 3:00 A.M. the mother subs took positions about ten miles west of the entrance channel and released the five midgets. According to Admiral Yamamoto's plan, the midgets were supposed to submerge and slip into the harbor prior to the carrier attack and contribute to the destruction of the Pacific Fleet.

When the *Ward*'s search proved fruitless, her captain, Lieutenant Commander William Outerbridge, contacted the *Condor* by radio for additional location data. In response, McCloy advised that the sub had been sighted in the channel. Their radio conversations took place over a fifteen-minute period and were conducted in plain language so that other warships and fleet command posts would be instantly alerted to submarine contacts. They followed orders issued by Admiral Kimmel a month earlier: "When American warships definitely know an enemy submarine is in the area then they are to broadcast the information in plain language in order to sound the alarm and alert the proper people and put them in a state of readiness." A twenty-four-hour communication watch was established and a special radio frequency was set aside so every Pacific Fleet unit could monitor submarine alerts.[26]

The fifteen-minute radio exchange between the *Condor* and the *Ward* did reach the Communication Watch Office of the Fourteenth Naval District. But the watch officer, Lieutenant Oliver Underkofler, was asleep and did not hear the loudspeaker report of the sub sighting.[27]

At 6:30 A.M. the *Antares*, a large supply vessel with a barge in tow, entered the channel, spotted a small submarine about 1500 yards off its starboard side, and asked the *Ward* to investigate. The *Ward* complied, and at 6:40 A.M. sighted a partially submerged submarine following the *Antares* into Pearl Harbor. A shouted call from the officer of the deck, "Captain, come up on deck!" reawakened Outerbridge, who had retired to his cabin after the *Condor*'s alert proved elusive. Outerbridge took one look at the object following the *Antares*, sounded general quarters, and at 6:45 opened fire on the sub, hitting its conning tower. Four depth charges dropped by the *Ward* finished off the sub, which sank in 1200 feet of water. Just to be sure, a PBY search plane, also guarding the Defensive Zone, dropped two more charges on the spot. Outerbridge saw black oil bubbling up on the water's surface. The first overt act by Japan, envisioned by McCollum in October 1940, had now taken place. The Empire had lost its first ship of war and two crew members to American defensive action.[28]

Outerbridge radioed an alert in plain language over the special frequency: "We have dropped depth charges upon subs operating in Defensive Sea Area." Believing his first message wasn't strong enough, he sent another: "We have attacked, fired upon, and dropped depth charges upon submarine operating in Defensive Sea Area." These plain-language messages woke up Underkofler, who rushed the *Ward*'s report to the senior duty officer for the Fourteenth Naval District, Lieutenant Commander Harold Kaminski. Now it was up to Kaminski to inform Rear Admiral Claude Bloch, the commandant of the Fourteenth District and the naval officer charged with protecting the fleet while at anchor in Hawaii. Kaminski received a busy signal when he dialed Bloch's aide. He then called Admiral Kimmel's office at the Submarine Base—a mile away—and reached the assistant duty officer, Lieutenant Commander F. L. Black.[29]

Kaminski did not, however, inform General Short, though there was an Army teleprinter connected to Fort Shafter for just such a purpose. Later, Kaminski said he didn't have time. The time was now 7:15 A.M. It was thirty-seven minutes before the first Japanese bomb would be dropped on American soil.

Black took the *Ward*'s report to Commander Vincent Murphy, the fleet duty officer, who had just awakened and was dressing. Acting with dispatch, Murphy telephoned Admiral Kimmel at his nearby residence and told him of the attack on the sub. "I'll be right down," Kimmel replied. The time was 7:35 A.M. Hawaii Time. Murphy's regular job was assistant war plans officer for Kimmel and he rotated the weekend duty officer position with other command officers.[30]

It is perhaps ironic that of all the commissioned naval officers in the United States, Vincent Murphy should end up being the decision maker for the Pacific Fleet, until Kimmel's arrival. Navy documents show that Murphy had accompanied Admiral Richardson to Washington during the week of October 7–12, 1940, when the admiral held the tumultuous meeting with Roosevelt, and also attended dinner conferences that week with senior naval officials including Chief of Naval Operations Harold Stark. Murphy had even been present at the naval conferences on American Pacific policy in November 1940. Murphy, in other words, was aware of the strategy to provoke an attack.

Chance had thrust Murphy into a decisive role at Zero Hour. Predictably, he would do little to upset the Washington policy that called for Japan to fire the first shot. Regardless, it was almost too late. By 8:00 A.M., the attack was in full force.

CHAPTER 15

THE ESCAPE WAS NORTH

ADMIRAL KIMMEL'S GOLF GAME WITH GENERAL SHORT ON SUNDAY, December 7, 1941, was set for 9:30 in the morning on the nine-hole Army course at Fort Shafter.[1] But the relaxation promised by the vistas of fairways and tees vanished with the 7:45 A.M. phone call from Commander Vincent Murphy, reporting the discovery of an enemy submarine in the Pearl Harbor entry channel. As Kimmel was preparing to leave his quarters bombs began to fall on his warships. The USS *Arizona* exploded in a giant fireball.[2] Kimmel witnessed the terrible destruction from the lanai of his home while he awaited his driver.

Most captains of the Pacific Fleet warships had remained on board during the weekend. Captain Charles "Savvy" Cooke, Jr., of the fleet's flagship, the USS *Pennsylvania*, slept aboard in his cabin. So did Captains Franklin Van Valkenburgh of the *Arizona*, Mervyn Bennion of the *West Virginia*,[3] and R. Bentham Simons of the light cruiser *Raleigh*. But not Rear Admiral Walter Anderson, who was in command of the seven battleships tied up to Ford Island and an eighth in dry dock. Anderson spent Saturday night, December 6, in his ocean-front residence on the Maui side of Diamond Head. His battleships bore the brunt of the raid: four were sunk, four others damaged. Loss of life aboard the *Arizona*, the flagship of Battleship Division One, was staggering. Between 80 and 90 percent of the personnel on board were killed, including Rear Admiral Isaac Kidd, commander of BATONE, and the ship's captain, Franklin Van Valkenburgh.

There were 2,476 Navy, Marine, Army, and civilian personnel killed in the Japanese attacks of December 7. The casualties stretched across the Pacific from Pearl Harbor to Wake Island and Guam. An additional 400,000 residents of the Hawaiian Islands were placed at risk. Japan seized 1,951 Americans as prisoners of war from the military and civilian populations on Guam and Wake, and many of those POWs died while in Japanese custody.[4]

Knocking out the warships of the US Pacific Fleet was Japan's primary aim in attacking Pearl Harbor. The six carriers of the First Air Fleet carried a total of 414 aircraft and launched 360 of them in two waves at Hawaii. Fifty-four Zero fighters were reserved for combat air patrol over the carriers in case American planes located the force and retaliated. There was no retaliation of the kind Japan expected. During the first attack wave, which lasted from 7:53 to 8:25 A.M., bombers, torpedo planes, and fighters crippled the American military forces on Oahu. First, Army, Navy, and Marine airfields were bombed and strafed, destroying most of the island's air defense. Commander Mitsuo Fuchida said that the air attack was designed to first immobilize the air bases on Oahu, then temporarily knock out the Pacific Fleet by "sinking battleships and aircraft carriers."[5] Enormous damage and a huge loss of life, delivered by 189 planes, occurred during the thirty-two minutes of the first wave. Battleship Row came under torpedo-plane assault at 7:55 A.M. From Hickam Field observers saw nine single-engine low-wing monoplanes aim at the seven battleships moored to quays on the Diamond Head side of Ford Island. Torpedoes, each equipped with a 1000-pound explosive charge, hit the battleships. One of the first was the USS *Oklahoma*, moored outboard of the USS *Maryland*, which took hits about 8:00 A.M. Huge gaps in her hull caused the warship to capsize at 8:32 A.M.

Battleship Row stood directly across the Pearl Harbor waters, about a mile from Admiral Kimmel's office. Had they been looking out on the scene, Kimmel's staff could have seen the crew of the *Maryland* prepare for 8:00 A.M. morning colors. On orders of their commanding officer, Captain D. C. Godwin, half the crew on board manned their battle stations, "just in case." High up in the foremast Seaman Lawrence McCutcheon, a seventeen-year-old native of Gridley, California, stood watch at his machine-gun post. At about 7:52 A.M. Lieutenant Jinichi Goto, leader of the *Akagi's* torpedo planes, led his pilots in the first attack on Battleship Row. Racing in from the Diamond Head side of Ford Island, Goto took aim at the *Oklahoma*. Low to the water—below the tops of the mainmasts of the two warships—he dropped his torpedo, then flew over both vessels firing his machine guns. At that instant a bullet tore into McCutcheon's heart, killing him instantly. His shipmates and family believe he was the first American killed that morning at Pearl Harbor.[6]

At 8:10 A.M. the forward powder magazine of the USS *Arizona* exploded, killing almost 90 percent of her crew. On the Ewa side of Ford Island, a separate torpedo attack hit the USS *Utah*, an old battleship converted for aerial gunnery practice. Her destruction was rapid. At 8:05 she took on a list of 40 degrees to port, then reached 80 degrees at 8:10. Two minutes later she capsized, trapping crew members in an air bubble that formed under the bottom plates. All along Battleship Row, Japanese torpedoes or bombs found their mark. The USS *California, Tennessee, West Virginia, Maryland,* and *Nevada* took hits. Of the capital ships, only the *Nevada* managed to get underway and head out through the channel to open seas. But she came under attack from the Japanese planes, and her captain beached the battleship at Waipio Point rather than risk foundering in the narrow channel. It was a fortunate choice, for a sinking in the channel would have bottled up all US Pacific Fleet warships inside Pearl Harbor.

Though the warships were in Condition X-Ray—a low state of alert—firing at the attackers began promptly at 7:55. Machine guns on the USS *Honolulu* focused on the attackers, and fired 2000 rounds of 30-caliber ammunition. The destroyer USS *Blue*, fully alert by 8:00 A.M., got underway and fired her main battery of five-inch AA guns, downing an attacker. A gunner on the *Blue*, listed in records as Smith, became famous as the inspiration for a World War II hit song, "Praise the Lord and Pass the Am-

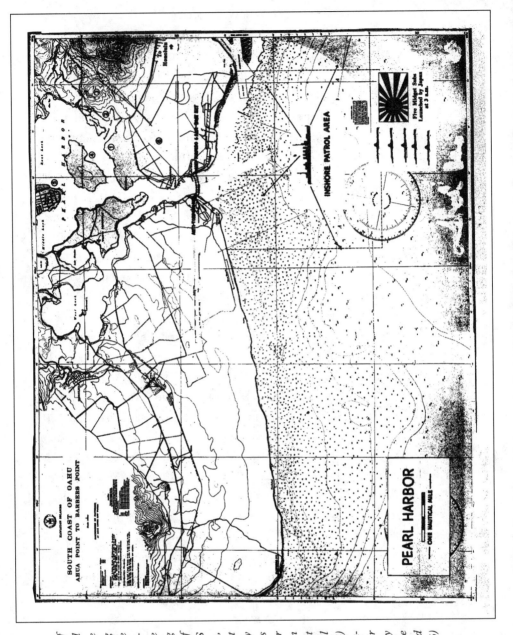

PEARL HARBOR
ONE NAUTICAL MILE ——

INSHORE PATROL AREA

Five Midget Subs
Launched by Japan
at 3 a.m.

SOUTH COAST OF OAHU
AHUA POINT TO BARBERS POINT

Japan's first overt act of war against the United States took place in the channel entrance leading to Pearl Harbor, when five midget submarines attempted to gain entrance to the anchorage during the early morning hours of December 7. The USS Ward, patrolling the area, sank one of the subs, but at least two gained entry when the antisub nets were left open (center right). Legend: (1) Station HYPO; (2) Pacific Fleet headquarters; (3) Admiral Kimmel's residence; (4) Battleship Row and adjacent Ford Island naval air station; (5) Pearl City peninsula, where Japanese spy Morimura watched fleet operations; and (6) Hickam Field.

munition," when his ammunition hoist became jammed: "Oh, Lord! Oh, Lord! Make this ammunition hoist work just this once." When the hoist was unjammed, gunners of the destroyer spotted a midget sub in the harbor, aimed the guns at the sub, and sank it.

Heroism ruled the morning throughout the Army, Navy, and Marine bases and the Pacific Fleet's warships. Acts of bravery and self-sacrifice by the sailors and soldiers of Oahu were awarded fifteen Congressional Medals of Honor, sixty Navy Crosses, five Distinguished Service Crosses, and sixty-five Silver Stars.

Rear Admiral Walter Anderson arrived on Battleship Row at about 9:00 A.M., as the second wave began. Though he had elected to spend Saturday night in the safety of his Diamond Head home, Anderson took charge, directed rescue efforts and damage control, and heaped praise on his officers and men: "I pay homage to the unusual exhibition of courage and magnificent fighting spirit by absolutely all the personnel of the battleships. Their conduct was in accord with the highest traditions of the service. Faced with the treacherous surprise attack on Pearl Harbor the battleship's ready guns opened fire at once." He said the anti-aircraft fire downed between fifteen and seventeen enemy planes. He praised the courageous crews' efforts to save the ships by fighting the large and menacing oil fires.[7]

Chief Boatswain's Mate Lewis W. Adkins of the *West Virginia* was among scores cited for heroism: "In charge of the after repair party, his leadership and heroic conduct while fighting the fires contributed much toward saving the ship from destruction. Throughout the attack he was in an exposed position and continued to fight the fires until they were brought under control."[8]

Uncommon bravery saved many lives. When the *Utah* capsized at 8:12 A.M., Fireman John Vaessen was trapped in the dynamo room, where he valiantly tried to keep the electricity flowing to the ship. As the ship began to roll over, Vaessen saw the lights dim, and then total darkness descended as he felt the battleship overturn. Trapped in an air bubble against the bottom of the hull—which was now facing skyward—Vaessen started banging on the steel. The tapping sound was heard by fellow crew members who had successfully abandoned ship and reached nearby Ford Island. Machinist S. A. Szymanski heard the tapped call for help, organized a rescue party, obtained a cutting torch, returned to the ship, and cut a hole in the bottom—where a grateful Vaessen climbed out to freedom.[9]

At 9:35 A.M. the Japanese ended the raid and began returning to their carriers. They left a heavy toll on Oahu: there were 2,273 Army and Navy dead, 1,119 wounded. Of the 101 warships in the anchorage, sixteen suffered major damage. Five were permanently out of World War II: *Utah, Oklahoma, Arizona, Cassin,* and *Downes.* The Army Air Force lost 96 planes and the Navy and Marine air bases lost 92.[10]

For Honolulu, the only American city ever subjected to an air raid, the human toll was equally heavy. The first civilian casualties were city firemen, called to Hickam Field in response to what they believed was a three-alarm fire: Captains John J. Carreiro and Thomas S. Macy, along with Hoseman Harry L. Pang, were killed and six other firemen were injured when their fire trucks arrived at Hickam and were hit in the second wave. Four of Honolulu's residential districts were hard hit—not by the Japanese, but by exploding five-inch shells fired from the US Navy's 232 anti-aircraft guns. According to Navy testimony given to Congress, 3,188 rounds of five-inch shells were fired at the attackers; many missed their marks and rained down on the streets of Honolulu. Very little city damage occurred during the first wave—probably because the five-inch guns were not yet manned. The Honolulu Fire Department received a call at 8:00 A.M. reporting a "bomb drop" on Hala Drive near the Bishop Museum. But as the Pacific Fleet warships gradually put their AA guns into action the toll mounted in the city's neighborhoods. Six hits were reported to the Fire Department during the forty minutes of the second wave—8:50 to 9:30 A.M.

But after the Japanese pilots had returned to their carriers the civilian toll increased. Fifteen civilians were killed and scores injured by fifteen shells (called "bombs" in 1941) between 9:35 A.M and 2:15 P.M. that afternoon. The worst was in an eight-block area surrounding McCully and South King Streets on the northern edge of Waikiki. Twelve people were killed, and homes and apartments were destroyed. Three unlucky civilian workers, rushing to their jobs at Pearl Harbor, died at 2:10 P.M. when a shell burst over their 1937 Packard sedan on Judd Street, near the Japanese consulate.[11]

Some historians have called the Japanese military strategy at Pearl Harbor brilliant. They cite the multifaceted plans: thirty full-size submarines with five midget subs poised to sink Pacific Fleet warships fleeing the anchorage from the air attack; the early Sunday morning timing when Hawaii's military was still in a peacetime mode. Japan's strategists shared a worldwide (but mistaken) belief that a nation's naval might could be destroyed or curtailed by sinking its battleships. Pearl Harbor's Battleship Row and its old dilapidated warships presented a mouth-watering target. But it was a major strategic mistake for the Empire. Japan's 360 warplanes should have concentrated on Pearl Harbor's massive oil stores of five million barrels and destroyed the industrial capacity of the Navy's dry docks, machine shops, and repair facilities. Oahu's electrical-supply grid was untouched. Had Japan destroyed the industrial base, the blow would have stunted American response in the Pacific, forced a retreat to the West Coast, and given the Japanese military another few months of offensive operations. By the Battle of Midway in June 1942, America had regained the offensive: repaired US warships, staged from the relatively undamaged Pearl Harbor naval base, sank four of the aircraft carriers that had attacked them six months earlier.

Once the Pearl Harbor raid was over, of course, the same large fleet that had attacked with such stunning success had to escape. Their chosen escape route was northward. Most of the 360 planes of Nagumo's First Air Fleet (which lost only 26) regrouped over Kaena Point at the northwest corner of Oahu and continued in that direction. Verification of this route came at midmorning during a spectacular twenty-minute dogfight when two of the US Navy's slowest airplanes shot down a speedy Japanese Zero fighter between Kaena Point and Kauai. It left a spiraling trail of smoke as it plunged into the waters off Kauai.

By 9:35 A.M., Japan had ended the attack. Admiral Nagumo moved his carrier fleet from the Prokofiev region toward the Mendelssohn Seamount, 200 miles northwest of Kauai. His planes followed their squadron leaders back north to their carriers. This large-scale movement of bombers and torpedo planes continued to be tracked by Army radar units as well as by Station H. Both intelligence facilities pinpointed the escape route. There was no doubt—the hostile aircraft came from, and escaped to, the north of Oahu.

Americans have never been given the full details of the First Air Fleet's escape to the north. However, bits and pieces of guarded testimony presented to various Pearl Harbor investigators between 1942 and 1946 show, when pieced together, that some American warplanes did chase after the First Air Fleet, and engaged Japanese planes in battle during the late morning and early afternoon of December 7. These dogfights extended over 150 miles of the North Pacific—from the Na Pali Coast of Kauai to near the Mendelssohn Seamount. Admiral Nagumo confirmed that the Pacific Fleet's planes pursued his force, but Admiral Kimmel never disclosed the full details of the pursuit—and missed a golden opportunity to establish himself as a forceful commander.[12]

Between 8:05 A.M. and noon, Station H radio operators and direction finder experts intercepted radio dispatches that clearly placed the First Air Fleet north of Oahu. The dispatches were originated by Nagumo, the carriers *Akagi, Kaga, Zuikaku, Hiryu,* and *Soryu,* and the battleships *Kirishima* and *Hiei.* First, Admiral Nagumo reported the successful attack to Tokyo at 8:05 A.M. Later, when a number of pilots became lost and couldn't find their way "home," the carriers broke radio silence and in plain language guided them north. Radioman First Class Donovan Chase, one of the operators at H, obtained the exact location of the carriers when the *Akagi*'s air officer talked over the radio and guided a lost pilot: "Head northwest and you will find us." Other carriers of the First Air Fleet repeated the directions to pilots unable to find their way home: "Head north." One pilot from the carrier *Kaga* radioed that his fuel would last ten minutes. Chase counted out the ten minutes then added a postscript to his log: "Outa gas I hope." Another *Kaga* pilot said flames were engulfing his plane and he planned to jump. Chase recorded these conversations in his radio log during the opening moments of the war. They are published here for the first time.[13]

The mass exodus of the Japanese planes registered on the radarscope at the US Army's Opana radar site. Again Army privates Joseph Lockard and George Elliott picked them up and tracked them on a northerly course headed for the general area of the Mendelssohn Seamount. According to

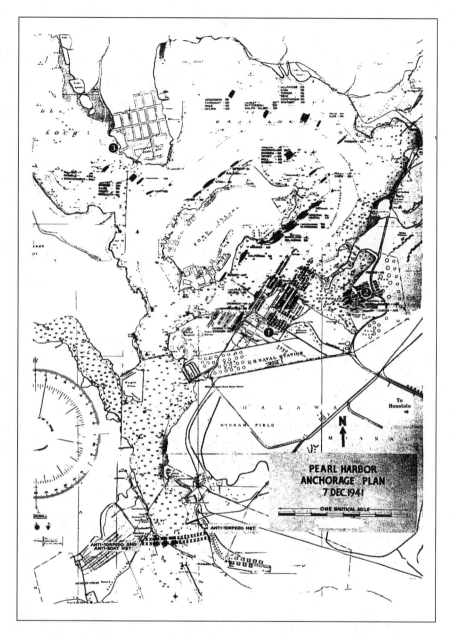

Source: General Short's papers, Hoover Archives, Stanford University, Stanford, California.

When the bombers, torpedo planes, and fighters of the First Air Fleet arrived over Pearl Harbor at 7:53 A.M. December 7, they found the warships of the Pacific Fleet neatly tied up to docks or buoys. Destroyers and light cruisers were anchored in East Loch (top); auxiliary vessels in Middle Loch [upper left]; the Pacific Fleet's flagship, USS Pennsylvania, along with other vessels were in overhaul berths in the Navy Yard (middle); seven other battleships were moored to Ford Island (center). Legend: (1) Station HYPO; (2) Pacific Fleet headquarters at the Submarine Base; (3) China Clipper base.

the Opana tracking chart, the planes appeared on the scope at 10:12 A.M. and went out of range at 10:39 A.M. when they were about 150 miles north of Oahu.[14] But as was the case three hours earlier, none of the north exodus reports were sent to General Short.

Japanese pilots continued to stagger back to their carrier flight decks throughout the late morning. But some pilots of the First Air Fleet ran into trouble. Two scout planes from the heavy cruiser USS *Northampton* encountered a straggler about 11:30 A.M. off the west coast of Kauai and, in a twenty-minute air battle, shot it out of the sky.[15]

On December 16, 1941, Admiral Kimmel was relieved of his command and demoted to rear admiral.

DESTROY ANYTHING IN WRITING

UNITED STATES CAPITOL

DECEMBER 1941

COMMANDER ARTHUR McCOLLUM'S PREDICTION OF OCTOBER 7, 1940, comes true throughout America on Monday, December 8, 1941. His Action F—keep the fleet in Hawaii—was one of the eight provocations that he said could lead to Japan committing an overt act of war, uniting America. And indeed unification was instant. Congress declared that a state of war existed with Japan, then three days later with Germany and Italy. There was one dissenter, Congresswoman Jeanette Rankin, who had also voted against United States participation in World War I. Young men ready to die for their country formed huge lines outside Army and Navy recruiting stations. Former isolationist leaders Henry Ford, Charles Lindbergh, and William Randolph Hearst joined the cry, "Remember Pearl Harbor!" Ford converted his auto factories to assembly lines for tanks. Lindbergh helped boost aircraft production and the Hearst papers championed the Administration's war efforts. America went from a peacetime economy to full war production virtually overnight. There was no military or moral limit to the

American resolve to destroy the Axis powers and win the war. But President Roosevelt sensed an underlying uneasiness stemming from Japan's devastating attack on Hawaii. The war was only ten days old when some congressional leaders, mostly Republicans, questioned why America's great military bastion in the Pacific had been unprepared. The *Chicago Tribune*, led by its publisher, Roosevelt-hater Colonel Robert McCormick, called for an independent inquiry that "can investigate in Washington." In Topeka, Kansas, *The Capital* suggested that the higher-ups in the War and Navy Departments should be investigated.[1]

On December 19, Republican leader Senator Robert Taft of Ohio sided with calls for an investigation: "Perhaps the fault at Hawaii was not entirely on the admirals and generals." A Democrat, Senator Tom Connally of Texas, while supportive of the Administration, said he was amazed and astounded by the attack and found its success "almost unbelievable." Senator Arthur Vandenberg (R., Michigan), one of the most powerful members of Congress, joined with the House Naval Affairs Committee and proposed a full inquiry into the Pearl Harbor raid. Vandenberg wrote to the President and recommended reestablishing the Committee to Conduct the War, modeled after a Congressional group that had functioned during the Civil War.[2]

Alarmed by the criticism leveled at the Administration and fearing that a congressional investigation would harm the war effort and provide political fodder for the 1942 elections, President Roosevelt sought a way to defuse the critics and called upon Supreme Court Justice Felix Frankfurter for advice.[3] Full disclosure of the pre–Pearl Harbor information—including McCollum's eight actions—would have compromised American codebreaking and disclosed the US success in solving the various Japanese cryptographic systems. Therefore the President headed off a proposed congressional inquiry by appointing a five-man board of inquiry, headed by Associate Justice Owen J. Roberts of the United States Supreme Court. Frankfurter endorsed Roberts as the most "forthright of men." But because of the need to maintain military secrecy the Roberts Commission was understandably unable to conduct a full examination or a public discussion of the Japanese naval intercepts. None of the US Navy's intercept operators testified or produced their radio logs and documents. Nothing was revealed about them.[4]

President Roosevelt approved the Roberts Commission's report on Saturday, January 24, 1942. It concluded that the attack was successful due to failures and errors of judgment by Admiral Kimmel and General Short. They were charged with dereliction of duty. At the same time the commission cleared General George Marshall and Admiral Harold Stark of any wrongdoing, saying they had fulfilled their command obligations. The 13,000-page report said that Japan's success "resulted largely from a sense of security due to the opinion prevalent in diplomatic, military and naval circles, and in the public press, that any immediate attack by Japan would be in the Far East." The United Press story, written by Joseph L. Myler,[5] received front-page play throughout the nation. Myler wrote of the report: "After thorough investigations in Washington and Hawaii, it told an amazing story of lack of preparation, arbitrary conclusions reached by Kimmel and Short in conflict with the advice from Washington."

Admiral James Richardson condemned the findings. "It is the most unfair, unjust, and deceptively dishonest document ever printed by the Government Printing Office. I cannot conceive of honorable men serving on the commission without greatest regret and deepest feeling of shame."[6] After the war ended in August 1945, Congress announced a comprehensive series of hearings intended to end all political speculation on Pearl Harbor. But in 1967, Max Freedman, the editor of Felix Frankfurter's correspondence, chided Washington: "To this day there is an obstinate suspicion in Congress, especially among those who sat on the investigating committees, that Congress never got the full story about Pearl Harbor."[7]

The key evidence of what really happened began to be concealed as early as December 11, 1941, only four days after the attack. The first step in the clean-up came from Rear Admiral Leigh Noyes, the Navy's Director of Communications. He instituted the fifty-four-year censorship policy that consigned the pre–Pearl Harbor Japanese military and diplomatic intercepts and the relevant directives to Navy vaults. "Destroy all notes or anything in writing," Noyes told a group of his subordinates on December 11.[8] Among the group was Commander Laurance Safford, head of Station US (appointed captain in January 1942). Though head of the Navy's cryptographic efforts, Safford reported to Noyes through Naval Communications, since it controlled all categories of service-involving communications. Safford implied that some destruction of records was carried out and added that he felt no shame or embarrassment in ordering his staff to destroy all unofficial notes.

At first Noyes denied ever issuing the destruction order, but later he admitted: "I may have instructed my subordinates to destroy personal memoranda. Nothing was said to destroy official records." Noyes was on shaky legal ground. Personal memoranda prepared in Navy offices by Navy personnel belong to the people of the United States if the files concern naval matters. They cannot be destroyed except by authority of Congress.

Noyes' destruction directive was issued just a few days before the formation of the presidential board of inquiries headed by Justice Roberts. His dictate set a policy that effectively excluded Japanese military intercepts from all Pearl Harbor investigations. Noyes said it was common practice to destroy "intercept stuff" after three or four months. However, some files escaped destruction. Every naval officer involved in the intercept and cryptographic operations (including those at outlying facilities) maintained a personal file at Station US for classified documents. The McCollum memorandum, for example, was discovered by the author in January 1995 in the personal classified file of Arthur McCollum.[9]

Two weeks after Japan surrendered in August 1945, the Navy blocked public access to the pre–Pearl Harbor intercepts by classifying the documents TOP SECRET. Even Congress was cut out of the intercept loop. The Navy's order was sweeping: it gagged the cryptographers and radio intercept operators who had obtained the Japanese fleet's radio messages during the fall of 1941. Fleet Admiral Ernest King oversaw the censorship. He threatened imprisonment and loss of Navy and veteran's benefits to any naval personnel who disclosed the success of the code-breaking. He prophesied that "writings of irresponsible people" would test the loyalty of all concerned. "The Navy Department does not intend to dignify any stories concerning successes in Ultra [code breaking] by official denials or confirmations. I repeat that it is most important that leaks and partial disclosures be not fortified or reinforced nor further discussion stimulated by additional statements of those who know the facts from the inside." King then reminded the code-breakers of the legal obligations embedded in their secrecy oath. The oath applied to all naval personnel, even those discharged: "The oath which you have taken must not be violated."[10]

When the congressional investigation into the Pearl Harbor attack began on November 15, 1945, Americans believed they would be given full details on breaking the Japanese code prior to the attack. Witnesses introduced intercepts into evidence and read decrypted messages to the senators and representatives of the Joint Committee. It was a total sham. None of the details involving the interception, decoding, or dissemination of the pre–Pearl Harbor Japanese naval messages saw the light of day. Only diplomatic messages were released. Republicans suspected a stranglehold but could not pierce King's gag order. Senator Owen Brewster (R., Maine) set off political fireworks when he was blocked from obtaining monitor records from the Navy's intercept stations. But all Brewster achieved was rhetoric; he never got testimony or records of the military intercepts.

In April 1995, at the urging of the Kimmel and Short families, the Senate and House of Representatives opened a miniprobe into the circumstances leading to Japan's attack.[11] Citing the fact that crucial Japanese intercept records had been denied to the Hawaiian commanders in 1941, both families sought to clear their loved ones' reputation. They asked Congress to posthumously restore Kimmel and Short to their 1941 ranks of Admiral and Lieutenant General. Senator Strom Thurmond, chairman of the Senate Armed Forces Committee, and Representative Floyd Spence, head of the House Armed Services Committee, conducted a one-day hearing and directed that the Pentagon conduct a thorough investigation. Thurmond asked John Deutsch, Deputy Secretary of Defense, for a speedy conclusion: "When I say speedy, though, I would not ask you to act until you feel you have completed all the investigation thoroughly and feel that you're ready to act." Deutsch replied: "Mr. Chairman, on behalf of the Secretary of Defense William Perry, myself, and Secretary of the Navy Dalton, you have my assurance that this matter will be examined without preconception, that the judgments will be made fair on the basis of fact and with justice, and that we will speedily arrive at the best judgment we can on this matter."

Steve Honigman, US Navy General Counsel, told Thurmond: "What I'd like to do is to state the official position of the Department today and that position is the following. In our view there are three principal reasons why Admiral Kimmel's rank should not be upgraded. The first, quite simply, is that the historical record does not establish convincingly that President Roosevelt, General Marshall, or others in Washington deliberately withheld information from Admiral Kimmel and General Short as part of a plan or a conspiracy to expose Pearl Harbor to attack in order to thrust America into the war." [12]

Thurmond then admonished the Pentagon to establish the truth and asked for "any information available anywhere that would help them [the families]." A seven-month investigation was then conducted by the Pentagon under the leadership of Undersecretary of Defense Edwin Dorn, who put together a team of civilians and military officers to thoroughly review the events leading to Pearl Harbor. The heart of their investigation centered on whether Hawaii was denied crucial intelligence.

On December 1, 1995, Dorn issued a 50-page report that rejected the petition of the Kimmel and Short families: "I cannot conclude that Admiral Kimmel and General Short were victims of unfair official actions and thus cannot conclude that the official remedy of advancement on the retired list is in order." Dorn said he agreed with conclusions drawn consistently over several investigations, that Admiral Kimmel and General Short committed errors of judgment. "As commanders, they were accountable." [13]

But Dorn's promised thorough review lacked crucial elements. His investigative team did not produce the Japanese naval intercepts, nor did they interview Captains Duane Whitlock and Homer Kisner, the US Navy's radio traffic experts in 1941. Dorn did not produce or reveal McCollum's memorandum listing eight actions that were allowed to proceed by President Roosevelt. Missing from Dorn's investigation was America's foremost expert on the Japanese naval intercepts, John Taylor, senior reseacher at Archives II. Taylor said neither Dorn nor his investigative team contacted him for documents. [14]

Why has it been so difficult to pry loose the truth of Pearl Harbor, this mystery that haunts American history? This book is certainly not the first time President Roosevelt's pre–Pearl Harbor strategy has been raised. Since September 1945, many authors and historians have expressed the belief that Roosevelt knew of the impending attack by the Japanese. What they didn't know—but is the heart of this book—was that a systematic plan had been in place long before Pearl Harbor that would climax with the attack.

As heinous as it seems to families and veterans of World War II, of which the author is one, the Pearl Harbor attack was, from the White House perspective, something that had to be endured in order to stop a greater evil—the Nazi invaders in Europe who had begun the Holocaust and were poised to invade England. There could be disagreement on whether the plan adopted was the right way to stop Hitler, but Roosevelt faced a terrible dilemma.

Despite his pleadings and persuasions, powerful isolationist forces prevented Roosevelt from getting into the European war. Roosevelt's advisors included American patriots such as General George Marshall, Rear Admiral Walter S. Anderson, and Commander Arthur H. McCollum who understood the need to arouse the United States from its isolationist position.

The wisdom and moral justification for the decision to provoke Japan into a bloody and terrible war that ultimately took millions of lives will be argued over for many years by people of good faith and from all political persuasions.

This book does not purport to resolve such dilemmas. What truths it uncovers from the distant past can only shed more light on a troubling time in our country's history.

The truth that has been told here does not diminish Franklin Delano Roosevelt's magnificent contributions to the American people. His legacy should not be tarnished by the truth. As with all American presidents, Roosevelt must be viewed in the total context of his administration, not just Pearl Harbor.

The real shame is on the stewards of government who have kept the truth under lock for fifty years. Had the facts uncovered in this book been known immediately after the war ended, and had Roosevelt explained his war strategies and tactics to the families who lost their sons at Pearl Harbor, how different American history might be viewed today. But President Roosevelt died in office on April 1945, four months before Japan surrendered. It may have been necessary for wartime security to withhold the truth about Pearl Harbor until the war ended, but to do so for more than half a century grossly distorted the world's view of American history.

Over that time, most of the US military leaders, cryptographers, and intercept operators who were either participants or witnesses to events leading to Pearl Harbor have died or their memories have faded with age. Because they were never called to testify for their country, we have been denied a full account of what happened from their perspectives.

To those heretofore silent survivors who are represented in this book, we owe an immeasurable debt.

AFTERWORD TO THE
PAPERBACK EDITION

In MAY 2000, TOO LATE TO INCLUDE THEM IN THE INITIAL HARDCOVER publication of *Day of Deceit*, the author unearthed over four thousand communications intelligence documents—all of them never before examined—that provide additional confirmation of America's foreknowledge of Japan's attack on Pearl Harbor and help to resolve two of the most contentious issues of the Pearl Harbor debate.[1]

Critics deny there was American foreknowledge of an attack. They make two assertions: (1) that America's radio cryptographers failed to solve Japanese naval codes, and (2) that even if the codes *were* successfully broken and translated, the American intelligence community could not know for sure where the blow would fall because Japan's admirals maintained radio silence and did not disclose the target as Pearl Harbor.[2]

These two assertions are demolished by the new documents. Overwhelming evidence contained in the May 2000 Freedom of Information Act release, reveals that by mid-November 1941, as Japanese naval forces headed for Hawaii, America's radio cryptographers *had* solved the principal Japanese naval codes and that Japan's top admirals went on the Japanese naval airwaves and in a series of radio messages disclosed that Pearl Harbor was the target of their raid. The documentation, closed to the American public and Congress for nearly sixty years, reveals an unambiguous truth: the messages of Japan's top admirals provided enormous intelligence as they were tracked by communications intelligence on their way to Pearl Harbor across the North and Central Pacific Oceans.

America's radio cryptographers were not asleep in 1941. Soon after Ambassador Joseph Grew learned through his own intelligence channels that Japan planned a carrier raid on Pearl Harbor, the formation of the Japanese carrier force was discovered by Station CAST on Corregidor. Intelligence confirmed Grew's January warning to the White House. The Japanese carrier force and its commander were fully identified. Chief Radioman Leroy Lankford provided the first details on April 22, 1941, when he correctly noted the carrier force command was centered aboard the 38,000-ton carrier HIJMS *Akagi*.

Lankford's information was unassailable. He had solved the secret radio identification code assigned to the admiral and tracked him as Japan organized her carrier force known as the First Air Fleet for the Pearl Harbor attack. Vice Admiral Chuichi Nagumo, Commander of the First Air Fleet aboard the *Akagi* spoke to every Japanese warship in the assault fleet while American cryptographers like Lankford listened and reported the intelligence to the White House. There was no escaping the electronic surveillance. Six US Navy monitor stations from Dutch Harbor, Territory of Alaska, Samoa, Hawaii, Corregidor, and two from San Francisco followed every move of Nagumo and the *Akagi*.

By November 16, 1941 (Manila Time), Lankford's colleagues at CAST reported another monumental breakthrough: they had solved the main operational code of the Japanese navy. The commanding officer of CAST, Lieutenant John M. Lietwiler, wrote Washington that his staff had succeeded in intercepting, decoding, and translating the Japanese naval operations code: "We are reading enough current traffic (messages) to keep two translators very busy." Lietwiler's admission that his cryptographers had broken the prime Japanese naval code has been kept in secret US Navy vaults until the May 2000 FOIA release. It was not listed in the US Navy index accompanying the records nor in the index prepared by Archives II.

Japan's admirals, believing that their naval codes were secure, filled the intelligence pipeline with messages that made clear their intentions during the weeks preceding Pearl Harbor. Four of these disclosures were radio messages originated between November 5 and December 2, 1941, by Admiral Osami Nagano, Chief of the Naval General Staff (similar to America's Chief of Naval Operations). In his messages Nagano violated every security rule. First, he issued radio orders making clear that Japan would attack America, Great Britain, and the Netherlands in the first part of December (transmitted November 5, 1941). Then, Admiral Isoroku Yamamoto, the operational chief of the Imperial Japanese Navy, was directed to use any strength if Japanese forces were challenged by US, British, or Dutch forces (transmitted November 21, 1941).

Nagano's radio orders continued to flow: Yamamoto would direct Vice Admiral Nagumo and the First Air Fleet to set sail from Hitokappu Bay on November 26, 1941 (Tokyo Time), proceed through the North Pacific, and refuel north of Hawaii (transmitted November 25, 1941); and finally, Nagano set the date for commencement of hostile action against the United States, the British Empire, and the Netherlands as December 8, 1941 (Tokyo Time; transmitted December 2, 1941). Based on these transmissions, President Roosevelt and General George Marshall predicted war with Japan would begin the first week of December. We would know even more about what FDR and his chief advisors thought, but the Japanese radio messages remain incomplete, still cloaked in American censorship. Though the author has filed Freedom of Information requests for all communication data concerning Nagano's messages, the information has not been released.

By continuing to classify Japanese naval intercepts and their communication and decoding data as "national defense secrets," the National Security Agency (NSA) has done a disservice to the excellent cryptographers and the radio intelligence obtained by monitor stations operated by the United States and her allies in 1941, as well as to history itself. The author estimates there are at least 143,000 Japanese naval intercepts plus supporting communication data that remain unseen in the 1941 US Navy files.

Nevertheless, the major secrets of Pearl Harbor are at last out in the open. After years of denial, the truth is clear: we knew.

Selected US Navy documents Uncovered in May 2000

New Year's Day, January 1, 1941: Chief Radioman O. C. Coonce, the traffic chief at Station CAST, Corregidor, reports intercepting messages in the Japanese navy's 5-num code. The messages detail the move of Japanese naval forces into French Indo China (Vietnam).[3]

January 20, 1941: Station CAST intercepts Japanese naval messages, and Coonce quotes directly from the intercepted and translated text: "Series of urgent messages Sunday from Bumil (Bureau of Military Affairs), Genl. Staff (Japanese Naval General Staff) indicated carriers, part of cruisers Second Fleet, aircraft from Formosa, may be sent French Indo China due unforeseen circumstances. Not confirmed by traffic this date. Will advise. *IDZUMO* (flagship of China Fleet) on South Coast Hainan. End."[4]

April 22, 1941: Chief Radioman Leroy Lankford, who relieved Coonce as traffic chief at CAST, reports that decrypted Japanese navy messages disclose the formation of a major new fleet, which places all ten of Japanese aircraft carriers under a single commander. Lankford learns the commander—secret radio code name MI KI 99—is aboard his flagship HIJMS *Akagi*, a 38,000-ton aircraft carrier with a full fleet staff and communications officer.[5]

April 23, 1941: CAST reports: *"Akagi* carries the new air command, MI KI 99."[6]

April 25, 1941: Station CAST aims its radio direction finder at the aircraft carrier *Akagi*, the flagship of the new air commander, Vice Admiral Chuichi Nagumo (MI KI 99) and reports their position to Washington. The procedure continues through December 6, 1941.[7]

April 30, 1941: Admiral Nagumo, as MI KI 99, originates radio dispatches while aboard the *Akagi*.[8]

May 1, 1941: In an attempt to foil American radio eavesdroppers and mask their vast preparations for war, Japan's naval command introduces an entirely new radio code system. The Imperial Navy calls it the *Yobidashi Fugo HYOO* 8 (radio call signs edition 8). It changes every radio address in the Japanese navy. Japan was positive it would protect the security of the warships, the identification of the officers of the high command who made the strategic and tactical decisions, and locations of shore stations/bases of the Combined Fleet.[9]

May 5, 1941: Lieutenant Rudolph J. Fabian, commanding officer of CAST, acquires photographic copies of the Imperial Japanese Army and Navy code books. He obtains 102 negatives of the Imperial Army's code system for General Douglas MacArthur, and

57 negatives of the Imperial Navy's 5-num code and sends them to Washington. In his written report, Fabian is specific: he secures key elements of the latest edition of the Japanese navy's 5-num code book. As this Afterword goes to press, secrecy still shrouds these code books. None of the 159 negatives or the photographic prints of the Japanese military code books obtained by Fabian have been released by the US Navy.[10]

May 11, 1941: Station CAST breaks into *HYOO 8* and identifies the *Akagi's* new radio call sign as HA MI 9. Then, using a radio direction finder, CAST locates the carrier operating near Sasebo Naval Base at the southwest corner of the island of Kyushu.[11]

May 17, 1941: Japan's Destroyer Division Seventeen, acting as plane guard (rescue of carrier pilots whose planes crash during sea operations) for the *Akagi*, requests Radio Tokyo to institute repeat-back communication procedures. It is the mother-hen-and-chickens method (see page 206 of this book). It also verifies that CAST could intercept, decode, and translate Japanese naval coded messages: "After 2130 hours, pass radio traffic for me through the *Akagi* (mother hen) or Kure (naval base)."[12]

June 15, 1941: Lieutenant Fabian continues to unmask Japan's carrier fleet operations. He dispatches a four-star priority message to the US Navy's Pacific commanders and a copy to Washington. It warns of and provides operational details of the new carrier command. Fabian adds a special request in the dispatch: "Show to Admiral Kimmel." There is no record it was shown to Kimmel.[13]

June 20, 1941: Intercepts show Nagumo and the *Akagi* in direct radio communications with the flagship of the Japanese submarine force, HIJMS *Katori*. Later, the radio contacts with the sub force will expand. On November 26, Nagumo and the sub force are heard in extensive radio communications while both are sailing on the high seas toward Pearl Harbor (see page 162).

August 1941: August was a defining month for America's Pacific radio monitor stations. Admiral Nagumo, the *Akagi*, and the entire operations of Japan's carrier force are under continuous electronic scrutiny by six US Navy monitor stations. The scrutiny continues right up to December 7, according to Robert Ogg, of San Francisco's naval intelligence office. *HYOO 8* backs up Ogg with a certainty. Two of the US Navy monitor stations were based on California's coastline and furnished direct radio surveillance of Nagumo and the *Akagi* to the Roosevelt administration. *HYOO 8* identifies the stations as Station TARE at Point St. George in Northern California, and Station X, still an American secret in the year 2000, but identified by Ogg and classified US Navy records as the British-owned radio facility of Mackay Radio and Telegraph on the San Francisco peninsula near Half Moon Bay, California.[14]

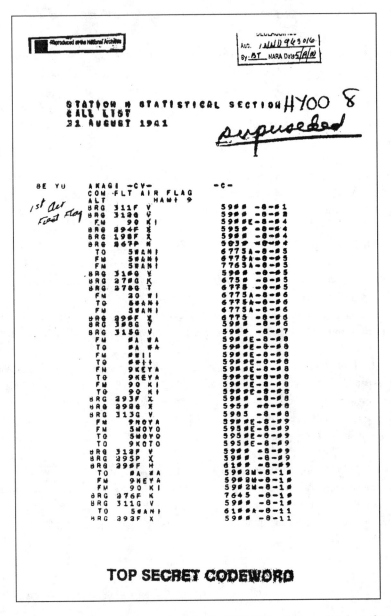

Source: RG 457, National Security Agency Records, Box 1315; Folder: Codes and Ciphers of Japan. Copied at Archives II by the author, May 19, 2000.

The widespread use of radio transmissions by Admiral Nagumo and their interception by US Navy monitor stations is verified by these pages under the heading 8 E YU, which was Nagumo's secret radio call sign issued in August 1941. This two-page listing was obtained by the author from HYOO 8, a communications intelligence report compiled by the Statistical Section of Station H, the Pacific Fleet's monitor station at Heeia, island of Oahu, Territory of Hawaii. It is published here for the first time and proves Admiral Nagumo's disregard for communication security. The left column lists radio direction finder bearings

BRG	270F	K		711#	-8-11
FM	#MOHA			59##E-8-12	
TO	1SEMI			59##E-8-12	
FM	1SEMI			59##E-8-12	
FM	5MOYO			59##E-8-12	
TO	5MOYO			59##E-8-12	
TO	9KEYA			59##E-8-12	
FM	9KEYA			59##E-8-12	
TO	9OKI			59##E-8-12	
FM	9OKI			59##E-8-12	
BRG	291F	X		59##	-8-12
BRG	193F	X		595#	-8-13
BRG	270F	K		583#	-8-12
FM	18EMI			59##E-8-13	
TO	5MOYO			595#E-8-13	
FM	5MOYO			595#E-8-13	
BRG	311G	V		59##	-8-13
FM	5MAYA			6##E-8-14	
BRG	292F	X		59##	-8-14
BRG	319G	V		59##	-8-14
TO	1SEMI			59##E-8-15	
FM	9KEYA			59##E-8-15	
FM	9OKI			59##E-8-15	
BRG	315G	V		595#	-8-15
BRG	292F	X		59##	-8-15
FM	18EMI			59##E-8-16	
TO	58OMU			59##E-8-16	
FM	9KEYA			59##E-8-16	
TO	9KEYA			59##E-8-16	
BRG	293F	X		59##	-8-16
TO	#MOHA			5915M-8-17	
FM	#MOHA			5915M-8-17	
TO	18EMI			5915M-8-17	
FM	18EMI			5915M-8-17	
TO	5TANI			5915M-8-17	
FM	5OANT			5915M-8-17	
TO	6MEU			5915M-8-17	
TO	2NEMA			596SM-8-17	
TO	3NIHI			596SM-8-17	
FM	3NIHI			596SM-8-17	
TO	5MOYO			596SM-8-17	
FM	5MOYO			596SM-8-17	
TO	9RETO			596SM-8-17	
BRG	312G	V		593#	-8-17
BRG	33#	B			8-18
BRG	316G	V		59##	-8-18
BRG	294F	X		59##	-8-18
BRG	3#9G	V		593#	-8-19
BRG	192F	X		5975	-8-19
BRG	294F	X		5975	-8-19
TO	2NEMA			5975E-8-2#	
FM	2NEMA			5975E-8-2#	
BRG	319G	V		59##	-8-21
BRG	33#	B			8-22
BRG	317G	V		59##	-8-22
BRG	295F	X		5975	-8-22
TO	5E	TI		5975E-8-23	
BRG	318G	V		59##	-8-23
BRG	29#G	X		595#	-8-23
BRG	315F	V		76##	-8-23
TO	9KOTO			595#E-8-24	
BRG	#2#	C			8-24

(BRG) and—in addition—warships intercepted in communication with Nagumo/Akagi. For example, the tactical radio call sign 9 O KI was assigned to the Akagi's sister carrier, HIJMS Kaga. Admiral Nagumo's tactical or operational war call sign at this time frame was 8 E YU—shown at top, far left. US Navy radio cryptographers used the term "number-kana-kana" to differentiate the tactical signs, such as 8 E YU, from administrative signs, which were kana-kana-number like HA MI 9.

Next on this chart is the listing for the monitor station that obtained the bearing: V = Station VICTOR, Vaitogi, American Samoa; K = Station KING, Dutch Harbor, Territory of Alaska; X = believed by the author to be radio station KFS of British-owned Mackay Radio and Telegraph, Half Moon Bay, CA; T = Station TARE, Point St. George, CA; H = Station H, Heeia, Territory of Hawaii; C = Station CAST, Corregidor, Philippines. At right is the kilocycle band used by Admiral Nagumo and the date of transmission/interception. The classification "TOP SECRET CODEWORD," added in the postwar period, kept this document under wraps for sixty years.

Station X made the difference. During August 1941, X uncovered Nagumo's secret operation call sign, 8 E YU, and located him and the *Akagi* seventeen times by radio direction finder. When combined with locations obtained by other Pacific monitor stations, Nagumo and the *Akagi* were intercepted 115 times at an average interception rate of 4.1 per day between August 1 and 28, 1941.[15] The intercepts disclosed continued radio association of Nagumo and his carrier fleet with the *Kyokuto Maru*, the flagship of Japan's naval refueling tankers. Nagumo's importance as a senior Japanese naval commander is documented by his extensive radio contacts.

August 5, 1941: Station TARE intercepts the *Akagi* transmitting on 6775 kilocycles, directs a radio direction finder beam on the carrier, and locates her at 278° from Point St. George. Another bearing obtained by Station KING at Dutch Harbor, Territory of Alaska, crosses the TARE's beam and positions the *Akagi* in the vicinity of Kyushu, Japan.[16]

August 9, 1941: Station X obtains direction finder location and reports the *Akagi* is in radio contact with the HIJMS *Nagato*, flagship of Admiral Isoroku Yamamoto, Commander of the Combined Fleet. X reports the *Akagi* was intercepted at 295°, using the radio frequency of 5900 kilocycles.[17]

August 12, 1941: *Akagi* again in radio contact with *Nagato* on 5900 kilocycles. Station X reports her position at 291°, indicating the carrier moved four degrees south in three days.[18]

August 23, 1941: Station X intercepts the *Akagi* at 298° from San Francisco in communication with the flagship of Japan's submarine fleet, the *Katori*. At nearly the same moment, the *Kyokuto Maru* transmits a message that is intercepted, decoded, and translated by CAST: "Departing communication zone of the *Akagi*, offing for Kure Naval Base." The *Kyokuto Maru*'s report was intercepted at 2200 hours on 8350 kilocycles, according to a written report by CAST.[19]

September 26, 1941: Japan changes the Nagumo/*Akagi*'s operational radio call sign to 8 YU NA. Station CAST detects the new call sign immediately. The change remains in effect through November 30 and establishes an *Akagi*/Nagumo intercept pattern for US Navy radio cryptographers.[20]

November 5, 1941: The author believes that two Japanese naval messages originated by Admiral Osami Nagano, Japan's top admiral, on November 5, 1941, and intercepted in Hawaii, were the intelligence source for statements attributed to President Franklin D. Roosevelt and General George C. Marshall, U.S. Army Chief of Staff in mid-November

1941. Both officials, using the information disclosed in paragraph one of those messages (reproduced on page 303 of this book), predicted that war with Japan would start the first part of December 1941.

Newly uncovered records confirm the author's belief. According to the intercept records of Station HYPO, Admiral Nagano originated two priority radio messages on November 5, 1941. Each was intercepted in Hawaii according to Lieutenant Commander Joseph Rochefort, head of Station HYPO, the Pacific Fleet's intelligence center at Pearl Harbor. Rochefort wrote that Nagano's original messages were in the Japanese navy's "Kana Code." Admiral Husband E. Kimmel initialed the report. It was up to Kimmel to request a decoding and translation of Nagano's messages. No record that he did so has come to light.[21]

November 16, 1941: Lieutenant John M. Lietwiler, co-commander of Station CAST, on Corregidor Island in Manila Bay, notifies naval headquarters in Washington that his radio cryptographers on Corregidor were intercepting, decoding, and translating Japanese naval messages.[22] Lietwiler bragged that his crypto yeoman, Albert E. Myers, Jr., had initiated a new technique that allowed the cryppie to "walk right across" the Japanese messages.[23]

November 25, 1941 [sic]: In a radio message transmitted to the First Air Fleet, then anchored at Hitokappu Bay, Admiral Isoroku Yamamoto orders the carrier force to open hostilities with the United States Fleet [sic] in Hawaii (see the dispatch, p. 302 of this book).[24]

Verification of Yamamoto's dispatch to the First Air Fleet—with a different originating date—appears five days earlier on the Station H Chronology for November 20, 1941. Under the heading Combined Fleet, Homer Kisner, the traffic chief at H, reports intercepting an "unusually large number of messages to the different Carriers and Carrier Commands." Kisner wrote: "This might be an indication of increased activity or movement of the Carriers." Kisner was correct. The six carriers and their supporting warships began to sortie to Hitokappu Bay during this five-day time frame.[25]

December 1, 1941: Elliott Okins, watch supervisor at Station H, reports intercepting a radio message originated by KO ME HA (Admiral Nagano). Okins wrote that the message was recorded verbatim on Station H message sheet 95678.[26] Nagano uses the impossible-to-mistake phrase "state of war" (see page 270).[27]

Based on Okins's report, the author has reconstructed the missing parts of this message and believes Admiral Nagano meticulously followed Japanese naval radio procedures and in the beginning of the original message authorized this coded radio address: "TI: YO WI ØØ, KE NO 8; DE: KO ME HA, To: Commander-in-Chief Combined Fleet, and Commander-in-Chief China Fleet, From: Chief Navy General Staff." Obviously,

---

THE CAMPAIGNS *of the* PACIFIC WAR

Japanese Naval Despatches Ordering Commencement of Hostilities

1 December 1941.

From: The Chief of Naval General Staff
To: CinC Combined Fleet
            CinC China Area Fleet

   1. It has been decided to enter into a state of war between the Imperial Government on one side and the United States, Great Britain and the Netherlands on the other during the first part of December.

   2. The CinC Combined Fleet will destroy the enemy forces and air strength in the eastern seas at the same time will meet any attack by the enemy fleet and destroy it.

   3. The CinC Combined Fleet will, in cooperation with the Commander of the Southern Army, speedily capture and hold important American and British Bases in Eastern Asia and then Dutch bases. Important strategic points will then be occupied and held.

   4. CinC Combined Fleet will in case of necessity cooperate with the operations of China Area Fleet.

   5. The time for activating the movements of forces in accordance with preceding articles will be given in a later order.

   6. Execution of details will be as directed by Chief of the Naval General Staff.

Source: United States Strategic Bombing Survey, The Campaigns of the Pacific War, (USGPO, 1946), p. 50.

Based on Japanese communication data gathered by Elliott Okins, the author believes this is Admiral Nagano's radio dispatch intercepted at Station H on December 1, 1941, as message sheet 95678. There is no record that this message/intercept was shown to Admiral Kimmel prior to the attack.

Okins was able to decode the original radio address, which has been omitted from the above document by US officials.[28]

Nagano's orders were followed immediately. No time was wasted. Yamamoto, in turn, transmitted: "Climb Mount Niitaka"—the start-the-war message in Japan's naval code.

McCOLLUM'S ACTION PROPOSAL

LIEUTENANT COMMANDER ARTHUR McCOLLUM'S
MEMORANDUM OF OCTOBER 7, 1940
Includes endorsement by Captain Dudley Knox

Lieutenant Commander Arthur McCollum's proposed eight actions, designed to provoke Japan into an overt act of war, were discovered by the author in Box 6 of a special US Navy collection in RG 38 in the Military Reference Branch of Archives II, January 24, 1995.

OP-16-F-2   ONI   7 OCTOBER 1940

~~CONFIDENTIAL~~

MEMORANDUM FOR THE DIRECTOR

SUBJECT: ESTIMATE OF THE SITUATION IN THE PACIFIC AND
            RECOMMENDATIONS FOR ACTION BY THE UNITED STATES.

1.   THE UNITED STATES TODAY FINDS HERSELF CONFRONTED
BY A HOSTILE GERMANY AND ITALY IN EUROPE AND BY AN EQUALLY
HOSTILE JAPAN IN THE ORIENT. RUSSIA, THE GREAT LAND LINK BETWEEN
THESE TWO GROUPS OF HOSTILE POWERS, IS AT PRESENT NEUTRAL, BUT
IN ALL PROBABILITY FAVORABLY INCLINED TOWARDS THE AXIS POWERS,
AND HER FAVORABLE ATTITUDE TOWARDS THESE POWERS MAY BE EXPECTED
TO INCREASE IN DIRECT PROPORTION TO INCREASING SUCCESS IN THEIR
PROSECUTION OF THE WAR IN EUROPE. GERMANY AND ITALY HAVE BEEN
SUCCESSFUL IN WAR ON THE CONTINENT OF EUROPE AND ALL OF EUROPE
IS EITHER UNDER THEIR MILITARY CONTROL OR HAS BEEN FORCED INTO
SUBSERVIENCE. ONLY THE BRITISH EMPIRE IS ACTIVELY OPPOSING BY
WAR THE GROWING WORLD DOMINANCE OF GERMANY AND ITALY AND THEIR
SATELLITES.

2.   THE UNITED STATES AT FIRST REMAINED COOLLY ALOOF
FROM THE CONFLICT IN EUROPE AND THERE IS CONSIDERABLE EVIDENCE
TO SUPPORT THE VIEW THAT GERMANY AND ITALY ATTEMPTED BY EVERY
METHOD WITHIN THEIR POWER TO FOSTER A CONTINUATION OF AMERICAN
INDIFFERENCE TO THE OUTCOME OF THE STRUGGLE IN EUROPE. PARADOXICALLY,
EVERY SUCCESS OF GERMAN AND ITALIAN ARMS HAS LED TO FURTHER
INCREASES IN UNITED STATES SYMPATHY FOR AND MATERIAL SUPPORT OF
THE BRITISH EMPIRE, UNTIL AT THE PRESENT TIME THE UNITED STATES
GOVERNMENT STANDS COMMITTED TO A POLICY OF RENDERING EVERY
SUPPORT SHORT OF WAR WITH THE CHANCES RAPIDLY INCREASING THAT
THE UNITED STATES WILL BECOME A FULL FLEDGED ALLY OF THE BRITISH
EMPIRE IN THE VERY NEAR FUTURE. THE FINAL FAILURE OF GERMAN
AND ITALIAN DIPLOMACY TO KEEP THE UNITED STATES IN THE ROLE OF
A DISINTERESTED SPECTATOR HAS FORCED THEM TO ADOPT THE POLICY OF
DEVELOPING THREATS TO U.S. SECURITY IN OTHER SPHERES OF THE WORLD,
NOTABLY BY THE THREAT OF REVOLUTIONS IN SOUTH AND CENTRAL AMERICA
BY AXIS-DOMINATED GROUPS AND BY THE STIMULATION OF JAPAN TO FURTHER
AGGRESSIONS AND THREATS IN THE FAR EAST IN THE HOPE THAT BY THESE
MEANS THE UNITED STATES WOULD BECOME SO CONFUSED IN THOUGHT
AND FEARFUL OF HER OWN IMMEDIATE SECURITY AS TO CAUSE HER TO
BECOME SO PREOCCUPIED IN PURELY DEFENSIVE PREPARATIONS AS TO VIR-
TUALLY PRECLUDE U.S. AID TO GREAT BRITAIN IN ANY FORM. AS A
RESULT OF THIS POLICY, GERMANY AND ITALY HAVE LATELY CONCLUDED
A MILITARY ALLIANCE WITH JAPAN DIRECTED AGAINST THE UNITED
STATES. IF THE PUBLISHED TERMS OF THIS TREATY AND THE POINTED
UTTERANCES OF GERMAN, ITALIAN AND JAPANESE LEADERS CAN BE BELIEVED,
AND THERE SEEMS NO GROUND ON WHICH TO DOUBT EITHER, THE THREE
TOTALITARIAN POWERS AGREE TO MAKE WAR ON THE UNITED STATES,
SHOULD SHE COME TO THE ASSISTANCE OF ENGLAND, OR SHOULD SHE
ATTEMPT TO FORCIBLY INTERFERE WITH JAPAN'S AIMS IN THE ORIENT AND,

FURTHERMORE, GERMANY AND ITALY EXPRESSLY RESERVE THE RIGHT TO DETERMINE WHETHER AMERICAN AID TO BRITAIN, SHORT OF WAR, IS A CAUSE FOR WAR OR NOT AFTER THEY HAVE SUCCEEDED IN DEFEATING ENGLAND. IN OTHER WORDS, AFTER ENGLAND HAS BEEN DISPOSED OF HER ENEMIES WILL DECIDE WHETHER OR NOT TO IMMEDIATELY PROCEED WITH AN ATTACK ON THE UNITED STATES. DUE TO GEOGRAPHIC CONDITIONS, NEITHER GERMANY NOR ITALY ARE IN A POSITION TO OFFER ANY MATERIAL AID TO JAPAN. JAPAN, ON THE CONTRARY, CAN BE OF MUCH HELP TO BOTH GERMANY AND ITALY BY THREATENING AND POSSIBLY EVEN ATTACKING BRITISH DOMINIONS AND SUPPLY ROUTES FROM AUSTRALIA, INDIA AND THE DUTCH EAST INDIES, THUS MATERIALLY WEAKENING BRITAINS'S POSITION IN OPPOSITION TO THE AXIS POWERS IN EUROPE. IN EXCHANGE FOR THIS SERVICE, JAPAN RECEIVES A FREE HAND TO SEIZE ALL OF ASIA THAT SHE CAN FIND IT POSSIBLE TO GRAB, WITH THE ADDED PROMISE THAT GERMANY AND ITALY WILL DO ALL IN THEIR POWER TO KEEP U.S. ATTENTION SO ATTRACTED AS TO PREVENT THE UNITED STATES FROM TAKING POSITIVE AGGRESSIVE ACTION AGAINST JAPAN. HERE AGAIN WE HAVE ANOTHER EXAMPLE OF THE AXIS-JAPANESE DIPLOMACY WHICH IS AIMED AT KEEPING AMERICAN POWER IMMOBILIZED, AND BY THREATS AND ALARMS TO SO CONFUSE AMERICAN THOUGHT AS TO PRECLUDE PROMPT DECISIVE ACTION BY THE UNITED STATES IN EITHER SPHERE OF ACTION. IT CANNOT BE EMPHASIZED TOO STRONGLY THAT THE LAST THING DESIRED BY EITHER THE AXIS POWERS IN EUROPE OR BY JAPAN IN THE FAR EAST IS PROMPT, WARLIKE ACTION BY THE UNITED STATES IN EITHER THEATER OF OPERATIONS.

3.   AN EXAMINATION OF THE SITUATION IN EUROPE LEADS TO THE CONCLUSION THAT THERE IS LITTLE THAT WE CAN DO NOW, IMMEDIATELY, TO HELP BRITAIN THAT IS NOT ALREADY BEING DONE. WE HAVE NO TRAINED ARMY TO SEND TO THE ASSISTANCE OF ENGLAND, NOR WILL WE HAVE FOR AT LEAST A YEAR. WE ARE NOW TRYING TO INCREASE THE FLOW OF MATERIALS TO ENGLAND AND TO BOLSTER THE DEFENSE OF ENGLAND IN EVERY PRACTICABLE WAY AND THIS AID WILL UNDOUBTEDLY BE INCREASED. ON THE OTHER HAND, THERE IS LITTLE THAT GERMANY OR ITALY CAN DO AGAINST US AS LONG AS ENGLAND CONTINUES IN THE WAR AND HER NAVY MAINTAINS CONTROL OF THE ATLANTIC. THE ONE DANGER TO OUR POSITION LIES IN THE POSSIBLE EARLY DEFEAT OF THE BRITISH EMPIRE WITH THE BRITISH FLEET FALLING INTACT INTO THE HANDS OF THE AXIS POWERS. THE POSSIBILITY OF SUCH AN EVENT OCCURRING WOULD BE MATERIALLY LESSENED WERE WE ACTUALLY ALLIED IN WAR WITH THE BRITISH OR AT THE VERY LEAST WERE TAKING ACTIVE MEASURES TO RELIEVE THE PRESSURE ON BRITAIN IN OTHER SPHERES OF ACTION. TO SUM UP: THE THREAT TO OUR SECURITY IN THE ATLANTIC REMAINS SMALL SO LONG AS THE BRITISH FLEET REMAINS DOMINANT IN THAT OCEAN AND FRIENDLY TO THE UNITED STATES.

4.   IN THE PACIFIC, JAPAN BY VIRTUE OF HER ALLIANCE WITH GERMANY AND ITALY IS A DEFINITE THREAT TO THE SECURITY OF THE BRITISH EMPIRE AND ONCE THE BRITISH EMPIRE IS GONE THE POWER OF JAPAN-GERMANY AND ITALY IS TO BE DIRECTED AGAINST THE UNITED STATES. A POWERFUL LAND ATTACK BY GERMANY AND ITALY THROUGH THE BALKANS AND NORTH AFRICA AGAINST THE SUEZ CANAL WITH A JAPANESE THREAT OR ATTACK ON SINGAPORE WOULD HAVE VERY SERIOUS RESULTS FOR THE BRITISH EMPIRE. COULD JAPAN BE DIVERTED OR NEUTRALIZED, THE FRUITS OF A SUCCESSFUL ATTACK ON THE SUEZ CANAL COULD NOT BE AS FAR REACHING AND BENEFICIAL TO THE AXIS POWERS AS IF SUCH A SUCCESS WAS ALSO ACCOMPANIED BY THE VIRTUAL ELIMINATION OF BRITISH SEA POWER FROM THE INDIAN OCEAN, THUS

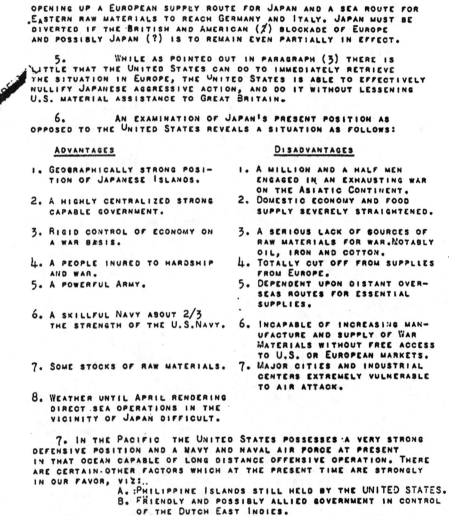

OPENING UP A EUROPEAN SUPPLY ROUTE FOR JAPAN AND A SEA ROUTE FOR EASTERN RAW MATERIALS TO REACH GERMANY AND ITALY. JAPAN MUST BE DIVERTED IF THE BRITISH AND AMERICAN (?) BLOCKADE OF EUROPE AND POSSIBLY JAPAN (?) IS TO REMAIN EVEN PARTIALLY IN EFFECT.

5. WHILE AS POINTED OUT IN PARAGRAPH (3) THERE IS LITTLE THAT THE UNITED STATES CAN DO TO IMMEDIATELY RETRIEVE THE SITUATION IN EUROPE, THE UNITED STATES IS ABLE TO EFFECTIVELY NULLIFY JAPANESE AGGRESSIVE ACTION, AND DO IT WITHOUT LESSENING U.S. MATERIAL ASSISTANCE TO GREAT BRITAIN.

6. AN EXAMINATION OF JAPAN'S PRESENT POSITION AS OPPOSED TO THE UNITED STATES REVEALS A SITUATION AS FOLLOWS:

ADVANTAGES	DISADVANTAGES
1. GEOGRAPHICALLY STRONG POSITION OF JAPANESE ISLANDS.	1. A MILLION AND A HALF MEN ENGAGED IN AN EXHAUSTING WAR ON THE ASIATIC CONTINENT.
2. A HIGHLY CENTRALIZED STRONG CAPABLE GOVERNMENT.	2. DOMESTIC ECONOMY AND FOOD SUPPLY SEVERELY STRAIGHTENED.
3. RIGID CONTROL OF ECONOMY ON A WAR BASIS.	3. A SERIOUS LACK OF SOURCES OF RAW MATERIALS FOR WAR, NOTABLY OIL, IRON AND COTTON.
4. A PEOPLE INURED TO HARDSHIP AND WAR.	4. TOTALLY CUT OFF FROM SUPPLIES FROM EUROPE.
5. A POWERFUL ARMY.	5. DEPENDENT UPON DISTANT OVERSEAS ROUTES FOR ESSENTIAL SUPPLIES.
6. A SKILLFUL NAVY ABOUT 2/3 THE STRENGTH OF THE U.S. NAVY.	6. INCAPABLE OF INCREASING MANUFACTURE AND SUPPLY OF WAR MATERIALS WITHOUT FREE ACCESS TO U.S. OR EUROPEAN MARKETS.
7. SOME STOCKS OF RAW MATERIALS.	7. MAJOR CITIES AND INDUSTRIAL CENTERS EXTREMELY VULNERABLE TO AIR ATTACK.
8. WEATHER UNTIL APRIL RENDERING DIRECT SEA OPERATIONS IN THE VICINITY OF JAPAN DIFFICULT.	

7. IN THE PACIFIC THE UNITED STATES POSSESSES A VERY STRONG DEFENSIVE POSITION AND A NAVY AND NAVAL AIR FORCE AT PRESENT IN THAT OCEAN CAPABLE OF LONG DISTANCE OFFENSIVE OPERATION. THERE ARE CERTAIN OTHER FACTORS WHICH AT THE PRESENT TIME ARE STRONGLY IN OUR FAVOR, VIZ:.

A. PHILIPPINE ISLANDS STILL HELD BY THE UNITED STATES.
B. FRIENDLY AND POSSIBLY ALLIED GOVERNMENT IN CONTROL OF THE DUTCH EAST INDIES.
C. BRITISH STILL HOLD HONGKONG AND SINGAPORE AND ARE FAVORABLE TO US.
D. IMPORTANT CHINESE ARMIES ARE STILL IN THE FIELD IN CHINA AGAINST JAPAN.
E. A SMALL U.S. NAVAL FORCE CAPABLE OF SERIOUSLY THREATENING JAPAN'S SOUTHERN SUPPLY ROUTES

ALREADY IN THE THEATER OF OPERATIONS.

F. A CONSIDERABLE DUTCH NAVAL FORCE IS IN THE
   ORIENT THAT WOULD BE OF VALUE IF ALLIED TO U.S.

8.   A CONSIDERATION OF THE FOREGOING LEADS TO THE
CONCLUSION THAT PROMPT AGGRESSIVE NAVAL ACTION AGAINST JAPAN BY
THE UNITED STATES WOULD RENDER JAPAN INCAPABLE OF AFFORDING ANY
HELP TO GERMANY AND ITALY IN THEIR ATTACK ON ENGLAND AND THAT
JAPAN ITSELF WOULD BE FACED WITH A SITUATION IN WHICH HER NAVY
COULD BE FORCED TO FIGHT ON MOST UNFAVORABLE TERMS OR ACCEPT
FAIRLY EARLY COLLAPSE OF THE COUNTRY THROUGH THE FORCE OF BLOCKADE.
A PROMPT AND EARLY DECLARATION OF WAR AFTER ENTERING INTO SUIT-
ABLE ARRANGEMENTS WITH ENGLAND AND HOLLAND, WOULD BE MOST EFFECTIVE
IN BRINGING ABOUT THE EARLY COLLAPSE OF JAPAN AND THUS ELIMINATING
OUR ENEMY IN THE PACIFIC BEFORE GERMANY AND ITALY COULD STRIKE
AT US EFFECTIVELY. FURTHERMORE, ELIMINATION OF JAPAN MUST SURELY
STRENGTHEN BRITAIN'S POSITION AGAINST GERMANY AND ITALY AND, IN
ADDITION, SUCH ACTION WOULD INCREASE THE CONFIDENCE AND SUPPORT
OF ALL NATIONS WHO TEND TO BE FRIENDLY TOWARDS US.

9.   IT IS NOT BELIEVED THAT IN THE PRESENT STATE OF
POLITICAL OPINION THE UNITED STATES GOVERNMENT IS CAPABLE OF
DECLARING WAR AGAINST JAPAN WITHOUT MORE ADO; AND IT IS BARELY
POSSIBLE THAT VIGOROUS ACTION ON OUR PART MIGHT LEAD THE
JAPANESE TO MODIFY THEIR ATTITUDE. THEREFORE, THE FOLLOWING
COURSE OF ACTION IS SUGGESTED:

A. MAKE AN ARRANGEMENT WITH BRITAIN FOR THE USE OF
   BRITISH BASES IN THE PACIFIC, PARTICULARLY
   SINGAPORE.
B. MAKE AN ARRANGEMENT WITH HOLLAND FOR THE USE OF
   BASE FACILITIES AND ACQUISITION OF SUPPLIES
   IN THE DUTCH EAST INDIES.
C. GIVE ALL POSSIBLE AID TO THE CHINESE GOVERNMENT
   OF CHIANG-KAI-SHEK.
D. SEND A DIVISION OF LONG RANGE HEAVY CRUISERS TO
   THE ORIENT, PHILIPPINES, OR SINGAPORE.
E. SEND TWO DIVISIONS OF SUBMARINES TO THE ORIENT.
F. KEEP THE MAIN STRENGTH OF THE U.S. FLEET NOW IN
   THE PACIFIC IN THE VICINITY OF THE HAWAIIAN ISLANDS.
G. INSIST THAT THE DUTCH REFUSE TO GRANT JAPANESE
   DEMANDS FOR UNDUE ECONOMIC CONCESSIONS, PARTI-
   CULARLY OIL.
H. COMPLETELY EMBARGO ALL U.S. TRADE WITH JAPAN,
   IN COLLABORATION WITH A SIMILAR EMBARGO IMPOSED
   BY THE BRITISH EMPIRE.

10.   IF BY THESE MEANS JAPAN COULD BE LED TO COMMIT AN
OVERT ACT OF WAR, SO MUCH THE BETTER. AT ALL EVENTS WE MUST BE FULLY
PREPARED TO ACCEPT THE THREAT OF WAR.

                                    A.H. McCOLLUM ✓

CC-OP-16
  OP-16-F
  FILE

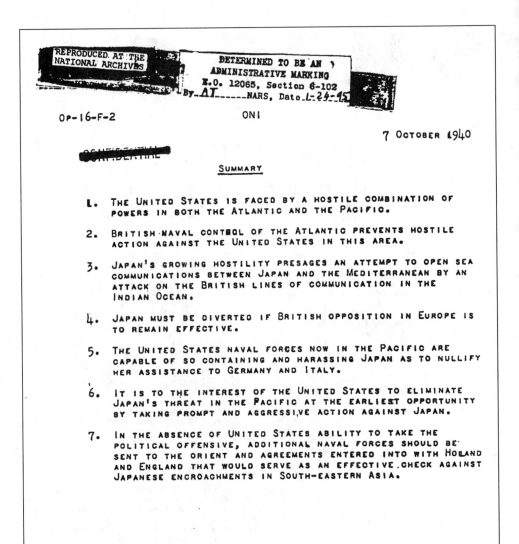

DETERMINED TO BE AN
ADMINISTRATIVE MARKING
E.O. 12065, Section 6-102
By AT   NARS, Date 1-24-45

OP-16-F-2   ONI

7 OCTOBER 1940

CONFIDENTIAL

SUMMARY

1. THE UNITED STATES IS FACED BY A HOSTILE COMBINATION OF POWERS IN BOTH THE ATLANTIC AND THE PACIFIC.

2. BRITISH NAVAL CONTROL OF THE ATLANTIC PREVENTS HOSTILE ACTION AGAINST THE UNITED STATES IN THIS AREA.

3. JAPAN'S GROWING HOSTILITY PRESAGES AN ATTEMPT TO OPEN SEA COMMUNICATIONS BETWEEN JAPAN AND THE MEDITERRANEAN BY AN ATTACK ON THE BRITISH LINES OF COMMUNICATION IN THE INDIAN OCEAN.

4. JAPAN MUST BE DIVERTED IF BRITISH OPPOSITION IN EUROPE IS TO REMAIN EFFECTIVE.

5. THE UNITED STATES NAVAL FORCES NOW IN THE PACIFIC ARE CAPABLE OF SO CONTAINING AND HARASSING JAPAN AS TO NULLIFY HER ASSISTANCE TO GERMANY AND ITALY.

6. IT IS TO THE INTEREST OF THE UNITED STATES TO ELIMINATE JAPAN'S THREAT IN THE PACIFIC AT THE EARLIEST OPPORTUNITY BY TAKING PROMPT AND AGGRESSIVE ACTION AGAINST JAPAN.

7. IN THE ABSENCE OF UNITED STATES ABILITY TO TAKE THE POLITICAL OFFENSIVE, ADDITIONAL NAVAL FORCES SHOULD BE SENT TO THE ORIENT AND AGREEMENTS ENTERED INTO WITH HOLLAND AND ENGLAND THAT WOULD SERVE AS AN EFFECTIVE CHECK AGAINST JAPANESE ENCROACHMENTS IN SOUTH-EASTERN ASIA.

CONFIDENTIAL

COMMENT BY CAPTAIN KNOX

It is unquestionably to out general interest that Britain be not licked — just now she has a stalemate and probably cant do better. We ought to make it certain that she at least gets a stalemate. For this she will probably need from us substantial further destroyers and air rienforcements to England. We should not precipitate anything in the Orient that would hamper our ability to do this — so long as probability continues.

If England remains stable, Japan will be cautious in the Orient. Hence our assistance to England in the Atlantic is also protection to her and us in the Orient.

However, I concur in your courses of action we must be ready on both sides and probably strong enough to care for both.

D.W.K.

Re your #6: — no reason for battleships not visiting west coast in bunches.

RESEARCH FOR *DAY OF DECEIT*

The principal archival sources for this book are in the Pacific War communications intelligence (COMINT) files of the United States Navy maintained by the US Navy Security Group Command, the successor of Station US—the Navy's communications intelligence headquarters in 1941. The author learned of the existence of the files in 1983, filed a FOIA request with the Navy, and specifically requested immediate declassification of the entire file pertaining in any manner to the Pearl Harbor attack. In 1983 these records were classified TOP SECRET CODEWORD and TOP SECRET CREAM—one of the highest classification categories of the US government. Except for a few documents, the author's request was denied.

The FOIA constituted a legal "information lien" on the classified COMINT documents. In June 1994, the Navy decided to declassify the records. The files were transferred by truck convoy from the Navy Security Group Command depository in Crane, Indiana, to Archives II, operated by National Archives on the campus of the University of Maryland at College Park, which is inside the Beltway that encircles Washington. Title to the records passed from the Navy to Archives II and the documents were free at last. The author's FOIA "information lien" on the records was honored by Clarence Lyons, then director of the Textual Reference Branch at Archives II. Lyons made a portion of the COMINT documents available to the author on January 23, 1995. The remaining records were in various stages of cataloguing.

As of 1999, these COMINT files are located in Record Group 38 of the Modern Military Records Branch at Archives II, and are known as the Station US Papers or Crane Files (after the depository). Timothy Nenninger, who replaced Lyons in 1998, estimated that the Station US papers contain over one million documents. As this book goes to press in 1999, declassification and cataloguing of the Station US papers continues under Nenninger's direction.

The Pacific War COMINT files in Archives II are not the last word on the subject. Three National Archives regional depositories—in Laguna Niguel and San

Bruno, California, and Seattle, Washington—contain important Pearl Harbor documents not found in the Archives II records.

At first glance some readers may puzzle over the intricacies of communications intelligence and the way it can reveal an opponent's strategy and tactics. It is very similar to listening to police and fire department radios in a newsroom. A din of routine transmissions generates a normal buzz—but if a major crime or fire is reported transmissions pick up and excited voices are heard. This jump from the normal gets attention and alerts the editor and reporters that major news is occurring. The same is true in military communications. When communications between units and commands suddenly increase manyfold and the increase is sustained, the alert intelligence command senses trouble. Captain Duane Whitlock, a radio traffic analyst at Station CAST on Corregidor, told the author that he received stacks of Japanese naval broadcasts during the last days of peace of 1941—way above normal: "It was not necessary to decipher the coded messages. I was fully convinced that Japan was gearing up for war based on the huge increase of orders transmitted to the warships and military commands."

This book's main archival sources are listed below.

Archives II, Modern Military Records Branch, 8601 Adelphi Road, Room 2400, College Park, Maryland

Archivists consulted: R. Michael McReynolds, Clarence Lyons, John Taylor, Timothy Nenninger, Richard A. von Doenhoff, Barry L. Zerby, Dick Mackay, JoAnn Williamson, Vernon R. Smith, Richard L. Boylan, Timothy P. Mulligan, Wilbert B. Mahoney, Richard H. Rayburn, Theresa Hammett. Superintendent of the Research Room: Calvin Jefferson.

National Archives filing policy is focused on Record Groups. The principal military record groups used by the author in researching Pearl Harbor records at Archives II were:

Pearl Harbor Liaison Office Files (PHLO), in Record Group 80

These comprise a declassified collection of documents gathered for the Pearl Harbor Joint Congressional Investigation Committee (JOINT) of 1945–46. President Harry S. Truman and Senator Alben Barkley (D., Kentucky), chairman of the investigating committee, set the national policy pertaining to testimony of witnesses and declassification of documents scheduled to appear before JOINT. In his first policy memorandum to the committee on the matter, dated August 28, 1945, President Truman curtailed presentation of evidence concerning the success of any US governmental cryptanalytic unit. His prohibition was directed to several officials of his Administration: the Secretaries of State, War, and Navy, the Attorney General, the Joint Chiefs of Staff, the Director of the Budget, and the Director of the Office of War Information: "Appropriate departments of the Government and the Joint Chiefs of

Staff are hereby directed to take such steps as are necessary to prevent release to the public, except with the specific approval of the President in each case, of: Information regarding the past or present status, technique or procedures, degree of success attained, or any specific results of any cryptanalytic unit acting under the authority of the US Government or any Department thereof" /ss/ Harry S. Truman.

Senator Barkley asked for a modification of the order on October 5, 1945. President Truman relented with a new memorandum on October 26 in which he eased the release of information concerning cryptanalytic activities: "The State, War and Navy Departments will make available to the Joint Committee on the Investigation of the Pearl Harbor attack, for such use as the Committee may determine, any information in their possession material to the investigation, and will respectively authorize any employee or member of the armed services whose testimony is desired by the Committee to testify publicly before the Committee concerning any matter pertinent to the investigation" /ss/ Harry S. Truman. [See the Truman-Barkley interchange, on file at the Truman Presidential Library, Independence, Missouri.]

During the course of the Truman-Barkley interchange, Fleet Admiral Ernest King attempted to prevent the intercepted Japanese 5-Num code dispatches and other communications intelligence activities from becoming public. King specifically asked Secretary of the Navy James Forrestal to override Truman's memorandum and prohibit witnesses [Navy intercept operators] from testifying either directly or indirectly concerning information obtained through cryptanalysis. [King to SECNAV, Oct. 1, 1945, Serial 8313, Station US Papers, MMRB, RG 38, Archives II.]

President Truman apparently became aware of King's directives attempting to curtail the testimony. Admiral King warned that any naval personnel who disclosed cryptographic information would be subject to naval discipline. Truman countered with a November 7, 1945, memorandum ordering protection for any witness before the Committee: "The testimony of any person in the armed services, and the fact that such person testified before the joint committee herein provided for, shall not be used against him in any court proceeding or held against him in examining his military status for credits in the service to which he belongs."

The President concluded his memorandum by requesting all Americans to come forward and provide any information of which they might have knowledge bearing on the subject of the Committee's investigation. Two days later he reiterated his request with another expanded memorandum, which called for all Americans to come forward and disclose information to the Committee. Truman added a caveat: "This does not include any files or written materials." But Fleet Admiral King prevailed. In the end, King won the battle of the memorandums. None of the Navy's intercept operators—the 165 members of the On The Roof Gang—testified. Not one of their military intercepts of Japanese naval radio broadcasts was introduced into evidence before the Committee. America's pre–Pearl Harbor success in obtaining, decrypting, and translating the Japanese naval messages in the 5-Num code was safe.

Most of the documents, evidence, and testimony heard by JOINT were reproduced in the official 39-volume transcript. But the most important records involving communications intelligence were omitted. None of the Station US papers—which contain the crucial Japanese military intercepts—were shown to Congress in either the 1945–46 or the 1995 Pearl Harbor investigations.

My original research into Pearl Harbor files began in Archives I, located at Seventh Street and Pennsylvania Avenue in downtown Washington. In 1994 the United States military history records were moved to a magnificent new depository on the campus of the University of Maryland at College Park, called Archives II. When Congress closed down the government in late 1994, funds for preserving records in the National Archives were curtailed. During research in the Archives I and II depositories, I noted rapid physical deterioration of the Pacific Fleet's Incoming and Outgoing radio message files (labeled SECRET and CONFIDENTIAL) for the pre–Pearl Harbor period. These records are fading and turning to dust because they were not properly stored in archival safe boxes. Cardboard boxes and some fiber products are unsuitable for archival storage because they contain toxins. Storage containers should have a neutral pH rating, which guarantees toxins are not present to destroy records. The pH safe boxes cost about $2 each.

The Pacific Fleet's radio message file was not printed in JOINT and constitutes some of the most crucial United States historical records of the pre–December 7, 1941, period. If not properly preserved in accordance with National Archives guidelines, the documents will be lost to future generations. I made an attempt to preserve some of the records by photographing the deteriorating documents with my Nikon 35-mm camera.

Station US Papers, a.k.a. **Crane Files, in RG 38**

The entire file is estimated to contain at least a million documents, according to Timothy Nenninger, Director of the Modern Military Records Branch. The original release of a portion of these documents—stored in 20 pH-safe boxes and three unsafe corrugated boxes—took place on January 23, 1995.

Other Record Groups consulted in the National Archives were:

Deck logs of US Navy vessels in RG 24.

Chief of Naval Operations files, 1940–41, RG 38.

Office of Naval Intelligence, RG 38.

Still Picture Branch, RG 80, for photographs.

Diplomatic Branch RG 59, State Department Decimal File.

President Jimmy Carter's limited release of the 1941 Japanese naval messages, with the blackouts, can be found in RG 457. The uncensored versions are in the Station US papers. Neither the censored nor the uncensored documents are arranged in chronological order or categorized by intercept stations. John Taylor, supervising archivist of RG 457, said the censored Carter documents were prepared and released to National Archives by the National Security Agency (NSA). Officials at NSA object to the use of the word *censored;* they prefer *redacted.*

Diplomatic Branch, Archives II, 8601 Adelphi Road, College Park, Maryland

These are State Department decimal files, 1940–44, in RG 59. They contain details of the removal of Japanese consulate members from Hawaii in spring 1942.

Department of Defense, The Pentagon

See *The Magic Background of Pearl Harbor,* originally printed by the US Government Printing Office. This is an eight-volume set of translations of communications intelligence involving intercepted Japanese diplomatic messages. It was published by Department of Defense (DOD) in 1977; no editor is listed. It lacks intercepts of Japanese naval communications, except incomplete references extracted from Daily Communications Summaries issued by Station HYPO. Volumes I and V combine appendix and narrative; Volumes II, III, and IV are separated into appendix and narrative.

The eight volumes lack crucial details concerning the interception of the diplomatic messages. There is no DOD explanation for the absence of the Japanese naval messages intercepted by US naval monitors in the Pacific. A foreword by the unnamed editor is misleading: "It was decided in the public interest to declassify the intelligence which the United States obtained from the communications of its World War II enemies." Japanese communications data pertaining to each message—usually included in such documents—are missing. There is no way to authenticate the intercepts.

National Archives, 24000 Avila Road, Laguna Niguel, California

Fred Close was archivist in charge of Pearl Harbor–era records.

See RG 181 for records of the Eleventh Naval District. Communications intelligence can be found in the A-6 files labeled SECRET and CONFIDENTIAL. They contain copies of communications intelligence records originated by various other naval districts and not found in other depositories.

National Archives, Pacific Sierra Region, 1000 Commodore Drive, San Bruno, California

Archivists: David Drake, Michael Anderson, Waverly B. Lowell, Gary Cramer, Kathleen M. O'Connor

Contains files of the Twelfth (San Francisco), Fourteenth (Hawaii and Central Pacific), and Sixteenth (Philippines) Naval Districts. See RG 181 and its A-6 file category in the SECRET and CONFIDENTIAL storage boxes. See Port Director file, San Francisco, for the mysterious SS *Lurline* controversy.

National Archives, 6125 Sand Point Way NE, Seattle, Washington

Archivists: Donald Piff, Joyce Justice, Janusz Wilczek, and Dwight Grinolds

See RG 181, subsection A-6, for SECRET and CONFIDENTIAL files of the Thirteenth Naval District. Contains files of the West Coast Communications Intelligence Network; Station KING, Dutch Harbor; Station AE, Sitka, Territory of Alaska; Station SAIL, Bainbridge Island, Washington. Every storage box in RG 181 must be checked to locate COMINT files, which were scattered haphazardly throughout the collection by Navy yeomen before their acquisition by the National Archives.

University of Hawaii, Manoa Campus, Honolulu, Hawaii

Pacific War Records Depository in the Hamilton Library. Personal accounts by Hawaiian residents of December 7, 1941. Radio logs of KGMB, KGU radio, Honolulu police, and Honolulu Fire Department files for December 7, 1941.

Franklin D. Roosevelt Presidential Library, Hyde Park, New York

Operated by National Archives

Archivists: William Emerson, Robert Parks, Raymond Teichman, Susan Elter, Mark Renovitch

> Original daily appointment schedules of President Franklin Roosevelt and First Lady Eleanor Roosevelt: the Usher Books chronicle the daily White House schedules; "Trips of the President," Diary and Itineraries detail his travel schedules, including names and affiliations of accompanying staff and news media. Both logs run continuously from March 1932 to the President's death in April 1945.
> The Diary of Adolf A. Berle, Jr.
> The photographic collection, originated by press services and volunteers. Roosevelt did not have an official White House photographer.

Columbia University, Butler Library, New York, New York

Oral History Program: Vice Admiral Walter S. Anderson.

United States Naval Institute, Annapolis, Maryland

Oral History Program:

> Reminiscences of Real Admiral Arthur H. McCollum
> Reminiscences of Real Admiral Charles Adair

Reminiscences of Captain Joseph J. Rochefort
Reminiscences of Captain Thomas Dyer

Federal Bureau of Investigation

There is no all-inclusive file. The author obtained portions of 61 FBI files concerning Japanese espionage by filing FOIA requests with the FBI's Freedom of Information Section in Washington, DC. In reply he received photocopies that were riddled with blackouts and censorship by the Bureau. In an attempt to override the blackouts and censorship, appeals were made to the Department of Justice, Attorney General Janet Reno and her public relations staff headed by Carl Stern, former US Supreme Court news reporter for NBC-TV. Except for minor variances, none of my appeals were granted. The 61 FBI file numbers are:

40-0	State Department visa file pertaining to Japanese diplomats in the United States, 1940–41 era.
61-4	Espionage at Japanese consulate, Honolulu; reports by special agent Frederick Tillman on Tadashi Morimura. Hoover alerts to FBI field offices.
61-5381	Unknown subject. Released to author based on FOIA inquiry concerning Tadashi Morimura and the *Nitta Maru*. But the so-called "released" pages are heavily censored and blacked out as a B-1 National Defense Secret.
61-7632	Transporation of obscene matter involving *Nitta Maru*.
61-10556	Japanese espionage, Honolulu; messages of Hoover to Berle. Some documents censored as B-1 National Defense Secrets.
62-33413	Possibly intercepts of Japanese COMINT involving espionage and subversive activities. Some Hoover-Anderson correspondence. Heavily censored.
62-60950	Involves 1941 reports of the Japanese liner *Taiyo Maru*, Honolulu and internal security of the United States.
62-66721	Complaints by the Japanese government concerning American treatment of consulate members who were moved from Hawaii to Dragoon, Arizona, in 1942.
65-0	Post-attack investigations of Japanese spy Tadashi Morimura.
65-2	Japanese espionage at Honolulu consulate.
65-286	Possible coded messages involving *Nitta Maru*. Not released.
65-414	Main espionage file on the Japanese consulate in Honolulu; includes wiretap file.
65-492	Not obtained. FOIA request not granted.
65-552	Unable to identify. Heavily censored as a B-1 National Defense Secret.

65-560	Japanese espionage suspects.
65-639	Japanese activities, Honolulu, 1941. Super secret file. No numbers or references assigned. Identification of Tadashi Morimura, but specific dates have been censored.
65-1574	German spy in Hawaii Otto Kuehn and his links to Japanese consulate.
65-1628	Tadashi Morimura espionage in Honolulu.
65-1841	Japanese espionage in Honolulu.
65-1843	Japanese espionage re *Nitta Maru*.
65-4374	Ordered from FBI by FOIA request. Not released to author.
65-5413	Espionage re *Nitta Maru*. Not released.
65-7267	Hoover alerts to Berle by special messenger. Involves the *Nitta Maru*, the liner that transported Morimura to Honolulu in March 1941. Heavily censored.
65-8946	Honolulu espionage file concerning *Nitta Maru*, April 1941. FOIA request filed but no part released.
65-9180	Honolulu espionage file involves Germany. Hoover alerts to Berle concerning Japan.
65-9748	Japanese espionage and activities in Hawaii, Washington, DC. Involves surveillance of Japanese Diet members while on visits to United States.
65-9873	Espionage file re *Nitta Maru*. October 1940.
65-10325	Special messages involving espionage reports from Hoover to Berle, 1940–41. Honolulu FBI field office reports from Robert Shivers.
65-10556	Extensive 1940–41 file on reports of Japanese espionage throughout United States. Involves Japanese consulate in Honolulu, Acting Consul-General Otojiro Okuda, and Secretary Kokichi Seki.
65-24238	Espionage file involving *Nitta Maru*, New York, San Francisco.
65-26112	Internal security re German espionage, with links to *Nitta Maru* and New York.
65-26142	Re: *Nitta Maru* and links to Atlanta, Georgia. Heavily censored.
65-26143	Re: *Nitta Maru*.
65-27565	Protection of Japanese consulate, Honolulu; espionage.
65-30500	Re: *Nitta Maru*. SAC Shivers' radiograms to Hoover sent via Navy radio facilities. Extraordinary FBI censorship blacks out dates, file numbers, and the text of documents as B-1 National Defense Secrets. Attorney General Janet Reno refused to declassify this file.
65-33780	Unable to identify the file subject due to FBI censorship.
65-36120	Cryptographic file involving Japanese espionage; contains intercepts. Some sent to Major General Edwin "Pa" Watson and marked as "Of interest to the President."

65-36220	Departure of Japanese consulate members from New York on SS *Gripsholm*, July–August 1942.
65-37803	1941–42 file. Japanese activities in Chicago, New Orleans. Wiretaps. Involves link to Assistant Secretary of State Adolf Berle, Jr. Entire file heavily censored.
65-39168	Japanese espionage. File never received by author.
65-41886	Japanese espionage file contains post-attack reports on Richard Kotoshirodo and Tadashi Morimura.
65-42398	Japanese espionage, Honolulu. 1942 FBI reports sent to Assistant Secretary of State Adolf Berle, Jr.
65-55473	A 1945 report of espionage with focus on German suspects and Japan, involving *Nitta Maru*.
66-03	FBI Bulletin file, 1941.
66-656	Intelligence Conferences with Hoover and military intelligence officials.
66-8603	Intelligence Conferences documents withheld as B-1 National Defense Secrets.
94-4	FBI surveillance in 1961 involving Morimura/Yoshikawa, Walter Cronkite, and CBS-TV news.
97-274	Japanese espionage, Honolulu.
100-0	Appears to be a special file on Morimura/Yoshikawa. Not released to author.
100-2	Japanese espionage in Honolulu.
100-97	Post-attack intelligence assessments by FBI dated after 1946. Confirms US Navy broke Japanese military codes prior to December 7, 1941. Contains Japanese diplomatic intercepts.
100-185	Espionage investigations of 1942 involving Kotoshirodo and Morimura.
100-687	Japanese espionage file for Honolulu. No details.
100-832	German espionage suspects en route from New York to San Francisco to board *Nitta Maru* in August 1940.
100-1387	Japanese espionage in pre–Pearl Harbor Honolulu area, 1943 reports.
100-2643	Japanese espionage pre Pearl Harbor, 1943 reports by US Army.
100-62229	FBI file on Nagao Kita, Japanese consul-general, Honolulu, 1941.
100-65558	Unknown. Not received by author.
100-111258	1942 files on Japanese espionage concerning pre Pearl Harbor.
100-141295	1943 era. Involves FBI agent Fred Tillman attempting to locate consulate clerk Richard Kotoshirodo and taxi driver John Mikami for trial.
190-152	Involves espionage activities at Honolulu Consulate. Not released to author.

Interviews and Personal Correspondence with the Author

I wish to acknowledge the enthusiastic assistance of the many dedicated US Navy intercept operators and cryptographers who, through letters or personal interviews, patiently explained their highly secret methods of tracking the Japanese naval units prior to December 7, 1941.

Station AE, Sitka, Alaska

Fred R. Thomson, Radioman-in-charge (Letters 1986–88).

Station M, Cheltenham, Maryland

Ralph Briggs, Navy intercept operator, interviewed by the author, Reno, Nevada, August 27, 1987.

Station King, Dutch Harbor, Territory of Alaska

Thomas E. Gilmore of Tacoma, Washington, RDF operator; letter of December 3, 1985.

Frank W. Hess of Chula Vista, California, RDF operator; letter of January 6, 1986.

Harry Hood of Philadelphia, Pennsylvania. RDF operator; letter of January 15, 1986.

Station CAST, Corregidor Island, Philippines

Duane L. Whitlock, traffic analyst. Taped audio interview with author, September 30, 1993, Danville, California; author-Whitlock telephone conversations and correspondence January–May 1999, Strawberry Point, Iowa.

Robert Dowd of Oakdale, California, Navy yeoman and Purple machine operator in 1941. Oakdale, California. Telephone and written correspondence with the author April–May 1999.

Station H, Heeia, Hawaii

Homer Kisner of Carlsbad, California, radio traffic chief. Author-taped audio interviews April 22, 23, 1988, Carlsbad, California. Videotaped interview Best Western Hotel, Sacramento, California, April 24, 1998. Extensive written correspondence between author and Kisner, 1988–1999.

Jerry Randle, intercept operator. Taped audio interview, Reno, Nevada, August 27, 1987.

Jack Kaye of Santa Ana, California, Navy intercept operator. Written correspondence and e-mail, April–May 1999.

Maynard Albertson of Spring Valley, California, Navy intercept operator. Written correspondence, April 1999.

Henry Garstka, of Edgewater, New Jersey, Navy intercept and RDF operator. Telephone conversation May 7, 1999.

Roy Lehman of Hawthorne, California, Navy intercept operator. Written correspondence with author, March 20, 1986, May 5, 1986. Taped audio interview, Hawthorne, California, December 2, 1987.

Elliott Okins of Chula Vista, California, Navy intercept supervisor. Written correspondence with author, June 7 and 20, 1986.

Donovan Chase, Santa Rosa, California, Navy intercept operator. Taped audio interview, January 15, 1988.

Hugh McGall of Magalia, California, Navy intercept operator. Written correspondence May 8 and September 2, 1986.

Joseph Christie Howard of Kent, Washington. Written correspondence and telephone interviews, May, June 1999.

Station HYPO, Administration Building, Fourteenth Naval District, Pearl Harbor Naval Yard, Hawaii

Rear Admiral Edwin Layton of Carmel, California, intelligence officer for the Pacific Fleet. Not an official part of HYPO, but spent considerable time with Rochefort and staff. Interviewed by the author November 29, 1982; written correspondence 1982–83.

Captain Thomas Dyer of Sykesville, Maryland, second in command and head of the cryptographic section. Written correspondence 1983.

Captain Forrest Biard of Long Beach, California, Japanese language officer, reported to Station HYPO November 1941. Taped audio interview at Long Beach, California, December 1, 1987, and subsequent written correspondence 1988; additional interview during visit to Midway Battle Symposium, Pensacola, Florida, April 1988.

Arnold Conant of Dunnellon, Florida, Chief Yeoman and cryptographer assistant to Dyer. Written correspondence May 4, 1986.

Durwood Rorie of Winter Springs, Florida, Chief Yeoman and head of physical security of the Station HYPO office. Written correspondence March 24, April 20, and May 23, 1986.

Irving Morris of Emeryville, California, yeoman in the ship movement section; interviewed at Emeryville, California, January 1993.

Captain Wilfred J. Holmes of Honolulu, Hawaii, ship movement section. Taped audio interview and correspondence, 1982–83.

I wish to acknowledge the utmost courtesy of Mrs. Janet Rochefort Elerding, daughter of Commander Joseph Rochefort, the commanding officer of Station HYPO, during my visit to Santa Ana, California, November 18, 1982.

Other Sources

I had the good fortune to benefit from the expertise of the following: William Seale, an architect-historian who provided details on the Roosevelt White House; Pulitzer Prize–winning historian John Toland and his wife Toshiko; Commander Sadao Seno of the Imperial Japanese Navy; the late Michi Weglen, an author and a victim of the Japanese Internment of 1942; author James Rusbridger; Lee S. Motteler, geographer, Honolulu; Ed Aber-Song, who served with US Navy Public Affairs in 1982; Donald Cleff, Chief Engineer City, and County of Honolulu, for maps of the Territorial Planning Board, 1939–41 era; Bertha Ihnat, Ohio State University at Columbus, and Kendrick D. McNulty of the *Daily News-Record*, Harrisonburg, Virginia, for details on Agnes Meyer Driscoll; and Bernard K. Zobrist, Director of the Harry S. Truman Library. Though I didn't always get what I asked for, personnel at the Naval Security Group Command at Washington, DC, at least tried: Christopher Gentile, Robert Sheer, Peg Feightner, Commander Irv Newman, the late George Henriksen, and Lieutenant Brian L. Blankenship. Grady Lewis, editor of *Cryptolog*, the official publication of the Naval Cryptologic Veterans Association, was gracious with his time and steered me to the Navy intercept operators. Carol Leadenham, Reference Archivist at the Hoover Institution Archives, Stanford University, Stanford, California, shared her extensive knowledge of the papers of Lieutenant General Walter Short. Captain Thomas Kimmel, his brother Edward, Husband E. Kimmel II and Thomas Kimmel Jr., grandsons of the admiral, shared their information. Jane Sween of the Montgomery County Historical Society, Rockville, Maryland; Richard Harnett, former United Press Bureau Chief in San Francisco; and Stephen A. Haller, Historian of the National Parks Service at the San Francisco Presidio, provided information on Station TWO. Dr. P. C. van Royen, Director of the Institute for Maritime History in the Netherlands, furnished details on Captain Johan Ranneft. Alma de Bisschop checked Dutch history records in Amsterdam and confirmed Dutch translations, as did the Dutch Consulate General in San Francisco. Paul Dane of the Society of Wireless Pioneers provided invaluable insights into the International Morse Code and its difference from Japanese radiotelegraphy. Marge Stromgren of Kaneohe, Hawaii, spent years tracing the records of Station H in the Kaneohe Library and took aerial photographs of the site.

Lieutenant Commander Cedric Brown of the Royal Navy corresponded with the author in 1985–86 and confirmed that a British cryptographic unit known as the Q Team intercepted Japanese communications on Stonecutter's Island in Hong Kong Harbor in 1941. William vanden Heuvel confirmed his diary report concerning William Donovan. Judges Vernon Moore and Robert Hughes gave me their legal insights on Arthur McCollum's provocative actions. Lynn Suter shared her knowledge of Navy–Congress relations.

Sean and Naemi McPherson served as the main Japanese translators for this book. I received additional translation input from Kimi and George Matsumoto, Kiyoko Yamada, and Gabriel Sylvian. I am indebted to Casey Murrow, son of Edward R. Murrow. In Oregon, Ann Witty of the Columbia River Maritime Museum and Dr. Charles F. Cardinell of the Oregon Maritime Center helped to locate the Bar Pilot records involving the Russian vessel *Uritski*. Daniel J. Lenihan, Chief of the Submerged Cultural Resource Unit of the National Parks Service, and his talented staff of divers and historians, detailed for me the damage to the USS *Arizona*. My thanks go to David Lotz and Bill Stewart of the War in the Pacific National Park on Guam. David Aiken shared many of his Japanese records. Max Bishop and H. Merrill Benninghoff, members of the 1941 American Embassy in Tokyo, shared their pre–Pearl Harbor experiences. Professor John Moore of California Polytechnic College, Pomona, supplied information on CBS radio newsman Cecil Brown.

The never-ending research involving Pearl Harbor began in 1982 and continues in 1999. It has taken a long time, and many people and organizations have helped me. If I have omitted your name it is an oversight and I apologize. I could not have written this book without the help of each and every one of you.

Special Acknowledgments

My wife Peggy, associate editor of the *Oakland Tribune*, who helped with professional guidance and insight along the long journey of getting this book done. She and my children kept my spirits up, Colleen and Dennis Badagliacco, Jim Stinnett, and grandchildren Robert and Laura Badagliacco have never wavered in their support of this project even though they often chorused: "When Will the Book Be Done?"

The Book Be Done people have been miraculous: Michael Larsen and Elizabeth Pomada, my literary agents, who believed in my project from the start; James O. Wade skillfully edited and guided the first manuscript drafts; Bruce Nichols, Senior Editor, Dan Freedberg, Carol de Onís, and Camilla Hewitt of The Free Press edited the final drafts and cleared the way for publication with warmth, humor, and enthusiasm. Their suggestions helped open up the manuscript for readers and guided me in explaining and simplifying the intricacies of code-breaking. For typing the manuscript there are no acknowledgments. I did it myself thanks to the two Steves, Jobs and Wozniak. Their Apple saw me through.

Any complaints concerning the book and my research must fall on me alone.

A SERIES OF WAR WARNINGS
ISSUED BY THE US GOVERNMENT

Source: RG 80, PHLO, MMRB, Archives II.

Prediction of a Japanese "surprise aggressive movement in any direction" came from Rear Admiral Royal Ingersoll, assistant chief of naval operations, on November 24, 1941. Upon receiving this message on the super secret US Navy CETYH circuit (see lower right), Admiral Husband E. Kimmel pulled the Pacific Fleet out of a North Pacific reconnaissance mission.

MEMORANDUM FOR DEPARTMENT ADJUTANT GENERAL:

....
(date)

Request that the following [*Secret *Confidential *XXXXXXXX] official radiogram be sent. This message does NOT cover subject matter previously sent in a message, either in the clear or having a different security classification.

This message is { *Priority. *XXXXXX *XXXXXX }

*Strike out words not applicable.

....
Signature and Title

Sent as Radiogram No.	Message Center No.	Time Filed	Check	Code Clerk

P1 WAR PRTY

WASHN DC 611 PM NOV 27 1941

CG

HAWN DEPT FT SHAFTER TH

Approved for Transmission:

....
Adjutant General

472 27TH NEGOTIATIONS WITH JAPAN APPEAR TO BE TERMINATED TO ALL PRACTICAL PURPOSES WITH ONLY THE BAREST POSSIBILITIES THAT THE JAPANESE GOVERNMENT MIGHT COME BACK AND OFFER TO CONTINUE STOP JAPANESE FUTURE ACTION UNPREDICTIBLE BUT HOSTILE ACTION POSSIBLE AT ANY MOMENT STOP IF HOSTILITIES CANNOT COMMA REPEAT CANNOT COMMA BE AVOIDED THE UNITED STATES DESIRES THAT JAPAN COMMIT THE FIRST OVERT ACT STOP THIS POLICY SHOULD NOT COMMA REPEAT NOT COMMA BE CONSTRUED AS RESTRICTING YOU TO A COURSE OF ACTION THAT MIGHT JEOPARDIZE YOUR DEFENSE STOP PRIOR TO HOSTILE JAPANESE ACTION YOU ARE DIRECTED TO UNDERTAKE SUCH RECONNAISSANCE AND OTHER MEASURES AS YOU DEEM NECESSARY BUT THESE MEASURES SHOULD BE CARRIED OUT SO AS NOT COMMA REPEAT NOT COMMA TO ALARM CIVIL POPULATION OR DISCLOSE INTENT STOP REPORT MEASURES TAKEN STOP SHOULD HOSTILITIES OCCUR YOU WILL CARRY OUT THE TASKS ASSIGNED IN RAINBOW FIVE SO FAR AS THEY PERTAIN TO JAPAN STOP LIMIT DISSEMINATION OF THIS HIGHLY SECRET INFORMATION TO MINIMUM ESSENTIAL OFFICERS

MARSHALL

TRUE COPY

O. M. Cutler

O M CUTLER
LT COL INFANTRY

116P/27

NOTE: This form to be used only for Radiograms and Cablegrams. One copy only to be submitted. The making of an exact copy of Secret or Confidential Radiograms is forbidden. Only such extracts as are absolutely necessary will be made and marked secret or confidential as the case may be. This copy will be safeguarded with the greatest care and when no longer required will be returned to the Records Division, Adjutant General's Office, without delay. (AR 380-5)

Form H.D. No. 1173 (Revised)—1664 Honolulu 10-10-40 5M.

Source: General Short's papers, Hoover Institution Archives, Stanford University, Stanford, California.

Though it is signed "MARSHALL," this November 27, 1941, war warning message was originated by Secretary of War Henry L. Stimson, acting on the orders of President Roosevelt. It directs the Hawaiian US Army commander, Lieutenant General Walter Short, to follow an official US government desire: "The United States desires that Japan commit the first overt act."

SEALED SECRET

NAVAL MESSAGE		NAVY DEPARTMENT	
PHONE EXTENSION NUMBER Op-12 Ext. 2992		ADDRESSEES	MESSAGE PRECEDENCE
FROM Chief of Naval Operations	FOR ACTION	CINCAF CINCPAC	PRIORITY X ROUTINE DEFERRED
RELEASED BY			
DATE November 27, 1941.			
TOR CODEROOM	INFORMATION	CINCLANT SPENAVO	PRIORITY ROUTINE DEFERRED
DECODED BY			
PARAPHRASED BY			

INDICATE BY ASTERISK ADDRESSEES FOR WHICH MAIL DELIVERY IS SATISFACTORY

GKVJL BVKLW 272337 0971

UNLESS OTHERWISE DESIGNATED THIS DISPATCH WILL BE TRANSMITTED WITH DEFERRED PRECEDENCE.
ORIGINATOR FILL IN DATE AND TIME FOR DEFERRED AND MAIL DELIVERY

DATE   TIME   GCT

HEELS

MM THIS DESPATCH IS TO BE CONSIDERED A WAR WARNING X NEGOTIATIONS
WITH JAPAN LOOKING TOWARD STABILIZATION OF CONDITIONS IN THE
PACIFIC HAVE CEASED AND AN AGGRESSIVE MOVE BY JAPAN IS EXPECTED
WITHIN THE NEXT FEW DAYS X THE NUMBER AND EQUIPMENT OF JAPANESE
TROOPS AND THE ORGANIZATION OF NAVAL TASK FORCES INDICATES AN
AMPHIBIOUS EXPEDITION PROBABLY AGAINST EITHER THE PHILIPPINES THAI
OR KRA PENINSULA OR POSSIBLY BORNEO X EXECUTE AN APPROPRIATE
DEFENSIVE DEPLOYMENT PREPARATORY TO CARRYING OUT THE TASKS ASSIGNED
IN WPL46X INFORM DISTRICT AND ARMY AUTHORITIES X A SIMILAR WARNING
IS BEING SENT BY WAR DEPARTMENT X SPENAVO INFORM BRITISH X

CONTINENTAL DISTRICTS GUAM SAMOA directed
take appropriate measures against sabotage MM

COPY TO WPD AND DEPT)

enc.phored calls

BY RAB
ELM-35

TOP SECRET

SEE NAV

MAKE ORIGINAL ONLY, DELIVER TO COMMUNICATION WATCH OFFICER IN PERSON

48425

The US Navy's war warning message of November 27, 1941, authored by Rear Admiral Royal Ingersoll (top left), omitted the crucial orders of President Roosevelt that called for US military forces to let Japan commit the first overt act. The omission was corrected the next day.

NAVAL MESSAGE   NAVY DEPARTMENT

PHONE EXTENSION NUMBER Op-12 Ext. 2092   ADDRESSEES | MESSAGE PRECEDENCE

FROM Chief of Naval Operations   COM PNHCP   PRIORITY X
RELEASED BY   COM PSNCP   ROUTINE
DATE November 28, 1941   DEFERRED

TOR CODEROOM _____   CINCPAC   PRIORITY
DECODED ?·_____   COM PHCF   ROUTINE
PARAPHRASED BY   DEFERRED

INDICATE BY ASTERISK ADDRESSEES FOR WHICH MAIL DELIVERY IS SATISFACTORY

290110

UNLESS OTHERWISE DESIGNATED THIS DISPATCH WILL BE TRANSMITTED WITH DEFERRED PRECEDENCE.
ORIGINATOR FILL IN DATE AND TIME FOR DEFERRED AND MAIL DELIVERY
                    DATE   TIME   GCT

TEXT

REFER TO MY 272338 X ARMY HAS SENT FOLLOWING TO COMMANDER WESTERN

DEFENSE COMMAND QUOTE NEGOTIATIONS WITH JAPAN APPEAR TO BE TERMINATED

TO ALL PRACTICAL PURPOSES WITH ONLY THE BAREST POSSIBILITIES THAT

THE JAPANESE GOVERNMENT MIGHT COME BACK AND OFFER TO CONTINUE X

JAPANESE FUTURE ACTION UNPREDICTABLE BUT HOSTILE ACTION POSSIBLE

AT ANY MOMENT X IF HOSTILITIES CANNOT REPEAT NOT BE AVOIDED THE

UNITED STATES DESIRES THAT JAPAN COMMIT THE FIRST OVERT ACT X THIS

POLICY SHOULD NOT REPEAT NOT BE CONSTRUED AS RESTRICTING YOU TO A

COURSE OF ACTION THAT MIGHT JEOPARDIZE YOUR DEFENSE X PRIOR TO

HOSTILE JAPANESE ACTION YOU ARE DIRECTED TO UNDERTAKE SUCH

RECONNAISSANCE AND OTHER MEASURES AS YOU DEEM NECESSARY BUT THESE

MEASURES SHOULD BE CARRIED OUT SO AS NOT REPEAT NOT TO ALARM CIVIL

POPULATION OR DISCLOSE INTENT X REPORT MEASURES TAKEN X A SEPARATE

MESSAGE IS BEING SENT TO CG NINTH CORPS AREA RE SUBVERSIVE

TOP SECRET

SEE ART. 76(4)
NAV REGS
MAKE ORIGINAL ONLY, DELIVER TO COMMUNICATION WATCH OFFICER IN PERSON
(page one of two)

Source: Rg 38, Station US papers, MMRB, Archives II.

On Friday, November 28, 1941, Admiral Harold Stark, the chief of naval operations, restored the previous day's omission by twice repeating that the United States desired that Japan commit the first overt act.

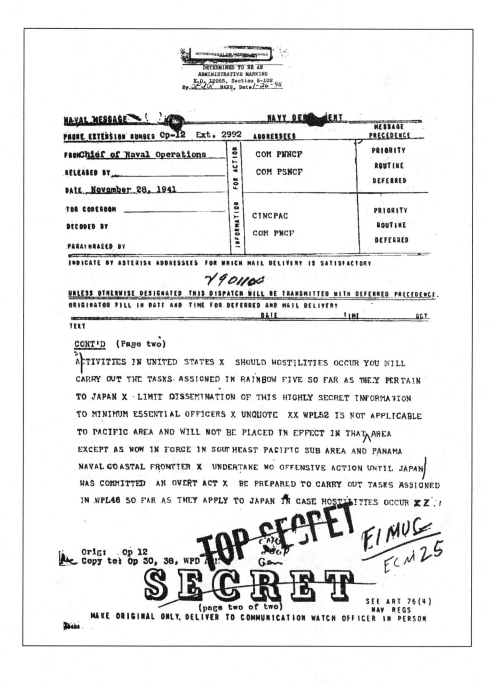

REPRODUCED AT THE NATIONAL ARCHIVES

DETERMINED TO BE AN
ADMINISTRATIVE MARKING
E.O. 12065, Section 6-102
By _____ NARS, Date _____

NAVAL MESSAGE ( )   **NAVY DEPARTMENT**

PHONE EXTENSION NUMBER Op-12 Ext. 2992		ADDRESSEES	MESSAGE PRECEDENCE
FROM Chief of Naval Operations	FOR ACTION	COM PWNCF	PRIORITY
RELEASED BY		COM PSNCF	ROUTINE
DATE November 28, 1941			DEFERRED
TOR CODEROOM	INFORMATION	CINCPAC	PRIORITY
DECODED BY		COM PNCF	ROUTINE
PARAPHRASED BY			DEFERRED

INDICATE BY ASTERISK ADDRESSEES FOR WHICH MAIL DELIVERY IS SATISFACTORY

190110

UNLESS OTHERWISE DESIGNATED THIS DISPATCH WILL BE TRANSMITTED WITH DEFERRED PRECEDENCE.
ORIGINATOR FILL IN DATE AND TIME FOR DEFERRED AND MAIL DELIVERY

	DATE	TIME	GCT

TEXT

CONT'D (Page two)

ACTIVITIES IN UNITED STATES X   SHOULD HOSTILITIES OCCUR YOU WILL
CARRY OUT THE TASKS ASSIGNED IN RAINBOW FIVE SO FAR AS THEY PERTAIN
TO JAPAN X LIMIT DISSEMINATION OF THIS HIGHLY SECRET INFORMATION
TO MINIMUM ESSENTIAL OFFICERS X UNQUOTE XX WPL52 IS NOT APPLICABLE
TO PACIFIC AREA AND WILL NOT BE PLACED IN EFFECT IN THAT AREA
EXCEPT AS NOW IN FORCE IN SOUTHEAST PACIFIC SUB AREA AND PANAMA
NAVAL COASTAL FRONTIER X UNDERTAKE NO OFFENSIVE ACTION UNTIL JAPAN
HAS COMMITTED AN OVERT ACT X BE PREPARED TO CARRY OUT TASKS ASSIGNED
IN WPL46 SO FAR AS THEY APPLY TO JAPAN IN CASE HOSTILITIES OCCUR X Z

TOP SECRET

SECRET

EIMUG
ECM25

CNO
Dep
Gen

Orig: Op 12
Copy to: Op 30, 38, WPD

SEE ART 76(4)
NAV REGS

(page two of two)
MAKE ORIGINAL ONLY, DELIVER TO COMMUNICATION WATCH OFFICER IN PERSON

HEAD QUARTERS HAWAIIAN DEPARTMENT
FORT SHAFTER, T. H.

MEMORANDUM FOR DEPARTMENT ADJUTANT GENERAL:

....
(date)

Request that the following { *Secret / *~~CONFIDENTIAL~~ / *~~RESTRICTED~~ } official radiogram be sent. This message does NOT cover subject matter previously sent in a message, either in the clear or having a different security classification.

This message is { *Priority. / *~~ROUTINE~~ / *~~Deferred~~ }

*Strike out words not applicable.

....
Signature and Title

Sent as Radiogram No.	Message Center No.	Time Filed	Check	Code Clerk

114 WAR KR 189 WD PRTY

WASHN DC   842P NOV 28 1941

Approved for Transmission:

....
Adjutant General

C G

HAWN DEPT FT SHAFTER T H

482 28TH   CRITICAL SITUATION DEMANDS THAT ALL PRECAUTIONS BE TAKEN IMMEDIATELY AGAINST SUBVERSIVE ACTIVITIES WITHIN FIELD OF INVESTIGATIVE RESPONSIBILITY OF WAR DEPARTMENT PAREN SEE PARAGRAPH THREE MID SC THIRTY DASH FORTY FIVE END PAREN STOP ALSO DESIRED THAT YOU INITIATE FORTHWITH ALL ADDITIONAL MEASURES NECESSARY TO PROVIDE FOR PROTECTION OF YOUR ESTABLISHMENTS COMMA PROPERTY COMMA AND EQUIPMENT AGAINST SABOTAGE COMMA PROTECTION OF YOUR PERSONNEL AGAINST SUBVERSIVE PROPAGANDA AND PROTECTION OF ALL ACTIVITIES AGAINST ESPIONAGE STOP THIS DOES NOT REPEAT NOT MEAN THAT ANY ILLEGAL MEASURES ARE AUTHORIZED STOP PROTECTIVE MEASURES SHOULD BE CONFINED TO THOSE ESSENTIAL TO SECURITY COMMA AVOIDING UNNECESSARY PUBLICITY AND ALARM STOP TO INSURE SPEED OF TRANSMISSION IDENTICAL TELEGRAMS ARE BEING SENT TO ALL AIR STATIONS BUT THIS DOES NOT REPEAT NOT AFFECT YOUR RESPONSIBILITY UNDER EXISTING INSTRUCTIONS

ADAMS

TRUE COPY

O M CUTLER
O M CUTLER
LT COL INFANTRY
NOTE: This form to be used only for Radiograms and Cablegrams. One copy only to be submitted. The making of an exact copy of Secret or Confidential Radiograms is forbidden. Only such extracts as are absolutely necessary will be made and marked secret or confidential as the case may be. This copy will be safeguarded with the greatest care and when no longer required will be returned to the Records Division, Adjutant General's Office, without delay. (AR 380-5)

Form H.D. No. 1173 (Revised)—1964 Honolulu 10-10-40 5M.

Source: Papers of Lt. Gen. Walter Short, Hoover Institution Archives, Stanford University, Stanford, CA.

A second warning to prepare for subversive activities and sabotage in Hawaii was issued to Lieutenant General Walter Short by the US Army Adjutant General, Emory Adams, on Friday, November 28, 1941. Adams warned Short not to precipate publicity or alarm.

HEADQUARTERS HAWAIIAN DEPARTMENT
FORT SHAFTER, T. H.

MEMORANDUM FOR DEPARTMENT ADJUTANT GENERAL:

.... (date)

Request that the following { *Secret / XXXXXXXXX / XXXXXXXX } official radiogram be sent. This message does NOT cover subject matter previously sent in a message, either in the clear or having a different security classification.

This message is { *Priority. / XXXXXXX / XXXXXXX }

/sgd/ Thomas H. Green,
THOMAS H. GREEN
Lt. Col. Signature and Title
Department Judge Advocate.

*Strike out words not applicable.

Sent as Radiogram No.	Message Center No.	Time Filed	Check	Code Clerk

THE ADJUTANT GENERAL
WAR DEPARTMENT
WASHINGTON D C

Approved for Transmission:

....
Adjutant General

RE YOUR SECRET RADIO FOUR EIGHT TWO TWENTY EIGHTH COMMA FULL PRECAUTIONS ARE BEING TAKEN AGAINST SUBVERSIVE ACTIVITIES WITHIN THE FIELD OF INVESTIGATIVE RESPONSIBILITY OF WAR DEPARTMENT PAREN PARAGRAPH THREE MID SC THIRTY DASH FORTY FIVE END PAREN AND MILITARY ESTABLISHMENTS INCLUDING PERSONNEL AD EQUIPMENT STOP AS REGARDS PROTECTION OF VITAL INSTALLATIONS OUTSIDE OF MILITARY RESERVATIONS SUCH AS POWER PLANTS COMMA TELEPHONE EXCHANGES AND HIGHWAY BRIDGES COMMA THIS HEADQUARTERS BY CONFIDENTIAL LETTER DATED JUNE NINETEEN NINETEEN FORTY ONE REQUESTED THE GOVERNOR OF THE TERRITORY TO USE THE BROAD POWERS VESTED IN HIM BY SECTION SIXTY SEVEN OF THE ORGANIC ACT WHICH PROVIDES COMMA IN EFFECT COMMA THAT THE GOVERNOR MAY CALL UPON THE COMMANDERS OF MILITARY AND NAVAL FORCES OF THE UNITED STATES IN THE TERRITORY OF HAWAII TO PREVENT OR SUPPRESS LAWLESS VIOLENCE COMMA INVASION COMMA INSURRECTION ETC STOP PURSUANT TO THE AUTHORITY STATED THE GOVERNOR ON JUNE TWENTIETH CONFIDENTIALLY MADE A FORMAL WRITTEN DEMAND ON THIS HEADQUARTERS TO FURNISH AND CONTINUE TO FURNISH SUCH ADEQUATE PROTECTION AS MAY BE NECESSARY TO PREVENT SABOTAGE COMMA AND LAWLESS VIOLENCE IN CONNECTION THEREWITH COMMA BEING COMMITTED AGAINST VITAL INSTALLATIONS AND STRUCTURES IN THE TERRITORY STOP PURSUANT TO THE FOREGOING REQUEST APPROPRIATE

NOTE: This form to be used only for Radiograms and Cablegrams. One copy only to be submitted. The making of an exact copy of Secret or Confidential Radiograms is forbidden. Only such extracts as are absolutely necessary will be made and marked secret or confidential as the case may be. This copy will be safeguarded with the greatest care and when no longer required will be returned to the Records Division, Adjutant General's Office, without delay. (AR.380-5)

-1-

Form H.D. No. 1173 (Revised)—1604 Honolulu 10-10-40 5M.

Source: Walter Short papers, Hoover Institution Archives, Stanford University, Stanford, CA.

General Short issued this reply to the three US Army war warnings sent him from Washington. Since two of the directives warned him to anticipate subversive and sabotage activities, Short followed orders.

HEADQUARTERS HAWAIIAN DEPARTMENT
FORT SHAFTER, T. H.

MEMORANDUM FOR DEPARTMENT ADJUTANT GENERAL:

(date)

Request that the following { *Secret *Confidential *Restricted } official radiogram be sent. This message does NOT cover subject matter previously sent in a message. either in the clear or having a different security classification.

This message is { *Priority. *Routine. *Deferred }

*Strike out words not applicable.

Signature and

Sent as Radiogram No.	Message No.

Approved for Transmission:

PAGE TWO

Adjutant General

MILITARY PROTECTION IS NOW BEING AFFORDED VITAL CIVILIAN INSTALLATIONS STOP IN THIS CONNECTION COMMA AT THE INSTIGATION OF THIS HEADQUARTERS THE CITY AND COUNTY OF HONOLULU ON JUNE THIRTIETH NINETEEN FORTY ONE ENACTED AN ORDINANCE WHICH PERMITS THE COMMANDING GENERAL HAWAIIAN DEPARTMENT COMMA TO CLOSE COMMA OR RESTRICT THE USE OF AND TRAVEL UPON COMMA ANY HIGHWAY WITHIN THE CITY AND COUNTY OF HONOLULU COMMA WHENEVER THE COMMANDING GENERAL DEEMS SUCH ACTION NECESSARY IN THE INTEREST OF NATIONAL DEFENSE STOP THE AUTHORITY THUS GIVEN HAS NOT YET BEEN EXERCISED STOP RELATIONS WITH F B I AND ALL OTHER FEDERAL AND TERRITORIAL OFFICIALS ARE AND HAVE BEEN CORDIAL AND MUTUAL COOPERATION HAS BEEN GIVEN ON ALL PERTINENT MATTERS

SHORT

ENC SEC BY
LT JOS ENGELHERTZ SC
2:45 P 29 NOV 41

TRUE COPY
O M Cutler
O M CUTLER
LT COL INFANTRY

NOTE: This form to be used only for Radiograms and Cablegrams. One copy only to be submitted. The making of an copy of Secret or Confidential Radiograms is forbidden. Only such extracts as are absolutely necessary will be and marked secret or confidential as the   may be. This copy will be safeguarded with the greatest care and no longer required will be returned to the Records Division, Adjutant General's Office, without delay. (Art 380

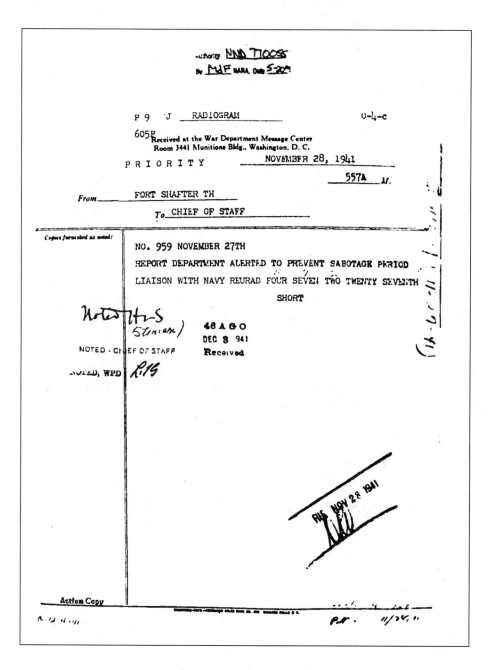

authority NND 710055
By MJF NARA Date 5-30-4

P 9 J   RADIOGRAM   O-4-c

605P
Received at the War Department Message Center
Room 3441 Munitions Bldg., Washington, D. C.

PRIORITY   NOVEMBER 28, 1941

                                        557A   1/.

From_____FORT SHAFTER TH

        To__CHIEF OF STAFF_____

Copies furnished as noted:

NO. 959 NOVEMBER 27TH

REPORT DEPARTMENT ALERTED TO PREVENT SABOTAGE PERIOD

LIAISON WITH NAVY REURAD FOUR SEVEN TWO TWENTY SEVENTH

                        SHORT

Noted HxS
      5(nicah)   46 A G O
                           DEC 3 941
NOTED - CHIEF OF STAFF   Received

NOTED, WPD LHS

FILE NOV 28 1941

Action Copy

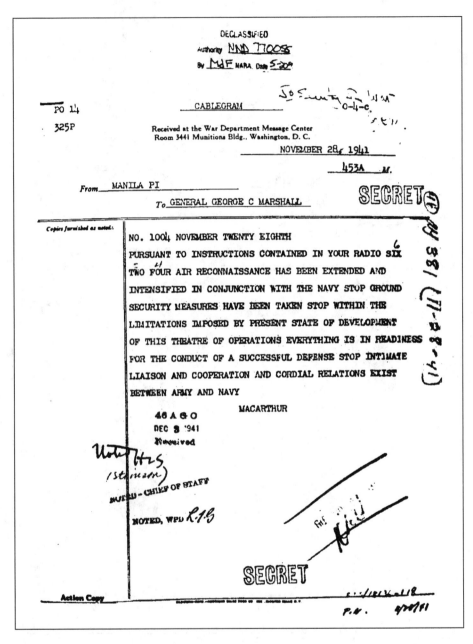

DECLASSIFIED

Authority NND 770055

By MJF NARA Date 5-30-

PO 14
325P

CABLEGRAM

Received at the War Department Message Center
Room 3441 Munitions Bldg., Washington, D. C.

NOVEMBER 28, 1941

453A M.

From MANILA PI

To GENERAL GEORGE C MARSHALL

SECRET

Copies furnished as noted:

NO. 1004 NOVEMBER TWENTY EIGHTH

PURSUANT TO INSTRUCTIONS CONTAINED IN YOUR RADIO SIX

TWO FOUR AIR RECONNAISSANCE HAS BEEN EXTENDED AND

INTENSIFIED IN CONJUNCTION WITH THE NAVY STOP GROUND

SECURITY MEASURES HAVE BEEN TAKEN STOP WITHIN THE

LIMITATIONS IMPOSED BY PRESENT STATE OF DEVELOPMENT

OF THIS THEATRE OF OPERATIONS EVERYTHING IS IN READINESS

FOR THE CONDUCT OF A SUCCESSFUL DEFENSE STOP INTIMATE

LIAISON AND COOPERATION AND CORDIAL RELATIONS EXIST

BETWEEN ARMY AND NAVY

MACARTHUR

46 A G O
DEC 3 1941
Received

(Stimson)

DUPLO - CHIEF OF STAFF

NOTED, WPD R.1.9

SECRET

Action Copy

P. N.

Source: RG80, PHLO, MMRB, Archives II.

General Douglas MacArthur assured Washington that he was not about to conduct offensive operations against Japan from his US Army command post in Manila. His reply to let Japan commit the first overt act was just what was desired by the White House: "Everything is in readiness for the conduct of a successful defense."

WAR DEPARTMENT **SECRET**
WAR DEPARTMENT GENERAL STAFF BY AUTHORITY OF A. C. OF S., WPD
WAR PLANS DIVISION
WASHINGTON

12/1/41. .....CK.7.........
Date   Initials

December 7, 1941.

MEMORANDUM FOR THE ADJUTANT GENERAL (Through Secretary, General Staff)

Subject: Far East Situation.

The Secretary of War directs that the following first priority secret radiogram be sent to the Commanding General, U.S. Army Forces in the Far East; Commanding General, Carribean Defense Command; Commanding General, Hawaiian Department; Commanding General, Fourth Army:

Japanese are presenting at one p.m. Eastern Standard time today what amounts to an ultimatum also they are under orders to destroy their Code machine immediately stop Just what significance the hour set may have we do not know but be on alert accordingly stop Inform naval authorities of this communication.

MARSHALL

Notice O.C.S.
12/7/41 JWB

L. T. GEROW,
Brigadier General,
Acting Assistant Chief of Staff.

Code messages
Sent by
Div

Radios as follows dispatched 11:52 AM, 12-7-41,
by Code Room, WDMC:
12.05 #733 to CG, USAFFE, Manila, P.I.;
12.17 #529 to CG, Haw. Dept., Ft. Shafter. TH.
12.00 #519 to CG, Crbn. Def. Cmnd., Quarry Heights, CZ.
12.11 # 16 to CG, Fourth Army, Pres. of San Fco., Cal.
ehb - 1705.

JAN - 3 1942
DAJ

SECRET

Source: RG 80, PHLO, MMRB, Archives II.

Hawaii was last on the US Army list to receive this warning that Japan had set a Washington, DC, deadline of 1 P.M., Sunday, December 7, 1941. The time corresponded to 7:30 A.M., Sunday December 7, 1941, in Hawaii—less than 30 minutes to the first Japanese bomb drop. This message did not reach Lieutenant General Walter Short until mid-afternoon, Sunday December 7, 1941, about 6 hours after the first bombs fell on Pearl Harbor.

SELECTED INTELLIGENCE
DOCUMENTS, 1940–41

25 November 1941

From: CinC Combined Fleet
To: First Air Fleet
          (Pearl Harbor Attack Force)

The task force, keeping its movement strictly secret and maintaining close guard against submarines and aircraft, shall advance into Hawaiian waters, and upon the very opening of hostilities shall attack the main force of the United States Fleet in Hawaii and deal it a mortal blow. The first air raid is planned for the dawn of X-day (exact date to be given by later order).

Upon completion of the air raid, the task force, keeping close coordination and guarding against the enemy's counterattack, shall speedily leave the enemy waters and then return to Japan.

Should the negotiations with the United States prove successful, the task force shall hold itself in readiness forthwith to return and reassemble.

Source: See Vice Admiral Homer N. Wallin, *Pearl Harbor* (Naval History Division, US Government Printing Office, 1968), p. 86. For a similar dispatch see United States Strategic Bombing Survey (Pacific) Naval Analysis Division, *The Campaigns of the Pacific War,* US Government Printing Office, 1946), p. 50.

This message, stripped of all communications data but following the form of the US Navy's intercept messages, was published in 1968 in a book written by Vice Admiral Homer N. Wallin. The message is from Admiral Isoroku Yamamoto, commander-in-chief of the Imperial Japanese Navy, to Admiral Chuichi Nagumo, commander of the First Air Fleet, Japan's carrier force. It indicates that Yamamoto broke radio silence and directed Nagumo to advance into Hawaiian waters and deal the United States Fleet in Hawaii a mortal blow. Wallin writes that the date is Tokyo Time, which would correspond to November 24, 1941, in the United States. On November 24, 1941, Admiral Kimmel called off an air and sea search for a Japanese carrier force and pulled the Pacific Fleet from the North Pacific when he was directed by Washington not to precipitate Japanese action. US Naval intercept records concerning November 24, 1941, Japanese naval dispatches have not been released.

THE CAMPAIGNS *of the* PACIFIC WAR

Japanese Naval Despatches Ordering Commencement of Hostilities

5 November 1941.

From: The Chief of Naval General Staff
To: CinC Combined Fleet

   1. In view of the fact that it is feared war has become unavoidable with the United States, Great Britain, and the Netherlands, and for the self preservation and future existence of the Empire, the various preparations for war operations will be completed by the first part of December.

   2. The CinC of the Combined Fleet will effect the required preparations for war operations.

   3. Execution of details will be as directed by Chief of the Naval General Staff.

5 November 1941.

From: The Chief of Naval General Staff
To: CinC China Area Fleet

   1. In view of the fact that it is feared war has become unavoidable with the United States, Great Britain, and the Netherlands, and for the self preservation and future existence of the Empire, the various preparations for war operations will be completed by the first part of December.

   2. The CinC Combined Fleet will effect the required preparations for war operations in accordance with Imperial Headquarters Order, No. 1.

   3. The CinC of the China Area Fleet will continue operations against China and at the same time effect required preparations for war operations.

   4. Execution of details will be directed by Chief of the Naval General Staff.

Source: United States Strategic Bombing Survey, The Campaigns of the Pacific War, (USGPO, 1946), p. 49.

These two radio dispatches originated by Admiral Osami Nagano, Chief of the Japanese Navy's General Staff, appear to be the possible source of statements delivered by General George C. Marshall during a secret press briefing on November 15, 1941. In his briefing, Marshall disclosed that the United States had broken Japanese codes, predicted that America was on the brink of war with the Japanese, and expected the danger period would include the first ten days of December 1941. See Nagano's period for the war's start in paragraph 1; see further details in chapter 10 herein.

NAVY DEPARTMENT
OFFICE OF NAVAL INTELLIGENCE
Office of the Chief of Naval Operations

In reply refer to No.

Op-16-F-2

WASHINGTON

16 September 1940.

Memorandum for the Chief of Naval Operations

SUBJECT: Gasoline and Oil Exports to Japan.

1. Highly reliable information has been received that on 20 August 1940 the Japanese Consul General at San Francisco informed his government that in spite of the restrictions on exports of petroleum products from the United States, no difficulty had been experienced in arranging for shipments of ordinary gasoline and of crude petroleum.

2. The Consul General at San Francisco informed his government in detail as follows:

(a) All the details connected with applications for export permits for petroleum products are being left in the hands of American agents by the Mitsui and Mitsubishi companies of San Francisco. These American agencies from whom the oil is bought go ahead and make suitable arrangements with the government authorities at Washington.

(b) The Mitsubishi agency at San Francisco has been notified by the local office of the Associated Oil Company that of the applications for export permits already filed in Washington by the Associated Oil Company export licenses have been granted for about 22,000 tons of Kettleman Hill crude oil and for a similar amount of other California crude oil. This material was applied for as "special blend" crude oil.

(c) Considering results so far, there would appear to be no chance of securing export licenses for aviation gasoline contracted for prior to 1 August nor that export permits will be issued for this material on the basis that exports should be permitted because the companies were under contract prior to the application of the export license system.

(d) Recently ordinary gasoline was loaded on board vessels of the Mitsui and Mitsubishi companies in the amount of some 85,000 barrels. Permits for the export of this gasoline were granted on application for the export of ordinary freight.

CONFIDENTIAL

Source: Station US papers, RG 38, MMRB, Archives II.

On September 16, 1940, President Roosevelt learned that Japan had found ways to evade his embargo on petroleum. Japan's consul-general in San Francisco claimed that there was no difficulty in arranging for purchase of ordinary gasoline or crude petroleum. A ton of oil equals 7.3 barrels. Though signed by Captain Walter S. Anderson, Director of the Office of Naval Intelligence, this report was originated by F-2, Commander Arthur McCollum.

-2-

(e) American oil dealers in the San Francisco area selling to Mitsui and Mitsubishi, of which the principal one is the Associated Oil Company, feel that there will be no difficulty about continuing the shipment of ordinary gasoline to Japan.

W.S. Anderson.

Original to Aide to the President.
CC — C.N.O.
       M.I.D.
       State
       File (2) ✓
       Treasury

CONFIDENTIAL

NAVY DEPARTMENT
Office of the Chief of Naval Operations
OFFICE OF NAVAL INTELLIGENCE
WASHINGTON

In reply refer to No.

Op-16-F-2

23 February 1940.

Memorandum for the Chief of Naval Operations

SUBJECT: Japanese Army Advisors to Bolivia.

     1.   Highly reliable information indicates that confidential conversations are in progress between Bolivia and Japan, having for their object the sending of a Japanese Military Mission to Bolivia to serve as instructors for the Bolivian Army. It is also proposed that a number of Bolivian Army officers be sent to Japan to study in Japanese Army schools. The Japanese Army is strongly in favor of concluding an agreement with Bolivia along the above lines.

W.S. Anderson.

Original to Aide to President.
CC — C.N.O.
     M.I.D.
     State
     File ✓

16 F Has seen

Source: RG 38, Station US Papers, MMRB, Archives II.

The first Japanese communications intelligence documents that can be verified as routed to President Roosevelt were originated in Arthur McCollum's F-2 office (above and following page) and signed by Captain Walter S. Anderson, Director of Naval Intelligence, on February 23, 1940. The notation "16-F Has seen" refers to Captain W. B. Heard, who was in overall charge of ONI foreign intelligence. The term "highly reliable information" is a synonym for communications intelligence, which in this case probably refers to Japan's Tsu series of codes—or possibly to their Red machine, which predated the Purple machine. The Purple Code was solved by United States cryptographers in September 1940.

NAVY DEPARTMENT
Office of the Chief of Naval Operations
OFFICE OF NAVAL INTELLIGENCE

In reply refer to No.

Op-16-F-2

WASHINGTON

23 February 1940.

Memorandum for the Chief of Naval Operations

SUBJECT: Japanese diplomatic pressure for oil rights in Portuguese
Timor.

1.   Highly reliable information has been received that the Japanese
have been engaged during the last year in diplomatic negotiations with Portugal
to obtain for SAPT, a company in Timor, the rights to drill for and produce oil
on the island of Timor. The Japanese have some connection with SAPT, probably
through the Japanese "South Seas Development Co." which has a branch in Timor.

2.   Indications are that Portugal, under pressure from Great Britain,
has granted or is about to grant monopoly rights for oil exploration in that part
of the island lying east of 125° E. longitude to the Timor Petroleum Company (believed to be Australian). Previous tests by Belgian interests proved the presence
of oil in this area.

3.   In December the Japanese Foreign Office informed its Lisbon representative that it was important that they contest the granting of monopoly rights
to the Timor Petroleum Company and get some compromise offer from Portugal.

4.   The Japanese Minister at Lisbon, in January, advised the Japanese
Foreign Office, "It is not only worthwhile but necessary for us, from the stand-
point of national policy, to force ourselves into the scene in order to acquire
rights even at the expense of straining Japanese-Portuguese relations. For this
purpose, I think there is no way of solving the difficulty except by application
of pressure backed by force."

W.S. Anderson.

Original to Aide to President
CC — C.N.O.
     M.I.D.
     State
     File

16 F Has seen

307

NAVY DEPARTMENT

OFFICE OF NAVAL INTELLIGENCE

WASHINGTON

In reply refer to No.
Op-16-F-2
776:777 (GZ-8)

8 February, 1941.

MEMORANDUM FOR THE CHIEF OF NAVAL OPERATIONS

Subject: Reorganization and intensification of
the Japanese intelligence activities in
the United States.

1.   A decision by the Japanese government to
appreciably strengthen its espionage activities in the
United States in cooperation with the Germans and Ital-
ians, is indicated by the attached memorandum which,
based on highly reliable information, gives the sub-
stance of two directives dated January 30, 1941, from
Foreign Minister Matsuoka to the Japanese Embassy in
Washington.

JULES JAMES,
Captain, U.S. Navy,
Acting Director of Naval Intelligence.

Distribution:

Naval Aide to the President : Original.
C.N.O.   : (1)
Secretary of State   : (1)
M.I.D.   : (1)
File   : (2)

Source: Station US Papers, RG 38, Modern Military Branch, Archives II.

On February 8, 1941, Lieutenant Commander Arthur McCollum sent to President Roosevelt an intelligence report outlining Japanese plans to change from propaganda activities to espionage activities in the United States. Japan's Foreign Minister, Yosuke Matsuoka, sent the strategy to Japanese missions in the United States, writing that the policy was instituted to prepare for the worst.

M E M O R A N D U M

From Foreign Minister Matsuoka
to Japanese Ambassador, Washington.
Dated January 30, 1941

These instructions classified as "Foreign Office Secret".

Heretofore, we have placed emphasis on publicity and propaganda work in the United States. In view of the critical situation in the recent relations between the two countries, and for the purpose of being prepared for the worst, we have decided to alter this policy. Taking into consideration the small amount of funds we have at our disposal, we have decided to deemphasize propaganda for the time being, and instead, to strengthen our intelligence work.

Though we must give the matter of intelligence work our further study - in this connection we are at present conferring with the Intelligence Bureau - we have mapped out a fundamental program, the outline of which is contained in my supplementary cable. (See below).

Please, therefore, reorganize your intelligence set-up and put this new program into effect as soon as possible.

Cable copies of this message, as "Minister's orders" to Canada, Mexico, (a copy to be relayed from Mexico to Mexicali), San Francisco, (copies from San Francisco to Honolulu, Los Angeles, Portland, Seattle, and Vancouver,) New York, New Orleans, and Chicago.

- -

LR4MY
HAVERECEIVED FROM BRITISH FOLLOWING IN A
PPROXIMATE NUMBERS REFERRING TO FIVE NUMERIC SYSTE
M EFFECTIVE DECEMBER TO FEBRUARY X FIVE HUNDRED BO
OK VALUE X FOUR THOUSAND SUBTRACTOR GROUPS X HALF
THOUSAND WORKSHEETS WITH CIPHER REMOVED X AND TWO
HUNDRED NINETY INDICATOR SUBTRACTORS FOR SMS NUMB
ERS X HAVE ARRANGED SECURE METHOD OF EXCHANGING FU
RTHER RECOVERIES BY CABLE X BRITISH EMPLOY THREE O
FFICERS TWENTY CLERKS ON THIS SYSTEM ALONE X THEYN
ARE DELAYING ATTACK ON CURRENT CIPHER TABLE UNTIL
MIDMARCH TO ACCUMULATE TRAFFIC AND OBTAIN FURTHER
BOOK VALUES FROM PROCEEDING PERIOD E DUE COLLATERAL
INFORMATION AVAILABLE HERE AND CAPABILITY RAPID EX
CHANGE WITH ENGLISH X CAVITE WILL ASSUME THIS SYSTEM
AS ONLY NAVY ASSIGNMENT X REQUEST DEPT FORWARD RE
SULTS TO DATE AND TECHNIGUE ADVICE IF CONSIDERED H
ELPFUL WPL

Source: This dispatch can be found in the Station US papers, RG 38, MMRB, Archives II.

A major controversy concerning whether America and her Allies had solved the Japanese Navy's 5-Numeral code system prior to Pearl Harbor has been under examination by journalists and historians since the end of World War II. If the system was solved prior to the attack, then the governments of the United States, Great Britain, and the Netherlands knew the precise plans for Japan's "surprise attack." Most Radio Tokyo transmissions directing Japanese warships to attack Hawaii were sent over radio waves in the 5-Number system and intercepted by US, British, and Dutch monitoring facilities in the Pacific.

On March 5, 1941, Admiral Thomas Hart, commander-in-chief of the US Asiatic Fleet, informed Admiral Harold R. Stark, FDR's Chief of Naval Operations, that the British monitor unit at Singapore had produced and exchanged solutions of the 5-Number code with the Asiatic Fleet. Hart said Station CAST on Cavite (he meant Corregidor) was in on the exchange and solution. A handwritten note at the middle-right asserts that OP20-A (Captain Joseph Redman, Assistant Director of Naval Communications) on March 5, 1941, authorized the removal of this dispatch from the Navy files and the substitution of a dummy message. (The note reads "3/5/41 OP20-A gave authority to remove this from code room and substitute dummy. Signed for by Coleman. No other appr." The first initial that follows is "A." The others are illegible.) This dispatch was not presented to Congress during the investigations of 1945–46 or 1995. Nor was it sent to Admiral Kimmel in Hawaii.

At the bottom, a handwritten note indicates the USS Sepulga *will bring United States solutions of the 5-Num code to Manila about March 26, 1941. Ensign Laurence Mac-Kallor, who transported the Purple machine to CAST on the* Sepulga, *carried the solutions to the 5-Num code. Apparently the reference is to the 5-Num code, additive version 6, in effect January 15, 1941, to July 1, 1941.*

Station CAST was ordered to furnish rapid translations of Japanese diplomatic messages to General Douglas MacArthur in this March 25, 1941, order from Rear Admiral Royal Ingersoll, Assistant Chief of Naval Operations. General George Marshall, Army Chief of Staff, received a copy (upper right). The initials at lower left indicate that Laurance Safford, 20-G, commander of Station US, and 20-A, Captain Joseph Redman, Assistant Director of Naval Communications, saw this dispatch. Initials EJK probably are those of Admiral Ernest J. King. A glaring omission is to be noted: nothing indicates this message was seen by Admiral Kimmel, the Pacific Fleet commander.

FT SHAFTER 5/6/41 AEM -36-

FR TOKYO MATUOKA
TO KOSHI BERLIN
5/5/41
-PURPLE-

NO. CA370

TR 5/6

              GJQMF BKVPV   IREMS
73-13 XX   15397

CAEUVVPPBBGLAACEGOLLEEUGA

AIXAZKIAOCNTJCCOBCCOAJPAI

TUKUFIFUUXWIPIKWFBTNOEUAH

EUJYIMUATAZBDFUSLWDKIWOOA

GOEIASCSNTAZPJMYOJKHBREGR

OUMISVAMJOEUPPIHAXRAZRBOV

LJIXUYISHEJEAZPILFFRPFVHG

Source: Station US papers. RG 38, MMBR, Archives II.

His fellow soldiers at Fort Shafter never informed Lieutenant General Walter Short that the Purple Code messages of the Japanese Foreign Ministry were being intercepted at Station FIVE, a US Army intercept facility just steps away from the Fort Shafter command post in Hawaii. This intercept of May 6, 1941, indicates that interception, decoding, and translation of Purple messages obtained by Station FIVE were speedy—they took only one day. The translation (next page) indicates that Foreign Minister Yosuke Matsuoka was concerned by a German report that the United States was reading his code messages and asked his ambassador to Germany, Baron Hiroshi Oshima, to check with the Berlin authorities.

From: Tokyo (Matsuoka)
To :   Berlin (Oshima)
5 May 1941
(Purple-CA)

#370   ▓▓▓▓▓▓▓▓▓▓▓▓▓▓▓▓▓▓▓▓▓▓▓▓▓▓
▓▓

        Please express our appreciation to
STAAMAA for the information in question and ask him if it
is not possible to give us the authority for the statement
that it has been fairly reliably established that the
U.S. government is reading our code messages, so that we
might take appropriate action.

        Reply requested.

*All copies destroyed except
(1) This original
(4 copy to Gen. Mauborgne*

314

Source: This TESTM dispatch can be found in the Station US papers, RG 38, MMRB, Archives II.

Cryptographers at CAST intercepted radio broadcasts involving the First Air Fleet five days before the attack. These broadcasts provide convincing evidence that carrier units violated radio silence; they were intercepted by American cryptographers and radio operators on Corregidor. The First Air Fleet's radio-call signs (**Yobidashi** Fugo) reserved for the Hawaii attack were obtained by Station CAST in advance of the raid, according to this report received at Station HYPO on December 5, 1941. The evidence is startling: HE HO 7, YO N 7, and YU NE 8, identified by CAST as the air (carrier) squadrons of Japan's Combined Fleet, were the exclusive radio-call signs assigned for the Hawaii force. This information could only be generated from radio broadcasts in the 5-Num code, additive version 7; it confirms the reports of the Twelfth Naval District and the SS Lurline of hearing Japanese transmissions from the North Pacific.

CAST's dispatch identified the twelve secret radio-call signs for Admiral Yamamoto: HO RI 2, FU MA 7, FU NE 4, KO NE 8, MA NO 8, RI HE 1, SE TU 7, TE KE 9, TU WI 4, U I 2, WA KA 3, and YO WI Ø. Japan's submarine fleet commander took to the airwaves, broke radio silence, and was uncovered as WA HI 8.

This information was transmitted to Station HYPO over the Navy's secret TESTM radio circuit. Rodney Whitten, of the HYPO staff, signed his initials to the dispatch and confirmed that it was received in Hawaii. Admiral Kimmel was never given this information.

JAPANESE CODES

4-22-71

TOP SECRET

MR. TOLSON:

RE: JAPANESE AND UNITED STATES
CODES DURING WORLD WAR II

Japanese Attack on Pearl Harbor

I have checked with L. Woodrow Newpher, Chief
of the Cryptanalysis-Translation Section of the Laboratory, and
William A. Branigan, Chief of the Espionage Section of the Domestic
Intelligence Division, both of whom were in the Bureau prior to
World War II and have knowledge of such matters. They advised
that to their knowledge the Japanese were never able to break
United States codes prior to Pearl Harbor or during the War.
Mr. Newpher also advised that a very reliable book, entitled
"The Code Breakers" by David Kahn on pages 582-585 also states
that Japan was not successful in breaking United States codes.

On the other hand, according to the above agents, the
U. S. Navy did break the Japanese military code prior to the attack
on Pearl Harbor and this directly attributed to the United States
victory in the battle at Midway Island and in Japanese Admiral
Yamamoto's being shot down in the Pacific. The Bureau also
broke an open code in one Japanese case which was handled by
our New York Office. During the War, Japan changed its codes
several times but the military services were able to break some
of them and they, as well as the Bureau, were able to read some
messages.

It is suggested that any details which could be made
available be obtained through the National Security Agency, which
assumed the cryptanalytic duties formerly handled by the military
services during the War.

REC-40 100-97-1-507

ST 104

R. R. BEAVER   18 MAY 25 1971

RRB:crt

* The logical person to contact at the office of
the National Security Agency is Dr. Louis W.
Tordella, Deputy Director, at Fort George G.
Meade, Maryland - telephone number

TOP SECRET 63

F-34
53 JUN 8 1971   JUN 1 1971

The FBI confirmed that the US Navy did break the Japanese military code prior to the attack. The information was passed on to Clyde Tolson, assistant to J. Edgar Hoover, by R. R. Beaver on April 22, 1971.

THIRTY-SIX AMERICANS CLEARED TO READ THE JAPANESE DIPLOMATIC AND MILITARY INTERCEPTS IN 1941

Thirty-six Americans were cleared for unrestricted access to decoded and translated Japanese diplomatic and military intercepts obtained by American cryptographic personnel in 1941. The following list of their names, compiled by the author from routing slips found in the Station US papers at Archives II, includes more officials than previously revealed:

President Franklin D. Roosevelt, Washington, DC

Secretary of State Cordell Hull, Washington, DC

Secretary of War Henry Stimson, Washington, DC

Secretary of the Navy Frank Knox, Washington, DC

General George Marshall, Chief of Staff, US Army, Washington, DC

Admiral Harold R. Stark, Chief of Naval Operations, Washington, DC

Rear Admiral Royal Ingersoll, Assistant Chief of Naval Operations, Washington, DC

Captain Theodore Wilkinson, fourth Director of Naval Intelligence in 1941 (October 1, 1941–December 7, 1941), Washington, DC

Captain Walter S. Anderson, Director of Naval Intelligence, Washington, DC

Captain Jules James, second Director of Naval Intelligence (January 15, 1941–March 1941), Washington, DC

Captain Alan G. Kirk, third Director of Naval Intelligence (March–October 1941), Washington, DC

Captain Laurance Safford, Commanding Officer, Station US, Washington, DC

Captain Leigh Noyes, Director of Naval Communications, Washington, DC

Captain Roland M. Brainard, Ship Movement Officer, US Navy, Washington, DC

General Douglas MacArthur, Commander US Army forces (Philippines), Manila

Brigadier General Sherman Miles, Army Intelligence, Washington, DC

Admiral Thomas Hart, Commander of the Asiatic Fleet, Manila

Colonel Rufus Bratton, US Army courier, Washington, DC

Lieutenant Commander Alwin Kramer, US Navy courier, Washington, DC

Captain John Beardall, naval aide to President Franklin D. Roosevelt, Washington, DC (May–December 1941)

Lieutenant Commander Joseph J. Rochefort, Commander, Station HYPO, Pearl Harbor Naval Yard (July–December 1941)

Lieutenant Rudolph Fabian, Co-commander, Station CAST, Corregidor, Philippines

Lieutenant John Lietwiler, Co-commander, Station CAST, Corregidor, Philippines

Captain William A. Heard, Far East Division, Office of Naval Intelligence, Washington, DC

Captain Howard Bode, Office of Naval Intelligence, Washington, DC

Rear Admiral Richmond K. Turner, Navy War Plans Officer, Washington, DC

Commander Arthur McCollum, head of Far East Section, Office of Naval Intelligence, Washington, DC

Lieutenant Commander Ethelbert Watts, assistant to McCollum, Office of Naval Intelligence, Washington, DC

Major Rodney Boone, USMC, assistant to Arthur McCollum, Office of Naval Intelligence, Washington, DC

Lieutenant Commander Edwin Layton, Pacific Fleet intelligence officer, Pearl Harbor

Lieutenant Robert Weeks, communications intelligence aide to Admiral Ernest J. King, commander-in-chief, Atlantic Fleet, Newport, Rhode Island

Agnes Meyer Driscoll, chief civilian cryptanalyst for the US Navy, Washington, DC

Ensign Prescott Currier, assistant to Driscoll, Washington, DC

Colonel William Friedman, US Army cryptanalyst, Washington, DC

Admiral Husband E. Kimmel, commander-in-chief, Pacific Fleet, Pearl Harbor (access restricted)

Lieutenant General Walter Short, commanding general Hawaiian Department, US Army, Fort Shafter, Oahu (access restricted)

Source: White House Route logs and Station US files, RG 38, MMRB, Archives II.

NOTES

A guide for quotations, sources, and events:
The principal end notes refer to:

PHPT (Pearl Harbor Part) A thirty-nine-volume transcript of eight official United States investigations of the Pearl Harbor attack that were held between December 22, 1941 and May 31, 1946. The volumes were numbered by the US Government Printing Office as parts 1 through 39 in the original publication at Washington, DC in 1946. Most major libraries in the United States carry the entire set. The eight investigations were:

1. Roberts Commission, December 22, 1941 to January 23, 1942 (Parts 22 through 25, PHPT 22–25).
2. Inquiry by Admiral Thomas Hart, February 12, 1944 to June 15, 1944 (PHPT 26).
3. Army Pearl Harbor Board Proceedings, August 7, 1944 to October 6, 1944 (PHPT 27–31).
4. Navy Court of Inquiry, July 24, 1944 to September 27, 1944 (PHPT 32–33).
5. Clarke Proceedings, September 20, 1944 to August 4, 1945 (PHPT 34).
6. Clausen Proceedings, December 1, 1944 to September 14, 1945 (PHPT 35).
7. Hewitt Proceedings, May 14, 1945 to July 11, 1945 (PHPT 36–38).
8. Hearings of the Joint Committee on the Investigation of the Pearl Harbor Attack, Congress of the United States, November 15, 1945 to May 31, 1946. Parts 1–11 are transcripts of testimony. Parts 12–21 are exhibits of JOINT.

During the course of research for this book between 1982 and 1999, the National Archives made major changes in its archival policy. A new facility called Archives II was constructed on the campus of the University of Maryland at College Park, Maryland, a community within the Beltway. In 1994 military records were split between Archives I (7th Street and Pennsylvania Avenue, Washington DC) and Archives II (College Park). Timothy Nenninger, head of military records at Archives II, provided details concerning the storage policy of United States military records for readers of this book: "The several hundred thousand cubic feet of permanently valuable military records accessioned by the National Archives, which date from the period of the American Revolution to the 1960s and 1970s, have been split between the National Archives Building in downtown Washington and the new archival facility Archives II at College Park, Maryland. Military records pre-dating World War II are housed in the National Archives Building in Washington; military records from World War II and after are stored in Archives II at College Park." Nenninger's office and his staff of archivists are located in Room 2400, A-II at College Park, 8601 Adelphi Road, College Park, Maryland 20740-6001. Telephone (301) 713-7250. The major Record Groups that Mr. Nenninger and his predecessor, Clarence Lyons, made available to the author through Freedom of Information Act requests (FOIA) are:

PHLO is a collection of documents obtained for the Joint Committee on the Investigation of the Pearl Harbor Attack, Congress of the United States, abbreviated in this book as JOINT. The investigation was conducted by a special committee appointed by the US

Senate and US House of Representatives in 1945–46. To facilitate acquisition of documents and witnesses for JOINT the US Navy established the Pearl Harbor Liaison Office headed by Lieutenant Commander John Baecher. The PHLO records are currently housed in Record Group 80, Modern Military Records Branch (MMRB), Archives II, College Park, Maryland.

Station US papers is a collection of approximately one million documents—some in original paper form, some in micro fiche—involving communications intelligence originally assembled by Station US and its successor the Naval Security Group Command. This collection can be found in RG 38, Modern Military Records Branch, Archives II. The author was given FOIA access to Boxes 1–20 on Monday, January 23, 1995 by Clarence Lyons, then head of what was called Textural Reference Branch, now known as Modern Military Records Branch. The January 1995 FOIA release contained about 6000 documents.

President Jimmy Carter's release of 1979 refers to over 300,000 decrypted and translated Japanese naval intercepts from the Pacific War dating from July 1941 to late fall 1945 and released as Record Group 457, SRN series (Special Research Navy). A major drawback for researchers: the collection is arranged by SRN numbers (starting at 1), not chronologically.

The author will deposit *Day of Deceit*'s entire research collection of cited documents, recorded audio and video tapes, photographs and graphics, including negatives, in his permanent collection housed at the Hoover Institution Archives, Stanford University, Stanford, California. This collection will be open for public use.

Japanese persons' names are reported in this book in US style, with the given name first, then the family name. In traditional Japanese usage, the family name comes first.

CHAPTER 1

1. Janet Murrow discussed the post-Pearl Harbor dilemma with Ann Sperber, author of *Murrow: His Life and Times* (Freundlich Publications Inc., 1986), p. 207; see also personal correspondence between author and Sperber in author's file.
2. For Murrow's Gunther quote, see Sperber, *Murrow*, p. 208. The White House Sunday night suppers were described by William Seale, White House historian, in personal communication to the author, August 31 and September 1, 1993 and August 28, 1995 in author's file.
3. For the Polo Grounds quote see Troy, *Donovan and The CIA* (University Publications of America, Inc., 1981), p. 115. James Roosevelt had joined Donovan's staff in August 1941 and worked from the Coordinator of Information office in the South Building, 25th and E Street NW in Washington. FBI chief J. Edgar Hoover, using special messengers, dispatched secret reports concerning Japanese espionage to Captain James Roosevelt at the COI building. See FBI file 61-10556-251; 380X, 448.
4. Donovan's account was confirmed by William J. vanden Heuvel of New York in telephone conversations with the author, January 22 and February 13, 1998. Mr. vanden Heuvel said he still has the diary.
5. Whitehead note, see Anthony Cave Brown, *Wild Bill Donovan: The Last Hero* (Times Books, 1982) pp. 6, 7. Brown's version of the meeting echoes some aspects of the October 7, 1940 memorandum of Lieutenant Commander Arthur McCollum. (See chapter 2 herein). Note Brown's reference to an "overt act" and FDR's concern for unification of America. For further details on T. North Whitehead see Joseph Lash, *Roosevelt and Churchill 1939–1941* (W. W. Norton, 1976), p. 291.
6. Ann Sperber to author, Dec. 1, 1992, in author's file. Sperber died in February 1994. John Chamberlain's article was in LIFE, September 24, 1945.
7. See Ann Sperber, *Murrow*, p. 207.
8. For Knox's report, see United Press story in *Honolulu Advertiser*, December 16, 1941.
9. For comments on the President's surprise, see Brown, *Wild Bill Donovan*, p. 6. Mr. vanden Heuvel confirmed to the author that he had allowed Brown access to the diary, see note 4 above.

CHAPTER 2

1. Memorandum from Lieut. Cdr. Arthur H. McCollum (promoted to Commander, Captain and retired as Rear Admiral) to ONI Director Captain Walter Stratton Anderson (promoted to Rear Admiral, Retired as Vice Admiral), dated October 7, 1940 in Arthur H. McCollum's classified personal file, RG 38, Station US papers, Box 6, folder 5750-15, Archives II, College Park, Maryland. Reproduced in full in Appendix A. In this book, McCollum's memorandum of October 7, 1940 will be referred to as the eight-action memo.

2. McCollum's oral history is the source for his early history, his adolescent years in Japan, his initial US Navy experience and his assignment to Prince Regent Hirohito. This information is found in volume 1 of *The Reminiscences of Rear Admiral Arthur H. McCollum, USN Ret.* (US Naval Institute, 1973), published in two volumes, softbound manuscript form, hereafter referred to as MACOH. The oral history interview starts December 8, 1970, and was conducted by John T. Mason, Jr., of the US Naval Institute. For McCollum's instructing Prince Hirohito see pp. 56, 58. Author's copy of the McCollum Oral History manuscript was prepared April 4, 1995 from original McCollum-Mason masters by Ann Hassinger, of the History Section of the USNI. In author's file.

3. Code names such as F-2 for intelligence officers are quite common.

4. The eight actions are found on page 4, section 9 of McCollum's memorandum. On page 4, the handwritten word "act" appears to have been added by pen to section 10 in the original typewritten copy, found by the author in RG 38, Archives II, College Park, Maryland. See copy in Appendix A. The phrase "overt act" involving Japan can be found in newspaper language. See an article in the *New York Times*, October 9, 1940 in which the *Times*'s Far East reporter Hallett Abend reports a Japanese "overt act" against China.

5. Captain Dudley Knox's comments will be found attached to McCollum's eight-action memo. See Appendix A.

6. "Not precipitate," Knox, loc. cit.

7. Capt. Walter S. Anderson's classified correspondence file, which would contain McCollum's original memorandum, has not been found in Archives II. McCollum and Anderson had a very close personal relationship: "I was Admiral Anderson's fair-haired boy," MACOH, p. 269. Two US government officials—Arthur H. McCollum, who authored the eight-action memo and Captain Dudley Knox, the endorser—saw the eight-action memorandum. President Roosevelt can be directly linked (see citations in Note 8 below) to six of McCollum's proposed actions: namely **Actions B and G, curtailing Japanese access to natural resources of Southeast Asia**—for he met with Dutch officials and received Japanese intercepts concerning Japan-Dutch negotiations in 1940–41; **Action C, aid to China:** FDR directed the Administration's China strategy which antagonized Japan's leaders who were engaged in war with China. On September 25, 1940 the Administration approved a $25 million loan to China's US-recognized government, headed by Generalissimo Chiang Kai-shek: see Breckenridge Long, *The War Diary of Breckenridge Long* (University of Nebraska Press. 1966), p. 132. On April 15, 1941, FDR issued an executive order authorizing US Army, Navy, and Marine Corps officers to voluntarily serve with the Flying Tigers Air Force, led by former US Army Air Corps Colonel Claire Chennault. The Flying Tigers openly trained in Burma for air battle with the Japanese. See John Toland, *The Rising Sun* (Random House, 1970), p. 127; Action C continued into the fall of 1941, when President Roosevelt sent his personal advisor, Henry F. Grady, to join a special US commission formed to provide additional support for China. The group was headed by Major General John Magruder, former US Army intelligence chief. See *The Magic Background of Pearl Harbor* (Department of Defense), Vol. III, narrative, p. 266, item 566. FDR's direct links to Actions D, F, and H are detailed in Note 8 below.

8. The conclusive evidence that links FDR or high-level administration officials to the eight action proposals is as follows. **Action A: Arrange for US use of British Pacific Bases.** Arrangements were made for US use of Rabaul's Simpson Harbor, a British possession in New Britain in the South Pacific, as USN Advance Pacific Base F. Orders came from Admiral Harold Stark, FDR's Chief of Naval Operations. See spe-

cial secret file NB/AB "F" (4), Special Advance Base—Pacific "F" in RG 181, Twelfth Naval District, National Archives, San Bruno, California. Base "F" leasing arrangements were in progress at time of Pearl Harbor. Japanese forces captured Rabaul in spring 1942 and ended US plans for Base "F." **Actions B and G: Urged the Dutch to cut off Japanese access to natural resources in Southeast Asia.** See summary of intercepted Japanese diplomatic dispatches routed to FDR, October 16, 1940. Lt. Cdr. Arthur McCollum entitled the summary: "Japanese Plans to Seize the Dutch East Indies," and routed it "Original to Aide to the President." See copy in Appendix D. FDR met with Dutch Foreign Minister Eelco Nicolaas van Kleffens and US Undersecretary of State Sumner Welles during a 70-minute conference in the Oval Office, March 19, 1941. See White House Usher Diary, 3/19/41, Franklin D. Roosevelt Library, Hyde Park, NY, hereafter FDRL. See photo of van Kleffens and Dutch Ambassador to the US Alexander Loudon—after concluding the presidential conference—outside the Oval Office and van Kleffens' comments to news reporters published in *Knickerbocker Weekly*, March 31, 1941, p. 13. For Dutch-Japanese negotiations see the account by Dutch negotiator H. J. van Mook: *The Netherlands Indies and Japan* (London: George Allen & Unwin Ltd., 1944). See **Action D: "Send cruisers"** in this chapter. **Action E: "Send US submarines to Orient."** See letter re dispatch of US subs to Manila, from Admiral Harold Stark to Admiral James O. Richardson, November 12, 1940, PHPT 14, p. 971, and US Assistant Secretary of State Breckenridge Long, *War Diary*, p. 155. Long writes that twelve submarines were sent from Honolulu to Manila. **Action F: Retain the US Fleet in Hawaiian waters.** See discussion in this and following chapters. See transcript of Oval Office audio tape of October 4, 1940, 48–61:1 (1) and (2) FDRL, in which President Roosevelt can be heard discussing "fool things that Japan might do."

THE PRESIDENT: "This country is, aah, ready to pull the trigger if the Japs do anything. I mean we won't stand any nonsense, public opinion won't in the country from the Japs, if they do some fool thing." (Position 322 on tape.)

THE PRESIDENT: "And the time may be coming when the Germans and the Japs will do some fool thing that would put us in. That's the only real danger of our getting in, is that their foot will slip." (Position 337 on tape.) Transcript by author from the October 4, 1940 tape using Sony cassette recorder, December 2, 1995. In author's file. The FDRL does not have an official transcript of FDR's Oval Office audio tapes, according to archivist Robert Parks. **Action H: A complete embargo of Japan.** A total embargo was issued by the President on July 26, 1941. See Executive Order 8832, Federal Register this date in National Archives I, 7th Street and Pennsylvania Avenue, Washington. For Japanese reaction to Action H, see (no editor) *The Magic Background of Pearl Harbor* (US Department of Defense, 1977), Vol. II, Appendix, p. A-226, item 447. See also discussion concerning Japanese embargoes by FDR, Secretary of State Cordell Hull, Undersecretary of State Sumner Welles, and Assistant Secretary of State Breckenridge Long in *War Diary*, October 10, 1940, p. 140.

9. See Secretary of War Henry L. Stimson's diary entry of Nov. 25, 1941, where the FDR war cabinet discussed "letting Japan fire the first shot." The cabinet believed this would unite the American people in the war effort; see PHPT 11, p. 5421.

10. The following (and probably more) knew of McCollum's eight-action policy that was adopted by FDR, according to direct and indirect evidence outlined herein: President Roosevelt; Lieutenant Commander Arthur H. McCollum; Captains Walter S. Anderson and Dudley Knox; Admirals Harold Stark, James O. Richardson, and William Leahy; General George Marshall; Commander Vincent Murphy. (Ranks listed as of the fall of 1940.) Parallels of "firing first shot" and "overt act of war" can be found in the United States war warnings of November 27 and 28, 1941, which directed America's Pacific commanders: "The United States desires that Japan commit the first overt act." See Appendix C.

11. Documentation that directly links FDR with McCollum's **Action D—sending US Navy cruisers in provocative moves against Japan** includes the following: first discussion in the White House Feb. 10, 1941. Present were President Roosevelt, Secretary of State Cordell Hull, Secretary of War Henry L. Stimson, Secretary of the Navy Frank Knox, General George Marshall, Army Chief of Staff, and Admiral Harold R. Stark, Chief of Naval Operations. Stark warned FDR that the cruises

"will precipitate hostilities," PHPT 16-2150 and PHPT 33, p. 1203. FDR advocated the cruises; see Stark in PHPT 33, p. 1203.

12. FDR called them "pop-up cruises" according to Admiral Stark. See B. Mitchell Simpson, III, *Admiral Harold R. Stark* (University of South Carolina Press, 1989), pp. 101, 102.

13. Admiral Husband E. Kimmel wrote to Stark on February 18, 1941 and said the proposed cruises were "most ill advised," PHPT 33-1199; "I fought but the decision may go against me," Stark to Kimmel, Feb. 10, 1941, PHPT 33-1197.

14. For Prime Minister Winston Churchill's advocating dispatch of US cruisers to Singapore see his message to FDR, October 4, 1940 in Warren E. Kimball, ed., *Churchill and Roosevelt: The Complete Correspondence*, (Princeton University Press, 1984) Vol.1, p.74. In this dispatch, Churchill wrote that sending American warships to Singapore might prevent spreading of the war. McCollum held a different view and used the Singapore proposal as one of eight provocations he thought would entice Japan into an overt act of war. Ultimately, no US warships were sent to Singapore.

15. Three pop-up cruises can be documented. (1) The first sailed during March 15-21, 1941. See testimony of Vice Admiral John H. Newton who led a task group of four USN cruisers: USS *Brooklyn*, USS *Savannah*, USS *Chicago*, and USS *Portland*. Together with a squadron of twelve destroyers sailed into the Central and South Pacific adjacent to Japanese territory. Newton told the Hart Investigation of Pearl Harbor that his orders were highly secret and directed to him verbally, PHPT 26-340. But the cruise was not too secret. The presence of the US warships in the South Pacific was leaked to Australian newspapers which announced the ships' arrival in news dispatches. The news reports were seen by the Japanese consulate in Honolulu and forwarded to Japan's Foreign Minister Yosuke Matsuoka in Tokyo. See the consulate's intercepted message to Matsuoka at PHPT 35, p. 431, and PHPT, 37, p. 1026. (2) A second cruise took US warships to Central and South Pacific regions adjacent to the eastern Japanese Mandates; see RG 24, deck logs of USS *Salt Lake City* and USS *Northampton*, July and Aug. 1941, Archives II. (3) For a pop-up cruise in Bungo Strait see US Naval attaché Tokyo Confidential Serial 220230 of Aug. 23, 1941, RG 38, Station US papers release of Jan. 1995, Archives II. A copy of Japan's protest was forwarded to FDR.

16. For Bungo Strait report, Serial 220230, loc. cit.

17. Ibid.

18. See *New York Times*, October 9, 1940, p. 1.

19. Reconstruction of the Oval Office meeting is based in three accounts: (1) Richardson's memoirs, *On The Treadmill To Pearl Harbor;* (2) Richardson's testimony to Congress starting at PHPT, 1, p. 253; and (3) secret Oval Office audio recordings of October 8, 1940, FDR Library in Hyde Park, NY. Roosevelt's voice is easily recognized on the Oval Office audio tapes which were originally recorded on an RCA recording device, then rerecorded on cassette tape for public use by FDRL. There are no minutes of the nearly three-hour luncheon meeting existing in the FDR Library files at Hyde Park, according to archivist Robert Parks. In addition to FDR and Richardson, Admiral William Leahy USN (Retired), then governor of Puerto Rico, participated. Leahy makes no reference to the meeting in his memoirs *I Was There* (New York: Whittlesey House, McGraw-Hill Book Company, Inc., 1950).

20. See James O. Richardson, *On The Treadmill to Pearl Harbor* (Washington, DC, Naval History Division, Department of the Navy, 1973), p. 435. Hereafter, cited as Richardson, *Treadmill*.

21. "Sacrifice of ship," "sooner or later," and "overt act." Richardson, *Treadmill*, ibid., p. 427.

22. See *Complete Presidential Press Conferences of Franklin D. Roosevelt* (DaCapo Press, 1972), Vol. 16, pp. 259–260.

23. *Kiplinger Newsletter* cited in Richardson, *Treadmill*, p. 402.

24. Nimitz "begged off," see E. B. Potter, *Nimitz* (US Naval Institute Press, 1976), p. 9.

25. See Richardson, *Treadmill*, for "did not give a damn," p. 442; Stark derelict, ibid., pp. 450-451.

26. See Husband E. Kimmel, *Admiral Kimmel's Story* (Henry Regnery Company, 1955); Roosevelt maneuvering, ibid. p. 2; "supply me promptly," ibid. p. 79.

27. For Richardson quotes of "Stark negligent," "kept advised," "fire it along," and "compounded," see Richardson, *Treadmill*, p. 450. Richardson never explained his failure to inform Kimmel of the Oval Office meeting of October 8, 1940. Stark clarified his nickname "Betty" to JOINT: "When I went to the Naval Academy the history that we studied there had the statement of old General John Stark, who was one of my forebears, that 'We win today or Betty Stark will be a widow tonight.' The histories that I had always studied at home were, 'We win today or Molly Stark will be a widow tonight.' Every time an upper classman came in my room when I was a plebe I had to get up and say, 'We win today or Betty Stark will be a widow tonight.' " See PHPT 5-2172.
28. Richardson, *Treadmill*, p. 450.
29. The military assistance portion of the Tripartite Pact is in Article 3: "Germany, Italy and Japan agree to cooperate in their efforts on the aforesaid basis. They further undertake to assist one another with all political, economic and military means, if one of the three Contracting Parties is attacked by a Power at present not involved in the European war or in the Chinese-Japanese conflict." PHPT 6-2852. See McCollum's correspondence with attorney Paul Freeman of Philadelphia, concerning whether President Roosevelt used Japan as a back-door approach to war, MACOH, Vol. 1, Appendix. During the Joint Congressional Investigation, Senator Scott Lucas (D., Illinois) asked McCollum if the Pacific Fleet had been used as a deliberate trick to decoy Japan into war. McCollum, apparently forgetting his Action F, replied, "No." MACOH, p. 799.
30. Strategic danger outlines, see Sections 1, 2, 3, 4, and 5 of McCollum's eight-action memo of October 8, 1940 in Appendix A.
31. "Ado," see Section 9, p. 4, ibid.
32. Long, *The War Diary*, p. 136.
33. See Richardson, *Treadmill*, p. 307 ff., where he provides background for basing the fleet at Pearl Harbor.
34. Called the American Committee for Nonparticipation in Japanese Aggression, this citizens' group advocated withholding war materials from Japan. It was headed by Roger Green and included such prominent Americans as Henry L. Stimson, later to be FDR's Secretary of War, Admiral Harry E. Yarnell, and Henry L. Harriman, former president of the US Chamber of Commerce; see report on activities of the Committee in Donald J. Friedman, *The Road from Isolation* (Harvard University Press. 1968). Prominent news executives William Allen White of the Emporia, Kansas *Gazette* and Jonathan Daniels of the Raleigh, North Carolina *News-Observer* were associated with the group. Green had notable connections in Washington, according to Friedman.
35. McCollum taught a Japanese language course in Tokyo; Edwin Layton, *And I Was There* (William Morrow and Company, 1985), p. 39.
36. On McCollum's delivery to FDR, see MACOH p. 708, and p. 4 of McCollum's letter of July 13, 1954 to Paul Freeman, a Philadelphia attorney who had questioned McCollum's review of a book in the *Saturday Review of Literature*, July 3, 1954: "The Secretary of War and the Secretary of the Navy when they were in Washington, as they usually were, were advised just as promptly as the President of the information contained in the Japanese telegrams." MACOH, Volume 1, Appendix.
37. Fourteen presidential routing indicators were found in Station US files: (1) "The President: Original," typed; (2) "P," rubber stamp; (3) "P" with a circle, rubber stamp; (4) "PR" with one star, rubber stamp; (5) "PR" with two stars, rubber stamp; (6) Routing block stamp for naval aide's initials; (7) "Special delivery to President" by Adm. Stark, typed; (8) "Special delivery to President," by Rear Admiral McIntyre (his physician), typed; (9) "Aide to President (Show)," typed; (10) "Aide to Pres. (Show)," typed; (11) "Aide to Pres," typed; (12) "NAVAIDE," typed and handwritten; (13) "Original to Aide to the President," typed, and (14) "Original to the Aide to the President," typed. See RG 38, Station US papers, Mod. Mil. Ref. Br., Archives II. Station US papers refer to the release, on January 23, 1995, of 20 boxes containing pre-Pearl Harbor communications intelligence records gathered by the US military pertaining to Japan; these released pursuant to a FOIA request filed by the author. The released files are kept in a separate research area at Archives II, according to Timothy Nenninger, head of the Modern Military Records Branch (MMRB), some-

times called Military Reference Branch. Arthur McCollum's eight-action memo is in Box 6. The National Security Agency refused to reveal the Japanese diplomatic code used in the intercepts delivered to the *Tuscaloosa*. Most likely it is the J series, probably J-15. All details of the routing system were shrouded in secrecy. Even as this book was being completed in 1999, thousands of these documents remained classified or unavailable for public examination. See "Trip of the President," White House Diary and Itineraries, February 14–March 2, 1940. FDRL. See RG 24, Deck Log of USS *Tuscaloosa*, February 25, 1940, in Archives II. The intercepts are in RG 38, Station US papers released January 23, 1995, Archives II, OP16-F-2, no serial number, dated February 23, 1940. Two destroyers, USS *Lang* and USS *Jouett*, escorted the President and carried fifteen members of the news media. Commander Daniel J. Callaghan, then forty-eight years old, was assigned as FDR's naval aide in June 1938 and remained in that post until May 1941. He became a presidential favorite, one of the boys. Roosevelt bragged of teaching "neophyte" Callaghan the techniques of deep sea fishing during a cruise to the Galapagos Islands in the summer of 1938, see Geoffrey C. Ward, ed., *Closest Companion* (Houghton Mifflin Company, 1995), p. 117. Later Callaghan was promoted to captain, then to rear admiral. He commanded Navy warships and task groups in the Pacific War following his White House assignment. Callaghan was held in high esteem by the officers and men of his command, according to naval historian Samuel Eliot Morison in his *History of United States Naval Operations in World War II* (Little, Brown and Company, 1949), Vol. V, p. 236. Daniel J. Callaghan was killed in action during a night battle with Japanese warships near Guadacanal on Friday, November 13, 1942.

38. FDR's "no foreign war" assurance was given at Philadelphia, October 23, 1940 and paraphrased in Boston, October 30, 1940. See Richardson, *Treadmill*, p. 435.
39. For "fight if attacked," see Robert Sherwood: *Roosevelt and Hopkins* (Harper & Brothers 1948), p. 191.
40. See PHPT 1, p. 467 and PHPT 2, p. 549. The United States Fleet was the major command of the United States Navy afloat prior to February 1, 1941. There was no Pacific Fleet or Atlantic Fleet. The commander-in-chief was known as CINCUS—an unfortunate acronym. CINCUS warships moved between the Atlantic and Pacific Oceans but under the single CINCUS command. A small group of warships separately stationed on the East Coast was known as the Atlantic Squadron. In the Pacific the warships at Pearl Harbor were called the Hawaiian Detachment. A small Navy command stationed in the Philippines was called the Asiatic Fleet.
41. Welles quote "diplomatic disaster" is in PHPT 2, p. 467.
42. Italy quote comes from Richardson, *Treadmill*, p. 307.
43. "Europe first," see ibid. pp. 332, 333.
44. For the objections to Hawaii, see ibid. pp. 324, 326, 327.
45. "It looks probable," ibid. p. 308.
46. " Nitwit," ibid. p. 309.
47. FDR's promise "not to send the fleet," see ibid. p. 384. Richardson sought transportation orders to Washington so he could protest the Hawaii policy direct to the Administration. During the period of July 5–17, 1940, Richardson and his war plans officer, Commander Vincent R. Murphy, flew to Washington traveling under assumed names: Richardson as Mr. Mandley, Murphy as Mr. McCleary. The admiral met with FDR for lunch on July 8, 1940. Later in the week meetings were held with Secretary of the Navy Frank Knox, Secretary of State Cordell Hull, Undersecretary of State Sumner Welles, Army Chief of Staff George Marshall, Senator James Byrnes, and Stanley Hornbeck, State Department Far East expert. It was the first of two meetings the admiral had with the President in 1940. The second was three months later, on October 8.
48. US naval strength was projected at 145,000 total according to 1940 figures, per Richardson *Treadmill*, p. 434; belligerent activity, ibid, p. 319.
49. Japan led by military men, *Treadmill*, ibid. p. 333.
50. San Francisco Japanese consulate report, September 16, 1940: see Appendix D, herein.
51. "No difficulty" intercept, see Appendix D, herein. Crude oil purchased in metric tons equals 7.33 barrels per metric ton according to a report in the 1997 edition of

the *British Petroleum Statistical Review;* courtesy American Petroleum Institute, Washington, DC.

52. For discussion concerning the US giving the green light to Japanese acquisition of petroleum products, see *Department of State, Foreign Relations of the United States: The Far East, 1940* (USGPO, 1955), Vol. IV, pp. 805, 806. Quoted in Jonathan Marshall, *To Have and Have Not* (University of California Press, 1995), p. 177.

53. See Tracking Chart 1 in insert herein. Original in RG 181, USN Secret A-6 files, National Archives, Seattle, WA.

54. For commercial facilities see Commandant, Eleventh Naval District, secret serial C-76 of April 4, 1940, RG 181, Box 196741, National Archives, Laguna Niguel, CA.

55. Tankers and their trans-Pacific routes are identified on Tracking Chart 1.

56. See Tracking Chart 1 in insert herein. For US Navy tracking of the tankers, see Tracking Chart 1, and for more details see Twelfth Naval District's (COM12) 1941 weekly tracking reports of foreign merchant vessels. The reports start with a January 14, 1941 letter from Admiral James O. Richardson, commander-in-chief of the US Fleet, who asked COM 12 to keep him informed of the tracking of the foreign merchant vessels "in the event of actual hostilities." The file, declassified for the author by Michael Anderson of San Bruno National Archives on November 1, 1984, covers January–December 1941 and is entitled "Foreign Merchant Ship-Movement Reports" found in RG 181-58-3223, QS1/EF(8), storage location 4006, Genl. Correspondence, Secret and Confidential, National Archives, San Bruno, CA.

For COM 12 named as coordinator see OPNAV Confidential Serial 016916 of February 17, 1940 in RG 181 classified records, National Archives, San Bruno, CA.

Kyokuto Maru was requisitioned by Japan's navy from a private shipping firm, hence, *Maru.* HIJMS *Shiriya* was a Japanese naval tanker and should be identified as His Imperial Japanese Majesty's Ship (HIJMS). Japanese *Marus* (merchant vessels) were assigned a permanent four letter commercial international radio call sign (RCS) by the Berne (Switzerland) International Radio Convention, known as the Berne List. All Japanese *Maru* commercial radio identification began with the letter J. The Berne List assigned JWTI to the *Kyokuto Maru.* The tanker used the call sign to contact American and worldwide radio sources. But in the secret Japanese naval communication scheme, the RCS for the *Kyokuto Maru* was I WI 2 during November 1941; see Special Research Navy (SRN) 115787 RG 457, Archives II. For the Berne List see Secret folder 077/01, RG 38, Station US papers, Archives II. The significance of the word *Maru* is similar to "red sails in the sunset" in Western culture. In Japanese, the word *maru* means "circle"; the Japanese believe that ships complete a circle and return loved ones home safely. Warships of the Imperial Japanese Navy are not called *Maru,* since they risk not completing a circle. (This explanation courtesy of Kimi and George Matsumoto of Oakland, CA.)

57. See chapter 5 of this book for a discussion on the Purple Code system.

58. A purple cover-binder, made by the ACCO Corp. of Chicago, enclosed the Navy's solution, hence the name. The Purple Code is not fully understood by some journalists and authors, who confuse it with the 5-Num code of the Japanese navy. See *Naval History,* December 1997, p. 37. Historian William Manchester made a similar mistake in referring to "Admiral Yamamoto's Purple Code" in *The Glory and the Dream* (Bantam Books, 1975), p. 269.

59. For confirmation of the 5-Num code designation assigned to the *Akagi,* see intercept SRN 115474 in Station US Papers, RG 38, MMRB, Archives II. Beware of the censored version of SRN 115474 in RG 457, Archives II, which blacks out the 5-Num code. For the 29 systems of the *Kaigun Ango,* see Kanya Miyauchi, *Niitaka Yama Nobore.* (Tokyo: Rikkyou Shuppan, 1976), p. 135. (Climb Mount Niitaka.)

60. For a copy of the original text of Admiral Ingersoll's secret letter, see RG 38, CNO Secret serial 081420 of October 4, 1940, SRN 355, Vol. 1, pp. 395–397, Archives II. Beware of the censored copy in Special Research History (SRH) 149, RG 38. Copies of both documents are available in author's file. Admiral Ingersoll's letter was prepared by Station US personnel, signed by Ingersoll, and forwarded to Admiral James Richardson, CINCUS; Admiral Thomas Hart, CinC Asiatic Fleet; Rear Admiral J. M. Smeallie, COM16; and Admiral Claude Bloch, COM 14. In 1940–41 America's major war plan was code-named Rainbow and each potential enemy was

designated by color. Orange was Japan. For a discussion of Rainbow war plans see Edward S. Miller, *War Plan Orange: The U. S. Strategy to Defeat Japan, 1897–1945* (US Naval Institute Press, 1991).

61. Ingersoll's secret letter, loc. cit.

62. Ibid. Decoding and translation of the Japanese Navy's 5-Num dispatches remain controversial as this book goes to press. Duane Whitlock, traffic analyst at Station CAST in 1941, wrote that "It was absolutely impossible for anyone in the United States to decode any of the JN-25 (*sic*) messages Station H intercepted in November 1941." See e-mail from Whitlock to author, May 22, 1999, author's file. For another viewpoint on American decoding of Japanese naval messages, see chapter 10, herein, where General George C. Marshall, head of the US Army in 1941, called a secret meeting in Washington, DC on November 15, 1941, and told select reporters that the United States had broken Japanese codes. Marshall informed the reporters that he expected a Japanese attack on the United States during the first ten days of December 1941, based on intercepted and decrypted Japanese messages.

CHAPTER 3

1. Roosevelt's 1940 presidential race with Wendell Willkie, the Republican nominee, was almost neck and neck on September 4, 1940, according to a Gallup Poll. See *New York Times (NYT)* p. 20. Roosevelt held a slim lead of 50 percent over Willkie's 49 percent, according to Gallup.

2. See Stefan Terzibaschitsch, *Aircraft Carriers of the U.S. Navy* (Annapolis: US Naval Institute Press. 1989), p. 304, which lists totals of CV (large carriers), CVL (light carriers) and CVE (escort carriers) built in the US for WWII.

3. For a description of the fistfight on the House floor the night of September 4, 1940 see *NYT*, September 5, 1940.

4. For Willkie's remarks on the destroyer deal, see *NYT*, September 7, 1940.

5. Nye quote is from *NYT*, September 2, 1940; Bridges was quoted in AP dispatch, *NYT*, September 2, 1940; editorial in St. Louis *Post-Dispatch* was excerpted in *NYT*, September 3, 1940; Ackerman was quoted in *NYT*, September 1, 1940.

6. Roosevelt spoke at Newfound Gap, Tennessee, September 2, 1940, during the dedication of Great Smoky Mountains National Park. See *NYT*, September 3, 1940, for full text.

7. Ibid.

8. For "Garden hose" press conference of December 17, 1940, see *Complete Presidential Press Conferences of Franklin D. Roosevelt* (DaCapo Press. 1972), Vol. 16, p. 354.

9. Bridges, prepared statement excerpt quoted by AP in *NYT*, September 2, 1940.

10. For discussion on the Oval Office recordings done in 1940 by President Roosevelt, see article by Professor Robert J. C. Butow in *American Heritage* (Feb./Mar., and Oct./Nov. 1982). Schlesinger discusses the President's reason for the recordings in ibid. p. 9.

11. On September 6, 1940, FDR discussed the Grant-Howard dispatch in audio tape 48-61:1 (3), transcribed by the author from cassettes furnished by FDRL. The sound quality is good, though some conversation is unintelligible. "Down and out physically and mentally" can be heard at tape location 19; "Wouldn't say anything more" is heard at tape location 59.

12. FDR scorns *NYT* editorial during Oval Office meeting with Speaker Sam Rayburn (D., Texas) and House Floor Leader John McCormack (D., Mass.). Meeting recorded on October 4, 1940, audio tape 48-61-1 (1) and (2) FDRL.

13. FDR's voice comes through loud and clear on his statement that the Axis Powers "want me licked on November fifth." Audio tape of October 4, 1940, 48-61-1 (1) and (2) starting at tape location 187.

14. Matthews article is in *NYT*, Oct. 4, 1940; editorial is in ibid.

15. Evidence of Axis directions, see Arthur McCollum's eight-action memo of Oct. 7, 1940, p. 1, item 2, first sentence, where he writes, "There is considerable evidence to support the view that Germany and Italy." See Appendix A herein.

16. FDR discussing "more worry" is heard on October 4, 1940 audio tape 48-61:1 (1) and (2) tape location 333.

17. Ibid.
18. Ibid. Apparently the President is discussing a United Press story distributed on Oct. 2, 1940. Roosevelt can be heard describing the story, which was published in all the Scripps Howard newspapers. The "God" quote is heard at tape location 333. The tape started with Roosevelt's saying "Hello"; FDR audio tape 48-61: 1 (2), Oct. 4, 1940.
19. FDR retreats to his study, see Helen Morris, ed., *At Random* (Random House, Winter 1993), p. 26. For 1940 election returns, see *NYT*, Nov. 5, 1940, p. 1.
20. FDR quote is from *NYT*, ibid. same date.
21. On British expectation of Japan-US war, see letter dated Nov. 12, 1940 from Admiral Harold Stark to Admiral Thomas Hart, Commander of the Asiatic Fleet: "British expect USA to be in the war a few days after reelection of Roosevelt," PHPT 16-2448.
22. Matsuoka "worst" quote is from intercept of January 30, 1941. See Appendix D, this book.
23. Matsuoka, ibid. The "worst" strategy change involved the ABCD powers (America, British, Chinese, Dutch). It was first revealed by Japanese diplomatic radio messages intercepted by US Army and Navy listening posts. See Matsuoka's message of January 30, 1941 in Appendix D where he used the "worst" word and writes that Japan is "being prepared for the worst."

    English translations of 1941 Japanese Foreign Office intercepts containing the word or phrase "worse," "worse comes to worse," and similar uses can be found in Department of Defense, *The Magic Background of Pearl Harbor* (USGPO, 1977).

    January 30, 1941 is Matsuoka's dispatch Vol. 1, p. A–76 item 118. Other examples follow.

    February 8, 1941: "Accompanying the worsening of Japanese-American relations" Vol. 1, p. A–105, item 190.

    March 11, 1941: "If the worst comes to worst the US will back up England." Vol. I, p. A–204, item 390.

    June 2, 1941: "If worse comes to worst, we consider Mexico City" Vol. II, p. A–192, item 384.

    July 7, 1941: "If worse comes to worse." Vol. II, p. A–185, item 369.

    July 12, 1941: Re Japanese merchant ship recall, "when the worse comes to the worst," Vol. II, p. A–171, item 340.

    July 23, 1941: "Whenever the situation should become worse," Vol. II, p. A–186, item 370.

    November 28, 1941: "When we are about to face the worst of situations," Vol. IV, p. A–250, item 526.

    American reaction to the "worse" policy (which meant war) can be found in the printed record of the Joint Congressional Committee:

    September 21, 1941: Washington dispatched an order to Admiral Kimmel listing ships to remain in Pearl Harbor "in case of worse conditions" and "would deal with the worse situation." See testimony of Admiral Richmond K. Turner, US Navy War Plans officer in 1941, to JOINT, PHPT 4, p. 2027.

    December 4, 1941 (Java Time): See Japan's "worse" policy revealed in radio intercept of the Winds Code sent by American Consul General Walter Foote in Batavia to the Secretary of State, December 4, 1941 (Java Time). Foote quotes the Japanese introduction to the Winds code: "When crisis leading to the worse," see PHPT 8, p. 3589.

    Bibliographical note: Volumes II, III, and IV of *Magic* have separate narrative and appendix volumes (The A distinguishes the appendix). Vols. I and V combine both narrative and appendix. "Worse" (sometimes translated as "worst") policy began as early as 1933. See Tokyo newspaper *Asahi*, February 27, 1933, in which the newspaper reported that Japan's withdrawal from the League of Nations had caused an increase in the spirit of war and "it is necessary for Japan to prepare for the worst." Reported in *Proceedings* (US Naval Institute, May 1933), p. 761.
24. See Hiroyuki Agawa, *The Reluctant Admiral* (Naval Institute Press. 1979), pp. 203 and 220 for Oikawa and Yamamoto.
25. For letter of Frank Knox to Secretary of War Henry L. Stimson, see PHPT 4-1939. Warnings to Pearl Harbor started flowing immediately from Washington following

the abrasive Oval Office luncheon with FDR and Admiral James Richardson. Three directives were dispatched by Admiral Harold Stark, the Chief of Naval Operations, to Rear Admiral Claude Bloch, Commandant of the Fourteenth Naval District (COM14) in Hawaii. Stark ordered improved air defenses to ward off a carrier air attack on Pearl Harbor. See Stark-Bloch dispatches of Oct. 9, 1940 (Serial 092135); Oct. 18, 1940 (Serial 182138), in RG 80, PHLO, MMRB, Archives II; and Stark to Bloch, Oct. 24, 1940, in PHPT 4-1939. On Dec. 30, 1940 Rear Admiral Bloch replied and agreed that aircraft attacking the base at Pearl Harbor would undoubtedly be brought by carriers. Bloch said the Japanese carriers would be repelled by (1) locating and destroying the ships, and (2) driving off the attacking planes with anti-aircraft fire; PHPT 33-1194.

26. All quotations here are from Max W. Bishop's letter to the author, Sept. 19, 1988, in author's file. A career State Department officer, Bishop arrived in Japan in 1935 and for a short time served as vice consul in Osaka. His five-year tour at an end, Bishop was under transfer to Washington, and was scheduled to depart via ocean liner at the end of January 1941–hence his money exchange efforts.

Bishop's written description of the meeting with Schreiber in the bank is contained in his letter to the author dated Sept. 19, 1988, in author's file. Japan prohibited two-way radio-wireless facilities in the American embassy. The most sensitive American government messages were encrypted in an "unbreakable code," then taken to the Japanese Telegraph Agency, which transmitted the messages to the radio facilities of the Fourth Marine Regiment in Shanghai, China, who then used Navy facilities to retransmit them to Washington. Japan's diplomatic missions in the United States used commercial firms such as RCA. Neither nation allowed the other radio transmitters. Each had the opportunity to read each other's mail, and did. On embassy radio facilities, see RG 38, Station US papers, SRH 355, Vol. 1, p. 347, MMRB, Archives II. On the "unbreakable" State Department code, see Joseph Grew's testimony PHPT 2, p. 582.

27. See the original copy of Grew's cablegram 125, as received by State Department at 6:38 A.M. on Monday, Jan. 27, 1941 (EST) in PHPT 14, p. 1042.

28. See Arthur McCollum dispatch, approved by Captain Jules James, interim ONI director, dictated Jan. 31, 1941 and transmitted to Admiral Kimmel on Feb. 1, 1941; confidential file, serial 09716, OP16-F-2 in RG 38, PHLO, MMRB, Archives II.

29. The exact time when message 301455 reached the White House is not clear. The six-digit number is the Navy's radio dispatch time recorded in Greenwich Mean Time, January 30, 1941 at 2:55 P.M. or 9:55 A.M. January 30 in Washington. Duane Whitlock, one of the traffic analysts at CAST in January 1941, told the author he wrote the dispatch and that it was based entirely on analyzing the Japanese naval communication procedures culled from the message. "We were not reading the actual text at CAST," Whitlock said in a telephone interview with the author in May 1999, notes in author's file. The time frame suggests an afternoon delivery to the White House. See CAST report serial 301455, RG 38, Station US papers, MMRB, Archives II.

The CAST report was initialed by Captain Daniel J. Callaghan in Washington sometime after 9:55 A.M. EST. The White House Usher Book does not list Callaghan as a visitor on Jan. 30, 1941. The President remained in the second floor Oval Study until 11:22 A.M., then went to the Oval Office until 1:15 P.M., then to the Blue Parlor and State Dining Room for the movie-star luncheon. He returned to the Oval Office at 3:00 P.M., see the White House Usher Book, Jan. 30, 1941, FDRL.

30. For the Gallup Poll of Jan. 30, 1941, see *NYT,* Jan. 31, 1941.

31. See James O. Richardson, *On The Treadmill to Pearl Harbor* (Naval History Division, Department of the Navy. 1973), pp. 402, 403, 420. A sea bag is the naval equivalent of a suitcase.

32. Richardson's quote is from Richardson, *Treadmill,* p.7.

33. For Stark's quotes, "not commit one inch" and "looking for new job," see his January 13, 1941 letter to Kimmel in PHPT 16-2144.

34. For Anderson's promotion to the Pacific Fleet as the number three commander, see his Oral History in microfiche form, p. 235, Oral History Research Office, Butler Library, Columbia University, New York; for "stars to Ernie King" see ibid.

35. For Knox-Anderson discussion re reporters, see Anderson's OH, ibid.
36. For Thomason quote see Ladislas Farago, *The Broken Seal* (Random House. 1967), p. 102.
37. On Anderson meetings with FDR see his OH, p. 230.
38. See Adolf Berle's diary entry of Oct. 4. 1940, at FDRL, copy in author's file.
39. Anderson lends McCollum to Hoover as consultant, see FBI report 62-33413-766, FBI headquarters, FOIA section, Washington, DC.
40. Anderson knew nothing about the Roosevelt-Richardson meeting of October 8, 1940 according to his OH, pp. 246-247. His lack of knowledge concerning the Oval Office meeting might be explained by his credo, given in his OH, on p. 231: "An intelligence officer should not write books or discuss in any detailed way their professional activity."
41. See photograph of the change of command ceremony aboard USS *Pennsylvania*, in the photo insert herein.
42. For Richardson's "lips sealed," see Richardson, *Treadmill*, p. 436.
43. Richardson told Kimmel of a "disagreement" in PHPT 6-2619. On June 9, 1941 Kimmel met with FDR and told him the fleet was vulnerable in Hawaii, but did not protest its basing at Pearl; White House Usher Book, FDRL. Richardson had close personal ties to both Kimmel and Lieut. Gen. Walter Short but there is no record that he told them of the Oval Office confrontation of October 8, 1940. Richardson had ample opportunity to confide in Short. While the general awaited his furniture from the mainland, he and his wife were house guests of Richardson and his wife.

    By naval tradition, command changes take place with incoming and outgoing officers reading their transfer orders to the assembled crew and invited guests. Battleship ceremonies were usually held on the fantail (rear deck of ship).
44. Anderson assumed title of Commander Battleships of the Pacific Fleet on January 31, 1941; see RG 24, Deck Log of USS *West Virginia*, Jan. 31, 1941, MMRB, Archives II. Anderson had changed his flagship to the USS *Maryland* by the time of the Pearl Harbor attack.
45. For Stark's, "The White House decides," see PHPT 16, pp. 2144–2146.
46. Stark "Our hand was forced," loc. cit.
47. For Richardson "little respect" quote, see Richardson, *Treadmill*, p. 7. See also ibid. p. 1, where Richardson objected to an FDR naval promotion slate of 1939 containing Anderson's name.
48. Anderson's address was 3671-A Diamond Head Road. He listed his telephone number as Honolulu 78450. See the Oahu telephone directory , fall 1941, p. 4. In 1996, his former residence still stood on the down slope toward the ocean.
49. Anderson commanded nine Pacific Fleet battleships. The USS *Colorado* was at Puget Sound Naval Yard, Seattle for overhaul and escaped the attack. The USS *Utah*, an ex-battleship, had been converted to an aerial target ship for training purposes.
50. On Anderson being home for the weekend and his return to his flagship *Maryland* at 0905 December 7, 1941, see Vice Admiral Homer N. Wallin, *Pearl Harbor: Why, How, Fleet Salvage and Final Appraisal* (Naval History Division, USGPO 1968), p. 153.
51. For Kimmel's "I may never understand," see Husband E. Kimmel, *Admiral Kimmel's Story* (Henry Regnery Company. 1955), p. 108. Shortly after Kimmel took command of the Pacific Fleet he questioned whether he was in the intelligence loop; see *Kimmel*, ibid. pp. 79 and 80.
52. See further discussion of the Purple Code in chapter 5.
53. For Kimmel to Stark, "no misunderstanding concerning intelligence," see PHPT 4, p. 1792.
54. For Stark's reply to Kimmel, see ibid.
55. For Kimmel's "cardinal principle," see loc. cit.
56. For US Navy ceasing to send decoded and translated Japanese intercepts acquired in Washington DC to Hawaii in July 1941, see testimony of Brigadier General Sherman Miles in PHPT 2, pp. 811, 812, 813. Station H on Oahu continued to intercept the Japanese navy's 5-Num dispatches up to the attack, but apparently did not have the means to decrypt the message text during the period of July 15 to December 7,

1941. Officials at Station US controlled the decrypting information and saw to it that none leaked out until after December 7, 1941. In 1999, the argument cannot be settled on whether American cryptographers could intercept, decode, and translate the 5-Num code in a timely manner in 1941. There is no way to prove or disprove the argument for the original coded intercepts obtained by Station H, and the decoding procedures necessary to unmask the Japanese text have not been publicly released. The author believes such an argument is moot for the answers to the argument are entirely clear. Officials in Washington did not want the Hawaiian commanders, Admiral Kimmel and General Short, to independently learn of Japan's plans to attack Hawaii and derail a clear-cut overt act of war by the Japanese.

CHAPTER 4

1. For McCollum's memo on actions B and G, see Appendix A of this book.
2. See Dr. H. J. van Mook, *The Netherlands East Indies and Japan* (London: George Allen & Unwin Ltd., 1944), p. 43 ff.
3. For Dr. van Mook's "preposterous" and Netherlands role as "supervisory" comments, see van Mook, ibid. p. 46.
4. For the October 16, 1940 Purple intercept routed to FDR, see RG 38, Station US papers in MMRB, Archives II.
5. See Admiral James O. Richardson's account concerning the question of war that he posed to FDR in PHPT 1, p. 266; see also James O. Richardson, *On the Treadmill to Pearl Harbor* (Naval History Division USGPO. 1973), p. 427.
6. For a copy of the October 30, 1940 intercept delivered by Arthur McCollum to Ranneft see RG 38, Station US papers, MMRB, Archives II. Notation on the report: "By D.N.I. (Director Naval Intelligence, Capt. Walter S. Anderson) order, above handed to Capt. Ranneft 2100, 30 Oct. by McC." Johan Ranneft was an experienced naval communications officer and would have understood the American techniques of acquiring the Japanese intercept. He was Director of Dutch Naval Communications 1934–38. He served in the United States as naval attaché from 1938–1947. Ranneft was born in Semarang, Java, Jan. 25, 1886, and died in Houston, Texas, January 20, 1982. USN intelligence reports based on Japanese naval intercepts were funneled to McCollum. He had two assistants, Major Rodney A. Boone, a US Marine Corps intelligence officer, and Lieutenant Commander Ethelbert Watts, a Japanese-language expert and a close friend of Joseph Rochefort, commander of Station HYPO. Starting in mid-November 1941, McCollum's F-2 operation alternated on eight-hour shifts around the clock forwarding the latest intelligence information to President Roosevelt and other American government leaders.
7. The American government has never publicly admitted to the exchange of pre-Pearl Harbor Japanese intercepted messages in the military and diplomatic codes with the Dutch and British governments. For confirmation of US exchange of Japanese intercepts with British and Dutch, see a letter dated November 8, 1941 from Knox to Hull; Secret serial 038513 in RG 38, PHLO, MMRB, Archives II. In 1941 the Dutch Navy assigned Commander H. D. Linder as COMINT liaison to Admiral Hart's staff in Manila, according to Hart's biographer, James Leutze, in *A Different Kind of Victory* (Naval Institute Press. 1981), pp. 199, 251, 252, 253. Batavia (Jakarta), the capital of the Dutch East Indies, was a major pre-Pearl Harbor source of US intelligence concerning Japan. Direct liaison between Batavia and Washington, DC was effected through the US Army's military attaché and the USN's naval attaché. Both officers were given access to Japanese diplomatic and military messages obtained by Dutch cryptographers who maintained an intercept facility at a Netherlands army post at Bandoeng, Java, under the cover name *Kamer* 14. A Purple Code machine was used in Batavia by the Japanese consul-general for communication with Tokyo and other diplomatic posts. Documents in the Station US papers indicate that Dutch officials in Batavia solved the Japanese naval operations code (the 5-Num code) and shared the information with Washington. Reciprocal intelligence exchanges were accorded Captain Johan Ranneft, the Dutch naval attaché in Washington. Most Pearl Harbor historians assert that communications

intelligence (COMINT) was a closely guarded secret disseminated only to a select list of high American government officials. The Station US papers in Archives II include documents labeled "1941 Netherlands raw traffic in the MH and NH Code," stored in Box 792. The documents have not been declassified as of the writing of this book in 1999.

8. On the FDR meeting with van Kleffens, see White House Usher Book for March 19, 1941, FDRL. Quote from van Kleffens is in *Knickerbocker Weekly*, March 31, 1941, pp. 12–13. Another agenda was on the Dutch minister's mind: He pressured Assistant Secretary of State Breckenridge Long, requesting that an LL.D degree be conferred on Netherlands Crown Princess Juliana by Princeton University; Long was an influential board member of the University. See Breckenridge Long, *War Diary of Breckenridge Long* (University of Nebraska Press 1966), p. 191.

9. For Abend's account, see Hallett Abend, *Japan Unmasked* (Ives Washburn, Inc. 1941), p. 142.

10. For Ranneft's diary accounts of December 2 and 6, 1941 see Johan E. M. Ranneft. *Dagboek* (Diary) 1938–1947. (The Hague Institute for Maritime History, Ministry of Defense, 1952), p. 39. For Ranneft's visit to ONI on December 2 and 6, 1941, see John Toland, *Infamy* (Doubleday & Company, Inc.), pp. 282, 298. A copy of Ranneft's diary was supplied to the author by Dr. P. C. van Royen, Director, Institute for Maritime History, on July 7, 1995; copy is in author's file.

11. For tracking Japanese Carrier Divisions Three and Four from Sasebo to the Southeast Asia/Palau (sometimes spelled as Palao by the navy cryptographers) region, and their continued association with the Third Fleet—not commander carriers—see Station H's daily Chronology for November 1–30, 1941 in Station US papers, RG 38, MMRB, Archives II, copies in author's file. The aircraft carrier HIJMS *Taiyo* was identified as the *Kasuga Maru* in the prewar Station H intercepts. The *Kasuga Maru*, a luxury passenger liner of the Nippon Yusen Kaisha (Known as the NYK Line or Japanese Steamship Company) was converted to an aircraft carrier during 1941 and that fall was commissioned as a 17,000-ton flattop. Since the conversion included the former liner's radio transmitters, USN cryptographers recognized her radio transmissions as that of the former luxury liner.

Note: For Japanese accounts on composition of Carrier Divisions Three and Four conflict, see Ikuhiko Hata, *Japanese Naval Aces* (Naval Institute Press, 1989). *Taiyo* was torpedoed and sunk by USS *Rasher* on August 18, 1944.

12. In Dutch: "*2-12-41. Bespreking op Navy Dept. men wijst mij op de kaart de plaats van 2 Japanese carriers uit Japan vertrokken met Oostelijke koers.*" The Netherlands Government provided two conflicting English translations for the author. Both agree that the two carriers were proceeding in an easterly direction from Japan. The conflict centers on the specific location of the departure of the Japanese carriers. A translation by the Netherlands consulate in San Francisco reads: "I was being shown the place on the map where the two Japanese carriers departed on an eastern course." A slightly different nuance—but with same meaning—appeared in a translation that the Ministry of Defense at The Hague prepared for the author. Translators at The Hague dropped "the place" and came up with: "Meeting at Navy Department, the location of two Japanese carriers leaving Japan with eastern course are pointed out to me on the map." The words "the place," "eastern," and "easterly" are critical here. A look at the map indicates that of the two, Sasebo or Hitokappu Bay, the latter is "the place" that offers a direct eastern (or easterly) departure. Asked by the author to clarify his Japanese carrier research concerning Ranneft, Toland wrote that Ranneft was referring to Japanese carriers, not Carrier Divisions. See Toland to author, July 19, 1995.

13. For Yamamoto's first dispatch see two sources: (1) Wallin, *Pearl Harbor*, p. 87; (2) Captain F. M. Trapnell, USN, Captain J. S. Russell, USN, and Lieutenant Commander J. A. Field, Jr., USNR, eds., *The Campaigns of the Pacific War* (United States Strategic Bombing Survey, Naval Analysis Division, USGPO Washington, 1946), p. 50.

14. For Yamamoto's second dispatch, see Wallin, *Pearl Harbor*, p. 86, *Campaigns*, supra. The Wallin version is reproduced in Appendix D of this book.

15. Vice Admiral Homer N. Wallin headed the US Navy's Pearl Harbor salvage operations, refloating battleships and other vessels sunk on December 7, 1941. The

US Strategic Bombing Survey was established by President Roosevelt on November 3, 1944. Its original mission was to survey effects of aerial bombing on Germany. On August 15, 1945, President Harry Truman requested that the Survey conduct a similar study of the aerial bombing of Japan. Truman named eleven directors headed by Franklin D'Olier, chairman. The other members were Paul H. Nitze, Walter Wilds, Harry L. Bowman, J. K. Galbraith, Rensis Likert, Frank A. McNamee, Fred Searls, Jr., Monroe Spaght, Dr. Louis R. Thompson, and Theodore P. Wright.

16. Yamamoto's thirteen missing radio messages can easily be documented by retrieving his SMS message numbers from the intercept file of Station H in RG 457, MMRB, of Archives II. Every Japanese naval commander, warship, and unit assigned a separate consecutive Secret Message Series (SMS) number to each radio dispatch they originated. It began at 001, advanced to 999, then repeated the sequence. Depending upon the number of dispatches, several series of 1000 messages could be issued per year for each command, etc. The author analyzed Yamamoto's message time frame in the Station H records. On November 24, 1941 at 1:00 P.M. Tokyo Time, he dispatched a fleet radio message using his call sign, RO SE 22. He numbered the message as 606 in the SMS Series. The next thirteen Yamamoto messages have disappeared from records released by the United States government. He reappears in SMS 620 which the admiral dispatched at 3:54 P.M., November 26, Tokyo Time, according to the Station H records. Again Yamamoto used his radio call sign of RO SE 22. (Prior to Pearl Harbor, a double-digit number always designated a commanding officer in Japanese naval dispatches.)

Obviously there are thirteen messages missing from the Yamamoto radio dispatch records of Station H—the principal US Navy monitoring unit for the Pacific Fleet. The missing dispatches include his explosive messages directing the carrier force to advance through the Northern Pacific and bomb Pearl Harbor. So where are the missing thirteen messages? Captain Homer Kisner, radio traffic chief for the Pacific Fleet in 1941, also wonders. He was in charge of the US Navy's intercept operations at Station H. In interviews with the author in 1988 and 1998, Kisner said his intercept operators rarely missed Japanese naval radio messages. "Even if some messages were missed during the first transmission, Japan's navy always repeated messages and we could obtain them on the second or third dispatch," Kisner told the author. Kisner said he and his men carefully monitored the SMS numbers: "We didn't want to miss a one."

Intercepted Japanese naval dispatches of the pre-Pearl Harbor era (July 15–December 7, 1941) are housed in MMRB at Archives II, College Park, Maryland as Record Group (RG) 457. They were released to National Archives by President Jimmy Carter's Executive Order 12065 of June 1, 1979 and labeled Special Research Navy (SRN).

Yamamoto's SMS 606 is filed as SRN 116780; 620 is SRN 117266 (SRN number is listed here as a finding aid, it has nothing to do with sequence of the messages). According to John Taylor, supervising archivist of RG 457 at Archives II, the thirteen missing Yamamoto radio dispatches, SMS 607 to SMS 619, were not released to the National Archives. The National Security Agency, at Fort George G. Meade, Maryland carried out President Carter's order. Before releasing the Japanese radio documents to the National Archives, NSA blacked out all reference to the 5-Num code. Some First Amendment scholars call the blackouts censorship; NSA refers to them as redactions. There are approximately 2,600 pre-Pearl Harbor Japanese naval intercepts mixed haphazardly together with about 300,000 intercepts of the Pacific War. The 2600 figure represents about 2 percent of the Japanese naval intercepts obtained by Station H operators between July 15 and December 7, 1941. Station H intercept operators intercepted about 1,000 Japanese naval messages per day in the pre-Pearl Harbor period, which, according to Kisner, totaled about 140,000 intercepts. The 2,600 intercepts released to the American public are not arranged chronologically, but mixed together, requiring a researcher to separate the pre-Pearl Harbor records from the lot. See the pre-Pearl Harbor intercepts—arranged in chronological order, in the author's file. All Japanese naval intercepts and radio logs monitored by American facilities were recorded in Tokyo Time. Japan's naval units used Tokyo Time no matter where they were located in the world.

17. As of 1999, the Kurile Islands are controlled by the Russian government. Etorofu is

called Ostrov Iturup. For coded movement reports of Japanese warships en route to Hitokappu Bay in November 1941, see the SRN documents in RG 457, MMRB, Archives II. The SRN documents in RG 457 indicate they were "trans" in 1945 and 1946.

18. During 1941 apparently 90 percent of the Japanese navy's coded movement reports were decoded and translated in Washington at Station US, according to an article written by US Navy cryptologist Captain Al Pelletier in *Cryptolog*, Summer 1992 issue, p. 5. But Duane Whitlock, a 1941 radio traffic analyst at Station CAST (the US Navy's cryptographic center for the US Asiatic Fleet on Corregidor island) said in a telephone interview with the author that his unit was not provided the means to decode Japan's ship movement code. "If Washington was reading Japan's ship movement code in 1941, that's news to me," Whitlock said in the interview. "We did not have the solution to the ship movement code at CAST" (Whitlock telephone interview, June 1999, notes in author's file). For Japanese radio orders directing warships to standby locations, see the Special Research Navy (SRN) file in RG 457, and the Daily Chronology of Station H, dated Nov. 15–30, 1941 in RG 38, MMRB, at Archives II. The reader is reminded that the English text in the SRN translations contained in RG 457 was "trans" in 1945 and 1946; the original intercepts were obtained in 1941. There is no reliable evidence, found by the author, that establishes how much of the 5-Num text could be deciphered, translated, and read by naval cryptographers in 1941.

19. For Layton's testimony that Japanese "carriers were never heard," see PHPT 10, pp. 4839 ff.

20. "The British "heard," see discussion throughout James Rusbridger, *Betrayal at Pearl Harbor* (Summit Books, 1991) ff.

21. Dutch heard and located Japanese warships "near Kuriles," see letter of Lieut. Gen. Hein ter Poorten, Commander of Netherlands East Indies Forces, dated July 23, 1960, Royal Netherlands Army Archives, The Hague; copy in author's file.

22. For Rochefort's report of a "large-scale screening maneuver," see his Communication Summary of Oct. 22, 1941, p. 2, in RG 80, PHLO, MMRB, Archives II. He said the maneuver would be eastward from the Kuriles. The Hawaiian Islands, Canada, and the United States lie eastward from the Kuriles. Rochefort's term "screening maneuver" is a military phrase that means to eliminate your enemy. It is a tactic similar to one used in football games, where the linemen protect the quarterback from charging opponents and screen them out by tackling them. "High-north" radio circuits meant north of Hokkaido to Horomushiru, a.k.a. Paramushiru.

23. For Admiral Harold Stark's testimony on Hitokappu Bay, see PHPT 5, p. 2253.

24. After analyzing a copy of the HITOKAPPU BAY intercept sent to him by the author in June 1999, Duane Whitlock, the radio traffic analyst at Station CAST, told the author in a telephone interview that he did not believe that Japan's naval radio transmitted the words HITOKAPPU BAY in plain Japanese as is noted on the United States version of the translated dispatch printed herein. "If the dispatch contained the words HITOKAPPU WAN (in actual transmission the Japanese word "wan"—for bay or harbor—would have been used) I would have spotted the security breach, realized the significance, and sounded the alarm bell" (Whitlock to author, telephone interview June 1999, notes in author's file).

25. For opposite view, see note 24 above.

26. The suffix 58 used in RI TA 358 was Japan's naval radio code for "chief of staff" it never changed prior to December 7, 1941. See Station H Code Movement reports for November 1941 and decryptions of Japanese naval call signs *(Yobidashi Fugo)*. For the censored version, see RG 457, SRN files, MMRB, Archives II; uncensored version is in RG 38, Station US papers, MMRB, Archives II. The SMS number that appears on most Japanese intercepts obtained by Station H refers to Secret Message Series. The SMS number, or Secret Message Series, was included within each 5-Num code message transmitted by Japan's navy in 1941. The SMS number was in the clear—meaning not encrypted. According to Homer Kisner, the traffic chief at Station H, the SMS number enabled the cryptographers to track the major Japanese commanders such as Admiral Isoroku Yamamoto, the commander-in-chief of the

Imperial Japanese Navy, and Vice Admiral Chuichi Nagumo, the commander of Japan's carrier force, the First Air Fleet. Yamamoto had his own SMS series, so did Nagumo, according to Kisner. (Author interview with Kisner April 1988, Carlsbad, California and April 1999, Sacramento, California; 1988 audio tape, transcript, photographs, follow-up written correspondence, notes; 1999 video tape interview, transcript, photographs, notes, in author's file.)

With Kisner's help in 1988, the author prepared an SMS analysis of Admiral Nagumo's daily radio messages in the SMS series for September through November 1941. The analysis is based on the 5-Num intercepts found by the author in RG 457, MMRB, Archives II. Nagumo's use of radio as he prepared his carriers for the journey toward Hawaii is dramatic evidence. In September 1941 he originated 2.8 radio messages per day. By November it was 14.8 messages per day, an increase of over 400 percent. See SMS analysis in author's file, also available from analysis of RG 457 at Archives II.

27. See the TESTM records for November and December 1941, in RG 38, Station US papers, MMRB, Archives II. RDF "fixes" must be recorded and evaluated on a Great Circle chart for accuracy. A TESTM report is reproduced in Appendix D of this book.

28. On November 1, 1941 the Japanese navy issued radio call list 9 *(Yobidashi Fugo)*, which completely changed all warship radio identities. For IJN radio call sign list 9, see SRN 117402 of September 3, 1941 in RG 457, Archives II; for Hawaii super radio call sign list see PHLO files, RG 80, MMRB, Archives II. Aware that USN cryptographers might solve list 9 and discover the warships headed for Pearl Harbor, the IJN prepared a second super secret list for vessels assigned to the Hawaii operation. The TESTM records disclose that the USN cryptographers at Station CAST solved portions of the Hawaii call list code prior to December 7, 1941. The super list was recovered from a downed Japanese aircraft on December 7, 1941 and proved CAST's solutions were correct. The shore-based Japanese high naval commands used a three-*kana* radio call sign that did not change at least through December 7, 1941. Example: the Chief of the Naval General Staff, Admiral Osami Nagano's call sign was KO ME HA, according to Station H records in RG 38, Station US files, MMRB, Archives II.

29. For further details on American cryptographers obtaining Japan's secret Hawaii radio call signs, see the TESTM reports in chapters 8, 9, 11, 12, and 13, herein.

30. For identifying spurious sounds emitted by Japanese naval radio transmitters, see interview between Robert Ogg and Commander Irwin G. Newman, SRH 255, pp.31 to 34, RG 457, MMRB, Archives II, copy in author's file; for "very easy to identify Japanese naval radio transmitters," see letter from Fred Thomson, radioman-in-charge at Station AE, Sitka, Territory of Alaska in 1941, to author dated January 29, 1986, p. 4, item h; p.11, item i; in author's file; see telephone discussion of June 30, 1999, between author and Robert Ogg concerning spurious sounds emitted by Japanese naval radio transmitters, notes in author's file. See also comments by Robert Fox, radioman-in-charge, Station KING, Dutch Harbor, Territory of Alaska, where he could distinguish Russian radio transmitters by their "hollow sound"; Station KING, monthly report, November 1941, RG 181, National Archives, Seattle, WA, copy in author's file.

31. Homer Kisner interviews, April 1988 and April 1998, author's files.

32. Ibid.

33. The Underwood code typewriter was officially known as Radio Intelligence Publication 5, or "RIP 5" by the US Navy because of the published instructions for its operation. It converted signals of the International Morse Code (IMC) to the Japanese naval *kata kana* telegraphic code. Laurance Safford and Joseph Rochefort, cofounders of Navy communications intelligence, persuaded John Underwood, president of the typewriter firm, to manufacture the special code typewriter in the mid-1920s. Later, Underwood developed code typewriters for Russian, German, and Italian intercepts. The typewriters cost the Navy $85 each. The RIPs were secret documents issued by Station US and contained decryption information on Japanese radio and cryptographic procedures. As an example when Station US broke the 1918 Japanese naval code it was published as RIP 2. A later revision became RIP 3. The IJN operations code (5-Num) was first published in 1941 as RIP 73 and RIP 80.

See SRH 355, Vols. I and II, in RG 457, and RIP 32 in Station US files, MMRB, at Archives II.

34. See Joseph Rochefort's Oral History (ROH) p. 99, supra; also Laurance Safford: "The best we had as far as experience and all-around skill was up at Pearl Harbor," PHPT 8-3560.

35. During interviews with the author in 1988 and 1998, Kisner said some historians— who never interviewed him—had misinterpreted his Daily Chronology, in which he said there was no change in carrier operations during the three week period the Pearl Harbor force assembled and headed for Hawaii. These historians interpreted Kisner's words "no change" to mean that the Navy had lost the carrier force destined for Hawaii. Kisner explained that "no change" meant that there was no Japanese communication intelligence which changed the operations of the "Carrier Divisions" with the cruiser *Tone* and the twelve ships of the destroyer squadron. "These warships remained together as a force throughout the period and never separated. That's what 'no change' means," Kisner said. See: Homer Kisner interview, author's file. For the Thanksgiving report of Carrier Commands and Divisions, see the Station H Chronology, November 20, 1941 in RG 38, Station US papers, MMRB, Archives II.

Kisner had two radio direction finders at his disposal. One was on the H property near the beach front on Kaneohe Bay, the other at the Lualualei Naval Radio Station on the northwest coast of Oahu. Additional bearings were obtained from RDF stations at Corregidor, Guam, Dutch Harbor, Samoa, Midway, and the West Coast Communications Intelligence Network. Station H property was acquired by the Navy from the Federal Telegraph Company, a firm originally engaged in trans-Pacific radio/telegraph operations.

36. English translations of the four Japanese naval broadcasts are found in RG 457 (for blacked out version), MMRB, Archives II, and RG 38, Station US papers, ibid, for uncensored version. (1) Plain language Hitokappu Bay SRN 116643; (2) For IJN submarine RO TU ØØ (Ø designates the number zero in radio telegraphy, O, letter) see SRN 117666, (3) for *I-19*, see SRN 11632, and (4) TAYU 88 see SRN 117675. Uncensored in RG 38, ibid. USN radio intercept operators placed their sine—a two initial identification—on each document. See Station H operator sine list, July 1941, RG 38, Station US papers, MMRB, Archives II. Sines SN and LF are unidentified as this book is being written.

37. Kisner would have warned Kimmel, Homer Kisner interview, Sacramento, CA, April 24, 1998, transcript, notes in author's files.

38. Britain's Japanese code-breaking unit the Far East Combined Bureau at Singapore also intercepted and reported the radio transmissions to Winston Churchill, according to Captain Eric Nave, RN in his (with co-author James Rusbridger) *Betrayal at Pearl Harbor* (Summit Books, 1991), pp. 137 ff. For letter of Secretary of Navy Frank Knox to Secretary of State Cordell Hull, see note 7, this chapter, supra.

39. Though Netherlands military forces in the Dutch East Indies destroyed the 1941 Japanese navy and diplomatic intercept files, copies may still exist. It appears that the Dutch intercepts shared with the American government by Ranneft and *Kamer* 14 have been preserved in the Station US papers in Archives II. An index or finders aid is part of the Station US papers and describes the contents of Box 792: "Netherlands Raw Intercepts of 1941," but includes no details. Censorship has prevented the author's access as of this writing; see copy of index in author's file.

40. For Ranneft's 100 percent quote, see Note 10 herein.

CHAPTER 5

1. On the "splendid arrangement," see testimony of Admiral Harold Stark, FDR's Chief of Naval Operations, in discussion with Senator Walter George (D., GA) re intercepted Japanese messages in PHPT 5, p. 2213.

2. For monitor stations and cryptographic control center locations, see map in this book on page 68.

3. For the early history of American communications intelligence, see SRH 355, in RG 457, MMRB, Archives II; also Herbert O. Yardley, *The American Black Chamber* (Bobbs-Merrill, 1931).

4. On Rochefort, see Joseph Rochefort's Oral History (ROH), pp. 4 ff. In 1970, a bound volume of *The Reminiscences of Captain Joseph J. Rochefort* was published by the United States Naval Institute, Annapolis, Maryland as part of their Oral History interview program. The interview was conducted by US Navy Commander Etta Belle Kitchen in 1969 and immediately classified as TOP SECRET CODEWORD by Naval Intelligence. When the author learned of its existence in 1983 he filed a FOIA request but the Navy refused to declassify. Naval censorship was bypassed when Rochefort's daughter Janet Rochefort Elerding made the manuscript available. Joseph Rochefort died in 1979.

5. Station US, the small cryptographic unit cofounded by Safford and Rochefort, has been known by several designations. In 1935 it was called the Communications Security Group. During World War II, as space requirements for the cryptographic operations expanded, the Navy purchased the Mount Vernon Seminary at 3801 Nebraska Avenue, N.W. in Washington, DC and renamed the former school campus and buildings as Station NEGAT (for Nebraska). The unit has gone through a series of name changes since World War II, and has moved to Fort George G. Meade, Maryland, where it is known as the Naval Security Group Command. For more details, see *A History of Communications Intelligence in the United States with Emphasis on The United States Navy* (Eugene, OR: Naval Cryptologic Veterans Association, 1982).

6. For history of Station CAST, see booklet, *"Intercept Station C"* (Naval Cryptologic Veterans Association, 1983). Lietwiler was scheduled to relieve Fabian in the fall of 1941, but due to the crisis both remained at CAST. Three other facilities contributed to the "splendid arrangement" at CAST: Station BAKER, an RDF station at Libugon, Guam; the FECB at Singapore; and *Kamer* 14 at Bandoeng, Java. See SRH 045 dated August 4, 1945, in RG 457, MMRB, Archives II, for limited information on Station SIX written by Lt. Col. Howard Brown, the noncommissioned officer-in-charge in 1941. Brown wrote that he personally delivered Japanese intercepts to MacArthur, and received a "Thank you, Son"; but Brown provides no details on the contents of the intercepts seen by the general. For US Navy decryption results at CAST, see John Lietwiler's memo in RG 38, Station US papers, MMRB, Archives II.

7. For US sharing Japanese communications with the British and the Dutch governments, see Note 6 above.

8. See ROH, pp. 25, 106, for Joseph Rochefort's intelligence credo.

9. See ibid., p. 100.

10. See Fourteenth Naval District Secret A-6-3 file, RG 181, NA, San Bruno. The reference to Lt. Gen. Walter Short's letter of Thursday, November 27, 1941, is in the naval routing slip received of COM 14, November 28; it bears Rochefort's initials, JJR. COM 14 was a cover name for Station HYPO in 1941. The second letter is in the same file dated January 1, 1942. Presumably the originals are in the Station US files at Archives II.

11. For Barkley's exchange with Gen. Short, see PHPT 7-3013. Emily Short, the general's daughter-in-law, said his treatment by the Army broke his heart and he was unable to present a spirited defense due to ill health. Telephone conversation with author, February 25, 1997, notes, transcript in author's file.

12. Assistant Secretary of State Adolf Berle, Jr., a principal advisor to FDR, arranged for the exchange of communications intelligence between Canadian WT (wireless/telegraph) stations and SAIL. See Berle to Knox, confidential memorandum July 21, 1941 in COM 13 file EF 13-39, RG 181, NA, Seattle.

13. For Oshima disclosing Hitler's Russian invasion plans, see Oshima message number 691 to Tokyo, Saturday, June 14, 1941, in *The Magic Background of Pearl Harbor*, Vol. II, p. A-335, item 659. See also ibid. item 660 of June 18, 1941. Presumably Oshima's message was delivered to the White House by FDR's naval aide Captain John Beardall, who saw Roosevelt at 11:18 A.M., on June 14, per White House Usher Book, FDRL. Beardall delivered intercepts to the President from mid-May 1941 to the time of Pearl Harbor.

14. David Kahn, *The Codebreakers* (Macmillan, 1967) and Cipher A. Deavours, *Machine Cryptography* (Artech House, 1985) are worth reading on cryptography theory. A formula offered by Deavours for partially solving Purple: $cS2\ bS1 = dS2\ cS1 = aS2$ $dS1 = bS2$. For an example of an original Purple intercept see RG 38, Station US files, folder 5830/75, MMRB, Archives II. It was intercepted at Station FIVE, Fort

Shafter, Hawaii on May 6, 1941, and forwarded by teleprinter to Washington, where it was initialed AHM by Arthur H. McCollum.

15. For the quote from Rear Admiral Leigh Noyes, see PHPT 10, p. 4714. On Colonel William Friedman's first purple decryption, see Ronald Clark, *The Man Who Broke Purple* (Little, Brown and Co., 1977), p. 144. The Japanese called the Purple machine *Obun Injiki* or electric typewriter. In the Pacific area, Japan issued Purple machines to its consulates in Manila, Hong Kong, Singapore, and Batavia, but not Honolulu. Pearl Harbor investigators were told that the Purple code was unknown to Hawaii's military officials in 1941, but the Station US papers prove otherwise. Lt. Cdr. Thomas Dyer, chief Navy cryptanalyst at Pearl Harbor's Station HYPO, wrote that he had received a descriptive write-up of the Purple system but was not provided with the necessary equipment for processing the messages between November 27 and December 7, 1941; Dyer is quoted by Rear Admiral Earl E. Stone in Top Secret Ultra Serial 0003048P20 of April 6, 1946, in RG 38, PHLO, MMRB, Archives II. Station US published secret instructions for operation of the Purple machine and its decoding techniques and sent them to the Pacific intercept stations, including Station HYPO, as Radio Intelligence Publication 77 (instructions). RIP 72—the prototype Purple machine—was not sent to Hawaii. Mysteriously, RIP 72 is missing from two RIP indices found by the author in the Station US papers, RG 38, MMRB, Archives II. At the request of the author, Cary Conn of the Archives FOIA staff began an investigation concerning the missing RIP 72 in September 1998.

16. See David Kahn, *Codebreakers*, supra, ff.

17. See Ensign Laurance MacKallor's handwritten note: "Facts concerning the 'Purple' machine as nearly as I can recall them," initialed LLM, in RG 38, Station US papers, MMRB, Archives II.

18. For Safford's dispatches listing the Purple sequence settings see OPNAV to COM SIXTEEN (CAST), Secret serial 060720, December 6, 1941; RG 38, Station US papers, MMRB, Archives II. At the end of the European War, British cryptographers seized a Purple machine found at the Japanese embassy in Berlin. According to MacKallor's note, CAST personnel destroyed the Purple machine in April 1942; but he gave no details. Robert Dowd and Duane Whitlock, who worked in the cryptographic tunnel at Station CAST in 1941 and 1942, told the author that the Purple machine was transported to Australia by a US Navy submarine in April 1942, when Japanese troops were about to seize Corregidor. Telephone interviews May 1999. In his telephone interview with the author, Dowd said he operated the Purple machine for the US Navy at CAST. At the time he was a yeoman second class assigned to the machine area of the cryptographic tunnel (see drawing of CAST in photo insert). Dowd said he received the encrypted Purple message from an intercept operator and then began the decryption process. First he set the rotor wheels for the correct sequence, then ran the message through the machine, which stripped off the encryption and produced plain Japanese text in Roman letters. Next he took the deciphered message to a Japanese-language officer, Lieutenant Commander S. A. Carlson, for translating to English. "I was never told of the contents of the Purple messages," Dowd said. " I didn't qualify under the need to know doctrine. So I never saw an English translation." Telephone conversations with author, May 1999. Dowd retired from the US Navy as a lieutenant commander.

19. For "within a day's time," see Safford testimony in PHPT 36, p. 67; also Lt. John Lietwiler's memo in Station US papers, RG 38, MMRB, Archives II. Lietwiler was co-commander of CAST from September 1941 until his evacuation from Corregidor in 1942.

20. On courier Fukuda, see PHPT 35-442; *Magic*, Vol. I, p. A-92, item 161. Twenty-one ports of call are listed including Los Angeles, New York, Washington, DC, plus cities in Central and South America.

21. See report of the *Yawata* $40,000 transaction written by Lt. Ellsworth Hosmer, DIO, COM 12, author's file, courtesy of his daughter, Patty Hosmer Rathbone, Loomis, CA.

22. A striking example of a US naval officer concealing British and American success in obtaining and solving Japanese code systems in 1941 can be found in the Station US records at Archives II. The concealment concerns elements of the Japanese navy's

operations code, known as the 5-Num or 5-Digit code. On March 5, 1941, Captain Joseph Redman, assistant director of naval communications, ordered that a radio dispatch sent by Admiral Thomas Hart, commander-in-chief of the Asiatic Fleet, be withdrawn from US Navy files and a dummy substituted in its place. In the secret message that Redman wanted withdrawn, Admiral Hart disclosed he was exchanging solutions of the 5-Num code with the British naval cryptology agency, the Far East Combined Bureau (FECB) at Singapore. "Combined" referred to Australian, New Zealand, and British officers working together. See Hart's message, secret serial 050535, March 5, 1941 in enclosure 2, FOIA release by Naval Security Group Command to author, August 31, 1993, in author's file. The Chinese government of Chiang Kai-shek may have been a part of the "splendid arrangement." Documents found by the author in Archives II, indicate that Chinese cryptographers solved Japan's 1941 military and diplomatic codes. American censorship in 1999 hides full details. Documents in Archives II provide a look at Chinese code-breaking success. On August 29, 1941, the British cryptology center in Singapore asked its air attaché in Chungking to obtain Japanese naval codes from Chinese cryptographers. According to the British, Chinese code-breakers had broken into the Imperial Japanese Navy's coded message texts (5-Num), radio frequencies, and coded call signs (Yobidashi Fugo) of the Japanese Naval Air Forces. See RG 38, Station US papers, SRH 406, Box 13, Folder 5830/115 MMRB, Archives II. But beware—avoid the sanitized version of SRH 406 in the so-called "open" file of RG 457 in Archives II. The true message is in the Station US papers. The reference to China breaking the Japanese codes is whited out in the "open" file. However, by holding the Aug. 29, 1941, whited out message to a light source a researcher can read the censored version. See also messages from the US Naval Attaché in Chungking (Chiang's wartime capital) for Sept. 11, Oct. 26 and 30, and Dec. 10, 1941. These four reports confirm that China had broken Japanese military codes. The September 11 message identifies Japanese Naval Air Groups 12, 13, and 15 and ties in with the earlier Singapore report. See folder containing Chungking USN attaché reports in RG 38, Station US papers, Archives II.

23. For a description of the Japanese naval code systems used in the Pacific War, see Kanya Miyauchi. *Niitaka Yama Nobore* (Climb Mount Niitaka) (Tokyo. Rikkyu Shuppan. 1976) pp. 135ff. Author's translation provided through courtesy of Commander Sadao Seno (Retired) of the Imperial Japanese Navy. For the US Navy's description of the Japanese navy code systems prior to November 1941, see RG 38, RIP 32, Station US papers, MMRB, Archives II. For Canada's WT (wireless/telegraph) Plan, see SECRET letter dated August 2, 1941 from HMC Dockyard Esquimalt, B.C., Canada to COM 13, in Folder EF13-39, Box 8155, RG 181, NA, Seattle, WA. See Note 6, supra.

24. In April 1943, American cryptographers learned of a Yamamoto inspection trip to bases in the South Pacific. The "unbreakable code" revealed his itinerary. American fighters were dispatched to the route and shot down the admiral's aircraft. The plane crashed, killing Yamamoto.

25. Whitlock's e-mail to author, May 22, 1999, in author's file. Re Admiral Thomas Hart, "Most of those dispatches that came in were kept very closely locked up, and I believe that Admiral Hart was about the only one who saw them, other than those that were doing the decrypting," Adair said in an oral history that was conducted in 1977 (hereafter referred to as Adair Oral History, AOH: *See Reminiscences of Rear Admiral Charles Adair*, US Naval Institute, 1977).

Q. But it was known that we were breaking the code.

ADAIR: They were, yes. As far as Washington knew, they knew everything that was going on at the time, that is, what the Japs were saying. (AOH p. 73).

Adair expanded on USN decoding procedures available to Admiral Hart from Station CAST and said that President Roosevelt was reading the Japanese intercepts: "I believe that the war was inevitable. It had to be because I think President

Roosevelt was bound and determined we were going to get into the war somehow. He had been unable to get our ships in the Atlantic attacked by the Germans. He was reading all the Japanese coded dispatches (AOH p. 76). Adair said Hart never confided in him but still conveyed the inevitable that we were going to get into this war, because of the dispatches he saw. "He (Hart) was getting dispatches and reading a lot of material that I don't think Washington knew he was getting at the time, because he did have some of those decoding machines which, I found out later, the Commander-in-Chief Pacific Fleet (Admiral Kimmel) did not have." (AOH p. 77). One of the decoding machines included JEEP IV used for solving the additive versions of Japan's naval code known to Americans as the 5-Num system. The JEEP IV decoding machine was brought to CAST by Lieutenant (j.g.) John W. Hess in early October 1941, according to a secret memo prepared by Lieutenant John Lietwiler, co-commander of CAST. See SRH 355, p. 433, in RG 457, MMRB, Archives II, copy in author's file.

For other confirmation on Washington's ability to read the intercepted Japanese military and diplomatic messages, see General George Marshall's statement to selected Washington, DC newsmen on November 15, 1941. In his meeting with the reporters, Marshall disclosed that the United States had broken Japanese codes and that he expected war with Japan would begin during the first ten days of December 1941; for full discussion see chapter 10 herein.

26. The author located 210 SM reports in the Station US files of RG 457, MMRB, Archives II. These, however, are apparently only a small portion of the SM reports obtained by Station H in 1941.

27. See Rudolph Fabian's original report of November 29, 1941, transmitted to Station US and Admiral Kimmel in Hawaii; converted to Presidential Monograph 70, RG 80, PHLO, MMRB, Archives II. The monograph is signed by Major R. A. Boone, a McCollum assistant. None of the original intercepted Japanese radio messages of Admiral Kondo, cited by Fabian, have been declassified and released to the public by Archives II. During a telephone interview with the author in May 1999, Captain Duane Whitlock (a radioman first class assigned to CAST in 1941) said that he wrote most of the intelligence dispatches sent to Hawaii and Washington in 1941. Whitlock denied that cryptographers at CAST had deciphered the SM code as suggested in Pelletier's article. "I was one of three radio traffic analysts assigned to CAST. None of the naval officers at CAST were trained in radio traffic analysis so the job fell on me or two other analysts, Charlie Johns or Tom Hoover (both chief radiomen). After writing the dispatches, I passed them to Fabian who had authority to release them for radio transmission."

Kondo's Second Fleet supplied battleships, cruisers, and destroyers for the protection of Japan's Southeast Asia invasion forces in December 1941. Two of his battleships *Hiei* and *Kirishima* were assigned to the First Air Fleet for the Hawaii attack.

28. During 1940 and 1941 Albert J. Pelletier, Jr., then a yeoman first class, served on the Navy's cryptographic team at Station US, headed by Agnes Driscoll. In his *Cryptolog* article (Summer 1992 issue), Pelletier wrote that he worked on the Japanese navy's 5-Num code in 1941; but he erroneously referred to the system as JN-25. Pelletier's work on the SM code can be traced to 1939 in Navy records. See RG 457, SRH 355, Vol. 1, p. 328, MMRB, Archives II. Pelletier retired from naval cryptology as a captain. In military use, according to Whitlock, *cryptology* refers to enemy codes; *cryptography* refers to friendly codes such as US Navy codes. Admiral James O. Richardson wrote that Station H obtained information on Japanese warship movements operating in the Central Pacific during May 10, 1940. He did not provide communication data, but indicated the information came from RDF bearings and "plain-language call signs of radio traffic." See James O. Richardson, *On The Treadmill to Pearl Harbor* (Naval History Division, Department of the Navy, USGPO, 1973), p. 331.

29. Agnes Driscoll is not listed on the US Navy's Cryptology Honor Roll. The roll, prepared by Admiral Chester Nimitz in June 1942, cited 65 men for their cryptographic efforts in using intercepted radio dispatches to penetrate the secret operations orders of the Japanese Fleet from July 1941 to June 1942. In their most famous feat the 65 honorees located the 177-warship Japanese Midway invasion force in May

1942. The northernmost islands in the Hawaiian chain, Midway was the initial target. Relying on information gained from naval intercepts, Admiral Nimitz's 49 warships ambushed the numerically superior Japanese force north of Midway, sank four of Japan's irreplaceable aircraft carriers, and in air battles caused the loss of her most experienced pilots. The three-day battle lasted from June 4 to 6, 1942. The ambush was the turning point of the Pacific War. Japan never regained the offensive. Agnes Meyer Driscoll's collection of 5-Num decrypting activities amassed after June 1939 has not been released. The 5-Num code was Japan's most important naval communications system. It was used to organize the attacks on Pearl Harbor and Midway, and throughout the four years of the Pacific War.

Driscoll's omission from the Cryptology Honor Roll is apparently intended to keep the spotlight off her discovery of the operations code on June 1, 1939. Driscoll was born Agnes May Meyer on July 24, 1889 in Westerville, Ohio, graduated from Ohio State University, Columbus in June 1911 with a Bachelor of Arts degree conferred by the College of Arts, Philosophy and Science; she was severely injured in an auto accident in October 1937 while en route to visit Thomas Jefferson's estate, Monticello in Virginia. Retired, age seventy, from Armed Forces Security Agency, July 31, 1959.

30. For Shakespeare commune, see William F. Friedman and Elizebeth S. Friedman, *The Shakespearean Ciphers Examined* (Cambridge University Press, 1958) ff. See also James R. Chiles, *"Breaking codes was this couple's lifetime career,"* (Smithsonian, June 1987), p. 128 ff.

31. Captain Duane Whitlock of Station CAST said he first recognized the change in Japan's naval operation code in June 1939 while he was serving as an intercept operator at Station H in Hawaii. "I copied the messages off the Japanese naval airwaves. We called the system the 5-Digit code," said Whitlock during a telephone conversation with the author in May 1999. Using the 5-Digit intercepts that had been obtained and forwarded to Washington, DC in 1939 by Whitlock and other naval intercept operators, Agnes Driscoll began solving the basic elements of the code. Her first breakthrough came in January 1940. According to Laurance Safford, commander of Station US, "Madam X crashed through with one of her strokes of inspiration last January (1940)." See Safford's letter to Joseph Wenger, September 10, 1940, in RG 38, Station US Papers, Box 6, folder 5750-81, MMRB, Archives II.

32. For Layton's quotes concerning Ms. Driscoll, see Edwin Layton, *And I Was There* (William Morrow & Co. 1985), p. 58.

33. For the 5-Num code similar to Spanish-American war codes, see Greg Mellen, editor, *Rhapsody in Purple: A New History of Pearl Harbor.* (Cryptologia, July 1982), p. 220. In 1941, the US Navy called the system the 5-Num code, not JN-25, according to Robert Hanyok, Center for Cryptologic History, Fort George G. Meade, Maryland.

34. For FBI confirmation, see FBI report 100-97-1-98.

35. As this book went to press in 1999, RIPs 73 and 80 have been reportedly declassified and are available at Archives II for researchers. Though the author filed FOIA requests with the US Navy and National Archives to see all RIP documents in 1987, RIPs 73 and 80 were never released.

36. For the Hawaiian journey of the elusive Navy transport carrying the latest solutions to the 5-Num code from Washington, DC, see SRH 355, Vol. 1, p. 399, RG 457, MMRB, Archives II. According to Japanese naval records, the 5-Num code in effect from July 1, 1941 to December 4, 1941 was known as *Ango Sho* D (Navy Code Book D), additive version 7. At midnight December 4, 1941 additive version 8 was placed in effect. For the effective dates that version 7 was in use, see SRN 116741 dated December 2, 1941, in RG 457, MMRB, Archives II, copy in author's file. For additive version 8, see loc. cit.; and discovery of additive version 8 by Station CAST, see the priority dispatch time-clocked at 1502 hours (3:02 P.M.) GMT, which corresponds to 10:02 A.M. in Washington, DC, and 4:30 A.M. on December 4, 1941 in Hawaii. Confirmed by enclosure 2 of US Naval Security Group Command FOIA release of August 31, 1993, copy in author's file. For Naval Regulations prescribing transport and stowage, see preamble to all RIP publications of the World War II era (in RG 38, Station US Papers, MMRB, Archives II): "This publication is SECRET and shall be handled and accounted for as prescribed in the Navy Regulations and the Regis-

tered Publication Manual. It shall be transported by officer messenger only and given Class A stowage." Except for the "slow boat," the policy was inviolate. When the 5-Num recoveries were transported to London and exchanged with the British in January 1941, four US military officers took turns guarding the package, two each from the Army and Navy.

37. Admiral Nagumo originated the three-page comprehensive report of December 16 as his SMS 845 and used the call sign NO SE 44. The report—decoded and translated—can be found in a collection of sixteen Station H intercepts dated between December 9 and 29, 1941, but vital communication data pertaining to the interception details has been omitted from No. 845. Apparently the omission is deliberate, intended to conceal the fact that the 5-Num dispatch was intercepted, decoded, and translated in Hawaii. Rochefort's Communication Summary (COMSUM) of December 16 confirms the interception of NO SE 44. The COMSUM indicates that Nagumo's flagship unloaded several dispatches including that of NOSE 4. At first Rochefort identified the radio call sign as a submarine unit, then later in the paragraph placed a question mark after NOSE 4. See pp. 2, 3, of COMSUM, December 16, 1941 under carriers, in RG 80, PHLO, MMRB, Archives II, copy in author's file.

38. For Rochefort's apparent decrypt of message 845, see page 257 of his COMSUM for December 19, 1941, in RG 80, PHLO, MMRB, Archives II, copy in author's file. The Japanese naval dispatch detailing American losses at Pearl Harbor appears to be an abbreviated decryption and translation of Admiral Nagumo's message SMS 845. All communication data have been stripped from the message translation/decryption.

In the COMSUM's English translation on p. 257 the Japanese originator is listed as "Tokyo Navy Department" and addressed to "Three unidentified addresses. (One of which is in the Saigon area)." The abbreviated translation of the text follows the identical syntax form of Nagumo's message SMS 845.

Two other examples of translated Japanese naval "decrypted traffic"—with some communication data—can be found on pages 250 and 251 of the COMSUM. On page 250 a message marked "from decripted (sic) traffic" details the sailing schedule for the Tairyu Maru in the Marshall Islands for November and December 1941. In the second example on page 251 the COMSUM cites the source as "from encrypted [sic] traffic"; the English translation indicates Commander Carrier Divison 5 (carriers Shokaku and Zuikaku were Carrier Division 5) will shortly be in Eastern Marshalls area."

In addition to these three decrypted/translated messages there are two extracts from US Coast Guard intercepts on page 254 dated December 17, 1941, Hawaii Time. See the COMSUMS in December 1941 file folder, PHLO, RG 80, MMRB, Archives II, copy in author's file. 27. At 8:05 A.M. on December 7, Admiral Nagumo transmitted a brief report to Tokyo that was intercepted at Station H by J. J. Perkins, radioman first class. Nagumo quickly reported the results of the attack to Japan. He said two American battleships were destroyed and four badly damaged and a great number of aircraft destroyed. The First Air Fleet lost thirty planes, according to Nagumo's report. Perkins' log notes that Nagumo originated the broadcast as SA FU 1, one of his alternate radio call signs. Three hours later, at 11:09 A.M. Nagumo was addressed in a radio dispatch as YO N 77 (a radio call sign identified four days earlier by CAST), according to Perkins' log entry. See Station H operator log for December 8, 1941, p. 147, Station US papers, RG 38, MMRB, Archives II. Logs are in Tokyo Time. The original Nagumo dispatches of December 7 have not been released by the US Navy.

39. On Thomas Dewey's knowledge of Japanese code interception prior to Pearl Harbor, see Gordon Prange, At Dawn We Slept, (McGraw Hill Book Company. 1981), p. 646.

40. On MacKallor's trip, see RG 457, SRH 355, Vol. I, p. 416; RG 24 for deck log of USS Sepulga, January to March 1941; his account of Purple is in RG 38, Station US papers, release of January 24, 1995, all in Archives II, copies in author's file.

41. On FDR's journey to Annapolis, see White House Usher Books, January 24, 1941, FDRL.

42. On the transfer of codes to Britain see David Kahn, Seizing the Enigma (Houghton Mifflin, 1991).

43. On Ens. Prescott Currier's assignment see SRH 355, Vol. 1, p. 376, in RG 457, MMRB, Archives II.
44. On Weeks aboard *Augusta*, see Deck Log of *Augusta*, RG 24, MMRB, Archives II.
45. For Admiral Hart's dispatch, the notation pertaining to Redman, and disclosure that MacKallor brought 5-Num solutions from Station US, see Appendix D of this book.
46. On Rear Admiral Royal Ingersoll, see OPNAV Secret 281500, March 25, 1941, RG 38, Station US papers, MMRB, Archives II. Three sets of initials are affixed to Ingersoll's dispatch; those of Redman and Safford are clearly read. However one set of initials that appear to be either AJK, AGK (Alan G. Kirk) or EJK (Ernest J. King) are smudged.
47. See Prescott Currier's letter dated September 7, 1988, in author's file. Currier retired as a Navy captain and lived in Damariscotta, ME. His death was reported in *Cryptolog*, Winter 1995 issue.
48. A cryptology (decodes of the enemy) blackout was aimed at the two Hawaiian commanders—Admiral Husband E. Kimmel and Lieutenant General Walter Short—in February 1941, soon after they assumed command. The cryptology blackout has been a contentious issue since the spring of 1941. For fifty-eight years either Admiral Kimmel or his surviving family members pressed for access to the Japanese intercepts. Finally on May 25, 1999 the US Senate by a narrow vote found that Kimmel and Short "were denied vital intelligence that was available in Washington." The Senate vote came nearly 58 years to the day after Admiral Kimmel asked that the US government establish a "cardinal principle" that would assure him of immediate access to information of a secret nature, the Japanese military and diplomatic intercepts. (See article on p. A-26 of *New York Times*, May 26, 1999: "Scapegoats of Pearl Harbor Are Cleared by a Split Senate.")

Kimmel was commander-in-chief of the Pacific Fleet, Short the commander of the Hawaiian Department of the US Army. Theoretically both were included members of the "splendid arrangement." Each had direct access to Army and Navy intercept stations that monitored Japanese diplomatic and military radio broadcasts: Kimmel had Station H (Navy), Short had Station FIVE (Army). Intercepts are worthless unless they can be decoded and translated at a processing center staffed by cryptographers and translators and delivered to the proper commander in a timely manner. Kimmel possessed the only Hawaiian military processing center, Station HYPO; Short had none. The record shows that of the two commanders, only Kimmel sensed he was a victim of the cryptology cutoff. Soon after assuming command of the Pacific Fleet on February 1, 1941, Kimmel sent two personal letters to Admiral Harold Stark, the Chief of Naval Operations, and requested guaranteed access to Japanese intercepts. (1) Paraphrase of Kimmel to Stark, February 18, 1941: "Let there be no misunderstanding, send me information of a secret nature" (PHPT 4, p. 1792). (2) Paraphrase of Kimmel to Stark, May 26, 1941: "Because of lack of information I am in a difficult position." Kimmel asked Stark to establish a cardinal principle and keep him informed (PHPT 4-1793). Stark replied that he was fully aware of the responsibility of "keeping you adequately informed." (See PHPT 4, p. 1792.) But Stark did not keep his promise because Station HYPO—the decoding and translation center for the Pacific fleet—was not provided with adequate instructions for decoding Japan's naval operations code—the 5-Num system—until a few days after the attack. Yet Japan's most strategic war secrets were intercepted in Hawaii throughout 1941. Japan's naval war strategy was disclosed in the 5-Num code messages intercepted by the thousands at the US Navy's Station H on Kaneohe Bay; her diplomatic strategy was revealed in the J Series of codes and the Purple Code which were intercepted by the hundreds at the US Army's Station FIVE at Fort Shafter.

The three Japanese systems in effect in the fall of 1941, 5-Num, J, and Purple had been solved by US Navy and US Army cryptographers in Washington, DC. There is no record that any of the Army and Navy officers or enlisted men involved in the interception of Japanese dispatches in Hawaii made any attempt to decode these vital messages and deliver the information to either Kimmel or Short. There was no call of alarm by the intercept personnel in Hawaii or by Army and Navy intelligence centers in Washington, DC. No timely attempt was made to deliver the solutions of the Japanese codes to Hawaii—except for the slow boat carrying the secrets of the 5-Num system. Still, military information was obtained from the 5-Num dispatches in Hawaii. According to Joseph Rochefort, the commander of HYPO, he and his staff culled military information from the 5-Num messages by a technique he called radio traffic analysis. Rochefort never explained his failure to obtain Washington's solution of the 5-Num code in an expeditious manner.

49. For the Winds Code controversy, see voluminous citation on testimony given to various Pearl Harbor investigations in 1944–46 in Stanley H. Smith, compiler, *Investigations of the Attack on Pearl Harbor. Index to Government Hearings* (Greenwood Press, 1990), pp. 41, 42.

50. The British intelligence unit at Singapore, known as the Far East Combined Bureau (FECB), was the source of the Winds Code intercept. See Admiral Thomas Hart's secret dispatch Serial 281430 of November 28, 1941, RG 38, Station US papers, MMRB, Archives II.

51. For the 1979 declassification of a portion of the pre-Pearl Harbor English translations of the 5-Num intercepts, see President Carter's Executive Order 12065, Federal Register of June 1, 1979. Carter also released Japanese naval intercepts that include the years 1942–45. There are two versions in Archives II, College Park, MD. One is in RG 457 and contains blackouts that paint out the pre-Pearl Harbor 5-Num code, mistakenly identified in the Carter documents as JN-25. An uncensored version (no words painted out in black) can be found in the Station US papers of RG 38, but with the JN-25 mistake.

On a CNN telecast during December 1991 commemorating the fiftieth anniversary of the Pearl Harbor attack, Pentagon correspondent Wolf Blitzer interviewed General Colin Powell, the chairman of the Joint Chiefs of Staff. Blitzer showed Powell some of the Japanese messages from the Carter release. Both apparently were unaware that they were looking at rigged documents.

52. Quotations from David W. Gaddy's letter of January 28, 1993 to British author James Rusbridger, in author's file.

CHAPTER 6

1. The description of Ted Emanuel's Boat Day comes from author's interview with Professors Yale Maxon and Denzel Carr, El Cerrito, California, May 9, 1983, in author's file. Emanuel's harbor surveillance had its beginnings in 1936 when Roosevelt authorized the Office of Naval Intelligence to conduct clandestine surveillance of Japanese merchant ships and tankers arriving at Hawaii ports. FDR acted on the advice of a special intelligence task force that included Lieutenant Colonel George S. Patton, Jr., a future Army commander in World War II in Europe. Patton's group detected Japanese "espionage" in Hawaii and warned the White House of spy voyages to Wake and Midway Islands and Honolulu by Japanese *marus*. On August 10, 1936, Roosevelt accepted the advice and ordered a continual ONI watch of all Japanese vessels calling at Hawaii ports; see RG 80, ONI secret serial A8-5EF37/EG12, dated June 30, 1936, Archives II. See also Roosevelt's Secret memorandum to CNO dated August 10, 1936, in FDRL.

2. The Navy's wiretap file on Morimura reveals that he took a Foreign Ministry examination for a consular position on March 8, 1941; see Japanese Foreign Office (JFO) Bulletin 463 in FBI file 65-414-7-1, Serial 394. On March 20, JFO Bulletin 464 said he would be ordered to serve in the Foreign Office telegraphic affairs section; see FBI file, 65-414-1A, serial 394. FBI Pearl Harbor files are available at the FBI's Washington, DC headquarters. Navy wiretaps on the consulate's telephone lines were first reported to Hoover by Shivers in a letter dated September 26, 1940. The letter said the Navy presently furnished the FBI with a day-by-day record of the wiretaps. Shivers promised to keep his boss fully informed on information obtained from the wiretaps; see FBI file 65-414-5.

3. For Morimura's "surprise attack" message of December 6, 1941 see facsimile of his message on p. 116 of this book.

4. See J. Edgar Hoover memorandum to Lieut. Gen. George Grunert, president of the Army Pearl Harbor Board, dated August 25, 1944, in RG 80, PHLO, Exhibit 70, pp. 5, 6, Archives II, copy in author's file.

5. For the arrival of the *West Virginia* at Ten-ten Dock, see RG 24, Deck Log of *West Virginia*, March 26, 1941, Archives II. This was the only time in 1941 when the battleship berthed at the Navy Yard dock; all her other moorings were at the isolated Battleship Row.

6. For Hoover's warning on Japanese naval officers as spies, see FBI file 65-414-28, para. C, dated Oct. 24, 1940, copy in author's file.

7. Robert Shivers letter dated October 31, 1940; see FBI file 65-414-22, p. 5, copy in author's file.

8. For J. Edgar Hoover letter of December 14, 1940 to Shivers, see p. 6 of Hoover's memorandum dated August 25, 1944, filed with Army Pearl Harbor Board as Exhibit 70; RG 80, PHLO, MMRB, Archives II, copy in author's file.

9. Attorney General Janet Reno did not release the complete *Nitta Maru* file because of its designation as a National Defense Secret. Her press relations official, Carl Stern, a former NBC-TV Supreme Court reporter, backed her up. He wrote that it was unfair for the author to accuse the FBI of stonewalling FOIA requests on Morimura. While at NBC-TV Stern, an attorney, succeeded in obtaining government documents by filing his own FOIAs; see Stern letters of May 25 and Aug. 2, 1994, author's file. Re the *Nitta Maru*, see FBI FOIA 292,385: six pages of the file are super secret and totally blacked out as this goes to press in 1999. Underscoring the secrecy attached to the six documents by the Department of Justice, neither Reno nor Stern would reveal the dates, serial numbers, or file numbers. The day before Morimura's arrival in Honolulu, Shivers addressed a letter to Hoover dated March 26, 1941. The letter concerned an ONI-FBI investigation, but the text is blacked out in FBI file 66-8603-165.

10. Interview of Frederick G. Tillman by the author, Fowler, California, March 26, 1990. Audio tape, transcript, and notes in author's file.

11. For Matsuoka's March 8, 1941 message to Honolulu re Morimura, see PHPT 37, p. 1101.

12. See the consulate's incoming message log for March 1941, in PHPT 35, pp. 403 ff.; the outgoing message log is on pp. 430 ff. A duplicate of the log is in PHPT 37, starting at page 1101. For Morimura's protocol (diplomatic passport) see FBI report 100-65558, item 1. For Morimura's arrival reported by Honolulu newspapers, *Hawaii Hochii, Nippu Jiji,* and *Star-Bulletin* for March 27, 1941. Station US kept a numerical log of the consulate's incoming and outgoing messages but none of the March 1941 Morimura dispatches could be located in the Station US numerical logs; instead there are blank spaces. For the Station US numerical logs concerning radio messages to and from the consulate, see RG 38, Station US papers, folder 5830/30 for March 1941, MMRB, Archives II. The J dispatches also disclosed that a new consul-general, Nagao Kita, was due to arrive in Honolulu March 14, 1941, a week before Morimura. By what is presumed to be pure coincidence, the *Star-Bulletin* on the same day carried a separate AP story headlined "Modern Spies Lack Oomph, Imagination." As of 1998, the original intercept of H-4 has not been declassified by Archives II. For information on the Mackay Radio dispatches of January 1941 see the "bulky enclosure" section of FBI file 65-414. "Bulky" is an FBI term for documents stored with many enclosures, annexes, etc.

13. For Okuda's Armistice Day statements, see Honolulu *Star-Bulletin*, November 11, 1940, byline by Lawrence Nakatsuka; also FBI file 65-414-30.

14. For Frederick G. Tillman's identification of Otojiro Okuda as involved in intelligence matters, see State Department decimal file 702.9411a/37, RG 59, Diplomatic Branch, Archives II. Hoover sent Tillman's comprehensive report on Japanese espionage activities in Hawaii to Adolf Berle on Oct. 6, 1941. Tillman prepared the report on August 22, 1941.

15. *Nitta Maru* was a 17,000-ton luxury passenger liner built for the Tokyo-Europe run. The ship's maiden voyage in June 1940 was diverted to San Francisco due to the European war. Admiral Yamamoto then conscripted the vessel for military transport. In November and December 1941 it transported aviators of the Eleventh Air Fleet to Takeo, Formosa for support of the amphibious landings in Southeast Asia. Then in January 1942 the ship transported reinforcements for the Japanese garrison that captured Wake Island. *Nitta Maru* was assigned to Carrier Division Three in March 1942 and converted to an aircraft carrier. As such she was commissioned in Novem-

ber 1942 and renamed HIJMS *Chuyo;* she was sunk by USS *Sailfish* on December 4, 1943, southeast of Tokyo Bay.

16. Lt. Denzel Carr, a prewar University of Hawaii professor and naval reservist, had taught previously in Japan at Otani and Wakayama Universities in Kyoto. After the war, he became a tenured professor and later chairman of the department of Oriental Languages, University of California, Berkeley. He was a Guggenheim Fellow in 1955. Carr "Known to Anderson"; see CNO confidential letter, Serial 0361316, Dec. 6, 1940 signed by W. S. Anderson, Director of Naval Intelligence. The letter included a November 1940 report by Captain W. S. Kilpatrick, the US Navy's Inspector-General, that praised Carr: "The work of Lieutenant Carr has special qualifications unequaled by anyone else in the United States naval service of intelligence." Praise was heaped equally on Emanuel's work as "outstanding." See Anderson's letter and Kilpatrick's report in RG 181, National Archives, San Bruno, CA. Carr was born in Kentucky in 1902 and died in Berkeley, CA. on Oct. 14, 1984. The mission of Carr's unit, the District Intelligence Office of the Fourteenth Naval District, was totally different from that of Station HYPO, Rochefort's organization located in the Pearl Harbor Naval Yard six miles distant. Station HYPO was concerned with combat intelligence derived from intercepted Japanese naval messages, while Carr and his associates dealt with domestic intelligence and espionage matters.
17. Okuda to escort Morimura, see Globe Wireless intercept of March 24, 1941, PHPT 35, p. 454, item 68. Duplicate in PHPT 37, p. 1094.
18. Queen Liliuokalani was a celebrated and accomplished composer. The Hawaiian monarchs supported the Royal Hawaiian Band as a public cultural legacy. After the Queen was overthrown in an 1893 cabal led by American economic interests, public subscriptions continued funding the band. The Royal Hawaiian Band is not connected with the Royal Hawaiian Hotel.
19. Denzel Carr interview with the author, El Cerrito, CA, May 9, 1983; in author's files.
20. For Theodore Emanuel's identification of Morimura, see COM 14 District Intelligence Confidential File A-8-5, dated March 28, 1941 included in FBI file 65-414 serial 67 1/2. Emanuel's report was signed by Captain Irving Mayfield, District Intelligence Officer for Hawaii. Ted Emanuel's photograph of Morimura has not been located in USN files at Archives II nor was it included in the FBI report serial 67 1/2 cited above. The FBI file copy has blacked out Mayfield's signature but left Theodore Emanuel's initials "TE" in the upper right corner. Photography of Japanese diplomats was a sore subject with the consulate. In April 1937, shortly after FDR issued the surveillance order, a "disguised" naval photographer, A. J. Carroll, created an international incident when he carried out the Roosevelt policy: Carroll in civilian clothes began photographing Japanese Consul-General Toyokichi Fukuma during a *bon voyage* send-off for the naval tanker HIJMS *Hayatomo.* Hearing the click of the camera's shutter, Fukuma's staff pummeled Carroll, then had him arrested and taken to the Honolulu police station. Though no formal charges were brought against Carroll, his cover was blown. Admiral O. G. Murphin, then commandant of the Fourteenth Naval District, protested the Japanese action to the Secretary of the Navy. See RG 187, National Archives, San Bruno, CA., COM 14 DIO, confidential file A-8-2 (2) of April 8–9, 1937. See also the newspaper *Hawaii Hochii* of April 9, 1937 for story and pictures of the incident. Carroll's surveillance duties were assumed by Chief Yeoman Theodore Emanuel.
21. Frederick G. Tillman interview with the author tape-recorded March 26, 1990, Fowler, CA. In author's file.
22. Ibid.
23. Washington, DC intelligence officials who admitted seeing the spy reports included Captain Theodore Wilkinson, Director of Naval Intelligence, and Brigadier General Sherman Miles, US Army intelligence; see their testimony in chapter 7 herein. For J. Edgar Hoover's reaction see Note 40, this chapter. Frederick Tillman not given intercepts: see his interview with author, Fowler, CA, March 26, 1990, in author's file.
24. From 1942 to 1944 America's top law enforcement officials investigated Richard Kotoshirodo. The investigation was spurred by J. Edgar Hoover, Director of the FBI, and involves Assistant Attorneys General Wendell Burge and Tom Clark; the latter became a justice of the US Supreme Court. The FBI main file number on Kotoshirodo is 65-41886; the file is available at the J. Edgar Hoover Building in Wash-

ington, DC. Copies of the file were obtained by the author through a FOIA request though much of the file is blacked out. In the interviews, Kotoshirodo details his spy excursions to Pearl Harbor, areas on Oahu, and neighboring islands of Kauai, Maui, and the Big Island (Hawaii). FBI report 65-41886-18 includes a 55-page report on Kotoshirodo's spy activities and concludes with a finding by investigators that Kotoshirodo willingly assisted Morimura, Okuda, and Seki. A Territorial Internee Hearing Board found that Kotoshirodo assisted Morimura and others to willingly commit the crime of espionage by observing and reporting US military installations. In connection with the Territorial Hearing Board action, Kotoshirodo gave this statement to Frederick G. Tillman of the FBI, on August 24, 1943: "I understood that I was gathering naval information for the Japanese Government when I made these trips, but I gave no thought as to what my superiors in the consulate were going to do with it" (FBI file 65-41886-32-5). In FBI report 65-41886-9-32-5, J. Edgar Hoover proposes prosecution of Kotoshirodo to Assistant Attorney General Wendell Burge. Attorney General Tom Clark's involvement is shown in FBI report 65-41886-41, p. 9. Prosecution of Kotoshirodo was denied by the US Attorney in Hawaii, G. Douglas Crozier, on March 18, 1944, in FBI report 65-41886-52.

Kotoshirodo's activities were not directly linked to Morimura until after the attack; see FBI report 65-41886-14. The 1941 US Navy wiretap transcript mentions Kotoshirodo's name but there is no hint of his spy activity. Seki emerges in the 1941 transcript as purchasing cameras, binoculars, maps, and film for the consulate. Frederick Tillman's initials on each wiretap indicate the date he read the transcript in 1941. Kotoshirodo and his wife, Joan, were interned at Topaz, Utah.

25. Station US ordered that diplomatic messages between Tokyo and overseas missions containing a five-numeral group at or near the beginning of messages and none at the end, and with a five-letter group of the form consonant-vowel-consonant-vowel-consonant, be forwarded immediately by teleprinter to Washington, DC. See OP-20-G, Secret serial 044320, Mar. 5, 1941 in COM 13, A6-2 files, RG 181, National Archives, Seattle, WA, copy in author's file.

26. Station TWO airmailed the intercepts to Washington for processing. The exact time and day that Station TWO discarded the slower airmail delivery and began forwarding intercepts by the faster teleprinter is in dispute. Army testimony claims that teleprinter transmission began Dec. 6, 1941. Col. Robert Schukraft, head of Army intercept stations, testified to the Joint Congressional Investigation that he used the teleprinter in a conference with Station TWO on Nov. 28, 1941; see PHPT 10, p. 4914. Records of Station US indicate that "AT" (Army teleprinter) was in use at Station TWO, May 12, 1941; see RG 38, Station US papers, Folder 5830/30, MMRB, Archives II. Fort Hunt, Virginia, known as Station SEVEN, intercepted one of Okuda's January messages. Fort Hunt is sixteen miles south of Washington on the Potomac River.

27. For the one-day decode of J series, see PHPT 36, p. 67.

28. See Oahu telephone directory, Spring and Fall 1941, Library of Congress, copy in author's file. The consulate buildings were demolished by Japan after the war and a new consulate built. But the stone gate used by Morimura still exists and faces outward on Kuakini Street near the corner of Nuuanu Avenue.

29. For "overzealous" critique, see Denzel Carr's interview with the author, May 9, 1983, El Cerrito, CA, in author's file. On Emanuel's home and activities in 1941, see interview with Denzel Carr and Yale Maxon, El Cerrito, CA, in author's file. Emanuel lived in Honolulu on Pacific Heights Road, according to FBI file 62-33413-1024, copy in author's file.

30. The Shunchoro restaurant was still in operation in 1994, in the same building and location, 2101 Aulii Street, Honolulu. Poinciana trees and neighborhood growth now obscure the Ewa views toward Pearl Harbor. The genial proprietor took the author on a tour of the two floors and said the premises were exactly the same as in 1941, except for a new kitchen. One policy change in service—no drop-in trade. Private parties only with reservations.

31. For description of the hired Packard limousine, and its "trips to the country," see FBI file 65-41886. The file is a post-attack investigation by the FBI and runs from item 1 to 75. All items of the file must be consulted as there are many cross-references to the espionage conducted from the Japanese consulate in 1941.

32. Teisaku Eto was the innocent sixty-seven-year-old proprietor of the soft-drink stand near the Pan American China Clipper base and the naval enlisted men's landing. For the location of the enlisted men's landing, see berthing chart of Pearl Harbor in PHPT 33, p. 1397, item 5. For description of Morimura and Kotoshirodo's visits to Eto's stand, see ONI Investigation Report, dated June 15, 1942, COM 14 file in RG 181, folder 58-3402, Box VOO9468, National Archives, San Bruno, CA. For quote that Morimura was amused by USN laxity, see ibid., p. 10, item 32. Eto was loyal to America and was not engaged in espionage. At that time American exclusion laws would not allow Eto or any other Japanese emigrant to obtain American citizenship.

The PAA terminal site could be seen in 1991. Foundations and cement lanais marked the historic Trans-Pacific Hawaii terminal at Franklin and Laniwai Avenues in Pearl City.

"Scuttlebutt" was navy slang for gossip.

Hawaiians rarely use traditional compass directions. Instead they say makai, toward the sea; mauka, toward the mountains; ewa (pronounced eh-vah), northwest of Pearl Harbor; Diamond Head, southwest of Pearl Harbor.

33. On Morimura's bank credit problem, see FBI file 65-414-2-2, serial 258. For Denzel Carr's "outside" note, see FBI file 65-414-3-1, serial 349.

34. Morimura's two phases of espionage reports can be documented through the Japanese consulate's outgoing message log, found in PHPT 35 starting on p. 430. A clear picture of Tadashi Morimura's activities can be traced by combining the incoming and outgoing message files, together with the English translations of the intercepts. To this information must be added the telephone calls—revealed by the wiretaps—to the Honolulu cable firms for a motorcycle messenger, and taxi and limousine charges for "trips to the country." By assembling and arranging this information into a daily basis, it is possible to reconstruct a day in the espionage life of Morimura on Oahu. For example, his arrival in Honolulu on March 27, 1941 can be documented through three sources: (1) the consulate's outgoing message file, in PHPT 35, p. 431, (2) the Mackay Radio message announcing his arrival, in PHPT 35, p. 441 and PHPT 37, p. 1026; (3) intercept by the US Army's Station TWO can be confirmed in the Station US diplomatic-intercept log found in RG 38, Station US papers, folder 5830/30, MMRB, Archives II.

Morimura left a paper trail when he filed his first bomb plot of Pearl Harbor on August 21, 1941. His "diary" can be reconstructed from three sources: (1) the outgoing message log in PHPT 35, pp. 437 and 439 and PHPT 12, p. 262, (2) a two-dollar charge for the Packard taxi in FBI file 65-41886-20, (3) proof that the bomb-plot message was intercepted at Station SEVEN and CAST can be found in RG 38, Station US papers, folder 5830/30, MMRB, Archives II. His drunken binge is confirmed by the wiretaps in FBI file 65-414, "bulky" section, "bulky" being an oversize archival filing method designed by the FBI. See Morimura's daily record of 1941 compiled by the author, in author's files. Mackay's Washington office as Station X is confirmed by Station US message log in RG 38, Station US papers, folder 5830/30 for January 11, 1941, Archives II.

35. Officials knew of Morimura: Hoover to Berle containing Tillman's "outside man" quote; Hoover to Maj. Gen. Edwin "Pa" Watson in FBI file 61-10556, serials 395, 399, 402, 405. Contents of Hoover's messages are classified as National Defense Secrets by the FBI in 1999, copies with FBI blackouts, in author's file.

36. Joint Investigative Committee reports were signed by these officials: Colonel James Lester of the War Department, Captain "CENSORED" of the Navy, and Edward Tamm, Assistant Director of the FBI and Hoover's third in command. See Report of the Committee of Intelligence Trends (an adjunct of the J.I.C. in FBI HDQ file 66-8603-165, p. 9. For Berle see p. 16. The FBI report blacked out the name of the USN captain for unknown reasons. Meetings of the J.I.C. alternated between the Munitions Building (US Army headquarters), Navy Department, and FBI headquarters. Roosevelt couldn't keep Directors of Naval Intelligence for long during 1941. Walter Anderson departed for Pearl Harbor in January. Then Captain Jules James briefly served until March. Next, Captain Alan Kirk stepped into the director's office. He departed rapidly when his friend, Admiral Adolphus Andrews, warned, "Get out of Naval Intelligence as fast as you can." See Kirk, *The Reminiscences of Alan Goodrich Kirk* (New York: Oral History Research Office, Columbia University,

1962), p. 182. Apparently Andrews, a former US Fleet commander, was aware of McCollum's eight-action policy. Kirk was gone by October 1941, relieved by Captain Theodore Wilkinson, one of Anderson's battleship commanders, who moved from command of the USS *Mississippi* to the ONI post.

37. For quote "out of all reasonable proportion," see item 3 in FBI memorandum dated April 29, 1941 in FBI file 8603, serial 180x, copy in author's file.
38. Ibid.
39. For mail cover order, see RG 59, State Department Decimal File, 702.9411A/35, Diplomatic Branch, Archives II, copy in author's file.
40. See *Complete Presidential Press Conferences of Franklin D. Roosevelt* (New York: Da-Capo Press. 1972), Vol. 17, pp. 401, 402.
41. For Hoover's be most "circumspect" order, see FBI file 66-8603, item 326, dated April 15, 1941, copy in author's file.
42. "No expulsion possible," see Berle diary, p. 196, June 3, 1941, FDRL, copy in author's file.
43. For reports sent to Berle by Hoover naming Morimura and Kita, see date August 7, 1941 in State Department Decimal File 702.9411A/35, item 35 in RG 59, Diplomatic Branch, Archives II, copy in author's file. For Morimura first being placed on the "most dangerous list," see Ted Emanuel's report in Note 20 of this chapter.
44. J. Edgar Hoover continued to pursue Morimura into the postwar years. In 1961, when Walter Cronkite and CBS-TV brought Morimura to Hawaii for the twentieth anniversary of the attack, Hoover saw another opportunity to arrest the spy for espionage. FBI agents tailed Cronkite and his TV crew when they photographed Morimura at Pearl Harbor. Hoover asked President John Kennedy's assistant attorney-general, J. Walter Yeagley, for permission to charge Morimura and was turned down. See FBI File 94-4-925 and 100-65558, copies in author's file.

CHAPTER 7

1. For bomb plots produced during Phase II, see the English version of Morimura's Japanese-language map recovered from a downed Japanese aircraft on December 7, 1941 in this chapter on p. 106. The original Japanese version found in the aircraft was not located by the author in Archives II.
2. See transcripts of the Japanese consulate's purchase of maps, postcards, cameras, and binoculars in FBI wiretap file 65-414, Subsections 2 through 4 serials 123 to 940. The author counted a total of 817 Honolulu consulate wiretap reports for 1941. Be aware that the wiretap was the work of naval intelligence in Hawaii which provided the file to the FBI.
3. Description of the August 21, 1941 spy trip is based on interrogation of Kotoshirodo by US Navy intelligence officers, see RG 181, COM 14 Confidential A-8-5 file, NA, San Bruno, CA, dated February 18, 1941 to April 30, 1942. See also the FBI interrogation of Kotoshirodo in chapter 6 of this book.

On June 21, 1941 Japan's Foreign Minister ordered a new version of the J code placed in effect, which US Navy cryptologists called J-19. Though Morimura's bomb plot message of August 21, 1941 has never been released publicly by the United States, its radiotelegraphy route from Honolulu to San Francisco to Washington to Tokyo can be traced in Japanese and American records. The bomb-plot-message day (August 21) involving both Richard Kotoshirodo and Tadashi Morimura can be reconstructed from FBI and US Navy records and from the Japanese consulate's outgoing message log: first the Packard taxi was ordered by telephone from John Mikami's Royal Taxi Stand. Mikami arrived at the consulate, picked up Kotoshirodo, and drove him to the heights overlooking Pearl Harbor. It was a two-hour spy trip and Mikami charged two dollars (FBI file 65-41886-20). Kotoshirodo briefed Morimura on the location of the US warships. The bomb-plot details were then encoded in the J-19 code system. Three copies were dispatched by RCA: (1) to the San Francisco Japanese consulate, (2) to Ambassador Kichisaburo Nomura in Washington, DC, and (3) to Foreign Minister Admiral Teijiro Toyoda in Tokyo, who replaced Matsuoka in the July 1941 shakeup of the Imperial Cabinet. Once the spy messages hit the RCA airwaves, they were intercepted at both Station SEVEN at Fort Hunt, Virginia, and Station CAST on Corregidor.

The outgoing Honolulu message log of the Japanese consulates is in PHPT 35, pp. 437, 439ff., and PHPT 37, pp. 1096ff.

For confirmation of US interception, see RG 38, Station US papers, folder 5830/30, MMRB, Archives II. See also FBI file 65-414, "bulky," which contains excerpts from the consulate's account book showing RCA charges. "Bulky" is a file term used by the FBI to indicate oversize, extra copies, enclosures, etc., attached to regular reports. FBI reports are filed by categories represented by a main file number. Example: 65-414-1 signifies that 65 is the category; 414 is the case number and the first report (or serial number) is 1. Subsections can be added. Voluminous records such as a 500-page supplementary report may be placed in a "bulky" file within 65-414.

4. Wiretapped conversations of August 21–23, 1941 are in FBI File 65-414, copies in author's file. For Okuda being worried about police matter on August 22, 1941, see subsection 4, serial 647, pp. 3ff. For the Nakatsuka interview with unnamed consulate employee August 23, 1941, see loc. cit. serial 654, pp. 1ff. Each wiretap transcription contains an FBI route stamp with initial T for Frederick G. Tillman, the FBI case agent assigned to investigate the consulate.

5. See Hoover-Berle correspondence, Aug. 7, 1941 in RG 59, State Department Decimal File 702,9411A/35, Diplomatic Branch, Archives II, copy in author's file. See FBI file 61-10556, serials 354, 355, 357, 361, 368 for the special messenger reports sent to Adolf Berle by Hoover. See FBI file 61-10556, serials 395, 399, 402, 405, which date from October 29 to November 13, 1941, copy author's file. Hoover forwarded the reports to FDR via the President's military aide, Major General Edwin "Pa" Watson. Eight "special messenger" reports, some containing British intercepts of Japanese messages, were delivered. One serial, 61-10556-399, dated November 13, 1941, contains 32 pages of British WT (wireless/telegraph, a British synonym for intercepts) intercepts of Japanese messages. Hoover wrote a directive by hand on serial 399 to his assistant, Clyde Tolson: "Get this to Watson, Berle, Miles and Wilkinson at once." Attorney General Janet Reno and her public affairs chief, Carl Stern, declined to declassify Serial 399 and labeled it a B-1 National Defense Secret under the provisions of the FOIA act.

6. For espionage underway, see Wilkinson's testimony in PHPT 4-1841.

7. See Adolf Berle's diary entry dated June 3, 1941, FDRL, copy author's file.

8. For Mackay messenger request by Honolulu consulate, see transcript of Navy wiretap in FBI file 65-414-Subsection A-4-serials 759, 780. For intercepts of the second bomb-plot message, see Station US intercept logs in RG 38, Station US papers, folder 5830/30, MMRB, Archives II, copy author's file.

9. See the Miles-Gesell exchange in PHPT 2, pp. 787, 794, 795, 797.

10. For Wilkinson exchange with Gesell, "I don't recall," see hearing testimony December 18, 1945 in PHPT 4, pp. 1748 ff. Two months after Wilkinson was questioned by Congress, he drowned when his car plunged off a ferryboat near Norfolk, Virginia.

11. For this lunch at the White House, see the Usher Book for October 14, 1941, FDRL, copies in author's file. For this FDR-Sarnoff exchange, see PHPT 20, p. 4468 ff; Sarnoff's cablegram sent from Honolulu and addressed to the President is on a White House cablegram form dated November 13, 1941. In a note at upper right of the cablegram FDR wrote by hand: "Steve to thank him." (Steve Early was FDR's press secretary.) For request for Forrestal-Kimmel to extend courtesies to Sarnoff, see RG 80, PHLO; CINCPAC flag file, Incoming Dispatches Serial 281812, October 26, 1941, MMRB, Archives II; in this document Assistant Secretary of the Navy James Forrestal asked Admiral Husband Kimmel and Rear Admiral Claude Bloch, commandant of Hawaii's Fourteenth Naval District, to extend every courtesy to David Sarnoff. In addition to RCA, Sarnoff was president of NBC, the National Broadcasting Company. Its radio news operation included KGU, the NBC affiliate in Honolulu. He was a skilled Morse Code operator and a real live newsman. In his youth he worked for Marconi Radio & Telegraph stations on the East Coast. On April 14, 1912, he picked up the SS *Titanic*'s SOS, and for the next seventy-two hours provided nonstop reports of the sinking and the rescue efforts to news organizations.

12. See Joseph Rochefort's discussion of Sarnoff's visit to Honolulu and the ability of Station HYPO to decode the messages: "We could read most of that stuff as it came

in. The simple ones we could read." PHPT 23, p. 686, given on January 2, 1942 during testimony before the Roberts Commission in Honolulu.

13. For the radio order to Captain Mayfield, see RG 80, PHLO, CINCPAC outgoing radio message files, microfiche form, MMRB, Archives II. When seen by the author this microfiche was in a state of serious deterioration, so the author photocopied the document so that there would be a readable record for future research; author's file. Lieut. Yale Maxon was an American interpreter for the Tokyo War Crimes trial after the war and translated interviews with Japan's wartime Premier, Hideki Tojo. Later Maxon became a professor at the Merritt Campus of Peralta Colleges, Oakland, California.

14. The original alert sent to Rochefort by Maxon is in the Rochefort Papers, held by his daughter, Janet Rochefort Elerding, of Santa Ana, CA. In 1982 she permitted the author to make a photocopy which was shown to and identified by Maxon and Carr during interviews at their homes in 1983, copy author's file. Neither Maxon nor Carr testified before any of the Pearl Harbor investigations.

15. For Morimura's spy message transmitted to the *Akagi* on December 2, 1941, see Mitsuo Fuchida, *The Japanese Navy in World War II* (US Naval Institute Press, 1969), p. 20. Beware of the scrambling of the message numbers by Woodward, for it can confuse any Pearl Harbor investigator. The Japanese consulate's outgoing log book numbered the message as 357 and it was transmitted by RCA as their radio message 363; see PHPT 35, p. 433 ff. For Woodward decoding before December 7, 1941, see his handwritten note in Exhibits and Illustrations of the Hewitt Inquiry, PHPT 38 item 153 ff. For his placing the question mark on RCA radio message 363, see ibid. item 151. The author believes numbers 357 and 363 are one and the same and represent the identical Morimura message that Fuchida received aboard the *Akagi* on December 2, 1941 (Tokyo Time). The original 5-Num transmission to the *Akagi* has not been released by the US government.

16. For cable companies refusing to turn over Japanese messages, see Shivers' report 65-414 dated December 26, 1941, in Record Group 59, US State Department decimal file 702.9411A/75, Diplomatic Branch, Archives II, copy author's file. Note that the cited Shivers report was not found in the FBI file 65-414 released by FOIA request to the author. For local radio firms refusing to hand over Japanese messages; see PHPT 36, p. 477. According to testimony given to Pearl Harbor investigators by Army, Navy, and FBI intelligence officers, the Hawaii RCA manager, George Street, declined to turn over the messages, claiming that the FCC Act of 1934 protected private communications. Robert Shivers said, "They flatly refused to turn over the wireless messages." Whether he knew it or not, Shivers' testimony muddled the truth because Army and Navy intelligence bypassed Street, ignored the FCC Act, and intercepted the espionage messages off the Tokyo-Hawaii radio circuits of RCA and Mackay. Each message was decoded and translated in Washington, but not forwarded to Hawaii.

17. For the testimony of Wilkinson, Layton, and Rochefort concerning cable company refusals, see PHPT 36 p. 477. As this book goes to press, there have been nine official Pearl Harbor investigations conducted in the United States: (1) Roberts Commission proceedings, 1942; (2) Admiral Thomas Hart's inquiry of 1944; (3) Army Proceedings, 1944; (4) Navy Court of Inquiry, 1944; (5) Clarke Investigation, 1944; (6) The Clausen Investigation 1944–45; (7) Admiral Henry Kent Hewitt investigation of 1945; (8) The Joint Congressional Investigation of 1945-46, and (9) Senator Strom Thurmond's investigation of 1995.

18. See the consulate's message log book in the Clausen investigation report, PHPT 35 starting on page 430. See the Station US log book in RG 38, Station US papers, Folder 5830/30, entitled Jap Dip. Trf. Logs (outgoing), 1941, MMRB, Archives II, and author's file. The USN log lists the place of the interception of the spy messages.

19. For Wilkinson's "fairly secure" quote, see PHPT 4, p. 1849.

20. Telephone conversation between author and Robert Dowd from Oakdale, California, May 13, 1999; transcript and notes in author's file. Japanese communications intelligence intercepted in the Pacific was encoded in COPEK or a sister system, CETYH, and dispatched over the US Navy's radio network. Encryption and decoding were done on an electric cipher machine (ECM), that was similar in concept to

Japan's Purple machine and Germany's Enigma machine. Six Navy commands held the "keys": CAST, HYPO, and Station US plus Admirals Hart, Kimmel, and King. The code systems, believed by the United States to be totally secure and unsolvable by enemies, were placed in operation on November 4, 1941 and carried the bulk of intercepted Japanese communications intelligence through December 7. For USN placing the COPEK system in effect, see OPNAV SECRET serial 042036 of November 4, 1941, Station US papers, MMRB, Archives II. Another similar Navy system, TESTM, transmitted radio direction finder data during November and December 1941. The two systems were used to transmit communications intelligence concerning Japanese military moves to the White House.

21. For Noyes quote, "could send to Honolulu," see PHPT 10, p. 4714.

22. Stations CAST and US held the solutions or "keys" to J-19 before the attack. Hawaii's ability to decode J-19 is murky. Thomas Dyer, Station HYPO's chief cryptographer wrote: "We did have [the ability to decode] J-19, but had no traffic to work." (Dyer letter to author, June 4, 1983, in author file.) Farnsley Woodward, HYPO's diplomatic cryptographer, testified to the Hewitt inquiry: "I did not work on J-19" (PHPT 36, p. 320). Morimura's J-19 dispatch to the *Akagi* on December 2, 1941 was in J-19, according to the consulate's log book, and was delivered to Woodward at Station HYPO on Friday, December 5, 1941, according to his written note. But four senior US naval officers gave varied answers when the J-19 decoding question was posed to them during the Joint Congressional Investigation of 1945–46. Leigh Noyes, the 1941 Director of Naval Communications was adamant: "We could not decrypt J-19 at Pearl Harbor" (PHPT 10-4714), Joseph Rochefort, commander of Station HYPO, testified that his cryptographers "could not decode J-19 without special equipment" (PHPT 10-4674). His testimony conflicted with what he gave to the Roberts Commission on January 2, 1942, see Note 12 in this chapter. Earl E. Stone, Chief of Naval Communications in 1945 was less sure: "No evidence has been found that J-19 could be processed in Hawaii." (See his letter to the Pearl Harbor congressional staff, dated February 28, 1946, serial 0003042P20 in RG 80, PHLO, MMRB, Archives II.) Joseph Wenger, an assistant to Stone, was more cautious when he wrote: "J-19 was not available at Pearl in registered publications," (Wenger to Pearl Harbor congressional staff, November 9, 1945 serial 00023P20. His letter was found in a special Pearl Harbor document release authorized by an FOIA and delivered to the author by the Naval Security Group Command, August 31, 1993, in author file). While the four naval officials provided nebulous information concerning the decoding of the J-19 system before December 7, 1941, their commander-in-chief, President Roosevelt, received decrypts in the system, according to Laurance Safford, head of Station US: "The naval aide (Captain John Beardall) saw Jig-19 and took the messages to the President." (See Safford testimony before the Hewitt Investigation, PHPT 36, p. 64.) The solutions to the Japanese code systems, both military and diplomatic, were distributed to the Pacific intercept stations and processing centers as Radio Intelligence Publications (RIP). Strict procedures were in place to assure the security of the code solutions. In 1941 each US naval base, ship, and station had a Registered Publications Office that accounted for the RIPs and other secret documents. The records of each RPO which show the status of the RIPs in 1941 at each monitoring station have not been declassified. Station CAST was regularly intercepting, translating, and reading J-19 during the fall of 1941, according to an affidavit filed with the Joint Congressional Investigation of 1945–46 by John Lietwiler, CAST's co-commander. Lietwiler said Station US regularly furnished his cryptographers with daily updates on the J-19 solution procedures. See his affidavit in RG 38, Station US Papers, MMRB, Archives II, copy in author's file. See the daily solutions to J-19 provided by Laurance Safford, commander of Station US, in RG 38, loc. cit., and in author's file. The testimony is overwhelming. At least five naval officers (Dyer, Woodward, Rochefort, Safford, and Lietwiler) and President Roosevelt were aware of the J-19 messages before the attack.

23. See Morimura's "opportunity for surprise attack" message and related items reproduced on p. 116 in this chapter. Members of the 1945–46 Congressional investigation heard about the Navy's failure to timely decode Morimura's message during the following exchange between investigator Gerhard Gesell (later appointed a federal

district judge in Washington, DC) and Theodore Wilkinson, the Navy's pre-Pearl Harbor intelligence chief:

GESELL: "It was tragic that that was not decoded before."

WILKINSON: "Yes sir."

GESELL: "How do you account for the fact that that was not decoded, when the decoders were decoding very rapidly and decoding messages in great number that day, the sixth?"

WILKINSON: "I do not account for it sir" (PHPT 4, p. 1854).

Since Morimura's message to the oncoming Japanese bombers and torpedo planes was in the simple PA code, the timely decoding procedures in Washington's Station US are of immense interest. Laurance Safford, commander of Station US, testified to the Hewitt investigation: "We had no difficulty in reading PA." (PHPT 36, p. 67)

24. See Morimura's "no barrage balloons and surprise attack" message on p. 116 of this chapter.

25. For consulate messages received, decoded, and translated before December 7, 1941, see PHPT 38, starting with item 149, which is the December 1941 RCA statement of toll charges for the Japanese consulate. See Farnsley Woodward's handwritten note "received 5 Dec. 41" on items 179, 178, 177, 176, 175. On Item 156 Woodward wrote: "Received on 5 Dec. 1941. Deciphered and translated prior to 7 Dec. 1941. Original message sent to Washington, translation retained by Pearl" /ss/ Woodward. For other messages received on December 5, 1941 by Woodward, see items 153, 154, 155 ff. Woodward identified a J-19 message sent over RCA on December 2. His handwritten note on the message reads: "J-19 K-10 transportation." Woodward circled the five-letter group HAHVK as the Japanese indicator for the J-19 system. (Item 249)

26. For Rochefort's quote, "cheap price," see *The Reminiscences of Captain Joseph J. Rochefort* (US Naval Institute Oral History Program, 1970), p. 163, copy in author's file.

27. See Joseph Finnegan's testimony before Pearl Harbor proceedings of Admiral Henry Kent Hewitt, June 8, 1945, PHPT 36. p. 251ff. Finnegan was then a Navy captain working at FRUPAC—the post–Pearl Harbor acronym given to Station HYPO which stood for Fleet Radio Unit Pacific. On December 7, 1941 Lieut. Finnegan was Flag Lieutenant for Rear Admiral Daniel Bagley, Commander of Battleship Division Two of the Pacific Fleet. In his testimony given to the Hewitt proceedings Finnegan said that Admiral Kimmel directed his temporary transfer to HYPO for translation duties. He received permanent orders on February 15, 1942. Finnegan was also a subordinate of Rear Admiral Walter Anderson, Commander Battleships.

CHAPTER 8

1. On Japanese males being drafted, see an estimate by British in PHPT 31, p. 3218, item FE-290. See also estimate of Colonel Harry Cresswell, US Army military attaché in Tokyo, PHPT 34, p. 186, serial 505.

2. For more on the China Incident, which is a Tokyo euphemism for Japan's aggression against China, see John Toland, *The Rising Sun* (Random House, 1970), pp. 37 ff.

3. For the total embargo against Japan advocated by McCollum's Action H, see where FDR signed Executive Order 8832 on July 26, 1941 (he announced the embargo on July 25) in Jonathan Marshall, *To Have And Have Not* (University of California Press, 1995), p.127; see also *The Magic Background of Pearl Harbor* (Department of Defense, GPO), Vol. II, p. A-226, item 447.

4. For Rochefort quote, see Rochefort's Oral History (in booklet form), *The Reminiscences of Captain Joseph J. Rochefort* (Annapolis: US Naval Institute Oral History Program, 1970), p. 65. His Oral History contains 307 pages transcribed from four interviews conducted by Commander Etta Belle Kitchen at Rochefort's home in Redondo Beach, California, August 14, September 21, October 5, and December 6, 1969.

5. For 100 aircraft carriers, see Stefan Terzibaschitsch. *Aircraft Carriers of the US Navy*, 2nd ed. (Naval Institute Press, 1989), p. 304.

6. For Japan's peacetime oil requirements, see Hiroyuki Agawa, *The Reluctant Admiral*

(Naval Institute Press 1979), p. 235; and Yale C. Maxon, *Control of Japanese Foreign Policy* (University of California Press. 1957), p. 168. To convert metric tons of crude oil to barrels multiply the number of metric tons by 7.3 barrels per ton, according to the American Petroleum Institute, Washington, DC. In an effort to conserve oil supplies Japan converted public transportation vehicles such as buses to coal-burning engines, according to George Matsumoto of Oakland, CA, who visited relatives on Kyushu during the summer of 1941; interview by the author in January 1999.

7. America's 1943 timetable was accurate. United States carrier task forces began the sustained assault on Japan in November 1943 with the invasion of Tarawa, when the first of the *Essex* and *Independence* class carriers, with their protective battleship, cruiser, and destroyer escorts reported to the Pacific Fleet.

8. For US carrier keels laid, see Francis E. McMurtrie, ed., *Janes Fighting Ships 1942* (Macmillan, 1943), pp. 450, 451.

9. For the start of Japan's China recall, see Rochefort's Daily Communication Summary, September 4, 1941, RG 80, PHLO, MMRB, Archives II.

10. The order of battle of Japanese Fleet was prepared by Duane Whitlock, a traffic analyst at Station CAST in 1941. Taped audio interview at Danville, California in September 1993, and in telephone interviews in May 1999, author's file.

11. During the pre-Pearl Harbor era, the Pacific Fleet was in the early stages of forming a Fast Carrier Force. In 1940, Vice Admiral Charles A. Blakely, a pioneer Navy aviator, organized the carriers USS *Enterprise, Saratoga, Yorktown,* and *Lexington* into a command known as the Aircraft Scouting Force. Blakely faced stiff opposition from the "battleship admirals," who distrusted air power. However, his concept of the fast carrier strike force was later adopted by Admiral Chester Nimitz. The Pacific War was essentially won by Navy task forces built around 16 aircraft carriers of the *Essex* and *Independence* classes supported by escort carriers called baby flattops.

12. For Yamamoto's radio silence order of November 25, 1941, see SRN 116866, RG 457, Station US papers, MMRB, Archives II. The order applied to all categories of Japanese naval units including the First Air Fleet, the carrier force assigned to the Pearl Harbor raid. During the Hawaii attack the First Air Fleet was combined with the Sixth Fleet. Japan named the force the *Kido Butai*. According to the Kenkyuska Dictionary, Harvard University Press, 1942: *Kido* means "have the entree," p. 936; *butai* means "fighting force," p. 129. Joseph Rochefort's translation from his Oral History, loc. cit., is, "Strike Force."

13. In this book, the term "US cryptographers" includes the Navy's radio intercept operators, who, by intercepting the Japanese naval messages, collectively participated in solving Japan's naval call sign code, the *Yobidashi Fugo*. Duane Whitlock, one of the three traffic analysts at Station CAST, explained to the author that the call sign system, combined with Japanese naval communication procedures and radio direction finder bearings, revealed Japan's military strategy. Whitlock insisted, that while the information he used in his 1941 analyses came from the 5-Num dispatches (he called them 5-Digit), none of the cryptologists at Station CAST had the means to read the encoded message text prior to Pearl Harbor because the solutions had not been received from Station US in Washington, DC. Whitlock told the author during a telephone interview in May 1999 that in 1941 he was unaware of three crucial US cryptographic breakthroughs: (1) Agnes Driscoll's team of cryptographers in Washington had solved the 5-Num code and published the solutions as Radio Intelligence Publication 73 (RIP 73); (2) his immediate boss, Lieutenant John Lietwiler, had brought 5-Num solutions to CAST in the fall of 1941; and (3) Admiral Thomas Hart had assured the Chief of Naval Operations on March 5, 1941 that the British cryptology unit at Singapore had provided the US Asiatic Fleet with solutions to portions of the 5-Num code. In the interview with the author, Whitlock indicated that the solutions of the 5-Num code described by Admiral Hart and RIP 73 had been rendered obsolete by changes to the code instituted by Japan later in 1941. Whitlock emphasized that prior to Pearl Harbor, all Japanese military information gained from the 5-Num intercepts at Station CAST came from analyzing the communications data and the radio call signs. Telephone interview of Captain Duane Whitlock by the author, May and June 1999, in author's file.

14. The American intercept operators knew the Japanese Bureau of Military Prepara-

NOTES

tions by its three-*kana* radio call sign, E O NO. Stations CAST and HYPO, using IBM statistical machines, established a normal rate of Japanese naval transmissions for each command, daily, weekly, etc. Every Japanese radio call sign intercepted by the cryptographers, such as E O NO, was punched into separate IBM cards for processing and the resulting tally established a norm. Rochefort said he used hundreds of thousands of the punch cards by December 7, 1941 (see his Oral History at US Naval Institute, loc. cit.). Readers can find the E O NO intercepts dated September to December 1941 in Record Groups 457 and 38, MMRB, Archives II, and in the author's files.

15. For examples of Japan's China recall dispatches obtained by Rochefort's staff, see Joseph Rochefort's Daily Communications Summaries (COMSUMS) issued between September 4 and 8, 1941 in RG 80, PHLO, MMRB, Archives II. He first noted the recall in his September 4, 1941 summary (see Note 9, this chapter). Admiral Kimmel usually initialed each summary. Abridged versions of Rochefort's Daily Communication Summary can be found in the 39 volumes of the *Joint Committee on the Investigation of the Pearl Harbor Attack, 1945–46.* The original complete set of summaries prepared and delivered each day to Admiral Kimmel between July 15, 1941 and December 6, 1941 was not published in its entirety. The original set can be found in RG 80, PHLO, MMRB, Archives II. An abridged version introduced before the Congressional investigators can be found in Exhibit 115 (PHPT 17, p. 2601 ff.), but it includes only November 1 to December 6, 1941. Exhibit 115-A contains December 9 and 10, 1941, ibid. p. 2673. Another abridged version can be found in PHPT 37, pp. 706 to 778 which contains breaks in continuity between pp. 729 and 739. While this book refers to the Rochefort summaries, each report reflects the combined efforts of the entire organization of the Mid-Pacific Communications Intelligence Network (MIDPAC). At Station HYPO, the headquarters of the MIDPAC network, traffic analysts Lieutenant Commander Thomas A. Huckins and Lieutenant John A. Williams generally wrote the summaries, according to Wilfred J. Holmes in *Double Edged Secrets* (Naval Institute Press, 1979), p. 18.

16. For Admiral Koga's message of September 1, 1941, see Station H intercept file, RG 457, MMRB, Archives II, SRN 117554; for a sample of other Japanese commands departing China, see SRN 117392 (Submarine Squadron Six's departure on September 4); SRN 117531 (commander-in-chief of Third Fleet's departure from China on September 5); SRN 117506 (arrival of Sea Plane Tender Division 12 at Sasebo on September 6), etc.

17. All of Japan's land-based naval air activity was concentrated in the Eleventh Air Fleet. About 564 aircraft were assigned, plus two seaplane squadrons which operated from sea-based tenders. At the start of the Pacific War the might of the Eleventh Air Fleet was concentrated in Air Flotillas 21, 22, 23, veterans of the China campaign, and Air Flotilla 24 based in the Central Pacific. See *Campaigns of the Pacific War* (United States Strategic Bombing Survey, USGPO 1946), p. 74.

18. At the time this book goes to press in 1999, English versions of the China recall messages issued by Japanese naval forces can be found (not in chronological order and with the naval code designator blacked out) in RG 457, MMRB, Archives II, in a file called SRN (Special Research Navy). A destroyer squadron is usually made up of four divisions, which contain four destroyers each. DESRON 5 then contained 16 destroyers plus a light cruiser as flagship, and supporting auxiliaries.

19. See Homer Kisner's audio tape interview with author, April 1988, at Carlsbad, California, transcript and tapes in author's file.

20. For the separation of Japanese carrier commands, see Station H Chronology, November 1941, supervised and written by Homer Kisner, traffic chief. A complete report containing Kisner's Daily Chronology, Supervisor Reports, Movement Reports, and Radio Call Signs can be found in RG 38, Station US papers, MMRB, Archives II. An abridged version comprising dates of December 1 to 6, 1941, is in PHPT 37, pp. 725 to 728. Kisner's interview with author at Carlsbad, California, April 1988, transcript and tapes in author's file.

21. See Arthur McCollum's merchant marine recall memorandum to all Navy commandants, Confidential Serial 016916 of February 17, 1940, in RG 181, COM 14 confidential file, National Archives, San Bruno, CA. McCollum used his secret code name F-2 on the memo. Declassified October 3, 1991 by author's FOIA request.

355

22. For the Berne List, see RG 38, Station US papers, MMRB, Archives II. American listening posts, operated by the US Navy, followed Tokyo Time when intercepting and recording Japanese naval communications. However, radio broadcasts originated by the US Navy were recorded in Greenwich Mean Time (GMT) in the pre-Pearl Harbor era.

23. For an example of the confusion on Japanese communication procedures by historians, see Telford Taylor, *New York Times Magazine*, April 29, 1984, p. 113. For identification of the *Akagi's* radio call signs—before the attack—see Station H report for November 1941; tactical call 8 YU NA p. 133; *Akagi's* administrative call SE YA Ø, p. 104; in RG 38, Station US papers, MMRB, Archives II.

24. For pre-Pearl Harbor intercept training concerning the On-the-Roof Gang, see RG 457, SRH 355 (Special Research History), Vols. 1 and 2, MMBR, Archives II.

25. For Stark's "probably involves war" warning, see CNO to CINCAF, CINCPAC, CINCLANT, COM 15, SPENAVO—London. Secret Serial 031939 of July 3, 1941 in FOIA released to author by US Navy Security Group Command, August 31, 1993, author's file (presumably also released to Archives II in January 1995); see also Admiral Kimmel acknowledging the warning in PHPT 6, p. 2629. SPENAV0 was the acronym for America's Special Naval Observer based in London, with liaison to the British Admiralty and Prime Minister Winston Churchill.

26. For Stark's message on the rapid withdrawal of Japan's merchant marine, see CNO dispatch Serial 142155 with information copies to COM 11, 12, 13, 14, 15, 16, in FOIA, Naval Security Group Command release, loc. cit. West Coast naval districts in 1941 included the Eleventh (COM 11), in San Diego, Vice Admiral Charles A. Blakely; Twelfth (COM 12) in San Francisco, Vice Admiral John Greenslade; and Thirteenth (COM 13) in Seattle, Vice Admiral Charles S. Freeman.

27. For Kimmel's written instruction to Layton concerning the *Heiyo Maru*, see RG 80, PHLO file, September 27, 1941, Pacific Fleet Incoming Message File in microfiche section, MMRB, Archives II. The message originator was COM 13 on September 27, 1941, see Serial 271911 with the Action address as OPNAV and the INFO addressees as COM 12 (San Francisco) and 14 (Hawaii) in CINCPAC Confidential Incoming Message File, PHLO, RG 80, MMRB, Archives II. The author found the image on a microfiche, which indicated rapid deterioration of the original. Congress cut National Archives funding in 1995, hampering efforts to preserve crucial Pearl Harbor documents. The author made 35-mm copies on Kodak T-Max black-and-white film of pertinent dispatches in the PHLO microfiche reels. The *Heiyo Maru* used three different radio call signs *(Yobidashi Fugo)* during this period. Station SAIL (Seattle) reported her using JRXB from the Berne list. Station BAKER (Guam) reported the vessel used call letters of SA TE Ø in October but changed to HE NU 2 on November 1, 1941; source: Station S monthly report for November 1941. The vessel was also heard by Stations AE (Sitka, Alaska) and ITEM (Imperial Beach, CA). See WCCI report in COM 13 files for November 1941, RG 181, National Archives, Seattle, WA. For Station BAKER TESTM of November 14, 1941, see TESTM files in RG 38, Station US papers, Archives II.

28. On the pouring in of building materials and laborers for construction of Japanese bases in Central Pacific, see Communications Summaries, September and October 1941, PHLO, loc. cit. Some historians assert that Japan began building war bases in the Central Pacific in the late 1930s and that aviatrix Amelia Earhart was sent to overfly the bases in 1937 and take photographs. However, according to Station H intercepts, Japan did not begin construction of the Central Pacific military bases until late 1940 and early 1941. See the intercepts in RG 457, SRN file, MMRB, Archives II for August through November 1941, also author's file.

29. For the "peculiar" 5-Num dispatch report of September 24, 1941, see COMSUM of that date in RG 80, PHLO, MMRB, Archives II, also author's file.

30. For Rochefort's "not to exploit" quote to Senator Ferguson, see PHPT 10, p. 4697.

31. For the *Keibii* report see the September 24, 1941 COMSUM, RG 80, PHLO, Box 41, MMRB, Archives II. The Japanese word *keibii* can mean defense; guard; guarding; police; a guard ship; a garrison, per *Kenkyuska New Japanese-English Dictionary* (Harvard University Press, 1942), p. 893. For the 5-Num message dates cited by Rochefort in his 1941 summaries, see the Communications Summaries in PHLO, RG 80, Box 41, MMRB, Archives II. But 28 years later in his 1969 interview with

Commander Kitchen (see Note 2 in this chapter) Rochefort switched gears and implied he and his staff only worked on a Japanese naval system he called AD: Rochefort (p. 109 of ROH): "Yes, you see, originally—without getting into too much of the details of it, some of it is still classified I would imagine—we were assigned responsibility when I took over there for one system which was not the system that Washington was working on. Washington and Cavite [sic, it was Station CAST on Corregidor] were working on what the Navy called the JN—for Japanese Navy, 25. This was the system" [sic, in 1941 the system was known as the 5-Num code, not JN-25].

Later in the series of interviews, Rochefort told Commander Kitchen that in 1941 he and his staff were assigned "a basic responsibility of solving the Japanese naval system which we called AD" (see ROH, p. 134). Rochefort's description of the AD code appears to be a cover story. According to Station US records, the AD code was used by Japan's navy for administrative matters, not operations. It was in effect from January 1, 1938 to November 30, 1940. (See Radio Intelligence Publication 54 A and B, RG 38, Station US papers, MMRB, Archives II, pp. 608, 609.) The AD code appears to have been discontinued by Japan's navy by December 1940. On October 31, 1941 Leigh Noyes, the Director of Naval Communications, wrote that the AD code was in effect until October 1940 and that it was used by all Japanese naval units for administrative matters not covered by special systems. Copies of the AD code's decryption details were sent to Stations CAST and HYPO, and to Admirals Hart in Manila and Kimmel in Hawaii. Noyes's letter is published in the US Navy's Radio Intelligence Publication 32 (RIP 32) which he released on October 31, 1941. See RG 38, Station US papers, RIP 32 file, section 23, MMRB, Archives II. There are no AD code messages in President Carter's document release of 1979 housed in RG 457, MMRB, Archives II.

Edwin Layton, in his book *And I Was There* (William Morrow, 1985), had a different account concerning Station HYPO's cryptographic efforts in the fall of 1941. He writes (p. 77) that Station HYPO concentrated on the Japanese navy's NL system until the second week of December 1941. He wrote that it consumed many thousands of valuable hours of cryptanalytic effort with no intelligence return. Layton's claim is not substantiated in President Carter's 1979 release of Japanese intercepts. There are no NL intercepts in Carter's release. According to Radio Intelligence Publication (RIP) 32 ibid., above, the NL code was the Japanese navy's encryption system for the Intelligence Office, Hydrographic Office, and Radio Stations of the South Sea Island Network (Central Pacific); see October 31, 1941 edition of RIP 32, p. 23.2, in RG 38, Station US papers, MMRB, Archives II. SMS 001 means "Secret Message Series number one" and indicates that it is the first radio message originated by the newly organized *Keibii* 52. The specific message was not found in President Carter's release of 1979.

None of the printed reports published by the nine Pearl Harbor investigations reproduced the entire set of Rochefort's Daily Communication Summaries (COMSUMS) which date from July 15 to December 31, 1941. The original and complete set, including the dates of September 24 and 28, 1941—which were initialed by Admiral Kimmel—can be found in the PHLO files, Box 41, MMRB, Archives II. It is complete from July 15, 1941 to December 6, 1941 but beware: the radio direction finder bearings for July, August, September, and October which were intended to be seen by Admiral Kimmel, have been crudely cut from the documents. Another set of the COMSUMS dated from October 14 to December 14, 1941—in printed form—is published in the Hewitt Investigation as PHPT 37, p. 739. RDF bearings are included from October 14 to 22, but missing from October 23–December 14, 1941. The Clausen Investigation printed the COMSUMS as Exhibit A dated from November 1 to December 6, 1941, as PHPT 35, p. 62. The RDF bearings are missing. The Congressional Investigation printed the COMSUMS as Exhibit 115 on PHPT 17, p. 2601. They are also dated November 1, 1941 to December 6, 1941; the RDF bearings are also missing.

32. For the COMSUM of September 28, 1941, see RG 80, PHLO, loc. cit. For background on Japanese troop movement to the Central Pacific, see intercept of September 8, 1942 Tokyo Time, Station H operator WK, who is unidentified as of the writing of this book, intercepted a message to the Fourth Fleet from the Tokyo Bureau of Military Affairs. The message provides military details on the composition of

Guard Divisions *(Keibii)* 51, 52 and 53. While there is no proof that the Japanese message text could be read in 1941, it indicates that each unit consisted of 16 warrant officers and 374 petty officers and men, listed their armament, and said the three units would be transported to the Central Pacific early in October. Rochefort did not specifically mention this dispatch in his September COMSUMS, though his knowledge of the *Keibii* units probably derived from this dispatch. See RG 457, SRN 117804, MMRB, Archives II.

33. For details on the Wake Island battle, see Stan Cohen, *Enemy on Island, Issue in Doubt* (Missoula, Montana: Pictorial Histories Publishing Co., 1983). On January 12, 1942, the *Nitta Maru* arrived at Wake, picked up American survivors, and transported them to POW camps.

34. For Rochefort reporting his interception of 5-Num code messages in September, October, and November 1941, see his COMSUM for those months in RG 80, Box 41, PHLO, loc. cit.

35. According to Rochefort's Oral History (ROH), he forwarded important Japanese naval intercepts to Washington by radio dispatch, others by US air mail. See ROH, US Naval Institute Oral History Program, Annapolis; copy in author's file.

36. See the intercepts of the *Heiyo Maru* in RG 457, SRN file for October and November 1941, MMRB, Archives II; also author's file.

37. See Note 27 in this chapter for monitoring stations that tracked the *Heiyo Maru*.

38. For the radio call signs, SA TE Ø and HE NU 2, see Note 27,in this chapter.

39. For proof that the *Heiyo Maru* originated the radio message on November 22, 1941, see the intercept by Jack Kaye (sine JK), SRN 117245 at 1546 hours Tokyo Time in RG 457, SRN file, MMRB, Archives II. In May 1999, Kaye, a retired US Navy captain, confirmed that his operator sine at Station H was JK in 1941. Kaye could not recall the intercept. "I was never told of the contents of the messages I intercepted. It was on a need to know basis and I didn't need to know." Kaye e-mail to author, May 1999, author's file.

40. For Washington, DC visits of Vincent Murphy, War Plans Officer for Admiral James Richardson in 1940 and later assistant war plans officer for Admiral Kimmel, see James Richardson, *On the Treadmill to Pearl Harbor* (Naval History Division, Department of the Navy, 1973), pp. 288, 307, 308, 383. For Murphy's meeting with Secretary of the Navy Frank Knox and Admirals Stark and Ingersoll in October 1940, see pp. 339, 400. Recalled to Washington by Admiral Stark in November 1940, see PHPT 14, pp 962, 980, 982, 983; see also letter Stark to Kimmel regarding Murphy's visits to Washington in PHPT 16, 2145.

41. For Rochefort's quote "concentrating far greater," see COMSUM of November 20 and 21, 1941 p. 2.

42. On Admiral Kimmel's concerns for the Japanese advance on Hawaii, see his alert sent to Washington, November 25, 1941 in chapter 10 of this book. See also a report dated November 25, 1941 concerning the arrival of Japanese Central Pacific landing forces together with arrival of *Marus* in the Marshall Islands, PHPT 14, p. 1365.

43. For the B-24 photo mission, see PHPT 7-2996; also PHPT 24-1780, 1781, 1826, 1827.

44. For confirmation that the B-24 was 100 percent destroyed, see PHPT 24-1833.

CHAPTER 9

1. See COM 14 secret serial Z-2051 of Oct. 8, 1941, in NA, Seattle, COM 13, A6-2 file of DCO route slip 029, declassified Oct. 9, 1985. All of Joseph Rochefort's written orders of 1941 carried the designator Z to indicate secret communications intelligence (COMINT) dictum.

2. For lookout for tankers, see Communications Summary (COMSUM), July 15, 1941 in RG 80, Box 41, PHLO, MMRB, Archives II.

3. For the *Katsuriki* in the Gilberts, see Station H, RDF bearings for October 1941, RG 38, Station US papers, Archives II.

4. See Joseph Rochefort's COMSUMs of Oct. 21 and 22, p. 2. Admiral Nishizo Tsukuhara assumed command of the Eleventh Air Fleet at Yokohama Air Station on September 10, according to Station CAST intercept, SRN 117447 in RG 457, SRN

file, MMRB, Archives II. Rochefort referred to the Eleventh Air Fleet as the Combined Air Force.

5. See COMSUM of October 21 and 22, 1941. loc. cit.
6. See PHPT 14, p. 1057; PHPT 2, pp. 560, 561, 679; also Joseph Grew, *Ten Years in Japan* (Simon & Schuster, 1944), pp. 470, 497. On the unnamed informant, see *The Magic Background of Pearl Harbor* (US Department of Defense, USGPO), Vol. IV, pp. N 11-13, items 14-17.
7. Japanese Foreign Ministers were in shaky political positions during 1941. Shigenori Togo was the third Foreign Minister appointed in 1941; Yosuke Matsuoka, January to July, Admiral Teijiro Toyoda, July to October, and Togo October onward.
8. For Smith-Hutton's schedule see RG 457, SRN 116271, Archives II, copy in author's file. Intercepted by Joseph Howard at Station H on Ocobert 31, 1941. After Smith-Hutton applied for a land travel permit from the Japanese Naval Ministry, Admiral Yamamoto was provided with Smith-Hutton's itinerary. The attaché was fluent in Japanese. His experience with the Japanese navy was unique. He was on personal and friendly terms with most of Japan's commanding naval officers. Smith-Hutton was closely associated with USN communications intelligence—he served at Station CAST in 1937 and was US Asiatic Fleet Intelligence Officer in 1938.
9. For Grew's "no substantial warning," see his testimony in PHPT 14, p. 1059.
10. See Rear Admiral Richmond K. Turner's discussion of the Vacant Sea order in PHPT 4, p. 1942. The significance of his admission that the North Pacific was cleared for the Japanese carrier force did not register with Congress or with the news media covering the 1945–46 investigation.
11. The Vacant Sea order was authored by Rear Admiral Royal Ingersoll, Assistant Chief of Naval Operations, and can be found in PHPT 12, p. 317. The order was issued after Admiral Kimmel disputed an earlier Vacant Sea order of Nov. 22, which interfered with his plans to have the Pacific Fleet patrolling the North Pacific waters starting Sunday Nov. 23. See Kimmel's protest: CINCPAC to OPNAV, Serial 220417 of Nov. 22, 1941 in RG 38, PHLO, Archives II.
12. Robinson Jeffers, "Pearl Harbor," in *Articles of War* (University of Arkansas Press, 1990). Reprinted by permission of the University of Arkansas Press.
13. See PacFleet employment schedule for Second Quarter, 1941–42 fiscal year, in PHPT 26, items section.
14. For Rear Admiral Richmond K. Turner's testimony that 25 years of US Army and Navy training taught that Japan would plan an air raid on Hawaii, see PHPT 4, p. 1963.
15. King's exercise was called Fleet Problem Nineteen and got underway March 14, 1938. See *Fleet Admiral King, A Naval Record* (W. W. Norton, 1952), pp. 281–282. For Alan Kirk's description of Fleet Problem 19, see his oral history, *The Reminiscences of Alan Goodrich Kirk*. (Oral History Office, Butler Library, Columbia University, NY 1962) p. 119, copy of entire OH, in author's file. Beware: Kirk has the wrong date for King's exercise. It was 1938, not 1937.
16. For Admiral Kimmel's Easy Cast Easy order, see CINCPAC order 37-41 of Nov. 5, 1941, Confidential A-4-3/FF12 [1], serial 01801, RG 313, Archives II. The report contains supporting files from various Pacific Fleet warships and commanders involved in Exercise 191, copy in author's file.
17. For quote of F. W. Purdy, see deck log of the USS *California* of Nov. 7, RG 24, PHLO, Archives II, copy in author's file.
18. "Catalina" was the name given to Navy twin engine patrol aircraft built by Consolidated and designated PBY. PB = patrol bomber; Y = Consolidated Aircraft Corp. See NOAA chart 19007 for "Classical" seamount locations, duplicate in author's file.
19. For Admiral Kimmel's "no radio" order of November 17, 1941, see PacFlt Flag file, RG 80, PHLO, Archives II.
20. For the scenario of Exercise 191, see CINCPAC Flag file serial 172118 of Nov. 17, 1941, RG 80, PHLO, and RG 313, Archives II, copies in author's file.
21. See Anderson-Greber memos, Nov. 19–21, in RG 313, Exercise 191 file A-16-3, Archives II, copy in author's file.
22. Ibid.

23. The USS *Tennessee* action report said the cancellation signal was FOX CAST DOG and was received at 3:47 P.M. Hawaii Standard Time. See RG 313, Exercise 191, file A-16-3, Archives II, copy in author's file.
24. The warning that halted the war games came from the Deputy Chief of Naval Operations, Rear Admiral Royal Ingersoll, who dispatched the order to Kimmel at 3:05 P.M., Washington time. According to Admiral Harold Stark, it reached Hawaii sometime after 1:35 P.M., Monday November 24, 1941; See PHPT 5-2438. For Greenwich Mean Time coordinated with the other time zones of the world, see time chart in PHPT 12, p. 340 ff.
25. See Admiral Stark's letter of September 23, 1941 to Admiral Kimmel advising of President Roosevelt's Pacific shooting policy, PHPT 33, p. 1168. Admiral Kimmel's comments, loc. cit.
26. See prediction of General George C. Marshall that a US-Japan war would break out during the first ten days of December 1941 in Chapter 10 herein.
27. See Admiral "Bull" Halsey's order 112-41 in RG 313, Archives II. The circumstances concerning the cancellation of Halsey's plan 112-41 have never been explained. He did not discuss the plan in his autobiography *Admiral Halsey's Story* (McGraw-Hill, 1947) nor did a separate biography, E. B. Potter, *Bull Halsey* (Naval Institute Press, 1985).
28. For Admiral Kimmel's disregard of Washington's injunction as faulty, see PHPT 6, p. 2713.
29. The USS *Lexington* and her battle group, composed of America's newest warships, was supposedly dispatched to Midway on a mission similar to Halsey's: deliver 18 fighter planes. She never delivered the planes. Normally the Navy's peacetime deck logs listed the specific destination of the vessel. According to the log entry by Lieutenant [j.g.] T. J. Nixon, the carrier was en route to "an assigned area." Between December 5 and 7 the log indicates the flattop remained in the Hawaii time zone [+10 1/2 GMT] until Monday morning, December 8 when she entered the +11 (GMT) time zone [Midway] at 10:50 A.M.

    The Task Force commander, Rear Admiral John Newton, testified before the Hart Proceedings that he canceled the Midway delivery on December 7 shortly after he learned of the Pearl Harbor raid. He did not explain what he was doing in the Midway area a day later, nor his reaction to the shelling of Midway by two Japanese destroyers on the night of December 7. For the *Lexington*'s deck log, see RG 24, MMRB, Archives II, copy in author's file. For Newton's account of canceling the flight to Midway, see PHPT 26-344 (Hart Proceedings).
30. For Senator Barkley's question to Stark, and for Stark's reply, "No specific dates," see PHPT 5, p. 2197.
31. For "transportation on aircraft carrier" dispatch from Stark, see serial 270038 of November 26, Washington Time, PHPT 17-2479. For Stark's documentation, see PHPT 5, pp. 2160-63. On October 17, Stark ordered Kimmel to take all practical precautions for the safety of airfields on Wake and Midway islands to protect flights of B-17 bombers headed for the Philippines. In compliance, Kimmel directed Halsey to plan for transporting 12 fighters to Wake and 18 to Midway. Instead, the transport plan was sidetracked on November 24 when Halsey planned to locate an enemy carrier force. But on November 26, Washington sidetracked the sidetrack and placed the deliveries to Wake and Midway back on the schedule; see PHPT 17-2534; PHPT 5-2160.
32. For Admiral Kimmel's directive to Layton/Rochefort, "Find The Carriers," see PHPT 10-4834. Testimony of Edwin Layton to JOINT, Feb. 18, 1946, questioned by Seth W. Richardson, general counsel.
33. For November identification of the *Akagi* as 8 YU NA, see Station H November 1941 report, p. 133; Station CAST made the identical ID in the TESTM reports, November 1941. Both reports in RG 38, Station US papers, MMRB, Archives II, and in author's file.
34. For Dutch cryptographers locating Japanese warships in the Kuriles, see Lt. General Hein ter Poorten's letter of July 23, 1960, Royal Netherlands Army Archives, The Hague, copy in author's file. In 1941 General ter Poorten was commander of the Dutch Army forces in the Netherlands East Indies.
35. General John Magruder was a former head of Army Intelligence and, at the time, an ally of the Navy's Intelligence Director, Walter Anderson. Both met with Roosevelt

in the Oval Office in 1939. Magruder's mission to China across the Pacific in September and October 1941 received full publicity and was dutifully reported to Tokyo by Honolulu Consul-General Nagao Kita.

36. Australia and the United States secretly set up Pacific Base F at Rabaul, New Britain on October 25, 1941; see CNO secret letter serial 0119912; also Navy Bureau of Ordnance A-16-a[2] PL, same date. On December 12, 1941 the development of Base F was indefinitely postponed by OPNAV serial 0134730. In RG 181-58-3223, NA, San Bruno, California. Japan seized Rabaul in the spring of 1942.

CHAPTER 10

1. The account of the US Army's secret conference held with selected members of the print media on November 15, 1941 at 10:15 A.M. in the Munitions Building is based on a memorandum written by *Time* magazine military correspondent, Robert Sherrod for his New York editor, David W. Hulburd, Jr. Sherrod wrote that the War Department invited the reporters to the secret conference. According to Sherrod's memo, General Marshall told the reporters he had called them together as "there were some things he had to tell to key press correspondents in order that their interpretations of current and forthcoming events did not upset key military strategy of the United States." After the war, Marshall told Hanson Baldwin, military writer for the *New York Times*, that the gist of Sherrod's account "is apparently correct." Reporters who complied with the secrecy rule were: Robert Sherrod, *Time;* Ernest K. Lindley, *Newsweek;* Charles W. B. Hurd, *New York Times;* Bert Andrews, *New York Herald Tribune;* Lyle P. Wilson, United Press; Edward Bomar, Associated Press; and Harold Slater, International News Service. None of the radio news reporters were invited to the conference. See Larry Bland, ed., *The Papers of George Catlett Marshall* (Johns Hopkins University Press, 1986), Vol. 2, p. 676 ff. For Short's questioning of Marshall's ethics in not telling him, see PHPT 7, p. 2960.

2. General Marshall did not disclose the specific source of his information to the correspondents that Japan would attack the United States during the first ten days of December 1941. Since Marshall revealed that his source was intercepted and decoded Japanese radio messages, the author looked for confirmation in Army and Navy communications intelligence records. On November 5 and 9, 1941, Admiral Osami Nagano, Chief of the Japanese Navy's General Staff (a title similar to the Chief of Naval Operations in the United States held by Admiral Harold Stark), sent radio messages to Admiral Isoroku Yamamoto, Commander-in-Chief of the Imperial Japanese Navy: "In view of the fact that it is feared war has become unavoidable with the United States, Great Britain and the Netherlands and for self-preservation and future of the Empire, the various preparation for war operations will be completed by the first part of December." Admiral Nagano also transmitted by radio a copy of the dispatch to the Commander-in-Chief of Japan's China Area Fleet, according to a US Navy publication, *The Campaigns of the Pacific War* (USGPO 1946), p. 49, published by the Naval Analysis Division of the United States Strategic Bombing Survey. None of Admiral Nagano's dispatches of the early November, 1941 time period intercepted by the United States monitor stations have been released to the National Archives, according to John Taylor, archivist in charge of the Japanese naval intercepts in Archives II. However, evidence found by the author in US navy records of Station HYPO indicates radio messages from Admiral Nagano were intercepted in Hawaii during the period of November 5 to 13, 1941. Joseph Rochefort, commander of HYPO, wrote in his Communications Summary (COMSUM) that his intercept operators obtained radio dispatches originated by the Chief of Japan's Naval General Staff (Admiral Nagano) addressed to at least three Japanese naval commands: 1. Admiral Isoroku Yamamoto, Commander-in-Chief of the Imperial Navy, 2. Commander-in-Chief of Japan's China Area Fleet, 3. chief of staff of Japan's carrier divisions, and other naval commands. Rochefort wrote that a series of high priority radio dispatches originated by Admiral Nagano were intercepted by his staff between November 5 and 13, 1941. See Rochefort's COMSUMS for November 5 and 13, 1941, pp. 198, 206, in RG 80 PHLO, MMRB, Archives II, copies in author's file.

Admiral Nagano sent two radio messages on November 5 in the Japanese Navy's "kana code," according to Rochefort's COMSUM on November 5, 1941, page 198. Apparently these two messages that indicated war with the United States would begin the first part of December were the source of Marshall's press briefing. On November 25, President Franklin D. Roosevelt announced to his War Cabinet that: "We were likely to be attacked perhaps (as soon as) next Monday (December 1), for the Japanese are notorious for making an attack without warning. . . ," according to the diary of Secretary of War Henry L. Stimson, in PHPT 11, p. 5433 (double parentheses by author). Nagano's messages of November 5, which indicated war would start by the first part of December, were forwarded to Station US in Washington for decryption and translation, according to US Navy communications intelligence policy. The communication circumstances of the November 5, 1941 Japanese naval intercepts, their forwarding to Washington, and their apparent decryption and translation while in the nation's capital fit into a time frame sufficient to reach General Marshall for his November 15 press briefing and for President Roosevelt's war discussion with his cabinet on November 25, 1941.

Between September 3, and December 8, 1941 (TT), Admiral Chuichi Nagumo originated 843 SMS messages, according to the RG 457 file of Japanese intercepts in Archives II seen by the author. The SMS series begins with number 40 on September 3, 1941, and ends with number 843 on December 8, 1941. Of the 843 SMS messages originated by Nagumo in this time frame, 78 (9.2 percent) were released by President Jimmy Carter in 1979. Therefore at least 765 (90.7 percent) are missing from National Archives files.

Please see the Afterword to this book in reference to Admiral Nagumo being first detected in radio broadcasts, April 22, 1941. The author believes Nagumo started his carrier command with the SMS number of 001 on or about April 22, 1941, reached the maximum number of 999 at the end of August 1941, and (per Japanese radio policy) started a new number series of 001. Therefore, about 1,765 of Nagumo's messages have not been declassified as of the year 2000.

3. On the visits of Princess Martha of Norway, see the White House Usher Book and Trips and Itineraries of the President under these dates: Princess Martha at the White House on June 15, 1941; see Trip of the President aboard the USS *Potomac* with Princess Martha, August 1941. Near Cape Cod Roosevelt left the *Potomac* and transferred to the USS *Augusta* for the Churchill meeting; dinner with Princess Martha on November 25, 1941. For the full schedule of Princess Martha's visits with President Roosevelt, see the White House Usher Book for 1940 through 1941. All recorded in the White House Usher Book, FDRL, Hyde Park, NY, copy in author's file.

4. See *Uritski* file, record card 1283; *Azerbaijan* card 3019, San Francisco Maritime Museum, San Francisco, California. See also Bar Pilots' records, Columbia River Museum, Astoria, Oregon, copies author's file. See radio message sent to Admiral Nagumo dated November 28, 1941 warning that his warships might encounter the *Uritski* and *Azerbaijan* in RG 457, SRN 16667, MMRB, Archives II, copy in author's file.

5. See Grace Tully, *F.D.R. My Boss* (Charles Scribner's Sons, 1949), pp. 23–24; FDR addressing the Princess as "child," p. 23, and Lieutenant Commander Fox as White House pharmacist p. 148, ibid. Princess Martha addressing the President as "Dear Godfather," see Joseph P. Lash, *Eleanor and Franklin* (W. W. Norton, 1971), p. 677. Information on Pooks Hill courtesy of Jane C. Sween, Montgomery County Historical Society, Rockville, MD.

6. The fortieth parallel of north latitude crosses the United States from Cape Mendocino, California, through Denver, Indianapolis, and Philadelphia. Nagumo's concentration of the carriers at the center offense of the Japanese fleet indicates that Japan's navy was years ahead of the US Navy in recognizing the military might of a Fast Carrier Task Force. Japan placed her carriers in the central position surrounded by other warships in outward formations for protective anti-aircraft roles. In pre-Pearl Harbor maneuvers USN battleships and cruisers were the stars of the fleet and moved separately from the carriers.

7. See Admiral Yamamoto's radio silence order SRN 116866 in RG 457, MMRB, Archives II, copy in author's file.

8. Commander Minoru Genda's written statement to the author dated November 22,

1982, author's file. After the war, Japanese voters elected him to the Diet (Parliament). Genda died on the forty-fourth anniversary of VJ-Day, Aug. 15, 1989.

9. For Edwin Layton on radio silence, see PHPT 10, p. 4904; see also Layton's comments on radio silence to the Roberts Commission, PHPT 23, p. 660.

10. Brig. Gen. Telford Taylor's article was published in the *New York Times Magazine*, April 29, 1984, p. 120. Taylor was US Chief of Counsel and prosecutor for the Nuremberg (Germany) War Crimes Trials of 1946–49. He died May 1998.

11. The Don Whitehead quote is from Don Whitehead, *The FBI Story* (Random House, 1956), p. 181.

12. Undated written report of Commander W. J. Sebald, COMINT aide to Fleet Admiral Ernest J. King, Chief of Naval Operations, folder 5830/6, RG 38, Station US papers, declassified January 28, 1995, MMRB, Archives II.

13. For interception of Admiral Nagumo's "extensive radio communications" as he departed Hitokappu Bay, see Joseph Rochefort's Communications Summary (COMSUM) of November 25, 1941, RG 80, PHLO, Box 41, Archives II. All of the original COMSUMS prepared by Station HYPO's staff for Admiral Kimmel and dated from July 15 to December 6, 1941 can be found filed together in Box 41, loc. cit. The PHLO files contain the original Kimmel copy with the admiral's notations and his initials, HEK.

14. For the tracking of Vice Admiral Mitsumi Shimizu, the commander of Japan's submarine fleet, from Japan, south past the Bonin islands, then eastward to the Marshall islands, see series of daily COMSUM, prepared by Rochefort and his staff, dated November 25 through December 6, 1941 in RG 80, PHLO, Box 41, loc. cit. See also the Code Movement Reports, Station H, Nov. 1941, p. 110 ff., in RG 38, Station US papers, MMRB, Archives II, and author's file.

15. Please note that the Chronology was prepared by Homer Kisner at Station H located on the windward side of Oahu; it differs from the Daily Communication Summary prepared at Station HYPO in the Pearl Harbor Navy Yard. The Chronology is a summary of the Japanese navy intercepts in the 5–Num code obtained by Station H during a 24-hour period from 8:00 A.M. to 7:59 A.M. For daily totals of Japanese naval message intercepts, see Station H report for November 1941, p. 110, under Nov. 25, 1941 [HST]. Estimate of 1225 intercepts is based on message sheets numbered 91932 to 93124 [1192 messages] and 78710 to 78743 [33 messages] RG 38, Station US papers, MMRB, Archives II. The Daily Chronology and its crucial supporting documents were overlooked by all Pearl Harbor investigations of 1944–46 and the Thurmond-Spence Pearl Harbor probe of 1995.

16. On Homer Kisner being unaware that FDR saw the results of communications intelligence, see Homer Kisner's interview with author, April 1988 and April 1999, author's file. Captain Kisner handled millions of Japanese intercepts during the war years and had forgotten the pre-Pearl Harbor dispatches. He and the author discussed the English translations of the pre-attack dispatches released by President Carter in 1979, but not the original Japanese versions that he (then a chief radioman) and his men acquired in 1941. The bulk of the original documents—about 98 percent—have not been released as this book goes to press in 1999. Kisner, promoted to commander, served as radio traffic chief and other communication intelligence duties for Admiral Chester Nimitz. He retired from the Navy as a captain.

17. For the November 25, 1941 movement report on Carrier Division Five, see Station H Chronology for November 1941, p. 110 under radio call sign of NA O Ø (The Ø distinguishes zero from the letter). For intercept of The Carriers (Kisner's term capitalized) on 4963 kilocycles, see Station H Chronology of November 26, 1941, Hawaii Time, p. 89. The intercept was made on the evening watch (4 P.M. to midnight) which would correspond to noon to 8 P.M., November 27, 1941 in Japan. Since The Carriers had been under way for over 24 hours, their location was about 200 miles east of Hitokappu Bay in the North Pacific. Full details on the intercept of the carriers is included on Station H message sheet 92095 of November 26, 1941. None of Station H's estimated 143,000 message sheets originated between July 15 and December 6, 1941, have been declassified by the US government as this book goes to press. See Station H Chronology, RG 38, Station US papers, MMRB, Archives II, copy in author's file.

18. See the author's written interview with Harry Hood, January 15, 1986, in author's

files. US Navy intercept operators and cryptographers were forbidden to discuss their work with journalists without the supervision of the Naval Security Group Command (NSGC), so the author submitted written questions to Hood in the fall of 1985. The written questions traveled by US Mail in a roundabout way to Hood through the NSGC (successor to Station US) then located on "Antennae Hill," 3801 Nebraska Avenue NW—a high ground point in Washington, DC. (It is called Antennae Hill because TV station WRC and the National Broadcasting Company's transmitting facilities were next door creating an antennae farm that could be seen from most points in the nation's capital. It would be interesting to learn what TV anchor Tom Brokaw and NBC sound technicians intercepted from the US Navy's antennae farm.) Two officials of the NSGC, Commander Irving Newman and George Henriksen, reviewed the author's questions and Hood's answers, then returned the complete interview to the author. Nothing in the written questions and answers was censored. Hood was living in Philadelphia in 1986.

19. For the "broad range of air operations" quote, see Rochefort's COMSUM of October 22, 1941, RG 80, PHLO, Box 41, MMRB, Archives II, and author's file.

20. Earlier in September, citing the "enemy's submarine menace," Rear Admiral Charles Freeman, Commandant of the Thirteenth Naval District (COM 13) in Seattle, wrote that he was ready to provide distant aerial reconnaissance of the North Pacific and the Alaska sector and asked Admiral Harold Stark, the Chief of Naval Operations, for permission to begin the search and "prevent a surprise attack." Freeman never received an OK. See RG 187, COM 13, Confidential Serial 121129 of September 17, 1941, in NA, Seattle, and author's file.

21. For Rochefort's testimony on tracking of Japanese submarines toward Hawaii, see his Daily Communication Summary, November 24, 25, 26, 1941, under sub-heading Fourth Fleet and Mandates. PHLO, RG80, MMRB, Archives II, copy in author's file.

22. See the Priority dispatch as received in Washington with Laurance Safford's initials, LFS, in RG 80, PHLO, MMRB, Archives II, and author's file.

23. Princess Martha bringing a bottle of Aquavit to the White House, see Grace Tully, *F.D.R. My Boss* (Charles Scribner's Sons, 1949), p. 23. For the time schedule of the President's dinner with Princess Martha, see White House Usher Book, November 25, 1941, FDRL, Hyde Park, NY, copy author's file. For description of the Oval Study dinners, see William Seale, *The President's House* (White House Historical Association. 1986), pp. 985–99.

24. The Rochefort-Kimmel-Bloch alert can be fully documented. It was written in Hawaii by Joseph Rochefort (see his testimony to Hart Proceedings, PHPT 26, p. 220, item 32) and dispatched by Radio Pearl Harbor to Washington DC at 1:10 A.M. November 26, 1941, GMT, which was 2:40 P.M., November 25, by Hawaii Time. Next it was received at Station US, where Commander Laurance Stafford initialed the copy shortly after 8:10 P.M. EST. Then Lieutenant Commander Ethelbert Watts, one of McCollum's assistants, prepared the Presidential Monograph 65 (published in PHPT 15, p. 1886 ff.). Secretary of War Henry L. Stimson wrote in his diary that he received a document from the Navy's secret service (his name for the US Navy's intercept operations) the evening of November 25, 1941 and sent it over to the White House. See Stimson diary entry for November 26, 1941 [EST], PHPT 11, p. 5434. See Edwin Layton, PHPT 26, p. 231, item 33, where he confirms that Kimmel authorized sending Rochefort's alert to Washington.

25. For missing monographs, see Richard von Doenhoff's letters to author, March 23, 1994 and April 27, 1995, author's file.

26. For President Roosevelt's daily schedule as recorded by Chief Usher Howell Crim, see White House Usher Book, FDRL, Hyde Park, NY, copy in author's file.

27. For Stimson's "secret service" quote see Note 21, this chapter. Brigadier General Sherman Miles, Army Chief of Intelligence, testified to the Joint Congressional Investigation that he received the message at 12:45 A.M. November 26, 1941. PHPT 14, p. 1366. For the presidential monographs 65, 66, see RG 80, PHLO files, Monographs 65, 66, Index Guide 901–200, dated November 26, 1941, MMRB, Archives II, copies in author's file.

28. For Captain John Beardall's delivery of Magic to FDR, see his testimony to the Joint Congressional Investigation of 1945–46 in PHPT 11, p. 5270.

29. For further confirmation of delivery of intercepted Japanese messages to FDR, see a November 12, 1941 "unofficial memorandum," marked *"Dissemination to White House,"* reportedly written by Lieutenant Commander Alwin D. Kramer (reportedly, see PHPT 11, p. 5475), the Navy's principal White House courier for communications intelligence, in RG 80, PHLO, MMRB, Archives II, copy in author's file.

30. For Kramer discussing delivery of "raw messages" to Roosevelt, see PHPT 9, pp. 3985, 3986. Captain Homer Kisner, radio traffic chief at Station H in 1941, believes Roosevelt did not literally mean "raw messages" for they would have been in Japan's naval 5–Num code or in clear Japanese language and either (1) unreadable or (2) untranslated. Instead, Kisner presumes FDR referred to the Communication Summaries (COMSUMS). See Kisner's taped interview with the author April 22, 1988, in author's files. See testimony of Kramer before Senator Homer Ferguson of the Joint Congressional Investigation of 1945–46. The two discussed delivery of Japanese "raw messages" to President Roosevelt before the attack (PHPT 9, p. 3986):

SENATOR HOMER FERGUSON: "Wasn't it your understanding that the President was personally receiving these raw messages to place his own evaluation on?"

LT. CDR. A. D. KRAMER: "Yes sir." For description of the leather pouch delivered to FDR, see memorandum of Captain W. B. Braun dated December 18, 1945 to Admiral Theodore Wilkinson in RG 80, PHLO, MMRB, Archives II, also in author's file.

31. For FDR meeting with Admiral King and later swim with Betsey Roosevelt, see White House Usher Book, November 27, 1941, FDRL, Hyde Park, NY, copy in author's file.

32. For Stimson's quote on his responsibility for carrying out the President's orders, see Stimson's written statement presented to the Joint Congressional Investigation of 1945–46, entitled "Statement of Facts as Shown by My Current Notes and My Recollection as Refreshed Thereby." Statement starts in PHPT 11, p. 5416; his account of carrying out Roosevelt's order will be found on p. 5425. See also Stimson dispatching the war warning order issued under authority of FDR and released for transmission by Brig. Gen. L. T. Gerow on Nov. 27, 1941: "The Secretary of War directs that following message be sent." Reproduced in Appendix C of this book.

33. For Admiral Ingersoll's war warning on November 27, 1941, see Appendix C of this book.

34. For the war warning by Admiral Stark on November 28, 1941, see Appendix C of this book.

35. For Admiral Thomas Hart not interfering with Japan's initial assault on the Philippines, see Clay Blair, *Silent Victory* (J. B. Lippincott, 1975), p. 158. See also the following observations from a biography of Hart, James Leutze's, *A Different Kind of Victory* (Naval Institute Press, 1981): he (Hart) had 27 subs submerged in Manila Bay, p. 235; it was Washington, not the Asiatic Fleet Commander (Hart) that directed the fleet to withdraw from Manila," p. 230; Hart was directed by Washington to send US Navy surface forces and submarines southeast toward Australia, p. 237. For examples of MacArthur and Stimson feuding with Hart over lack of US Navy submarine action: MacArthur asked the admiral: "What in the world is the matter with your submarines?" p. 242; MacArthur complained that Hart's inactivity allowed Japan's navy freedom of action, p. 234; according to Stimson, MacArthur felt that Hart's ships and submarines were ineffectual, not because Japan controlled the air but because Hart had lost his courage, p. 240; Hart's reaction to MacArthur's brickbats: "He (MacArthur) is inclined to cut my throat and perhaps the Navy in general," p. 240.

36. For the replies of Generals Andrews and DeWitt, see Papers of Lt. Gen. Walter Short, Hoover Archives, Stanford University, Stanford, CA.

37. For General Short's comments on alarming Honolulu civilians see PHPT 7, p. 2985, PHPT 27, p. 283; and targets to shoot, see PHPT 7, pp. 2946, 3015. See also Chapter 4 of *The General's Lady*, an unpublished manuscript, by Florence Isabel Short, the general's wife, in the Hoover Institution Archives, Stanford University, Stanford, CA, copy in author's file. Ms. Short usually went by the name Isabel.

38. For Adjutant General Adams' dispatch to General Short of November 28, 1941, see Appendix C of this book. For Adams' original War Department dispatch 482, as re-

ceived by Short, see his personal papers, Hoover Institution Archives, Stanford University, copy in author's file.

CHAPTER 11

1. Lester R. Schulz was interviewed in writing by the author, Schulz' letters are in the author's file.
2. In 1941 Thanksgiving was celebrated by the nation on November 20. Congress changed the holiday to the third Thursday of November to provide more Christmas shopping days.
3. See the Stimson diary quotes—the original 1941 quotes in PHPT 11, pp. 5433–5435, and an elaboration of the diary provided to the Joint Congressional Investigating Committee in 1945–46, pp. 5421–5427.
4. Ibid.
5. Ibid.
6. On FDR sending a special message to Emperor Hirohito, see Joseph Grew, *Ten Years in Japan* (Simon & Schuster, 1944), p. 486.
7. For wording of FDR's dispatch to Emperor Hirohito, see ibid., p. 487.
8. For FDR's quote on "fighting by next Thanksgiving," see the *New York Times*, November 30, 1941, p. 1.
9. Steve Early quote from *New York Times*, ibid.; see also Grace Tully, *F.D.R. My Boss* (Charles Scribner's Sons, 1949), pp. 250, 251.
10. See Grace Tully, *F.D.R. My Boss* (Charles Scribner's Sons, 1949), p. 205, where the *Ferdinand Magellan* was designated US Number One. The presidential car was bullet-proof and built of armor plate for the President by the Pullman Company and the American Association of Railroads. According to Tully, the car was placed in service after 1940. On FDR's return to White House, see Tully, *F.D.R. My Boss*, p. 250.
11. Hoisting a dark gray ball above railroad tracks was a standard procedure of American railroads in 1941. It directed all trains to secondary tracks or sidings for emergency passage of US Number One. In the Jet Age, similar procedures were adopted for Air Force One that clear air traffic routes and airport runway traffic for the presidential aircraft. During the Joint Congressional Investigative Hearing of 1945–46, Congressman Bertrand Gearhart (R., CA) questioned the high-ball return. Undersecretary of State Sumner Welles (the number two man) tried to provide an answer in State Departmentese (PHPT 2, p. 540).

    GEARHART: Why did FDR return from Warm Springs so unexpectedly, so precipitously?

    MR. WELLES: The instructions given me by the President to communicate the memorandum he had sent me to the two Japanese Ambassadors was one of the reasons, in my judgment at that time, as it is now, which required the President's return in order that he himself could take charge of the communication.
12. See Foreign Minister Shigenori Togo's messages in PHPT 12, pp. 195 (Togo to Ambassador Nomura in Washington, "Don't give impression negotiations broken off," Nov. 28, 1941), 204 (a two-part message from Togo to Ambassador Oshima in Berlin, "Say to Hitler that there is extreme danger war will break out with United States," Nov. 30, 1941), 206 (Togo to Ambassador Oshima in Berlin, "The United States regards Japan as an enemy," Nov. 30, 1941), and 208 (Togo to Ambassador Nomura in Washington, "To keep United States from becoming unduly suspicious say negotiations are continuing," December 1, 1941).
13. For FDR's requests for a copy of the "extreme danger" dispatch, see Herbert Feis, *The Road To Pearl Harbor* (Princeton University Press, 1950), p. 336.
14. For Rear Admiral Richmond K. Turner's quote, "indication of war," see see PHPT 4, p. 2002.
15. For Joseph Rochefort's "looked damn bad" testimony, see Admiral Hart's Proceedings in PHPT 23, p. 687.
16. For observations of Captain Charles McMorris and Commander Vincent Murphy that Pearl Harbor is unlikely to be attacked by Japan, see PHPT 36, p. 455.
17. For Japan's military intercepts available to President Roosevelt, see the SMS series of secret radio transmissions of the Japanese fleet, compiled from SRN series in RG 475, Archives II by the author; in author's file.

18. See Rochefort's Daily COMSUMS from Dec. 1 to 6, 1941 in RG 80, PHLO, Box 41, MMRB, Archives II, and author's file.
19. For Yamamoto's radio messages to the Carriers, see COMSUM of December 6, 1941, RG 80, PHLO, Box 41, MMRB, Archives II, also in author's file.
20. See also Homer Kisner's Chronology for Dec. 5, 1941, which contains the long-distance warning; it may be found in RG 38, Station US papers, MMRB, Archives II, and in author's file. Beware of copies printed in the Joint Congressional Hearings; they contain typos. Homer Kisner interviews with the author, April 1988 and 1998, transcripts in author's file.
21. Ibid.
22. Duane Whitlock taped audio interview with author, Danville, California, September 30, 1993, transcript and tapes in author's file.
23. According to the Station US papers in Archives II, there were at least three super-secret US Navy code systems for radio dispatch of intercepted Japanese communications intelligence in use in late 1941. Kimmel and Hart held keys for these: COPEK, CETYH, and TESTM. Admiral King of the Atlantic Fleet held keys to COPEK and CETYH and possibly TESTM. Manila Time, not GMT, was used for the CAST TESTM dispatches sent to Hawaii, according to Duane Whitlock. Messages sent to MacArthur by CAST were fully decrypted, translated, and delivered to the general's headquarters in Manila by naval officer messenger.
24. For roster of Station H personnel as of July 1941, see Station H monthly report in RG 38, Station US papers, MMRB, Archives II, copy in author's file.
25. For identification and location of the Japanese carriers *Akagi, Zuikaku, Hiryu* and the battleship *Kirishima*, see TESTM dispatches in RG 38, Station US papers, MMRB, Archives II, and in author's files.
26. See transcript of Duane Whitlock's interview, September 30,1993, Danville, California, audio tape and transcript in author's file; the author conducted additional telephone interviews with Whitlock at Strawberry Point, Iowa, May and June 1999.
27. See transcript of Whitlock interview, loc. cit.
28. See *Intercept Station "C"*, authored and published by the Naval Cryptographic Veterans Association for the roster of Station CAST for December 1941. When Japanese troops overran the Bataan Peninsula and threatened Corregidor in the spring of 1942, the CAST personnel were evacuated by Navy submarines to Melbourne and linked up with codebreakers of the Royal Australian Navy. The unit became Fleet Radio Unit Melbourne, with the acronym FRUMEL. Before evacuating Corregidor, they burned all intelligence records and reportedly destroyed their Purple machine by throwing it into Manila Bay.
29. For operations of the Purple machine at Station CAST, see author's telephone interview with Captain Duane Whitlock at Strawberry Point, Iowa, May, June 1999, in author's file. For same subject on Purple machine, see telephone interview between author and Lieutenant Commander Robert Dowd, Oakdale, California, May and June 1999, notes in author's file. Dowd told the author that he operated the Purple machine at CAST. For quote that Station CAST personnel worked from same cryptographic quarters, is from Captain Jack Kaye, Santa Ana, California, e-mail to author, June 1999, author's file. In 1941, Kaye worked as intercept operator at Station CAST, then transferred to Station H in Hawaii in October 1941. Kaye to author, e-mail, ibid.
30. See the original "most reliable order" in Secret serial 242239, 10:39 P.M., GMT or 5:30 P.M., EST, both Nov. 24, 1941, PHLO, RG 80, Archives II. Order bears McCollum's initials at top: sent to Admiral Hart (CINCAF) for action and information to CINCPAC and the US Navy attachés in Shanghai, Chungking, and Tokyo. Beware of the reprint of the message in PHPT 36, p. 650, which dropped McCollum's initials as originator and has minor typos.
31. See Kisner interview with author, April 1988, transcript, notes, audio tape, photographs, author's file.
32. See Presidential Monograph file, PHLO, RG 38, MMRB, Archives II. On the night of December 7 (EST), Station CAST located the *Akagi* in Okinawa and sent the report to Station US. It was an erroneous report, of course, because the *Akagi*, after attacking Pearl Harbor, escaped to the North Pacific. McCollum routed the report to FDR sometime after 11 P.M. EST. There is no record of its delivery to the White House. Captain Duane Whitlock, one of the traffic analysts at Station CAST, said he did not send

the erroneous *Akagi*/Okinawa report to Washington and did not recall its existence (interviewed by the author September 30, 1993). The author was unable to locate the erroneous *Akagi* dispatch in President Jimmy Carter's 1979 release of Japanese naval intercepts to Record Group 457 at Archives II. There is no record of Station H intercepting the carrier in the Okinawa region on December 7, 1941, Hawaii Time. Instead, the Station H records show interceptions of the *Akagi*, north of Oahu on December 7. See Station H operator logs for December 8, 1941 (Tokyo Time) RG 38, Station US papers, MMRB, Archives II. The erroneous report: "DF bearing indicates *Akagi* moving south from Empire. Now in Nansei Islands area," was sent by radio dispatch to Admiral Kimmel as an information address. It was dispatched from Station CAST at 3:33 A.M. on December 8, 1941, GMT, which is 5:03 P.M. on December 7, 1941 in Hawaii, nine hours after the attack on Pearl Harbor. The erroneous *Akagi*-bearing report can be found in RG 80, PHLO, Pacific Fleet incoming classified message file, microfiche section, MMRB, Archives II, copy in author's file.

CHAPTER 12

1. See John Toland, *Infamy* (Doubleday, 1982). For accuracy, RDF bearings must be plotted on great circle charts, not Mercator projections. Electronic signals do not follow a Mercator projection. A great circle chart establishes the shortest distance between any two points on the earth's curved surface; see Merriam Webster's Collegiate Dictionary, 10th edition. Example: the shortest air distance between Chicago and San Francisco is through Laramie, Wyoming, not through Denver, Colorado, as a Mercator map would indicate.
2. See reconstruction of the track chart by Robert Ogg on p. 191 of this book.
3. Robert Ogg, interviewed by the author, 1984–1999; transcripts, notes and correspondence in author's files. Later in the war, Ogg served on the radio communication staff of Admiral Nimitz for the Central and North Pacific campaigns. After the war ended, Ogg entered the US Navy Reserve, and was executive officer of the destroyer USS *Shields*. He is an emeritus trustee of the University of California (UC) Foundation; chairman of the Finance and Audit Committees, Advisory Board University Research Expedition; Member UC Nimitz Lectureship Committee, Member of UC Chancellor's Circle; Honorary Fellow California Academy of Sciences; Life Fellow, Explorers Club. He is a ninth descendant of John Howland of the *Mayflower*. He retired from the Navy Reserve as a lieutenant commander. See also Ogg's oral history, Regional Oral History Office, The Bancroft Library, UC Berkeley.
4. According to Webster's Collegiate Dictionary, 10th edition, a williwaw is a "violent gust of cold land air, common along mountainous coasts of high latitudes." A good name for a cold strong drink.
5. For Lieutenant Ellsworth Hosmer's direct link to Station US, see FBI report 62–33413, item 766, copy in author's file.
6. "Be on the lookout for carriers": for confirmation, see Edwin Layton's statement: "Intense watch began Nov. 25, 1941," in PHPT 10, p. 4908.
7. For Ogg's statement, "The best of my memory is that this was in the 4 megacycle range" (i.e., the 4,000-kilocycle band) see his oral history interview of May 4–6, 1983, pp. 35, 39, 42, conducted by Commander Irwin G. Newman of the Naval Security Group Command and published by the US Navy as SRH 255 in RG 457, MMRB, Archives II; also in author's file. See also interviews of Ogg by the author, 1984 to 1999, telephone, correspondence, author's file.
8. On those transmissions being identified in Japan's *kana* code, see Ogg's comments in SRH 255, loc. cit., pp. 18, 22, 23, 25.
9. Admiral Greenslade, Commander of the Western Sea Frontier and Commandant of the Twelfth Naval District, held keys to GUPID, a Navy communications intelligence system similar to COPEK, CETYH, and TESTM. For selected dispatches to and from Greenslade in the GUPID system dated November and December 1941, see RG 80, PHLO "reels file," MMRB, Archives II, and author's file. See Gerhard Gesell's comments regarding deletions of Navy code systems from the official records in PHPT 4, p. 1911, and confirmation of their deletion by Commander John F. Baecher, the Navy's liaison officer for the Joint Committee on June 7, 1946 in PHLO file, RG 80, ibid., copy in author's file.

10. For McCullough's sending the intelligence data to the White House via a secure method, see Ogg's comments p. 40, SRH 255, RG 457, MMRB, Archives II.

11. Lieutenant Ellsworth Hosmer's original Navy memorandum and other papers are in the custody of his daughter, Patty Hosmer Rathbone, of Loomis, California. Mrs. Rathbone confirmed that she had custody of her father's documents in a telephone conversation with the author on April 17, 1998, notes in author's file; copies furnished to the author by Ogg, in author's files. After filing his memo, Hosmer transferred to the District's communication office on December 27, 1941. In his memo, Hosmer alludes to a dispute with Lieutenant Commander Eugene Kerrigan over locating the Japanese force north of Hawaii. Commander Kerrigan headed the investigative section of the District's intelligence office. "Kerrigan became enraged when told of the location of the force. He said I was wasting my time and instructed me to keep away," Hosmer wrote. Hosmer filed his sealed statement and papers with Lieutenant Commander Selim Woodworth, Chief Administrative Officer of the intelligence office, according to his daughter, Patty Rathbone.

12. See Robert Ogg interview, in RG 457, SRH 255, loc. cit., for: commercial radio facilities, see pp. 19, 35, 36, 38; Japanese telegraphic *kana* code,which is not a secret code, pp. 18, 22, 23, 25. Telephone interviews of Ogg by the author in 1999, notes, transcriptions in author's file.

13. For Ogg's quote concerning Japanese radio transmissions on 4 megacycles, see SRH 255, ibid., p. 35, "odd frequencies," pp. 35, 39, 42.

14. For the radio direction finder intercept of the *Akagi* using the radio call sign of 8 YU NA, see Station KING, monthly report for November 1941 in RG 181, Commandant 13th Naval District, Secret A-6 files, NA, Seattle, WA, copy author's file.

15. For Station H report, "The Carriers are using secret calls on 4963 kcs.," see H Chronology p. 89 of November 26, 1941 in RG 38, Station US papers, MMRB, Archives II, copy in author's file. The three-point gap in kilocycles is infinitesimal. The radio call sign 8 YU NA was a secret call or tactical call for the *Akagi* in November 1941. In communications procedures, whenever the Japanese navy placed the number before the *kana* it signaled a secret radio message originated by the unit. In administrative calls assigned to mobile units, the number followed the *kana*.

16. See Station ITEM report in COM. 13 Secret A-6 files, RG 181, NA Seattle. Tokyo Radio addressed the vessel as FU ME 8 which was the *Kirishima*'s radio call sign for November 1941, according to Station CAST's TESTM report, November 1941 in RG 38, Station US papers, MMRB, Archives II, copy in author's file. Vandenberg transferred from Station H to Station ITEM in June 1941 when he was relieved by Homer Kisner. Vandenberg was the Navy's senior radio traffic chief on the West Coast.

17. See Leslie Grogan's reconstructed *Lurline* log dated December 10, 1941. The Matson Navigation Company, San Francisco furnished copy to author. Grogan reconstructed the log after the Navy seized the original on December 10, 1941. Grogan did not list or define the "lower marine frequency in the reconstructed log." Grogan died August 4, 1974.

18. For quote, "signals were being repeated back," see *Lurline*'s reconstructed log, loc. cit.

19. For "bold repetition," see *Lurline*'s reconstructed log, loc. cit. Grogan reported hearing the blasts aimed at the North Pacific for five days. Theoretically the blasts were among at least 5,000 naval messages transmitted by Japan during the five days. But in President Jimmy Carter's Japanese intercept release of 1979, only 102 Japanese intercepted messages from this time frame were made public. That left 4898 unreleased which surely must be considered as part of what Grogan called "blasts." Homer Kisner, the Pacific Fleet's traffic chief, and his operators intercepted a minimum of 1,000 Japanese radio dispatches per day.

20. For commercial radio call signs not used for warships, see letter from Commander Fred R. Thomson to author, dated January 29, 1986, p. 1, item d., author's file. In 1941 Thomson was radioman-in-charge of the Navy's intercept facility, Station AE, Sitka, Territory of Alaska.

21. For quote about "a mighty serious situation," and presenting transcript to Lieutenant Commander Pease, see the *Lurline*'s reconstructed log, loc. cit..

22. See the *Lurline* log withdrawal slip in RG 181, Twelfth Naval District, Port Director file, NA, San Bruno, CA.

23. Kathleen O'Connor interview with the author, September 24, 1991, also written confirmation from Ms. O'Connor, June 16, 1999 in author's file. See photo of her taken by author in the San Bruno National Archives research room with the suspect withdrawal slip, in author's file.

24. See Station ITEM intercept report of December 4, 1941, RG 181, A-6 file, NA, Laguna Niguel, CA, copy in author's file; "Strong signals" heard by Station SAIL, see COM 13 dispatch to OPNAV serial 031825 in PHLO file, RG 80, MMRB, Archives II, copy in author's file.

25. For Station H confirming the ITEM report, see Operator Log of H, December 4, 1941, p. 51, as UTU 8571, NR 888 (which is the same NR heard at ITEM. The NR number refers to Japan's naval radio station serial number), in RG 38, Station US papers, MMRB, Archives, copies in author's file.

26. When he copied the Japanese navy's communication procedures into his log, Henry Garstka recorded what he heard on the airways. Using the RIP 5 code typewriter he typed that HO MI 3 (Radio Yokosuka) called NU TO 4 (Hawaii radio call sign for the heavy cruiser *Tone*) at 10:20 A.M. and 10:45 A.M. (December 5, 1941, Tokyo Time or 2:50 P.M., and 3:15 P.M. respectively Hawaii Time, December 4, 1941. Since Japan's navy operated on Tokyo Time, all US Navy Japanese intercept logs were recorded in Tokyo Time). Radio Yokosuka asked the *Tone* in *kata kana:* KAN? KAN? ("Do you have messages for me?"). See Henry F. Garstka log entry, Station H for December 5, 1941, Tokyo Time, pp. 93 and 94, RG 38, Station US papers, release of Jan. 1995, Archives II, copy author's file (parentheses by the author). In May 1999 Garstka, then living in Edgewater Park, NJ, confirmed to the author that he worked at Station H and frequently copied Japanese comments in his log; telephone interview with author, May 1999.

27. For example of a Japanese UTU log, see Station H Operator Logs, December 3 to 8, 1941, Tokyo Time (the only pre-Pearl Harbor logs so far released) in RG 38, Station US papers, MMRB, Archives II, also author's file.

28. For Kisner's "drastic action" quote, see Station H Chronology, p. 2, dated December 4, 1941, RG 38, Station US papers, copy in author's file. A typeset copy of the Chronology for December 1–6, 1941, is published in PHPT 37, pp. 725 to 728. Radio traffic chief, Homer Kisner analyzed the communication data in the batch on intercepts and concluded that Japan's navy was preparing for drastic action: "The large number of high-precedence messages and general distribution might indicate that the entire Navy is being instructed to be prepared for drastic action."

29. Garstka did not record any radio response from the cruiser *Tone* in his Station H logbook. See Note 26 supra.

30. For "The Carriers" remaining in vicinity of Kyushu, see Station H Chronology of December 4, 1941, RG 38, Station US papers, MMRB, Archives II, copy author's file.

31. Homer Kisner, interviewed by the author in April 1988 (audiotape at Carlsbad, California) and April 1998 (video interview during Kisner's visit to Sacramento, California). Transcripts of audio and video interviews, plus correspondence, notes, and telephone interviews between April 1988 and April 1998, are in author's file.

32. See Station H Chronology of November 20, 1941 (p. 81 loc. cit.), which associates Japanese warships of Cruiser Division Eight and Destroyer Squadron One with what Kisner called the Carrier Divisions (Kisner's capitalization). He included different Carrier Commands and Carriers for emphasis. These warships were associated together by Station H from early November onward as they trained together in air operations, refueling at sea drills and moving to the assembly point, Hitokappu Bay during the period of November 20–24, 1941, Tokyo Time. On November 17, Kisner reported "DesRon One seems to be operating with the Carriers and that the Commander Carriers (Admiral Nagumo) was aboard the *Akagi*." (See p. 79 of H Chronology.) There was one apparent error in Kisner's analysis. He reported that the battleship *Kirishima* was "believed" to be at the Yokosuka Navy Base (southeast of Tokyo) on November 25, 1941, when actually the warship was at Hitokappu Bay on that date (see p. 88 of the H Chronology). See H Chronology, RG 38, Station US papers, MMRB, Archives II, copy in author's file.

33. Kisner's report on "war time basis," see Station H Chronology, p. 2. December 6, 1941 under General, RG 38, Station US papers, MMRB, Archives II.

34. For Kisner's conclusion, "They are going to jump us," is in a video interview with the author, April 1998, Sacramento, CA, in author's file.
35. For Japanese radio deception, see Captain Sadatoshi Tomioka, quoted in PHPT 1, p. 238.
36. For Admiral T. B. Inglis' testimony regarding Japanese radio deception, see PHPT 1, p. 185.
37. For Edwin Layton's description of Japanese radio deception, see his book, *And I Was There* (William Morrow, 1985), p. 228.
38. See Paul Seaward's intercept of Japanese naval air stations in Station H operator log December 6, 1941, Tokyo Time, p. 123. RG 38, Station US papers, MMRB, Archives II. Seaward wrote in the log: "Note Air Sta's 9 KE KU, 1 NI KU and others working just below 8040 (kilocycles)." Seaward did not copy any messages from the air stations, according to the log. Seaward, one of the watch supervisors at Station H and an experienced intercept operator, did not suggest deception was involved, but the fact that he did not see fit to copy the messages involving the Air Stations is significant.
39. See Fred Thomson report, Station AE, December 1941 report, p. 5, under "Radio Deception." RG 181, NA, Seattle, copy in author's file.
40. See Joseph Rochefort's Oral History, *The Reminiscences of Captain Joseph J. Rochefort* (US Naval Institute, Oral History Office, 1970), p. 157, copy in author's file.

CHAPTER 13

1. For Admiral Kimmel's quote, "if I had anything," see PHPT 6–2632.
2. For Rochefort's quote, "cheap price," see *The Reminiscences of Captain Joseph J. Rochefort* (US Naval Institute Oral History Division, 1970), p. 163.
3. For Thomas Dyer's quote, " There is not the slightest. . . ," see his letter to the author, June 4, 1983, author's file. See also written statement submitted to the Joint Congressional Committee on the Pearl Harbor attack by Captain Laurance Safford, commanding officer of Station US in 1941: "The 5–Num system yielded no information which would arouse even a suspicion of the Pearl Harbor raid either before or afterward." See RG 80, PHLO, Box 49 MMRB, Archives II. Quoted by Edwin Layton in *And I Was There* (William Morrow, 1985), p. 548, note 27.
4. For the weather message sent to the First Air Fleet by Radio Tokyo on November 27, 1941 warning of typhoon conditions in the North Pacific, see RG 457, SRN 116668, MMRB, Archives II, copy in author's file. Tokyo Radio said the storm's winds reached from 15 meters to 26 meters (34 m.p.h. to 58 m.p.h.) Conversion courtesy Dan Plumlee, Geography Department, University of California, Berkeley.
5. *Kuroshio* translates as Black Current, so-called because its waters carried the black-hulled ships of foreign nations, including those of the United States–Japan Expedition of 1854, commanded by Commodore Matthew Perry. The Perry expedition opened trade between Japan and America. Lieutenant Silas Bent, navigator for Perry, described the *Kuroshio* as 75 km wide with a depth of 900 meters. He said it originated in the East China Sea and formed two branches. The more powerful skirted the east coast of Japan, then turned northeast at about 40° N, 143° E. Its speed of 35–40 miles per day permitted fast sailing time. See Bent's report and his chart of the *Kuro-Siwo* (1857 spelling) in Francis L. Hawks, *Narrative of the Expedition of an American Squadron to the China Seas and Japan* (D. Appleton & Co., New York, 1857), p. 495. A black-ship festival is held at Shimoda, Japan, site of the first American trade center, according to the Tourist Industry Bureau, Ministry of Transportation, ed., *Japan The Official Guide* (Japan Travel Bureau, 1962), p. 367.
6. See Iki Kuromoti, written description of his journey to Pearl Harbor aboard the light cruiser HIJMS *Abukuma*, flagship of Destroyer Squadron One. His account is part of the Exhibits of the Joint Congressional Committee in PHPT 13, 516 ff. A note on the translation suggests Kuromoti might be the nom de plume of an enlisted man aboard the *Abukuma*. Kuromoti describes the departure from Hitokappu Bay, the fierce storm that washed men overboard, etc. In the western Pacific, fierce ocean storms that are called hurricanes in the eastern Pacific are called typhoons.
7. On the *Akagi*'s transmitter being tuned to 4960 kilocycles, see the interception of the

Japanese radio call sign of 8 YU NA (November call sign of *Akagi*) in contact with another Japanese warship in a report by Robert Fox, radioman-in-charge at Station KING, Dutch Harbor Naval Air Station, Territory of Alaska, November 1941 monthly report, p. 3, RG 181, Commandant of Thirteenth Naval District (COM 13) A-6 report, National Archives, Seattle, WA; declassified October 9, 1985 by Donald Piff, Director of National Archives, Seattle, WA, copy in author's file. According to a general alert sent by Station SAIL to the Dutch Harbor RDF intercept station on December 3, 1941, these Japanese radio transmissions were executed in less than ten seconds in an attempt to lessen chance of discovery and interception by British and American cryptographers. See RG 181, NA, Seattle; COM 13 Secret file, Serial 202210, dated 12/3/41.

For identification of 8 YU NA as the *Akagi* (with a question mark), see Station H Chronology of November 28, 1941, secret call list for November 1941, p. 133, copy in author's file. Station H, the intercept facility for Station HYPO, issued a monthly report consisting of at least four sections: (1) a daily Chronology listing important Japanese naval intercepts; (2) identification of secret (sometimes referred to as tactical, meaning that the unit was involved in operations as opposed to purely administrative matters) Japanese call signs and warship addresses for naval units originating radio transmissions; (3) Code Movement reports, with radio direction finder bearings locating Japanese warships and *marus;* (4) individual supervisor reports from each eight hour watch. The November 1941 Station H monthly report totaled 134 numbered pages and was released to the author by the Naval Security Group Command under a FOIA request in 1985. Another crucial and separate part of the Station H records is the operator logs (HOPSLOGS) that recorded every intercepted Japanese naval transmission. About 65 intercept operators shared the work load of eight hours on, sixteen hours off, and kept a running account of the Japanese communication data in the logs. A separate log, called Message Sheets, documented the text of each message. It went on 24 hours a day without letup from July 1 to the attack of December 7, 1941. In this book, these operator logs are abbreviated as HOPSLOGS. But again beware. The Navy has released only five days of the pre-Pearl Harbor HOPSLOGS: December 4, 5, 6, 7, and 8, 1941. Since the logs were kept in Tokyo Time the dates correspond in part to December 3–7, 1941, Hawaii Time. None of the HOPSLOGS prior to December 3, 1941 have been released. None of the estimated hundreds of thousands of Message Sheets that record the Japanese navy's original text have been declassified and released to the public.

The Station H records were transferred to Archives II, College Park, Maryland in 1994 as part of the Station US collection and placed in Record Group 38. A limited release of the Station H records took place in January 1995 at Archives II and those records no longer require a FOIA request. The November and December Station H Monthly Reports can be found in Box 9 of the January 1995 release. But please note: the entire Station US collection which contains the Station H records, is estimated to include over 1,000,000 documents; these are in various stages of declassification and cataloguing. The author found he could examine about 300 documents per day. An examination of the entire collection, working 365 days per year, would cover 109,500 records. At that rate, plan on at least nine years for examining the entire collection.

For further identification of 8 YU NA as the *Akagi*, see two TESTM reports of Station CAST, November 14, 1941, secret serial 141522, and November 27, 1941, secret serial 281511, in RG 38, Station US papers, TESTM file, MMRB, Archives II, copy in author's file. See also Station H report of hearing carriers transmitting on 4963 kilocycles on November 26, 1941 in HMORPT, p. 89; see Station HYPO Communication Summary (COMSUM) of November 30, 1941 which reports hearing the *Akagi* on tactical radio circuits in contact with several *marus*, in RG 80, PHLO, Box 41, MMRB, Archives II. See Edwin Layton's contrary view (without confirming details) that the *Akagi* was misidentified, in his biography *And I Was There* (William Morrow, 1985), p. 227. Homer Kisner's placement of the HIJMS *Hiryu* relied on radio direction finder bearings submitted by Station CAST. Kisner placed the carrier *Hiryu* in Japan's Inland Sea near the city of Kure on November 29, 1941. Kisner apparently based his estimate on CAST's RDF bearing taken on November 26 (Hawaii Time) when the *Hiryu* was about a day out of Hitokappu Bay.

CAST did not place the carrier at Kure, but reported the bearing as 30 degrees from Corregidor—a northern bearing line that takes in the offshore waters of Hitokappu Bay (see the Great Circle Chart on p. 191 of this book. Technically the great circle bearing of 30 degress could also be southward from Corregidor—through the South China Sea and Indian Ocean—an illogical location for the carrier). For the *Hiryu* bearing by CAST, see the TESTM report, secret serial 281511, in RG 38, Station US papers, MMRB, Archives II, copy in author's file.

There were 31 warships in the First Air Fleet proceeding through the North Pacific, plus two more in the Central Pacific known as the Midway Neutralization Unit (sometimes translated as the Midway Destruction Unit) according to figures prepared by Rear Admiral Sadatoshi Tomioka, Operations Chief, Navy General Staff, cited in Gordon Prange, *At Dawn We Slept* (McGraw Hill, 1981), p. 416.

8. Solar storms affecting radio/telegraph and voice transmissions in the winter of 1941–42 were predicted several months in advance in 1941, in bulletins issued by the United States Department of Commerce, National Bureau of Standards (NBS) entitled *Radio Transmission Handbook* (NBSHB). Each bulletin (and addendum), updating solar storm conditions as predicted by the NBS, was forwarded to all naval commandants and Navy radio facilities, including the intercept stations. See the *Radio Transmission Handbook, Frequencies 1000 to 30,000 KC* (prepared by the National Bureau of Standards, Washington, DC, under the sponsorship of the Communications Section National Defense Research Committee). Selected NBS comments taken from the *Handbook* by the author follow: the range of the radio waves is accelerated over ocean waters because of the greater electrical conductivity of the ocean (p. 15); ionosphere storms are most severe in northern latitudes and decrease in intensity toward the equator (p. 13). High frequency radio waves—above 2000 kcs—are given a boost by the storms (p. 9). Ionosphere is the region 30 to 300 miles above the earth's surface that reflects radio waves (p. 5). See the looseleaf *Handbook*, in RG 181, Box 196506, NA, Laguna Niguel, CA, copy in author's file. The solar storm over the weekend of Nov. 28–Dec. 1, 1941 reached "disaster" proportions on December 1, when the NBS rated the storm at 8 on a scale of 0 to 9. See NSB report in RG 181, COM 14 files, San Bruno, CA for Dec. 1941 to Feb. 1942, copy in author's file. For use of frequencies in the 4960–4980 kilocycle range to overcome radio interference by solar storms (a.k.a., the Dellinger effect), see SRH-355, pp. 273–275, RG 457, Station US papers, MMRB, Archives II. Solar storm interference varies throughout the northern latitudes, and by time of year, daylight versus night; radio transmission bounce can last from minutes to hours.

9. In naval parlance, "type command" refers to vessels of all same military purposes: battleships are a type; ditto cruisers, carriers, etc. See two Homer Kisner interviews with author April 1988 in Carlsbad, California (audio tape, still photographs, transcript and follow up correspondence), and in April 1999 in Sacramento, California (video tape, still photographs, transcript). Both interview sessions were augmented by telephone conversations and correspondence during a ten year span from 1988 to 1998; transcripts and correspondence are in author's file.

10. For identification of the *Kyokuto Maru* and its close radio association with the Commander Carriers, see Communication Summary of October 9, 1941 in RG 80, PHLO, Box 41, MMRB, Archives II, copy in author's file.

11. For the *Kyokuto's* code movement reports obtained by Station H in November 1941, see November 1941, Chronology of Station H, pp. 96, 99, 100, and identification of its secret radio call sign of 4 U I, see p. 128 in RG 38, Station US papers, MMRB, Archives II; also in author's file.

12. The commanding officer of the *Kyokuto Maru* placed aboard the aircraft carrier HIJMS *Kaga*, see Communication Summary for October 27, 1941, loc. cit. For Admiral Kimmel examining COMSUMS each morning at 8:15 A.M., see Layton testimony at PHPT 10 p. 4833. The *Kaga* served as the temporary flagship of Admiral Nagumo while the *Akagi* was refitting at the Yokosuka naval base.

13. For Kimmel's question to his intelligence chief Edwin Layton, "Where are the carriers?" see PHPT 36, p. 128. See Layton's book *And I Was There* (William Morrow, 1985), p. 243. Layton's *Akagi* intercept testimony to the Congressional investigation on February 18, 1946: "The fact that *Akagi* was that day (November 30, 1941) exercising with several *marus* was brought to my attention and the admiral noted it also.

He asked me what I thought, as I recall it, and I said the *Akagi* was probably talking to some tanker *marus, marus* being merchant ships and probably going to get oil." PHPT 10, p. 4836. Layton then testified, "Since the middle of November the association of forces, the tying together of your task forces, the commander of carriers, or carrier division commander, with the exception of Carrier Division 3, were not addressed, were not associated, and apparently were entirely aloof from the whole proceeding," PHPT 10, p. 4837. Layton repeated that neither the carriers, the carrier division commanders, or the carrier commander in chief were ever addressed, "not even once," PHPT 10, p. 4839. Layton on the disappearance of the carriers: "My own personal opinion was that the carriers were remaining in home waters preparing for operations so that they would be in a covering position in case we moved against Japan," PHPT 10, p. 4840.

14. For an additional statement by Edwin Layton that the Japanese carriers had neither sent nor originated radio messages since mid-November 1941, see his book *And I Was There*, p. 243: "There was no traffic—or traffic analysis—to or from these carriers or their commanders."

15. For Joseph Rochefort's testimony that he didn't lose the carriers but found them in a negative sense, see exchange with Congressman John Murphy (D., PA) on February 15, 1946 during the Joint Congressional Investigation, found at PHPT 10, p. 4681. But see his answer to a follow-up question posed by Murphy: "Is it the usual plan, when you have a war warning and you cannot account for carriers, that you prepare for the worst?" Rochefort: "Yes, sir." PHPT 10, p. 4682.

16. See a letter from Richard A. von Doenhoff to the author NNRM93–RVD, July 9, 1993, in author's file. For the original Communications Summaries (COMSUMS) prepared by Station HYPO in 1941 that were read and initialed by Admiral Kimmel, see RG 80, PHLO, Box 41 (includes the mutilated copies), Archives II, duplicate copy in author's file.

17. See Stephen E. Ambrose, *Pearl Harbor Revisited* (St. Martin's Press, 1995), pp. 99–100. Ambrose repeated this charge in a *Wall Street Journal* opinion piece on May 27, 1999: "The real problem was that American intelligence was terrible (sound familiar?)" (Parentheses by Ambrose.) Homer Kisner told the author that Stephen Ambrose never contacted him for comment on the Navy's 1941 communications intelligence operations.

18. Duane Whitlock interviewed by the author in Danville, California, September 1993, audio tape, transcript, notes, in author's file. Follow up telephone calls, notes and correspondence and e-mail in May and June 1999 with Whitlock at Strawberry Point, Iowa, author's file. Author's interview of Homer Kisner, April 1988 (audiotape transcript, still photographs, notes), in author's file. A second interview with Kisner while he was on a family automotive tour, video taped at Sacramento, California, April 1998 (still photographs, notes, and video tape transcript), in author's file.

   With the guidance of Captain Homer Kisner, the 1941 radio traffic chief for the Pacific Fleet, and Captain Duane Whitlock, traffic analyst for Station CAST, the author located evidence of the carriers and commands originating and receiving radio messages between November 15 and December 6, 1941. Both Navy captains have impeccable professional reputations. Both were cited for their intercept and cryptographic skills between July 1941 and June 1942 and placed on the Midway Cryptographic Honor Roll by Admiral Chester Nimitz. In 1941–42, both were chief radiomen and later advanced to commissioned officers. As of this writing, both are retired; Kisner lives in California, Whitlock in Iowa. For over fifty years, both these giants in American naval cryptography have been ignored by Congress and every Pearl Harbor investigation, excluded by historians, and the media. Yet they were in on all of the major intelligence events of the Pacific War.

19. See the TESTM reports originated by Station CAST in November and December 1941 and received at Station HYPO initialed by Lieutenant Commander Thomas Huckins and Radioman Rodney Whitten of Station HYPO, in RG 38, Station US papers, MMRB, Archives II, copy in author's file.

20. For the documentation of the 129 Japanese naval intercepts involving the carriers and warships of the First Air Fleet between November 15 and December 6, 1941, see the author's compilation based on intercepts found in RG 457 in the SRN intercept series; the TESTM reports of Station CAST; and Station H code movement re-

ports in RG 38, MMRB, Archives II, compilation in author's file. The Station CAST TESTM radio direction finder reports involving the carriers were discussed with Captain Duane Whitlock, at Danville, California, in September 1993; notes, transcript, photographs, audiotape interview in author's file. Intercepts, code movement reports were discussed with Captain Homer Kisner, at Carlsbad, California, in April 1988 (notes, taped audio interview, transcript, and photographs in author's file), and at Sacramento in April 1998; notes, video tape, transcript and photographs, in author's file).

The author arranged the 129 intercepts into seven categories and labeled them from A to G for the purpose of analyzing them for this book: (A) Vice Admiral Chuichi Nagumo, commander-in-chief of the First Air Fleet, originated 60 transmissions in his Secret Message Series (SMS) between November 15 and December 7, 1941 (Hawaii Time); see special booklet prepared by the author and labeled "SMS series, Vol. 1," in author's file. It is a compilation of Nagumo's SMS messages based on the SRN series in RG 38 and 457, Archives II, also in author's file; (B) for the 24 messages dispatched to various First Air Fleet vessels, see RG 38 and 457, loc. cit.; (C) for the 20 transmissions originated by six carriers, see RG 38 and 457, loc. cit.; (D) for the twelve messages originated by the Carrier Division Commanders, see RG 38 and 457, loc. cit.; (E) eight warships attached to the First Air Fleet (not carriers) originated 12 messages, see RG 38 and 457, loc. cit.; (F) the Midway Neutralization Unit (HIJMS *Shiriya* and two destroyers) originated four messages, RG 38 and 457, loc. cit.; and finally (G) there was one message addressed to Carrier Division Four. Entire compilation based on Station US papers, RG 38, 457, Station H code movement reports, Station CAST TESTM files, Archives II, copies in author's file.

21. See article by Koiichi Shimada in *The Japanese Navy in World War II*, Raymond O'Connor, ed., (US Naval Institute Press, 1969), p. 34. The correct title of the command was Imperial Navy General Headquarters. According to Joseph Rochefort's cryptographers at Station HYPO, Admiral Nagano held two titles, Chief of the Navy General Staff (NGS) and Chief of the Imperial Navy General Headquarters (IHQ). When Nagano convened his staff on the palace grounds it became IHQ; at the naval ministry, NGS. According to Station H records, Nagano used different radio call signs to distinguish the commands; see RG 457, SRN series, and RG 38, Station US papers, MMRB, Archives II, copies in author's file. There were six messages transmitted to Japanese naval communications officers in the Formosa/South China area by Radio Tokyo on December 4, 1941 (Tokyo Time), according to Station H records. Three were addressed to units of the Eleventh Air Fleet (AF); two are unidentified as this book goes to press; one was addressed to the China Fleet. See Station H operator log (HOPSLOG), December 4, 1941 (Tokyo Time) for radio call signs: HA O 249 (UNID), KI NE 549 (AF), RE HE 849 (AF), SA HA 049 (UNID), SI HA 149 (AF), TA KE 649 (China), in RG 38, Station US papers, MMRB, Archives II, author's file. The suffix 49 designated radio officers.

22. For identifications of the radio call signs of the Eleventh Air Fleet immediately prior to the attack, see TESTM dispatch with secret serial 051533 of December 4, 1941 (Tokyo Time) found in RG 38, Station US papers, MMRB, Archives II, copy in author's file. The initials RW that appear on the dispatch belong to Rodney Whitten of Rochefort's staff, which confirms that it was received at HYPO.

23. For CU's intercept record of SI HA 149, see the HOPSLOG of December 4, 1941 (Tokyo Time), p. 51, as UTU 8591. CU made the intercept at 3:15 A.M. (or 7:45 A.M., December 3, 1941, Hawaii Time) on 8310 kilocycles.

24. Of Japan's Hawaii force of about 30 fleet submarines (I-boats), eleven were equipped with small float planes. A hangar, catapult, and a service crane for lifting the plane (called an E-14Y by Japan, and Glen by the US Navy) out of the water were installed on the broad afterdeck of each sub. After a flight, the wings of the Glen were dismantled and, along with the fuselage, stored inside the compact hangar. A Glen from the sub *I-25* bombed the Oregon coast near Brookings in September 1942—the only air bombing of the US mainland in World War II. See Dorr Carpenter and Norman Polmar, *Submarines of the Imperial Japanese Navy* (Naval Institute Press, 1986), pp. 5, 6, 7, and 13.

25. For Joseph Rochefort's testimony that he "never received RDF from Samoa," see

the Army Pearl Harbor Proceedings, PHPT 28, p. 868. See SECRET file of Lieut. Cmdr. Thomas Huckins, Confidential Serial ADCO14/12–10, p. 3, RG 38, Station US papers, MMRB, Archives II. For the 300 pages of RDF bearings taken by Station VICTOR between July and December 1941, see the index of Station US papers, folder 3270/5, RG 38, MMRB, Archives II; see the Station VICTOR document tracing RDF to Rochefort in RG 181, file A-6, Samoa, found in NA, San Bruno, CA, copies in author's file.

26. For the PSIS report, see file 500–1, Japanese Submarine Operations, Vol. 1, p. 2, RG 80, PHLO, MMRB, Archives II. For the intercept report (but not its text) of Admiral Shimizu by Stanley Gramblin, see the Station H operator log for December 4, 1941, Tokyo Time, p. 52; RG 38, Station US papers, MMRB, Archives II, copy in author's file.

27. Vice Admiral Shigeyoshi Inoue used his radio call sign RI RO ØØ, according to the log entries of Henry Garstka and LF. See operator logs, Station H, pp. 100 (Garstka), 120 (LF), December 6, 1941 Tokyo Time; RG 38, MMRB, Archives II, copy in author's file. For the English message text of Admiral Inoue's declaration-of-war message, with omissions, see RG 457, SRN 115368, MMRB, Archives II, copy in author's file.

28. For the repeat of Admiral Inoue's war declaration intercept by LF, see Station H operator log, December 6, 1941, p. 120, as RI RO ØØ, NR 951 (Garstka's intercept was NR 952) on 6665 kilocycles at 6:48 P.M. Tokyo Time or 11:18 P.M. December 5, 1941 in Hawaii; see Station US papers, RG 38, MMRB, Archives II, copy in author's file. The letters NR apparently refer to accounting numbers of Japan's dispatching radio station.

29. For Rear Admiral Ugaki's premature release of the Imperial Rescript, see the Station H operator log of December 6, 1941 at 11:20 P.M. (Tokyo Time), which is 3:40 A.M. Saturday, December 6 in Hawaii. Station H intercept operator Maynard Albertson (sine SU) recorded Ugaki's message as number 92. Then 55 minutes later, at 12:15 A.M. (on December 7, Tokyo Time, or 4:45 A.M., on December 6, Hawaii Time), Albertson intercepted Admiral Yamamoto's version as number 93. For the intercept details of Emperor Hirohito's Imperial Rescript, jointly issued with Admiral Yamamoto and received in Hawaii during the early dawn hours of December 6, 1941 (Hawaii Time), see Station US papers, Station H operator log, pp. 101 for Ugaki's number 92, and 124 for Admiral Yamamoto's version, in RG 38, Archives II, copy in author's file. Ugaki used his radio call sign of SE TU 758; Yamamoto used YO WI ØØ which is the same call sign he used for the Climb Mount Niitaka dispatch on December 2. For the English version of the Imperial Transcript intercepted by Albertson, see RG 457, SRN series, SRN 115370 (Rescript), 115371 (Yamamoto's introduction), MMRB, Archives II, copy in author's file. The Emperor also issued separate Rescripts to the Japanese army and navy ministers and to the citizens of Japan. Transmission details have not been disclosed as this book goes to press.

30. Emperor Hirohito's Imperial Rescript was received aboard the cruiser HIJMS *Aoba* on December 7, 1941 (Tokyo Time). See JICPOA item 4986, pp. 3, 15, RG 181, National Archives, San Bruno, CA, copy in author's file.

31. For the the misleading English language version of the Hirohito/Yamamoto Rescript message, see SRN 115371 in RG 457, MMRB, Archives II, copy in author's file. A notation on SRN 115371 claims that the intercept is available only in captured form and is dated December 7, 1941, implying that the Japanese transmission took place after the attack. The transmission date listed is actually Tokyo Time. The censorship has skewed historians' accounts of Emperor Hirohito's message. According to historian Robert J. C. Butow, the Emperor's "annihilate the enemy" rescript was not issued until more than eight hours after the Pearl Harbor attack. See Robert J. C. Butow, *Tojo and the Coming of the War* (Stanford University Press, 1961), p. 408 n. 5. Of the approximately 1,000 intercepts collected by operators of Station H during the period 8:00 A.M. December 5 to 8:00 A.M. December 6, 1941 (Hawaii Standard Time), only six have been declassified by the National Security Agency (NSA). Since Jesse Randle's intercepts did not enter the pipeline until the morning of December 7, they are not included in this discussion.

32. On carriers operating with Japanese Cruiser Division Eight and Destroyer

Squadron One, see Station H Chronology for November 20, 1941, p. 81, RG 38, Station US papers, MMRB, Archives II, copy in author's file.

33. For Kisner quote, "the only time I forecast war," see transcript of Kisner's video interview by the author, Sacramento, CA, on April 24, 1998, in author's file.

34. For quote by Thomas Dyer, "no warm bodies," see Dyer's letter to the author, June 4, 1983, in author's file.

35. Confirmation of the decoding and translation of complete Japanese warship movement reports is murky. Captain Al Pelletier, a Station US cryptologist in 1941, wrote that 90 percent of the text of the Japanese navy's ship movement code could be read in Washington prior to December 7, 1941; see *Cryptolog*, Summer 1992, p. 5. Hawaii's Navy cryptographers could also decrypt the code, according to Joseph Rochefort, commander of Station HYPO. Rochefort testified to the Congressional Investigating Committee on February 15, 1946 that his staff could handle and translate the ship movements. See his testimony in PHPT 10, p. 4678. If so, a question still lingers: why didn't Pelletier at Station US and Rochefort at HYPO decrypt and translate the *Shiriya*'s message for Admiral Kimmel? The Pacific Fleet and the sailors of Battleship Row needed to know. There has never been an answer to the Navy's failure to divulge the *Shiriya*'s intercept. The intercept was never introduced before any Pearl Harbor investigation so none of the investigators could get answers. Homer Kisner did not recall the *Shiriya* report, but did remember obtaining position reports of Japanese war ships between Hawaii and the Empire, and concluded that Japan was "going to jump us"; video interview of Kisner by the author, April 24, 1998, Sacramento, CA, transcript, videotape, still photographs, notes, and correspondence, in author's file. *Shiriya* filed eight code movement reports in November that appear to have been decrypted at Station H. See Monthly Report of Station H, November 1941, RG 38, Station US papers, MMRB, Archives II, copy in author's file. Captain Minoru Togo of the *Shiriya* was the son of Admiral Heihachiro Togo, Japan's famed hero and the victor of the Russian fleet battle, May 1905.

36. On Vice Admiral William Halsey's search in the area of Wake Island, see the Deck Log of the USS *Enterprise*, Halsey's flagship, for December 1 to 7, 1941, RG 24, MMRB, Archives II, copy in author's file. Flight operation schedules show that Halsey conducted daily morning and evening reconnaissance flights.

37. See the radio frequency charts issued by the US Department of Commerce, National Bureau of Standards, November 1941 to February 1942. The Bureau of Standards radio section suggested using radio frequencies that were capable of reaching radio receivers operating in the open ocean waters of the North Pacific at various hours of the day and night during that time frame. By coincidence, the National Bureau of Standards used the 40° N for the North Pacific open ocean communication baseline—the approximate west to east route used by Japan's First Air Fleet on its Hawaiian journey. Included among the recommended frequencies were those that ranged from 11,000 to 16,000 kilocycles. A first day communications intelligence student, aware that Radio Tokyo and Radio Ominato were transmitting to warships using the 11,000 to 16,000 kilocycle range, could consult the Bureau's charts and could approximate—if not pinpoint—the position of the vessels. The frequency charts were seasonal and published by the Bureau throughout 1941; they took into account the solar storm activity that disrupted radio communications in the Northern Hemisphere. For the November 1941 to February 1942 charts, see RG 181, Eleventh Naval District, A-6 radio files, Box 196506, National Archives, Laguna Niguel, California, copy in author's file. Operators at Station H who heard Tokyo calling the tankers (but no replies were heard) were Roy Lehman, William Eaton, and Charles Southerland. See the Station H Log Book, RG 38, Station US papers, MMRB, Archives II, copy in author's file.

38. For reaction to the so-called United States ultimatum of November 26, 1941, see *The Reminiscences of Joseph Rochefort*, p. 66 ff. See also the comment on the ultimatum by Ensign Kazuo Sakamaki, the Japanese midget sub commander captured as Prisoner of War Number 1 when his sub ran aground on Oahu on December 7: "Your honorable 'have' country placed an economic blockade on the 'have not' country." PHLO, RG 80, MMRB, Archives II. On Cordell Hull's *modus vivendi*, see PHPT 14, p. 1157. FDR's handwritten note is in the same location at p. 1142.

39. For Secretary of State Hull's *modus vivendi*, see PHPT 14, p. 1150; see also discussion on the *modus vivendi* in Harry Elmer Barnes, *Perpetual War for Perpetual Peace* (Caxton Printers, 1953), p. 344, ff.

40. For copy of FDR's handwritten note to Hull, see PHPT 14, p. 1142.

41. Since the Climb Mount *Niitaka* message was sent to some Japanese naval commands that lacked cryptographic expertise, Admiral Yamamoto couldn't take a chance on encrypting the message in the complicated Code Book D (5–Num). Smaller commands—picket boats, coastal lookouts, and other smaller units needed to get the word, but didn't have the sophistication or the trained cryptologists to decipher Code Book D (the 5–Num code). They would have been out in the cold, unable to decipher the D-code messages. So apparently, according to some Japanese historians and Edwin Layton, the intelligence chief for the Pacific Fleet, Admiral Yamamoto decided to use Code Book A—the hidden-word code. From the A code book, he chose "*Niitaka Yama Nobore* 1208": "Climb Mt. *Niitaka* December 8." Japan's foreign ministry, army, and navy each had a special hidden word code for the war's start. "East Wind Rain," served the foreign ministry; "The black kite, eagle, and hawk will fly December 8" was the code for the Imperial Army. See the *Niitaka* dispatch reproduced on p. 221 of this book.

42. Joseph Christie Howard arrived in Hawaii from Station US on March 6, 1941. He had acquired the latest skills on Japanese naval radio communications and code procedures from his Washington, DC instructor Anton Novak, one of the US Navy's brightest code breakers. Novak is on the Midway Cryptographic Honor Roll. The author's twelve-year search for Joseph C. Howard in the naval records was difficult. He was carried on the official Navy roster of Station H as James C. Howard. Finally in May 1999 the author located him, living happily with his wife in Kent, Washington. Howard apologized for the name mix up but said it wasn't his fault; it was the Navy's. "And they had the guts to ask me for six thousand dollars to change the wording on a plaque at the Naval Security Group Command Headquarters from the misnamed James to Joseph," Howard said in a telephone interview with the author.

43. Edwin Layton provided four versions concerning the transmission (or lack thereof) of the *Niitaka* message to the 1945–46 Joint Congressional Committee investigating Pearl Harbor. He began by stating: (1) "I am being honest with you. The message was never transmitted by the Japanese" (to Senator Ferguson [R., MI], on the evening of Feb. 18, 1946. PHPT 10, p. 4906); then he said, "The message was broadcast in plain language" (to Rep. Murphy [D., PA], PHPT 10, p. 4908); then, "Message never heard or intercepted in Hawaii" (to Rep. Murphy PHPT 10, 4909); and then "We did not have the message in Hawaii" (to Rep. Murphy, PHPT 10, 4908). A fifth version appeared in his book: "[The message] was intercepted at Station SAIL and thus not available in Hawaii" (Edwin Layton, *And I Was There*, p. 242). His sixth version emerged at his Carmel, California home, November 29, 1982, when the author interviewed him for this book. The interview went well until the author asked him about these inconsistencies and his failure to pass the *Niitaka* dispatch to his boss, Admiral Kimmel. Layton became visibly angry, quickly rose from his chair, and indicated that the interview was over.

44. Author's telephone interviews, correspondence, and notes with Joseph Christie Howard, Kent, Washington, June 1999, in author's file. Howard said his sine XT which appears on all his 1941 Navy intercepts, was adopted from his grandfather's shorthand; the latter abbreviated Christie as XT (similar to Xmas).

45. See: Hiroyuki Agawa, *The Reluctant Admiral* (Naval Institute Press, 1979), p. 244. The *Niitaka* message was drafted aboard Admiral Yamamoto's flagship, HIJMS *Nagato*, on December 2, 1941, and released for radio transmission at 1500 (3:00 P.M. Tokyo Time) by his chief of staff, Rear Admiral Matome Ugaki. Yamamoto had been called to Tokyo to receive an Imperial Rescript from Emperor Hirohito. The message was transmitted by the Tokyo Navy Signals Unit, whose call letters were HA FU 6. By not using the *Nagato*'s transmitter, Japan hoped to conceal Yamamoto's identity as the originator of the message. The ruse did not work. His most secret radio call sign, YO WI ØØ, was heard and identified at Stations CAST and H on December 2 and 6. Transmission of the message to the entire Japanese Navy took most of the night hours; see Kanya Miyauchi *Niitaka Yama Nobore 1208* (Tokyo: Rikkyou Shuppan, 1976), p. 19. In his four-volume history of the Pacific War, Takushiro Hattori

writes that the *Niitaka* dispatch was sent in "clear text." See Takushiro Hattori, *Dai-Toa Senso Zenshi* (Complete History of the Greater East Asia War), 4 vols, (Tokyo: Masu Shobo, 1953), pp. 345–349 and 362. On December 2, Tokyo Time, the Imperial Japanese Army also notified its commands of the war's start using the agreed-language (hidden-meaning) code: "The black kite, eagle, and hawk will fly December 8"; see Hattori, loc. cit., pp. 348, 349. Translations for this book were made by Sean and Naemi McPherson, Japanese language translators, University of California at Berkeley.

46. In his correspondence and telephone interview with the author, Howard confirmed that he worked the midnight to eight A.M. watch on Tuesday, December 2, 1941. At the conclusion of the shift he turned over his intercepts to the watch supervisor, Elliott Okins. That was the last he saw of the intercepts until 58 years later, in June 1999 when the author asked him to authenticate the English version of his famed intercept as found in Archives II. Howard instantly recognized his sine that he had copied from his grandfather, but could not recall whether the original message was in plain Japanese or the 5–Num code. "It's been too long. I do recall copying a few Japanese plain language messages in the weeks before Pearl Harbor but I can't confirm this *Niitaka* message was among them." Howard agreed that the message was probably the most historic of World War II, for it catapulted the United States into what had been called a European war. Congress declared war on Japan, December 8, followed with declarations against Germany and Italy on December 11, 1941. Throughout the globe, it was World War II. Howard said the mystery of whether Admiral Yamamoto's start-the-war order was in plain language or in 5–Num code could easily be solved by examining the message sheet on which he typed the original text. He recalled he had worked two of the Underwood code typewriters, called RIP 5's. "One was for my operator log; the other, for the message text, was on a stand with casters that I could roll about for convenience." Telephone interviews of Joseph C. Howard by the author, June 1999, notes in author's file.

47. See author's FOIA requests directed to Admirals Studemann, McConnell, and Stevens as well as FOIAs to National Security Agency and National Archives, in author's file.

48. See author's interviews with Homer Kisner, April 1988 and April 1998, transcript, notes, audio tapes in author's file.

49. See RK's comments in SRN 115376, RG 457, Archives II. Beware of the blacked out version. Item Time, written on the intercept that is reproduced in this book on p. 221 by RK, refers to Japan Time. The ninth letter of the alphabet refers to nine hours subtracted from Greenwich Mean Time, England, hence the minus-nine time. Mount *Niitaka* is on Formosa; its 13,075–foot peak is 500 feet higher that Mount *Fuji* in Japan.

50. In telephone interviews with the author on June 15 and 28, 1999, Howard estimated it took less than five minutes to record Admiral Yamamoto's war start order directed at the United States and her allies in his log book and on the message sheet. He said that if the message was in plain language it was called Romanji by the operators at Station H. "We did not refer to the letters as *kana* in 1941," Howard said. Station CAST obtained a radio direction finder bearing on a Yamamoto radio call sign of YO WI ØØ on December 2. The identical call sign appears on the *Niitaka* message intercepted at Station H and provides circumstantial evidence that the message was available to MacArthur and Hart in Manila, see TESTM file, Station US papers, Archives II, copy in author's file. According to the Station H operator logs, Admiral Yamamoto only used the call sign, YO WI ØØ, twice during the week of December 1 to 6; once for the *Niitaka* message on December 2, the other for a message on December 6. Obviously Station CAST identified Yamamoto's call sign of YO WI ØØ from the *Niitaka* message; this indicates that it was intercepted on Corregidor by one of the operators on duty.

A major historical question is then raised: Did General MacArthur and Admiral Hart receives copies of *Niitaka*? (For MacArthur's access to intercepts obtained by Station CAST, see Note 53 below.) Captain Duane Whitlock who was one of three radio traffic analysts at CAST in December 1941, agreed that if the message was in plain Japanese he or the other analysts/cryptographers would have instantly recognized its impact and would have sounded the alarm, but he could not recall the *Niitaka* message during telephone interviews with the author in May and June 1999, notes in author's file.

Whitlock, a radioman first class in 1941, had no recollection of seeing Admiral Yamamoto's start-the-war order. Later, Whitlock, then stationed in Melbourne, Australia, was part of the American cryptographic team that in 1943 intercepted and decoded an air-flight itinerary for Admiral Yamamoto and directed US Army Air Force fighters to its path in the Solomon Islands. There the admiral's twin-engine bomber was shot down; Yamamoto died in the crash.

51. See Elliott Okins' report in Station H monthly report under date of December 2, 1941, in RG 38, Station US papers, MMRB, Archives II, copy in author's file.

52. See Communications Summary for December 2, 1941, p. 2, RG 80, PHLO, MMRB, Archives II, copy in author's file.

53. On March 25, 1941, Station CAST was directed to coordinate its intercept activities involving the Japanese army, navy, and diplomatic code systems with General MacArthur's intercept unit, Station SIX on Corregidor. In turn, MacArthur was ordered to use rapid means to furnish copies of all Japanese diplomatic intercepts to Station CAST, whose translators would furnish English translations directly to him. The order by Army Chief of Staff General George Marshall was: "Deliver exact translation of this message to MacArthur." See: OPNAV, released by Admiral Ingersoll, and dispatched in the Navy's GATOF code system as SECRET serial 251500, March 25, 1941, RG 38, MMRB, Archives II, copy in author's file.

54. On the conversion of the Del Monte airfields on Mindanao Island to landing strips for B-17 bombers, see the files of the MacArthur Memorial, MacArthur Square, operated by the City of Norfolk, Virginia.

55. On McMorris's "Never" comment, see PHPT 22, p. 526. For McMorris's action plan, see RG 80, PHLO file, MMRB, Archives II, and PHPT 33, p.1348.

CHAPTER 14

1. See Cecil Brown, *Suez to Singapore* (Halcyon House, 1943), p. 284. Kimmel wrote that he obtained news from "the radio and newspapers," see Husband E. Kimmel, *Admiral Kimmel's Story*, Henry Regnery Company, 1955), p. 94. See also Admiral Kimmel's testimony to the 1944 Navy Court of Inquiry: "I got a major part of my diplomatic information from the newspapers," PHPT 32, p. 237.

2. For contrasting Admiral Kimmel's statements concerning the lack of long range air search plans and the so-called unavailability of scouting aircraft on the morning of December 7, 1941, see the actual status of the long-range planes that were available to him at Pearl Harbor that morning in PHPT 24, p. 1367. He discusses Hawaiian long range search activities in his book *Admiral Kimmel's Story*, pp. 14 ff. and 65 ff., but does not explain grounding the 54 planes that were available for long-range reconnaissance on December 7, 1941. Critics have blasted Kimmel for what they see as his perceived failure to place reconnaissance aircraft in the air. But he had an ideal defense to the charge: His orders from Washington were explicit: Stand aside and permit Japan to commit the first overt act of war. See *Admiral Kimmel's Story*, p. 15 where he intimates that he expected Japan's air attack would come from the North Pacific: "The type of air attack the Japs actually made was considered the most probable form such an attack would take."

3. Unlike Japanese military messages which were hidden from Congress, the two Foreign Office messages indicating war with America and Britain on pp. 225–26 were introduced before the Joint Committee on the Investigation of the Pearl Harbor Attack (JOINT) in 1945–46.

4. General Marshall's December 7 message was dispatched by Western Union landlines in the United States from Washington to Oakland, California, then by RCA wireless facilities on the headlands of Marin County, north of San Francisco, to Honolulu. It reached RCA's South King Street office in Honolulu at 7:33 A.M. An attendant telephoned to Short's headquarters asking for delivery instructions. No one answered the phone, so the message was dispatched by motorcycle messenger to Fort Shafter. The messenger arrived at the US Army's Fort Shafter at 11:45 A.M. Decoding delays ensued and the message was not delivered directly to General Short until 2:58 P.M. He then sent a copy to Admiral Kimmel, who threw it in a wastebasket: "It is not of the slightest interest to me now." For delivery time to Fort Shafter in

Honolulu, see PHPT 9, p. 4404; see also General Walter Short's papers, Hoover Institution Archives, Stanford University, Stanford, CA.

5. Foreign Minister Shigenori Togo's memo was dated Tokyo Time. See PHPT 12, p. 238.

6. The "thirteen-part" message was actually one message, broken into thirteen parts by the wireless firms for transmissions purposes; see the thirteen-part message 902 in PHPT 12, pp. 239–245. In 1941, wireless messages were divided into groups of fifty words (or code groups) for ease of transmission, then dispatched over the airwaves. Apparently the thirteen-part message contains 650 words or encoded groups of five letters each. In their testimony given to the 1945–46 Joint Congressional Investigation into Pearl Harbor, neither Kramer nor Schulz fully described the items contained in their presidential deliveries, nor did they clarify whether or not there were military intercepts in the pouch. In 1941 the naval aide's office was located in the mail room of what is now the Old Executive Office Building, adjacent to the west wing of the White House.

7. See PHPT 12, pp. 239 ff., for a complete English translation of the fourteen-part message. For Francis M. Brotherhood's testimony on intercepts 380 and 381, see PHPT 33, pp. 843 ff. See also Station SAIL December 1941 report, p. 2, RG 187, A-6 secret file, National Archives, Seattle, copy in author's file.

8. For Lester Schulz' testimony to the Joint Congressional Investigating Committee in 1946, see PHPT 10, p. 4663.

9. During the Congressional hearings in 1946, Senator Homer Ferguson praised Lieut. Cmdr. Kramer: "At least we had someone running that night," see PHPT 9, p. 4043.

10. For the English text of message 381 (Part 14), see PHPT 12, p. 245.

11. See John Beardall, PHPT 11, pp. 5287 ff. Chief White House Usher Howell Crim did not record the Saturday night visit of Lester Schulz. Instead the White House Usher Book records the Roosevelts as hosting a dinner for 34 persons, highlighted by a violin concert by Arthur LeBlanc, which ended at 10:55 P.M. The December 7 Usher Book does not record Beardall's 10:00 A.M. arrival/delivery. The record begins at 12:30 P.M. listing a visit by the Chinese Ambassador. FDR and Harry Hopkins were served lunch in the Oval Study at 1:15 P.M. which was 7:45 A.M. in Hawaii. The first bomb drops were ten minutes away. White House Usher Books, FDRL, copy in author's file.

12. Admiral Stark's version of the midnight telephone call is suspect. During his initial testimony to the Congressional investigation, he denied having a telephone conversation with the President Saturday night: "To the best of my knowledge and belief, the President did not call me that night," PHPT 11, p. 5157. But when his flag secretary contradicted Stark's account, the admiral admitted his telephone conversation with Roosevelt. Throughout his Congressional Pearl Harbor testimony Stark was evasive and defensive on 343 occasions using such phrases as "I do not know" and "I'm not clear, I'm hazy." He invoked "I can't recall" 160 times. The author's compilations are based on Stark's testimony before the Joint Congressional Investigating committee on December 31, 1945 and January 2, 3, 4, and 5, 1946, in PHPT 5, p. 2096; April 9, and 11, 1946, PHPT 11, p. 5153. For President Roosevelt's reported quote, "Relations with Japan are very critical," see PHPT 11, pp. 5543, 5546, 5557.

13. See testimony of Colonel Rufus Bratton to the Joint Congressional Investigating Committee, February 1946 PHPT 10, p. 4615 ff.

14. For the Army Pearl Harbor Board's conclusion regarding General Marshall, see PHPT 3, p. 1469.

15. See the sworn affidavit of General Walter Bedell Smith dated June 15, 1945 at Frankfurt am Main, and included as part of the Clausen Pearl Harbor Investigation, in PHPT 35, p. 90.

16. For the Keefe-Murphy quarrel of December 13, 1945, see PHPT 3, p. 1560.

17. For the Army Pearl Harbor Board testimony of Pvt. George Elliott, see PHPT 27, pp. 517 ff., for Pvt. Joseph Lockard, see loc. cit., p. 526 ff.

18. For the testimony of Pvt. Joseph McDonald, see PHPT 29, pp. 2121 ff.

19. For Lieutenant Kermit A. Tyler's testimony on hearing Hawaiian music over a local radio station about 4:00 A.M. on Sunday December 7, 1941, see his testimony to the Navy Court of Inquiry, August 17, 1944, PHPT 32, p. 344. Tyler's claim that an unnamed Hawaiian radio station provided a beacon for arriving US mainland aircraft

NOTES

by broadcasting music during the early morning hours is suspect. Both Honolulu radio stations went off the air at their regular closing time of 11:00 P.M. Saturday night. They resumed broadcasts at 6:00 A.M. Sunday morning with public service programing that included church services, according to the technician logs of KGMB and KGU and schedules published in the *Star-Bulletin* on December 6, 1941. See the KGMB and KGU technician logs, Hamilton Library, Manoa Campus, University of Hawaii, Honolulu.

20. For Lieutenant General Walter Short's directive placing US Army early warning radar in operation at 4:00 A.M. on Sunday December 7, 1941, see standing operating procedure, US Army Hawaiian Department, dated 5 November 1941, pp. 1–20 in the Walter Short papers, Box 1–2, Hoover Institution Archives, Stanford University, Stanford, California. See also testimony concerning the hours of operation of the US Army's Hawaiian early warning radar by Colonel Bernard Thielen to the Joint Committee Investigation of the Pearl Harbor Attack, November 15, 1945, PHPT 1, p. 39.

21. For Lt. Gen. Walter Short's "most dangerous time" quote, see the Hoover Institution Archives, Stanford University.

22. For Kermit Tyler's quote "only officer present," see his testimony to the Roberts Commission, January 1942, PHPT 22, pp. 220 ff., also his testimony to the Army Pearl Harbor Board in 1944, PHPT 27, pp. 566 ff.

23. For Major Kenneth Berquist's statement that his mind was not clear on what he did the morning of December 7, 1941, see his testimony to the Roberts Commission, PHPT 22, p. 231 ff.

24. Lt. General George Grunert's "cock-eyed" quote followed Kermit Tyler's testimony concerning the Opana radar debacle. See the Army Pearl Harbor Board Proceedings of August 17, 1944, PHPT 27, pp. 571, 572:

GRUNERT: Then it appears that the organization seemed to be faulty, and its instruction faulty, and there seemed to be a lack of organization and common sense and reason on this. You went up there to do duty as a pursuit officer in the information center. There was nobody to do the work with, because the controller was not there, and the Navy liaison man wasn't there, and probably some others were missing, so you couldn't do your duty, as a pursuit officer, because there was nobody to do duty with; and then, at the end of the tour at 7 o'clock, everybody disappeared except the telephone operator and you, and the telephone operator remained there for apparently no reason. You had no particular duty, did you?

TYLER: No sir; we hadn't.

GRUNERT: It seems all cock-eyed to me and that, on the record, too.

25. For details on USS *Ward* and USS *Condor* sighting and depth-charging a Japanese midget sub, see PHPT 39, p. 496. For the radio report on the depth charge by USS *Ward*, see PHPT 37, p. 704.

26. For the testimony of William Outerbridge of USS *Ward*, see PHPT 36, pp. 55 ff.

27. For the "broken out of bunk" testimony of Lieut. Oliver Underkofler, see PHPT 36, p. 276.

28. For a discussion of the total loss of the five Japanese midget subs, see PHPT 23, p. 1034.

29. For the testimony of Lt. Cdr. Harold Kaminski, duty officer of the Fourteenth Naval District, see PHPT 11, p. 5293.

30. For Admirals Kimmel and Bloch being notified of the submarine report, see PHPT 13, p. 491.

CHAPTER 15

1. For Kimmel and Short's golf date, see PHPT 32, p. 283.

2. Death toll on the *Arizona* was 1,177 persons killed; for the Navy damage report, see PHPT 24, p. 1603.

3. At least seven torpedoes and two bomb hits struck the *West Virginia*, killing Captain Bennion. For damage to the *West Virginia*, see Vice Admiral Homer N. Wallin, *Pearl Harbor: Why, How, Fleet Salvage and Final Appraisal* (USGPO Naval History Division, 1968), p. 233; for death of Bennion, see ibid., p. 155.

4. Some 2,334 persons were killed in Hawaii by the December 7 attack, per the US

Naval Chronology World War II (USGPO, 1955), p. 13. A revised US Navy casualty figure was released by Fleet Admiral Ernest J. King in 1946 (but dated April 23, 1944) listing US Navy and Marine Corps losses at 2117 persons killed and 960 persons missing; see Fleet Admiral Ernest J. King, *The US Navy At War* (USGPO US Navy Department, 1946), p. 11. There were 68 deaths on Guam, per the report of Captain George J. McMillin (Navy governor of Guam in 1941, taken as a POW by Japan) to the Secretary of the Navy, dated September 11, 1945. McMillin wrote that there were 427 American military and 381 Guamanians involved in the island's defense on December 8, 1941 (Guam Time). For McMillin's letter and enclosures, see Guam file, RG 80, PHLO, MMRB, Archives II, copy in author's file. For casualties at Wake, see report of Edwin Layton to Admiral Chester Nimitz, dated September 17, 1942 in RG 80 PHLO, MMRB, Archives II. POW deaths are not included here, nor are Philippine casualties.

5. For account of the attack given by Commander Mitsuo Fuchida to Lieutenant Commander James A. Field, Jr., on October 10, 1945, see the transcript in United States Strategic Bombing Survey, *Interrogations of Japanese Officials*, Volume I (USGPO, 1946), p. 122.

6. On Lawrence McCutcheon, see Rich Pedroncelli, "Pearl Harbor, The First to Fall," *Naval History*, (December 1996), p. 56. See also Gordon Prange's interview with Jinichi Goto in *At Dawn We Slept* (McGraw Hill Book Company, 1981), pp. 509, 819. For the attack on the *Maryland*, see PHPT 1, p. 45.

7. For Rear Admiral Walter Anderson's account of December 7, 1941, see Wallin, Pearl Harbor, pp. 152 ff.

8. For Chief Boatswain's Mate Lewis W. Adkins, see ibid., pp. 157, 326.

9. For heroic actions of John B. Vaessen, see ibid., pp. 148, 178.

10. For damage details, refloating warships etc., see ibid. See also the testimony of Rear Admiral T. B. Inglis and Colonel Bernard Thielen to the Joint Committee on the Investigation of the Pearl Harbor Attack, in PHPT 1, p. 26 ff.

11. See December 7, 1941 logs of the Honolulu Fire and Police Departments, Hawaiian War Records, Hamilton Library, Manoa Campus, University of Hawaii, Honolulu, copies in author's file. For civilian deaths and injuries, see the Honolulu *Star-Bulletin*, 1st, 2nd, and 3rd extra editions, University of California, Doe Library, newspaper room, Berkeley, California, also copies in author's file. Wallin, *Pearl Harbor*, lists sixteen capital ships with major damage: USS *California, West Virginia, Pennsylvania, Oklahoma, Arizona, Utah, Maryland, Tennessee, Raleigh, Curtiss, Oglala, Shaw, Vestal, Honolulu, Downes*, and *Cassin*. Under the category of "destroyed or never to fight again": *Arizona, Utah, Shaw*, and *Oklahoma*. Machinery was removed from the *Downes* and the *Cassin* and installed in new hulls at Mare Island Navy Shipyard, Vallejo, California.

12. For the US Army radar plot indicating Japanese aircraft were tracked north, see testimony of Colonel Bernard Thielen in PHPT 1, pp. 141 ff. For Admiral Nagumo's disclosure that Pacific Fleet aircraft pursued the First Air Fleet, see his report transmitted to Admiral Yamamoto on December 17, 1941 in RG 457, SRN 115372, MMRB, Archives II, copy in author's file.

13. For Radioman 1/c Donovan Chase's written comments, see the Station H operator log for December 8, 1941, Tokyo Time, pp. 144 ff., RG 38, Station US papers, MMBR, Archives II. According to Chase's log, the Japanese pilots transmitted on 6581 kilocycles and used plain Japanese, not navy code. Chase translated Japanese to English in the log. Author interview with Donovan Chase, January 15, 1988, Santa Rosa, California, audio tape and transcript in author's file. At about this time, Airman 1/c Shigenori Nishikaichi, a fighter pilot on the *Hiryu*, crash-landed on Niihau, a privately owned 18–mile-long island off Kauai's west coast. Nishikaichi briefly seized the island but an unarmed resident, Ben Kanahele, grabbed the pilot and threw him against a rock wall. The airman died instantly. See Alan Beekman, *The Niihau Incident* (Heritage Press of Pacific, 1982), pp. 25 ff.

14. See the original copy of the US Army's Opana tracking chart, General Walter Short Papers, Hoover Institution Archives, Stanford University, Stanford, California. The Opana site was located on Kahuku Point at the northeast corner of Oahu. See the map of Oahu on p. 64 of this book.

15. For reports on the shooting down of a Japanese fighter by two scout planes from the USS *Northampton*, see PHPT 1, p. 61; PHPT 24, p. 1607; PHPT 37, pp. 955, 1220, 1252.

EPILOGUE

1. See report in *Chicago Tribune*, December 18, 1941; see report in *The Capital*, December 19, 1941.
2. For Senator Vandenberg's proposal, see an abridged version of a letter written by Vandenberg to FDR on December 15, 1941, Arthur H. Vandenberg Jr., ed. *The Private Papers of Arthur Vandenberg* (Houghton Mifflin, 1953), p. 24; for Vandenberg's Civil War quote excised from the December 15, 1941 letter just cited, see PHPT 24, p. 1298. Vandenberg, briefly an isolationist candidate for president, survived the 1940 New Deal election sweep.
3. See Max Freedman, ed., *Roosevelt and Frankfurter* (Atlantic Little, Brown, 1967), p. 644, entry of January 17, 1942.
4. For the full report entitled *Proceedings of the Roberts Commission*, see PHPTs 22 and 23 (testimony) and 24 (exhibits) printed in the *Report of the Joint Committee on the Investigation of the Pearl Harbor Attack* (Congress of the United States, 1946). Available at most major libraries.
5. See the United Press story by Joseph L. Myler, that appeared in the *Oakland Tribune* and other major Sunday papers, on January 25, 1942.
6. For condemnation of the Roberts Report by Admiral James Richardson, *On The Treadmill to Pearl Harbor* (Department of the Navy, Navy History Division, 1973), p. 453.
7. Congress "never got the full story," see Max Freedman, ed., *Roosevelt and Frankfurter*, p. 645.
8. For Admiral Leigh Noyes's "destruction order" see PHPT 10, p. 4739; Captain Laurance Safford testified that Admiral Noyes was concerned with spread of rumors and, according to Safford, told him, "If you have got any notes or anything in writing, destroy them because somebody might see them and start something which you don't intend," PHPT 8, p. 3571.
9. See McCollum's memorandum printed in Appendix A of this book.
10. For Fleet Admiral Ernest King's order see CNO Serial 182206, September 17, 1945; RG 38, Station US papers, MMRB, Archives II, copy in author's file.
11. See Proceedings of the Thurmond-Spence hearing, April 27, 1995, tape and official transcript by the United States Senate Armed Services Committee, transcript furnished author by Husband E. Kimmel II, grandson of the Admiral.
12. For Honigman's testimony, see transcript of the Thurmond-Spence probe, April 27, 1995, p. 9 ff., copy in author's file.
13. See the report dated December 15, 1995, issued by Undersecretary of Defense Edwin Dorn, Department of Defense, The Pentagon, copy in author's file. On May 25, 1999, the US Senate in a split vote "cleared" Admiral Husband E. Kimmel and Lieutenant General Walter C. Short of dereliction of duty charges. See *New York Times*, p. A-26, May 26, 1999.
14. For John Taylor not listed or reported as a witness, see ibid.

AFTERWORD

1. The documents were found in Record Groups 38 and 457 of the Modern Military Records Branch of Archives II, College Park, MD. They document the final countdown-to-war based on communications intelligence that started January 1, 1941. The condition of the documents, many covered with a layer of dust and bow-tied with a curious waxed string, indicated that no one had examined most of them since 1941. Timothy Wilford, master's degree candidate at the University of Ottawa, Canada, traveled to Archives II in March 2000 and uncovered a portion of the Station CAST records. Wilford said his interest in Pearl Harbor history was piqued when he read the first edition of *Day of Deceit*.
2. For critics, see *Cryptologia*, April 2000, Vol., XXIV, by Philip H. Jacobson, p. 110, et al. See *New York Review of Books*, November 2, 2000, by David Kahn, p. 59, et al.

3. See Coonce's report in CAST Daily Chronology, RG 38, Crane Files, Inactive Stations Philippines, Boxes 15, 16, 17, 18. Some historians claim the 5-Numeral code was called JN-25 by the US Navy in 1941. For their claim, see Note 2, supra. US Navy files of 1941 do not confirm their thesis. There were three radio traffic chiefs at Station CAST in 1941 who supervised the US Navy's eavesdropping operations: O. C. Coonce, from January to March; Leroy Lankford, April; Antone Novak, May to December. Each was a chief radioman.

4. CAST TESTM dispatch, January 20, 1941, Secret Serial 201540, RG 38, Crane Files, ibid. Copy in author's file. Parenthesis by author.

5. See Station CAST, April 1941, Monthly Report, RG 38 Crane Files, ibid.

6. CAST Monthly Report, April 1941, p. 92, ibid.

7. See CAST Monthly Report, April 1941, p. 93, ibid.

8. See CAST Monthly Report for April 1941, p. 97, ibid.

9. See the *HYOO 8* file in RG 457, National Security Agency records, Box 1315, Folder: Codes and Ciphers of Japan, MMRB, Archives II. Copy, author's file. *HYOO 8* contains 530 pages, dated May to October 31, 1941, compiled by the statistical section of Station H, Heeia, Territory of Hawaii. A RIP 5 typewriter, identified by its unique typeface, was used by Navy yeomen to type the report. Station HYPO was not issued a RIP 5 in 1941. Some portions of *HYOO 8* appear to have been updated in 1946, by unknown. Station H moved from Heeia to new quarters in the town of Wahiawa, on the lee side of Oahu, in January 1942 and was renamed Fleet Radio Unit Pacific (FRUPAC). Station CAST also prepared a smaller version of *HYOO 8*. See RG 38, Crane Files, ibid.

10. For Fabian's May 5, 1941 letter, see RG 38, Crane Files, Box 15, MMRB, Archives II, copy author's file.

11. See CAST Monthly Report, May 1941, p. 69, RG 38, Crane Files, Boxes 15, 16, 17, 18. MMRB, Archives II. Copy, author's file.

12. See CAST Monthly Report, May 1941, RG 38, ibid. Copy in author's file. In November 1941, Japan's repeat-back communication system disclosed the *Akagi* and her "chickens" in the North Pacific.

13. See Fabian's report, Secret serial 150700, in RG 38, Crane File release of January 25, 1995, MMRB, Archives II, copy in author's file. Note: Not to be confused with release of May 2000. For "not shown Kimmel," see letter dated July 1, 1998, from Husband E. "Ned" Kimmel II, grandson of the admiral and family spokesman. Further confirmed in Kimmel II to author, telephone conversations 1999. Notes in author's file.

14. Mackay's radio station call letters were KFS; had branch in San Francisco Bay mud flats near Palo Alto, CA. KFS ceased operations in July 1999, per *Oakland Tribune*, July 13, 1999. Four of Ogg's colleagues in the Navy's San Francisco intelligence office confirmed he was involved in assembling Japanese communications intelligence for the Twelfth Naval District during 1941. They are retired US Naval Reserve officers: Commander Charles Black and Lieutenant Commander A. William Barkan, luncheon with author, May 30, 2000, San Francisco; Captain A. James McCollum, USNR (Ret.), nephew of Rear Admiral Arthur H. McCollum, luncheon with author, April 13, 2000, Oakland, CA; and former US naval chief photographer Ron Partridge, telephone conversation with author, Berkeley, CA, May 2000.

Black, then an ensign, clearly recalled events at San Francisco's Twelfth Naval District in November and December 1941: "We all knew that navy radio cryptographers were breaking into Japanese communications. We were aware of the results. It was common knowledge." Black in telephone interview with author, February 14, 2000, notes in author's file.

Barkan, also an ensign, confirmed the comments of Black: "Washington knew what was going on," letter Barkan to author, September 10, 2000, copy in author's file. Barkan said Washington, DC naval headquarters authorized the Twelfth Naval District to secretly obtain naval code books from Japanese merchant ships calling in San Francisco. "We dressed as US Customs officials, boarded the Japanese vessels and obtained the codes." Barkan interview, May 30, 2000, notes in author's file.

15. Compiled by author from two US Navy reports: (1) *HYOO 8*, and, (2) CAST Monthly Report, August 1941, RG 38 Boxes 15, 16, 17, 18, ibid. Compilation dated August 7, 2000, (Rev.) in author's file.

16. See *HYOO 8*, RG 457, ibid.
17. Ibid.
18. When this and other reports of Japan's using the 5900 radio spectrum reached Hawaii, Commander Joseph Rochefort, head of Station HYPO ordered all Navy monitor stations to do a "Scoop Watch" and intercept every radio message carried on 5900 kcs., and similar frequencies. See Rochefort's order, p. 139 of this book.
19. For bearing, see *HYOO 8*, RG 457, ibid. For interception and translation of *Kyokuto Maru*, see Station CAST Monthly Report, August 1941, ibid.
20. For unmasking as 8 YU NA by CAST, see *HYOO 8*, September 26, 1941, RG 457, ibid. For American interception of 8 YU NA in November 1941 by Dutch Harbor, see p. 195 and note 7, p. 371 of this book. For extensive communications, see p. 163 of this book. As 8 YU NA, Nagumo/*Akagi* broke radio silence between November 26 and November 30, and were located in the North Pacific by the direction finder beams of the US Navy's Pacific monitor stations (see chapters 12, 13, this book). Nagumo's radio link with *Katori* surfaced on November 26 (TT), when Nagumo, aboard the *Akagi*, departed Hitokappu Bay for Hawaii and held extensive radio communications with Vice Admiral Mitsumi Shimizu, commander of the Japanese submarine fleet, who was aboard the *Katori*.
21. See Communication Summary of Fourteenth Naval District, dated November 5, 1941, RG 80, PHLO, Box 41, MMRB, Archives II. Copy in author's file. Rochefort capitalized "Kana Code" but did not specify the US Navy's designator for the "Kana Code." The author believes Rochefort refers to Japanese Naval Code Book "KO," assigned for radio use of Japan's commanding admiral's. (For Japanese naval code systems, see Kanya Miyauchi. *Niitaka Yama Nobore*. Tokyo, Rikkyu Shuppan, 1976. pp. 135 ff.) There are numerous references to a "Kana Code" in the pre–Pearl Harbor US naval cryptographic records. Station CAST reported that a "Nine character Kana Code with a period separator" was introduced by Japan on June 1, 1939 (see CAST Monthly Report, June 1939, RG 38, Crane files, Inactive Stations, Philippines, MMRB, Archives II). US Navy records are vague, but indicate the so-called "Nine character Kana Code" was designated as the "AD" Code. The main crypto task for Rochefort's Station HYPO in the fall of 1941 was solving the AD code (see *The Reminiscenses of Captain Joseph J. Rochefort*. United States Naval Institute. Annapolis, 1970, p. 134). In July 1927, Rear Admiral Osami Nagano led a Japanese naval training squadron in a visit to San Francisco. Nagano and his sailors were feted during a civic reception held at the Fairmont Hotel. See *Oakland Tribune*, July 26, 1927.
22. Lietwiler to Lee W. Parke, RG 38, Crane Files, Inactive Stations Philippines, Box 15, Folder 3200/1. MMRB, Archives II, copy in author's file. Lietwiler arrived on Corregidor in August 1941 to relieve Lieutenant Rudolph Fabian, who was due for rotation back to the States. As the crises intensified and his wife lay critically ill in the States, Fabian reluctantly remained on Corregidor and continued as co-commander of the monitor facility. Fabian's work was crucial to the war effort. CAST was a principal supplier of Japanese military and diplomatic intelligence for America's top command: President Franklin D. Roosevelt, the Philippine commanders, General Douglas MacArthur, and Admiral Thomas Hart. CAST also sent copies to Hawaii's commanders, but no record has ever surfaced that confirms the copies reached them. According to Lietwiler, the personnel at Station HYPO at Pearl Harbor complained directly to him of not receiving intelligence information. In mid-August, while en route by train/ship from Washington to Corregidor, Lietwiler heard the complaints from unnamed key HYPO personnel when he stopped off in Hawaii to discuss communications intelligence. See Lietwiler to LCDR Robert Densford, RG 38, Crane File, Box 15, August 30, 1941, MMRB, Archives II, copy in author's file. Parke headed the US Navy's uniform personnel in cryptography in November 1941. He was promoted to captain in 1944 and transferred to head the US State Department's Division of Cryptography.
23. Myers—and his expertise with the 5-Num Code—was transferred to Station CAST from Parke's office at Station US, and arrived on Corregidor September 1941. Transferred with Myers was Lieutenant John Hess who brought the latest decryption device for recovering the Five-Num Code. The device was invented in Washington, D.C., by Parke and called JEEP IV by USN cryptographers. It enabled the cryppies to recover the current (July to December 4, 1941) additives and subtractors

for the 5-Num code which the Japanese navy called *Ango Sho D, Ippan 7* (Code Book D, Edition 7). For a description of JEEP IV, see SRH 355, Vol. 1, p. 433, RG 457, MMRB, Archives II, copy in author's file. The device/machine and its ability to aid in solving the Japanese Navy's Operation Code (5-Num) was first described to Navy officials by Rear Admiral Royal Ingersoll on october 4, 1940 (see page 23 of this book).

24. Yamamoto's message reproduced herein apperas to have been reconstructed from the memory of Japanese radio operators in 1945. See explanation of the reconstruction in PHPT 13, p. 415.

25. For Kisner's report of November 20, 1941, see RG 38, Crane File, MMRB, Archives II, Chronology of Station H, p. 81. Between November 17 and November 25, 1941, Admiral Yamamoto dispatched eighty-three messages consecutively numbered in his Secret Message Series (SMS) radio log, an average of 9.2 messages per day. The SMS numbers begin with 531 on November 17 to 614 on November 25, 1941. Eleven of these SMS dispatches (13.2 percent) have been released to Archives II, and seventy-two (86.7 percent) have not been released. See the SMS log compiled by the author from Station H Chronology, November 1941, author's file.

26. See Okins report, in Station H Monthly Report, supervisor section, p. 14, in RG 38, Crane Files, MMRB, Archives II, copy in author's file. The author has filed a Freedom of Information request for release of all Station H intercepted messages, including those originated by Admiral Nagano. Neither the message sheet nor communication data concerning this message have been released. For history of the Nagano messages reported herein, see Note 24, supra. According to the Japanese radio call sign code, Nagano's code name was KO ME HA, Admiral Yamamoto RO SE 22, and Koga, HA NA 33, on November 5, 1941. For identification of KO ME HA as Chief of the Naval General Staff, see RG 457, SRN 115627, November 7, 1941, serial 70425, MMRB, Archives II, copy in author's file. For Yamamoto and Koga, see *HYOO 9* (Japanese navy radio call sign list, edition 9) in RG 457, National Security Agency, Box 1315, Codes and Ciphers of Japan, AHA 45704, MMRB, Archives II, copy in author's file. See confirmation in Station H Monthly Report, issued November 1941, copy in author's file.

Admiral Nagano survived the war and was promoted to Fleet Admiral. On November 20, 1945, he was "interrogated" in Tokyo by Rear Admiral Ralph A. Ofstie, head of the Naval Analysis Division of the United States Strategic Bombing Survey. Fleet Admiral Nagano was described as "thoroughly co-operative, was keenly alert and intelligent, and seemed anxious to develop American friendship." Ofstie obliged. Journalists will recognize Ofstie's questioning methods. In the year 2000, the technique is called soft-ball questioning. Nagano was not asked about his explosive radio messages of November 5 through December 3, 1941. Ofstie did not seek out the original messages in US Navy communications intelligence files; instead, he obtained "reconstructions" of the Nagano messages with all communication data removed. An example of a leading question suggesting an answer: OFSTIE: "Admiral, what do you think was the major mistake made by the Japanese High Command? Would you say that the senior officers were too old or that they were not air minded, or that they weren't broadly enough experienced? Was there some major item like that that was important in decreasing the efficiency, let us say, of the military forces? NAGANO: "Apropos of your comment about being too old, it is quite possible the Chief of the Navy General Staff was too old." For Nagano's interrogation, see p. 352; for assessment of Nagano's demeanor during interrogation p. 562. *Interrogations of Japanese Officials*, Vol. II, Washington, DC. USGPO, 1946.

27. For Japan's identical use of the phrase "state of war," see *Associated Press*, Tokyo report printed in Second Extra of *Honolulu Star-Bulletin*, p. 1, December 7, 1941,

28. For identification of Admiral Yamamoto's December 1941 radio call sign of YO WI ØØ, see p. 315, this book. For ID of China Area Fleet as KE NO 8, see RG 457, Box 1284; Folder, Codes and Ciphers of Japan *HYOO 10*, p. 40 in MMRB, Archives II, copy in author's file.

INDEX